The Routledge Handbook on Extraterritorial Human Rights Obligations

The Routledge Handbook on Extraterritorial Human Rights Obligations brings international scholarship on transnational human rights obligations into a comprehensive and wide-ranging volume.

Each chapter combines a thorough analysis of a particular issue area and provides a forward-looking perspective of how extraterritorial human rights obligations (ETOs) might come to be more fully recognized, outlining shortcomings but also best state practices. It builds insights gained from state practice to identify gaps in the literature and points to future avenues of inquiry. The Handbook is organized into seven thematic parts: conceptualization and theoretical foundations; enforcement; migration and refugee protection; financial assistance and sanctions; finance, investment and trade; peace and security; and environment. Chapters summarize the cutting edge of current knowledge on key topics as leading experts critically reflect on ETOs, and, where appropriate, engage with the *Maastricht Principles* to critically evaluate their value 10 years after their adoption.

The Routledge Handbook on Extraterritorial Human Rights Obligations is an authoritative and essential reference text for scholars and students of human rights and human rights law, and more broadly, of international law and international relations as well as to those working in international economic law, development studies, peace and conflict studies, environmental law and migration.

Mark Gibney is the Belk Distinguished Professor at the University of North Carolina-Asheville, USA, and an Affiliated Scholar at the Raoul Wallenberg Institute in Lund, Sweden.

Gamze Erdem Türkelli is a Tenure Track Research Assistant Professor at the University of Antwerp, Law and Development Research Group, Belgium.

Markus Krajewski is Professor at the University of Erlangen-Nürnberg, and Director of the Centre for Human Rights Erlangen-Nürnberg (CHREN), Germany.

Wouter Vandenhole holds the Human Rights Chair at the Law Faculty of the University of Antwerp, Law and Development Research Group, Belgium.

"The editors have been working on extraterritorial human rights obligations for years and have brought their collective experience to bear on this welcome volume. Up to the moment, wide-ranging and with specialist coverage, this is an extremely valuable compendium that assesses international law beyond borders as if people matter."

Margot Salomon, *London School of Economics, UK*

"While the general area of extraterritoriality is relatively new, and at times described as 'metaphysics of human rights law', this volume takes the discourse to new heights in covering novel areas such as digitalisation, cyber operations, arms control, climate change and refugee rights in the context of extraterritorial human rights obligations. Written by some of the pioneers of the field of extraterritoriality, the book is a great addition to the emerging literature on the topic. What is equally impressive about this book is its coverage of global as well as regional human rights systems, both in theory and practice."

Takele Soboka Bulto, *Legal Adviser, Peace and Security Department, African Union*

"This rich and comprehensive collection of different aspects of the extraterritorial application of human rights treaties is a welcome addition to the academic discourse. Through its variety of subjects and perspectives, the book will help in understanding the complexities of the topic and move the thinking about the development of the law further."

Fons Coomans, *Maastricht University, The Netherlands*

The Routledge Handbook on Extraterritorial Human Rights Obligations

Edited by Mark Gibney, Gamze Erdem Türkelli, Markus Krajewski and Wouter Vandenhole

Routledge
Taylor & Francis Group
LONDON AND NEW YORK

Cover image: © Getty Images

First published 2022
by Routledge
4 Park Square, Milton Park, Abingdon, Oxon OX14 4RN

and by Routledge
605 Third Avenue, New York, NY 10158

Routledge is an imprint of the Taylor & Francis Group, an informa business

British Library Cataloguing-in-Publication Data
A catalogue record for this book is available from the British Library

Library of Congress Cataloging-in-Publication Data
Names: Gibney, Mark, editor.
Title: The Routledge handbook on extraterritorial human rights obligations / edited by Mark Gibney, Gamze Erdem Türkelli, Markus Krajewski and Wouter Vandenhole.
Other titles: Handbook on extraterritorial human rights obligations
Description: Abingdon, Oxon ; New York, NY : Routledge, 2022. | Series: Routledge international handbooks | Includes bibliographical references and index.
Identifiers: LCCN 2021020272 (print) | LCCN 2021020273 (ebook) | ISBN 9780367546489 (hardback) | ISBN 9780367546571 (paperback) | ISBN 9781003090014 (ebook)
Subjects: LCSH: International law and human rights. | Exterritoriality. | International law and municipal law.
Classification: LCC KZ1266 .R68 2022 (print) | LCC KZ1266 (ebook) | DDC 341.4/8–dc23
LC record available at https://lccn.loc.gov/2021020272
LC ebook record available at https://lccn.loc.gov/2021020273

ISBN: 978-0-367-54648-9 (hbk)
ISBN: 978-0-367-54657-1 (pbk)
ISBN: 978-1-003-09001-4 (ebk)

DOI: 10.4324/9781003090014

Typeset in Bembo
by KnowledgeWorks Global Ltd.

Contents

Contributors

Marina Aksenova is Professor of Comparative and International Criminal Law at IE University in Madrid. She holds PhD from the European University Institute, MSc from the University of Oxford, and LLM from the University of Amsterdam. She authored a number of publications in the area of public international law and international criminal justice, including a monograph entitled *Complicity in International Criminal Law* (Hart 2016). She also manages Art and International Justice Initiative (artij.org).

Daniel Augenstein works as Associate Professor in the Department of Public Law and Governance at Tilburg Law School. His research focuses on the legal and policy framework governing the relationship between international human rights protection and global business operations. Daniel has published widely on issues relating to business and human rights. He has conducted numerous policy studies on this topic for international organisations and national governments, and occasionally contributes work to NGO campaigns and cross-border litigations for corporate-related human rights violations.

Stephan Backes is a human rights activist and practitioner. He holds an MA in English and German Philology and in Human Rights. At FIAN International, he has been working on accountability, European policies and social movement processes, TNCs, and ETOs (currently in charge of the Secretariat of the ETO Consortium). He co-authored 'Land Grabbing and Human Rights: The Involvement of European Corporate and Financial Entities in Land Grabbing outside the European Union' (Borras et al. 2016) and 'Democracy not for Sale: The struggle for food sovereignty in the age of austerity in Greece' (Backes et al. 2018).

Antal Berkes (PhD, Paris 1/ELTE Budapest; LLM, CEU) is currently a Lecturer in Law in the School of Law and Social Justice at the University of Liverpool. Antal's research interests encompass international law, especially international human rights law, humanitarian law and refugee law in areas outside the effective control of the state. In 2019, Antal was a postdoctoral research fellow at the University of Pretoria, where he prepared his book entitled *International Human Rights Law in Areas beyond State Territorial Control* (CUP 2021).

Clara Burbano-Herrera is a research professor of human rights law and director of the Programme for Studies on Human Rights in Context at the Faculty of Law and Criminology of Ghent University. Previously, she was a Fulbright Researcher at Harvard and a Postdoctoral Researcher of the Flanders Research Foundation. Her research relates to the role of international monitoring organs in preventing human rights violations, especially as to vulnerable groups. Clara holds a PhD in Law (Ghent University), an LLM in Fundamental Rights

(Universidad Carlos III, Spain), a Postgraduate in Constitutional Law (Universidad Nacional de Colombia), and a Master of Laws (Universidad de Los Andes, Colombia). She is the co-editor of *Human Rights Behind Bars: Tracing vulnerability in prison populations from a multidisciplinary perspective* (Springer, forthcoming) and *The Inter-American Court of Human Rights: Theory and Practice, Present and Future* (Intersentia, 2015).

Giacomo Capuzzo is lecturer at the Department of Law of the University of Perugia (Italy). He is a member of the Italian Association of Comparative Law and board member of the Coordination of Italian Law Clinics. He has published several essays in national and international journals on comparative law, comparative jurisprudence, European private law, property law, and urban space. He is a member of the International Scientific Committee of the Semaine Doctorale Intensif/Intensive Doctoral Week, organised by Science Po Paris – School of Law, University of Perugia, University of Turin, SOAS, University of Is there a space missing? Tel-Aviv, Birkbeck University, Erik Castren Istitute – Helsinki. He has carried out research and teaching activities at Science Po Ecole de Droit of Paris (2016) and Florida International University (2020).

Lilian Chenwi is Professor of Law at the School of Law, University of the Witwatersrand, South Africa. Her areas of research are international human rights law, socio-economic rights, housing rights, death penalty from a human rights perspective, public international law, and international criminal law. Her publications include being co-editor of *Extraterritorial Human Rights Obligations from an African Perspective* (Intersentia 2018). She is an editor of South African Journal on Human Rights. She is a member of the ETO Consortium and a signatory to the *Maastricht Principles* on Extraterritorial Obligations of states in the area of Economic, Social, and Cultural Rights.

Joshua Curtis is a lecturer in law at the Adelaide Law School, University of Adelaide. His research and consulting work address the fields of human rights, international economic law and development economics. His most recent publication is *Ending Childhood Obesity: A Challenge at the Crossroads of International Economic and Human Rights Law* (Edward Elgar 2020 – co-edited with Amandine Garde and Olivier De Schutter). His monograph on *Human Rights and Foreign Investment: Cooperation and Coherence in Global Law-Making* is forthcoming with Cambridge University Press. He has advised the Irish Department of Foreign Affairs, the Government of Oman, the Irish Cancer Society, Amnesty International, and the International Federation for Human Rights. He is an academic member of the ETO Consortium.

Stéphanie de Moerloose is a Swiss National Science Foundation Post-Doctoral Fellow at Humboldt University of Berlin and Affiliated Professor at Universidad Austral, Argentina. Dr. de Moerloose's research focuses on law and development, with a particular interest in sustainability, Human Rights and international financial institutions. Her publications include *World Bank environmental and social conditionality as a vector of sustainable development* (Schulthess 2020) and, as a co-editor, *Encyclopedia of Law and Development* (Edward Elgar 2021). Her current work investigates international financial institutions' interpretation of Free, Prior, and Informed Consent as well as the private turn of development finance, especially within the World Bank Group.

Nicoletta Dentico is a journalist with a longstanding expertise in global health and international cooperation. She coordinated the International Campaign to Ban Landmines (ICBL) in Italy from 1993 to the end of 1999, achieving a national ban on these weapons (Italy was then a major producer and exporter of landmines). She directed Doctors Without Borders in Italy from 2000 to 2004, when she joined the internatioonal team engaged in the MSF Campaign for Access to Essential Medicines first and then Drugs for Diseases Initiative (DNDi). She worked as WHO consultant in the EMRO Region and then in the Geneva HQ on issue of intellectual property rights and public health. She is one of the founding members of the Italian Global Health Watch. She led the international department of the Lelio Basso Foundation from 2015 to 2018, and served as board member of the Italian Ethical Bank from 2013 to 2019. Since 2019 she leads the global health programme of Society for International Development (SID). She has extensively written about disarmament issues, and the right to health. Her recent publications include: *Geopolitica della Salute: COVID-19, OMS e la Sfida Pandemica* (Rubbettino 2021), The World Needs Health Commons, the monographic issue of the SID Development Journal (Palgrave 2020), *Ricchi e Buoni? Le trame oscure del filantrocapitalismo* (EMI 2020), OMS e Diritto alla Salute: Quale Futuro (2015), *Salute e Globalizzazione* (Feltrinelli 2004).

Mohammed El Said is a legal consultant and Professor in International Trade and Intellectual Property Law at the School of Justice, the University of Central Lancashire (UK). He worked as a resource person extensively with international organisations including the UNDP, WIPO, UNITAID, and WHO in the field of IP policy, IP and development, public health, and access to medicines. El Said has several books and publications in the area of intellectual property, public health, and access to medicines.

Gamze Erdem Türkelli is a Tenure Track Research Assistant Professor at the University of Antwerp Law and Development Research Group. Dr. Türkelli holds a PhD in Law from the University of Antwerp and Master's degrees from Université Paris 1 – Panthéon Sorbonne and Yale University, where she was a Fulbright Fellow. Her current research interests include transnational human rights obligations and legal responsibility, children's rights, and the links between law and sustainable development, and new and old economic actors in development financing and governance. She is the author of *Children's Rights and Business: Governing Obligations and Responsibility* (Cambridge University Press 2020), co-author of *Children's Rights: A Commentary on the Convention on the Rights of the Child and its Protocols* (Edward Elgar 2019), and co-editor of *Encyclopedia of Law and Development* (Edward Elgar 2021).

Thomas Gammeltoft-Hansen is Professor in legal science with special responsibilities in migration and refugee law at the University of Copenhagen, iCourts Centre for Excellence. He received his PhD (in international law) from Aarhus University, MSc (in refugee studies) from the University of Oxford, and MA (in political science) from the University of Copenhagen. His research focuses on migration and refugee law, international human rights law, and the relationship between international law and politics. Thomas Gammeltoft-Hansen has consulted for a number of international organisations, governments, and NGOs, and previously served as member of the Danish Refugee Appeals Board. At the University of Copenhagen, he directs the Nordic Asylum Law & Data Lab which combines legal and data science methods to study refugee and migration law.

Mark Gibney is the Belk Distinguished Professor at the University of North Carolina-Asheville and an Affiliated Scholar at the Raoul Wallenberg Institute in Lund, Sweden. From 2014 to 2016, he served as the inaugural Raoul Wallenberg Visiting Professor of Human Rights and Humanitarian Law at the Faculty of Law, Lund University and the Raoul Wallenberg Institute. Gibney is one of the founding members of the Extraterritorial Obligations (ETO) Consortium and he serves on the Board of Editors of *Human Rights Quarterly, the Journal of Human Rights*, and *the International Studies Journal* (Iran). Since 1984, Gibney has directed the Political Terror Scale

(PTS) (PoliticalTerrorScale.org), which measures levels of physical integrity violations in more than 190 states and this work has recently been expanded to include the SocietalViolence Scale (SVS), which provides a comparative analysis of human rights violations by non-state actors. His recent book publications include: *International Law: Our Common Future* (2020); *International Human Rights Law: Returning to Universal Principles* (2015, 2d ed.); *Litigating Transnational Human Rights Obligations: Alternative Judgments* (2014); *the Handbook of Human Rights* (2014); and *Watching Human Rights: The 101 Best Films* (2013).

Hannah Ghulam Farag is an academic assistant at the Research Group Contextual Research in law (CORE) of the Free University of Brussels and a Research Associate in the Programme for Studies on Human Rights in Context at Ghent University. Hannah holds an LL.M. from the University of Cambridge (2021, first class honours) and a Master of Laws of Ghent University (2020, summa cum laude, receiving the award for best student). At Ghent University she participated in multiple research projects in the Programme for Studies on Human Rights in Context and in the Human Rights Centre. In Cambridge she led a research team on the question of continuous state obligations regarding historical enforced disappearances for the Cambridge University Pro Bono Project. Presently, Hannah's interest lie on the intersection between international human rights law, public international law and labour law.

Kristof Gombeer is a fellow of the Research Foundation, Flanders (FWO) and a PhD candidate at the Vrije Universiteit Brussel and Leiden University researching the interaction between human rights law and the legal regime on search and rescue at sea.

Elspeth Guild is a Jean Monnet Professor ad personam in law at Queen Mary University of London and Emeritus Professor at Radboud University, Nijmegen, Netherlands. Prof. Guild is also a partner at the London law firm Kingsley Napley. She regularly advises EU institutions on migration and asylum in particular the European Parliament. She also advises the Council of Europe. In 2017, she co-edited with Stefanie Grant and Kees Groenendijk *The Human Rights of Migrants in the 21st Century* directed at the UN Global Compact for Safe, Orderly, and Regular Migration.

Yves Haeck is a professor of human rights law and director of the Programme for Studies on Human Rights in Context at the Faculty of Law and Criminology of Ghent University, and a visiting professor at the Universities of Geneva and Pretoria. Prior to this, he was an assistant professor at Utrecht University. Yves holds a PhD in Law (Ghent University) and a Master of Laws (Ghent University). He is the co-editor of *The Inter-American Court of Human Rights: Theory and Practice, Present and Future* (Intersentia, 2015) and *Human Rights Behind Bars: Tracing vulnerability in prison populations from a multidisciplinary perspective* (Springer, forthcoming). Yves is co-founder of the Human Rights Centre of Ghent University. His research focuses on substantial and procedural issues before human rights adjudicators, especially admissibility conditions and urgent measures.

Roman Herre is a human rights activist. He is working for over 13 years for the German section of the human rights organisation FIAN International on specific cases of human rights violations with a focus on food and land rights and the role of development cooperation. He holds an MA in Geography. His publications include 'Fast track agribusiness expansion, land grabs and the role of *European private and public financing in Zambia. A right to food perspective*' (FIAN 2013) and co-authoring '*Rogue Capitalism and the Financialization of Territories and Nature*' (FIAN, TNI, Focus on the Global South 2020).

Ademola Oluborode Jegede (LLM, UP; LLD, UP) is a Professor of Law in the School of Law, University of Venda, Thohoyandou, South Africa. He holds degrees from Obafemi Awolowo University Ile-Ife, University of Ibadan, and the Centre for Human Rights, Faculty of Law, University of Pretoria. He has been a research visitor to the Centre for International Environmental Law, USA and Human Rights Institute at Abo Akademi, Finland. His research focuses on the interface of climate change with human rights of vulnerable groups and general international human rights law. His writings on these themes include the book: *The climate change regulatory framework and indigenous peoples' lands in Africa: Human rights implications* (Pretoria University Law Press 2016).

Matthias C. Kettemann (PD Mag., LLM (Harvard)) is professor of innovation, theory and philosophy of law at the Department of Theory and Future of Law at the University of Innsbruck, senior researcher at the Leibniz Institute for Media Research | Hans-Bredow-Institut (HBI) and head of its research programme on rule-making in online spaces. He is research group leader for Global Constitutionalism and the Internet at the Alexander von Humboldt Institute for Internet and Society (HIIG), Head of Section, International Law and the Internet, Max Planck Institute for Comparative Public Law and International Law, research group leader for Platform and Content Governance at the Sustainable Computing Lab of the Vienna University of Economics and Business and associated researcher at Germany's Research Centre Social Cohesion. He has been a consultant for internet law and digital rights for a number of international organisations, including the Council of Europe and the Fundamental Rights Agency, national governments, ministries and legislatures, including the Federal Foreign Office, the Ministry of Economy and the German Bundestag, and international companies and foundations. His most recent books are Kettemann, *The Normative Order of the Internet: A Theory of Rule and Regulation Online* (OUP 2020), (as editor) *Navigating Normative Orders: Interdisciplinary Perspectives* (Campus 2020), and (with W. Benedek), *Freedom of Expression and the Internet* (2nd ed.) (Strasbourg 2020).

Markus Krajewski is professor of public and international law at the University of Erlangen-Nürnberg and Director of the Centre for Human Rights Erlangen-Nürnberg (CHREN). He also chairs the Board of Trustees of the German Institute for Human Rights, Germany's national human rights institution. Before taking up his current position, Markus taught at King's College London and the Universities of Potsdam and Bremen. His research focuses on human rights law as well as international trade and investment law.

Pauline Maillet is a graduate of Wilfrid Laurier's Ph.D. programme in Global Governance (Canada). She holds an LLM in Public International Law from the London School of Economics.

Rod Michelmore is a doctoral candidate at the University of Sydney, where he completed a Master of Law and International Development. His professional practice as a Senior Crown Prosecutor in London and a litigation barrister and attorney in the British Overseas Territory of Bermuda, triggered his interest in the interface between internationally mobile capital and extreme poverty. His research has largely focused on the developmental concept of tax-related illicit financial flows, and its application to international human rights law obligations and international tax transparency agreements, as they relate to the Least Developed Countries.

Marko Milanovic is Professor of Public International Law at the University of Nottingham School of Law. He is co-editor of EJIL: Talk!, the blog of the European Journal of International Law, as well as a member of the EJIL's Editorial Board, and was formerly Vice-President and member of the Executive Board of the European Society of International Law. He held visiting professorships at Michigan Law School, Columbia Law School, Deakin Law School, and the Geneva Academy of International Humanitarian Law and Human Rights.

Sofia Monsalve Suárez is the Secretary General of FIAN International, a human rights organisation working for the realisation of the right to food and nutrition. Prior to her appointment as Secretary General in 2016, she coordinated FIAN's program on land and natural resources for more than 15 years. This work included field research to twenty countries; close collaboration with peasants, fishing communities, indigenous peoples, and rural workers; research and conceptual work on the intersection between human rights and natural resource governance in collaboration with various academic institutions; and advocacy work in the UN human rights system as well as with several UN agencies.

Khulekani Moyo is a Senior Lecturer in the School of Law, University of the Witwatersrand. Khulekani received his doctoral degree in Public Law from Stellenbosch University, an LLM in Public International Law from the University of Oslo, Norway and an LLB (Hons) from the University of Zimbabwe. He also holds two diplomas in the International Protection of Human Rights and the Justiciability of Economic, Social, and Cultural Rights from Åbo Akademi University in Finland. He has held the positions of Head of Research at the South African Human Rights Commission, Senior Lecturer at the Nelson R. Mandela School of Law, University of Fort Hare and Researcher at the Norwegian Centre for Human Rights. His research interests include international law, international human rights law; business and human rights; intellectual property law and human rights; international criminal law; constitutional law; and regional integration law.

Angela Müller, PhD/Dr. des., is currently Team Lead Policy & Advocacy at AlgorithmWatch and AlgorithmWatch Switzerland. Prior to that, she was a Research Associate at the Faculty of Law of the University of Zurich, where she wrote her PhD thesis on extraterritorial human rights obligations, funded by the Swiss National Science Foundation. She was a visiting researcher at Columbia University, New York, and Hebrew University, Jerusalem, and obtained her MA in Political and Economic Philosophy from the University of Berne. She is also the Vice-President of the UN Association Switzerland. Previously, she held positions at a think tank on foreign policy, the Federal Department of Foreign Affairs, Lucerne University of Applied Sciences and Arts, and the University of Berne.

Anne Oloo is a teaching assistant in the field of human rights and a PhD researcher within the Law and Development Group at the University of Antwerp. Her PhD research is on algorithmic human rights accountability and online global platform governance. She holds a Bachelor of Laws degree (LLB) from the University of Nairobi and an LLM in International and European Law from Ghent University. Her research interests include human rights, digital rights, public international law, and sustainable development

Elena Pribytkova is a Postdoctoral Fellow at the Faculty of Law of the National University of Singapore. She received a JSD degree from Columbia Law School and a PhD degree from the Russian Academy of Sciences. She is a Habilitation candidate at the Faculty of Law of the University of Basel. Her research focuses on the role of human rights in reducing poverty and inequality and promoting social, global, and environmental justice, and sustainable development. Elena held various appointments at leading universities and research institutes, including

Columbia Law School, University of Oxford, European University Institute, Max Planck Institute for Comparative Public Law and International Law, Swiss Institute of Comparative Law, University of Basel, and New York University School of Law. She has more than 50 publications in English, German, French, and Russian.

Emma Luce Scali is Lecturer in Law at Birmingham City University's School of Law and Roma Tre University's Department of Political Science, where she teaches, among others, a course on the 'crisis' of human rights. Her current research interests and publications centre around human rights, sovereign financing and the global economic order. Her first monograph on *Sovereign Debt and Socio-Economic Rights Beyond Crisis: The Neoliberalisation of International Law* is forthcoming with Cambridge University Press (January 2022).

Joseph Schechla coordinates the Geneva- and Cairo-based Housing and Land Rights Network (HLRN) of Habitat International Coalition (HIC), the civic movement founded in 1976 to support and develop the UN Habitat Agenda. HLRN builds the Coalition's capacity to advocate habitat-related human rights, including adequate housing, water and land, in international forums, foremostly the UN Human Rights System. Living in the Middle East/North Africa (MENA) for 25 years, he also has represented OHCHR in Palestine and Tunisia. Since graduate school (Georgetown University), Joseph's academic interests include research, writing, and teaching on foreign policies toward MENA vis-à-vis states' human rights obligations.

Sara L. Seck (PhD) is an Associate Professor and Associate Dean Research at the Schulich School of Law, Dalhousie University where she is a member of the Marine & Environmental Law Institute. She has researched in the areas of public and private international law, international environmental and human rights law, business and human rights, and sustainable development law since becoming an academic in 2007. Among recent contributions, she is co-editor of the *Cambridge Handbook on Environmental Justice and Sustainable Development* (2021), co-editor of a forthcoming Handbook on *Climate Change Loss & Damage*, and is a director with GNHRE.

Jennifer Sellin (PhD, Maastricht University) is an assistant professor in international (human rights) law at the Department of International & European Law, Faculty of Law, Maastricht University in the Netherlands. Her research interests encompass socio-economic human rights with a focus on access to medicines, the right to health and the right to benefit from science. From February until July 2019, Jennifer was a visiting professor at the Dalla Lana School of Public Health, University of Toronto, Canada. There she collaborated with Prof. Lisa Forman on the topic of access to medicines. Jennifer is also a member of the Advisory Council of Farma ter Verantwoording.

Philip Seufert is a human rights practitioner who works at FIAN International – an international organisation that has been advocating for the human right to food and nutrition for over 30 years. He works with social movements of small-scale food producers, Indigenous People's organisations, and other civil society organisations supporting them to assert and advance their rights at local, national, and international levels. His main areas of work are the control over land, fisheries, and forests, and biodiversity. He also works on financialisation as well as on the impacts of digitalisation on the right to food and nutrition.

Sigrun Skogly is Professor of Human Rights Law at Lancaster University, UK. Her work has largely focused on human rights obligations, both of states and non-state actors, and on the content of such obligations in particular related to economic, social, and cultural human rights. She was a founding member of the Extraterritorial Human Rights Obligations Consortium in 2008, and is currently a member of the steering group working on Principles on Human Rights for Future Generations. For a number of years, she was a visiting professor at University of Bergen, Norway; and also the University of South East Norway.

Stefaan Smis is currently professor of international and human rights law at the Faculty of Law & Criminology of the Vrije Universiteit Brussel. At the University of Westminster (UK – London), he also has a part-time position as a reader in International Law. He has been invited as guest lecturer at various universities in Europe, Africa, Middle-East, and USA. Prof. Dr. Stefaan Smis is secretary of the Belgian Branch of the International Law Association (ILA), was a member of the ILA Committee on the Rights of Indigenous Peoples and is currently alternate member of the Committee on Human Rights in Times of Emergency.

Anna Sophia Tiedeke (Ass. jur.) is currently a Research Associate at the Leibniz Institute for Media Research | Hans-Bredow-Institut (HBI) in the research programme on rule-making in online spaces and a PhD candidate at the Humboldt University in Berlin. In her PhD thesis, she engages with the concept of the state under international law in times of digitality. She is a member of the editorial board ofVölkerrechtsblog.

Vito Todeschini (PhD, Aarhus University) is a Legal Adviser at the Middle East and North Africa Programme of the International Commission of Jurists, where he focuses on Libya and Palestine/Israel. His research interests include international humanitarian law, human rights law, and the law on the use of force. The chapter was written in a personal capacity; the views expressed cannot be attributed to the International Commission of Jurists.

Wouter Vandenhole is a human rights and law-and-development scholar. He holds the human rights chair at the Law Faculty of the University of Antwerp, and is a member of the Law and Development Research Group. Between 2007 and 2018, he also held the UNICEF Chair in Children's Rights. His research interests include children's rights, economic, social, and cultural rights, and the relationship between human rights law and development. Over the last 15 years, he has extensively researched extraterritorial human rights obligations.

Tara Van Ho is a Lecturer in the School of Law and Human Rights Centre, University of Essex, UK. She is co-president of the Global Business and Human Rights Scholars Association, and her research focuses broadly on business and human rights, including the intersection of investment law and human rights. She has a particular interest in these issues within the context of conflict and post-conflict states. A co-director of the Essex Business and Human Rights Project, she advises states, nongovernmental, and intergovernmental organisations on the impact of investment agreements, business practices and legal standards on human rights.

Ralph Wilde is an expert in international law. His book *International Territorial Administration: How Trusteeship and the Civilizing Mission Never Went Away* (OUP 2008) was awarded the Certificate of Merit (book prize) of the American Society of International Law. De. Wilde previously served on the executive bodies of the American and European Societies of International Law, and the International Law Association, and at the latter he is currently a member of the International Committee on Human Rights in Times of Emergency. https://www.ucl.ac.uk/laws/people/ralph-wilde.

Preface

The genesis for this project began with a three-day meeting at the Raoul Wallenberg Institute (RWI) in the spring of 2016. Special thanks go to Morten Kjaerum, the Director of RWI and Rolf Ring, the Deputy Director, for providing us with funding, facilities, and great enthusiasm.

An important impetus to the fruition of this project has been given by the Scientific Research Network (SRN) "Extraterritorial Human Rights Obligations in Practice". This SRN is funded by the Research Foundation Flanders (FWO), and has allowed partners from the Universities of Antwerp, Brussels and Ghent, together with the University of North Carolina and the Friedrich-Alexander Universität Erlangen-Nürnberg to pull together an amazing amount of scholarship from across the globe to contribute to this research Handbook.

The research Handbook is made available Open Access with funds from Friedrich-Alexander-University Erlangen-Nürnberg in order to make the most contemporary scholarship on ETOs compiled in this volume accessible to the broadest possible audience of scholars, students, civil society and policy-makers around the globe, particularly in developing countries.

We are grateful to the publisher, and in particular to Andrew Taylor and Sophie Iddamalgoda, for their enthusiasm and support throughout the project.

Antwerp – Asheville – Erlangen-Nürnberg
January 2021

Introduction

Wouter Vandenhole, Gamze Erdem Türkelli, Mark Gibney and Markus Krajewski

The *Maastricht Principles* ten years on

The year 2021 marked the tenth anniversary of the adoption of the *Maastricht Principles* on Extraterritorial Obligations in the Area of Economic, Social, and Cultural Rights (*Maastricht Principles*). The *Maastricht Principles* is a landmark document that seeks to set out legal principles on extraterritorial human rights obligations (ETOs). This Handbook is testament to how the notion of extraterritorial human rights obligations has challenged and fundamentally changed our understanding of human rights.

Human rights have traditionally been framed in a vertical perspective (state-individual), with the duties of states confined to individuals on their territory. Obligations beyond this 'territorial space' have been viewed as either non-existent or at best, minimalistic. This territorial paradigm has achieved particular prominence in the interpretation of international human rights conventions, although there is language in many of these treaties that would provide a broader scope of application (Gibney and Vandenhole 2014; Skogly 2006). As the cover image of this volume suggests, territorially conceptualised human rights obligations often act as an arbitrary wall, beyond which new threats to human rights arise in extraterritoriality (as symbolised by the bird of prey). ETOs provide a window through which to see, assess, and deal with these new threats and, also a window to a more expansive understanding of human rights, as depicted by blue skies.

Today, however, the territorial paradigm is seriously challenged. For one thing, the ability of states and other actors to impact human rights far from home – both positively and negatively – has never been clearer. Perhaps the most direct means by which states act extraterritorially is by placing their own troops on the ground in another state, especially in a conflict situation. Likewise, states may use surveillance beyond their borders. States may intercept migrants in international waters before these migrants arrive at their borders. States may pollute the land, water, or air with cross-boundary impacts or contribute to climate change through high levels of carbon emissions. In addition, the regulatory role of states may be invoked when businesses domiciled in their territory undertake transnational operations or when states need to take measures to fight and prevent corruption and bribery.

When the four editors of this volume convened a meeting at the Raoul Wallenberg Institute in the spring of 2016, our initial goal was to bring together a group of like-minded human rights

DOI: 10.4324/9781003090014-1

scholars to analyse actual state practice. This was five years after the signing of the Maastricht ETO Principles and the foremost question was how states acted in the world. Quite simply, do they follow the same kinds of human rights standards as they do at home? Or, instead, do they act in a way that would be viewed as both immoral and illegal if performed within their own domestic realm? At the outset, this group focused on a relatively small number of topics where one state's ability to affect the human rights protection of individuals in other countries was seemingly incontrovertible – e.g., arms sales or economic sanctions. However, it soon became clear that the importance, but also the challenge, of this extraterritorial dimension could be found in a wide array of topics, which, at least to some extent, are reflected in this Handbook. Of course, a systematic survey of state practice remains on the ETO research agenda.

This research Handbook seeks to take stock of progress made over the last decade, since the adoption of the *Maastricht Principles*, in applying the principles, and proposes ways forward. We have identified five thematic clusters in which extraterritorial human rights obligations have become most pertinent: migration; financial assistance and sanctions; investment, finance, and trade; peace and security; and environment. These thematic parts are preceded by two introductory parts, which cover the conceptualisation and theoretical foundations as well as the enforcement of ETOs at the global and regional level.

Each chapter combines a thorough analysis of a particular issue area as it now stands, but it also provides a forward-looking perspective of how ETOs might come to be more fully recognised. Where appropriate, the authors engage with the *Maastricht Principles* and critically evaluate their value ten years after their adoption in various areas of the law and policy, both with respect to and beyond economic, social, and cultural rights. The chapters also seek to address state practice, outlining shortcomings but also best practices.

The Handbook's outline

Part I – Conceptualization and theoretical foundations

This opening section is intended to introduce what extraterritorial obligations are, how (and why) the concept arose, and to provide some sense of how recognition of such obligations changes our entire understanding of "human rights". In his chapter the "Historical Development of Extraterritorial Obligations," Mark Gibney explains how a little more than two decades ago, human rights scholars first began to push against the dominant "territorial" interpretation of international human rights law, mainly due to the enormous gaps in protection this approach often resulted in. Following this, in 2007 the Extraterritorial Obligations Consortium (ETOC) was formed, and although it initially focused on economic, social, and cultural rights (ESCR), the notion that states have human rights obligations beyond their own territorial borders soon was applied to all human rights, as evidenced by the array of chapters in this Handbook. At the present time, ETO Principles generally – and the Maastricht ETO Principles in particular – are now commonly referenced in United Nations and in various other international law fora, and there is even some evidence of a growing recognition of these principles by states (Heupel 2018).

Sigrun Skogly explores the foundation and the scope of "Global Obligations," and catalogs how such obligations are firmly grounded in international law. The starting point is the UN Charter, which lists as one of its purposes: "To achieve international co-operation in solving international problems of an economic, social, cultural, or humanitarian character, and in promoting and encouraging respect for human rights and for fundamental freedoms ..." Similarly, the Universal Declaration of Human Rights (UDHR) underscored this principle of state cooperation, while other international conventions, most notably the International Covenant on Economic, Social, and Cultural Rights (ICESCR), demands that states engage in "international assistance and cooperation." Although the legal foundation for "global obligations" is quite solid, a more challenging problem involves determining the means of implementing cooperative measures.

Gamze Erdem Türkelli analyses state responsibility within the context of extraterritorial human rights obligations, and she makes the argument that in this particular area of international law there is a pressing need for going beyond strict causation. Erdem Türkelli focuses on three different situations of possible state responsibility: a state's own acts; the conduct of international organisations that the state is a member of; and finally, the conduct of some other entity the state is associated with, including non-state actors. After surveying various approaches to state responsibility, she proposes a polycentric model that would not only reflect contributions to the commission of an internationally wrongful act, but also the ability and interest in addressing structural injustices moving forward.

The debate on whether states have extraterritorial human rights obligations has in large part been confined to the legal realm. Angela Müller brings a much-needed ethical perspective to this issue, taking the reader through the various strands of international relations theory as a way of testing the obligations that one state might have to individuals in some other state.

Almost by definition, the term "extraterritorial" indicates an area outside a state's own territorial borders. In a fascinating twist to this, Pauline Maillet examines the converse, namely, when a state treats a certain part of its land mass – the Charles de Gaulle airport in her case study – as being extraterritorial as a way of restricting certain legal protections. The final chapter in Part I looks at "digitalization," a phenomenon that, one could argue, has seemingly taken over the world, and if not that, at least the lives of so many of us. While human beings are vastly more "connected" to one another than at any time in history, the downside is the inability of an individual state – or even the international community – to undertake any form of meaningful regulation, and the problems this poses for the protection of human rights.

Part II – Enforcement

This part maps the extent to which extraterritorial human rights obligations (ETOs) have been recognised by global and regional human rights monitoring bodies. There are four chapters. Pribytkova's chapter focuses on some of the UN human rights treaty bodies. She distinguishes between what she calls remedial ETOs and global obligations, and applies her typology of global obligations to the work of the treaty bodies. This chapter shows how the UN human right treaty bodies have made an important contribution to the conceptualisation and enforcement of ETOs, while there are also areas in which further progress could be made, such as strengthening individual complaints procedures and expanding ETOs to transnational obligations, that is, direct human rights obligations for international organisations and non-state actors. The other three chapters in this part cover the European, Inter-American, and African regional systems of human rights protection. Each of these three regional chapters follows a similar pathway of analysis: they look both into the attribution of extraterritorial human rights obligations (in most cases through the prism of jurisdiction) and into the nature and scope of these obligations.

Haeck, Burbano Herrera, and Ghulam Farag map the case law of the European Court of Human Rights along the lines of the personal and spatial model of jurisdiction, and look into the question of concurrent jurisdiction in instances in which both the territorial state and a foreign state exercise jurisdiction simultaneously. They conclude that the Court has given an expansive reading to jurisdiction in its rich jurisprudence on the topic, extending extraterritorial jurisdiction beyond the legal space of the Council of Europe. Nonetheless, the expansion has been situated mainly within the personal model of jurisdiction. Also, critics have proposed a third model – that of functional jurisdiction. The authors wonder how much traction – if any – that third model can be given by the European Court, given strong opposition from states parties to a further expansion of extraterritorial jurisdiction.

As Haeck and Burbano Herrera explain in their chapter on the Inter-American system, the Inter-American Commission and Court have gone beyond the personal and spatial model of jurisdiction, to recognise a new extraterritorial jurisdictional link based on control over domestic activities with extraterritorial effect (functional or cause-and-effect jurisdiction). The latter model of jurisdiction has so far been applied to environmental pollution, but could be extended to home state's responsibility for the extraterritorial human rights violations by one of its (transnational) companies, the authors contend. Oloo and Vandenhole in their chapter on the African human rights system scrutinise whether a unique African perspective has been adopted on ETOs. The cases available do not allow for any definitive conclusion, but it looks like the African Commission on Human and Peoples' Rights is willing to endorse the three models of jurisdiction mentioned before.

Oloo and Vandenhole suggest that regional obligations, that is, global obligations as defined in Principle 8 of the Maastricht Guidelines but applied to the African context, would give a unique African touch to ETOs. These regional obligations would take on particular meaning with regard to the collective human rights to free disposal of wealth and natural resources and to development. The lack of explicit jurisdiction clause in the ACHPR additionally provides an opportunity to move beyond existing approaches to extraterritoriality.

In sum, three models of jurisdiction have taken shape, that is, the personal, spatial, and cause-and-effect model, although the amount of case law on the latter is more limited and the notion is yet to be fully clarified. Beyond these extraterritorial obligations in a strict sense, based on a notion of causality, global and regional obligations may be the next frontier for ETOs. Such global and regional obligations do not draw on causation of harm, but on notions of true universality of human rights, regardless of territorial location.

Part III – Migration and refugee protection

Migration and refugee protection is a key area in which extraterritorial human rights obligations are of utmost relevance. Migration and refugee protection is by definition about boundaries, sovereignty, and the crossing of borders. With the growth of policies that seek to exercise transnational migration control, the extraterritorial human rights obligations of states that set up or support such transnational migration control have been foregrounded too. This part contains four chapters.

Gammeltoft-Hansen introduces in a general review of the field the initial 'human rights turn' in transnational migration control and current challenges to reframe and redirect extraterritorial human rights claims. Somewhat surprisingly perhaps, the inclusion of migration issues in ETO case law happened rather late in the gradual development of ETOs. But the effect of being fairly late has been positive, since migrant and refugee cases have been able to benefit from precedents in other areas. On the other hand, migration cases are now at the forefront of new challenges for extraterritorial jurisdiction and shared responsibility. Gammeltoft-Hansen proposes two new turns. The first is to reframe existing approaches to ETOs to move beyond the status quo of current human rights jurisprudence. The second is to redirect accountability claims towards other legal regimes (such as international criminal law) and institutional settings (such as national courts in the Global South). The second chapter hoovers in on externalisation and outsourcing of migration control in particular. It explains the practices, maps state practice, and examines which role ETOs have played so far. Gombeer and Smis argue that the second wave of externalisation of migration control is more difficult to tackle, which leads them to plea for innovative understandings of jurisdiction so as to capture the actual relations of power. They too suggest that ETOs may not be sufficient, and that we may have to look closer at questions of ancillary forms of state responsibility (like complicity) too, and the implications for standing of affected migrants.

Two other chapters look into specific topics, i.e. that of climate change displacement and that of diplomatic asylum. Oluborode Jegede seeks to articulate the extraterritorial link of climate change displacement and socio-economic rights of the child under key instruments of the African human rights system, and explores how ETOs may be of help in addressing the adverse effects of climate displacement. He points out how in addition to the acts and omissions of African states, the acts or omission of actors from the Global North in their territories and in states within Africa impact on the human rights of children in Africa. Oluborode Jegede submits that provisions in African human rights instruments that deal with international cooperation and assistance support the position that states in the Global North have a remedial role to play in climate induced displacement of children in Africa.

Wilde submits that diplomatic asylum should be seen as an invocation of the idea that states have extraterritorial obligations. He equates diplomatic asylum with the operation of the notion of *non-refoulement* as applied in a state's embassy in a foreign country, hence the extraterritorial nature of any human rights obligations that a state has in that context. More generally, he challenges the common understanding that the European region has led developments on extraterritoriality. He suggests that it was rather the Latin American region that laid the foundation for extraterritorial human rights obligations, exactly through its much earlier normative commitment to diplomatic asylum. In this light, Wilde's chapter is also a nice example of decolonising human rights law.

Part IV – Financial assistance and sanctions

The initial interest in extraterritorial human rights obligations, certainly from the UN human rights treaty bodies like the CESCR and the CRC Committee, was mainly visible in their comments on (the lack of) development cooperation. This part engages with what used to be considered North-South or development issues. Even if that terminology may meanwhile have become problematic, what the chapters in this part continue to have in common is the very unequal bargaining power and power imbalances that characterise so strongly the relationship between so-called first- and third-world countries, between the Global North and the Global South. Several framings of the relationship between human rights and development have been undertaken, such as that of a human right to development; a human rights-based approach to development (HRBAD); a right to development; human rights conditionality for development cooperation; and an obligation under human rights law to provide development cooperation. In this part, some of these framings are revisited from an overall perspective of extraterritorial obligations: a HRBAD; sovereign debt; financialisation of development cooperation; and sanctions.

Chenwi looks into a HRBA in the context of development assistance, while also pointing out the need to address power inequalities to avert the risks of conditionalities and neocolonialism. In her chapter, she explores the nature and scope of ETOs in the context of development assistance across the spectrum of obligations to respect, protect, and fulfill rights. Chenwi concludes that a HRBAD provides a framework for consideration of ETOs in development assistance, so that states abide more operationally with their ETOs in the context of development aid.

Herre and Backes look into development finance in particular and apply an ETO lens to two aspects of the financialisation of public development cooperation, that is, its impact on substantive and procedural ETOs. They strongly argue in favour of assigning human rights obligations to private financiers as well as of strengthening state accountability for human rights violations related to development finance.

In her chapter on sovereign debt, Luce Scali focuses on another aspect of finance, i.e. sovereign financing. Sovereign financing has evolved into a primarily debt- and market-based practice. She examines the nature and relevance of ETOs in relation to sovereign debt as well as the usefulness of jurisdictional models developed so far. Luce Scali concludes that the cause-and-effect jurisdictional test may be relevant for sovereign debt, although the ETO framework shows some persistent limitations due to its focus on states as duty-bearers; difficulties in attributing conduct in complex multilateral activities; a difficult relationship with the public international law notion of jurisdiction; and the necessity and proximity of harm requirements.

Schechla's chapter moves away from finance and takes us to the question of economic sanctions. ETOs are relevant in the context of sanctions, in particular for states imposing sanctions, collectively or individually. Collective sanctions regimes raise the difficult question how to attribute obligations (and responsibility in case of violations) to all actors involved.

Part V – Finance, investment, and trade

The regulation of international trade, investment, and financial regulations as well as rules addressing the accountability of transnational corporations are of a genuine extraterritorial character as they concern policy fields which are, by definition, transnational. Therefore, one could assume that integrating extraterritorial human rights obligations into these policy fields would seem natural. However, it must also be noted that international human rights law and international economic law have always been considered as antagonistic, sometimes even, directly opposite fields of law – the former aiming at protecting and promoting human rights and other humanitarian aspirations, but the latter focusing on economic efficiency, transnational business expectations, and a general support of the global market.

The section starts with a fresh look at extraterritorial human rights obligations and International Financial Institutions (IFIs) by Stéphanie de Moerloose, Gamze Erdem Türkelli, and Joshua Curtis. As these institutions finance and support development projects or macroeconomic policy reforms, they have a significant impact on the realisation of human rights. While this has been subject to public and academic debates for more than three decades, the discussion increasingly employs the language of extraterritorial obligations. The authors identify two axes in this context: obligations of states as members and owners of IFIs on the one side and obligations of IFIs themselves on the other. Regarding the first axis, the authors suggest that despite the separate legal personality of IFIs, member states retain responsibility for their involvement in the IFIs decision-making processes. Concerning direct human rights obligations of IFIs, the chapter shows that the scholarly literature remains divided, but treaty bodies started to formulate direct expectations of IFIs. After an analysis of internal and external accountability mechanisms, the authors conclude with a number of proposals for further research and political development, including the modification of the charters of IFIs to restrict their immunity in case of human rights violations.

In the following chapter, Daniel Augenstein focuses on home-state regulation of corporations as a possible indication of the home state's extraterritorial human rights obligations. The chapter reviews current legislative trends in the area of home-state regulation of corporations in light of states' international legal obligations to prevent and redress business-related human rights violations outside their borders. Augenstein finds the basis for these obligations in the UN Guiding Principles on Business and Human Rights (UNGP) and assesses both transparency regulations such as the UK Modern Slavery Act as well as due diligence legislation including the French Loi de Vigilance and the Dutch Wet Zorgplicht Kinderarbeid. The chapter traces a convergence between these regulatory models arguing that it suggests the emergence of a new legal consensus on business and human rights, according to which states' regulation of the impacts of business enterprises on human rights should be anchored in international legal obligations towards foreign victims of business-related human rights violations.

While the human rights impact of IFIs and transnational corporations constitute classic topics of the debate on extraterritorial human rights obligations, the next two chapters on tax transparency and corruption address more recent elements of the discourse. Rod Michelmore argues that tax-related illicit financial flows from Least Developed Countries (LDCs) are a fundamentally important human rights issue in particular due to the impact of this loss on poverty. The chapter shows that many LDCs face systemic barriers in accessing the international tax cooperation needed to administer and enforce revenue laws against those who illicitly transfer income and capital offshore. Michelmore claims that states implicated in the regulation of offshore wealth management are required by extraterritorial human rights obligations to take the necessary steps to prevent domestic private actors from concealing tax-related illicit financial flows as these drain scarce public revenues from the most vulnerable countries.

Subsequently, Khulekani Moyo explores the developments of extraterritorial human rights obligations in the field of anti-corruption and anti-bribery laws. He examines international and regional treaties and instruments adopted to curb corruption and assesses the extent to which these instruments impose obligations on states beyond their territorial borders to adopt legislative, investigative, adjudicatory, and other measures combatting bribery and corruption. Although corruption impedes the realisation of human rights, human rights instruments do not address corruption directly and monitoring bodies have failed to bring conceptual clarity to the question of how corruption can potentially be construed as a human rights violation. However, such an approach would, as Moyo argues, improve enforcement of anti-corruption regulations at national and international levels.

Moving to international investment law as a traditional topic of international economic law, but a new topic for human rights law, Tara Van Ho develops an innovative argument which not only places a duty to respect and protect human rights on the parties of a specific international investment agreement, but also on third states. While there is a general agreement in academia shared by many treaty bodies and human rights experts that international investment agreements reduce the regulatory space for states to fulfill their human rights obligations and that states should reform or abandon their investment agreements, Van Ho argues that also states which are not parties to the respective agreements have an obligation to assist and cooperate with the treaty parties to ensure that investment agreements do not lead to negative impacts on human rights. Such third states obligations can be built on the obligation to international assistance and corporation enshrined in Article 2 (1) ICESCR and would be applicable in the context of World Bank policies towards investment protection or UNCTAD activities aimed at developing new model treaty language which would avoid or at least reduce the negative impact of investment agreements on human rights.

The final chapter in this section turns to a much-debated issue – access to medicines and the World Trade Organization's Agreement on Trade-Related Aspects of Intellectual Property Rights (TRIPS) – which became a current topic again in light of the controversies about access to COVID-19 medication and vaccines. Jennifer Sellin argues that access to essential medicines is a global and shared responsibility and that states have extraterritorial human rights obligations to respect, protect, and fulfill access to medicines. However, international intellectual property regimes, particularly TRIPS, may impede access to medicines and negatively impact states' ability to comply with their human rights obligations. The chapter demonstrates the value and importance of health-related extraterritorial obligations to facilitate and contribute to achieving universal access to medicines. Selin shows that it is possible to identify specific reform options with regards to access to medicines concerning TRIPS as well as so-called TRIP+ measures in free trade agreements based on the extraterritorial dimension of health-related human rights.

Part VI – Peace and security

One of the great ironies involving extraterritorial obligations is that at the same time that the "territorial" approach first began to be challenged and ETO principles developed, the "war on terror" was announced, and one of the most disturbing policies of this was the practice of extraordinary rendition, where a suspected terrorist is abducted in one country and then sent to some other state for detention and "enhanced interrogation" (torture). As Elspeth Guild examines in her chapter, extraordinary rendition was essentially a blueprint for how states (and particularly the United States) made use of the blind spots of a "territorial" interpretation of international human rights law as a way of avoiding responsibility for the human rights violations that were carried out, but almost always in another country and at the hands of foreign actors.

Another component of the "war on terror" was the greatly increased capacities of states to engage in both domestic and extraterritorial surveillance. Yet, absent Edward Snowden's shocking revelations, the full extent of these practices would never have become known, and arguably, are still not known to the fullest extent. Marko Milanovic's chapter explores the tension between state surveillance practices that truly know no national boundaries against a regulatory and enforcement regime that has been slow to escape the confines of the territorial paradigm it has placed itself in.

The world's booming arms trade is certainly international in scope as Western sellers are continually on the lookout for purchasers of these wares in all corners of the globe. Like some of the other practices under scrutiny in this section, arms sales also make profit (literally) when the selling state can use the sovereign of the receiving state as a way of avoiding any responsibility for its own actions. The common rationale is that the seller merely provides the weapons, and how the recipient makes use of these weapons is determined by this other sovereign state. Of course, this gives arms-selling states – mainly comprised of Western states, particularly the United States – license to sell to even the most horrible and notorious regimes. One central question addressed by Marina Aksenova in her chapter 'Arms Trade and Weapons Export Control' is whether the Arms Trade Treaty, which went into effect in late December 2014, will change any of this.

One of the enduring questions raised by the recognition of extraterritorial human rights obligations is the relationship between international human rights and international human rights law, a topic that Vito Todeschini provides extensive treatment to in his chapter 'Extraterritorial Military Action.' While Todeschini deals with traditional forms of warfare, Matthias Kettemann and Ana Sophia Tiedeke address the specter of a new form of warfare: cyberwarfare. Although it is widely, if not universally, recognised that cybersecurity is in the interests of all, what has in large part prevented this is the complete mismatch between an extraterritorial phenomenon of cyberwarfare, on the one hand, and enforcement mechanisms that remain tethered to national borders.

Part VII – Environment

The section on Environment and Extraterritorial Human Rights Obligations (ETOs) features three chapters on climate justice, cross-border pollution, and biodiversity. These three issue areas are at the forefront of the ETO debate with respect to the environment. Another chapter on ETOs and the use of common waterways was envisaged but did not materialise. The section of course has limitations in terms of the topics covered. For instance, although the biodiversity chapter links to the importance of ecosystems, ecosystems conservation is not directly addressed. Similarly, though climate change and cross-border pollution indirectly address the right to a healthy and sustainable environment and clean air and water resources, these topics do not have their own chapters.

Sara Seck's chapter on climate justice inquires whether the *Maastricht Principles* have contributed to clarifying human rights obligations beyond borders in relation to climate change and takes issue with the use of "extraterritoriality" as a concept when referring to human rights, which may reinforce territorial boundaries in ways detrimental to human rights protection. Seck points to overtures being made through the recognition of substantive environmental rights such as an autonomous right to a safe, clean, healthy, and sustainable environment with implications for human rights related to climate change and corresponding obligations. Finally, Seck argues for a relational conceptualisation of human rights obligations related to climate change coupled with international cooperation duties and concludes on a positive note, reminding that we are all 'ecologically embedded relational individuals.'

Antal Berkes tackles ETOs and cross-border pollution, namely the direct or indirect transboundary introduction of hazardous substances into the components of the environment, air, land, water, and the atmosphere. Berkes credits the *Maastricht Principles* for setting a good baseline for ETOs for human rights harms linked to cross-border pollution and surveys the obligations to respect, protect, and fulfill. Berkes argues that the progressive development of international law that prescribes more punctual threshold criteria for harm in cross-border pollution will enhance human rights protections.

Philip Seufert and Sofia Monsalve Suárez evoke the close relationship between biodiversity and the realisation of human rights. They focus on the right to food as a gateway to their discussion on the need for "cross-fertilization" between environmental law and human rights law. In this cross-fertilization, Seufert and Monsalve Suárez call on states to prioritise the rights of marginalised and disadvantaged individuals and groups. They also argue for the recognition of biodiversity as a global commons to be protected as a common concern for mankind in order to realise human rights related to biodiversity.

Part I

Conceptualization and theoretical foundations

1

The historical development of extraterritorial obligations

Mark Gibney

The year 2021 marks the ten-year anniversary of the signing of the *Maastricht Principles* on Extraterritorial Obligations in the Area of Economic, Social, and Cultural Rights (Maastricht ETO Principles), and this Handbook is testament to how the notion of extraterritorial human rights obligations has challenged and fundamentally changed our understanding of 'human rights'. A simple way of framing these issues is this: while international law regulates the (horizontal) relationship between sovereign states, and international human rights law regulates the (vertical) relationship between a state and its own citizens – ETOs are concerned with the 'diagonal' relationship between a state and individuals living in other countries. Or to put this in even more basic terms: what human rights obligations (if any) do states have to individuals who are outside its territorial borders (Skogly and Gibney 2002)?

One other introductory remark relates to terminology. At one point, scholars employed a variety of terms to describe what was essentially the same phenomenon: transnational; third state; transborder; international; cross-border; global; and so on. However, the most commonly used term was 'extraterritorial' and that is the term that has gained general acceptance and is used here (Gibney 2013). Still, there are several problems with this term, most notably that 'extraterritorial' might seem to refer to human rights obligations that are separate and distinct – in a word, extra – from those a state is already bound by in its domestic sphere. Because this is a misnomer, the better term would be to simply refer to a state's 'human rights obligations', with the understanding that these obligations have both an international and domestic application. Unfortunately, international law has not yet progressed to this point. Thus, 'extraterritorial' is used to describe a state's legal responsibilities to individuals living in other lands.

This introductory chapter is divided into two sections. Following this brief introduction, Part I analyzes some of the perceived shortcomings in human rights protection that have ensued from a 'territorial' reading of international human rights law. Particular focus is given to two rulings of the International Court of Justice (ICJ) – *Nicaragua v. United States* (1986) and *Bosnia v. Serbia* (2007) – both of which involve a state providing massive levels of military and economic assistance to paramilitary forces located in another country that carried out gross and systematic human rights violations (ICJ 1986) or genocide (ICJ 2007), and the question was whether the state providing such assistance had thereby acted in violation of international law. In both cases, the Court ruled that the 'assisting' state had not. The landmark ruling of the European Court of Human Rights (ECtHR) in the *Bankovic* case presents yet another 'territorial' reading of

DOI: 10.4324/9781003090014-3

international human rights law. Finally, although these cases involve war and the violation of civil and political rights (CPR), similar issues, with similar results, have also arisen in the context of economic, social, and cultural rights (ESCR).

One of the great ironies at work here is that international human rights law has been heralded for the manner in which it has pierced the shell of state sovereignty in that states can no longer hide their egregious practices from international scrutiny on the grounds that this constituted a 'domestic' matter. However, what repeatedly happens in the extraterritorial context is that one state uses the state sovereignty of another state as a way of avoiding any responsibility for its own actions.

Part II provides a brief overview of the growing acceptance of Extraterritorial Obligations (ETO) principles. One of the central roles in all this was the establishment of the Extraterritorial Obligations (ETO) Consortium in Heidelberg, Germany in 2007, an initiative led by Rolf Kunnemann of FIAN, which is where the ETO Secretariat has been placed ever since. Later that same year, the first global ETO conference was held in Geneva and since then Consortium membership has continued to expand not only in terms of size but also in terms of global coverage.

No doubt the crowning achievement of the ETO Consortium was the adoption of the Maastricht ETO Principles by a group of eminent international lawyers in 2011. There is only space in this chapter to provide a brief overview of these principles; however, it is important to emphasize at the outset that these constitute *lex lata* (law as it is) and are not *lex ferenda* (law as it should be). In short, for the signatories of the Maastricht ETO Principles, extraterritorial human rights obligations exist under present international law.

Still, there is little question that the "territorial" approach continues to dominate the interpretation of international human rights law. For one thing, there is not a single state that has been willing to publicly acknowledge having extraterritorial human rights obligations. In addition, and making specific reference to the ICJ rulings mentioned above, there is a continued hesitancy to move away from a territorial interpretation of international law. Yet, international human rights law is changing, and given the growing recognition of the manner in which a state can have an enormous effect (both positive and negative) on human rights practices and protections in other countries, it is indeed noteworthy that ETO principles have come to be widely accepted by the U.N. treaty bodies and in other international law venues as well (Wilde 2013).

Territory and human rights

Although human rights are declared to be "universal", until fairly recently it was commonly accepted that a state's human rights obligations extended no further than its own territorial borders. There are at least two reasons for this. The first involves the international law principle that while a state can always lawfully act within its own territory, it must have permission to act in another state, otherwise it will be violating this other state's sovereignty.

The second reason comes from international human rights law itself. Although there are slight variations in terminology, human rights treaties oftentimes make reference to a state's 'territory' or to its exercise of 'jurisdiction' (or both) as a way of limiting the nature and scope of state's obligations. For example, Article 2 (1) of the International Covenant on Civil and Political Rights (ICCPR) provides: 'Each State Party to the present Covenant undertakes to respect and to ensure to all individuals within its territory and subject to its jurisdiction the rights recognized in the present Covenant…'. Article 2 (1) of the Torture Convention employs similar language: 'Each State Party shall take effective legislative, administrative, judicial or other measures to prevent acts of torture in any territory under its jurisdiction'. The final example comes from Article 1 of the European Convention on Human Rights, which references 'jurisdiction' but makes no mention of 'territory'. 'The High Contracting Parties shall secure to everyone within their jurisdiction the rights and freedoms defined in … this Convention'.

What has evolved is a sharp divide between states, on the one hand, and various U.N. institutions. Seemingly without exception, states continue to act as if their human rights obligations are confined to their own domestic borders. In contrast to this, the U.N. treaty bodies and a number of Special Rapporteurs have interpreted international human rights law more broadly. For example, notwithstanding the restrictive language quoted above, both the ICCPR and the Torture Convention have been given an extraterritorial reading by the treaty bodies that monitor their implementation.

The Human Rights Committee (HRC) in its General Comment 31 (2004) on the scope of the ICCPR:

> States Parties are required … to respect and to ensure the Covenant rights to all persons who may be within their territory and to all persons subject to their jurisdiction. This means that a state party must respect and ensure the rights laid down in the Covenant to anyone within the power or effective control of that state Party, even if not situated within the territory of the state Party.

Similarly, in its ruling in *Lopez v. Uruguay* (HRC 1981), the HRC unanimously rejected the position put forth by Uruguay that its treaty obligations did not apply to its actions in another state (Argentina), instead holding that the key was the 'relationship between the individual and the state in relation to a violation of any of the rights set forth in the Covenant, wherever they occurred'. Employing even stronger language, in an individual opinion, Christian Tomuschat noted that Uruguay's territorial interpretation of the ICCPR would naturally lead to 'utterly absurd results'. Going even further, Tomuschat argues:

> Never was it envisaged … to grant states parties unfettered discretionary power to carry out willful and deliberate attacks against the freedom and personal integrity against their citizens abroad. Consequently, despite the wording of article 2 (1), the events which took place outside Uruguay come within the purview of the Covenant.

The Committee Against Torture (CAT) has taken a similar position, most notably in its General Comment 2:

> Article 2 (1) requires that each state party shall take effective measures to prevent acts of torture not only in its sovereign territory but also 'in any territory under its jurisdiction'. The Committee has recognized that 'any territory' includes all areas where the state party exercises, directly or indirectly, in whole or in part, *de jure* or *de facto* effective control, in accordance with international law.

This same difference in interpretation also has arisen with respect to the International Covenant on Economic, Social and Cultural Rights (ICESCR) as well. Article 2 (1) of ICESCR provides:

> Each state Party to the present Covenant undertakes to take steps, individually and through international assistance and co-operation, especially economic and technical, to the maximum of its available resources, with a view to achieving progressively the full realization of the rights recognized in the present Covenant by all appropriate means, including particularly the adoption of legislative measures.

Note that neither 'territory' nor 'jurisdiction' are referenced in the treaty itself (the Optional Protocol does refer to 'jurisdiction') and the states parties are also obligated under the Convention to engage in 'international assistance and cooperation' (Skogly 2006). In addition, the Committee on Economic, Social, and Cultural Rights has repeatedly affirmed that the Convention has an extraterritorial application (Wilde 2013).

Still, states continue to resist acknowledging ETOs of any kind. One of the most revealing examples of this was the country study of Sweden conducted by the former Special Rapporteur on the Right to Health (Paul Hunt). It is well known that Sweden has long been one of the most generous countries in the world in terms of the amount of foreign assistance it provides. However, when government officials were asked whether, as a state party to the ICESCR, there was a legal obligation to provide such aid, Swedish government officials demurred. In his report, Hunt soundly rejects such a position:

> If there is no legal obligation underpinning the human rights responsibility of international assistance and cooperation, inescapably all international assistance and cooperation is based fundamentally upon charity. While such a position might have been tenable 100 years ago, it is unacceptable in the twenty-first century.
>
> *(Hunt 2007, p. 28)*

As a final word on this, it is by no means clear that Hunt's scathing criticism brought about any change in state policy or practices – either in Sweden or in any other country. Instead, 'territory' has become the default position even for a treaty where there is no mention of this.

Security issues

When human rights scholars began to question the primacy of "territory", it was generally on the basis of the kinds of inconsistent results this so often led to. As an example, one of the most widely recognized principles in international law is *nonrefoulement*: a state has an obligation not to send an individual (usually a foreign national who has arrived at its borders seeking refugee protection) back to a country where this person's life or freedom would be threatened. Yet, while there is strong adherence to this principle (at least in theory), at the same time international law seems to allow states to pursue policies that can have devastating consequences for those living in other states. One such example has been the ability to sell massive amounts of military equipment to countries that then use these weapons against civilian populations.

The ostensible difference between these two scenarios is that, in the first case, the foreign national is at some point on this other state's territory. This, among other things, helps explain how and why states are now making such efforts to prevent refugees from being able to reach their national borders in the first place (Gammeltoft-Hansen; Gombeer and Smis, this volume). In the scenario involving arms sales, no territorial link is present. Based on this distinction, in the first case the state has a legal obligation to provide human rights protection, while in the second case, at least under a territorial interpretation of international human rights law, the sending state has no obligations outside its borders. One question is whether the Arms Trade Treaty (ATT), which went into effect in December 2014, will significantly change this (Aksenova, this volume). The same issue arises with respect to the Responsibility to Protect (R2P) initiative, which places a duty on the international community to intervene in countries experiencing gross and systematic human rights violations (Gibney 2011). Still, the 'territorial' interpretation of international human rights law remains dominant.

This is not to suggest that states are able to act outside their own national borders with impunity. The clearest cases arise when a state acts directly in another state, as was the case in the

ICJ's rulings in the *Namibia Advisory Opinion* (ICJ 1970), the *Wall Advisory Opinion* (ICJ 2004), and *DRC v. Uganda* (ICJ 2005) (Wilde 2013). The Court took a similar position in *Nicaragua v. United States* (ICJ 1986) when it ruled that the United States had acted in violation of international law when U.S. agents acted directly against the ruling government in that country, including mining Nicaragua's harbors.

However, the more vexing question is when a state does not act directly but through local proxies instead. This was the second question of state responsibility raised in the *Nicaragua* case and the ICJ ruled that the United States was not responsible for any of the widespread atrocities carried out by the Contra rebel forces, notwithstanding the substantial levels of military, political, and economic support provided by the United States. According to the Court, in order for such responsibility to arise it would have to be established that the U.S. government had exercised 'effective control' over the Contras. It remains unclear when this standard is met; however, at one point the Court framed the issue in these terms:

> In light of the evidence and material available to it, the Court is not satisfied that *all* the operations launched by the contra force, at *every* stage of the conflict, reflected strategy and tactics *wholly* devised by the United States.
>
> *(ICJ 1986, para. 106 (emphases supplied))*

There are a number of questions raised by this case (Gibney, Tomasevski, and Vedsted-Hansen 1999). One simply is the strong disincentive that states will have of exercising 'effective control' over another state or an entity in another state, thereby opening itself up to a finding of state responsibility for any resulting harms carried out by the recipient. A second problem is the near impossibility of ever meeting the 'effective control' standard in the first place. The Contras were essentially creatures of the U.S. government and the relationship between the two was extraordinarily close, something the ICJ itself readily acknowledged. Still, the Court ruled that in order for the United States to be responsible for the human rights violations carried out by the Contras, the U.S. would have to control virtually every activity these paramilitary forces engaged in. Finally, under the Court's approach, state responsibility is treated as being either-or: either a state has exercised 'effective control' over the foreign entity and is therefore fully responsible for its human rights violations – or, much more likely, it has not exercised that level of control (purposely or otherwise), in which case it will not bear any responsible at all.

What is missing in such an approach is any sense of the nature and level of support that is provided, as well as the foreseeability or likelihood of harm occurring because of this assistance. Reflecting many of these concerns, the International Criminal Tribunal for the (Former) Yugoslavia (ICTY) described the ICJ's 'effective control' standard as not being consonant with the 'very logic of the entire system of state responsibility', and also 'at variance with judicial and state practice'. Rather than employing this standard, the ICTY relied on an 'overall control' standard instead.

> In order to attribute the acts of the military or paramilitary group to a state, it must be proved that the state wields overall control over the group, not only by equipping and financing the group, but also by coordinating or helping in the general planning of its military activity. Only then can the state be held internationally accountable for any misconduct of the group. However, it is not necessary that, in addition, the state should also issue, either to the head or to members of the group, instructions for the commission of specific acts contrary to international law.
>
> *(ICTY 1999, para. 131)*

More than two decades after its decision in *Nicaragua*, the ICJ returned to the issue of extraterritorial state responsibility in *Bosnia v. Serbia* (ICJ 2007). Similar to *Nicaragua*, the key issue in this case was whether Serbia was responsible for genocide that had been carried out by various Bosnian Serb paramilitary forces it was allied with. By the time this case arose, the U.N. International Law Commission had completed its (Draft) Articles on State Responsibility (ASR) (Crawford 2002) and the ICJ relied heavily on these. The first issue it addressed was whether the Bosnian Serb forces were acting as 'state agents' for the Serbian state. Interpreting Article 4 ASR, the Court held that there was no evidence they were *de jure* state agents, and in order to be considered as *de facto* state agents of Serbia it would have to be established that these paramilitary forces had 'complete dependence' on the Serb government, which it concluded had not been established.

The second issue was whether, under Article 8 ASR, the Serbian government had 'directed and controlled' the actions of the Bosnian Serb forces at the time genocide was carried out. Taking direct aim at the ICTY's ruling in *Tadic*, the Court invoked the 'effective control' test from its *Nicaragua* decision, holding that in order to achieve this standard it must be shown 'that this "effective control" was exercised, or that the state's instructions were given, in respect of each operation in which the alleged violations occurred, not generally in respect of the overall operations taken by the persons or groups of persons having committed the violations' (ICJ 2007, para. 400). Making reference to what it perceived as 'differences' between the Bosnian Serbs and the Serbian government following the overthrow of Srebrenica when most acts of genocide had taken place, the Court ruled that this requisite level of 'effective control' had not been achieved.

The final issue was whether Serbia was responsible for being complicit in genocide and the ICJ applied Article 16 of the Articles on State Responsibility, which reads:

> A state which aids or assists another state in the commission of an internationally wrongful act by the latter is internationally responsible for doing so if:
>
> - (a) That state does so with knowledge of the circumstances of the internationally wrongful act; and
> - (b) The act would be internationally wrongful if committed by that state.

The Court rejected the claim that Serbia was 'complicit' in genocide on the grounds that it had not been proven 'beyond any doubt' that Serbia possessed the specific intent (*dolus specialis*) required by the Genocide Convention.

> A point which is clearly decisive in this connection is that it was not conclusively shown that the decision to eliminate physically the adult male population of the Muslim community from Srebrenica was brought to the attention of the Belgrade authorities when it was taken; the … decision was taken shortly before it was actually carried out, a process that took a very short time (essentially between 13 and 16 July 1995), despite the exceptionally high number of victims. It has therefore not been conclusively established that, at the crucial time, the FRY supplied aid to the perpetrators of the genocide in full awareness that the aid supplied would be used to commit genocide.
>
> *(ICJ 2007, para. 423)*

In sum, notwithstanding the widespread atrocities suffered by the Bosnian Muslim population and despite the extraordinarily close ties between the Bosnian Serb forces and the Serbian government, the ICJ ruled that the Serbian Republic was not 'responsible' in any manner for the acts of genocide that occurred following the fall of Srebrenica (Gibney 2007). However, in a part of the *Bosnia* ruling that has received only minor attention, the Court held that Serbia had failed to meet its obligations to 'prevent' genocide and to 'punish' those who had engaged in it. The former was based on the apparent ability of the Serb state to 'influence' the actions of its Bosnian Serb allies, and the latter on the basis that Serbia had failed to fully cooperate with the ICTY.

To be clear, in neither of these two cases did the ICJ announce that it was basing its decision on a 'territorial' interpretation of international law. Yet, one way of understanding that this is exactly what the Court has done is to look at a situation where a government provides similar forms of assistance – but to a domestic group rather than to an entity in some other country. One such example would be the relationship between the government of Sudan and the Janjaweed, a domestic paramilitary group that has engaged in all manner of human rights atrocities, including ethnic cleansing. The Sudanese government has worked closely with the Janjaweed forces, but certainly no closer than the United States with the Contras or the Serbian government with various Bosnian Serb allies. And yet, Sudan's responsibility goes unquestioned. The only difference is that in *Nicaragua* and *Bosnia* territorial borders were crossed, while this is not the case in the Sudan.

Before turning to situations involving ESCR, the last security case to be mentioned is the ECtHR's landmark ruling in *Bankovic v. Belgium et al.* (ECtHR 2001), which was based on a North Atlantic Treaty Organization (NATO) bombing mission over Serbia (before it was a state party to the European Convention) that harmed and/or killed a group of civilians, who then brought suit against the NATO members. The key issue was whether these individuals were within the 'jurisdiction' of these states at the time these events occurred. As noted earlier, Article 1 of the European Convention reads: 'The High Contracting Parties shall secure to everyone within their jurisdiction the rights and freedoms defined in … this Convention'. In a Grand Chamber decision, the ECtHR ruled these individuals were not within the jurisdiction of any of the state parties and dismissed the case as inadmissible (Lawson 2004; Orakhelashvili 2003).

In arriving at its conclusion, the ECtHR noted that the original version of Article 1 had included the term 'territory', and although this was removed in the final draft, the ECtHR maintained that the Convention remained territorial – or what it described as being 'essentially' or 'primarily' territorial – and that because of this the Convention only applied extraterritorially under 'exceptional circumstances'. It remains unclear when an 'exceptional circumstance' exists. However, what we do know from the result in this case is that killing or harming civilians in foreign lands by means of an aerial bombardment (somehow) does not meet this standard.

Since *Bankovic*, the ECtHR has backtracked, at least to some degree, from its ruling (Milanovic 2012). Still, with extraordinarily rare exception, when the state parties act outside of Europe – as they do almost as a matter of course – they will not be regulated by the strictures of the European Convention. Instead, there is one set of human rights standards within Europe – and another set of standards when these states operate outside of 'Europe' (Roxstrom, Gibney, and Einarsen 2005).

Non-security issues

As we have seen in the analysis above, issues of extraterritorial human rights obligations might arise at times in the conduct of security operations. However, the more common situation occurs far from the field of battle. Yet, even here there has been a strong tendency to read international human rights law in a territorial fashion, as we will see in the following two case studies.

The first was developed by the Crowley Program in International Human Rights at Fordham University Law School (Hoodbhoy, Flaherty, and Higgins 2005), and it centres around what has been termed the Mexico City Policy ('Global Gag Order') and the human rights consequences this U.S. law has had on healthcare practices in Kenya (and, presumably, other developing countries as well). By way of background, the Mexico City Policy was an Executive Memorandum issued by President George W. Bush on 22 January 2001 that reinstated a set of restrictions prohibiting foreign non-governmental recipients of U.S. family planning funds from promoting or advocating abortion as a means of family planning in situations other than that of protecting a woman's health. These restrictions bind U.S. Agency for International Development (USAID), the principal conduit through which U.S. funding for healthcare is provided to Kenya and other developing countries. At the time the Global Gag Rule was issued in 2001, USAID provided 16 percent of all healthcare funding to Kenya and 28.4 percent of the Ministry of Health's development budget. What also has to be noted is that although the United States has signed the ICESCR, it has never ratified the treaty. Still, as a signatory it has obligated itself not to violate the Convention's provisions. And as mentioned earlier, the ICESCR makes no mention of either 'territory' or 'jurisdiction'.

The Fordham study focused on two Kenyan family planning organizations that refused to sign the required pledge not 'to perform or actively promote abortion', and USAID responded by cutting off funding to both, which ultimately resulted in the closure of a number of family planning clinics and outreach programs. The end result of all this is that the number of Kenyan women receiving family planning services was severely reduced, leading to a serious deterioration of maternal health in that country. In sum, there is a direct link between the reduction of U.S. aid and ESCR violations in Kenya. The (legal) question is whether the U.S. has thereby committed an internationally wrongful act. Another way of framing this is to ask whether the U.S. has any human rights obligations to women in Kenya and whether it has violated these obligations by eliminating family planning funds as it did.

The second case involves the Canadian mining corporation TVI Pacific and its operations on the island of Mindanao in the Philippines (Seck 2008). In 2004, a delegation of community members from Mindanao traveled to Canada and met with Canadian lawmakers about the environmental devastation and health consequences brought about by TVI Pacific's operations. In March 2005, two community members presented additional evidence to a parliamentary committee, which then endorsed a proposal to establish 'clear legal norms' to regulate Canadian multinational corporations (MNCs) in their operations in countries outside of Canada. However, such legislation was not pursued any further at that time because of governmental concerns that the international community is still in the early stages of defining and measuring corporate social responsibility, especially in the area of human rights.

Not to be overlooked, the government of the Philippines has failed to protect its own citizens and has therefore committed a human rights violation itself. However, what about Canada and other countries whose MNCs are operating in the world, oftentimes with limited regulation? Although there have been some recent domestic efforts to regulate MNCs, international law continues to struggle with this issue, and one important reason is the great hesitancy in recognizing that states have human rights obligations beyond their own territorial borders.

The extraterritorial challenge

As we have seen in the previous section, although a 'territorial' interpretation of international human rights law continues to dominate, it is important to note that seldom is a strictly territorial approach taken. For example, in the *Nicaragua* case, the ICJ not only ruled against the United States for harmful acts carried out directly by U.S. agents in Nicaragua, but it also ruled that the U.S. would bear responsibility for human rights violations carried out by the Contras – so long as it exercised 'effective control' over them. Similarly, in the *Bankovic* case, the ECtHR did not adopt a strictly 'territorial' approach. Rather, it held that the European Convention could apply outside of 'Europe' – but only under 'exceptional circumstances'.

Aside from the problem of knowing when these standards happen to be reached (let alone where they came from) what both of these adjudicatory bodies appear to be doing is hedging their bets: international human rights treaties are territorial (for the most part). This is easier to see in *Bankovic*. The ECtHR noted that the original draft of the Convention included a reference to 'territory' in Article 1, and although this term was removed in the final draft, the ECtHR maintained the position that the territorial basis of the Convention had not been changed. On the other hand, and for whatever reasons, the ECtHR found it necessary to allow for certain exceptions and in that way interpreted the treaty as being 'primarily' or 'essentially' territorial. The problem is that a treaty cannot be both territorial and non-territorial or semi-territorial at the same time.

Around the turn of the century, scholars and members of civil society organizations began reacting to the inconsistencies in these rulings and the manner in which human rights were left unprotected under a territorial approach. In addition, what also became evident is that many states that adhered to human rights standards at home tended to ignore these same standards when they operated in the world.

In the Spring 2003, sympathetic members of the U.N. Committee on Economic, Social, and Cultural Rights met with some human rights practitioners and scholars to discuss ETOs and what recognition of such obligations would mean in the area of ESCR. In 2007, a group of five convened in Heidelberg, Germany and established the Extraterritorial Obligations (ETO) Consortium. Later that same year, the first global ETO conference was held in Geneva.

In 2011, 40 prominent international lawyers signed the Maastricht ETO Principles in the Area of Economic, Social, and Cultural Rights (de Schutter et al. 2012). The Maastricht ETO Principles are a clear articulation that, under present international law, all states have ETOs. As General Principle 3 reads: 'States have obligations to respect, protect and fulfil human rights, including civil, cultural, economic, political and social rights, both within their territories and extra-territorially'. Furthermore, Article 9 entitled *Scope of Jurisdiction* provides:

> A state has obligations to respect, protect and fulfil economic, social and cultural rights in any of the following:
>
> a) situations over which it exercises authority or effective control, whether or not such control is exercised in accordance with international law;
> b) situations over which state acts or omissions bring about foreseeable effects on the enjoyment of economic, social and cultural rights, whether within or outside its territory;
> c) situations in which the state, acting separately or jointly, whether through its executive, legislative or judicial branches, is in a position to exercise decisive influence or to take measures to realize economic, social and cultural rights extraterritorially, in accordance with international law.

One way to get a sense of the nature and scope of the Maastricht ETO Principles is to contrast its reading of international law regarding the regulation of MNCs with the *Guiding Principles on Business and Human Rights: Implementing the United Nations 'Protect, Respect and Remedy' Framework* (U.N. High Commissioner for Human Rights 2011). Principle 2 of the Guiding Principles reads: 'States should set out clearly the expectation that all business enterprises domiciled in their territory and/or jurisdiction respect human rights throughout their operations'. However, as the commentary makes clear, such regulation of business operations in other states is permissive but not required.

> States are not generally required under international human rights law to regulate the extraterritorial activities domiciled in their territory and/or jurisdiction. Nor are they generally prohibited from doing so, provided there is a recognized jurisdictional basis. Within these parameters some human rights treaty bodies recommend that home states take steps to prevent abuse abroad by business enterprises within their jurisdiction.

In contrast to this, under the Maastricht ETO Principles not only does the 'home' state have an obligation to regulate its own MNCs, but so do other states that are in a position to do so. Principle 24 *Obligation to Regulate* reads:

> All states must take necessary measures to ensure that non-state actors which they are in a position to regulate … such as private individuals and organizations, and transnational corporations and other business enterprises, do not nullify or impair the enjoyment of economic, social and cultural rights. These include administrative, legislative, investigative, adjudicatory and other measures. All other states have a duty to refrain from nullifying or impairing the discharge of this obligation to protect.

ETO Principles are now frequently referenced by the U.N. treaty bodies in General Comments and Concluding Observations to state reports. In addition, a number of U.N. Special Rapporteurs have explicitly acknowledged states' ETOs (ESCR-Net 2015).

Beyond this, in June 2014, the Human Rights Council adopted a resolution backed by Ecuador and South Africa to establish an Inter-Government Working Group with the mandate to elaborate a legally binding instrument on Transnational Corporations and Other Business Enterprises with Respect to Human Rights. A second revised draft of a treaty was completed in August 2020. It is important to note that the draft treaty would still place regulatory responsibility only on states parties. A proposal that would go much further than this in protecting human rights would be to explicitly recognize that MNCs have human rights obligations (Erdem Turkelli 2020).

Conclusion

Although human rights are declared to be universal, the responsibility to protect such rights has long been confined by territorial considerations. In that way, while a state has human rights obligations to its own citizens, what remains contested is whether it has any obligations to those living in other countries. One reason for this is the international law principle that a state is not to infringe on the sovereignty of another state. A second reason is that many international human rights treaties contain language that reifies territorial limitations. Yet, even treaties that make no reference to 'territory' have quite often been given a territorial interpretation, particularly by states themselves.

Two decades ago, scholars first began to challenge the primacy of territory, mainly on the basis that this often led to situations where human rights were left unprotected. Moreover, there was also a certain degree of irony in that so many states that adhered to human rights principles at home were so willing to abandon, or at least turn a blind eye toward, these very same principles when they acted outside their national borders.

The word 'development' in the title of this chapter is a bit misleading because the notion of ETOs has not progressed in any kind of linear or systematic fashion. For one thing, states (or at least developed states) have been quite resistant to this idea, although there are at least some indications of cracks in the sovereignty wall. On the other hand, most segments of the United Nations support an extraterritorial interpretation of international human rights law. However, two of the major impediments are U.N. agencies: the International Law Commission and the International Court of Justice.

The European Court of Human Rights has also taken a puzzling route on this matter. Prior to its landmark ruling in *Bankovic*, the ECtHR readily recognized the extraterritorial application of the European Convention (Roxstrom, Gibney, and Einarsen 2005). *Bankovic* changed this dramatically, although the ECtHR also provided some leeway for the geographic expansion of Convention protection. Still, as shown by the active involvement of so many European governments in various aspects of the extraordinary rendition program (see Guild, this volume), assigning state responsibility for human rights harms that occur outside of 'Europe' will be difficult at best.

Almost as a matter of course, states have used 'territory' as a way of avoiding their own human rights obligations. To reaffirm the principle set forth at the outset of this chapter: all states have human rights obligations and these obligations apply both at home and abroad.

References

Arms Trade Treaty (ATT) (2013) Adopted and opened for signature, ratification and signature by General Assembly resolution 67/234B 2 April 2013, *Entry into force* 24 December 2014.

Committee Against Torture (CAT) (2008) GC 2 on the implementation of article 2 by states parties, U.N. Doc CAT/C/GC/2.

Convention against Torture and Other Cruel, Inhuman or Degrading Treatment or Punishment (1984) Adopted and opened for signature, ratification and accession by General Assembly resolution 39/46 of 10 December 1984, *Entry into force* 26 June 1987.

Crawford, J. (2002) *The International Law Commission's Articles on State Responsibility: Introduction, Text and Commentaries*, Cambridge University Press.

De Schutter, O. et al. (2012) 'Commentary to the *Maastricht Principles* on Extraterritorial Obligations of States in the Area of Economic, Social and Cultural Rights', *Human Rights Quarterly* 34, 1084–1169.

Erdem Turkelli, G. (2020) *Children's Rights and Business: Governing Obligations and Responsibilities*, Cambridge University Press.

ESCR-Net. (2015) 'Human Rights Law Sources: UN Pronouncements on Extra-Territorial Obligations', https://www.escr-net.org/resources/human-rights-law-sources-un-pronouncements-extra-territorial-obligations [accessed DATE].

European Convention for the Protection of Human Rights and Fundamental Freedoms (1950) Nov. 4, 1950, 213 U.N.T.S. 222.

European Court of Human Rights (ECtHR) (2001) *Bankovic et al. v. Belgium et al.*, Application no: 52207/99.

Gibney, M. (2007) 'Genocide and State Responsibility', *Human Rights Law Review* 7, 760–773.

——— (2011) 'Universal Duties: The Responsibility to Protect, the Duty to Prevent (Genocide), and Extraterritorial Human Rights Obligations', *Global Responsibility to Protect* 3, 123–151.

——— (2013) 'On Terminology: Extraterritorial Obligations' in Langford, M., Vandenhole, W., Scheinin, M. and van Genugten, W. (eds). *Global Justice, State Duties: The Extraterritorial Scope of Economic, Social, and Cultural Rights in International Law*, Cambridge University Press.

Gibney, M., Tomasevski, K. and Vedsted-Hansen, J. (1999) Transnational State Responsibility for Violations of Human Rights, *Harvard Human Rights Journal* 12, 267–296.

Human Rights Committee (HRC) (1981) *Sergio Euben Lopez Burgos v. Uruguay*, Communication No. R.12/52, U.N. Doc. Supp. No. 40 (A/36/40).

_______ (2004) GC 31 on the nature of the general legal obligation imposed on states parties to the Covenant, CCPR/C/21/Rev.1/Add. 1326.

International Court of Justice (ICJ) (1970) *Legal Consequences for States of the Continued Presence of South Africa in Namibia (South West Africa) Notwithstanding Security Council Resolution*, Advisory Opinion.

_______ (1986) *Case Concerning Military and Paramilitary Activities in and against Nicaragua (Nicaragua v. United States)*.

_______ (2004) *Legal Consequences of the Construction of a Wall in the Occupied Palestinian Territories*, Advisory Opinion.

_______ (2005) *Case Concerning Armed Activities on the Territory of the Congo (Democratic Republic of the Congo v. Uganda)*, Judgment.

_______ (2007) *Application of the Convention on the Prevention and Punishment of the Crime of Genocide (Bosnia and Herzegovina v. Serbia and Montenegro)*, Judgment.

International Covenant on Civil and Political Rights (ICCPR) (1966) Adopted and opened for signature, ratification and accession by General Assembly resolution 2200A (XXI) of 16 December 1966, *entry into force* 23 March 1976.

International Covenant on Economic, Social and Cultural Rights (ICESCR) (1966) Adopted and opened for signature, ratification and accession by General Assembly resolution 2200A (XXI) of 16 December 1966, *entry into force* 3 January 1976.

International Criminal Tribunal for the (Former) Yugoslavia (ICTY) (1999) *Prosecutor v. Tadic*, Case No. IT-94-1-A, Judgment.

Hoodbhoy, M., Flaherty, M.S. and Higgins, T.E. (2005) 'Exporting Despair: The Human Rights Implications of U.S. Restrictions on Foreign Health Care Funding in Kenya', *Fordham International Law Journal* 29, 1–118.

Hunt, P. (2007) *Report of the Special Rapporteur on the Right of Everyone to the Enjoyment of the Highest Attainable Standard of Physical and Mental Health*, Addendum, Mission to Sweden. U.N. Human Rights Council, Al/lHRC/4/28/Add.2.

Lawson, R. (2004) 'Life After *Bankovic*: On the Extraterritorial Application of the European Convention on Human Rights' in Coomens, F. and Kamminga, M.T. (eds). *Extraterritorial Application of Human Rights Treaties*, Intersentia.

Milanovic, M. (2012) 'Al-Skeini and Al-Jedda in Strasbourg', *The European Journal of International Law* 23, 121–139.

Office of the High Commissioner for Human Rights (2011) *Guiding Principles for Business and Human Rights*.

Optional Protocol to the International Covenant on Economic, Social and Cultural Rights (2008) 10 December 2008.

Orakhelashvili, A. (2003) 'Restrictive Interpretation of Human Rights Treaties in the Recent Jurisprudence of the European Court of Human Rights', *European Journal of International Law* 14, 529–568.

Roxstrom, E., Gibney, M. and Einarsen, T. (2005) 'The NATO Bombing Case and the Limits of Western Human Rights Protection', *Boston University International Law Journal* 23, 55–136.

Seck, S. (2008) 'Home State Responsibility and Local Communities: The Case of Global Mining', *Yale Human Rights and Development Law Journal* 11, 177–206.

Skogly, S. (2006) *Beyond National Borders: States' Human Rights Obligations in International Cooperation*, Intersentia.

Skogly, S. and Gibney, M. (2002) 'Transnational Human Rights Obligations', *Human Rights Quarterly* 24, 781–798.

Wilde, R. (2013) 'Human Rights Beyond Borders at the World Court: The Significance of the International Court of Justice's Jurisprudence on the Extraterritorial Application of International Human Rights Law Treaties', *Chinese Journal of International Law* 12, 639–677.

2

Global human rights obligations

Sigrun Skogly

Introduction

At the end of the cold war about 30 years ago, the international community experienced a brief period of reduced political conflict and a more conciliatory approach to international collaboration. The world returned to some of the visions that had inspired the establishment of the United Nations. These visions, as expressed through the Preamble of the UN Charter, reflected the conviction that peace and security in the world is dependent upon the universal respect for human rights and fundamental freedoms. However, the more conciliatory period was short-lived: the terrorist attacks on 9 September 2001, the subsequent international reactions in Afghanistan and Iraq, the global financial crisis in 2008/09, and other events have led to a far more polarised world where multilateralism and international cooperation have suffered. The four years of the Trump administration in the United States with its slogan 'America First' and disregard for international cooperation and institutions significantly increased tensions in the international community.

State practice related to human rights is often considered in light of big international events reflected above, or in the way individual states comply or ignore their human rights obligations. Often, the headlines are dominated by the situations where states fail to comply with obligations, or where they deny the existence of legal obligations. However, state practice also includes their behaviour in intergovernmental organisations, their bilateral interactions with other states, and their engagement with new soft and hard law developments.

It is against this backdrop that the current chapter will address global human rights obligations.

With the adoption of the UN Charter in 1945, human rights protection moved from being a national issue to a 'matter of legitimate international concern' (Vienna Declaration, para. 4). The experience of the Second World War made the drafters of the Charter recognise that certain human values were not adequately protected by individual states alone, but rather that the international community of states had a central role to play to ensure that individuals' human rights were protected. Despite the tensions in the international community described above, the global community of states is now more integrated than ever, and the changes in technology, population growth, depletion of natural resources, climate change, refugee flows, migration, and persistent poverty are current challenges that transcend national borders and require collective

DOI: 10.4324/9781003090014-4

actions by states. These and other problems in the international community have had a significant impact upon individuals' ability to enjoy their human rights. Hence, global action to ensure respect for and promotion of human rights requires states to engage collectively.

The questions that will be addressed in this chapter are whether global human rights obligations exist; whether they are legally binding, and if so, what their content may be. In the discussion, the human rights framework can be considered 'a normative basis' (Pribytkova 2020b) for global obligations. From a moral philosophical perspective, it can be argued that all actors in the international community, including private enterprises and individuals, have obligations related to the human rights enjoyment of individuals globally (Pribytkova 2020a). However, this chapter will focus on states' obligations in this regard.

The chapter will address the definition and legal foundation for global obligations in Section 1. Section 2 will be devoted to a discussion of the content of the obligations, including the meaning of international assistance and cooperation, and how the tripartite classification of obligations to respect, protect, and fulfil may assist our understanding. Finally, Section 3 will address the question of causality and whether this is a useful concept for apportioning responsibility for human rights problems in the global community. The chapter concludes with some reflections on the challenges ahead for compliance with global human rights obligations.

Section 1 – Definition and Legal Foundation

In this chapter I will use the term 'global obligations' in the meaning of states' 'collective legal obligations' (Vandenhole 2018, p. 666) in the international community. Global obligations do not have an agreed definition, but for the purposes of the current work, I will use the term as expressed in the *Maastricht Principles* on Extraterritorial Obligations of states in the Area of Economic, Social, and Cultural Rights (*Maastricht Principles*):

> Obligations of a global character that are set out in the Charter of the United Nations and human rights instruments to take action, separately, and jointly through international cooperation, to realize human rights universally.
>
> *(Principle 8(b))*

Some will argue that extraterritorial human rights obligations in general, and 'global obligations' more specifically, represent a radical departure from the traditional human rights paradigm where states hold human rights obligations within their jurisdiction only (often equated with their physical territory). As is elaborated elsewhere in this volume, the question of jurisdiction and territoriality related to human rights obligations is a complex one, and much debate has been carried out amongst academics and other commentators. However, international actors, including human rights courts and treaty bodies, have accepted that jurisdiction and human rights obligations reach further than a state's territory. Nevertheless, global obligations have not been subject to adjudication in the same manner as states' individual extraterritorial obligations have been. Hence, the question of whether these obligations are legally binding has been debated.

To analyse the question of whether 'obligations of global character' are legally binding or merely an expression of moral principles, it is necessary to consider the sources from which these obligations arise.

It is clear that the *Maastricht Principles* are not legally binding *per se*; they are an expression of expert opinions regarding the status of extraterritorial human rights obligations in international law. Still, while the Principles themselves do not represent a separate source of law, they were explicitly 'drawn from international law [...] with a view to advancing and giving full effect to the object of the Charter of the United Nations and international human rights' (*Maastricht Principles*, Preamble). Consequently, Principle 8b refers to the UN Charter as the source of obligation, and this would be the starting point for an evaluation of the legal character of such obligations.

The central provisions in the UN Charter that provide for human rights protection are to be found in Article 1 that lists the purposes of the organisation, and more specifically in Article 1(3), which provides that

> The Purposes of the Organisations are ....To achieve international co-operation in solving international problems of an economic, social, cultural, or humanitarian character, and in promoting and encouraging respect for human rights and for fundamental freedoms for all without distinction as to race, sex, language, or religion.

The obligations related to the purpose as detailed in Article 1(3) were further elaborated in Articles 55 and 56 of the UN Charter. These provisions hold that the member states of the UN 'pledge themselves to take joint and separate action in co-operation with the Organization [...]' to promote 'universal respect for, and observance of, human rights and fundamental freedoms for all [...]'.

In spite of the content of these provisions, some of the early commentators on the Charter held that the wording was ambivalent with the requirement of protecting human rights and fundamental freedoms, on the one hand, and the commitment to refraining from interference in domestic affairs on the other (UN Charter, art. 2(7)), and therefore the human rights provisions could not be seen as firm legal obligations (Kelsen 1951). Others held that the Charter imposed a legal duty on member states to respect and observe human rights and fundamental freedoms (Lauterpacht 1950).

Writing in 1965, Henkin argued that the provisions of the Charter were imprecise, and 'hortatory', trying to convince the member states of idealistic goals (Henkin 1965, p. 511). However, he conceded that

> Article 1 proclaims international cooperation to promote human rights as one of the purposes of the United Nations; Articles 55 and 56 make the achievement of universal respect for human rights *one of the few explicit undertakings* of United Nations membership.
>
> *(Henkin 1965, p. 504)*

Others have questioned the legal bindingness of the human rights provisions by pointing to the lack of international accountability structures in case states fail to comply with the provisions of the UN Charter (Langford 2013). However, it should be noted that the International Court of Justice (ICJ) in its Advisory Opinion on *the Legal Consequences for States of the Continued Presence of South Africa in Namibia* found that 'distinctions, exclusions, restrictions and limitations exclusively based on the grounds of race, colour, descent or national or ethnic origin [...] constitute a denial of fundamental human rights. This the Court views as a flagrant violation of the purposes and principles of the Charter of the United Nations' (ICJ 1971, para. 131). Consequently, the Court found the Charter to provide a source of law for international human rights obligations, and one to which member states of the UN could be held accountable.

It is important to take developments since the adoption of the United Nations' Charter into account. International human rights law has grown significantly in that time, and the understanding of its implications has deepened. This, combined with the recognition of human rights as an issue of legitimate international concern, as well as mainstreaming efforts of human rights throughout the UN system (UN Development Group's Human Rights Working Group), and initiatives such as the Responsibility to Protect (ICISS 2001), all point towards greater acceptance of the legal importance of the human rights provisions in the Charter.

Following the entry into force of the UN Charter, the Universal Declaration on Human Rights (UDHR) was adopted in 1948. This declaration provides a detailed interpretation of the content of the provisions in the UN Charter providing human rights protection (Stavrinides 1999). While focusing much on individual human rights, one article in the UDHR provides the goal for what global obligations should achieve. Article 28 states that 'Everyone is entitled to a social and international order in which the rights and freedoms set forth in this Declaration can be fully realized'. No individual state will be in a position to establish or create a 'social and international order', and the achievement of this is logically dependent on global cooperation. According to Eide, this article requires 'that social and international conditions be so structured as to make possible' the equal enjoyment of the rights provided in the UDHR (Eide 1999, p. 597). Consequently, Article 28 envisages a structure of the international community that is conducive to the full implementation and enjoyment of human rights, which reflects an obligation as per the United Nations' Charter.

These provisions in the Charter and the UDHR represent the foundation for global human rights obligations. As such, 'global obligations' have a raison d'être in themselves, namely an obligation for the states collectively to promote an international society that ensures the human rights enjoyment of individuals across the world. In operationalising this obligation, the attention has been given to international assistance and/or cooperation and how this shall be applied to achieve the human rights compliance. Practically, many commentators will translate global obligations to obligations of international (assistance and) cooperation (Pribytkova 2020b). Theo van Boven holds that 'human rights are placed by the Charter in a system of international cooperation' (van Boven 1997, p. 5). This international cooperation represents a state obligation to 'fulfil in good faith the undertakings they have assumed on the basis of the Charter of the United Nations and other relevant international instruments' (ibid). Consequently, the obligation of international cooperation becomes a means by which these obligations are implemented in a global setting.

Following the entry into force of the UN Charter and the adoption of the UDHR, global obligations have had their expression in individual human rights treaties, declarations, UN resolutions, and other soft law instruments. The requirement of international cooperation (and assistance) to achieve the full realisation of human rights has been explicitly recognised in many international human rights treaties *inter alia* in Article 2(1) of the Covenant on Economic, Social, and Cultural Rights (ICESCR), in the Preamble and Art. 4 of the Convention on the Rights of the Child (CRC); and the Preamble and Arts. 4 and 32 of the Convention on Rights of Persons with Disabilities (CRPD). In 1986, the UN General Assembly adopted the Declaration on the Right to Development (1986), which places the duty of international cooperation centrally in the text, for instance, in Articles 4 and 6. More recently, through the Millennium Declaration, and the Agenda 2030 with the Sustainable Development Goals, the UN General Assembly has adopted soft law instruments that reiterate the global commitments to cooperate for the promotion of human rights.

Furthermore, states have demonstrated that they accept human rights obligations stemming from the Charter and the UDHR, through the adoption of the Universal Periodic Review (UPR) procedure under the auspices of the Human Rights Council. The procedure was adopted by the General Assembly in 2006 (UN General Assembly Resolution 2006), when the Human Rights Council was established. Through this resolution, the General Assembly decided that the Council shall 'Undertake a universal periodic review, [...] of the fulfilment by each state of its human rights obligations and commitments in a manner which ensures universality of coverage and equal treatment with respect to all states' (UN General Assembly Resolution 2006, para. 5 (e)). The UN Charter and the UDHR represent the legal foundations for the mandate of this procedure, and all states members of the UN are subject to review under this procedure. The UN emphasises that the 'human rights obligations addressed are those set out in the UN Charter, the UDHR, and those pertaining to the treaties that each individual state has ratified, voluntary pledges and commitments, and relevant international humanitarian law' (Human Rights Council 2007, para. 1). Consequently, the obligations stemming from the UN Charter are global obligations to 'take joint and separate action' to promote 'universal respect for, and observance of, human rights and fundamental freedoms for all without distinction as to race, sex, language, or religion' (UN Charter, arts. 55 and 56) and are the foundations of the UPRs mandate.

To summarise, global human rights obligations have their legal foundations in the UN Charter, and have been further developed through subsequent international human rights instruments. These developments are clear expressions of state practice that confirm the global commitment to human rights protection. I will argue that to disregard the human rights obligations as provided in the Charter would weaken the legal significance of the whole treaty and put in doubt the other obligations it contains as well, such as the obligation to maintain international peace and security as provided in Article 1(1). Hence, all states that are members of the United Nations have ratified the UN Charter and committed to perform this treaty 'in good faith' (UN Vienna Convention on the Law of Treaties (VCLT), art. 26). Consequently, for the 193 states that are members of the United Nations, international cooperation to achieve the goals of the organisation is not a choice but a legally binding commitment that they have made (Salomon 2013a). The fact that states, particularly in the last 20 years, have been reluctant to expressly accept global human rights obligations does not remove the obligations based on international law. This reluctance reflects the difference between compliance with or breaches of international law obligations. Legal obligations entered into by ratifying treaties are not altered by states taking different views in different political realities. Furthermore, as has been argued above, state practice is expressed in different ways, and states' willingness to promote human rights through the United Nations' procedures and institutions contribute to their commitment.

Section 2 – Content of Global Human Rights Obligations

Having proposed that there is a firm legal foundation for global obligations in the UN Charter and subsequent treaties, the question to be addressed is what the content of these obligations are. In this section, I will discuss the concepts of international assistance and international cooperation and how they relate to each other. I will also apply the tripartite obligations' classification of *respect, protect,* and *fulfil,* to make the content of global human rights obligations more concrete.

International assistance and cooperation

On the basis of what has been discussed above, international assistance and cooperation are means by which the global human rights obligations can be complied with. This raises the question of the content of the requirements of international assistance and cooperation. The end goal of this cooperation is to comply with the global human rights obligations as set out in the UN Charter and confirmed through the International Bill of Rights.[1] As not all forms of cooperation will necessarily be compliant with these obligations, there is a requirement of certain qualities of such cooperation (Skogly 2006).

The international instruments mentioned so far use two terms: international assistance and international cooperation. The UN Charter uses international cooperation, the International Covenant on Economic, Social, and Cultural Rights applies the term 'international assistance and cooperation' (ICESCR, art. 2(1)), while the Convention on the Rights of the Child and the Convention on the Rights of Persons with Disabilities both use the term 'international cooperation' (CRC, art. 4; CRPD, arts. 4 and 32). In the debate regarding the legal significance of these provisions, much of the attention has been given to whether they imply a legal obligation for richer countries to provide assistance to poorer countries. The obligation to provide international assistance has often been raised with respect to the commitment to allocate a minimum of 0.7% of GDP to development assistance, and whether this is a legal obligation or a political goal (Salomon 2013a). It has also been raised in terms of a possible legal obligation to provide disaster relief (Sandvik-Nylund 2003; UNCESCR, General Comment no. 14, para. 40), and more specifically to contribute to the development of scientific knowledge in developing countries (UNCESCR, General Comment no. 25), and to share such scientific progress.

In a world that is marked by global disparities related to human rights enjoyment and states' abilities to tackle these problems due to financial and structural impediments, the need for international assistance is evident. In addition to bilateral commitments, such international assistance is important on multilateral levels as means to implement global obligations. Hence, support for the UN Specialised Agencies and other global institutions that provide assistance necessary for the fulfilment of the substantive content of human rights is essential.

The UN Committee on Economic, Social, and Cultural Rights (CESCR) holds in its General Comment no. 3 that 'the phrase "to the maximum of its available resources" [in Article 2(1)] was intended by the drafters of the Covenant to refer to both the resources existing within a state and those available from the international community through international cooperation and assistance' (CESCR, General Comment no. 3, para. 13). The Committee continues in the same General Comment to refer to Articles 55 and 56 of the UN Charter, and holds in paragraph 14 that 'international cooperation for development and thus for the realization of economic, social and cultural rights is an obligation of all states'. With this phrasing, the Committee clearly sees international cooperation as a means to be applied for human rights' realisation by all states members of the UN. This is important, as the General Comment in the next sentence refers to assistance as part of this international cooperation in holding that 'It is particularly incumbent upon those states which are is in a position to assist others in this regard' (ibid). Consequently, 'the reference to international assistance and cooperation has been understood by the UN treaty bodies as imposing an obligation for developing countries to seek, and for developed countries to offer, development assistance' (Vandenhole 2020, p. 227).

However, this discussion only addresses one element of 'international assistance and cooperation', and from the perspective of global obligations, perhaps not the most important one. International cooperation is so much more than international assistance, and the content of such international cooperation should have human rights as a primary objective to comply with the obligations stemming from the UN Charter. Writing from the perspective of the ICESCR, Sepúlveda holds that 'the purpose of the reference to international assistance and cooperation in the Covenant is to emphasise that such cooperation must be oriented, as a matter of priority, to the realization of all human rights, in particular economic, social and cultural rights' (Sepúlveda 2006, p. 275). Yet, we commonly see that international cooperation is not conducive to human rights compliance globally. The structures that underpin the international community's operation in today's globalised society are characterised by a 'particular model of the creation and distribution of wealth that is serving to enrich some, and not others' (Salomon 2007;Vandenhole 2018). A compelling example of this has been shown by Sekalala in addressing the right to health in the context of access to Anti-Retroviral Drugs for HIV/AIDs sufferers. She demonstrates clearly how the international law provisions relating to intellectual property in areas of global health are structured in manners that make it very hard for many developing countries to provide medication for their population and to comply with their obligations related to the right to the highest attainable standard of health (Sekalala 2017). In a series of reports, Inclusive Development International (IDI) demonstrates how the International Finance Corporation (The World Bank's private sector institution) has moved from direct loans to projects and programmes in developing countries, to using for-profit financial intermediaries. This has, according to IDI, led to great harm being inflicted upon people, and 'IFC intermediaries have financed companies that have forcibly evicted and impoverished hundreds of thousands of people. They have contributed to climate change, ravaged forests, polluted the oceans and rivers, and killed endangered species. Activists who have dared to resist them have been jailed, beaten and even murdered' (IDI, no date).

Such examples show that the quality of international cooperation is essential. The way in which states cooperate in areas such as trade, security, environment, and finance may contribute to human rights enjoyment, or it may be detrimental to human rights globally. Current structures and realities such as those detailed above are contrary to Article 28 of the UDHR as the 'social and international order' is not one in which 'the rights and freedoms in the Declaration can be fully realized' (UDHR, art. 28). To counter this reality, the *Maastricht Principles* prescribe that states, through international cooperation, must take 'deliberate, concrete, and targeted steps [...] to create an international enabling environment [to universally fulfil] economic, social and cultural rights' (*Maastricht Principles*, no. 29) by specifically mentioning areas of bi- and multilateral trade, investment, taxation, finance, environmental protection, and development cooperation. This demonstrates the point made above that the requirement for human rights conducive international cooperation relates to all areas where states cooperate internationally. This position has been confirmed by the CESCR, *inter alia*, in General Comment no. 14 on the right to health where it holds that 'states Parties have an obligation to ensure that their actions as members of international organisations take due account of the right to health' (para. 39).

It was mentioned above that part of international assistance and cooperation is encouraged through the adoption of soft law instruments adopted by the member states of the UN. The most recent such instrument is the Agenda 2030 with its Sustainable Development Goals (UN General Assembly 2015). These Goals have been framed in language that incorporates references to human rights in that the Preamble holds that the Goals 'seek to realize the human rights of all', and the respect for human rights is mentioned on a few occasions (see *inter alia* paras. 3, 10, 19 and 35) in the Resolution introducing the SDGs. However, human rights provisions are not incorporated into the 17 Goals with their 169 targets, with the exception of one mention in Goal 4 on gender equality. Soft law instruments such as the SDGs may be part of the way in which states comply with their global human rights obligations (Sekalala 2017). However, to do so requires more than a brief mention of human rights, and that they recognise human rights requirements in a constructive manner by, for instance, including cross-cutting human rights principles of transparency, participation, non-discrimination, and accountability. As the SDGs currently stand, they give no clear indication as to how people can participate in the achievement of the Goals, or how they can hold anyone accountable for lack of progressive realisation of their rights through the fulfilment of the SDGs. It would lead too far in the present chapter to give a full assessment of these questions. However, there are a number of other soft law instruments that suffer from the same lack of specificity, and perhaps even more important, a specific recognition of the differentiated and/or collective responsibility for lack of compliance.

To summarise, the global human rights obligations are operationalised through international assistance and cooperation. Under the ICESCR, state Parties are under an obligation to seek assistance if necessary, and to provide assistance if able to. Obligations related to international cooperation involve quality criteria that require compliance with human rights standards, and in particular standards of economic, social, and cultural rights. As will be further elaborated in Section 3 below, it is important to recognise that states have global obligations whether or not they have the resources to contribute financially. Or in other words, the availability of resources is not 'an appropriate normative basis for allocating global obligations' (Pribytkova 2020a). In terms of global human rights obligations, international cooperation can be seen as an overarching principle, with international assistance as an element of such cooperation.

Levels of obligations

The tripartite classification of obligations to respect, to protect, and to fulfil human rights treaty provisions is now commonly accepted. These levels have been confirmed and detailed for extraterritorial human rights obligations (including global obligations) in the *Maastricht Principles* (Principle no 3). This tripartite classification relates to the negative and positive obligations states have to refrain from violating human rights and to take action to promote human rights.

The *Maastricht Principles* have detailed the content of the global obligations of states for all three levels in Principles 19, 23, and 28. Regarding the obligation to respect, it is confirmed that states have 'the obligation to refrain from conduct which nullifies or impairs the enjoyment and exercise of economic, social and cultural rights of persons outside their territories' (Principle 20). For global obligations, this would imply that international cooperation should be conducted in a way that is not harmful to human rights. The Commentary to the *Maastricht Principles* confirms that 'a state confronted with a situation that could implicate risks to economic, social, and cultural rights is required to undertake positive measures to ensure its actions do not nullify or impair the enjoyment of these rights outside the national territory' (de Schutter et al. 2012). This would be the case for states when carrying out bi- or multilateral international cooperation.

The obligation to protect with respect to extraterritorial obligations is framed in terms of the obligation to regulate the conduct of non-state actors over which states have regulatory authority (Principle 24). While much of the implementation of this obligation will relate to how states regulate the conduct of non-state actors over which they have direct legislative or other regulatory control, as part of their global obligations, states would also be expected to cooperate in international regulation of non-state actors to ensure that they 'do not impair the enjoyment of the economic, social and cultural rights of any person. This obligation includes measures to prevent human rights abuses by non-state actors, to hold them to account for any such abuses, and to ensure an effective remedy for those affected' (Principle 27). Furthermore, the Maastricht Guidelines on Violations of Economic, Social, and Cultural Rights confirm that 'the obligations of states to protect economic, social and cultural rights extend also to their participation in international organizations, where they act collectively' (Guideline no. 19). While these Guidelines come from soft law instruments, the CESCR has confirmed this principle in a number of General Comments.[2] An example of how states can comply with their global obligations to protect would be to take an active and constructive part in the drafting process of the 'Legally binding instrument to regulate, in international human rights law, the activities of transnational corporations and other business enterprises', which is currently ongoing.

For global obligations, the *Maastricht Principles* are most detailed with respect to the positive obligation to fulfil (Principles 28–35). With clear reference to Article 28 of the UDHR, the *Maastricht Principles* – under the heading of 'Obligations to create an international enabling environment' – hold that states must take 'deliberate, concrete and targeted steps, separately, and jointly through international cooperation, to create an international enabling environment conducive to the universal fulfilment' of the relevant rights (Principle 29). In this Principle, it is also confirmed that such international cooperation is not only relevant for specific human rights programmes or human rights cooperation, but rather that this action includes 'matters relating to bilateral and multilateral trade, investment, taxation, finance, environmental protection, and development cooperation'. Consequently, the global human rights obligation to fulfil is clearly comprehensive and touches all forms of international cooperation amongst states. The list provided of areas where this obligation is relevant is not exhaustive, but rather indicative, and other areas may well be equally relevant (de Schutter et al. 2012, p. 1148). The CESCR has also confirmed that the obligation to create an international enabling environment would include addressing structural causes for human rights problems internationally, such as structural causes of food crises and the 'underlying causes of food insecurity, malnutrition and undernutrition' (UNCESCR, statement 2008, para. 12).

Thus, the *Maastricht Principles* detail the content of global human rights obligations, and in particular to the obligation to fulfil. The detailing of global obligations makes it clear that they set a quality marker on all international cooperation, not only cooperation that is undertaken specifically in the name of human rights promotion. Much of the content of the provisions of the *Maastricht Principles* relates to the way in which states should carry out their international cooperation, and as such this reflects obligations of conduct (UNCESCR, General Comment no. 3). However, as has been shown, the international cooperation is aimed at certain goals that reflect the quality of the cooperation. This requirement for a certain level of quality is determined by the impact (positive and negative) on human rights enjoyment of international cooperation among states, and as such represents obligations of result (Skogly 2006).

Section 3 – Causality and Equal or Differentiated Responsibilities

The above sections have addressed the legal foundations for global obligations and detailed how we understand the content of these obligations. What will be considered in this section is the question of responsibility related to global non-fulfilment of internationally guaranteed human rights. The *Maastricht Principles* have been criticised for not providing a clear division of responsibility between states individually and collectively, as they do not 'establish a regime of shared responsibility for violations of the global obligations' (Vandenhole 2018, p. 666). This shows that the *Maastricht Principles* were not able to develop the accountability principles that, according to some commentators, were missing already from the UN Charter. The clarification of shared responsibility for collective global obligations is therefore still an important task to enable better accountability for states' failures to provide an international enabling environment for human rights enjoyment. If global human rights obligations are obligations that states hold collectively, does this mean that the responsibility for actions and omissions to ensure that the rights are respected, protected, and fulfilled are equally distributed? Commonly when states violate human rights provisions to which they are bound through international legal provisions, they may (dependent upon acceptance of certain procedures) be held responsible through a variety of national and international accountability mechanisms. In this respect, for traditional human rights litigation, the question of causality is central: has the state caused the human rights problem, or could they have prevented the human rights problem through regulation or other forms of due diligence? In order to determine the causal link between state acts or omissions and a human rights violation, it is necessary to determine which acts or omissions that led to the human rights breaches. It is also necessary to identify the international legal obligations that made the acts or omissions unlawful (Vandenhole 2018). However, establishing such levels of causality is rarely easily done with respect to the collective legal obligations of states (Skogly 2013). When states work together in international cooperation, the individual responsibility for the negative outcome of such cooperation is hard to assign. Salomon holds that

> To ignore the legal implications of the need for remedial international action would be to hollow out the value of the positive obligation of international cooperation for the realisation of socio-economic rights completely. It is difficult, however, to determine when an obligation of international assistance and/or cooperation has been breached, thereby giving rise to a claim of international legal responsibility, because there is a paucity of judicial elucidation as to what would indicate that a given state was required to act in this area.
>
> *(Salomon 2013b, p. 279)*

However, the fact that it is harder to establish a causal link between an act or omission when states act through international cooperation, and that act/omission leads to human rights violations, does not mean that global human rights obligations do not exist or should not be complied with.[3] Salomon argues that 'states acting singly or jointly need not have caused harm in order to be under a positive duty to address the nonfulfillment of socio-economic rights elsewhere, nor in order to be held responsible for an internationally wrongful act derived from a failure to comply with an obligation to assist or cooperate internationally' (Salomon 2013b, p. 281).

While all states have obligations based on the legal sources discussed in Section 2 above, and these obligations reflect negative and positive obligations based on the principles of respect, protect, and fulfil human rights, it is not a given that the content of these obligations is equal for all states in the international community. Will the responsibility for rectifying problems be the same for Mali or Fiji as it is for the United States or for Germany? While the UN Charter Article 2(1) clearly recognises each state's sovereign equality in the international community, it does not necessarily imply that all states have equal amounts of obligations globally. Or put differently, states – depending on their size (territory, population, economy) – may be affecting the lives and living conditions of individuals around the world in different ways, and therefore the actual content of a state's obligation may differ. Other elements that may come into consideration are a state's history, economic power, contribution to problems, and its ability to influence decision-making in international institutions. As an example, it is clear that the five permanent members of the UN Security Council have more power to influence international action/inaction that can affect individuals' enjoyment of human rights than do other UN member states. Less formalised influence distinguishers can also be found in factors such as a state's history as a colonial power, military capabilities, or host to large multinational corporations. In short, states are different in terms of their abilities to influence state and non-state actors (including influence over institutions such as the International Monetary Fund, the World Bank, and the World Trade Organisation), and those states that have the opportunity should 'exercise such influence, in accordance with the Charter of the United Nations, and general international law [...]' (*Maastricht Principles*, no. 28). In addition to differentiation in influence or power, there are also differences in terms of benefiting from a system that perpetuates inequalities (Salomon 2007).

Reflecting these differences, principles have developed whereby obligations can be considered through a lens of 'common but differentiated responsibility' (CBDR) (Vandenhole 2018, p. 662). With origins in international environmental law (Shelton 2009), this principle recognises that states' history and ability to influence differ. Shelton holds that the CBDR principle 'provides a corrective justice basis for obliging the developed world to pay for past harms as well as present and future harms' (ibid, p. 67). Writing in the context of international environmental law, she argues that 'even though the responsibility for protecting the environment is to be shared among all nations, countries should contribute differently to international environmental initiatives depending on their capabilities and responsibilities. Common but differentiated responsibility calls broadly for developed countries to take the lead in solving existing global environmental problems, in particular because of their contributions to the creation of these problems' (ibid).

Salomon addresses the CBDR principle from a global obligation for international human rights perspective and holds that

> While all states are to cooperate in order to contribute to the common objective of eradicating world poverty, the responsibility of a state for the creation of a just institutional economic order should be in accordance largely with its weight and capacity in the world economy.
>
> *(Salomon 2007, p. 193)*

She continues that in the context of international cooperation for human rights the CBDR 'provides the basis for four indicators that may assist in determining responsibility [...]', which can be summarised as: a) the contribution that a state has made to the emergence of the problem; b) the relative power of influence a state has at the international level over the direction of finance, trade, and development; c) whether the given state is in a position to assist; and d) determination of which states benefit most from the existing distribution of global wealth and resources (ibid).

Thus, the arguments based on the CBDR are not based on an assessment of the direct causality between a state's action and the resulting human rights problems. As has been indicated, global human rights obligations that are implemented through international assistance and cooperation do not lend themselves easily to a direct causality relationship. Under human rights obligations, states have a negative duty to refrain from deteriorating the human rights situation and a positive duty to work for the improvement of human rights globally (*Maastricht Principles*, no. 28). Such obligations are not dependent upon establishing an individual state's responsibility for causing the human rights problem in the first place (Salomon 2013a). The CBDR principle is a way in which equity can be addressed, whereby historic influence as well as ability to contribute is taken into account (Shelton 2009).

On the other hand, the CBRD principle does not remove the obligations for financially poorer and less influential states. Constructive cooperation to avoid human rights problems will not necessarily require resources more plentiful in developed countries, but rather a political will to make decisions that are conducive to an improved international environment for human rights protection and enjoyment. As already mentioned, availability of resources is not a basis for allocation of obligations but may be a basis for ability to contribute. The ability to influence differs among states, both from a *de facto* and a *de jure* perspective. In the Security Council, the five permanent members have veto powers that no other members of the United Nations have, and consequently they have more responsibility than other states to engage constructively in international cooperation to carry out the UN mandate. Furthermore, in certain international institutions such as the World Bank and the International Monetary Fund, the member states have weighted voting power based on their financial contributions to the institutions. Hence, the greater financial powers (such as the G7) have significantly more influence on the policies and programmes that the institutions pursue.[4] From a CBDR perspective, the dominant states in these institutions would have more responsibility for furthering human rights constructive international cooperation in these institutions.

Conclusions

In this chapter, the legal foundations for global human rights obligations have been discussed. Stemming from treaty obligations undertaken by the member states of the United Nations, it is concluded that the global human rights obligations as reflected in the Charter's Articles 1(3), 55, and 56 are legally binding. These provisions of the Charter have been followed by a significant development in human rights law and practice that support this conclusion.

The chapter details the content of global human rights obligations and argues that the sources of such obligations are to be found in the UN Charter and subsequent international human rights law. The Charter requires that ratifying states comply with the overall global obligations as detailed in its provisions, while international assistance and cooperation are means through which these obligations can be implemented. Furthermore, the content of the obligations has been analysed from the tripartite classification perspective of *respect, protect,* and *fulfil.*

One of the remaining difficulties that needs further elaboration is the question of apportioning of responsibility among states in the international community. It is argued that states do not have equal obligations when it comes to international assistance and cooperation. Related to assistance, it is a matter of which states have the ability to assist; related to international cooperation, the responsibility is heavier for those states that are in a position to influence. In the discussion of these matters, the principle of 'common but differentiated responsibility' is helpful in explaining how the differences may be addressed.

In terms of state practice, it is important to consider this from three distinct perspectives: the firm legal commitments stemming from ratification of international treaties, such as the UN Charter and international human rights law conventions and covenants; the political commitments states make in international fora, such as the UN General Assembly; and finally, the behaviour between and among states in other bi-and multilateral relations. While it is easy to find examples where states do not behave in a manner consistent with their global human rights obligations, it has been argued above that this does not imply that obligations do not exist, but rather that such behaviour represents non-compliance, or breach, of the obligations. Furthermore, the contribution to the compliance with global obligations through participation in international fora should not be underestimated. Soft law instruments emerge from such activities, for example, the *Sustainable Development Goals*, or the *Responsibility to Protect* principles. Such soft law instruments are expressions of states' political will to further human rights conducive global initiatives and strengthen the commitment to the content of global obligations. Still, such initiatives and soft law instruments need to be critically analysed and potentially improved to ensure that the cross-cutting human rights principles (participation, transparency, non-discrimination, and accountability) is brought to bear, and that the focus remains on the individual person who may or may not have their human rights situation improved through international assistance and cooperation.

Notes

1. The International Bill of Rights is a common label for the Universal Declaration on Human Rights and the two International Human Rights Covenants from 1966.
2. See for example, UN CESCR General Comment no. 12 (1999), para. 38; UN Human Rights Committee (HRC), CCPR General Comment No. 25, art. 25 (Participation in Public Affairs and the Right to Vote), The Right to Participate in Public Affairs, Voting Rights and the Right of Equal Access to Public Service, 12 July 1996, CCPR/C/21/Rev.1/Add.7, para. 77.
3. It should be noted that much of international cooperation that states take part in is conducted through international institutions, such as the United Nations, the World Bank, or NATO. This institutional construct adds to the complexity in apportioning responsibility, as such international institutions composed of states are also separate legal entities with their own responsibilities. However, the division of responsibility between the member states and the international institutions is not the focus of this article. In this chapter, the attention is devoted to the role of the state in international cooperation, and even if the institutions themselves may have responsibilities, that does not mean that individual states working collectively will lose their original human rights obligations.
4. The G7 consists of Canada, France, Germany, Italy, Japan, the United Kingdom and the United States. The G7 represent 41.26% of all the cotes in the IMF; The United States having 16.5% on their own.

References

De Schutter, et al. (2012) 'Commentary to the *Maastricht Principles* on Extraterritorial Obligations of States in the Area of Economic, Social and Cultural Rights', *Human Rights Quarterly* 34(4), 1084–1169.

Eide, A. (1999) 'Article 28' in Alfredsson, G. and Eide, A. *The Universal Declaration of Human Rights: A Common Standard of Achievement*, Martinus Nijhoff Publishers.

Henkin, L. (1965) 'The United Nations and Human Rights', *International Organisation* 19(3), 504–517.

Inclusive Development International (2020) 'Outsourcing Development - Lifting The Veil On The World Bank Group's Lending Through Financial Intermediaries', https://www.inclusivedevelopment.net/what-we-do/campaigns/outsourcing-development/ [accessed 12 February 2021].

International Commission on Intervention and State Sovereignty (2001) 'The Responsibility to Protect', December 2001. The Responsibility to Protect: Report of the International Commission on Intervention and State Sovereignty, 2001 - Global Centre for the Responsibility to Protect (globalr2p.org) [accessed 18 July 2021]

International Court of Justice (ICJ) (1971) 'Advisory Opinion on the Legal Consequences for States of the Continued Presence of South Africa in Namibia', 21 June 1971, Judgments, Advisory Opinions and Orders | International Court of Justice (icj-cij.org)[accessed 18 July 2021]

Kelsen, H. (1951) *The Law of the United Nations*, Stevens and Sons.

Langford, M. et al. (eds). (2013) *Global Justice, State Duties*, Cambridge University Press.

Lauterpacht, H. (1950) *International Law and Human Rights*, Stevens and Son.

Maastricht Principles on Extraterritorial Obligations of States in the Area of Economic, Social and Cultural Rights (2011) '*Maastricht Principles* on Extraterritorial Obligations of States in the Area of Economic, Social and Cultural Rights', https://www.etoconsortium.org/nc/en/main-navigation/library/maastricht-principles/?tx_drblob_pi1%5BdownloadUid%5D=23 [accessed 12 February 2021].

Pribytkova, E. (2020a) 'What Global Obligations Do We Have?', *Chicago Journal of International Law* 20(2), 384–449.

Pribytkova, E. (2020b) 'Global Obligations for Sustainable Development: Harmonizing the 2030 Agenda for Sustainable Development and International Human Rights Law', *University of Pennsylvania Journal of International Law* 41, 1031–1136.

Salomon, M.E. (2007) *Global Responsibility for Human Rights*, Oxford University Press.

Salomon, M.E. (2013a) 'From NIEO to Now and the Unfinishable Story of Economic Justice', *International and Comparative Law Quarterly* 62, 31–54.

Salomon, M.E. (2013b) 'Deprivation, Causation and the Law of International Cooperation' in Langford, M. et al. (eds). *Global Justice, State Duties*, Cambridge University Press.

Salomon, M.E. (2014) 'How to Keep Promises: Making Sense of the Duty Among Multiple States to Fulfil Socio-Economic Rights in the World', *SHARES Research Paper* 53, SHARES-RP-53-final.pdf (sharesproject.nl) [accessed 18 July 2021]

Sandvik-Nylund, M. (2003) *Caught in Conflicts: Civilian Victims, Humanitarian Assistance and International Law*, Åbo, Institute for Human Rights.

Sekalala, S. (2017) *Soft Law and Global Health Problems: Lessons from Responses to HIV/AIDS, Malaria and Tuberculosis*, Cambridge University Press.

Sepúlveda, M. (2006) 'Obligations of "International Assistance and Cooperation" in an Optional Protocol to the International Covenant on Economic, Social and Cultural Rights', *Netherlands Quarterly of Human Rights* 24(2), 271–303.

Shelton, D. (2009) 'Describing the Elephant: International Justice and Environmental Law' in Ebbesson, J. and Okowa, P. *Environmental Law and Justice in Context*, Cambridge University Press.

Skogly, S. (2006) *Beyond National Borders: States' Human Rights Obligations in International Cooperation*, Intersentia.

Skogly, S. (2013) 'Causality and Extraterritorial Human Rights Obligations' in Langford, M. et al. (eds). *Global Justice, State Duties*, Cambridge University Press.

Stavrinides, Z. (1999) 'Human Rights Obligations under the United Nations Charter', *The International Journal of Human Rights* 3, 38–48.

UN Committee on Economic, Social and Cultural Rights (CESCR) (1990) GC 3 on the Nature of States Parties' Obligations (Art. 2, Para. 1, of the Covenant), 14 December 1990, E/1991/23.

_______ (1999) GC 12 on the Right to Adequate Food (Art. 11 of the Covenant), 12 May 1999.

_______ (2000) GC 14 on the Right to the Highest Attainable Standard of Health (Art. 12 of the Covenant), 11 August 2000, E/.12/2000/4.

_______ (2008) World Food Crisis: Statement, 20 May 2008, UN Doc. E/C.12/2008/1.

_______ (2020) GC 5 on science and economic, social and cultural rights (article 15 (1) (b), (2), (3) and (4) of the International Covenant on Economic, Social and Cultural Rights, 30 April 2020, E/C.12/GC/25.

UN Committee on Human Rights (HRC) (1996) CCPR GC 25 on Article 25 (Participation in Public Affairs and the Right to Vote), The Right to Participate in Public Affairs, Voting Rights and the Right of Equal Access to Public Service, CCPR/C/21/Rev.1/Add.7.

UN General Assembly (UNGA) (1966) International Covenant on Economic, Social and Cultural Rights, United Nations Treaty Series, 16 December 1966, 993.

_______ (1986) Declaration on the Right to Development: resolution/adopted by the General Assembly, 4 December 1986, A/RES/41/128.

_______ (1989) *Convention on the Rights of the Child*, United Nations Treaty Series, 20 November 1989, vol. 1577.

_______ (1993) Vienna Declaration and Programme of Action, 12 July 1993, A/CONF.157/23.

_______ (2006) Resolution, 15 March 2006, UN Doc A/RES/60/251.

_______ (2007) Convention on the Rights of Persons with Disabilities: resolution/adopted by the General Assembly, 24 January 2007, A/RES/61/106.

_______ (2015) Transforming our world: the 2030 Agenda for Sustainable Development, 21 October 2015, A/RES/70/1.

United Nations, Human Rights Council, *Basic Facts about the UPR*, https://www.ohchr.org/EN/HRBodies/UPR/Pages/BasicFacts.aspx

United Nations, Human Rights Council, *Institution-building of the United Nations Human Rights Council*, 18 June 2007, A/HRC/RES/5/1(1).

United Nations (UN) (1986) Charter of the United Nations, 1 UNTS XVI.

_______ (1996) Vienna Convention on the Law of Treaties, United Nations Treaty Series, vol. 1155.

University of Minnesota Human Rights Library (1997) 'Maastricht Guidelines on Violations of Economic, Social and Cultural Rights', adopted by a group of experts in 1998, http://hrlibrary.umn.edu/instree/Maastrichtguidelines_.html [accessed 18 July 2021]

van Boven, T. (1997) 'Introduction' in United Nations. Manual on Human Rights Reporting, UN doc. no. HR/PUB/91/1 (Rev.1).

Vandenhole, W. (2018) 'De-Growth and Sustainable Development: Rethinking Human Rights Law and Poverty Alleviation', *Law and Development Review* 11(2), 647–675.

Vandenhole, W. (2020) 'Towards a Division of Labour for Sustainable Development: Extraterritorial Human Rights Obligations' in Kaltenborn, M. et al. (eds). *Sustainable Development Goals and Human Rights (Interdisciplinary Studies in Human Rights, 5)*, Springer.

3

Extraterritorial human rights obligations and responsibility under international law[1]

Gamze Erdem Türkelli

International law on responsibility and ETOs: The state of the art

Extraterritorial human rights obligations (ETOs) pose important challenges in the current framework of public international law (IL) as regards how responsibility for internationally wrongful acts ought to be attributed and distributed, especially in cases where the obligations breached are shared by different types of actors. The responsibility of extraterritorial states for human rights violations may take on three forms: 1. responsibility for their own acts or omissions resulting in human rights violations, including the acts of state agents, or a failure to abide by their global obligations; 2. human rights violations originating from the acts or omissions of international organisations (IOs) to which they are members; 3. Finally, when any entity, such as a business enterprise, that they have obligations to regulate engage in acts or omissions resulting in human rights violations. In many of these cases, the human rights violations in question involve one or more states and one or more types of non-state actors (NSAs). Such scenarios necessitate the consideration of shared responsibility, firstly through the attribution of responsibility to multiple duty-bearers and consequently, the distribution of responsibility among these duty-bearers. The parameters of shared responsibility, particularly when they involve situations of multiple duty-bearing, involving not only states but also IOs and NSAs remain contentious. This chapter first takes stock of the law on responsibility in the context of ETOs, particularly in relation to state responsibility, the responsibility of IOs and shared responsibility. The chapter then provides a critique of existing legal constructs around responsibility with respect to ETOs, identifying gaps. The chapter finally offers alternative sociological and political conceptualisations of shared responsibility.

Basic tenets of the law on responsibility: Attribution of conduct, wrongfulness and enforcement

Any normative discussion on responsibility for breaches of ETOs needs to start with an assessment of the law on state responsibility, which relates to secondary norms as to outcomes when primary norms (rights and obligations for participants in IL) are violated. The law on responsibility, therefore, responds to the need to enforce these secondary norms when actors

DOI: 10.4324/9781003090014-5

breach primary norms and relies on the articulation of state responsibility, through the Articles on State Responsibility for Internationally Wrongful Acts (ARSIWA) and the responsibility of IOs through the Articles of Responsibility of International Organisations (ARIO) of the International Law Commission (ILC). According to Art. 2 ARSIWA and Art. 4 ARIO, responsibility is engaged for any action or omission attributable to a state or IO that is in breach of any international obligation, as defined by IL, undertaken by that given state or IO (ILC 2001; ILC 2011a). Law on responsibility is thus not specifically a responsibility regime for human rights violations.

The enforcement of responsibility for internationally wrongful acts begins with the attribution of the conduct (action or omission) to a state or an IO. State responsibility is engaged, according to ARSIWA, when the conduct can be attributed to state organs (art. 4), 'persons or entities exercising elements of governmental authority' (art. 5), organs of third states at the disposal of the said state (art. 6) even if those organs, persons or entities are acting in contravention of instructions or excess of the authority they possess (art. 7) as well as the conduct of person(s) that act on the instructions, direction or control of the state (art. 8), or conduct acknowledged by the state as its own (art. 11). In relevant situations, acts of actors exercising governmental authority or elements thereof (art. 9), or the conduct of insurrections that later become governments (art. 10) are attributed to that state under IL. According to art. 1.2 ARIO, states may additionally incur responsibility for 'internationally wrongful act[s] in connection with the conduct of an international organisation' (ILC 2011a).

The wrongfulness of conduct is gauged when the said conduct is 'not in conformity with what is required' of the state by the obligation (art. 12), in so far as the state is bound by that international obligation at the time of the conduct (art. 13) (ILC 2001). According to ARSIWA, responsibility is triggered by the act of the breach of obligation even if the effects continue over time (art. 14.1), except when the act causing violations (breaches of obligations) has a continuing character (art. 14.2). According to ARSIWA, wrongfulness may be precluded by valid consent, lawful self-defence, countermeasures, force majeure, distress, necessity and compliance with an obligation arising from *jus cogens* (arts. 20–24). Of course, state responsibility is also engaged when a state is in serious, meaning gross or systematic, breach of peremptory norms of IL (arts. 40–41).

The current articulations of the law on responsibility also extend to 'aid or assistance', or what may be more broadly referred to as complicity, by attributing responsibility to a state or IO when they aid or assist in committing the internationally wrongful act 'with the knowledge of the circumstances' of that wrongful act, and when that act would have been unlawful if committed by itself (ILC 2001, art. 16; ILC 2011a, art. 14). In its *Bosnia and Herzegovina v. Serbia and Montenegro* judgment, the IJC noted that Art. 16 ARSIWA on aid and assistance reflected the customary IL on state responsibility for complicity (ICJ 2007). Of course, what the ICJ reaffirmed was the existence of such a customary principle but not what that principle required in terms of attribution (Lanovoy 2016). State complicity does not need to be limited to the ARSIWA definition, for instance when it is based on specialised regimes under IL such as Art. 3(e) of the Genocide Convention (Aust 2011). In addition, Aust (2011) posits that obligations on state conduct that can be likened to complicity (such as the *non-refoulement* obligation under international refugee legal regimes), or positive obligations under human rights conventions may give rise to complicity considerations.

According to ARSIWA, the consequences arising from a state being attributed responsibility for an internationally wrongful act include cessation and non-repetition (art. 30) and reparation (art. 31), which may include restitution – re-establishing the situation before the breach (art. 35), compensation – for all losses (art. 36) or satisfaction when restitution and compensation are not possible, including through acknowledging the violation, issuing a statement of regret or a formal apology (art. 37).

Gaps and critiques

ARSWIA and ARIO, as general public IL frameworks on responsibility, are not sufficient to address human rights responsibility. For instance, their primary limitation is the focus on strict causality, through a fixation on conduct as a single act or omission that triggers a breach. Gauged against real-world human rights violations, strict causality focuses only on one very small part of the overall picture. Often, it is difficult to make the single and strict causal connection between the victim of a human rights violation and the abuser. For instance, 'a single event [could] generate multiple violations by a range of actors' (Clapham 2010, p. 56). In addition, violations of economic, social and cultural (ESC) rights may entail the compounded effect of a number of different acts or omissions, possibly by different duty-bearers. For instance, when states or IOs impose austerity measures or structural adjustment plans on a third state, underfunded health or education systems in the third state that violate human rights will not be readily attributable to a single causal act. Of course, the limitations of strict causality are a relevant consideration for all human rights, not only for ESC rights. The Inter-American Court of Human Rights (IACtHR) held in *Velásquez-Rodríguez v. Honduras* that states may be held legally responsible for human rights violations resulting from the acts of private or unknown actors if they fail their duty of due diligence to prevent the violation (IACtHR 1988). More recently, in *Munaf v. Romania*, the UN Human Rights Committee noted that states may be held responsible for violations of the International Covenant on Civil and Political Rights (ICCPR) beyond their borders if they are 'a link in the causal chain' that enables said violations in another state when the risk of violations is a result of the 'necessary and foreseeable' result of their conduct (UN HR Committee 2009). Law on responsibility, if it is to have relevance in the human rights arena, needs to become 'relevant to the nature of contemporary human rights violations' (Salomon 2007, p. 182).

Another important shortcoming of the existing frameworks on responsibility is linked to the limited purview they accord for the existence of multiple duty-bearers to be addressed in relation to a violation. ARSIWA and ARIO recognise that several states and IOs can jointly be responsible for a wrongdoing if they are both bound by the international obligation in question, and if they can both be attributed the conduct leading to the wrongdoing. Beyond the considerations of 'aid or assistance', the frameworks are unable to resolve issues of legal responsibility involving multiple duty-bearers that are not states or IOs (Nollkaemper and Plakokefalos 2016). Independent responsibility, on which current international law is based, arises when responsibility for a wrongdoing is attributed to each duty-bearer independently of other duty-bearers and exclusively (Nollkaemper and Jacobs 2013). Beyond independent responsibility, violations by a multiplicity of actors can amount to responsibility for collective and concerted action as well as responsibility where different actors contribute to a harm with individual actions but not in any collective or concerted way, which requires apportioning responsibility.

Responsibility for violations of ETOs: Beyond the ILC's articles

Responsibility for ETOs necessitates moving beyond conceptualising violations as strict causation. A state's responsibility for ETOs should be considered in relation to at least three situations: first, for its own acts or omissions giving rise to the violations of its ETOs; second, for the conduct of IOs to which it is a member; third, for the conduct of another entity, such as an NSA.

State responsibility for its own acts or omissions in breach of ETOs

The practical implementation of state responsibility for human rights violations under IL through courts has largely rested on a territorial model of attributing obligations, with exceptions made for effective control over territory, persons or situation (Milanovic 2011). The European Court of Human Rights (ECtHR), for instance, has consistently applied this territorial model, where the domestic state is considered the primary and often sole duty-bearer in relation to human rights on its territory, with exceptions for effective control over territory (ECtHR 1996; ECtHR 2011b) or over persons (ECtHR 2011a; ECtHR 2014a). In these exceptional circumstances, State B replaces State A as the duty-bearer and breaching these duties is then the basis for the attribution of responsibility to that state. The Inter-American Commission on Human Rights (IACmHR 2002) has considered states' human rights obligations not to be constrained by the territory they control but as extending to all persons over whom the state has 'authority and control' (para. 44), giving rise to responsibility if these are breached.

The ECtHR has also dealt with cases where a state does not have complete control over its internationally recognised territory. In the cases on Transnistria (*Ilaşcu, Catan and Mozer*) the ECtHR found that, both Moldova that did not have effective control in the area and Russia that aided and assisted the self-proclaimed Moldavian Republic of Transnistria had breached their obligations and bore responsibility for the human rights violations in question. Moldova was only considered to have limited positive obligations to 'take the diplomatic, economic, judicial or other measures that it is in its power to take and are in accordance with international law' (2004, paras. 330–331) and only attributed responsibility if that positive obligation was not discharged, whereas Russia was found to be exercising jurisdiction and therefore attributed responsibility over the specific violations in question. The issue of the attribution of responsibility to multiple states also arose in *Jaloud v. the Netherlands*, where the ECtHR noted, in addition to the Netherlands having jurisdiction over Mr Jaloud who had been shot and killed by a Dutch military personnel, that the UK which controlled the part of Iraq where the events occurred could have 'concurrent jurisdiction' (ECtHR 2014b, para. 153). The joint responsibility of the Netherlands and the UK was not invoked by the Court since the UK was not a respondent state in the case. Yet, from a conceptual perspective, if concurrent jurisdiction by more than one state is found to exist over a situation that entails the same human rights obligation, the breach of the obligation could give rise to responsibility of each of these states.

In contrast, the scope of state responsibility under the *Maastricht Principles* covers all conduct violating its human rights obligations 'whether within its territory or extraterritorially' that is attributable to a state 'acting separately or jointly with other states or entities' (art. 11). In addition, state responsibility is engaged when states engage in acts or omissions with foreseeable real risk of jeopardising ('nullifying or impairing') the enjoyment of ESC rights beyond their territory (art. 13).

State responsibility for the acts or omissions of IOs in breach of ETOs

ARIO states that IOs bear responsibility for the breaches of international legal obligations they have undertaken, while member state responsibility for the acts or omissions of IOs has been considered exceptional (Higgins 1995; Ryngaert and Buchanan 2011). Nonetheless, IOs and states may have joint responsibility for the same internationally wrongful act, if responsibility can be attributed to an IO 'in connection with' the act of a state, or if responsibility can be attributed to a state 'in connection with' the act of an IO (ILC 2011b, art. 48, commentary para. 1). As an illustration, in the case *European Parliament v. Council of the EU*, the Court of Justice of the European Union (CJEU) noted that in areas where the EU and its member states had joint competences, the EU and its member states were 'jointly liable' for the obligations assumed by the EU based on the terms of the obligation that had been undertaken (CJEU 1994, para. 29). This responsibility is normally individual but may also be subsidiary when the primary responsibility that has been invoked does not lead to reparation (ILC 2011b, art. 48.2).

When IOs are attributed responsibility for human rights violations, responsibility may also be attributed to member states of the institution for their role in a wrongful act and thus, a breach of their ETOs. There is contention over whether invoking member state responsibility based on membership alone can endanger an IO's independence and effectiveness (as argued by Ryngaert and Buchanan 2011) or not (Stumer 2007). Sarooshi (2005) argues that the extent to which states may be attributed responsibility for the acts of IOs as members depends on the extent of conferred, delegated or transferred powers. For instance, states using IOs as agents retain responsibility for the acts of the agent if they fall within the powers conferred to the agent, but member states which delegate competences to IOs that they also continue to exercise contemporaneously with IOs would not be responsible for the breaches of the IOs (Sarooshi 2005).

The ECtHR has shied away from accepting joint or concurrent responsibility of member states alongside IOs, concerning claims surrounding the actions of the NATO Kosovo Force (KFOR) and of UN Interim Administration Mission in Kosovo (UNMIK), when it declared the cases inadmissible against the respondent states. The Court asserted that the acts in question were attributable to UN, over which it did not have *rationae personae* jurisdiction (ECtHR 2007). This has led to sidestepping the real issue of how responsibility ought to be attributed in cases where state and IO act and jurisdictions overlap (Sari 2008). In *Al-Jedda v. the UK,* however, the ECtHR found that responsibility could be attributed both to an IO and its members, in so far as the member states have not completely delegated the authority over the action to the IO (ECtHR 2011a).

The *Maastricht Principles*, on the other hand, clearly note that states retain responsibility for their conduct, as it affects their human rights obligations both inside and beyond their territory and have an obligation to 'take all reasonable steps to ensure that [an IO to which it transfers competences or in which it participates] acts consistently with [its] international human rights obligations' (art. 15). This duty and the responsibility for its breach exist independently of any obligations and the subsequent responsibility IOs have independently under IL (art. 16). Similarly, General Comment (GC) 16 of the UN Committee on the Rights of the Child notes that states retain their children's rights obligations as members of IOs, including IOs working in development, finance and trade (2013).

State responsibility for the acts or omissions of NSAs

The issue of state responsibility for the acts and omissions of NSAs is at the core of responsibility for ETOs. This is also the part of the law on responsibility that is the most contested and underdeveloped. Scholars have argued that states should be attributed responsibility for complicity in a corporation's commission of an international crime (Clapham 2004), or for the breach of an extraterritorial due diligence obligation when they fail to oversee and prevent the adverse extraterritorial human rights impacts of their corporations (McCorquodale and Simons 2007). state responsibility according to the *Maastricht Principles* covers responsibility for conduct (acts or omissions) of NSAs that are 'acting on the instructions or under the directions or control of the state' as organs of the state (art. 12(a)) or those that are 'empowered by the state to exercise elements of governmental authority' when these actors in fact act in that capacity (art. 12(b)). Similarly, the UN Committee on Economic, Social and Cultural Rights' (CESCR) GC 24 on state Obligations in the context of business activities recalls that direct international responsibility of states may be invoked in relation to the conduct (acts or omissions) of private actors under three conditions: if that private actor is under its instructions, control or direction, if that private entity is exercising governmental authority, or 'if and to the to the extent that the state party acknowledges and adopts the conduct as its own' (CESCR 2017, para. 11). Beyond those conditions, also enumerated under ARSIWA, state responsibility for the conduct of private actors is not widely recognised.

There are no clear legal frameworks to gauge how international legal responsibility might be attributed directly to NSAs, given the ongoing debate on the nature of their 'duties' under IL. It is also unclear whether NSAs will incur direct legal responsibility under IL for human rights violations, given the contestations over unhelpful parameters, such as international legal personality (Erdem Türkelli 2020). For instance, while the norms of due diligence and remediation continue to become more legalised overtime in the case of business enterprises (Erdem Türkelli 2020), states are likely to be confronted with responsibility for failures to regulate the extraterritorial activities of businesses domiciled or headquartered in their territory. Karavias (2015) suggests that home and host state breaches of due diligence obligations, in regulating corporate conduct extraterritorially or within the state's territory, can be considered a basis for the attribution of responsibility. Similarly, CESCR's GC 24 notes that responsibility for violations of ESC rights is invoked when a state fails to carry out its obligation to protect, by taking all reasonable measures to prevent the violation. Even when the responsibility for the conduct also befalls on other actors, including NSAs, provided that the violation was 'reasonably foreseeable' based on the risks presented by the circumstances surrounding the conduct, not having foreseen the violation does not absolve the state from responsibility (2017, para. 32). GC 24 thus expresses a broad due diligence obligation for state parties in relation to the activities of private entities, including business enterprises. Similar breaches of due diligence obligations may also give rise to responsibility, such as when states fail to take adequate measures to protect individuals by preventing violations of human trafficking by NSAs (Gallagher 2016).

Multiple duty-bearers and shared responsibility

The enforcement of human rights, through international human rights law, designates the domestic state as the primary human rights duty-bearer in its own territory. For that reason, any consideration of responsibility for violations of ETOs necessitates – at the very least – a consideration of shared responsibility between the domestic state and extraterritorial state(s). More broadly, the violation of ETOs may engage shared responsibility among several states, one or more IOs as well as NSAs.

Attribution of responsibility to multiple duty-bearers

The attribution of responsibility to multiple duty-bearers under ARSIWA and ARIO is foreseen in cases when more than one state engages in the conduct, causing an internationally wrongful act (art. 15 ARSIWA), or when that conduct is a composite act of an IO and one or more member states (art. 12 ARIO). Of course, scenarios of complicity (or 'aid or assistance') would also necessitate a consideration of the attribution of responsibility to multiple duty-bearers. The application of ILC articles to multiple duty-bearers is found to be problematic, in terms of how these norms are interpreted and implemented through various independent responsibility mechanisms (Gallagher 2016). The ILC's frameworks on the law on responsibility do not respond to the real-world situations, where the complexity of governance regimes and economic transactions often mean that, multiple duty-bearers are involved in various ways, and to different degrees in a wrongdoing or in multiple wrongdoings that result in human rights violations (Erdem Türkelli 2020).

Nollkaemper argues that causal contributions to an internationally wrongful act could also trigger shared responsibility among various duty-bearers, but while such causal contributions are 'necessary' conditions to responsibility they are not 'sufficient' (2014, p. 9). The Guiding Principles on Shared Responsibility in IL, an outcome of the EU-funded SHARES project at the University of Amsterdam, look at attributional aspects of shared responsibility to several international persons (states or IOs) to 'an indivisible injury' based either on 'individual, concurrent or cumulative' contribution (Principle 2.2) where contribution requires a causal relationship (Principle 1(d)) (Nollkaemper et al. 2020). Accordingly, the injury may arise from a single internationally wrongful act (Principle 3) or multiple acts (Principle 4). Reaching 'beyond the scope of the ARSIWA and the ARIO', the Guiding Principles allow for responsibility to be owed to individuals or other persons, not only to other states and IOs (ibid., p. 22).

Distribution of responsibility

While ARIO and ARSIWA recognise the need to attribute responsibility to multiple duty-bearers, they do not set out the parameters of how that responsibility is to be apportioned or distributed. Of course, as a fundamental distinction, responsibility to multiple duty-bearers may be attributed on the basis of independent responsibility of each actor, or on the basis of shared responsibility jointly attributed to duty-bearers.

The Guiding Principles on Shared Responsibility distinguish three types of causal relationship to shared responsibility: individual contribution where the contribution is the cause of the injury itself; concurrent contributions where 'each of the contributions could have caused the injury' by themselves; and cumulative contributions where 'conduct of multiple international persons together results in an injury that none could have caused on their own' (Nollkaemper et al. 2020, p. 25). What remains missing are situations where contributions take the form of complicity as well as when the initial act or omission leading to the harm is attributable to one actor but others contribute to the continuation of the harm, or where that breach and the resulting harm are a function of the socioeconomic conditions, to which various actors have contributed as opposed to a single discernible act or omission (Erdem Türkelli 2020).

Theoretically, shared legal responsibility can be distributed on the basis of the strength of primary norms (obligations) incumbent upon the actors, causal relationship (causation), nature and strength of contributions to the harm, the role of relative power wielded over other actors, as well as fairness (Nollkaemper and Jacobs 2015). Yet, in cases necessitating shared responsibility, the rights-holder may not be able to distinctly identify the actor or actors, to whom the acts or omissions resulting in the harm can be traced. The tort law principle of joint and several liability has been suggested as a solution in cases when the different contributions of a diverse set of actors leads to a wrongdoing, including when the shared responsibility of an IO and its member states is engaged (Stumer 2007; Ahlborn 2013). In that scenario, rights-holders would bring the entirety of their claims against one of the duty-bearers, and that duty-bearer would then seek to recover the contribution of other duty-bearers (Stumer 2007). Applying the joint and several liability model to the enforcement of responsibility for breaches of international legal norms in practice would be challenging, because there is no clarity as to how one duty-bearer would be able to enforce the distribution of responsibility it has incurred against others (Ahlborn 2013). Without endorsing joint and several liability as it exists in domestic settings, the Guiding Principles on Shared Responsibility also envisage that full reparation be made by any of the responsible parties to the injured person(s), without the injured person(s) having to justify the attribution of responsibility to specific parties (Principle 10). The exception is when the contribution to the injury is negligible as not to justify full reparations; in those cases, partial reparations may be sought (Nollkaemper et al. 2020). In line with joint and several liability, a responsible party that has made a full reparation for the injury has a right of recourse against the other responsible parties to share the responsibility (Principle 12).

A way forward based on alternative visions: Polycentric governance of responsibility[2]

The effective enforcement of responsibility under IL for breaches (including breaches of ETOs) that result from the collective or cumulative actions, or omissions of a number of actors may be difficult, given the limitations of the existing frameworks on international legal responsibility. What we may need to embrace, for the time being, is a polycentric governance of responsibility (Ostrom 2009; Prenkert and Shackelford 2014) that is firmly grounded in a recognition of ETOs but attempts to resolve the question of responsibility in a governance model that includes private, governmental and third-sector venues at the local, national and international levels (as proposed by Keohane and Nye 2000). '[E]xisting [enforcement] landscape for responsibility' for human rights violations is already one based – however imperfectly – on polycentricism (Erdem Türkelli 2020, p. 290), and responsibility for breaches of ETOs would fit squarely within this landscape. The polycentric governance of responsibility for violations of ETOs in particular necessitates a notion of responsibility that transcends the frameworks suggested under the ILC Articles, or those confined to using doctrinal understanding of duty-bearing based on territorial jurisdiction or personhood (Erdem Türkelli 2020). Such conceptualisations may rely on alternative legal visions and inspiration on responsibility from outside of the legal field.

Alternative legal visions

Alternative and more comprehensive legal visions of legal responsibility, particularly relevant to responsibility for breaches of ETOs also exist. Clapham (2006) explored the notion of 'complementarity' (a physics notion that he applied to human rights responsibility) which asserts that how an event is observed depends as much on the viewing apparatus as the observer. For instance, '[t]he jurisdictional filter of an international or national court' might end up seeing the responsibility of one state but not of the other actors involved in the wrongdoing (Clapham 2010, p. 56). Yet, the notion of complementarity allows viewer to identify an actor both as private and public, to see multiple duty-bearers and to discern the wrongdoings leading to multiple breaches of IL (Clapham 2006). Of course, complementarity does not clarify how that responsibility ought to be distributed. In the specific case of ETOs, complementarity allows for extraterritorial states to coexist with the domestic states as well as other potential duty-bearers, such as IOs and NSAs as regards the attribution of responsibility.

Tort law may also provide insights, besides the joint and several liability model, with respect to how responsibility may be distributed from an ETO perspective, particularly in relation to human rights violations. The Principles of European Tort Law (PETL 2005) define causation in a much broader way, noting that it is linked to conduct without which the harm (damage) would not have taken place. PETL also defines 'concurrent causes' of damage, which means that '[i]n case of multiple activities, where each of them alone would have caused the damage at the same time, each activity is regarded as a cause of the victim's damage' (art. 3:102). In addition, when rights-holders (victims) have experienced 'personal injury; or injury to human dignity, liberty, or other personal rights', the 'gravity, duration and consequences' of the victim's grievance should be considered in the establishment of non-pecuniary damages as well as possibly, the 'degree of fault' of the tortfeasor under the exceptional circumstances where 'it significantly contributes to the grievance of the victim' (art. 10:301(1) and (2)). Hence, responsibility may be distributed on a differentiated scale, where contributions to the wrongdoing causing more harm or injury may give rise to a bigger share of legal responsibility. From the perspective of ETOs, this would mean that the traditional human rights law tenet that domestic states are the primary duty-bearers as regards human rights in their territory, and thus the primary locus of responsibility may be challenged depending on the specific circumstances of a harm or injury, if, for instance, the action or omission of an extraterritorial state were found to be more significant in causing the harm or injury.

Responsibility for systemic or structural violations of global obligations, such as those linked to global justice and alleviation of poverty, necessitates looking beyond strict and direct causality. In this regard, Salomon's proposal (2007) which links responsibility to failures of acting with adequate due diligence and standards of care is particularly important. Salomon puts forth a framework based on 'common but differentiated responsibilities' based on the 'contribution … to the emergence of the problem', 'relative power … manifested as influence over the direction of finance, trade, and development', being in a 'position to assist' and 'benefit[ing] … from the existing distribution of global wealth and resources' (2007, p. 193 [footnotes omitted]).

Of course, legal responsibility for violations that centres on wrongful conduct, injury and reparations is only a limited part of the broader concept of accountability linked to IL (Brunée 2005). The concept of accountability involves the 'justification of an actor's performance vis-à-vis others, the assessment or judgment of that performance against certain standards, and the possible imposition of consequences if the actor fails to live up to applicable standards' (Brunée 2005, p. 4 [footnote omitted]). Accountability has preventive and corrective functions, by involving standards, principles and mechanisms applicable to the performance and conduct of actors (OHCHR and Center for Economic and Social Rights 2013). 'Shared accountability', a broader concept than shared responsibility, can respond to circumstances currently situated beyond the scope of existing international legal norms, and hence do not give rise to international responsibility (Nollkaemper and Jacobs 2013). For ETOs, the question of accountability that can be enforced politically and socially is indeed an important one, especially when mechanisms to hold extraterritorial states legally accountable are absent.

Alternative visions from outside of the law

The question of how 'responsibility' ought to be shared between multiple contributors is not specific to the legal field as such. Philosophy and political theory have also dealt with the question of how responsibility can and should be attributed and distributed for actions or omissions of multiple actors.

Larry May, in *Sharing Responsibility*, calls for a 'partial rather than full responsibility for participation in a joint venture' which 'divid[es] responsibility for a harm' in contrast to the joint and several liability approach (1992, pp. 37–38). May's model foresees the attribution of responsibility not only for an actor's direct contributions to harm but also indirect contributions, for instance when an actor shares attitudes that lead to harmful outcomes which allow for the facilitation of acts that result in harm (1992, p. 37). The model does not restrict responsibility to causal relationships and can thus cover situations where 'all parties played a necessary causal role in the harm, and that no one party played a sufficient role' (May 1992, p. 39). Of course, May's focus is on responsibility for natural persons (individuals) in social interactions rather than responsibility of actors that participate in international legal processes. Extrapolating insights from May's concept of shared responsibility, actors participating in international legal processes may be found to share attitudes or perpetuate structures, resulting in harms and should correspondingly incur responsibility. For instance, when private and public actors further agendas that allow unchecked financial and corporate interests to reign over economic and social policies at the expense of public interest, and create conditions that render the violations of ESC rights more likely, these social interactions at the global level may in fact form the basis for shared responsibility. What is important is that May does not see the overall responsibility in relation to a fixed whole, meaning that those in leadership positions being apportioned a higher share of responsibility results in the overall responsibility assigned to the harm increasing and not the share of other actors decreasing. For ETOs, this would mean that those actors exercising more decisive roles having differentiated and higher levels of responsibility.

The late political theorist Iris Marion Young, who based her work on responsibility for global injustices on May's social interaction model of responsibility, distinguished two models of responsibility: the liability model of responsibility and the political model of responsibility. The liability model, which links responsibility to 'guilt or fault for harm' in the form of punishment or compensation is applied to events that have already taken place, based on causal connections to the harm (Young 2004, p. 368). Young, who attempted to devise a theory to respond to the question of who bears responsibility for the labour conditions in sweatshops, noticed that beyond the direct liability of factory owners and managers, those farther away in the upper end of the supply chains from sweatshops were too removed. In the shared responsibility model that she believed was necessary, each actor (an individual person or group of persons like in May's approach) would bear partial personal responsibility 'for outcomes or the risks of harmful outcomes' that result from group action (Young 2004, p. 380). Consequently, Young devised the forward-looking theory of political responsibility for structural injustices to complement the liability model, by focusing on the future action of actors (2006). The model is based on the variables of power ('power or influence over the processes … produc[ing] the outcomes'), 'relative privilege' held or gained as a result of structural injustice, 'interest' in keeping or changing the existing social structures and 'collective ability' in influencing structures (Young 2006, pp. 127–129). The combination of these variables determines the level of political responsibility of an actor in the global structures of injustice in a given issue area. Using the sweatshop example, Young noted that the workers who have the most interest in challenging the status quo would have the least amount of power, privilege and collective ability, while high street retailers benefitting from the system but also able to recover losses by cancelling orders when economic downturn looms on the horizon (IndustriALL 2020) have the most amount of power, privilege, collective ability but the least amount of interest (2006). Using Young's political responsibility model as complementary to the *strictu sensu* legal responsibility for ETOs would allow to bypass the limitations of territorial jurisdiction and international legal personality as well as direct causality as required by existing international legal responsibility frameworks (Erdem Türkelli 2020).

A final word

A polycentric governance framework for responsibility for the breaches of ETOs involves the use of existing legal mechanisms for responsibility such as domestic courts based on civil and criminal law, international and regional courts enforcing IL or human rights law as well as human rights treaty bodies (Erdem Türkelli 2020). Polycentricity also necessitates, where they are found to be lacking, the 'construct[ion]', of 'regulatory and political institutions' that can deal with social injustices (Young 2004, p. 388), including violations of specific human rights, or of global human rights obligations. Being able to tackle responsibility for human rights violations through multiple domestic and international venues enables access for rights-holders and facilitates the future development of ETOs, by overcoming constraints linked to territorial conceptions of jurisdiction.

Notes

1. This chapter draws on my doctoral work, my doctoral dissertation (2017) 'Corporate and Corporate-like Actors and Children's Rights: Obligations and Responsibility in Theory and in Practice' (University of Antwerp, Faculty of Law) and my book (2020) *Children's Rights and Business: Governing Obligations and Responsibility,* Cambridge University Press.
2. This section draws on Chapter 5 of my book (2020) *Children's Rights and Business: Governing Obligations and Responsibility*, Cambridge University Press.

References

Ahlborn, C. (2013) 'To Share or Not to Share? The Allocation of Responsibility between International Organizations and their Member States', *SHARES Research Paper* 28 *Die Friedens-Warte/Journal of International Peace and Organization* 88 (3-4), 45–75.

Aust, P.H. (2011) *Complicity and the Law of State Responsibility*, Cambridge University Press.

Brunnée, J. (2005) 'International Legal Accountability through the Lens of the Law of State Responsibility', *Netherlands Yearbook of International Law* 36(1), 21–56.

Clapham, A. (2004) 'State Responsibility, Corporate Responsibility, and Complicity in Human Rights Violations' in Bomann-Larsen, L. and Wiggen, O. (eds). *Responsibility in World Business: Managing Harmful Side-Effects of Corporate Activity*, United Nations University Press.

Clapham, A. (2006) *Human Rights Obligations of Non-State Actors*, Oxford University Press.

Clapham, A. (2010) 'The Subject of Subjects and the Attribution of Attribution' in Boisson de Chazournes, L. and Kohen, M. (eds). *International Law and the Quest for Its Implementation: Liber Amicorum Vera Gowlland-Debbas*, Brill Nijhoff.

Committee on Economic, Social and Cultural Rights (CESCR) (2017) GC 24 on State Obligations under the International Covenant on Economic, Social and Cultural Rights in the context of business activities, E/C.12/GC/24.

Committee on the Rights of the Child (CRC) (2013) GC 16 on State obligations regarding the impact of the business sector on children's rights, CRC/C/GC/16.

Court of Justice of the EU (CJEU) (1994) *European Parliament v. Council of the European Union* (Action for annulment - *Act* of the Council - Lomé Convention), Case C-316/91.

Erdem Türkelli, G. (2017) *Corporate and Corporate-like Actors and Children's Rights: Obligations and Responsibility in Theory and in Practice*, University of Antwerp, Faculty of Law (Doctoral Dissertation).

Erdem Türkelli, G. (2020) *Children's Rights and Business: Governing Obligations and Responsibility*, Cambridge University Press.

European Court of Human Rights (ECtHR) (1996) *Loizidou v. Turkey*, Application no: 15318/89, Judgment (Merits).

_______ (2004) *Ilascu et al. v. Moldova and Russia* [GC], no. 48787/99, § 317, 8 July 2004 (Judgment).

_______ (2007) *Behrami and Behrami v. France and Saramati v. France, Germany and Norway*, Applications no. 71412/01 and 78166/01 (Admissibility Decision).

_______ (2011a) *Al-Jedda v. the United Kingdom*, Application no: 27021/08, Judgment.

_______ (2011b) *Al-Skeini and Others v. the United Kingdom*, Application no: 55721/07, Judgment.

_______ (2014a) *Hassan v. The United Kingdom*, Application no: 29750/09, Judgment.

_______ (2014b) *Jaloud v. the Netherlands*, Application no: 47708/08, Judgment.

European Group on Tort Law (2005) 'Principles of European Tort Law' (PETL).

Gallagher, A.T. (2016) 'The Practice of Shared Responsibility in Relation to Human Rights and Human Trafficking' in Nollkaemper, A. and Plakokefalos, I. (eds). *The Practice of Shared Responsibility in International Law*, Cambridge University Press.

Higgins, R. (1995) *Legal Consequences for Member States of the Non-fulfilment by International Organizations of Their Obligations toward Third Parties, Session of Lisbonne*, Extract from Institute of International Law – Yearbook 66-I.

IndustriALL. (2020) 'ACT Brands Commit to Responsible Business Practices in Bangladesh', 31 March 2020, http://www.industriall-union.org/act-brands-commit-to-responsible-business-practices-in-bangladesh [accessed 1 September 2020].

Inter-American Commission on Human Rights (IACmHR) (2002) 'What is Terrorism? Report on Terrorism & Human Rights', OEA/Ser.L/V/II.116 Doc. 5 rev. 1 corr.

Inter-American Court of Human Rights (IACtHR) (1988) *Case of Velásquez-Rodríguez v. Honduras*, Series C No. 4. Case 7.615, Judgment.

International Court of Justice (ICJ) (2007) Application of the Convention on the Prevention and Punishment of the Crime of Genocide (*Bosnia and Herzegovina v. Serbia and Montenegro*), Judgment.

International Law Commission (ILC) (2001) 'Articles on the Responsibility of States for Internationally Wrongful Acts (ARSIWA)', Annex to General Assembly resolution 56/83 of 12 December 2001, and corrected by document A/56/49(Vol. I)/Corr.4.

_______ (2011a) 'Articles on the Responsibility of International Organisations' (ARIO), https://legal.un.org/ilc/texts/instruments/english/draft_articles/9_11_2011.pdf (accessed 16 July 2021).

_______ (2011b) 'General Commentary to the DARIO', Draft articles on the responsibility of international organizations, with commentaries, https://legal.un.org/ilc/texts/instruments/english/commentaries/9_11_2011.pdf (accessed 16 July 2021).

Karavias, M. (2015) 'Shared Responsibility and Multinational Enterprises', *Netherlands International Law Review* 62, 91–117.

Keohane, R.O. and Nye, Jr., J.S. (2000) 'Introduction' in Nye, Jr., J.S. and Donahue, J.D. (eds). *Governance in a Globalizing World*, Brookings Institution Press.

Lanovoy, V. (2016) *Complicity and Its Limits in the Law of International Responsibility*, Hart Publishing.

May, L. (1992) *Sharing Responsibility*, University of Chicago Press.

McCorquodale, R. and Simons, P. (2007) 'Responsibility beyond Borders: State Responsibility for Extraterritorial Violations by Corporations of International Human Rights Law', *The Modern Law Review* 70(4), 598–625.

Milanovic, M. (2011) *Extraterritorial Application of Human Rights Treaties: Law, Principles, and Policy*, Oxford University Press.

Nollkaemper, A. (2014) 'Introduction' in Nollkaemper, A. and Plakokefalos, I (eds), *Principles of Shared Responsibility in International Law: An Appraisal of the State of the Art*, Cambridge University Press, 2014

Nollkaemper, A. and Jacobs, D. (2013) 'Shared Responsibility in International Law: A Conceptual Framework', *Michigan Journal of International Law* 34, 359–438.

_______ (2015) 'Introduction: Mapping the Normative Framework for the Distribution of Shared Responsibility' in Nollkaemper, A. and Jacobs, D. (eds). *Distribution of Responsibilities in International Law*, Cambridge University Press.

Nollkaemper, A. and Plakokefalos, I. (2016) 'Conclusions: Beyond the ILC Legacy' in Nollkaemper, A. and Plakokefalos, I. (eds). *The Practice of Shared Responsibility in International Law*, Cambridge University Press.

Nollkaemper, A. et al. (2020) 'Guiding Principles on Shared Responsibility in International Law', *European Journal of International Law* 11(11), 15–72.

Office of the High Commissioner for Human Rights (OHCHR) and Center for Economic and Social Rights (2013) 'Who will be Accountable? Human Rights and the Post-2015 Development Agenda', https://www.ohchr.org/Documents/Publications/WhoWillBeAccountable.pdf (accessed 16 July 2021).

Ostrom, E. (2009) 'A Polycentric Approach for Coping with Climate Change', *World Bank Policy Research Working Paper No. 5095*, 2-54, https://documents1.worldbank.org/curated/en/480171468315567893/pdf/WPS5095.pdf (accessed 16 July 2021).

Prenkert, J.D. and Shackelford, S.J. (2014) 'Business, Human Rights, and the Promise of Polycentricity', *Vanderbilt Journal of Transnational Law* 47, 451–500.

Ryngaert, C. and Buchanan, H. (2011) 'Member State Responsibility for the Acts of International Organizations', *Utrecht Law Review* 7(1), 131–146.

Salomon, M.E. (2007) *Responsibility for Human Rights: World Poverty and the Development of International Law*, Oxford University Press.

Sari, A. (2008) 'Jurisdiction and International Responsibility in Peace Support Operations: The Behrami and Saramati Cases', *Human Rights Law Review* 8, 151–170.

Sarooshi, D. (2005) *International Organizations and Their Exercise of Sovereign Powers*, Oxford University Press.

Stumer, A. (2007) 'Liability of Member States for Acts of International Organizations: Reconsidering the Policy Objections', *Harvard International Law Journal* 48(2), 553–580.

UN Human Rights (HR) Committee (2009) *Munaf v. Romania*, CCPR/C/96/D/1539/2006.

Young, I.M. (2004) 'Responsibility and Global Labor Justice', *The Journal of Political Philosophy* 12(4), 365–388.

_______ (2006) 'Responsibility and Global Justice: A Social Connection Model', *Social Philosophy & Policy Foundation* 23(1), 102–130.

4

Justifying extraterritorial human rights obligations

An ethical perspective

Angela Müller

Introduction[1]

Today, opportunities for states to affect human rights abroad abound: Global phenomena like climate change, migration, trade, or terrorism multiply the scope of individuals a state can affect—at home as well as abroad. New technologies such as automated weapon systems open up novel ways to infringe human rights without even setting foot on a territory, and intelligence strategies like extraordinary renditions, or 'terror by proxy' that intend to exploit 'legal black holes' abroad are on the rise.

In light of these developments, spotlighting the obligations states are subject to when affecting people on foreign territories is an urgent and timely task. So far, such *extraterritorial human rights obligations* (ETOs) have mostly been discussed within legal scholarship. In philosophy, only little attention has been paid to the analysis of *normative reasons* for such obligations, i.e. for the assumption that *human rights law* should oblige *states* with respect to *individuals abroad*.[2]

Given the level of sophistication the legal ETO debate has achieved over the last two decades, one might suggest that it can reasonably proceed on the presumption that such conceptual work is no longer required and move on to focus on technical legal details in concrete cases. However, this move might be not only premature but also ill-timed: In scholarship, critiques of the general idea of universal human rights are on the rise, stemming from a variety of theoretical outlooks (e.g., Posner 2014; Moyn 2018). In the political realm, nationalist agendas are gaining grounds all over the world, and many of them are openly critical of the idea of duties to strangers abroad. Most importantly, to a certain extent, such a move conflicts with state practice: Many states still—generally and/or in concrete cases—oppose the extraterritorial applicability of human rights law.

Against this background, this contribution starts from the assumptions: (i) That establishing a firmer normative basis of ETOs could ultimately improve their standing in practice, too, and (ii) that this requires a systematic analysis of the grounds on which the persistent *opposition* to ETOs rests: The concerns behind this opposition must be discerned and engaged with. The chapter begins by, first, pointing to two common threads in legal practice: Courts' struggle for consistency when extraterritorially applying human rights law and the territorial paradigm that continues to underlie this legal field. Second, it presents selected theories—associated with moral, political,

DOI: 10.4324/9781003090014-6

and legal philosophy and related fields—that could stand behind skeptic positions on ETOs, and it reconstructs the arguments they could provide for such skepticism. Based on a critique of these arguments in its third section, it then, fourth, turns to the normative justification of ETOs and, lastly, indicates how these ethically oriented reflections could be considered at the legal level.

As a last preliminary remark, it is important to clarify that, while the following reflections focus on international human rights law (IHRL), the basic assumption is that the *moral foundation* of fundamental rights enshrined in domestic law (or in European supranational law) does not essentially differ from the former's.

Two tendencies in legal practice

Due to its normative focus, this chapter will not include a legal analysis of ETOs (for such analyses, see other contributions in this volume). The following section limits itself to asserting two tendencies that can be observed across a range of legal regimes, and it does so by way of an illustrative example: The case law on the *European Convention of Human Rights* (ECHR).

First, courts struggle with developing consistent approaches to how and when states are bound by human rights norms when their acts or omissions have effects abroad. In IHRL, where *jurisdiction* functions as the key threshold for the applicability of many treaties (e.g., ECHR, art. 1), this typically boils down to the question of how and when states exercise jurisdiction abroad. The European Court of Human Rights denied jurisdiction in cases in which individuals abroad had been severely affected by the actions of Member states (e.g., ECtHR 2001, paras. 54–82), while confirming it without any (or any thorough) discussion in other extraterritorial situations where the link between the applicant and the foreign state appeared, at least *prima facie*, to be less direct (e.g., ECtHR 2014). In still other cases, it applied the Convention abroad, but still emphasized the 'essentially territorial' nature of jurisdiction (e.g., ECtHR 2012, paras. 71–72). So far, it has failed to settle on a principled approach to what jurisdiction means in situations abroad. It has tried to develop such principles in some cases (e.g., ECtHR 2011, paras. 133–142), while at the same time referring to the need to decide the issue on a case-by-case basis (e.g., ECtHR 2019, para. 190; 2012, para. 74).

Second, the Court reveals its skeptic stance on extraterritorial applicability of the Convention, by including the above-cited dictum on the territorial nature of jurisdiction and the exceptionality of its extraterritorial exercise in almost all relevant case law (e.g., ECtHR 2020, paras. 98–100). This illustrates the territorial paradigm that continues to underlie IHRL: It stems not only from the fact that IHRL forms part of public international law, which was built on Westphalian-inspired conceptions of territorial sovereignty, but also from the central role assigned to jurisdiction and its potential for ambiguity. In IHRL, the question must be whether jurisdiction was *de facto* exercised, deviating from its *de jure* understanding in general public international law (e.g., Milanović 2013, p. 26). Its ambiguous nature contributes to the difficulties judicial bodies seem to have in addressing this central concept (cf. ECtHR 2001, paras. 59–61).

These tendencies are epitomized by, but not limited to the jurisprudential body on the ECHR. While other IHRL courts and treaty bodies—such as the Inter-American Court of Human Rights or the Human Rights Committee (HRC)—have recognized a wider scope of extraterritorial applicability, controversies continue and claims about the essentially territorial nature of human rights obligations persist. Moreover, while this chapter spotlights IHRL, and while the applicability of domestic protection regimes is not regulated by the threshold of *jurisdiction*, it is informative that the two tendencies can also be observed in domestic contexts: For example, they are mirrored by the jurisprudence of the US Supreme Court, which takes a restrictive approach to the extraterritorial reach of constitutional protection (US Supreme Court 1990, 494 US 259), struggles with providing coherent principles on it, and tends to avoid this 'sensitive' and 'far reaching' question (US Supreme Court 2017, 582 US ___, slip. op. at 5). Lastly, and most importantly, ETOs continue to face resistance on the part of duty-bearers at stake, i.e., states (cf. illustratively HRC 2018 and there e.g., the statements of The Netherlands, para. 29; or United States, paras. 13 and 15; also, France 2019, para. 18).

These two common threads point to the need for further research on the normative background of ETOs. If the territorial paradigm shall be won over, and if coherent approaches to extraterritorial applicability shall be developed, they need firmer grounding.

Concerns behind skepticism towards extraterritorial human rights obligations

In the philosophical debate on global justice, two strands of theories stand for contrary perspectives on the reach of duties to individuals. *Cosmopolitan* theories typically take a universalist starting point, assuming that any *limitations* to the universal reach of such duties need to be justified. In contrast, *statist* theories diagnose an elemental difference between the domestic and the global sphere, asserting that the burden of proof lies with those that aim at *expanding* obligations beyond national boundaries. The next section provides a (non-exhaustive) list of statist theories and suggests how they could be deployed for developing arguments against ETOs. Even though, so far, many of these theories have not explicitly been linked to the ETO debate, and even though more moderate exponents associated with them often refrain from thoroughly denying any obligations to outsiders, their skeptical views on the general moral idea of universal human rights and on their legal codification contain premises that could furnish such arguments against ETOs—at least in their more radical versions. Hence, they provide clues to the concerns that may stand behind the persistence of the territorial paradigm.

First, the legitimacy of ETOs could be denied from a perspective of *International Relations (IR) Realism*—a theory that, as its name says, is typically associated with the field of IR but that has had important reverberations in political philosophy. It goes back to authors like *Morgenthau* (1949) or *Waltz* (1979) and has recently been revived as an alternative to the liberalist picture (e.g., Williams 2005; Geuss 2008). According to the realist, the international sphere—strictly differing from the domestic one—is marked by constant threat and prone to conflicts. In this anarchical setting, the state functions as the central agent and power as its main instrument. States primarily (or exclusively) pursue national self-interest and the relations among them are not governed by morality but by standards of rationality and effectiveness. In contemporary versions, liberal universalist ideas like human rights, the triumph of which had marked the years after the Cold War, are said to have arrived at their end point.

Realists tend to reject the moral idea of universal human rights and their legal codification in general, which they declare incompatible with the setup of the international sphere. Adopting this perspective, the mere idea of ETOs—i.e., of legally introducing diagonal obligations of a state to individuals abroad—must be regarded as naïve, given that states' motives simply do not depend on the content of international norms but on national interest. Respect for the former is always conditional upon its congruency with the latter. Direct duties to persons abroad would illegitimately limit states' pursuit of self-interest in foreign affairs (Morgenthau 1949, p. 210; see also US Supreme Court 1990, 494 US 259, 273–275).

Second, in this view, it is hypocritical to incorporate moral concerns—like the one behind human rights—into transnational relations and international law, considering that states would only hide their real motivation behind such efforts—their self-interests—behind the façade of the former (e.g., Morgenthau 1979, pp. 4–7). Applying this view to the issue of ETOs, realists could thus assert that if there was a general system positing norms on other states' territories that do not stem from the latter's sovereign decision, this would increase the opportunities to imperialistically inflict standards of hegemonic states onto others.

Communitarianism—a theory rooted in moral philosophy but often applied to political theory—provides a second potential strand of skepticism. Communitarians oppose the liberalist individualistic perspective, asserting that individual identity is essentially determined by social bonds (e.g., Taylor 1985, pp. 187 ff.). Humans attach great significance to similarity and otherness, they are naturally partial to the near and dear and motivationally incapable of expanding solidarity to distant strangers. Particularity—the fact that someone is *my* sister or *my* compatriot—is of intrinsic importance to us, generating *sui generis* moral reasons that are not reducible to impartial and universalist moral concerns, the source of which would lie outside the community. Applied to national or political communities, it is the mutual sharing of values, history, culture, and traditions that makes membership of them such an essential value for individuals, their identity, socialization, moral education, and flourishing (e.g., MacIntyre 1984; Walzer 1983, pp. 31–63 and p. 314). They are perceived as essentially involving a network of exclusive obligations to co-members (or at least special obligations to prioritize them). From a hard communitarian position, it could be derived that there are no grounds for subjecting the state to obligations that are based on universalist ideas and that expand beyond its own community—thus, that there are no grounds for ETOs.

Related concerns stand behind *neo-republicanism*, a prominent approach in political theory, which assigns central value to *freedom* from others' control. Freedom can be defined as *non-domination*, i.e., the guarantee of not being subject to the arbitrary will of others (Pettit 1997). As a prerequisite for realizing freedom, *collective self-determination* is of particular significance: Individual freedom requires internal freedom of one's political community, i.e., collective self-determination—and the latter requires freedom of the state from external agents: It must only act upon standards on which its members have autonomously agreed and that reflect the will of the community (Pettit 2016).

With respect to individual rights protection, the neo-republican must generally hold that if such norms exist, they can only result from the activity and the consent of the community. Based on this perspective, she could add that *extraterritorially applying* IHRL norms in order to protect *non-members* cannot reflect the will of members but rather mirrors external and universal standards. Accepting such standards would be equal to subjecting the state to the arbitrary will of outside agents and thus result in domination. This can be combined with a voluntarist view on the authority of international law, which describes participation in the latter as a fully voluntary undertaking, rooted in sovereign consent that reflects members' will.

From a similar perspective, *Nagel* promotes a specific version of a political theory of justice, arguing that justice is not a pre-institutional concept but only (and necessarily) arises within the context of institutions and among members of the corresponding community (2005). In his account, it only pertains within 'thick' institutional frameworks characterized by, first, *coerciveness* over members and, second, the fact that members at the same time *participate as co-authors* of the coercive structure, i.e., the state acts *in their names*. According to Nagel, it is this unique combination that generates duties of justice (pp. 128–130)—and that, at least as of today, only exists in the context of the *domestic state*. He regards the international order as categorically different: Neither is it structured by coercion (but by consent of its subjects, i.e., states), nor can individuals act as co-authors (as its norms are not enacted by them but by the state) (pp. 137–143). Hence, justice obligations do not apply here. Thus, on condition that human rights duties can be classified as duties of justice,[3] Nagel's approach entails that they only hold within the domestic context, obliging the state vis-à-vis insiders but not vis-à-vis outside non-members.

A further cluster of concerns springs from moral *relativism*—in particular, from the relativist critique of universal human rights. According to cultural relativism, values and principles—including conceptions of individual rights—are defined relative to the particular historical, social, religious, and cultural context. To this descriptive thesis, the moral relativist adds the normative premise that, given this fact, all sets of values and principles deserve equal respect.

According to the relativist critique, what is today referred to as 'human rights' does not flow from a universally shared but from a specific modern, Western, and liberal value set (e.g., Brown 1997), which is incompatible with, for example, *Asian values* that attach great significance to collectivity. Declaring the former universally valid results in an ethnocentric, parochial, imperialistic, neo-colonialist, or neo-liberalist imposition of values onto others who do not share them (from a postcolonial perspective, e.g., Mutua 2002; Koskenniemi 2018; for the neo-liberalist critique, Hardt and Negri 2000; from the perspective of pragmatism, Rorty 1989). When applying their general critique of human rights to the question at issue, relativists could argue that equipping human rights law with extraterritorial reach would introduce a system that adds to the illegitimate nature of the enterprise. The duties a state has must be derived from its particular context-specific conceptions and only hold vis-à-vis its members. When states act abroad, the norms they are subject to must stem from the territorial context on which they are acting. Other societies have 'wholly dissimilar traditions and institutions' (US Supreme Court 1990, 494 US 259, 278 (Kennedy J., concurring)), and a political community cannot simply inflict its way of fundamental rights protection on territories abroad.

Why skepticism is unfounded

After this summarized listing of several concerns that could motivate the persistence of the territorial paradigm, this section focuses on the weaknesses of these objections—an analysis that in turn will help identify aspects relevant to the normative justification of ETOs.

The empirical analysis of *IR Realism* certainly points to important features of the international sphere. At the same time, there is reason to doubt that states only act on self-interest, that human rights law does not make any difference, and that a firm judicial recognition of ETOs would not influence states' conduct at all. Of course, some states notoriously fail to comply with IHRL, and its introduction has not resulted in the global demolition of injustices. However, it has certainly had some—and not only minor—achievements, be it at the level of compliance, adjudication, or awareness-raising. Furthermore, the *empirical* realist analysis does not by itself have implications for the *normative legitimacy* of extraterritorially applying human rights norms: There is a gap between *Is* and *Ought*. If some states tend to ignore human rights when affecting people abroad, this does not yet mean they are justified in doing so. Morality applies whenever human-controlled actions have effects on other sentient beings, regardless of the acceptance of its applicability by its subjects, the confrontative and decentralized nature of the setting, and the territorial location of these effects (Caney 2006, p. 276).

Second, the concept of national interest—vague as it is—need not be in contradiction with a concern for human rights. On the one hand, compliance with human rights both at home and abroad can contribute to international stability and thereby promote domestic interests, too. On the other hand, states also have non-instrumental interests in taking human rights, as common concerns of humankind, seriously (Ryngaert 2015, pp. 102–111). This is what basic constitutional principles routinely assert by declaring human rights constitutive parts of the national value set (e.g., *Grundgesetz für die Bundesrepublik Deutschland,* art. 1). But if this is the case, then their value cannot simply evaporate when this very state's acts have effects beyond its national borders.

A nationalist argument against ETOs based on a hard *communitarian* position is equally unconvincing. First, if one's personal and moral *identity develops* within a specific context, that does not yet mean that *moral norms only apply* within this context. For example, to see how one's communal structure treats non-members and to learn that the latter also have legitimate claims form central parts of moral education. Moreover, various real-life counterexamples prove that humans are not virtually incapable of solidarity to strangers. Likewise, one should avoid overstating the uniformity *within* and the differences *among* communities (Langford and Darrow 2013, pp. 422–423). It has always been the case—and today's globalized world just more evidently illustrates it—that values and interests are shared across territorial boundaries, and so are the social bonds that individuals hold dear. What co-members of anonymous political communities share is unlikely as thick and uniform as nationalist communitarians portray it. This indicates that the general strategy of drawing normative implications from the analogy between personal and political relationships is mistaken: These are two very distinct phenomena. While the latter may be instrumentally valuable for realizing individual goods, their value is not of an intrinsic kind. Moreover, individuals are doubtlessly social animals, but they are not reducible to their social bonds—and it is this very idea that human rights as rights of human beings that do not depend on membership (except for membership of humanity) reflect.

Second, partiality is certainly not something that *states*, in the area of human rights, cannot overcome. Second-level impartiality, which applies to institutions like the state and is ensured by law, might precisely define and enable legitimate degrees of first-order partiality, i.e., for individuals to act partial to their personal concerns. The discussion at issue concerns the principles by which *international law* should oblige *states* when it comes to actions that affect *individuals' human rights*. At least in this area and for this actor, *being mine* does not make a foundational difference.

Again, members *factually* perceiving the state as having exclusive obligations to its members does not mean that such obligations are *normatively* justified. If insiders always get priority (or exclusive concern), outsiders get at least *less* (or no) concern. This raises justification conditions of such prioritizing considerably, especially if what is at stake for the outsider is of a fundamental nature—such as in the case of human rights. This is especially problematic in situations where states are acting abroad: Downplaying or denying the duty of a state agent located abroad not to violate human rights of local residents by referring to its special duties to compatriots at home comes close to denying human rights at all.

The *neo-republican* concerns toward ETOs are, first, in tension with contemporary reality: In today's world, where threats to individual goods are increasingly of a global nature—be it climate change, transnational crime, or cyber attacks—maximizing states' external freedom is unlikely to guarantee internal freedom for their members. Rather, securing the latter often depends on states' participation in cooperative global efforts to tackle these challenges. Plus, a voluntarist take on international law opens the door to unpredictable unilateralism (Criddle and Fox-Decent 2019, p. 291), whereas the reliable application of norms like those of IHRL to all domains and locations of state conduct fosters predictability—and thereby precisely reduces the risks of insecurity and arbitrariness.

Second, *within* the community, collective freedom does not guarantee individual freedom. Individuals, especially those belonging to minorities, precisely rely on protections in the form of constitutional or—as a backstop—international rights, should the will of the majority threaten to undermine their freedom. Moreover, while it is certainly crucial for individuals to participate in some exercise of autonomy at the collective level, it is not crucial for them that this collective autonomy includes being free from duties to non-members and disregarding non-members' claims to freedom and autonomy. If individual freedom is so significant, then it must be significant for all human beings, regardless of their territorial location.

The pertinence of Nagel's account to the issue of ETOs depends on the adequacy of defining human rights duties as a category of justice obligations. This is a substantial assumption that will need to be explicated when the discussion turns to the normative justification of ETOs. At this point, the critique proceeds from this assumption, spotlighting two main problems of employing Nagel's approach as an argument against ETOs.

First, institutional obligations—i.e., obligations *of institutions*—do not have to be associative obligations: They are not only directed at those who formally classify as the respective institutions' members but at *everyone affected* by this institutional structure. If institutions are essentially charged with the protection of justice concerns, then these concerns do not become irrelevant when institutional conduct affects non-members. Justice regulates institutions, not *vice versa*: It is not the particular institutional community that defines what justice demands. Justice principles—including human rights—set substantive constraints on institutions that are not contingent, neither on domestic decision-making nor on geographical facts. As *Kumm* puts it, if state conduct has negative externalities abroad that touch upon justice-relevant concerns—such as human rights—they cannot be left to states' sovereign decision but must be regulated by international law, whether states have explicitly consented or not (2013, p. 613).

Moreover, outsiders typically do not have the judicial, political, and societal means paradigmatically available to insiders, to defend themselves against infringements of basic rights. In other words, while they can be *exposed* to *coercive* acts of foreign states, they lack the means to participate as *co-authors*. Human rights—especially internationally guaranteed rights—exactly provide crucial means of protection for whom it is more difficult or impossible to rely on domestic mechanisms.

What stands behind both the neo-republican and the institutionalist skepticism toward universal human rights is the worry of an unresolvable tension between genuine popular sovereignty and being constrained by such universal norms, assuming that the latter reflect standards that do not derive from the will of those subjected. This suspicion is mistaken. Subjugation to regimes of basic rights protection (at domestic or international levels) does not undermine popular sovereignty but, on the contrary, likely increases its legitimacy. The idea of democratic self-determination is not only a procedural but also a substantive one, including preconditions that cannot be made the objects of the decision-making process—such as, centrally, fundamental rights. These are not external standards that compromise popular sovereignty; rather, they enhance individuals' capacity for autonomy, freedom, and living a life in dignity. Their source is not the arbitrary will of an outside agent but lies in each and every individual, within or beyond borders.

Second, it is *empirically* questionable whether Nagel is correct in asserting that 'thin' international institutions categorically differ from domestic ones. For example, contemporary international law amounts to an expansive (even if not yet fully comprehensive) legal system with at least some coercive structures, which recognizes individuals as direct legal subjects, enables at least indirect participation (even if mediated by individuals' ability to participate domestically), and is increasingly accompanied by the evolution of a global civil society. International norms, politics, and agents have actual and potential, direct and indirect impacts on individuals' lives. As of today, some international institutions might be *gradually* thinner but not all of them are *categorically* distinct to domestic ones (the EU being a paradigmatic example).

On closer inspection, the general *relativist* critique of universal human rights itself takes a universalist moral position: It relies on the implicit premise that it is—universally—wrong to impose own norms to others, implying a universal principle of tolerance and ascribing normative superiority to cultural diversity. Moreover, its claim about the hypocrite nature of human rights efforts, which ETOs would multiply, is only valid insofar as the assumption of the universal justifiability of human rights is *wrong*. Only then could obeying them abroad mean illegitimately imposing foreign standards. In addition, it is important to underline that foundationally universally justified principles can still be formulated (e.g., in positive law) or applied (e.g., by judicial bodies) in context-sensitive ways.

The relativist overstates the dichotomy between Western and non-Western values and ignores the wide convergence on values and principles across the globe—especially on core principles behind IHRL (Sen 1996). Moreover, the conception behind IHRL attaching significance to individual autonomy neither contradicts community concerns nor undermines cultural diversity: Autonomy-based norms can precisely serve as a means to protect diversity (cf. Coomaraswamy 2013, p. 53), and their extraterritorial extension could actually contribute to protecting the diverse needs and interests of outsiders.

Lastly, human rights have certainly been misused to conceal other (sometimes imperialist) motives—by both Western and non-Western regimes. However, this does not render the concept itself an illegitimate instrument of the powerful. It is precisely in extraterritorial settings, too, where human rights are crucial for protecting individuals who are exposed to foreign state acts and have only limited other means of protection available. At the very least, a firm legal recognition of ETOs would entail a common set of expectations that if foreign interventions are made, human rights must not be left behind.

Normatively justifying extraterritorial human rights obligations

The above discussion of the concerns that might motivate skepticism towards ETOs now allows for identifying aspects relevant to the normative justification of these obligations.

The first cluster of such aspects concerns the *core idea behind human rights obligations*, which correspond to rights assigned by virtue of *being human*. This 'being human' refers to a distinct core of human nature, which is universally shared. This conception of universally shared rights sketches the core idea behind human rights. If it is denied, it is not clear how one could still speak of *human* rights. And, as alluded to when discussing Nagel's approach, human rights are foundationally a justice-relevant domain: It is the basic idea of justice to treat everyone equally who is equal with respect to the relevant aspects at issue. Consequently, it is a demand of justice to apply the foundational norms that are assigned by virtue of the universally shared core of human nature—human rights—to everyone equally as well (Mahlmann 2008, pp. 447–453 and pp. 518–519). And it is this basic moral idea that stands behind the legal protection of human rights—at the international level and, arguably, also at the domestic level.

However, as rights do not only consist of claims but also of obligations, the universality of rights suggests the universality of obligations (Skogly 2010, pp. 833–834). At the very least, the legitimate starting point is the general assumption that human rights *obligations* hold universally, too. In other words, the point of departure for the debate on their reach should be a universalist one, namely the assumption that states are, in principle, bound by them *whenever* and *wherever* they affect human beings. Thus, the burden of proof does not lie with those who wish to expand duties beyond states' borders but with those who would want to constrain them to these very borders.

As it seems, it is already this basic moral idea behind human rights that is in tension with asserting that states are only bound with regard to part of their actions or omissions with effects on individuals, namely those the effects of which happen to materialize on their territory.

The second cluster of considerations relevant to the justification of states' ETOs concerns the *nature of the duty-bearer* at stake here. As the paradigmatic human rights duty-bearer, the state is the actor that means the biggest threat to human rights and, at the same time, that can most reliantly and effectively protect human rights. This ambiguity stems from the multifaceted nature of this institution, which can both positively and negatively affect people in major ways, not only through unique means of normative, legal authority but also through its enormous *de facto* power and resources. At the same time, states are institutions set up in the service of individuals (ICJ 2010, Separate Op. Cançado Trindade, para. 239; even if, evidently, not every factual state lives up to this demand). This ambiguity mirrors the basic insight behind human rights, namely that human beings need to be protected from states' extraordinary power (requiring states to respect human rights) and at the same time must rely on this powerful agent set up for them (obliging states to also protect and fulfil human rights). Accordingly, human rights obligations must *normatively delimit and define* the space of legitimate state action.[4] While statehood is not a necessary condition for being a human rights duty-bearer, it certainly amounts to a *sufficient condition*.

This directly bears on the question of ETOs. It entails that human rights obligations bind states by virtue of their mere statehood and, consequently, with regard to all their conduct that affects human beings—*at home or abroad*. For these duty-bearers, being subject to human rights obligations means being subject to substantive restrictions on their freedom of action (including negative duties to refrain from acting as well as positive duties to act), which do not depend on the location of the effects of their acts or on other contingencies—unless this can be justified.

It is true that, given the global *status quo*, it is often the domestic state on the protection of which individuals most urgently depend: Typically, it is my state of residence that can most easily violate my rights as well as most efficiently protect them. However, this does not make membership a *necessary* condition for human rights obligations to apply. Today, people are routinely exposed to the effects of foreign states' actions, too. While outsiders' vulnerability is not necessarily greater than that of insiders—typically, the opposite is the case—it evolves within a special context, given that outsiders' means to defend themselves tend to be more limited. It is often more arduous for them to challenge a foreign state's violations in its domestic courts, to influence foreign state conduct by participating in decision-making, or to raise awareness on and demand justifications for this conduct in public debate. In this diagonal relation, in which other means of protection are often limited, ETOs provide critical protection. If human rights standards essentially regulate relationships between states and individuals, then they must also govern diagonal relationships between states and foreign individuals (Müller 2020). In other words, while membership of political communities, collective self-determination, or co-authorship can certainly be of moral and legal relevance, what must be denied is that they serve as necessary thresholds for the applicability of human rights duties.

Lastly, ETOs are certainly demanding requirements. Yet, the institution state, which comes with a legal system, precisely has the intention of and capacity for discharging such demands. One of the crucial points behind normative systems like morality and law is to ensure impartiality as the foundational touchstone of regulating human interactions. They do so, *inter alia*, by dividing moral labor and allocating demanding, impartial, and universal duties to institutions like the state, leaving more leeway for individuals to act on personal concerns.

To sum up, foundationally, at least in this domain (*human rights*) and at least for this actor (*the institution state*), the point of departure must be that obligations hold universally. Thus, it is not their universal reach but, on the contrary, their limitation to territory that bears the burden of proof.

How to approach jurisdiction

Moral norms are not necessarily directly translatable to legal ones, but there are domains in which ethical theory should crucially inform the content or interpretation of the latter. This nexus is particularly strong in the area of human rights, the legalization of which is based on their basic moral idea. At the same time, ethical reasoning cannot ignore legal reality—*inter alia*, it must consider the content of positive law. Thus, the idea here is that the normative idea behind human rights obligations should guide the interpretation of corresponding legal norms and their applicability conditions as enshrined in positive law—such as, in IHRL, of *jurisdiction*.

That said, the universalist starting point argued for above can only serve as a first approximation to jurisdiction: It must be translated into legally workable criteria of how to interpret this central notion (e.g., promising guidelines based on a universalist starting point are provided by the *Maastricht Principles on Extraterritorial Obligations of States in the Area of Economic, Social, and Cultural Rights*). The following limits itself to pointing to selected aspects the above reflections entail for a coherent interpretation of jurisdiction.

First, it must capture the ambiguous and multifaceted nature of states as human rights duty-bearers: They can exercise jurisdiction by acting as bearers of legal authority but also by making use of their factual power, whether in lawful or unlawful ways. That said, states cannot be obliged to do the impossible. The effects over which they can reasonably be said to exercise jurisdiction cannot include distant side-effects they could not have foreseen or altered by lawful and proportionate means.

Second, the multifaceted nature of states must also be mirrored in the multidimensionality of ETO. In this respect, it is important that jurisdiction and corresponding obligations can be divided and tailored, especially as in extraterritorial situations, it is often the case that many states are involved.

Third, the interpretation of jurisdiction must still account for the fact that it is—*not necessarily* but *typically*—the domestic state on the protection of which individuals most urgently depend, without thereby assigning foundational significance to relations of membership or territory. Rather, these relations serve as a mere 'rule of coordination' (Shany 2013, p. 69). Given the contemporary statist system, there might be *instrumental* reasons for allocating primary obligations to the domestic state: This then serves as an efficient instrument of realizing the overall universalist aim—but there is nothing more behind the domestic relation.

Fourth—and this point goes beyond the question of how to interpret jurisdiction—it must be ensured that human rights protection provides a reliable mechanism in light of outsiders' limited means. *Inter alia*, ETOs must be accompanied by measures enabling or enhancing the enforceability and justiciability of these—doubtlessly complex—norms. This includes, among many other things, enabling outsiders' access to domestic and international courts by removing formal and practical barriers, or equipping judicial bodies with the adequate means to analyze situations that occurred far away (cf. also *Maastricht Principles*, pp. 36–41).

In sum, a coherent model of how to interpret jurisdiction must translate the foundational moral insight—namely that states, as institutional tools for humans and in light of their multifaceted role, are universally bound by human rights norms—into a practicable criterion sensitive to legal reality. Such a criterion must be coherent and principled, but it is clear that it will, to a certain extent, remain an abstract standard that, eventually, has to be put into practice by judicial bodies—which is, however, a task such bodies are essentially and routinely entrusted with. And in undertaking this task, they should be guided by the universalist normative idea behind human rights obligations.

Moreover, while jurisdiction—so reinterpreted—might be able to cover ETOs *sensu stricto* (Vandenhole 2012, p. 5), it will still leave many transnational rights concerns unanswered. It is unlikely to capture what normative considerations also point to: That there are, in addition, obligations to the entire human community that do not depend on any underlying jurisdictional link. Such *global obligations to work toward the universal realization of human rights* (cf. *Maastricht Principle* 8b; Skogly in this volume) also have a firm normative standing, even if they cannot fully be captured by current positive human rights law, the applicability of which is, to a large extent, conditioned on the notion of jurisdiction. In this area, a comprehensive implementation of ETOs might not be achievable *exclusively* through *reinterpretation* of positive human rights law—even though some current regimes could account for such global obligations. Here, the normative idea behind human rights obligations suggests that positive law might also have to evolve.

Conclusion

The present chapter has concluded that, taking seriously the idea behind human rights, the legitimate starting point as to states' human rights obligations is a universalist one. Thus, it is not their universal reach but rather any territorial limitations of such obligations that bear the burden of proof.

In times of globalization, the introduction of new technological means that allow for causing distant harm at the push of a button, the academic revival of statist and nationalist accounts, the success of their political derivatives all over the world, and the rising human rights critique in both academia and practice, the debate on ETOs is timelier than ever. The present contribution has sought to contribute to strengthening the justificatory basis of these duties, which, as state practice indicates, continues to be a major task. Such theoretically oriented background work can hope to contribute to greater coherence and ultimately to the growing acceptance of ETOs in scholarship, jurisprudence—and, ultimately, among the duty-bearers at stake, namely states.

Notes

1. This contribution formed part of a research project on «The Legal Philosophy of Extraterritorial Applications of Human Rights» (2018–2021), funded by the Swiss National Science Foundation and led by Prof. Matthias Mahlmann at the University of Zurich.
2. This gap in normative theorizing is not without notable exceptions on the part of legal scholars (*inter alia* Langford and Darrow 2013; Milanović 2013; Gibney 2016; Raible 2020).
3. Nagel might object that his theses only concern *positive duties of socioeconomic justice*, as he grants that a 'minimal humanitarian morality' could apply beyond the domestic context (2005, pp. 126–132). However, Nagel's 'minimal humanitarian morality' is well below contemporary IHRL: It is restricted to negative duties not to commit atrocities and of an ethically *humanitarian* kind, differentiating it to stringent *moral* and *legal human rights obligations* (Cohen and Sabel 2006, p. 173).
4. Compliance with human rights is certainly not a sufficient condition of state conduct to be legitimate. Moreover, many state actions do not concern fundamental rights issues. Hence, it is only suggested that legitimate state conduct *must not involve human rights violations*.

References

Brown, C. (1997) 'Universal Human Rights: A Critique', *The International Journal of Human Rights* 1(2), 41–65.

Caney, S. (2006) *Justice beyond Borders: A Global Political Theory*, Oxford University Press.

Cohen, J. and Sabel, C. (2006) 'Extra Rempublicam Nulla Justitia?', *Philosophy & Public Affairs* 34(2), 147–175.

Coomaraswamy, R. (2013) 'Universalism of Human Rights and Cultural Relativism' in Sheeran, S. and Sir Rodley, N. (eds). *Routledge Handbook of International Human Rights Law*, Routledge.

Criddle, E.J. and Fox-Decent, E. (2019) 'Mandatory Multilateralism', *American Journal of International Law* 113(2), 272–325.

European Court of Human Rights (ECtHR) (2001) Banković and Others v. Belgium and Others, Application no: 52207/99, Decision.

_______ (2011) *Al-Skeini and Others v. United Kingdom*, Application no: 55721/07, Judgment.

_______ (2012) *Hirsi Jamaa and Others v. Italy*, Application no: 27765/09, Judgment.

_______ (2014) *Gray v. Germany*, Application no: 49278/09, Judgment.

_______ (2019) *Güzelyurtlu and Others v. Cyprus and Turkey*, Application no: 36925/07, Judgment.

_______ (2020) *M.N. and Others v. Belgium*, Application no: 43599/18, Decision.

France (2019) 'Observations de la France présentées en vertu de l'article 40, paragraphe 5, du Pacte', https://www.ohchr.org/Documents/HRBodies/CCPR/GCArticle6/Observations_France_apres.pdf [accessed 7 September 2020].

Geuss, R. (2008) *Philosophy and Real Politics*, Princeton University Press.

Gibney, M. (2016) *International Human Rights Law: Returning to Universal Principles* (2nd ed.), Rowman & Littlefield.

Hardt, M. and Negri, A. (2000) *Empire*, Harvard University Press.

Human Rights Committee (HRC) (2018) 'Call for Comments on Article 6 – Right to Life', https://www.ohchr.org/EN/HRBodies/CCPR/Pages/GC36-Article6Righttolife.aspx [accessed 25 September 2020].

International Court of Justice (ICJ) (2010) 'Accordance with International Law of the Unilateral Declaration of Independence in Respect of Kosovo', ICJ Reports 2010 (22 July), 403, Advisory Opinion.

Koskenniemi, M. (2018) 'Rights, History, Critique' in Etinson, A. (ed). *Human Rights: Moral or Political?*, Oxford University Press.

Kumm, M. (2013) 'The Cosmopolitan Turn in Constitutionalism: An Integrated Conception of Public Law', *Indiana Journal of Global Legal Studies* 20(2), 605–628.

Langford, M. and Darrow, M. (2013) 'Moral Theory, International Law and Global Justice' in Langford, M. et al. (eds). *Global Justice, State Duties: The Extraterritorial Scope of Economic, Social and Cultural Rights in International Law*, Cambridge University Press.

MacIntyre, A. (1984) *Is Patriotism a Virtue?*, The Lindley Lecture, University of Kansas.

Mahlmann, M. (2008) *Elemente einer ethischen Grundrechtstheorie*, Nomos.

Milanović, M. (2013) *Extraterritorial Application of Human Rights Treaties: Law, Principles, and Policy*, Oxford University Press.

Morgenthau, H.J. (1979) *Human Rights and Foreign Policy*, Council on Religion and International Affairs.

(1949) 'The Primacy of the National Interest', *The American Scholar* 18(2), 207–212.

Moyn, S. (2018) *Not Enough: Human Rights in an Unequal World*, Belknap Press of Harvard University Press.

Müller, A. (2020) 'Security Measures Abroad and Extraterritorial Human Rights Obligations' in Fritsche, R. et al. (eds). *Unsicherheiten des Rechts*, ARSP Beihefte 162, Franz Steiner.

Mutua, M. (2002) *Human Rights: A Political and Cultural Critique*, University of Pennsylvania Press.

Nagel, T. (2005) 'The Problem of Global Justice', *Philosophy & Public Affairs*, 33(2), 113–147.

Pettit, P. (2016) 'The Globalized Republican Ideal', *Global Justice: Theory Practice Rhetoric* 9(1), 47–68.

(1997) *Republicanism: A Theory of Freedom and Government*, Oxford University Press.

Posner, E.A. (2014) *The Twilight of Human Rights Law*, Oxford University Press.

Raible, L. (2020) *Human Rights Unbound: A Theory of Extraterritoriality*, Oxford University Press.

Rorty, R. (1989) *Contingency, Irony, and Solidarity*, Cambridge University Press.

Ryngaert, C. (2015) *Unilateral Jurisdiction and Global Values*, Eleven.

Sen, A. (1996) 'Thinking about Human Rights and Asian Values', *Human Rights Dialogue* 1(4), 1–4.

Shany, Y. (2013) 'Taking Universality Seriously: A Functional Approach to Extraterritoriality in International Human Rights Law', *The Law & Ethics of Human Rights* 7(1), 47–71.

Skogly, S.I. (2010) 'Extraterritoriality: Universal Human Rights without Universal Obligations?' in Joseph, S. and McBeth, A. (eds). *Research Handbook on International Human Rights Law*, Edward Elgar.

Taylor, C. (1985) *Philosophy and the Human Sciences: Philosophical Papers 2*, Cambridge University Press.

United States Supreme Court (1990) *United States v. Verdugo-Urquidez*, 494 US 259.

(2017) *Hernández v. Mesa*, 582 US ___ (slip. op.).

Vandenhole, W. (2012) 'Emerging Normative Frameworks on Transnational Human Rights Obligations', *EUI Working Papers, RSCAS* 2012/17, http://cadmus.eui.eu/handle/1814/21874 [accessed 17 September 2020].

Waltz, K.N. (1979) *Theory of International Politics*, McGraw-Hill.

Walzer, M. (1983) *Spheres of Justice: A Defense of Pluralism and Equality*, Basic Books.

Williams, B. (2005) *In the Beginning Was the Deed: Realism and Moralism in Political Argument*, Princeton University Press.

5

Nowhere countries: When states use extra-territoriality at home to circumvent legal, human and refugee rights

Pauline Maillet

Introduction

The opening statement of the *Maastricht Principles* laments the fact that, 'despite the universality of human rights, many states still interpret their human rights obligations as being applicable only within their own borders'. Concurring with the *Maastricht Principles*' observation, this chapter discusses how two states have redrawn their borders in order to escape or lessen their legal, human and refugee rights obligations. Contrary to the other contributors, I am concerned with the protection that states owe to individuals located *within* their geographical boundaries, on pieces of land *declared* extra-national. I use the term 'extra-territoriality' (with a hyphen) to refer to exclusionary practices taking place within states' territories. More precisely, this term refers to the designation, by a state, of a piece of its territory as 'not national territory', for certain categories of people: non-citizens *depicted* as undesirable. The term 'nowhere countries', coined by French activists, aptly describes these spaces *deemed* extra-territorial for non-citizens categorized as undesirable. Nowhere countries can be established and thrive on any part of a state territory, but international zones at airports and islands have been spaces of choice for these zones of exclusion. Nowhere countries have been used by some states to curtail access to domestic legal rights as well as access to human and refugee rights granted by international law. While the other contributors to this volume explore the duties of states outside of their territorial boundaries, this chapter reaffirms states' obligations to individuals located within their territories, in places *labelled* extra-territorial.

Drawing from the French and the Canadian cases, I argue that exclusion from rights through extra-territoriality may take two main forms. Under the first configuration of extra-territoriality, state authorities consider non-citizens to be not physically located on the state's territory. Exclusion from rights is triggered by geography and legal absence: situated in a geographical space *construed* as non-national, some incoming people are denied access to the legal, human and refugee rights attached to sovereign territory. Under this first configuration, the non-citizens in question are placed in a legal limbo: they are left outside of applicable legal frameworks, both at the domestic and international levels. This is what happened to non-citizens stranded in the

DOI: 10.4324/9781003090014-7

international zone at Paris' airports in France in the 1980s and early 1990s: the government instructed border authorities to disregard the applicable domestic legal framework and its associated rights. Foreign nationals were refused the protection of the law on account of their location in a space *portrayed* as extra-territorial. Similarly, people from the Fujian Province who arrived off the Canadian coast of British Columbia in 1999 were taken to the Esquimalt naval base on Vancouver Island, a place *depicted* as 'Not-Canada' (Mountz 2010). Canadian authorities declared the naval base a 'port of entry' claiming that the Chinese people were still walking the tunnels of an international airport, not yet landed in Canada. This trick allowed the Canadian government to deny access to lawyers during processing at the base: migrants being assessed at a port of entry did not have the right to legal counsel under Canadian law. This first configuration of extra-territoriality attracted widespread criticism from human and refugee rights activists, lawyers and courts, and may have forced states to resort to a subtler configuration.

The second form of extra-territoriality (the second and the first form not being mutually exclusive) is less manifest: when physically located in spaces *deemed* extra-territorial, non-citizens are not refused legal protection. Instead, they are subjected to a less protective regime compared to that granted to foreign nationals who are not located in spaces *construed* as extra-national. Exclusion from the regular rights regime is triggered by geography *and* a legal technique. Although non-citizens receive the exclusionary status when located in a space *declared* extra-territorial, the exclusionary regime follows them well after they leave this space. Once non-citizens are assigned to the French legal regime of exclusion, they carry it with them wherever they go. The waiting zone has created a particular legal space of lesser rights that always accompanies the individual, no matter his or her location. Practitioners explain that non-citizens carry the waiting zone status like a 'backpack' or are in a waiting zone 'bubble'.

Importantly, alternate legal regimes may be enshrined in the law or exist *de facto*, as evidenced by the Canadian case. The Chinese boat people's location on Esquimalt naval base, a space *declared* extra-territorial, triggered a less protective legal regime that was not engraved in Canadian law. While the asylum seekers were granted due process on paper, in practice their access to rights was altered by their passage through a place considered as 'Not-Canada'. The second form of exclusion from rights through extra-territoriality allows states to appear engaged in the global refugee regime while subverting it. Both configurations of extra-territoriality enable states to tailor the border to suit their immigration goals and to evade their obligations under the Refugee Convention. While the state practices hereby described are not limited to France and Canada, this chapter will only be able to cover that of the two aforementioned states.

First configuration of extra-territoriality at home: Exclusion from rights through geography and a legal absence

The case of the international zone at French airports in the 1980s and 1990s

International airports are interesting sites where legal and cartographic borders do not map onto one another (Lochak 1992). There, borders are created at the heart of states' territories, without a territorial delimitation between states. This creation of borders *ex nihilo*, or what Del Valle Galvez (2005) refers to as the 'legal fiction of the interior border', is permissible under international law, as there is no human right to enter a country, except one's own. The admission of an individual to a country is a state's discretionary act. However, as Del Valle Galvez (2005) explains, this 'legal fiction of the interior border' can easily lead to an 'extra-territorial legal fiction' (hyphen added). France implemented this extra-territorial legal fiction in the 1980s and early 1990s. The French government considered individuals in international zones to be not on French territory for they had not gone through police control and customs. Thus, France transformed the legal distinction between *de facto* entry and formal entry (that characterizes the 'legal fiction of the interior border') into the dichotomy formal entry/no formal entry.

At the time, the status of the international zone, also called 'transit zone', was not well defined. International law did not *explicitly* state whether or not transit zones were part of a state's territory or what laws applied to passengers located in these spaces. Originally, Annex 9 to the Chicago Convention's definition of a 'direct transit area' (First edition, 1950) did not include passengers. At first, it was 'a special area established in connection with an international airport, approved by the public authorities concerned and under their direct supervision for accommodation of traffic which is pausing briefly in its passage through the Contracting state'. In 2004 the Facilitation Division of the International Civil Aviation Organization proposed to broaden this definition to mention that 'passengers can stay during transit or transfer without being submitted to border control' in the direct transit area (FAL/12-WP/6, 12/11/03). This international legal instrument did not, and still does not, specify the perimeter of the direct transit area. It became apparent in 1993, at a conference gathering lawyers and activists from Europe and North America, that countries delineated airport transit zones' perimeter differently (Anafé 1993). This lack of consensus allowed the French government to claim that the international zone included hotels.

Nevertheless, it does not mean that airports' transit zones were not covered by international law in the 1980s. As previously mentioned, Annex 9 to the Chicago Convention established that the transit zone *was directly supervised or controlled by the public authorities of the state concerned.* This meant that the state in question exercised its territorial sovereignty over the transit zone. As Labayle (1993, p. 48) explains, a state exercising its sovereignty over a territory is competent both to create and implement rules. As soon as international legal scholars, international human rights courts and treaty monitoring bodies turned to the matter of the international or transit zone, they clearly stated that this space was integrally part of the state's territory. Under international law, airports' transit zones are not extra-territorial spaces.

In the years preceding the Law on the Waiting Zone (July 6, 1992), French law provided for the detention of non-citizens turned away at the border and equipped them with legal safeguards. The 1945 Ordinance (art. 35 bis) allowed detention of non-admitted individuals in administrative facilities for a maximum of seven days – time period deemed necessary for them to be returned. However, detention was to take place 'in case of absolute necessity' during 'the time strictly necessary for the departure' of the foreign national. While the decision to detain was taken by an administrative agent, detainees had to be presented to a liberty and custody judge after 24 hours. On an exceptional basis, the judge could extend the duration of detention to six more days, bringing the maximum amount of time spent in confinement to seven days in total. After this time, if return had not occurred, the non-citizen had to be set free. The judge's decision could be appealed and the public prosecutor (immediately informed of the detention decision) always had the possibility of checking detention conditions. Important rights were attached to Article 35 bis, including the rights to see a doctor and a counsel and to communicate with the consulate or any person of the detainee's choosing. Non-French speakers had to be notified of the aforementioned rights by an interpreter.

Claiming that international zones were extra-national spaces allowed the French government to circumvent domestic and international laws. According to the newspaper *Le Monde* (Bernard 1992), 10,000 travellers per year were denied entry into France due to missing or improper travel documents. Less than 1% of these travellers were placed in administrative detention under the legal rules applicable at the time. Therefore, in the 1980s and the early 1990s, the bulk of the non-citizens rejected at the border were held in the international zone in a legal vacuum. Detention outside of the 1945 Ordinance allowed the border police to keep non-admitted foreign nationals for more than seven days and, generally, to deny them the safeguards provided by Article 35 bis of the same Ordinance. Rejected passengers were left outside of the protective reach of domestic laws.

As far as asylum seekers were concerned, French legislation did not permit their detention. Indeed, the 1945 Ordinance authorized detention *only once a non-admission decision was made, not before.* At the time, a decree (May 27, 1982) stated that only the Ministry of the Interior could decide to deny entry to asylum seekers, after consulting with the Ministry of Foreign Affairs. From September 1991 refugee agency representatives were delegated to the borders to hear claimants and advise the Ministry of Foreign Affairs before it offered its opinion to the Ministry of the Interior (Lochak 1992, p. 680). Importantly, France was already a party to the 1951 Refugee Convention and to its 1967 Protocol. As such, the French state had to honour its *non-refoulement* obligation and could not impose criminal sanctions against refugees for illegal entry (respectively arts. 33 and 31 of the Refugee Convention). The duty of *non-refoulement* is the cornerstone of refugee law: it 'prohibits states from exposing a refugee "in any manner whatsoever" to the risk of being persecuted for a Convention reason' (Hathaway and Gammeltoft-Hansen 2015, p. 238). Domestic legislation acknowledged the obligation to take international conventions into account in entry decisions (1945 Ordinance, art. 5). Under domestic and international law, asylum seekers could not be denied entry for lack of travel documents. They could only be refused access for security reasons, under Article 5 of the 1945 Ordinance: threat to the public order, previous banishment from territory or deportation order.

In practice, those seeking international protection could be confined for days or weeks in the international zone while the refugee agency, the Ministry of Foreign Affairs and the Ministry of the Interior decided on their cases. Some claimants also experienced *refoulement.* To justify these practices, the French government argued that the international zone had extra-territorial status. As explained by Hoop de Scheffer, Council of Europe rapporteur, who visited Roissy-Charles de Gaulle (CDG) Airport on November 20, 1989:

> Asylum-seekers are detained in a so-called international zone at the airport, which means that they are not yet on French territory and the French authorities are therefore not under a legal obligation to examine the request as they would be if a request was made by someone already on French territory. The international zone has no legal background and must be considered as a device to avoid obligations [...]. No legal basis for detention exists and a maximum term is not prescribed by law.
>
> *(Lord Mackie of Benshie 1991, p. 7)*

French authorities at Charles de Gaulle Airport assumed that they were under no legal obligation to examine asylum seekers' requests in international zones, on the basis that they were not on French territory yet. While French authorities insisted that the duration of detention was limited to a week, some asylum claimants told the Council of Europe Rapporteur that they had been waiting for six weeks in the international zone (Lord Mackie of Benshie 1991, p. 7).

Those denied admission or waiting on an admission decision at French airport borders were detained in small holding rooms in the airport's international zone and/or in nearby hotels, which were construed as an extension of the international zone. The employees working for Paris' Airports or airline companies were tasked with guarding the non-citizens in holding rooms. Distressed by the plight of detainees, trade unionists contacted lawyers and NGOs defending human and foreign nationals' rights.

Activist lawyers started to sue the Ministry of the Interior from 1988 for arbitrary detention of foreign nationals in the international zone. Lawyers coined the term 'legal fiction' to debunk the government's extra-territorial theory according to which non-nationals present in the international zone were deemed outside of France (interview with Serge Slama, law professor, Paris, July 2014). It is not a legal term and therefore cannot be found in legal textbooks (interview with Danièle Lochak, law professor, Paris, July 2014). Activist lawyers using the term 'legal fiction' did not define it. According to the Oxford online English dictionary (accessed December 7, 2014), a fiction is 'an invention or fabrication as opposed to fact'. The expression 'legal fiction' was precisely meant to convey the idea that the government fabricated the international zone as a lawless area. Activists found it useful to denounce the exclusion of individuals located in the international zone from the guarantees offered by French law and international human rights and refugee law.

The lawyers' goal was to obtain a ruling that would release the asylum seekers in question from the international zone on the grounds that detention in this space was tantamount to arbitrary sequestration and therefore resulted in severe infringement upon a fundamental liberty (Lochak 1992, p. 682). The judge who heard the cases had a limited mandate: putting a stop to an illegal administrative practice resulting in a severe violation of fundamental rights. The judge could therefore only order the government to put an end to confinement in the international zone. Until November 1991, these trials did not affect the government, which always instructed border authorities to return or admit to the territory the foreign national in question before the hearing took place.

The newspaper *Le Monde*, dated November 21, 1989, described one of these trials (Peyrot 1989). Isabelle arrived at Charles De Gaulle from then Zaire on November 4, 1989. She had fled her country where she had been imprisoned, beaten and raped by soldiers on account of her religious opinions. In spite of presenting a regular passport, visa and financial means, she was denied entry at the border and detained at the Arcade hotel at Charles De Gaulle Airport. Her counsel, Bourguet, paid her a visit on November 11 and immediately forwarded a refugee status request to the refugee agency. As his client remained deprived of liberty, Bourguet sued the Ministry of the Interior before the Paris Court of First Instance. He pleaded that his client's arbitrary detention had severely infringed upon her fundamental rights. However, the judge could not rule on 'a situation that had ended', as Isabelle had been released just before the hearing. The newspaper notes that the government had already resorted to the same manoeuvre several times. The Ministry of the Interior had consistently made sure that the non-citizen was no longer held in the international zone at the date of the hearing. Since the foreign national had either been sent back to the country of departure or admitted to French territory, the point of contention had disappeared (Bourguet 1992). Therefore, the judge had no other option but to declare that he lacked jurisdiction. This strategy on the part of the government endured for a few years after Isabelle's case.

The situation finally changed when the Paris Court of First Instance issued a very unusual ruling. On November 22, 1991, the Court allowed a Haitian asylum seeker to sue the Ministry of the Interior for 'arbitrary sequestration' and monetary compensation even though he had been admitted to France in the meantime. The plaintiff had landed in Charles De Gaulle on November 6, 1991 where he had been refused entry. He had been confined for two days in the international zone and six days at the Arcade Hotel. He had been informed that he was to be put in the next available plane to Port-au-Prince. The court hearing took place on February 26, 1992 and also dealt with the similar cases of four other asylum seekers (three Haitians and one Zairian) who had landed in Charles de Gaulle Airport on November 19, 1991 (Bernard 1992). Their lawyers had also been authorized by the same Court of First Instance on November 26,

1991 to pursue the cases on their merits. At the hearing, the Ministry of the Interior acknowledged the following: their deprivation of liberty was not based on any legal document, a legal framework existed but was not applied, and *lastly, the order was expressly given to civil servants not to detain foreign nationals at the border under the existing legal framework* (Paris Court of First Instance 1992a).

The hearing revealed that the plaintiffs' right to seek asylum had been violated. France did not uphold its *non-refoulement* obligation, as decisions were made to return the asylum seekers in question to Kinshasa and Port-au-Prince. Their return was stopped in extremis when the Court heard their case. The asylum seekers also faced obstacles when filing their claim: only two plaintiffs could have their claim registered while the other two were treated as regular migrants failing to fulfil entry conditions.

The Court ruled on March 25 (Paris Court of First Instance 1992b), rejecting the government's extra-territoriality thesis. It found that there was no domestic or international document giving extra-territorial status to all or part of the Arcade hotel where asylum seekers had been held. The Court agreed that the international zone constituted a 'legal fiction' and ruled that holding at the Arcade hotel constituted a deprivation of liberty.

What would become the landmark European Court of Human Rights case, *Amuur v. France* (ECtHR 1996), started at the domestic level the following day, on March 26, 1992, when lawyers Dominique Monget-Sarrail, Laurence Roques and Pascale Taelman first brought the case to the Créteil Court of First Instance. As previously stated, the day before the Paris Court of First Instance had rejected the government's extra-territoriality thesis, according to which the government argued that the Arcade hotel at Charles De Gaulle Airport was part of the international zone and, as such, had extra-territorial status. The *Amuur* case was part of a series of trials that activist lawyers launched against the French government from the late 1980s.

Four Somali siblings arrived on March 9, 1992 at Paris Orly Airport from Syria where they had spent two months after fleeing from Somalia via Kenya. They alleged their lives were at risk in Somalia after the fall of President Siyad Barre. The border police refused them entry on the basis that their passports were forged. They were placed at the Arcade hotel, which was considered an extension of the international zone. On March 12, the Ministry of the Interior examined their request to enter France to claim asylum. By March 14, 18 other Somali nationals (among which 11 children) had arrived at Orly from Syria and Egypt. Of these 18 Somali citizens, 5 were cousins of the Amuur brothers and sister. They were all members of the Darob Marhan tribe, which was in power during the regime of President Mohamed Siyad Barre. They explained that several members of their family had been murdered. After obtaining legal aid, they wrote a letter to the refugee agency on March 25, requesting refugee status according to the Geneva Convention of 1951. On March 26, their case was referred to the Court of First Instance at Créteil on the grounds that their deprivation of liberty was arbitrary. Lawyers Monget-Sarrail, Roques and Taelman transferred the case of the 22 plaintiffs to the European Commission of Human Rights on March 27, 1992.

The European Commission of Human Rights then referred the case of the four Amuur siblings to the European Court on March 1, 1995. The plaintiffs had argued that several articles of the European Convention on Human Rights had been violated (arts. 3, 4, 5, 6, 13 and 25), but the Commission rejected all of the alleged violations save the one based on Article 5 (right to liberty and security). In its observations to the European Commission (transmitted on July 7, 1992), the French government claimed that the plaintiffs' 'holding' (*maintien*) in the international zone did not amount to deprivation of liberty: they were not arrested or detained. They were instead 'staying' (*séjourner*) in the international zone as they were free to leave for any other destination than France (Council of Europe: European Commission of Human Rights, October 18, 1993).

The European Court of Human Rights (ECtHR 1996) rejected this claim and concluded that the applicants had indeed suffered a deprivation of liberty in the international zone. Their detention was found to be unlawful as it had had no legal basis in domestic law: France was declared to have violated Article 5 by illegally depriving the Somali asylum claimants of liberty. As the court explicitly stated, 'despite its name, the international zone does not have extraterritorial status'. The court remarked that the French Constitutional Council had not challenged 'the legislature's rights to lay down rules governing the holding of aliens in that zone'. In other words, the court observed that France exercised jurisdiction over the international zone at Orly Airport. This is how a manual of International Law (Shaw 2017) defines jurisdiction:

> Jurisdiction concerns the power of the state under international law to regulate or otherwise impact upon people, property and circumstances and reflects the basic principles of state sovereignty, equality of states and non-interference in domestic affairs. Jurisdiction is a central feature of state sovereignty, for it is an exercise of authority which may alter or create or terminate legal relationships and obligations. It may be achieved by means of legislative, executive or judicial action.

The case of *Amuur v. France* illustrates the fact that a state cannot decide to exercise jurisdiction selectively; laws must apply homogeneously to all individuals under jurisdiction. As jurisdiction cannot be withdrawn at will, the non-citizens in the international zone at Orly Airport were subjected to French law, even though French authorities claimed the opposite. Manipulations of jurisdiction are not valid under international law, and, therefore, states cannot evade their obligations by labelling a piece of their territories 'extra-territorial'.

Yet, just a few years after the *Amuur v. France* ruling was passed, another state resorted to such an extra-territorial legal fiction to deprive non-citizens of rights. Interestingly, the Canadian government used the arguments developed by the French government (i.e. the idea that the international zone at airports was an extra-territorial space).

The case of the Esquimalt Naval Base in Canada in 1999

Mountz (2010) pursued research with the Department of Citizenship and Immigration Canada (CIC) in the wake of the interceptions of 599 individuals from China off the coast of British Columbia in July 1999 by Canadian authorities. She documented how the Canadian authorities developed the 'long tunnel thesis' to claim that the Chinese people placed at the Esquimalt naval base had not reached Canadian soil yet, in spite of them being physically located on Canadian territory.

The non-citizens, who had been smuggled, arrived in four different boats over the course of six weeks (Mountz 2010). At the time, tens of thousands of smuggled non-citizens were arriving at Canadian airports every year, making this figure of 599 individuals rather unremarkable. Yet, the non-citizens from the Fujian Province were treated differently compared to those arriving by land or air. Their boats were towed, and they were taken by ship or by bus to the Esquimalt naval base on Vancouver Island, which was declared a 'port of entry'.

At the naval base, the non-citizens were considered inside the tunnels of an international airport, not yet landed in Canada. The construction of the Esquimalt naval base as 'Not-Canada' carried deep implications for the boat people's access to rights. Firstly, like in French airports in the 1980s, the non-citizens were denied access to rights. During processing at the base, they were refused access to lawyers. Indeed, the CIC, the federal agency in charge of managing immigration, refugee claims and border enforcement, wanted to gather as much information as possible about the boat people's journeys and their smugglers before allowing lawyer access.

CIC was wary of lawyers, as they might have advised their clients to claim refugee status and to present their stories accordingly. In order to delay access to lawyers, the Canadian government temporarily designated the Esquimalt base as a port of entry. This designation carried important consequences, since migrants in detention did have the right to legal counsel under Canadian law, whereas migrants being processed at a port of entry did not. Lawyers observed that the Chinese people were undeniably detained, as evidenced by the presence of barbed wire, guard dogs and guards on the military base. Some individuals spent up to 14 days at the Work Point Barracks at Esquimalt, in 'processing'. During this time, immigration officials conducted preliminary interviews with the non-citizens with no legal counsel being present. The Canadian and the French case are very similar in the sense that both states resorted to the two configurations of extra-territoriality to exclude non-citizens from rights. After refusing to treat the non-citizens according to the laws in force at the time of their arrival, Canadian and French authorities placed them under less protective legal regimes (these alternate legal regimes are either enshrined in law or exist *de facto*).

Second configuration of extra-territoriality at home: Exclusion from rights through geography and an alternate legal regime

The French waiting zone from July 6, 1992 to nowadays

The ruling issued by the Paris Court of First Instance on November 22, 1991 apparently unnerved the French Ministry of the Interior. The court had allowed the Haitian asylum seeker to sue the Ministry of the Interior for 'arbitrary sequestration' and monetary compensation, even though he had been admitted to France in the meantime. Faced with challenging upcoming litigation, Philippe Marchand, the Socialist Minister of the Interior at the time, decided to draft a legal provision addressing the situation of non-admitted foreign nationals and asylum seekers in the international zone, which he renamed 'transit zone'. This provision on the transit zone finally came into being through the Law on the Waiting Zone of July 6, 1992.

Non-citizens in the international zone ceased to be detained in a legal void as of July 6, 1992, when the Law on the Waiting Zone was finally passed. The Socialist government presented this new legislation as significant progress: France was setting a fine example in terms of rights protection. Yet, the Law on the Waiting Zone offered a less advantageous legal framework to non-citizens compared to the one previously in place that the government had refused to apply (i.e. 1945 Ordinance, art. 35 bis). Under this new law, detainees were to be presented to a judge after four days in the waiting zone (compared to one day previously) and could not spend more than 20 days in the waiting zone (confinement was limited to seven days previously).

Furthermore, the Law on the Waiting Zone established a parallel and less protective system of rights based on the distinction between physical and legal entry. Before the Law on the Waiting Zone came into existence, the same legislative provisions applied to all foreign nationals detained for immigration control purposes: the law did not establish any distinction between those at French borders and those already deemed to be on French territory. Non-citizens all benefited from the same rights. This equality before the law ended in 1992, with the Law on the Waiting Zone. Since this time, non-citizens arriving at the border have been subjected to a watered-down legal framework compared to the one applicable to those already deemed to be on French soil (who are either applying for asylum or are to be removed after staying illegally in the country). This less advantageous legal regime was precisely premised on the idea that international zones, renamed 'transit zones' and then 'waiting zones', were somehow extra-territorial spaces.

When the Law on the Waiting Zone came into force in July 1992, the *overt* mechanisms of exclusion shifted in the sense that the law itself (and not the absence thereof) created a less protective regime than that applicable to the same groups regarded as being on French territory. Exclusion, in other words, was reinvented: instead of individuals being placed outside of the law, the law *itself organized* exclusion. The waiting zone's exclusionary legal framework builds on the premise that groups at the border find themselves from a legal standpoint at the threshold of, but not yet having entered, French sovereign territory. They find themselves, instead, in territorial border zones where the state establishes the distinction between physical and legal entry: physical presence proves insufficient and only lawful admission amounts to entry into the territory (Basaran 2011). In the 1980s, exclusion was triggered by geography and legal absence: it started from the moment the non-citizen set foot in the geographical location of airports' international zones. Today, under the Law on the Waiting Zone, exclusion is triggered by a combination of geography and law: an individual is placed under the waiting zone framework when arriving in the border's physical location and after being refused entry or registered as an asylum seeker. Although physically in France, rejected non-citizens and asylum seekers at the border are not present from a legal standpoint, for they have not crossed yet 'law's admission gate' (Shachar 2007).

The Law on the Waiting Zone governs foreign nationals denied admission into French or Schengen territory or claiming asylum at a French border arriving by train, boat or airplane (CESEDA 2016, arts. L221-1 to L224-4). Those assigned the waiting zone status are detained during the time necessary for them to be returned or, if they are claiming asylum, to determine whether or not their claim is inadmissible or 'manifestly unfounded'. Individuals located in the waiting zone are not governed by ordinary laws, but instead subjected to its particular legal regime. Two groups particularly suffer from the eroded rights attached to the waiting zone status: asylum seekers and minors (especially when unaccompanied). Indeed, the regular refugee determination procedures do not apply to asylum seekers at the border. Only asylum seekers passing through this initial sieve will be entitled to enter French territory where claims will be examined on their merits. The number of claimants able to file a claim has varied greatly over the years. In 2011, the French refugee agency (OFPRA) reviewed the case of 1857 claimants (for all waiting zones) and recommended that 188 be admitted to the territory: about 10% of claimants got access to refugee status determination (OFPRA 2012). In 2012, this number was 13.1% (OFPRA 2013) but increased to 40.5% in 2019 (OFPRA 2020). As for unaccompanied minors, they are denied due process rights that children in France enjoy (HRW 2014). All unaccompanied minors who are not asylum claimants are detained in waiting zones. As for those seeking asylum, the law provides for their detention in waiting zones under many circumstances (Maillet 2019).

Since July 1992, the scope of the Law on the Waiting zone has been extended significantly, following litigation 'crises'. At first, those denied entry or seeking asylum were geographically circumscribed by an administrative authority (*le préfet*) to waiting zones, which ran between points of boarding or disembarkation and border checkpoints. These zones could include accommodation located on or nearby the airport, port or train station. When the Law on the Waiting Zone was first passed in July 1992, it read that the waiting zone 'runs between the points of embarkation and disembarkation to the border checkpoints', therefore covering the area of the 'international zone'. The law also specified that the waiting zone could include nearby hotel-like accommodations. The geographical space of the waiting zone therefore mapped onto that of the international zone and onto what the government construed as its extension, i.e. hotels close by. The perimeter of the waiting zone is now larger than that of the international zone, as it encompasses any place where the person goes for administrative or medical reasons. As a result, the waiting zone status now accompanies the individual, even kilometres from the point of arrival. Trapped by the waiting zone framework, foreign nationals 'are not expelled by the border, they are forced to *be* the border' (Khosravi 2010, p. 99). In the French case, the legal regime of the waiting zone has been engraved in law. The Canadian case shows us that these alternate legal regimes providing individuals subjected to them with diminished protection can also exist *de facto*.

The Canadian de facto *alternate legal regime in 1999*

In Canada, on Vancouver Island, the non-citizens' location in a space declared extra-territorial triggered a less protective legal regime. On paper, the Chinese non-citizens were accorded the regular protection of the law. After processing, 500 of the 599 non-citizens asked for refugee status. The asylum seekers were granted due process under the Canadian Charter of Rights and Freedoms: their cases were heard, and they could exhaust all appeals procedures. However, *in practice*, they experienced diminished protection. While claimants from the first boat were released after processing on Vancouver Island, those from the second, third and fourth boats were detained. At the time, detention of non-citizens in Canada for immigration purposes was quite rare. Many claimants from the first boat did not attend their refugee hearings; they were considered to have left Canada to work in Chinatown in New York City. Yet, as Mountz (2010, p. 77) notes, the fact that many boat people absconded did not justify the massive use of detention. After all, many non-citizens entering Canada by air or land also vanished after their release:

> The reasons this group was treated differently through detention en masse went largely unexplained. Officials cited the involvement of organized crime, the failure of claimants to provide identity documents and the fact that they were likely to flee. The same could be said, however, of many arriving at airports and land borders who were released during the same time period.

Claimants from the second, third and fourth boats were detained in a provincial prison in the small city of Prince George, in the interior of the British Columbia Province. In this remote location, that stood ten hours away by car from Vancouver, the claimants experienced isolation from refugee lawyers, interpreters, human rights monitors and the Chinese community. Their cases were heard inside the prison, in provisional tribunals, and adjudicated by Immigration and Refugee Board officers especially brought to the prison. The claimants attended their hearings wearing prison outfit and handcuffs. Refugee lawyers and advocates argued that the claimants had not benefited from the regular rights regime, as the government used the data that was obtained in the absence of legal counsel at the military base to point to contradictions in the claimants' stories. Lawyers also deplored the fact that claimants were not identified and treated as individuals but as a homogeneous group. Furthermore, refugee advocates argued that Immigration and Refugee Board members, who were temporarily accommodated in Prince George, were in a hurry to decide on the cases, as they were keen on returning home.

Almost all of the claims that were heard in Prince George were ultimately rejected. Only 24 asylum seekers had their claims accepted out of the 577 claimants. At the time, asylum seekers from China had a 58% approval rate. By contrast, the approval rate dropped to less than 5% for the claimants who arrived by boat in 1999. The majority of those who were conferred refugee status had not been detained in the regular criminal system in Prince George but had been hosted or detained in the surroundings of Vancouver in youth facilities or prisons. There, they enjoyed access to experienced refugee lawyers, and their claims were heard in a more individualized manner at the regional headquarters of Citizenship and Immigration Canada. Claimants that were detained in Prince George did not enjoy the same quality of access to the refugee determination process. One lawyer argued that they experienced 'skeletal justice', by opposition to the 'thick justice' taking place in Vancouver. Many of the claimants who had been detained were deported back to China in 2000 after they exhausted all legal recourses. The media, public opinion and the government depicted the asylum claimants as illegal migrants trying to abuse Canada's generous refugee system. The inscription of the 'bogus refugee' identity to the Chinese claimants triggered their detention in 'Not-Canada' and in the remote location of Prince Georges as well as the subsequent subversion of the access to the regular rights' regime. As Mountz (2010, p. 113) puts it: 'the narrative of *who* these migrants were explains *where* they were located and vice versa'.

Conclusion

To conclude, states have created 'nowhere countries' at the very heart of their territories. In other words, they have engaged in elaborate manoeuvres to redraw their territorial boundaries, in the hope of selectively relinquishing jurisdiction over some parts of their territories. The very fact that states have gone to such lengths to manipulate their borders suggests that they still entertain a very territorial conception of their rights obligations – as if the assignment of an 'extra-territorial' character to some parts of their land magically lifted or diminished the protection owed to individuals thereby located. Yet, 'nowhere countries' do not exist under international law. Despite states' efforts to practice what could be called 'selective sovereignty', islands and international zones at airports are all part of the state's territory. This is a fact that *cannot* be changed by domestic law (Hathaway 2005). States' obligations towards all individuals falling within their jurisdiction must be urgently reiterated.

References

Anafé (1993) *Frontières du droit, frontières des droits: l'introuvable statut de la 'zone internationale'*, L'Harmattan.

Basaran, T. (2011) *Security, Law and Borders: At the Limits of Liberties*, Routledge.

Bernard, P. (January 21, 1992) *'"L'amendement Marchand" à nouveau devant les parlementaires. Des demandeurs d'asile contestent la "zone internationale" prévue par le Ministère de l'Intérieur'*, *Le Monde*.

Bourguet, C. (1992) "La notion de frontière dans les aéroports ou 'le pays de nulle part'. *Autres Temps. Les cahiers du christianisme social.* 33–34, 24–31.

Del Valle Galvez, A. (2005) 'Las zonas internacionales o zonas de tránsito de los aeropuertos, ficción liminar fronteriza', *Revista Electrónica de estudios internacionales* 9, 1–18.

European Court of Human Rights (ECtHR) (1996) *Amuur v. France*, Application no: 19776/92, Judgment.

French Office for the Protection of Refugees and Stateless people (OFPRA) (2012) Rapport d'activité 2011.

_______ (2013) Rapport d'activité 2012.

_______ (2020) Rapport d'activité 2019.

Hathaway, J.C. (2005) *The Rights of Refugees Under International Law*, Cambridge University Press.

Hathaway, J.C. and Gammeltoft-Hansen T. (2015) 'Non Refoulement in a World of Cooperative Deterrence', *Columbia Journal of Transnational Law* 53(2), 235–284.

Human Rights Watch (HRW) (2014) France: Unaccompanied Children Detained at Borders. 500 a Year Held in Transit Zones.

International Civil Aviation Organization (ICAO) (1944) Convention on International Civil Aviation ('Chicago Convention').

_______ (2003) Facilitation Division, Twelfth Session, FAL/12-WP/6, 12/11/03.

_______ (2005) Annex 9 to the Convention on International Civil Aviation, 12th edition, July 2005.

Khosravi, S. (2010) *'Illegal' Traveller: An Auto-Ethnography of Borders*, Palgrave Macmillan.

Labayle, H. (1993) 'Réglementation et souveraineté des Etats' in Anafé (ed.). Frontières du droit, frontières des droits: l'introuvable statut de la 'zone internationale', *L'Harmattan*.

Lochak, D. (1992) 'Bulletin de jurisprudence française', *Journal du droit international*.

Lord Mackie of Benshie (1991) Report on the arrival of asylum seekers at European airports, Report N 6490, Parliamentary Assembly of the Council of Europe.

Maillet, P. (2019) *Nowhere Countries: Exclusion of Non-Citizens from Rights Through Extra-Territoriality at Home*, Brill Nijhoff.

Mountz, A. (2010) *Seeking Asylum: Human Smuggling and Bureaucracy at the Border*, University of Minnesota Press.

Paris Court of First Instance (1992a) First Chamber, Hearing.

_______ (1992b) Ruling.

Peyrot, M. (November 21, 1989) 'La situation juridique de la zone internationale de l'aéroport de Roissy. Prisonnière au pays de nulle part', *Le Monde*.

Shachar, A. (2007) 'The Shifting Border of Immigration Regulation', *Stanford Journal of Civil Rights and Civil Liberties* 3(2), 165–193.

Shaw, M. (2017) *International Law*, Cambridge University Press.

UN General Assembly (1951) Convention Relating to the Status of Refugees.

_______ (1967) Protocol Relating to the Status of Refugees.

6

Digitalization: The new extraterritorial challenge to extraterritorial obligations

Nicoletta Dentico, Mohammed El Said and Giacomo Capuzzo

> Governments have certainly not regulated the tech industry as if human rights were at stake, and the technology sector remains virtually a human rights-free zone.
>
> *Philip Alston, UN Rapporteur on extreme poverty and human rights*

The good, the bad, and the ugly of the digital revolution

More than ever, digitalization is all around us. For years, carried away by the fascination with digital gadgets and technologies, we have been allured to blindly enter a world of sophisticated machines without taking into consideration where this journey would take us and how it would revolutionize our existence – to the extent of taking over our human ability to control life. In such unaware mood, we have ceded much of our decision-making power to sophisticated invisible digital systems that have penetrated our daily lives. Only in recent months, since the outburst of COVID-19 has halted our ordinary lives, have we been able to get a better sense of the reality of transformation we have been in for some time. The internet has eased lockdown life for millions, digitalization and the web have been the critical unifying forces enabling work from home, school through online classrooms, social activities and mutual support and solidarity at a healthy distance. Policymakers have managed the unprecedented situation, and their international negotiations, through virtual meetings.

What do we mean with the term *digitalization*? Digitalization is a concept that lacks a single clear definition (IGI Global 2018), and is fraught with ambiguity. Brennen and Kreiss define it as 'the way in which many domains of social life are restructured around digital communication and media infrastructures' (Brennen and Kreiss 2016, p. 3). The Gartner Glossary focuses on business models rather than social interactions and describes digitalization as 'the use of digital technologies to change a business model and provide new revenue and value-producing opportunities; it is the process of moving to a digital business' (Gartner Glossary). We propose a third definition: 'the ongoing adoption of digital technologies across all possible societal and human activities' (IGI Global 2018).

For good or bad, the new coronavirus pandemic has accelerated and will further accelerate the shift towards digitalization globally. This historic jump reanimates the dilemma between law and technology, and risks creating *itself* significant human rights challenges. Governments have

DOI: 10.4324/9781003090014-8

to keep up with technology to play the role they must, with *any* industry. But as often the case, national and international laws lag behind technological developments, intellectual property being a recent example: after 20 years of negotiation, in 1995 the Trade Related Aspects of Intellectual Property Rights (TRIPS) Agreement at the World Trade Organization (WTO) was born deficient as it did not address the rise of the internet. State regulators are now struggling with insurmountable obstacles in dealing with apps that are reshaping the world at incredible speed, with rampant extraterritorial dynamics. Platforms like Google Alphabet, Facebook, or TikTok operate outside the jurisdiction of most countries, while the few regulatory frameworks in place lack the agility to accommodate the increasing pace of digital development. Moreover, digitalization deeply challenges the way governments regulate as it can easily bail out enforcements, transcend administrative boundaries domestically and internationally (OECD 2019), hence exposing less powerful countries to a digital wild west. While it spurs new regulatory needs, digitalization cannot be dealt with using old rules.

States have obligations to limit any potential unintended negative consequences, but the reality is that digital tools are already being used to crack down on civil and political rights. According to accredited analysts, automation, robotics, drones, and remote sensing will bear the undesirable consequences of a high-tech dystopia providing cover for those ready to implement a raft of oppressive social practices associated with the tech industry (Klein 2020). In many countries, systems of social protection and assistance are increasingly driven by digital data and technologies used to automate, predict, identify, surveil, detect, target, and punish (Burgess 2020). The process is neutrally denominated 'digital transformation', but the inoffensive term should not be allowed to conceal the revolutionary legal and political connotations of such innovation, leading to the expansion of a new form of governance, with extraterritorial implications. At the dawn of the Fourth Industrial Revolution electronic voting, technology-driven surveillance including through facial recognition programs, algorithm-based predictive policing, the digitalization of justice (Marr 2020) and immigration systems (Blix 2017), online submission of tax returns and payments (OECD 2018), and many other forms of electronic interactions between citizens and different levels of government have become an irresistible attraction. With the avatar of *the internet of things*, the embrace of digital welfare is pursued in the name of efficiency and with a reduction of public spending (Marsh 2019), but UN Rapporteur Philip Alston alerts that it risks 'becoming a Trojan Horses for neoliberal hostility towards social protection and regulation [...] and a complete reversal of the traditional notion that the state should be accountable to the individual' (Alston 2019b). The policy bias proclaims the benign intention of an interconnected *open society* that promotes responsibility and fosters individual autonomy, but through the processing of immense quantities of digital data, it relies on automated predictions/decision-making, gradually distancing and *de facto* removing the human factor. As Philip Alston points out, 'citizens become ever more visible to their governments, but not the other way round' (Alston 2019b).

States' obligations painfully struggle with the digital acceleration being under the primary control of private entrepreneurs whose main interest is to operate in an environment with minimum legal constraints. Regulators fail to get a deeper understanding of the emerging technologies' institutional and transboundary challenges, and their potential consequences for society. Meanwhile tech titans generate endless profits through their platforms, as we are seeing in pandemic times (Mattioli 2020). They benefit from the 'networks effects': size begets size. In providing the infrastructure for the digital convergence, they don't compete in the market. They *are* the market.

Is it too late, to ring the alarm? Difficult to tell. While possibly nothing more extraterritorial exists than digital technology, regulating this sector in the mismatch between its transboundary nature and the regulatory fragmentation undermines the effectiveness of any action and may generate barriers to the spread of beneficial digital innovations. Solutions limited to domestic domains are not an option. Specific, extraterritorial institutional responses are urgently required. Even more so following the pandemic.

Unequal access to digital rights, and digital tools used against human rights

Almost the entire world population lives within reach of a mobile network; still, a gross digital divide still holds back roughly half of the planet (ITU 2020). A huge digital rights gap marks the line between those who have internet access and those who don't. The three-decades-long drive to connect the planet was relatively easy in the high-income countries, where financial availability, good education, and dense urban centres smoothened the way to connectivity. Getting the rest of the nations online will be far more difficult[1], despite apparent political attention and the Sustainable Development Goal (SDG) 9 which aims to 'significantly increase access to ICT and strive to provide universal and affordable access to the internet in least developed countries by 2020' (SDG, target 9c)[2].

In fact, the pace of growth of internet across the globe has slowed down significantly since 2015: from 19% in 2007 to less than 6% in 2017 (Sample 2018); the digital revolution will continue to be a hard option for the most marginalized people. Digital disparity hits Africa, where only 1/4 people can access the web[3], the hardest. Investments by operators have either stalled or declined in recent years, and the level of costs for internet access remains a key driver of the digital inequality. The UN Target for affordable internet is 2% of monthly income for one gigabyte of data – the threshold deemed to permit basic internet access. Only the richest 20% of South Africans can actually afford this. For the poorest 60% of the people in South Africa, such basic access costs between 6% and 21% of their monthly earnings. In Mozambique, one of the poorest nations, practically nobody can afford the internet (A4AI 2014). Universal access will not be realistic before 2050 or later (Sample 2019).

Literacy is the other stumbling block, and another reasons of women's exclusion. Men are 21% more likely to have online access, and 52% in the lowest income countries (Iglesias, Web Foundation 2020). The digital gender gap continues to grow, particularly in Arab States, Asia and the Pacific, and Africa (ITU 2020, p.4). Against this asymmetry, digitalization has engineered new forms of violence against women and fueled new abuses of women's bodies. Web violence against women has taken up a disproportionate level of pathology, with new pandemic forms: from cyber-stalking to revenge porn, from doxing to sexting. The international human rights law provides standards to govern state and company approaches to online expression (A/HRC/38/35), yet the pervasiveness of the phenomenon in the digital environment actually hinders the process of advancing its conceptual and juridical definition, as illustrated by the European Commission work on hate speech online[4]. The intersection of online hate speech, freedom of expression, and inequality should provide space for governments' human rights legislation but, as UN Rapporteur David Kaye remarks:

> New laws that impose liability on companies are failing basic standards, increasing the power of those same private actors over public norms, and risk undermining free expression and public accountability. Companies likewise are not taking seriously their responsibilities to respect human rights. It is on their platforms where hateful content spreads, spurred on by a business model and algorithmic tools that value attention and virality.

> They have massive impact on human rights and yet all fail to articulate policies rooted in human rights law, as the UN Guiding Principles on Business and Human Rights call upon them to do.
>
> *(Kaye 2019)*

In 2020, COVID-19 has exposed the digital divide like never before. Among the many inequalities revealed by the pandemic, this manifestation is one of the starkest and most surprising. It stretches well inside the wealthiest nations, where access to internet infrastructures is definitely lower than we might have assumed before COVID. In the US, roughly 12 million children are estimated to live in homes without broadband connectivity (US Congress 2017). In the UK, 60,000 children have no internet at home (UK Children's Commissioner 2020) and many more were prevented from online learning with schools closed (Montacute 2020). Ultimately, while we all inhabit this brave new world of digital data, not everybody experiences it in the same way. Lack of access and tools is one side of the coin. Not the only one.

As more services are moving online, the divide is growing because digitalization has increasingly been used, like previous technological innovations, with the purpose of smothering economic and social rights, through profiling and containing marginalized groups. In the absence of national or international legal instruments to discipline the operations of digital tools – particularly algorithms – within the decision-making processes of private and public actors, and the potential discriminatory effects resulting from such use[5], the riveting sequence of precarious lives *vulnerated* by bad data, software errors, and unfit bureaucrats in Virginia Eubanks' powerful book is but the display of the hideous outcome (Eubanks 2018). Addressing the sources of discrimination and remedying the corresponding deficiencies in the law is not only technically difficult, but challenging also from a legal and political perspective. Yet, the skyrocketing precariousness for millions of people after the 2008 global financial crisis has been chaperoned by an equally swift increase of sophisticated data-based technologies like predictive algorithms, automated eligibility systems, risk models in public administration services that are being rationalized in the name of efficient social protection, so as to *better help those who are really in need*. The uptake of these technologies is rampant at a time when social schemes that serve the impoverished working class and other segments of society are as unpopular as they have ever been (Buchanan 2019), not by coincidence. In terms of litigation outcomes, victories in these cases are based on claims that challenged the lack of notice, explanation, and ability to comment or contest the changes to public benefit systems. This was especially relevant for the plaintiffs, individuals with intellectual or developmental disabilities:

> However, as systems become more widely adopted and accepted across different jurisdictions and domains, and affect different demographics, these challenges may be harder to bring, at least on grounds that challenge lack of notice. It is also worth noting that these challenges and the resulting mitigation efforts are extremely resource intensive, which can serve as an additional barrier for advocates.
>
> *(AI Now Institute 2018, p.8)*

Meanwhile, the increasing number of poor face higher levels of electronic scrutiny when they are processed for access to public benefit services or the healthcare system, when they walk highly policed neighborhoods or cross national frontiers, unknowingly entering a new digital infrastructure of poverty relief: 'a "low rights environment" where there are few expectations of political accountability and transparency' (Eubanks 2018, p.8). A 'digital poorhouse that hides poverty and gives society the needed ethical distance to design and implement inhumane policies' (Eubanks 2018, pp. 174–200).

Artificial intelligence and the digital anthropomorphic metamorphosis

In his investigation on artificial intelligence, French philosopher Éric Sadin argues that we have definitely entered a post-digital era or, more precisely, a digital technology's anthropomorphic era (Sadin 2019). We cannot grasp it yet, but given the power currently held by digital technologies it is urgent that we recognize how their features and functions entirely define a break from their original conceptualization. Tech anthropomorphism is peculiar: modelled on human cognitive capacities but enhanced to be more rapid, reliable, and efficient; fragmented, to solely perform specific tasks; enterprising and extreme, capable not only to interpret data, but also to start automatically goal-oriented actions.

We are confronted with the inexorable insurgence of an algorithmic *aletheia* (truth), which is literally in the hands of Western tech monopolies, determining the trajectory of digital research, and interpreting any single life moment as a beneficial opportunity for never-ending capital generation (and accumulation). Their models are 'black boxes' whose contents are fiercely guarded corporate secrets (Szymielevicz 2020). Beyond their aura of genial creative rebellion (Giridharadas 2019), tech titans escape tax bills alongside regulations and are accused to be 'BAAD – big, anti-competitive, addictive and destructive to democracy' (The Economist 2018, p.11). Preaching the idea of 'building a new global community' (Zuckerberg 2017), they run their business of math-powered applications driving the data economy and the instauration of *a new order of things* based on maximum reactivity and return. An order to which all segments of society – individuals and their life style, workforce, public institutions, hospitals, schools, transport networks, companies – must adapt and respond, almost outside of any territorial jurisdiction.

The anthropomorphist orientation of algorithmic sciences is – for the first time in human history – trying to endow digital artefacts with the human capacity to evaluate situations and extract conclusions. Modelled on the human brain, computational architectures are enabled to improve their competence via algorithms that help them rapidly retain and stock any new elements and data, thus asserting *their* truth in orienting human actions. Their improved ergonomic features allow them to get closer to human bodies and minds (to exercise their incremental 'powers of enunciation': incentivizing, imperative, prescriptive, and coercive (Sadin 2019, pp. 65–92).

Their incentivizing power thrives through the deployment of 'conversational interfaces' and voice-controlled personal assistants (*chatbots*) that may be installed anywhere, to map our tropisms and interests, in unpredictable forms of *daily body contacts* that imperceptibly mark the slow shift from control to a psychological relation of surrender and addiction (Dilci 2019). Chatbots form the backbone of the 'conversational commerce' featuring the *economy of attention* – attention being the digital age's most valuable asset (Mintzer 2020).

The imperative enunciation dominates justice digitalization, the automated management of people's profiles and the credit score system used in selection processes, used for behavioral modification (AI Now Institute 2018, p.10). The prescriptive stage grows in the decision-making capacity of precision medicine and in police surveillance procedures, while the coercive vocation moves in the military industry's digitalization of the battlefields (ICRC 2017) and in companies' warehouses, where expert systems tell human personnel which items to pick up from which shelves, which fastest routes to take to optimize time (reorienting their route if humans autonomously decide otherwise). Coercive are the irregular working schedules intentionally adopted with low-waged workers, where algorithms treat people as cogs in a machine (O'Neil 2016, pp.123–140).

Artificial intelligence: definitions (Serokell 2020)

Artificial intelligence (AI) studies ways to create computers and machines capable of solving problems through intelligent behavior. Some researchers make a distinction between 'narrow AI' and 'general AI'.

Narrow AI focuses on a single subset of cognitive abilities and advances in that spectrum, like computer systems that are better than humans at specific tasks (generating images, diagnosing diseases, playing chess).

General AI allows a machine to apply knowledge in different contexts, more closely mirroring human intelligence, by providing opportunities for autonomous learning and problem-solving, with generalized learning capabilities. Research progress is facilitating the transition from narrow AI to general AI, i.e. decision-making processes without explicit instructions.

Machine learning (ML), a subset of artificial intelligence, focuses on teaching computers how to automatically learn and improve without being programmed for specific tasks. ML aims to create algorithms that learn and make predictions based on data (neural networks). By using these neural architectures, it can reach out to higher levels of complexities.

Deep learning (DL) has steered the most significant breakthroughs in AI recently. It is a subset of machine learning that 'learns' from unsupervised and unstructured data processed through algorithms with brain-like functions, neural networks. Neural networks can develop through training (using different algorithms and improving them over time though incorporating new data sources) and inference (when a machine can identify which data sources are needed to make predictions).

The paradigm shift is supported by a robust rhetorical structure, blindly unchallenged. A new sophisticated lexicon has been crafted (Malabou 2017) to borrow the jargon from cognitive sciences, linked to the increasing ergonomic qualities of the products, towards a ***techno-ideology*** which allows the mix between cerebral processes and socio-economic logics. We need to re-conceptualize international legal protection in this field: human enhancement through such technologies is the primary human rights challenge of our time.

The automated invisible hand: The challenge for states' regulatory obligations

AI is the new gold rush. Governments and private companies are engaged in the global race to the AI podium, as the promising route for the next economic expansion. The race appears crowded with runners, but few are the real champions in this arena, indeed a national security concern with many geopolitical implications. In 2017 Vladimir Putin declared that 'whoever becomes the leader in this sphere will become the ruler of the world' (Allen 2017). The US has long steered public and private artificial intelligence research and development (R&D); investments by venture capitalists have skyrocketed in less than a decade, with a financial wave that has molded several US organizations into relatively sophisticated AI users (Loucks, Jarvis and others 2019). But it is no longer alone. Despite lack of technological maturity, the Chinese government is determined to become the world's leading AI innovator by 2030, leapfrogging global competition with tens of billions of dollars investments in AI R&D (Deloitte 2019). US and China together account for 90% of the market capitalization value of the world's 70 largest digital platforms (UNCTAD 2019); preoccupation is mounting about this concentration morphing into a duopolistic race between two digital superpowers[6], where countries may one day have *to choose sides*, with potentially significant geopolitical implications. The European Commission's concern is about the leadership of the European digital economy, as expressed in its thriving sequence of initiatives in this field (Hilty 2018): Germany aims to accelerate the AI development and adoption with a holistic strategy, focused also on the need for a responsible use of the technology and its impact on the German workforce (Loucks, Jarvis and others, Deloitte 2019). France's 'AI for Humanity' reflects plans to transform the country into a global AI hub (Loucks, Jarvis and others, Deloitte 2019). The UK is exuberantly betting on the future of AI, like Israel, Japan, and South Korea. Saudi Arabia has created a ministry on artificial intelligence. In the promises of the Fourth Industrial Revolution, AI is the new golden calf, but there is hardly any Moses willing to grind the idol into the powder of its complexity.

Rather, the opposite. In 2017, the 73rd session of the UN General Assembly invited robot Sophia[7] to address governments about 'the future of everything', making it the first humanoid celebrity in history[8]. After Sophia's interaction with member states at the UN, Saudi Arabia granted citizenship to the genderless robot (Walsh 2017), while still depriving human women of their basic rights and criminalizing LGBTIQ. In this state of euphoric confusion, the UN Secretary General decided to create a high-level panel on digital cooperation in 2018, appointing tech tycoon Jack Ma and Melinda Gates as co-chairs (UN Digital Cooperation 2018).

The lack of global governance mechanisms for the use of digital technologies – including in the public domain – and their commercialization remains one of the toughest issues (Daño and Prato 2019). Big tech companies of course work hard to increase their footprint in the digital space and keep the scenario that way, based on the assumption that the ability to innovate demands freedom. The Facebook founder's early call for the tech industry to 'move fast and break things' epitomizes the relevance attached to removing legal and governmental constraints. As mentioned earlier, the traditional notion of liability is at stake, including the attribution of responsibility for harm caused to end users, particularly when dealing with the transversal challenges raised by digitalization. Ownership of the knowledge created by AI affiliated technologies is also a major threat. Gathering patients' details and commercializing them in the health industry, for example, has very controversial legal implications, since the medical knowledge owned by public institutions should be treated as a public good and used as such. Another uncomfortable question is how current legal regimes are to deal with *machines as creators of knowledge*. The intellectual property (IP) regime grants protection to a known inventor: how will the patent be managed if the machine is the inventor of a new antibiotic, for instance? In the fragmentation of regulatory jurisdictions, who will enforce these rights and how, across borders?

The international initiatives recently undertaken to provide principles and guidelines[9], especially in using artificial intelligence, reveal the mounting sense of alert but do not yet really attack the regulatory roots of the problem. The European Union has embarked in the process of constructing a complex set of regulations for establishing and supporting a digital single market (DSM)[10] among the most crucial structural policies currently in train (European Commission 2020), with the primary intent of recalibrating the current legal frameworks. A case in point is the General Data Protection Regulation (GDPR) (European Union 2016), to confer all EU residents more control over their data. However, how will GDPR interact with AI and machines obtaining, processing, and producing data? Centralization, the backbone of the digital economy's regulation in Russia, does not seem quite compatible with the requirements of a digital scenario (Shatkovsskaya, Epifanova et al. 2018). Determining appropriate policy approaches is inherently difficult, the dynamic pace of technological change proceeds faster than legislative solutions and the key resources of the digital economy – intelligence and data – are invisible to current regulatory texts. Piecemeal regulatory efforts, like huge fines or sanctions, have failed to make any significant dent; 'the problem here may be that the regulators are trying industrial era remedies on digital age problems. Digital economy paradigm must be understood in its significant discontinuities with the industrial age. Regulation of digital economy needs to focus on the central role of data and data-derived intelligence' (Jeet Singh 2020, pp. 20–21). It has been highlighted that the outbreak of the new coronavirus reveals a digital governance emergency of international concern (McDonald 2020a), in a 'technological wild west' that deepens inequalities (Saez and Zucman 2019) and allows a bare handful of powerful CEOs to determine the disquieting sense of direction societies will take (Zuboff 2019). This emergency affects low- and middle-income countries (LMICs) disproportionately. Meanwhile, the debate on the human rights obligations of domestic states, foreign states, and transnational corporations, on who are *the new duty bearers* and *the right holders*, is painstakingly developing in official diplomatic fora; but attention to the legal uncertainty enveloping digital transformation remains limited[11].

The Hippocratic Oath reloaded

Digital technologies have been hailed in recent years as *the* most promising solution to tackle health challenges and help address healthcare inequalities, and they have gained, if possible, new impetus with COVID-19, in the public health response to the pandemic worldwide. Digital epidemiological surveillance, online data sourcing for early detection, contact tracing, rapid case identifications, and data-visualization tools for decision support are being extensively harnessed and combined[12], leveraging a significant breadth of innovation and investments. While technologies are obviously crucial to the disaster response, the digital hype against COVID-19 should not obfuscate the fact that technologists' blind spots and biases have already generated poisonous systems (Chesney and Citron 2018); the science community must ask itself a few fundamental questions to avoid that the tech rush may add to the chaos and ultimately injure the fight against the new coronavirus (Kalluri, Gillespie et al. 2020). The riddle goes beyond COVID: 'the way that we enable, administer and check the exceptional surveillance and social powers that each government exerts to contain COVID-19, especially as implemented through technology systems, will frame an important part of the future of state power in a world with increasing emergencies' (McDonald 2020b).

The future of public health is bound to become digital, in a swirling kaleidoscope of progress, expectations, limitations, and dilemmas (Budd et al. 2020): computational systems are quickly becoming the new frontier in healthcare, creeping out of their labs and making their way into supporting *real* people take *real* medical decisions. Despite their reputation for impartiality, they hammer complexity into simplicity and they always reflect goals and ideology: hence, their unflinching verdicts need serious scrutiny. At the Winterlight Labs, a Toronto-based startup that uses speech technology to assess cognitive health (for diseases like Alzheimer, Parkinson, and multiple sclerosis) language was the built-in bias – it only worked for English speakers of a particular Canadian dialect, leaving everyone else behind (Narayan 2019). A striking racial bias was identified in an algorithm used across America by hospitals and insurance companies to predict which patients were most likely to need follow-up care (Obermeyer, Powers et al. 2019). Hospitals and health systems are increasingly being structured on the premise that *these systems are the future*, gathering 'a bunch of data on previous patients, and use it to predict what will happen when a new patient steps in the door' (Gershgorn 2018). The clinical validity of this approach remains theoretical. From a human rights perspective, it means that the most vulnerable and powerless in society are subject to demands and forms of intrusiveness without accountability (Hawi, Samaha, Griffiths 2019) (Kickbush 2020).

Since the '90s, the progressive introduction of digital instruments and recording for medical exams has transformed medicine into a data generating practice, a trend that has formidably enhanced precision medicine (PM) and its armamentarium. PM methods seek treatments or prevention measures that are *specifically tailored* to an individual's disease process and symptoms and has received multibillion dollars in the last decade, to the detriment of key potential investments in population-based preventive programs that consider the behavioral, environmental, or social determinants of health (Ramaswami, Bayer, and Galea 2018). The first human genome sequenced in 2001 has stimulated the development of DNA-sequencing methods that have contributed to massive data availability and to a revolution in medical work and drug discovery, catering to the needs of high-income countries, where most research is conducted. The co-optation of medical and biological abilities as data hounds has been accepted by healthcare providers as an inevitable evolution, and the cheerleading medical literature has flourished to announce the provision of new instruments to better promote diagnosis, treatment, rehabilitation, and recovery. While there is no way to deny the real life improvement of this booming phenomenon, it is necessary to dig into some of its downsides for the right to health. The hyper-individualization of medicine supported by digital tools has further skewed health towards pharmaceutical approaches and forged a culture of personalized outcome improvements that are used by the private sector, especially the insurance industry, leaving behind key concerns for population health and the industry regulations required to this end. High costs are associated with digital health innovation, be it for individual users or societies; while commercial actors always reap heavy rewards, the solutions are not necessarily cost-effective for public authorities. Moreover, very few of the health apps comply with regulatory processes or have had their effectiveness formally assessed (Duggal, Briddle, and Bagenal 2018).

From a human rights' angle, digital devices have exacerbated existing power relations replicating and even reinforcing inequalities in very different ways, depending on their context of implementation (Al Dahdah 2019, pp.101–119; Al Dahdah 2020, pp. 39–69). In some countries, health data are used to structure public welfare programs and establish social credit scores; in others, they serve to sell goods and market services based on 'the starting assumption that the individual is not a rights-holder but rather an applicant' who must satisfy eligibility criteria (Alston, A/74/48037 2019, p. 14). For example, employers engaged in the constant quest for lowering costs have new tactics to fight growing insurance premiums – in the US these are encouraged by the Affordable Care Act (Obamacare) (Cawley 2014, pp. 810–820) – which involve greater workers' surveillance. The good justifications for the so called 'wellness programs' aimed to incentivize health conceal new forms of intrusion and coercion for the worker, who must follow a host of health behavioral dictates. Those who cannot reach the company's targets are compelled to pay extra contributions (fines?) to their insurance company, or likely undergo humiliating practices triggered by a mysterious proprietary algorithm (O'Neil 2016, pp. 173–178).

More disquieting challenges are looming. With new technologies such as synthetic biology and gene editing techniques, researchers are starting to court the idea of making better performing humans. A new technological myth of the superhuman is cherished (Warwick 2020). By using preferred gene variants preserved in computer databases and by unlocking genetic codes, it is possible to overcome the current biological boundaries of human performance and identify traits like disease resistance, powerful muscle, intelligence, that can be associated with real-life superheroes. As if the spark of life were migrating out of the human body and into the lab, it may soon be possible through selection and editing of genetic variants to intervene on living organisms and on the human body to produce genetic sequences that provide human embryos with the traits of the outliers, or create babies immune from diseases (Metzl 2019). How the traditional paradigm of human rights obligations may help prevent or mitigate such future dystopic scenarios is to be seen (Metzl 2020).

Conclusions: Towards a 'Digital New Deal'?

It seems that we are confronted with systemic threats from all angles in this 21st century. Like climate change, digital technologies present unprecedented human rights dilemmas. Digitalization was supposed to be an equalizer of access, opportunities and resources, the condition for enhanced community-making and democracy-building. Instead, it prosecutes exacerbating extractive and exclusionary social outcomes and consolidating the totalizing pattern of neoliberal economic globalization, in the absence of international normative cooperation. There should be no excuses for further lethargy: data and digital systems are not going away, with considerable cross border effects.

COVID-19 has highlighted the state's pivotal function and the public notion of economic interest. The shaping of institutional frameworks and governance processes of data and digital systems will mark the battle ground between the hegemony of the few and the democratic future of the many. It is possible to move towards a 'Digital New Deal' akin to Roosevelt's Keynesian revolution (Just Net Coalition and IT for Chance 2021), whereby the state regulatory capacities are strengthened, to tackle the opacity of tech companies' business operations and to tighten the privacy rules of already vulnerable individuals, particularly because during the pandemic public health has been used to justify a rollback of existing legislations. Supranational entities might consider leveraging access to the markets of their members to force tech companies into compliance with such regulations – a possible blueprint of this approach may be the EU Digital Service Act regulation. The state fiscal capacities also need to be enhanced, possibly with the introduction of a 25% global minimum effective corporate tax rate on all profits earned by tech multinationals, as proposed by the Independent Commission for the Reform of International Corporate Taxation (Ocampo 2020). Finally, time has come for an intergovernmental negotiation on a new treaty – a Convention for Data and Cyberspace – which should contain explicit principles for extending well-established offline legal obligations to the online world (Hill 2021).

We need to engage and direct the purpose of data-based intelligence towards the ideal of digital public goods, if we are to reaffirm the chant of human intelligence, its diversity and divergence. Ultimately, the reasons of human rights law.

Notes

1. At the end of 2019, 67% of the global population had subscribed to mobile devices, of which 65% were smartphones— with the fastest growth in Sub-Saharan Africa (GSMA, *The mobile economy 2020*, https://www.gsma.com/mobileeconomy/). In 2019, 204 billion apps were downloaded, with impressive growth in China (https://techcrunch.com/2020/01/15/app-stores-saw-record-204-billion-app-downloads-in-2019-consumer-spend-of-120-billion/), and as of January 2020, 3.8 billion people actively used social media (Simon Kemp, Digital 2020: Global Digital Overview, in *Data Reportal,* 30 January 2020, https://datareportal.com/reports/digital-2020-global-digital-overview/). But these numbers should not lead to hastily optimistic conclusions.
2. United Nations Development Programme (UNDP), Sustainable Development Goal 9: Industrial Innovation and Infrastructure, https://www.undp.org/content/undp/en/home/sustainable-development-goals/goal-9-industry-innovation-and-infrastructure.html, accessed 14 August 2020.
3. In developed countries, most people are online, with close to 87% of individuals using the internet. This number drops to a meagre 19% in the least developed countries (LDCs); see https://www.itu.int/en/ITU-D/Statistics/Documents/facts/FactsFigures2019.pdf.

4. Women were absent as a hate-specific target group in the taxonomy of the research conducted by the European Commission, in compliance with the Code of Conduct on Countering Illegal Hate Speech Online released in May 2016.
5. Several studies exist in relation to the potential discriminations associated to the use of artificial intelligence and particularly algorithms. Among the many, we highlight Hard M. (2014), 'How big data is unfair. Understanding unintended sources of unfairness in data driven decision making', *Medium*, 26th September 2014, https://medium.com/@mrtz/how-big-data-is-unfair-9aa544d739de; Barocas S. and Selbst A. (2016), 'Big Data's Disparate Impact', *California Law Review,* 104:671, 2016, http://dx.doi.org/10.2139/ssrn.2477899; Jon Kleinberg J., Ludwig J. et al. (2018), 'Discrimination in the age of algorithms', *Journal of Legal Analysis*, Volume 10, 2018, pp. 113:174, https://academic.oup.com/jla/article/doi/10.1093/jla/laz001/5476086, accessed 29th December 2020.
6. In her first speech as Managing Director of the International Monetary Fund, Kristalina Georgieva alluded to a "digital Berlin Wall" the forces countries to choose between either technology systems. https://www.imf.org/en/News/Articles/2019/10/03/sp100819-AMs2019-Curtain-Raiser.
7. Sophia is a social humanoid robot developed by Hanson Robotics, based in Hong Kong. It was first activated on 14th February 2016, and made its debut in mid-March 2016, in Austin, Texas. Sophia robot is capable to display over 50 facial expressions, https://en.wikipedia.org/wiki/Sophia (robot).
8. https://www.youtube.com/watch?v=BqB4ZOdNY7s
9. See the Asilomar Principles initiative (2017), to the OECD Council Recommendations on Artificial Intelligence (2019), to the Human-Centred AI Principles by the G20 (2019).
10. The DSM directive is merely regulating the status quo created by the unrestrained actions of big corporations such as Google, curbing the rights and protections of authors of online contents and smaller operator. See on this, Bridy A. (2020), "The Price of Closing the "Value Gap": How the Music Industry Hacked EU Copyright Reform", in 324 *Vand. Journal of Entertainment. & Technology Law*, Vol. 22, pp. 323-358.
11. See the diplomatic process around a Binding Treaty on transnational corporations' business activities and human rights at the UN Human Rights Council (UNHRC) https://www.ohchr.org/en/hrbodies/hrc/wgtranscorp/pages/igwgontnc.aspx.
12. https://www.nature.com/articles/s41591-020-1011-4/figures/1

References

AI Now Institute (2018) *Litigating Algorithms: Challenging Government Use of Algorithmic Decision-Making*, an AI Now Institute Report, in collaboration with Centre on Race, Inequality and the Law Electronic Frontier Foundation.

Al Dahdah, M. (2019) 'When Digital Giants Care for Africa: The Mobile Phone as a New Global Health Tool', *Politique Africaine* 156(4), 101–119.

_______ (2020) 'Mobile Phones, Promoters of Behavioural Health in the Global South', *Réseaux* 219(1), 39–69.

Allen, G.C. (2017) 'Putin and Musk are right: Whoever masters AI will run the world', *CNN*, 5 September 2017, https://edition.cnn.com/2017/09/05/opinions/russia-weaponize-ai-opinion-allen/index.html [accessed 17 August 2020].

Alliance for Affordable Internet (A4AI) (2014) 'A4AI Mozambique Multi-stakeholder Forum', 29 June 2014, https://a4ai.org/mozambique-africa/ [accessed 12 August 2020].

Alston, P. (2019a) 'Report of the UN Special Rapporteur on extreme poverty and human rights', 74th Session of the General Assembly, A/74/48037, available at https://www.ohchr.org/EN/NewsEvents/Pages/DisplayNews.aspx?NewsID=25156 [accessed 4 August 2020]

_______ (2019b) Statement by Prof. Philip Alston, Special Rapporteur for extreme poverty and human rights, 74th Session of the General Assembly, Third Committee, Item 7 (c), 18 October 2019, http://statements.unmeetings.org/media2/21999189/sr-extreme-poverty-ga-3rd-cttee-statement-f.pdf [accessed 7 August 2020].

Blix, M. (2017) *Digitalization, Immigration and the Welfare State*, Edward Elgar Publishing, https://www.elgaronline.com/view/9781786432940/9781786432940.xml [accessed 22 August 2020].

Brennen, J.S. and Kreiss, D. (2016) 'Digitalization', *The International Encyclopedia of Communication Theory and Philosophy,* 28 October 2016, 1–11.

Buchanan, M. (2019) 'Poverty in the UK is "systematic" and "tragic", says UN special rapporteur', *BBC News*, 22 May 2019, https://www.bbc.com/news/uk-48354692 [accessed 13 August 2020].

Budd, J. et al. (2020) 'Digital technologies in the public health response to COVID-19', *Nature Medicine* 26, 1183–1192, 7 August 2020, https://www.nature.com/articles/s41591-020-1011-4 [accessed 23 August 2020].

Burgess, M. (2020), 'Co-op is using facial recognition tech to scan and track shoppers', *Wired,* 10 December 2020, https://www.wired.co.uk/article/coop-facial-recognition [accessed 16 August 2020].

Cawley, J. (2014) 'The Affordable Care Act Permits Greater Financial Rewards For Weight Loss: A Good Idea In Principle, But Many Practical Concerns Remain', *Journal of Policy Analysis and Management* 33(3): 810–820, doi: 10.1002/pam.21767 [Accessed 29 August 2020].

Chesney, R. and Citron, D. (2018) 'Deepfakes: A Looming Crisis for National Security, Democracy and Privacy?', *Lawfare*, 21 February 2018, https://www.lawfareblog.com/deepfakes-looming-crisis-national-security-democracy-and-privacy [accessed 26 August 2020].

Children's Commissioner (2020) 'Tackling the disadvantage gap during the Covid-19 crisis', Briefing note, April 2020, https://www.childrenscommissioner.gov.uk/wp-content/uploads/2020/04/cco-tackling-the-disadvantage-gap-during-the-covid-19-crisis.pdf [accessed 18 August 2020].

Daño, N. and Prato, S. (2019) 'The Real Technology Revolution: Technology Justice', *Development* 62(1–4), October 2019, https://doi.org/10.1057/s41301-019-00230-3 [accessed 17 August 2020].

Dilci, T. (2019) 'A Study on Validity and Reliability of Digital Addition Scale for 19 Years or Older', *Universal Journal of Educational Research* 7(1), January 2019, https://www.hrpub.org/journals/article_info.php?aid=7641 [accessed 23 December 2020].

Duggal, R., Briddle, I. and Bagenal, J. (2018) 'Digital Healthcare: Regulating the Revolution', *BMJ*, 360: k6, https://doi.org/10.1136/bmj.k6 [accessed 22 August 2020].

The Economist (2017) 'The World's Most Valuable Resource is No Longer Oil but Data', 6 May 2017, https://www.economist.com/leaders/2017/05/06/the-worlds-most-valuable-resource-is-no-longer-oil-but-data [accessed 10 August 2020].

_______ (2018) 'Taming the titans: Google, Facebook and Amazon are increasingly dominant. How should they be controlled?', *The Economist* 426(9075).

Eubanks, V. (2018) *Automating Inequality: How High-Tech Tools Profile, Police and Punish the Poor*, Picador Paperbacks.

European Commission (2020) 'Shaping Europe's Digital Future', *The European Data Market Study Update,* 6 July 2020, https://ec.europa.eu/digital-single-market/en/news/european-data-market-study-update [accessed 22 December 2020].

European Union (2016) Regulation 2016/679 on the protection of natural persons with regard to the processing of personal data and on the free movement of such data, and repealing Directive 95/46/EC (General Data Protection Regulation), 27 April 2016, https://eur-lex.europa.eu/legal-content/EN/TXT/?uri=CELEX:32016R0679 [accessed 28 August 2020].

Gartner Information Technology (n.d.) 'Digitalization', Gartner *Glossary*, https://www.gartner.com/en/information-technology/glossary/digitalization [accessed 28 December 2020].

Gershgorn, D. (2018) 'If AI is going to be the world's doctor, it needs better textbooks', *Quartz*, 6 September 2018, https://qz.com/1367177/if-ai-is-going-to-be-the-worlds-doctor-it-needs-better-textbooks/ [accessed 20 August 2020].

Giridharadas, A. (2019) *Winners Take All: The Elite Charade of Changing the World*, Allen Lane, Penguin Random House.

Hawi, N.S., Samaha, M. and Griffiths, M.D. (2019) 'The Digital Addiction Scale for Children: Development and Validation', *Cyberpsychology, Behaviour and Social Networking* 22(12), 12 December 2019, https://www.liebertpub.com/doi/10.1089/cyber.2019.0132 [accessed 23 December 2020].

Hill, R. (2021) 'A New Convention for Data and Cyberspace', *A Digital New Deal: Visions of Justice in a Post-COVID World*, January 2021, 181–200, January 2021, https://itforchange.net/digital-new-deal/ [accessed 15 January 2021].

_______ (2018) 'Big Data: Ownership and Use in the Digital Age', in Seuba, X., Geiger, C. and Pénin, J. (eds). *Intellectual Property and Digital Trade in the Age of Artificial Intelligence and Big Data*, CEIPI-ICTSD Publications Series, (5). https://blogs.bmj.com/bmj/2020/01/14/ilona-kickbusch-the-dark-side-of-digital-health/ [accessed 12 August 2020].

Human Rights Council (HRC) (2018) Report of the Special Rapporteur on the promotion and protection of the right to freedom of opinion and expression, A/HRC/38/35, June-July 2018, agenda item 3, https://documents-dds-ny.un.org/doc/UNDOC/GEN/G18/096/72/PDF/G1809672.pdf?OpenElement [accessed 23 December 2020].

IGI Global (2018) 'What is Digitalization', *IT Strategy Follows Digitalization*, https://www.igi-global.com/chapter/it-strategy-follows-digitalization/183799 [accessed 28 December 2020].

Iglesias, C. (2020) 'The gender gap in internet access: using a women-centred method', *Web Foundation Blog*, 10 March 2020, https://webfoundation.org/2020/03/the-gender-gap-in-internet-access-using-a-women-centred-method/ [accessed 12 August 2020].

International Committee of the Red Cross (ICRC) (2017) 'Digital Technology and War', *International Review of the Red Cross*, March 2017, https://international-review.icrc.org/articles/digital-technology-and-war [accessed 22 December 2020].

International Telecommunication Union (ITU) (2019) 'Measuring Digital Development: Facts and Figures 2019', *ITU Publications*, https://www.itu.int/en/ITU-D/Statistics/Documents/facts/FactsFigures2019.pdf [accessed 10 August 2020].

The Just Net Coalition and IT for Change (2021) 'A Digital New Deal:Visions of Justice in a Post Covid World', January 2021, https://itforchange.net/digital-new-deal/ [accessed 15 January 2021].

Kalluri, R., Gillespie, R. et al. (2020) 'If We're Not Careful, Tech Could Hurt the Fight against COVID-19', *Scientific American*, 18 May 2020, https://blogs.scientificamerican.com/observations/if-were-not-careful-tech-could-hurt-the-fight-against-covid-19/ [accessed 24 August 2020].

Kaye, D. (2019) 'Report of the UN Special Rapporteur on the promotion and protection of the right to freedom of opinion and expression', 74th Session of the UN General Assembly, A/74/486, 9 October 2019, https://www.ohchr.org/Documents/Issues/Opinion/A_74_486.pdf, [accessed 27 December 2020].

Kickbush, I. (2020) 'The dark side of digital health', *The British Medical Journal Blog*, 14 January 2020.

Klein, N. (2020) 'Screen New Deal: Under Cover of Mass Death, Andrew Cuomo Calls in the Billionaires to Build a High-Tech Dystopia', *The Intercept*, 8th May 2020, https://theintercept.com/2020/05/08/andrew-cuomo-eric-schmidt-coronavirus-tech-shock-doctrine/, [accessed 12 August 2020].

Loucks, J., Hupfer, S. et al. (2019) 'Future in the Balance? How countries are pursuing an AI advantage', *Insights from Deloitte's State of AI in the Enterprise*, 2nd Edition Survey, Deloitte, 1 May 2019, https://www2.deloitte.com/us/en/insights/focus/cognitive-technologies/ai-investment-by-country.html [accessed 17 August 2020].

Malabou, C. (2017) *Métamorphoses de l'intelligence. Que faire de leur cerveau bleu?*, Presses Universitaires de France.

Marr, B. (2020) 'The future of Lawyers: Legal Tech, AI, Big Data and Online Courts', *Forbes*, 17th January 2020, https://www.forbes.com/sites/bernardmarr/2020/01/17/the-future-of-lawyers-legal-tech-ai-big-data-and-online-courts/?sh=51b885bff8c4 [accessed 13 August 2020].

Marsh, S. (2019) 'One in three councils using algorithms to make welfare decisions', *The Guardian*, 15 October 2019, https://www.theguardian.com/society/2019/oct/15/councils-using-algorithms-make-welfare-decisions-benefits [accessed 17 August 2020].

Mattioli, D. (2020) 'Big Tech Companies Reap Gains as Covid-19 Fuels Shift in Demand', *The Wall Street Journal*, 29 October 2020, https://www.wsj.com/articles/amazon-sales-surge-amid-pandemic-driven-online-shopping-11604003107 [accessed 17 August 2020].

McDonald, S. (2020a) 'Coronavirus: a Digital Governance Emergency of International Concern', *Centre for International Governance Innovation*, 2 March 2020, https://www.cigionline.org/articles/coronavirus-digital-governance-emergency-international-concern [accessed 20 August 2020].

_______ (2020b) 'The Digital Response to the Outbreak of COVID-19', *Centre for International Governance Innovation*, 30 March 2020, https://www.cigionline.org/articles/digital-response-outbreak-covid-19 [accessed 13 August 2020].

Metzl, J. (2019) 'Making Babies in the Year 2045', *The New York Times*, 10 April 2019, https://www.nytimes.com/2019/04/10/opinion/genetic-testing-privacy.html?auth=login-email&login=email [accessed 20 December 2020].

_______ (2020) *Hacking Darwin: Engineering and the Future of Humanity*, Sourcebooks.

Mintzer, A. (2020) 'Paying Attention: the Attention Economy', *Berkeley Economic Review*, 31 March 2020, https://econreview.berkeley.edu/paying-attention-the-attention-economy/ [accessed 17 August 2020].

Montacute, R. (2020) 'School Closures and Disadvantaged Students', *The Sutton Trust*, 19 March 2020, https://www.suttontrust.com/news-opinion/all-news-opinion/school-closures/ [accessed 14 August 2020].

Narayan, S. (2019) 'An Inconvenient Truth – The Problem with Data Quality In MedTech AI', *Medium*, 18 October 2019, https://medium.com/@swethaxnarayanan/an-inconvenient-truth-the-problem-with-data-quality-in-medtech-ai-476d7486dae0 [accessed 20 August 2020].

Obermeyer, Z., Powers, B. et al. (2019) 'Dissecting racial bias in an algorithm used to manage the health of populations', *Science* 366(6464), 447–453, 25 October 2019, https://science.sciencemag.org/content/366/6464/447 [accessed 18 August 2020].

Ocampo, J.A. (2020) 'Fiscalité: Il est impératif d'introduire un taux effectif minimum global d'imposition des multinationales d'au moins 25%', *Le Monde*, 20 November 2020, https://www.icrict.com/icrict-in-thenews/2020/11/26/fiscalit-il-est-impratif-dintroduire-un-taux-effectif-minimum-global-dim-position-des-multinationales-dau-moins-25- [accessed 15 January 2021].

Office of the High Commissioner for Human Rights (OHCHR) (2019) 'Governments and Internet companies fail to meet challenges of online hate', 21 October 2019, https://www.ohchr.org/en/NewsEvents/Pages/DisplayNews.aspx?NewsID=25174&LangID=E [accessed 28 December 2020].

O'Neil, C. (2016) *Weapons of Math Destruction: How Big Data Increases Inequality and Threatens Democracy*, Penguin Books.

Organisation for Economic Co-operation and Development (OECD) (2018) 'Tax and Digitalization', *OECD Paper*, October 2018, https://www.oecd.org/tax/beps/tax-and-digitalisation-policy-note.pdf [accessed 3 October 2020].

_______ (2019) 'Regulatory effectiveness in the era of digitalization', June 2019, https://www.oecd.org/gov/regulatory-policy/Regulatory-effectiveness-in-the-era-of-digitalisation.pdf [accessed 22 December 2020].

Ramaswami, R., Bayer, R. and Galea, S. (2018) 'Precision Medicine from a Public Health Perspective', *Annual Review of Public Health* 39, 153–168, 1 April 2018, https://pubmed.ncbi.nlm.nih.gov/29166244/ [accessed 13 August 2020].

Sadin, E. (2019) *Critica della Ragione Artificiale: Una Difesa dell'Umanità*, Luiss University Press.

Saez, E. and Zucman, G. (2019) *The Triumph of Injustice: How the Rich Dodge Taxes and How to Make Them Pay*, W.W. Norton & Co.

Sample, I. (2018) 'Exclusive: dramatic slowdown in global growth of internet access', *The Guardian*, 18 October 2018, https://www.theguardian.com/technology/2018/oct/18/exclusive-dramatic-slowdown-in-global-growth-of-the-internet [accessed 12 August 2020].

_______ (2019) 'Universal internet access unlikely until at least 2050, experts say', *The Guardian*, 10 January 2019, https://www.theguardian.com/technology/2019/jan/10/universal-internet-access-unlikely-until-2050-experts-say-lack-skills-investment-slow-growth [accessed 12 August 2020].

Serokell (2020) 'Artificial Intelligence vs. Machine Learning vs. Deep Learning: what's the Difference', *Medium*, 10 April 2020, https://medium.com/ai-in-plain-english/artificial-intelligence-vs-machine-learning-vs-deep-learning-whats-the-difference-dccce18efe7f [accessed 12 August 2020].

Shatkovsskaya, T.V., Epifanova, T.S. et al. (2018) 'A Legal Mechanism for Regulating the Digital Economy', CBU International Conference on Innovations in Science and Education, 21–23 March 2018, *CBU Journal*, October 2020, https://ideas.repec.org/a/aad/iseicj/v6y2018i0p763-767.html [accessed 27 August 2020].

Singh, J. P. (2020) 'Breaking up Big Tech: Separation of its Data, Cloud, and Intelligence Layers', *IT for Change*, Working Paper 9, June 2020, https://itforchange.net/sites/default/files/add/Regulating_data__cloud_and_intelligence_-_Paper_9-21.pdf [accessed 20 August 2020].

Szymielevicz, K. (2020) 'Black-Boxed Politics: Opacity is a Choice in AI Systems', *Medium*, 17 January 2020, https://medium.com/@szymielewicz/black-boxed-politics-cebc0d5a54ad [accessed 14 August 2020].

UNCTAD (2019) 'Digital Economy Report 2019', *UNCTAD Publications*, https://unctad.org/en/PublicationsLibrary/der2109_overview_en.pdf [accessed 20 August 2020].

United Nations (2018) 'Secretary General's High-Level Panel on Digital Cooperation', July 2018, https://www.un.org/en/digital-cooperation-panel/ [accessed 17 August 2020].

US Congress Joint Economic Committee (2017) 'America's Digital Divide', September 2017, https://www.jec.senate.gov/public/_cache/files/ff7b3d0b-bc00-4498-9f9d-3e56ef95088f/the-digital-divide-.pdf [accessed 21st August 2020].

Walsh, A. (2017) 'Saudi Arabia grants citizenship to robot Sophia', *Deutsche Welle*, 28 October 2017, https://www.dw.com/en/saudi-arabia-grants-citizenship-to-robot-sophia/a-41150856 [accessed 17 August 2020].

Warwick, K. (2020) 'Superhuman Enhancements via Implants: Beyond the Human Mind', *Philosophies, MDPI*, 5, 14, 10 August 2020, https://www.mdpi.com/2409-9287/5/3/14/htm [accessed 22 December 2020].

Zuboff, S. (2019) *The Age of Surveillance Capitalism: The Fight for a Human Future and the New Frontier of Power*, Public Affairs.

Zuckerberg, M. (2017) 'Building Global Community', *Facebook*, 16 February 2017, https://www.facebook.com/notes/mark-zuckerberg/building-global-community/10154544292806634/ [accessed 14 August 2020].

Part II
Enforcement

7

Extraterritorial obligations in the United Nations system: UN treaty bodies

Elena Pribytkova[1]

Introduction

The United Nations is a complex system exhibiting a number of various approaches to regulating, governing, and enforcing extraterritorial obligations (ETOs). This chapter focuses on the activity of five UN treaty bodies mandated to monitor the implementation of the core international human rights treaties – the *International Covenant on Economic, Social and Cultural Rights* (ICESCR); the *International Covenant on Civil and Political Rights* (ICCPR); the *Convention on the Rights of the Child* (CRC); the *Convention on the Elimination of all Forms of Discrimination Against Women* (CEDAW); and the *Convention on the Rights of Persons with Disabilities* (CRPD) – the Committee on Economic, Social, and Cultural Rights (CESCR), the Human Rights Committee (HRC), the Committee on the Rights of the Child (UN CRC), the Committee on the Elimination of Discrimination Against Women (UN CEDAW), and the Committee on the Rights of Persons with Disabilities (UN CRPD)[2] and the manner in which they have reformed international law relating to ETOs.

Based on an analysis of the treaty bodies' major outputs – General Comments/General Recommendations (GC/GR); Concluding Observations (COBs); Statements; and Individual Communications – the chapter seeks to identify their approach to ETOs. The study embraces descriptive and normative components. It explores practices of the treaty bodies concerning ETOs and outlines some directions for further development of these practices.

The chapter is structured as follows. First, it provides a general overview of the treaty bodies' interpretation and classification of ETOs as well as their definition of remedial ETOs. Following that, it explores the treaty bodies' approach to regulating and enforcing global obligations, including obligations of extraterritorial cooperation and assistance. Then, their methods of assigning ETOs to states and non-state actors (NSAs) are analysed. The final section examines the treaty bodies' role as accountability mechanisms capable of holding states responsible for breaching their ETOs.

Extension of states' human rights obligations beyond their borders

The treaty bodies have developed a common approach to ETOs, although some differences emerge due to a number of factors. First, the treaty bodies' activities are determined by the

DOI: 10.4324/9781003090014-10

different UN conventions themselves, the implementation of which they are designed to monitor.[3] Second, the Committees have diverse experience of work. The HRC (1976), the CESCR (1985), the UN CEDAW (1982), and the UN CRC (1990) are more sophisticated in comparison to the relatively 'young' UN CRPD (2008).[4]

International law proceeds from a presumption, expressed in the *Vienna Convention on the Law of Treaties*, that international treaties are binding upon state parties within their territory (art. 29). Although the ICCPR and the CRC contain jurisdictional clauses,[5] the ICESCR, the CEDAW, and the CRPD have no such restrictions. Moreover, the ICESCR, the CRC, and the CRPD explicitly recognise that states have ETOs corresponding to socio-economic rights in provisions on obligations of international assistance and cooperation (ICESCR, art. 2; CRC, art. 4, art. 24 para. 4, and art. 28 para. 3; CRPD, art. 4 para. 2 and art. 32).

The treaty bodies appeal to personal and spatial models of jurisdiction, according to which a state's jurisdiction extends to situations beyond its borders when it exercises effective control over individuals or territory (Milanovic 2011, Ch. 4). For instance, in concluding observations on Israel, various treaty bodies have asserted that jurisdiction includes all territories and populations under a state's effective control (CESCR 1998, para. 8; HRC 1998, para. 10; UN CRC 2002, paras. 2, 5, and 57–58; UN CEDAW 2005, para. 23; see also HRC 2004a, para. 10; HRC 2019, para. 63). Additionally, jurisdiction extends to situations where states' acts or omissions affect the enjoyment of human rights abroad. Thus, the HRC determines that jurisdiction concerns the 'relationship between the individual and the state in relation to a violation of any of the rights set forth in the Covenant' (HRC 1981a, para. 12.2; see also HRC 2019, paras. 22 and 63).

One can distinguish between *remedial ETOs* for the negative impact of global actors on the enjoyment of human rights and *global obligations*, which arise when human rights deprivations cannot be attributed to any particular actors or institutions. A criterion used for this classification is the possibility of establishing a causal link between acts or omissions of global actors and human rights abuses.[6] It is important to emphasise that both types of ETOs – remedial ETOs and global obligations – correspond to all types of human rights, which has been reaffirmed by the treaty bodies.

The treaty bodies have paid significant attention to states' remedial ETOs for various human rights violations relating to military occupations and peacekeeping operations; killings, sexual abuse, torture or other cruel, inhuman, or degrading treatment; kidnapping and arbitrary detention; discrimination on various bases; abusive international trade, investment, financial secrecy, tax, and agricultural policies; extractive industries; environmental damage and climate change impact, etc. The treaty bodies have also addressed remedial ETOs for states' non-compliance with global obligations to respect, protect, and fulfil human rights (UN CRC 2020a), including obligations of international cooperation and assistance (CESCR 2014, para. 12; CESCR 2016b, para. 15) and obligations to protect against extraterritorial human rights violations caused by private entities having a 'reasonable link' with these states (see Section on attributing ETOs to states and non-state actors).[7]

The treaty bodies have set forth two conditions for attributing remedial ETOs. The first is *causation*, i.e., the existence of a causal link between an actor's activity and human rights impacts. The HRC asserts that 'a state party may be responsible for extra-territorial violations of the Covenant, if it is a link in the causal chain that would make possible violations in another jurisdiction' (HRC 2009, annex para. 14.2). As the CESCR specifies, states bear remedial ETOs 'even if other causes have also contributed to the occurrence of the violation' (CESCR 2017, para. 32). The second condition involves the *reasonable foreseeability* of extraterritorial human rights violations occurring. According to the HRC, 'the risk of an extra-territorial violation must be a necessary and foreseeable consequence and must be judged on the knowledge the state party had at the time' (HRC 2009, annex para. 14.2). The CESCR has held that the state is responsible even if it 'had not foreseen that a violation would occur, provided such a violation was reasonably foreseeable' (CESCR 2017, para. 32; see also HRC 2019, paras. 22 and 63).

Remedial ETOs embrace *interactional* and *institutional* aspects. Interactional remedial obligations are aimed at realising the right to effective and affordable remedies and adequate (full and effective) reparation for particular victims of extraterritorial human rights violations. They call for measures of comprehensive, long-term, needs-based, victim-centred protection and assistance to victims. Institutional remedial ETOs include obligations to guarantee the availability of efficient accountability mechanisms at national, regional, and international levels necessary to secure remedies for the victims, including measures of non-repetition, restitution, compensation, satisfaction, and rehabilitation (CESCR 2000, para. 59; HRC 2014, paras. 5 and 9; UN CEDAW 2016d, para. 13). States and other members of the international community should cooperate in order to 'prevent contradictions and inadequacies in the remedies and sanctions' (Commission on Human Rights 1997, para. 131).

Global obligations

In an earlier work, I proposed a classification of *global obligations*. It includes global obligations of result, which embrace *interactional obligations to realise human rights universally* and *institutional obligations to create and maintain a just global order*, as well as global obligations of conduct, consisting of *obligations to cooperate* and *obligations to assist* (Pribytkova 2020). Under both hard and soft international law (*UN Charter*, art. 1 paras. 2–3 and arts. 55–56; *Maastricht Principles*, Principles 8 and 29), there is a tendency to interpret all global obligations as obligations of conduct, focusing on efforts and processes, rather than obligations of result, addressing achievements and outcomes. The ICESCR and the CRPD also treat global obligations as duties of conduct (ICESCR, art. 2 para. 1; CRPD, art. 4 para. 2). However, the CESCR and the UN CRPD assert that general legal obligations corresponding to socio-economic rights involve both obligations of conduct and obligations of result. Although many global obligations of result corresponding to socio-economic rights are supposed to be implemented progressively, they aim at achieving a concrete goal – the full realisation of socio-economic rights universally (CESCR 1990, para. 1; UN CRPD 2016, para. 40). Some global obligations are obligations of immediate effect.[8]

According to a tripartite theory of human rights obligations, three types of obligations (to respect, protect, and fulfil) correspond to each human right (Shue 1996; Sepúlveda 2003). The treaty bodies acknowledge *global obligations to respect, protect,* and *fulfil* human rights, which embrace interactional and institutional aspects.[9] First, the treaty bodies demand that states 'refrain from interfering directly or indirectly with the enjoyment' of human rights abroad (CESCR 2017, para. 29; UN CEDAW 2017, paras. 14–15). Institutional global obligations to respect human rights imply, in particular, obligations to create mechanisms for systematic and efficient human rights impact assessments (HRIAs) as well as gender, child rights, environmental, and social impact assessments with the participation of all stakeholders, especially vulnerable individuals and social groups (UN CEDAW 2018a, paras. 29–30; UN CRC 2019b, para. 18; UN CRPD 2019b, para. 67). Second, the treaty bodies recognise states' obligations to regulate and influence the conduct of NSAs and individuals to prevent extraterritorial violations of human rights and ensure victims' access to effective remedies. Global institutional obligations to protect require establishing efficient national and international monitoring and accountability mechanisms, and not only when these mechanisms are unavailable or inefficient in states where extraterritorial activity takes place (CESCR 2017, paras. 30–35; UN CRPD 2018b, para. 94(c);

UN CEDAW 2016b, paras. 24–25). Third, global obligations to fulfil combine obligations to *facilitate, provide,* and *promote.* Obligations to facilitate demand removing structural impediments to a just international order and creating the enabling environment necessary for the universal realisation of human rights. ETOs to promote involve interactional and institutional duties to produce, and ensure access to, educational programs, knowledge, and information about human rights globally and, thereby, supporting people in making informed choices. Global obligations to provide presuppose guaranteeing access to resources and services indispensable for leading a decent life to those who are unable to secure this access by themselves; they also embrace interactional and institutional obligations of extraterritorial assistance (CESCR 2000, paras. 33, 36–37 and 39; UN CRC 2013b, para. 29).

The treaty bodies address both *global obligations of relational justice* that presuppose guarantees of all individuals' full-fledged and meaningful participation in key global institutions and practices, including important decision-making processes (UN CRPD 2018a, para. 72; UN CEDAW 2015, para. 25), and *global obligations of distributive justice* that call for a fair allocation of certain social goods or resources indispensable for enjoying a decent life (CESCR 2017, para. 37; UN CRC 2013b, para. 29). For instance, the UN CRPD defends a new model of 'inclusive equality' which embraces relational (recognition and participative) and distributive components.[10] In accordance with the principles of 'ownership of development' and 'leaving no one behind', global actors should ensure effective and meaningful participation, inclusion, and consultation with disadvantaged individuals and social groups and their representatives 'in the design, implementation, monitoring and evaluation' of all extraterritorial programs and projects (UN CRPD 2019a, para. 60; UN CRPD 2019c, para. 62; UN CEDAW 2013a, para. 42).[11] In the time of pandemic, the CESCR pays special attention to primary distributive obligations of states and NSAs to ensure universal, affordable, equitable, and non-discriminative access to treatment for and vaccines against COVID-19, which are 'safe, effective and based on the best scientific developments', for all individuals, especially those from the least developed countries (CESCR 2020b; CESCR 2021).

The treaty bodies have established that states have legal obligations to cooperate with other public and private actors and to assist in the realisation of their obligations to respect, protect, and fulfil human rights universally.[12] As the UN CRC states, '[w]hen states ratify the Convention, they take upon themselves obligations not only to implement it within their jurisdiction, but also to contribute, through international cooperation, to global implementation' (UN CRC 2003, para. 5). The CESCR stresses that without an active and efficient program of international assistance, which is more important than ever during a pandemic, the full realisation of socio-economic rights 'will remain an unfulfilled aspiration in many countries' (CESCR 1990, para. 14; CESCR 2020a, para. 19). In particular, the treaty bodies determine that key components of the right to an adequate standard of living – the rights to adequate food, water, sanitation, housing, and health – give rise to international obligations to assist (CESCR 1991, paras. 10, 13, and 19; CESCR 1999a, paras. 36, 38, and 40; CESCR 2000, paras. 38–40, 45, and 63; CESCR 2003, paras. 30 and 34; UN CRC 2003, section J; UN CRC 2013b, para. 41). The current practice of developed states reporting on their implementation of international obligations to assist within the treaty bodies periodic reporting procedure may be interpreted as a recognition of these legal obligations (CESCR 2019; UN CRC 2017, para. 29; UN CRC 2018, paras. 41–43). Moreover, territorial human rights obligations of social support and ETOs to assist are considered to be simultaneous: states are not exempt from obligations to provide extraterritorial assistance because their domestic obligations are not fully realised.[13]

Though international human rights law has not yet acknowledged the obligations of the state to seek international assistance if it is unable to guarantee the full realisation of human rights within its jurisdiction, the treaty bodies often encourage states to seek international assistance (CESCR 2011b, para. 4; UN CRC 2011a, paras. 19 and 23). The treaty bodies appeal to the UN 0.7% GDP target for official development assistance (ODA) and request developed countries to take all measures to achieve this target (CESCR 2016a, paras. 7–8; UN CRC 2003, para. 61). However, the treaty bodies' references to the 'position to assist', 'maximum of available resources', and 'progressive realisation' clauses in the context of obligations to assist obscure rather than shed light on their nature, content, and scope, as they are often used by states as 'escape clauses' giving reasons to withdraw from the (full) realisation of their obligations (Alston and Quinn 1987, pp. 172–180).[14]

The treaty bodies address the obligations of both parties of extraterritorial relations of assistance – donors and recipients – to provide efficient assistance and to use it effectively for the realisation of human rights. On the one hand, they note that very often international assistance provided by donors is insufficient, inefficient, and causes serious human rights violations in recipient countries (CESCR 2014, para. 12; CESCR 2016b, para. 14; UN CRPD 2015a, para. 74). They also rightly criticise unjustified conditionalities of assistance, recalling that donor states should not impose duties that adopt retrogressive measures in violation of recipient states' human rights obligations (CESCR 2016c, paras. 9–11). The treaty bodies demand applying a human rights-based approach to international cooperation and assistance policies that implies creating efficient monitoring mechanisms for systematic, independent, and participatory *ex ante* and *ex post* HRIAs, taking remedial measures when necessary, and guaranteeing accessible complaint mechanisms (CESCR 2014, para. 12; UN CRPD 2019b, para. 67; CESCR 2016c, para. 11). In addition, they urge states to mainstream the most disadvantaged individuals and their organisations through international cooperation and assistance programs (UN CRPD 2015b, paras. 59–60; UN CRPD 2013, paras. 71–72).

On the other hand, the treaty bodies have noted the many cases of corruption, 'mismanagement of international cooperation aid', and 'unbalanced budgetary allocations', including low allocations to the 'social sectors', and 'the limited effectiveness of the use of foreign funds' that constitute 'serious breaches' of states' territorial obligations (CESCR 2002, para. 11; CESCR 2009a, para. 16). They stress the obligations of states receiving international assistance to use it efficiently to empower the local poor and to realise their human rights, while prohibiting the use of assistance to perpetuate inequalities, discrimination, and segregation (UN CRPD 2014, para. 47; UN CRPD 2017, para. 96). Recipient states should combat corruption and increase transparency and consultations with the most vulnerable individuals and social groups at all levels of decision-making concerning the distribution of funds, as well as the monitoring and evaluation of aid's impact (CESCR 2002, para. 30; CESCR 2009a, para. 16; UN CRPD 2018b, paras. 72, 78, 92, and 94(r)).

It is important to note that extraterritorial assistance implied by the treaties is state-centred. That is why the treaty bodies monitor the implementation of obligations of *international* assistance, which are addressed to states and aimed at supporting them in realising their human rights obligations within their territory, rather than obligations of *global* assistance specifically directed to those in need (Pribytkova 2019, pp. 276–282). In this context, the main agents of assistance are developed states. However, the UN CRPD goes beyond these limitations and urges states to ensure direct access of persons with disabilities and NGOs representing them to foreign development aid, i.e., to guarantee their independence and autonomy from the state and promote their right to seek and receive assistance from 'international sources, including private individuals and companies, civil society organisations, states parties and international organisations' (UN CRPD 2018b, paras. 64 and 94(b,p)). This may be interpreted as an expression of the awareness that state-centred international assistance is insufficient and the recognition of the right of disadvantaged individuals and social groups to direct *global assistance*.

Attributing ETOs to states and non-state actors

International human rights instruments acknowledge not only states but also intergovernmental organisations (IGOs), NSAs, and individuals as bearers of human rights obligations. For example, the UDHR proceeds from the assumption that 'every individual and every organ of society' should strive to promote respect for human rights and to 'secure their universal and effective recognition and observance' through progressive national and international measures (pmbl., art. 29 para. 1 and art. 30). This provision is reaffirmed by the ICESCR (art. 5 para. 1). Relatedly, the CRPD determines the obligations of states to cooperate with international and regional organisations and civil society (art. 32). The treaty bodies also clarify that human rights bind all global actors and encourage states to cooperate with public and private actors for human rights realisation (see previous Section).

Without paying significant attention to direct obligations of other global entities, the treaty bodies address obligations of states in their triple role. First, states have *direct ETOs* which embrace global obligations to respect, protect, and fulfil and remedial ETOs (see two previous Sections). Second, *as members of IGOs*, including international financial institutions (such as the World Bank, the IMF, and regional development banks), states have ETOs to refrain from coercing other IGO members into violating human rights (CESCR 2016c, paras. 9–10) and to ensure that human rights are implemented through the policies of the IGOs (CESCR 1999b, para. 56; CESCR 2008, para. 58; UN CEDAW 2013a, paras. 12 and 14).[15]

Third, states should *regulate and influence the conduct of NSAs and individuals* (HRC 2004a, para. 8; CESCR 2017; UN CRC 2013b; UN CEDAW 2010, para. 36).[16] The treaty bodies used to emphasise the primacy of host states' obligations to regulate NSAs and protect their citizens from the negative impact as part of their territorial obligations (CESCR 2010, para. 10; UN CRC 2011b, para. 21; UN CRC 2013b, para. 42). This focus often exceeded the ability of developing countries to control more powerful NSAs (especially transnational corporations (TNCs)) affiliated with developed states; it also failed to encourage the acceptance of direct human rights obligations by NSAs and their home states (Vandenbogaerde 2016, p. 78). More recently, the treaty bodies have been requiring home states to govern the extraterritorial conduct of NSAs registered or domiciled in their territory (CESCR 2011a, para. 5; HRC GC 36, para. 22; UN CEDAW 2016a, paras. 18–19).

The treaty bodies call for the implementation of the *UN Guiding Principles on Business and Human Rights* (*UN Guiding Principles*), according to which TNCs possess only obligations to respect human rights (along with remedial ETOs), while obligations to protect and fulfil human rights fall on the state (Principle 11). Generally following this pattern, the treaty bodies demand that TNCs act 'with due diligence to prevent human rights violations and provide effective remedies for human rights violations connected to their operations' (UN CEDAW 2018b, para. 48; UN CRC 2021b, paras. 35–36, 38, 48). At the same time, some treaty bodies go beyond the *UN Guiding Principles* and stipulate that TNCs also have obligations to protect human rights as well as certain obligations to fulfil human rights, making impact on their 'effective enjoyment and exercise' (UN CEDAW 2018b, para. 48; UN CRC 2010a, para. 31; UN CRC 2010b, para. 19; UN CRPD 2016, para. 76; UN CRC 2021b, para. 36).[17] In the context of pandemic, the CESCR claims that TNCs should only 'at a minimum' respect human rights while having more extensive obligations corresponding to the human right to health, in particular obligations to contribute to guaranteeing universal, fair, and affordable access to medicines, vaccines, diagnostic tools, and health-care technologies (CESCR 2020b, para. 7; CESCR 2021, para. 8). The treaty bodies demand states to take several measures in relation to TNCs. First, they should establish and strengthen their regulatory framework, especially a national action plan on business and human rights, and monitoring mechanisms, including HRIAs, and demand TNCs to exercise due diligence, consult with local populations and receive their informed consent prior to implementing any projects (HRC 2015, para. 6; UN CEDAW 2016c, para. 41; UN CRC 2019a, para. 17). Second, states should provide effective and independent judicial and non-judicial mechanisms to investigate complaints against TNCs and secure remedies and reparations for victims, particularly through supporting the work of the National Contact Points established under the *OECD Guidelines for Multinational Enterprises* (CESCR 2018, paras. 16–17; HRC 2011, para. 11; HRC 2012, para. 16; UN CEDAW 2014a, paras. 14–15).

The treaty bodies consider civil society to be an important global actor possessing obligations to respect human rights and to prevent and/or minimise possible harm resulting from its activity, including assistance projects (UN CEDAW 2018b, para. 50). They encourage states to cooperate with NGOs 'in order to benefit from their expertise in human rights monitoring, reporting and analysis, policy development and implementation and all related capacity development in international cooperation' (UN CRPD 2015c, para. 51; see also UN CRC 2021b, para. 34).

UN treaty bodies as accountability mechanisms

The treaty bodies have not developed any special procedures for monitoring the realisation of ETOs. States may be held accountable for extraterritorial human rights violations through the treaty bodies' general procedures, including periodic reporting, inquiry procedures, and interstate and individual complaints; though, in practice, not all of these procedures have been used for this purpose. The treaty bodies have different experiences of functioning as accountability mechanisms: while the HRC (1976) has elaborated a solid case law, including the one related to ETOs, the communication procedures of the UN CEDAW (2000), the UN CRPD (2008), the CESCR (2013), and the UN CRC (2014) are still in development. Since the treaty bodies' accountability mechanisms are state-centred, NSAs cannot be held accountable through them even in case of their complicity with states in human rights violations.

As demonstrated in previous Sections, within the *periodic reporting procedures*, the treaty bodies concentrate on a set of questions surrounding extraterritorial human rights violations relating to international trade, investment and tax policies, military occupations and peacekeeping operations, surveillance activities, corporations' extraterritorial activities, and environmental damage. They also address breaches of global obligations, including obligations of cooperation and assistance. Through periodic reporting on their implementation of ETOs, which should be submitted every four or five years by states, the latter express their recognition of these obligations as legally binding (see Section on global obligations). Parallel reports from civil society, encouraged and considered by the treaty bodies, play an important role in holding states accountable. Though the treaty bodies' concluding observations provide a significant normative framework for ETOs influencing both theory and practice, they are criticised for being often inconsistent, using 'soft', 'general', and political rather than legal language, formulating non-obligatory recommendations and, therefore, not being taken seriously by states and having a limited impact (Langford and King 2008, p. 503; Vandenbogaerde 2016, p. 50). Additionally, periodic reporting procedures (along with inquiry procedures) usually focus on general problems rather than on concrete cases and are not aimed at holding certain actors responsible and providing remedies for particular victims.

Despite their potential to serve as accountability tools for ETOs, inquiry procedures and inter-state communications have not been used for this purpose. Through *inquiry procedures*, the CESCR, the UN CRC, the UN CEDAW, and the UN CRPD examine information which can be submitted by any actor, including those unable to submit individual communications for 'practical constraints or fear of reprisals',[18] about states' 'grave and systematic' violations of human rights (the *Optional Protocol to the International Covenant on Economic, Social, and Cultural Rights* (OP-ICESCR), art. 11; the *Optional Protocol to the Convention on the Rights of the Child on a Communications Procedure* (OP-CRC), art. 13; *the Optional Protocol to the Convention on the Rights of Persons with Disabilities* (OP-CRPD), art. 6; the Optional Protocol *to the Convention on the Elimination of All Forms of Discrimination against Women* (OP-CEDAW), art. 8). The CESCR's, the HRC's, and the UN CRC's *inter-state communications* mechanisms allow states to complain about human rights violations carried out by another parties (OP-CESCR, art. 10; ICCPR, arts. 41–43; OP-CRC, art. 12). One possible difficulty of using inter-state communications procedures relates to their optional character (states should declare whether they agree applying this mechanism to themselves). In addition, individuals rarely benefit from these procedures because inquiry procedures have a very high threshold ('grave and systematic' violations), while using inter-state communications is considered by states to be an 'unfriendly act' towards other states (Vandenbogaerde 2016, p. 184).

Since there is no judicial body addressing individual complaints at the international level, the significance of *individual communications procedures* provided by the treaty bodies cannot be overstated.[19] With regard to ETOs, this mechanism has so far been most commonly used by the HRC. Individual communications procedures have been applied to hold states accountable in various extraterritorial cases, including kidnapping and unlawful detention by security forces on the territory of another state (HRC 1981a; HRC 1981b; HRC 2009); discrimination in paying pension allowances on the basis of nationality/race (HRC 1989); states' refusal to issue/renew passports to their citizens living abroad because of their political views (HRC 1980a; HRC 1980b; HRC 1983b; HRC 2004b); alleged violation of the right to vote of citizens residing abroad (HRC 2003a); discriminatory denial of a migrant's visa (HRC 2003c); state's responsibility for human rights violations during an individual's custody in another state and for executing the sentence of a foreign state (HRC 2016); responsibility of states for human rights violations committed by private corporations overseas (HRC 2017); and failure to repatriate children whose parents are linked to terrorism activities (UN CRC 2020a; UN CRC 2021a).

The treaty bodies also consider numerous territorial cases with the so-called 'indirect extraterritorial effect' (Skogly 2006, p. 155; Da Costa 2012, p. 57), such as extraditions or other removals of asylum seekers, refugees, migrant workers, and prisoners to states where their human rights may foreseeably be seriously violated or they may face real and personal violence or a more severe punishment, including the death penalty (HRC 1994; HRC 1993; HRC 2003b; UN CEDAW 2013b; UN CEDAW 2013c; UN CEDAW 2014b; UN CEDAW 2014c; UN CRC 2019c; UN CRC 2019d; UN CRC 2019e; UN CRC 2020c). Additionally, treaty bodies also consider communications from individuals who fled a state because of the human rights violations happening in its territory and reside abroad (HRC 1982; HRC 1983a; HRC 1983c; HRC 1984).

It is necessary to point to the limitations of some individual complaint mechanisms in relation to ETOs.[20] First, although there are no jurisdictional limitations in the ICESCR, the CEDAW, and the CRPD, the Optional Protocols to these instruments, which allow individual communications, impose the criterion of jurisdiction (OP-ICESCR, art. 2; OP-CEDW, art. 2; OP-CRPD, art. 1). These jurisdictional restrictions contradict the very nature of states' obligations under the treaties, narrow the scope of application of these instruments, and impose on claimants the burden of proof that a human rights violation occurred within the jurisdiction of the state (Courtis and Sepúlveda 2009, pp. 57–58). Second, individual communications may be submitted to the HRC, the CESCR, the UN CRC, the UN CEDAW, and the UN CRPD only against states that have ratified relevant Optional Protocols. Since states have been quite reluctant to do so, for most individuals in the world, these mechanisms are still not available.[21] Additionally, states can make reservations and thereby limit individuals' capacities to complain about violations of certain human rights. Third, the subject-matter jurisdiction of individual communications procedures is restricted to states' remedial obligations and there might be difficulties with claiming breaches of global obligations through them.[22] For instance, according to the OP-ICESCR, 'communications may be submitted by or on behalf of individuals or groups of individuals, under the jurisdiction of a state Party, claiming to *be victims of a violation* of any of the economic, social and cultural rights set forth in the Covenant by that state Party' (art. 2; emphasis added). Non-compliance with global obligations that is not deemed to be a violation of human rights cannot, therefore, be claimed through this mechanism. Communications submitted by subjects other than victims may be considered only if they raise 'a serious issue of general importance' (art. 4).

Conclusion

The role of the UN treaty bodies in the interpretation and enforcement of ETOs can hardly be overestimated – they are significant global norm-setters and institution-designers and provide major international monitoring and accountability mechanisms. Among the most important contributions of the treaty bodies in relation of ETOs are the following:

First, the treaty bodies have extended states' human rights obligations, both remedial ETOs and global obligations to respect, protect, and fulfil human rights, beyond their borders. Additionally, they have specified interactional and institutional as well as relational and distributive ETOs, while emphasising obligations to guarantee the full-fledged and meaningful participation, inclusion, and consultation with disadvantaged individuals and social groups and their representatives in the design, realisation, and monitoring of all extraterritorial projects and programs.

Second, the treaty bodies call for the application of a human rights-based approach to extraterritorial assistance as well as a substantial improvement of contemporary mechanisms and practices of international assistance in order to integrate several essential ETOs: obligations to increase the effectiveness of assistance and ensure its sufficiency; obligations to seek assistance if states cannot fully realise the human rights of its people; obligations to conduct systematic HRIAs of assistance programs with the participation of the most vulnerable individuals and social groups; and remedial ETOs for violations of human rights through foreign aid projects. Moreover, the UN CRPD has recognised the principal limitations of state-centred international assistance and suggested its supplementing with human-centred global assistance addressed directly to those in need.

Third, the treaty bodies have clarified states' obligations to regulate the extraterritorial activities of private and public NSAs, with which they have a 'reasonable link', and to cooperate with them for the realisation of human rights. In addition, they have acknowledged that ETOs binding various NSAs (IGOs, TNCs, and civil society) go beyond obligations to respect human rights (including obligations to exercise human rights due diligence and consult with local communities before conducting any extraterritorial projects) and obligations to provide effective remedies to victims in case of human rights violations connected to their activity; NSAs' ETOs also embrace certain obligations to protect and fulfil human rights.

Fourth, through periodic reporting and individual communications procedures the treaty bodies have substantially increased the international accountability of states for extraterritorial violations of human rights and breaches of their ETOs.

Despite general state-centrism of their approach and certain limitations, the UN treaty bodies have a potential to contribute to the shift from a state-centred to a human-centred and polycentric global order. This would require several significant steps: first, further attribution of direct ETOs to IGOs and NSAs (in particular through demanding states to regulate the ETOs of these actors); second, the reconceptualisation of international assistance, i.e., the recognition that people, not states, are the actual addressees of assistance and should be empowered to participate in and control over the processes of international assistance, and its supplement with direct global assistance to vulnerable individuals and social groups; and third, removing the existing restrictions of individual complaint mechanisms to ensure their effectiveness in providing remedies for victims and holding states accountable for extraterritorial violations of human rights and breaching their global obligations.

Notes

1. I would like to thank the editors and other authors of this volume for their valuable comments and suggestions.
2. Other UN treaty bodies include the Committee on the Elimination of Racial Discrimination, the Committee against Torture, the Committee on Migrant Workers, and the Committee on Enforced Disappearances.
3. Two general instruments – the ICESCR and the ICCPR – recognising fundamental rights of all human beings, designate the basic focus of the CESCR and the HRC on ETOs corresponding to social, economic, cultural, civil, and political rights. Since three special conventions – the CRC, the CEDAW, and the CRPD – determine additional measures of protection for children, women, and persons with disabilities, the UN CRC, the UN CEDAW, and the UN CRPD concentrate on ETOs towards these most vulnerable categories of right-holders. It is important to add that the treaty bodies' output concerning ETOs reflects their general intention to prioritise the interests and needs of the most disadvantaged individuals and social groups, including minorities, indigenous people, Roma, those in poverty, refugees, asylum seekers, migrants, older people, and conflict-affected populations, which has been recently reaffirmed in the context of the global pandemic (CESCR 2020a, para. 19; UN CRC 2020b, para. 7; UN CEDAW 2020a & 2020b; UN CRPD 2020).
4. Being 'younger' in this context means not only having less practice but also a capacity to be more progressive; cf., e.g., the UN CRPD's model of 'inclusive equality' and recognition of global obligations to assist (see the next Section).
5. 'Each State Party to the present Covenant undertakes to respect and to ensure to all individuals within its *territory* and *subject to its jurisdiction* the rights recognized in the present Covenant' (ICCPR, art. 2(1), emphasis added). The HRC interprets components of this clause disjunctively, i.e., territory *or* jurisdiction. The CRC's jurisdictional clause does not mention territory: 'States Parties shall respect and ensure the rights set forth in the present Convention to each child within their *jurisdiction* without discrimination of any kind' (CRC, art. 2(1), emphasis added).
6. The *Maastricht Principles on Extraterritorial Obligation of States in the area of Economic, Social, and Cultural Rights* (*Maastricht Principles*) classify '*obligations relating to the acts and omissions* of a state, within or beyond its territory, that have effects on the enjoyment of human rights outside of that state's territory' and '*obligations of a global character* that are set out in the Charter of the United Nations and human rights instruments to take action, separately, and jointly through international cooperation, to realize human rights universally' (Principle 8, emphases added).
7. 'Reasonable link' means that a NSA 'has its centre of activity, is registered or domiciled' or has the main place of its substantial activities in the state (UN CRC 2013b, para. 43).
8. Applying the CESCR GC 3 to ETOs, the immediate ETOs of conduct and result are the following: obligations aimed at eliminating discrimination; obligations to 'take steps', in particular, to cooperate and assist (para. 2); minimum core obligations (para. 10); relatively low-cost targeted programs for vulnerable individuals (para. 12); obligations corresponding to human rights that are not subject to progressive realisation (para. 5).
9. *Interactional* and *institutional global obligations* are based on two fundamental entitlements embedded in the *Universal Declaration of Human Rights* (UDHR): first, the entitlement of an individual 'to realization, through

national effort and international co-operation and in accordance with the organization and resources of each state, of the economic, social and cultural rights indispensable for [individual's] dignity and the free development of [individual's] personality' (art. 22); and second, the entitlement 'to a social and international order in which the rights and freedoms set forth in this Declaration can be fully realized' (art. 28).

10. Inclusive equality embraces: '(a) a *fair redistributive dimension* to address socioeconomic disadvantages; (b) a *recognition dimension* to combat stigma, stereotyping, prejudice and violence and to recognize the dignity of human beings and their intersectionality; (c) a *participative dimension* to reaffirm the social nature of people as members of social groups and the full recognition of humanity through inclusion in society; and (d) an accommodating dimension to make space for difference as a matter of human dignity' (UN CRPD 2018a, para. 11, emphasis added).
11. Cf.: any system of support should be based on 'giving effect to the rights, will and preferences of those receiving support rather than what is perceived as being in their best interests' (UN CRPD 2018a, para. 49(b)).
12. Obligations to assist are interpreted as an integral part of obligations to cooperate. For example, the CRPD states that obligations of international cooperation involve duties of technical and economic assistance (CRPD, art 32 para. 1) that is reaffirmed by the UN CRPD (2018b, paras. 92, 94(r)). Even if it is not specified in the ICESCR and the CRC, the CESCR and the UN CRC treat obligations to assist as part of obligations to cooperate (CESCR 1990, paras. 13–14; UN CRC 2013a, para. 88).
13. Thus, the CESCR recommended to Spain that it 'redouble its efforts to increase official development assistance to at least 0.7 per cent of GDP, in line with the goals assumed at the international level' despite austerity measures adopted by the state (CESCR 2012, para. 10). The CESCR also emphasises simultaneous character of territorial and global obligations to ensure universal and affordable access to vaccines against and treatment for coronavirus disease (CESCR 2020b; CESCR 2021).
14. Elsewhere, I demonstrated the inadequacy of these clauses for determining the scope of ETOs to assist and suggested using instead the principles of sufficiency and a decent minimum sacrifice, which may be balanced through a fair distribution of the burdens of assistance among all members of the international community (Pribytkova 2019, pp. 289–299).
15. The CESCR requires states to report on how their participation in the decision-making and norm-setting of IGOs affects the enjoyment of socio-economic rights worldwide (CESCR 2009b, para. 3).
16. States' obligations to regulate and influence the conduct of NSAs and individuals should not be confused with states' responsibility for the conduct of NSAs and individuals in cases when the latter are directed and controlled by the state (International Law Commission 2002, art. 8).
17. As opposed to the *UN Guiding Principles*, the *UN Norms on the Responsibilities of Transnational Corporations and Other Business Enterprises with Regard to Human Rights* acknowledge that TNCs, 'as organs of society', should protect and 'promote and secure the fulfilment' of human rights (pmbl., arts. 1, 13–14).
18. Christian Courtis and Magdalena Sepúlveda suggested that the CESCR's inquiry procedure 'might prove to be the best mechanism to supervise compliance with the extra-territorial obligations under the ICESCR' (Courtis and Sepúlveda, p. 63).
19. The two world courts, the International Court of Justice and the International Criminal Court are able to act only on the basis of applications made by states (or other special subjects) and not individuals. As the Office of the High Commissioner for Human Rights affirms, 'the ability of individuals to complain about the violation of their rights in an international arena brings real meaning to the rights contained in the human rights treaties' (OHCHR).
20. For further critique, see Vandenbogaerde and Vandenhole 2010.
21. For instance, only 26 states have ratified the OP-ICESCR meaning that 172 states cannot be held accountable through the CESCR individual complaint mechanisms. The OP-CRC is ratified by 48 states; the OP-CRPD – by 99 states; the OP-CEDAW – by 114 states; and the OP-ICCPR – by 116 states.
22. The possibility of bringing individual claims regarding states' non-compliance with their obligations to cooperate and assist was discussed in the process of elaboration of the OP-ICESCR. Committee members asserted that though the CESCR had never considered such cases, 'in theory' they might arise (Commission on Human Rights 2004, para. 45; Commission on Human Rights 2005, para. 79).

References

Alston, P. and Quinn, G. (1987) 'The Nature and Scope of states Parties' Obligations under the International Covenant on Economic, Social and Cultural Rights', *Human Rights Quarterly* 9, 156–229.

Committee on Economic, Social, and Cultural Rights (CESCR)

CESCR (1990) GC 3 on the nature of states Parties' obligations (art 2., para. 1 of the Covenant), E/1991/23.

_______ (1991) GC 4 on the right to adequate housing (art. 11(1) of the Covenant), E/1993/23.

_______ (1998) COBs: Israel, E/C.12/1/Add.27.

_______ (1999a) GC 2 on the right to adequate food (Art. 11), E/C.12/1999/5.

_______ (1999b) GC 13 on the right to education (Art. 13), E/C.12/1999/10.

_______ (2000) GC 14 on the right to the highest attainable standard of health (Art. 12), E/C.12/2000/4.

_______ (2002) COBs: Georgia, E/C.12/1/Add.83.

_______ (2003) GC 15 on the right to water (Arts. 11 and 12 of the Covenant), E/C.12/2002/11.

_______ (2008) GC 19 on the right to social security (Art. 9), E/C.12/GC/19.

_______ (2009a) COBs: the Democratic Republic of the Congo, E/C.12/COD/CO/4.

_______ (2009b) Guidelines on treaty-specific documents to be submitted by states parties under articles 16 and 17 of the International Covenant on Economic, Social and Cultural Rights, E/C.12/2008/224.

_______ (2010) COBs: Columbia, E/C.12/COL/CO/5.

_______ (2011a) Statement on the Obligations of States Parties Regarding the Corporate Sector and Economic, Social and Cultural Rights, E/C.12/2011/1.

_______ (2011b) COBs:Yemen, E/C.12/YEM/2.

_______ (2012) COBs: Spain, E/C.12/ESP/5.

_______ (2014) COBs: China, including Hong Kong, China and Macao, China, E/C.12/CHN/CO/2.

_______ (2016a) COBs: France, E/C.12/FRA/CO/4.

_______ (2016b) COBs: United Kingdom of Great Britain and Northern Ireland, E/C.12/GBR/CO/6.

_______ (2016c) Statement on Public Debt, Austerity Measures and the International Covenant on Economic, Social and Cultural Rights, E/C.12/2016/1.

_______ (2017) GC 24 on State obligations under the International Covenant on Economic, Social and Cultural Rights in the context of business activities, E/C.12/GC/24.

_______ (2018) COBs: New Zealand, E/C.12/NZL/CO/4.

_______ (2019) Sixth periodic report submitted by Norway under articles 16 and 17 of the Covenant, E/C.12/NOR/6.

_______ (2020a) Statement on the coronavirus disease (COVID-19) pandemic and economic, social and cultural rights, E/C.12/2020/1.

_______ (2020b) Statement on universal and equitable access to vaccines for the coronavirus disease (COVID-19), E/C.12/2020/2.

_______ (2021) Statement on universal affordable vaccination against coronavirus disease (COVID-19), international cooperation and intellectual property, E/C.12/2021/1.

Commission on Human Rights (1997) The Realization of Economic, Social and Cultural Rights, Final Report on the Question of the Impunity of Perpetrators of Human Rights Violations (Economic, Social and Cultural Rights), prepared by Mr. El Hadji Guissé, Special Rapporteur, E/CN.4/Sub.2/1997/8.

Commission on Human Rights (2004) *Report of the Open-Ended Working Group to Consider Options Regarding the Elaboration of an Optional Protocol to the International Covenant on Economic, Social and Cultural Rights on Its Second Session*, E/CN.4/2004/44.

Commission on Human Rights (2005) *Report of the Open-Ended Working Group to Consider Options Regarding the Elaboration of an Optional Protocol to the International Covenant on Economic, Social and Cultural Rights on Its Second Session*, E/CN.4/2005/52.

Committee on the Elimination of Discrimination Against Women (UN CEDAW)

UN CEDAW (2005) COBs: Israel, CEDAW/C/ISR/3.

_______ (2010) General Recommendation no. 28 on the core obligations of states parties under article 2 of the Convention on the Elimination of All Forms of Discrimination against Women, CEDAW/C/GC/28.

_______ (2013a) General Recommendation no. 30 on women in conflict prevention, conflict and post-conflict situations, CEDAW/C/GC/30.
_______ (2013b) *M.E.N. v. Denmark*, CEDAW/C/55/D/35/2011.
_______ (2013c) *M.N.N. v. Denmark*, CEDAW/C/55/D/33/2011.
_______ (2014a) COBs: India, CEDAW/C/IND/CO/4–5.
_______ (2014b) *N. v. Netherlands*, CEDAW/C/57/D/39/2012.
_______ (2014c) *S.O. v. Canada*, CEDAW/C/59/D/49/2013.
_______ (2015) COBs: Spain, CEDAW/C/ESP/7–8.
_______ (2016a) COBs: Canada, CEDAW/C/CAN/8–9.
_______ (2016b) COBs: France, CEDAW/C/FRA/CO/7–8.
_______ (2016c) COBs: Switzerland, CEDAW/C/CHE/CO/4–5.
_______ (2016d) General Recommendation no. 34 on the rights of rural women, CEDAW/C/GC/34.
_______ (2017) COBs: Norway, CEDAW/C/NOR/CO/9.
_______ (2018a) COBs: Australia, CEDAW/C/AUS/CO/8.
_______ (2018b) General Recommendation no. 37 on the gender-related dimensions of disaster risk reduction in the context of climate change, CEDAW/C/GC/37.
_______ (2020a) Guidance Note on CEDAW and COVID-19.
_______ (2020b) Call for Joint Action in the Times of the COVID-19 Pandemic.

Committee on the Rights of Persons with Disabilities (UN CRPD)
UN CRPD (2013) COBs: New Zealand, C RPD/C/NZL/CO/1.
_______ (2014) GC 2 on Article 9: Accessibility, CRPD/C/GC/2.
_______ (2015a) COBs: European Union, CRPD/C/EU/CO/1.
_______ (2015b) COBs: Germany, CRPD/C/DEU/CO/1.
_______ (2015c) COBs: Turkmenistan, CRPD/C/TKM/CO/1.
_______ (2016) GC 4 on the Right to Inclusive Education, CRPD/C/GC/4.
_______ (2017) GC 5 on living independently and being included in the community, CRPD/C/GC/5.
_______ (2018a) GC 6 on equality and non-discrimination, CRPD/C/GC/6.
_______ (2018b) GC 7 on the participation of persons with disabilities, including children with disabilities, through their representative organizations, in the implementation and monitoring of the Convention, CRPD/C/GC/7.
_______ (2019a) COBs: Australia, CRPD/C/AUS/CO/2–3.
_______ (2019b) COBs: India, CRPD/C/IND/CO/1.
_______ (2019c) COBs: Iraq, CRPD/C/IRQ/CO/1.
_______ (2020) Statement on COVID-19 and the Human Rights of Persons with Disabilities.

Committee on the Rights of the Child (UN CRC)
UN CRC (2002) COBs: Israel, CRC/C/15/Add.195
_______ (2003) GC 5 on general measures of implementation for the Convention on the Rights of the Child, CRC/GC/2003/5.
_______ (2010a) COBs: Ecuador, CRC/C/ECU/4.
_______ (2010b) COBs: Sri Lanka, CRC/C/LKA/CO/3–4.
_______ (2011a) COBs: Cambodia, CRC/C/KHM/CO/2–3.
_______ (2011b) COBs: Cuba, CRC/C/CUB/CO.2.
_______ (2013a) GC 15 on the right of the child to the enjoyment of the highest attainable standard of health (art. 24), CRC/C/GC/15.
_______ (2013b) GC 16 on state obligations regarding the impact of the business sector on children's rights, CRC/C/GC/16.
_______ (2017) Combined fourth and fifth reports submitted by Singapore under article 44 of the Convention, CRC/C/SGP/4–5.
_______ (2018) Combined fifth and sixth periodic reports submitted to the CRC by Australia under article 44 of the Convention, CRC/C/AUS/5–6.
_______ (2019a) COBs: Australia, CRC/C/AUS/CO/5–6.

_______ (2019b) COBs: Republic of Korea, CRC/C/KOR/CO/5–6.

_______ (2019c) *D.D. v. Spain*, CRC/C/80/D/4/2016.

_______ (2019d) *R.K. v. Spain*, CRC/C/82/D/27/2017.

_______ (2019e) *Z.H. and A.H. v. Denmark*, CRC/C/82/D/32/2017.

_______ (2020a) *L.H. et al v. France*, CRC/C/85/D/79/2019–CRC/C/85/D/109/2019.

_______ (2020b) The Committee on the Rights of the Child warns of the grave physical, emotional and psychological effect of the COVID-19 pandemic on children and calls on states to protect the rights of children.

_______ (2020c) *V.A. v. Switzerland*, CRC/C/85/D/56/2018.

_______ (2021a) *F.B. et al v. France*, CRC/C/86/D/R.77/2019.

_______ (2021b) GC 25 on children's rights in relation to the digital environment, CRC/C/GC/25

Courtis, C. and Sepúlveda, M. (2009) 'Are Extraterritorial Obligations Reviewable under the Optional Protocol to the ICESCR?', *Nordic Journal of Human Rights* 27, 54–63.

Da Costa, K. (2012) *The Extraterritorial Application of Selected Human Rights Treaties*, Martinus Nijhoff Publishers.

Human Rights Committee (HRC)

HRC (1980a) *Guillermo Waksman v. Uruguay*, CCPR/C/OP/1.

_______ (1980b) *Samuel Lichtensztejn v. Uruguay*, CCPR/C/18/D/77/1980.

_______ (1981a) *Delia Saldias de Lopez (on behalf of Lopez Burgos) v. Uruguay*, CCPR/C/13/D/52/1979.

_______ (1981b) *Lilian Celiberti de Casariego v. Uruguay*, CCPR/C/13/D/56/1979.

_______ (1982) *Carmen Amendola Massiotti and Graciela Baritussio v. Uruguay*, CCPR/C/16/D/25/1978

_______ (1983a) *Elena Quinteros Almeida and Maria del Carmen Almeida de Quinteros v. Uruguay*, CCPR/C/19/D/107/1981.

_______ (1983b) *Mabel Pereira Montero v. Uruguay*, CCPR/C/18/D/106/1981.

_______ (1983c) *Miguel Angel Estrella v. Uruguay*, CCPR/C/18/D/74/1980.

_______ (1984) *Antonio Viana Acosta v. Uruguay*, CCPR/C/21/D/110/1981.

_______ (1989) *Ibrahima Gueye et al. v. France*, CCPR/C/35/D/196/1985.

_______ (1993) *Kindler v. Canada*, CCPR/C/48/D/470/1991.

_______ (1994) *Chitat Ng v. Canada*, CCPR/C/49/D/469/1991.

_______ (1998) COBs: Israel, CCPR/C/79/Add.93.

_______ (2003a) *Dáithi Ó Colchúin v. Australia*, CCPR/C/77/D/1038/2001.

_______ (2003b) *Roger Judge v. Canada*, CCPR/C/78/D/829/1998.

_______ (2003c) *Sunil Dixit v. Australia*, CCPR/C/77/D/978/2001.

_______ (2004a) GC 31 on the nature of the general legal obligation imposed on states Parties to the Covenant, CCPR/C/21/Rev.1/Add.13.

_______ (2004b) *Loubna El Ghar v. Libyan Arab Jamahiriya*, CCPR/C/82/D/1107/2002.

_______ (2009) *Mohammad Munaf v. Romania*, CCPR/C/96/D/1539/2006.

_______ (2011) COBs: the Republic of Korea, CCPR/C/KOR/CO/4.

_______ (2012) COBs: Germany, CCPR/C/DEU/CO/6.

_______ (2014) COBs: the United States of America, CCPR/C/USA/CO/4.

_______ (2015) COBs: Canada, CCPR/C/CAN/CO/6.

_______ (2016) *David Hicks v. Australia*, CCPR/C/115/D/2005/2010.

_______ (2017) *Basem Ahmed Issa Yassin v. Canada*, CCPR/C/120/D/2285/2013.

_______ (2019) GC 36 on Article 6 of the International Covenant on Civil and Political Rights, on the Right to Life, CCPR/C/GC/36.

International Law Commission (2002) ILC Articles on Responsibility of States for Internationally Wrongful Acts, A/RES/56/83

Langford, M. and King, J.A. (2008) 'Committee on Economic, Social and Cultural Rights: Past, Present and Future' in Langford, M. (ed.). *Social Rights Jurisprudence, Emerging Trends in International and Comparative Law*, Cambridge University Press.

Milanovic, M. (2011) *Extraterritorial Application of Human Rights Treaties: Law, Principles, and Policy*, Oxford University Press.

Office of the United Nations High Commissioner for Human Rights (OHCHR) (n.d.) 'Human Rights Bodies - Complaints Procedures', http://www.ohchr.org/EN/HRBodies/TBPetitions/Pages/HRTB-Petitions.aspx [accessed 24 January 2021].

Pribytkova, E. (2019) *Global Human Rights Obligations Relating to a Decent Standard of Living*, J.S.D. dissertation, Columbia University.

_______ (2020) 'What Global Human Rights Obligations Do We Have?', *Chicago Journal of International Law* 20, 384–449.

Shue, H. (1996) *Basic Rights: Subsistence, Affluence and U.S. Foreign Policy*, 2nd ed, Princeton University Press.

Skogly, S. (2006) *Beyond National Borders: States' Human Rights Obligations in International Cooperation*, Intersentia.

Sepúlveda, M. (2003) *The Nature of the Obligations under the International Covenant on Economic, Social and Cultural Rights*, Intersentia.

Vandenbogaerde, A. (2016) *Towards Shared Accountability in International Human Rights Law. Law, Procedures and Principles*, Intersentia.

Vandenbogaerde, A. and Vandenhole, W. (2010) 'The Optional Protocol to the International Covenant on Economic, Social and Cultural Rights: An Ex Ante Assessment of its Effectiveness in Light of the Drafting Process', *Human Rights Law Review* 10(2), 207–237.

8

Extraterritorial obligations in the inter-American human rights system

Clara Burbano-Herrera and Yves Haeck

Introduction

The conduct of states may affect the human rights of individuals located outside their borders. In the inter-American human rights system (IAHRS), the scope of extraterritorial obligations is linked to the universality principle and the jurisdiction clause. States are internationally responsible for not only human rights violations that were attributed to them within their own territory, but also for actions or omissions perpetrated outside their territory but within their jurisdiction. This chapter explores the criteria developed by the Inter-American Commission on Human Rights (IACmHR; Commission) and the Inter-American Court of Human Rights (IACtHR; Court) to establish the international responsibility of states in the framework of extraterritorial obligations in specific cases and identifies the types of situations in which extraterritorial responsibility has been established. First, following some background on the IAHRS, the provisions related to extraterritorial jurisdiction and obligations will be dealt with. Second, the Commission's and Court's case-law under the Declaration and/or the Convention will be examined. We will end with some conclusions.

Brief background to the inter-American system

The IAHRS has three protection levels: states which have not ratified the ACHR have obligations under the Declaration and are supervised by the Commission; states having ratified the ACHR are obligated under it and are supervised by the Commission; states having ratified the Convention and having accepted the IACtHR's jurisdictional competence are obligated under the Convention and are supervised by the Commission and Court.

The Charter of the Organization of American States (OAS), the American Convention and the IACmHR Statute provide that the Commission is an OAS organ created to promote the observance and defense of human rights. The Commission interprets not only the American Convention (1969), but also the American Declaration (1948). The Declaration is not a treaty, but it imposes indirectly obligations upon all 35 states, through their OAS membership. The

DOI: 10.4324/9781003090014-11

IACmHR was created through a political decision of the Ministers of Foreign Affairs of the American states (1959). The Commission started to document violations and promote human rights applying the Declaration, being the only existing regional instrument at that time. Subsequently, the Commission was granted competence to examine individual petitions alleging human rights violations (1965). Thus, the Commission, when examining the complaints, also started to apply the jurisdiction clause to all OAS states (see *infra*). The Convention, which entered into force in 1978, has not been ratified by all OAS states (e.g., the US; Canada; some Caribbean states), while others have even denounced it (e.g., Trinidad/Tobago). The Convention created the IACtHR, which started to work in 1979 but only began to exercise its judicial competences in earnest in 1988.

In general terms, the international obligations of the states to the IAHRS are contemplated in Articles 1 and 2 ACHR, and can be classified into: (i) Obligation to respect human rights; (ii) Obligation to guarantee human rights; (iii) Obligation to adapt the domestic law. These obligations are sufficient to structure the responsibility of the states. Besides, the rights under the Declaration are also a source of similar international obligations for the OAS states.

In the Americas, the supervisory bodies connect the extraterritorial application of human rights with the recognition of the principle of universality and the so-called jurisdiction clause. The universality principle affirms that all people must enjoy all human rights anywhere in the world, while the jurisdiction clause indicates under which circumstance states are obligated beyond their territory. While the Declaration does not explicitly contain a jurisdiction clause, the American Convention does.

Extraterritorial obligations in the American Declaration

The Declaration does not include an explicit mention of limitation of its territorial scope, nor any other explicit jurisdiction clause. Curiously, the Declaration drafts prepared by the Inter-American Juridical Committee did contain a jurisdiction clause. Article XVIII 1945 Draft linked it to the principle of equality. The 1947 final Draft Declaration of the Committee submitted to the Bogota Conference still contained the reference to jurisdiction in the equality clause (Art. XVIII(2)). Eventually, the reference to jurisdiction was deleted in the renumbered Article II:

> All persons are equal before the law and have the rights and duties established in this Declaration, without distinction as to race, sex, language, creed or any other factor.

The Working Group Human Rights chose not to include the duties (of the state), concluding that to do so would exceed its mandate and that it would detract from the forcefulness and clarity of the Declaration (Report Rapporteur, in Buergenthal and Norris 1982–1983, p. 16).

The general human rights obligations on OAS states under the Declaration and the absence of a reference to jurisdiction have not precluded the IACmHR from using the provision as the basis for assessing the extraterritorial responsibility of states under the Declaration. In the IAHRS, most cases concerning extraterritorial application have been decided by the Commission under the Declaration, applying the universality principle together with the (implicit) jurisdiction clause.

Extraterritorial obligations in the American Convention

The American Convention does not contain a provision on extraterritorial human rights obligations, but contains an explicit jurisdiction clause, which is almost identical to that in the European Convention on Human Rights. Article 1(1) says:

> The states Parties to this Convention undertake to respect the rights and freedoms recognized herein and to ensure to all persons *subject to their jurisdiction* the free and full exercise of those rights and freedoms, without any discrimination for reasons of race, color, sex, language, religion, political or other opinion, national or social origin, economic status, birth, or any other social condition (emphasis added).

An IACmHR draft, adopted by the OAS Council (12 October 1968), was based on three drafts. The subsequent draft Convention adopted by the OAS Council in 1968 referred to 'all persons within their territory and subject to their jurisdiction' and its similarity to Article 2(1) ICCPR was mentioned in the IACmHR's annotations on the draft Convention. The IACmHR and the US agreed with the text and did not propose any amendments, and the IACmHR did not even comment on the wording of the phrase concerned.

During the San Jose Conference, the main change proposed by a Working Group of Committee I was the deletion of the words 'within their territory'. Panama wanted to delete the phrase in order to protect the human rights of residents in the Panama Canal Zone which was subject to US jurisdiction but was not US territory, and the US apparently did not oppose.

The draft Working Group text of Article 1(1) was subsequently unanimously adopted by the Committee.

The interpretation of the jurisdiction clause in the Convention and the implicit clause in the Declaration, as developed by the Commission and Court through country reports, the individual and interstate petition system procedure, precautionary measures and an advisory opinion, will now be examined. As will be shown, a broad range of rights and freedoms have been given extraterritorial application by the IACmHR (Cassel 2004, p. 176), while the IACtHR has until now only done this in a single situation.

Extraterritorial obligations under the American Declaration and Convention in practice

The Commission has adopted the same interpretation regarding extraterritorial obligations and therefore extraterritorial responsibility with respect to states that have ratified the Convention and those which have not yet done so. In other words, these cases are not decided differently from the ones submitted under the American Declaration (Cerna 2004). Moreover, the Commission has held that in order to establish state responsibility for extraterritorial human rights violations, it is necessary to prove the exercise of state jurisdiction and therefore there needs to be 'authority and effective control'. Overall, the essential tool in determining jurisdiction and establishing the responsibility of a state for acts committed by its agents abroad, is the 'exercise of authority over persons' by state agents, without necessarily requiring the existence of a formal, structured and prolonged legal relation in terms of time. The Commission has indicated that a state's international responsibility may refer to extraterritorial actions when the person is present in the territory of a state but is subject to the control of another state, generally through the actions of that state's agents abroad. It has therefore recognized the exercise of extraterritorial jurisdiction in cases relating to military interventions, operations in international airspace and on the territory of third states, as well as in detention facilities outside a state's territory.

In *Saldaño*, the first petition decided by the Commission on extraterritorial responsibility in the framework of the American Convention, an Argentinian sentenced to death in the US, argued that during the trial certain rights under the Declaration (rights to life; liberty and personal security; fair trial; petition; due process of law) and the Convention had been violated. Under the latter, the petitioner alleged that Argentina had an obligation to present an interstate complaint against the US, and the failure of doing this rendered it responsible for human rights violations (rights to life; fair trial; judicial protection). The Commission held:

> (...) a state party to the American Convention may be responsible under certain circumstances for the acts and omissions of its agents which produce effects or are undertaken outside that state's own territory.
>
> *(IACmHR 1999a, para. 17)*

> Furthermore, (...) *the understanding of jurisdiction* and therefore responsibility for non-compliance with international obligations (.) *is a notion linked to authority and effective control, and not merely to territorial boundaries* (emphasis added).
>
> *(Ibid, para. 19)*

In casu, there was no proof that Argentina had exercised authority or control over Saldaño under Article 1(1) ACHR, and he was thus not within Argentinian jurisdiction prior/subsequent to his arrest in the US, or that Argentina had exercised authority or control over the local US officials involved in the subsequent criminal proceedings, and the mere bond of being Argentinian was not sufficient either (ibid, paras. 21–23). Argentina also had no Conventional obligation to lodge an interstate complaint against the US (ibid, paras. 1–3 and 32–34).

Extrajudicial killings and harassment by state agents

The Commission has implicitly established the extraterritorial scope of the Declaration and the responsibility of OAS states for extrajudicial killings and harassment by state agents in a Country Report on Chile (1985) and another one on Suriname (1985), when fulfilling its general monitoring function (Cerqueira 2015, p. 19).

In the Chile Report, the Commission referred to the murder on Chileans outside Chile, more specifically two former high-ranking officials of the Allende government, namely, the former Minister of state and Ambassador Orlando Letelier, and the former commander-in-chief of the army, general Carlos Prats (IACmHR 1985a, paras. 80–91), respectively, in Washington DC and Buenos Aires, by Chilean secret agents (right to life). The Commission explicitly held that the seriousness of these events '(...) lies in the method used in the respective crimes and in the fact that they took place beyond the frontiers of Chile' (IACmHR 1985a, para. 80).

Similarly, in its Suriname Report, the Commission referred to the attacks on and harassment of Surinamese in the Netherlands by Surinamese agents. The Commission took special note of '(...) the numerous and serious allegations made by Surinamese citizens both in the Netherlands and Suriname that the Government of Suriname, through its Consulate at the Hague and through its agents in the emigrant community, [had] threatened members of the refugee community with reprisals against their relatives remaining in the country if their anti-government activities didn't cease'. The Surinamese citizens were prevented from obtaining passports and returning home (right to a passport) if they were considered to be opponents (IACmHR 1985b, Chapter V, Introductory Section).

Use of force by state agents during military operation/intervention

The extraterritorial scope and the responsibility of OAS states under the Declaration was first implicitly and later explicitly recognized by the Commission in cases concerning US military interventions in Grenada/Panama, as well as Ecuadorian and Colombian military operations on each other's territory.

Disabled Peoples' International (DPI), the first petition submitted against a state in the Americas alleging extraterritorial responsibility under the Declaration, was filed following the US intervention in Grenada in 1983 (IACmHR 1987) and more specifically the bombing of a psychiatric institution, killing 16 and injuring 6 persons (rights to life; preservation of health and well-being). The applicants held that, since Article 112 OAS Charter provides that the Commission's main function was to promote the observance and protection of human rights, the complaint was within the Commission's competence.

The Commission declared the petition admissible in 1986, indicating that it had jurisdiction to examine the allegations, without explicitly touching upon the extraterritorial jurisdiction issue, as none of the parties had alleged anything in that regard (IACmHR 1987).

The US position was that the Commission lacked competence because the facts concerned a country with an internal armed conflict, and the Commission is only allowed to apply the Declaration but not the Fourth Geneva Convention which regulates actions within the political context concerned – a position maintained ever since (infra). Eventually, the merits of the case were not assessed because a friendly settlement was reached (IACmHR 1996, Background para. IV).

Coard was also related to US military actions during its intervention in Grenada, but this time the petition was submitted by 17 Grenadian petitioners who had been actively involved in deposing the government (IACmHR 1999b). In October 1983, rival members of the prime minister's party murdered the Grenadian prime minister and some government members and established a Revolutionary Military Council (RMC). Some days later, the US and Caribbean armed forces invaded Grenada, deposing the RMC. During the US-led operation, the petitioners had allegedly been unlawfully detained by US forces, held incommunicado for many days and ill-treated, and they contended that the US corrupted the Grenadian judicial system thereby depriving them of their right to a fair trial (ibid, paras. 2–4 and 17–20). In 1994, the Commission admitted the case (IACmHR *Coard* 1994, unpublished).

In order to determine US jurisdiction, the Commission considered the 'effective control and authority over the presumed victims' ('personal jurisdiction model'), thereby reading into the Declaration a state jurisdiction requirement which is actually not included into the text itself. Geographic location and territorial jurisdiction did not play a (decisive) role. Indeed, while the petitioners were detained on US military ships, which could basically be seen as bringing the persons concerned under US jurisdiction, the Commission did not say a word on this, nor did it hold that from the moment that the petitioners had been detained, US military had already gained full control over Grenada. As a reason for its standpoint, it held that 'individual rights inhere simply by virtue of a person's humanity'. More specifically, the Commission said:

> While the extraterritorial application of the American Declaration has not been placed at issue by the parties, (...) jurisdiction over acts with an extraterritorial locus will not only be consistent with, but required by the norms which pertain. The fundamental rights of the individual are proclaimed in the Americas on the basis of the principles of equality and non-discrimination (...). Given that individual rights inhere simply by virtue of a person's humanity, *each American state is obliged to uphold the protected rights of any person subject to its jurisdiction. While this most commonly refers to persons within a state's territory, it may, under given circumstances, refer to conduct with an extraterritorial locus where the person concerned is present in the territory of one state, but subject to the control of another state usually through the acts of the latter's agents abroad.* (...) the inquiry turns not on the presumed victim's nationality or presence within a particular geographic area, but on whether, under the specific circumstances, *the state observed the rights of a person subject to its authority and control* (emphasis added).
>
> *(IACmHR 1999b, para. 37)*

Given that the victims had been subjected to the extraterritorial authority and control of the US authorities, the US was found in violation of the Declaration (rights to life; protection of juridical personality; protection from arbitrary arrest), in view of the victims '(being) held in the custody (...) for approximately nine to twelve days, including six to nine days after the effective cessation of fighting', while 'the petitioners were not afforded access to a review of the legality of their detention with the least possible delay' (ibid, paras. 60–61). Furthermore, the Commission reiterated the legal basis of its competence deriving from the OAS Charter, its Statute and Regulations (ibid 1999, paras. 9 and 36). The US once again contested the admissibility of the case asserting the Commission's lack of competence to examine the legal validity of its military actions in Grenada as this fell beyond the scope of its mandate, particularly with regard to a non-state party to the Convention. The Commission (IACmHR *Coard* 1994) dismissed the US objections related to the alleged lack of competence to examine the US actions and reiterated that the Declaration 'is a source of international obligation for member states not party to the American Convention', and that its Statute authorizes it to examine complaints under the Declaration, an approach which it has maintained ever since.

In a subsequent case decided under the Convention related to the alleged extra-judicial execution of an Ecuadorian by the Colombian army on Ecuadorian territory (IACmHR 2010), the Commission explicitly stated that

> (...) [u]nder Inter-American human rights law, each American state is obligated (...) to respect the rights of all persons within its territory and of those present in the territory of another state but subject to the control of its agents.
>
> *(Ibid, para. 91, referring to IACmHR 1999c; further: IACmHR 2011b, para. 23; IACmHR 1993)*

Rejecting the Colombian argument that the alleged victim was not subject to Colombian jurisdiction, the Commission held that according to the Vienna Convention the term jurisdiction in Article 1(1) must be interpreted in good faith and be understood and applied in its ordinary meaning as a term of international law, because it is clear that the parties did not intend otherwise (IACmHR 2010, para. 88; Vienna Convention on the Law of Treaties, Art. 31(1) and (3)(c)). Also, the Convention's drafting history did not indicate that the parties intended to give a special meaning to 'jurisdiction' (ibid, para. 89). Moreover, they omitted the reference to 'territory', thereby widening the scope of protection to the extent that the states not only may be held internationally responsible for the acts and omissions imputable to them within their territory, but also for those acts and omissions committed wherever they exercise jurisdiction (ibid, para. 90).

In its case law, the Commission stresses that it had to be established whether there was a causal link between the extraterritorial conduct of a state through the actions or omissions of its agents and/or persons who have acted under its orders or acquiescence and the alleged violation of the rights and freedoms (rights to life; humane treatment; fair trial; due process) of an individual (IACmHR 2010, para. 99; also: IACmHR 2011b; IACmHR 2018).

Downing of civilian airplanes by state agents

In *Armando Alejandre Jr*, which involved the 1996 downing in international airspace of two unarmed civilian light airplanes belonging to the organization 'Brothers to the Rescue' by the Cuban military resulting in the immediate death of four persons on board, the Commission reaffirmed – implicitly – that it was clearly competent with respect to the alleged human rights violations committed by Cuba despite the fact that Cuba was not a state party to the American Convention (IACmHR 1999c, paras. 1 and 23).

Following its jurisprudence in the US-related cases, the Commission held that although a state's jurisdiction *ratione loci* is primarily territorial, exceptions exist in limited circumstances based on the principle of universality and when the victims were under the control or authority of the foreign agents. The Commission held more specifically:

> (…) the Commission is competent to consider reports alleging that agents of an OAS member state have violated human rights protected in the inter-American system, even when the events take place outside the territory of that state. (…) Because *individual rights are inherent to the human being, all the American states are obligated to respect the protected rights of any person subject to their jurisdiction. Although this usually refers to persons who are within the territory of a state, in certain instances it can refer to extraterritorial actions, when the person is present in the territory of a state but subject to the control of another state, generally through the actions of that state's agents abroad.* In principle, the investigation refers not to the nationality of the alleged victim or his presence in a particular geographic area, but to whether, in those specific circumstances, the state observed the rights of a person *subject to its authority and control* (emphasis added).
>
> *(Ibid, para. 23)*

The Commission considered that the victims died as a consequence of direct actions taken by Cuban state agents in international airspace (ibid, para. 25). It was clear that the power and control exercised by the state agents had provoked jurisdiction. The Commission said:

> (…) The fact that the events took place outside Cuban jurisdiction does not limit the Commission's competence *ratione loci*, because, as previously stated, *when agents of a state, whether military or civilian, exercise power and authority over persons outside national territory, the state's obligation to respect human rights continues*, in this case the rights enshrined in the American Declaration. The Commission finds conclusive evidence that agents of the Cuban state,

> although outside their territory, placed the civilian pilots of the 'Brothers to the Rescue' organization under their authority (emphasis added).
>
> *(Ibid, para. 25)*

The Commission declared Cuba responsible for violating the Declaration with respect to the four persons who had died as a result of the direct actions of its agents while flying through international airspace (rights to life; freedom of movement).

Use of force by state agents when arresting and/or abducting a person

The *Alikhani* case, which concerns a transnational abduction, allowed the Commission to assert that such abduction cases also amount to the exercise of extraterritorial jurisdiction by an OAS state.

The petitioner, a dual citizen of Iran and Cyprus, was lured to the United States by US agents from an airport in the Bahamas on the false premise that he would be flying to another Bahamian island for a business meeting and some fishing. After the plane had left the runway, the petitioner was arrested for violating US sanctions against Libya. The applicant held that the Bahamas had not authorized his arrest on its territory. In its admissibility report, the Commission asserted its competence *ratione loci,* given that:

> The petition indicates that Mr. Alikhani was under the jurisdiction of the United States at the time of his arrest, detention and subsequent criminal proceedings.
>
> *(IACmHR 2005, para. 42)*

While the case has been declared admissible with regard to the rights to life, residence and movement, right to petition, protection from arbitrary arrest and due process of law, the case has not yet been decided on the merits.

Use of force by state agents when detaining persons on board of naval vessels on the high seas, sending them to an overseas detention centre or returning them to country of origin

In *Haitian Centre for Human Rights*, the exercise of extraterritorial jurisdiction over persons detained and/or deported by a state on the high seas was implicitly but clearly established. In establishing the jurisdiction of the US, the Commission used the control over person's test.

The petition alleged that Haitians fleeing their country had been stopped at sea (interdicted), taken on board US vessels and returned to Haiti or Guantanamo Bay, thereby preventing them from landing on US shores and acquiring certain procedural rights to apply for asylum and thus without affording them an opportunity to establish whether they qualified as refugee (IACmHR 1997).

The Commission found that the US act of interdicting Haitians on the high seas and placing them in vessels under its jurisdiction, sending some of them to Guantanamo and returning others to Haiti and leaving them exposed to acts of brutality by the Haitian military and its supporters, amounted to a violation of the right to security of the Haitians, as well as the rights to life; liberty; equality before the law; fair trial; and asylum under the Declaration (IACmHR 1997, paras. 171 and 183).

Subsequently, the US responded by letter, stating that '(...) the Commission's analysis is legally flawed. For example, it was error to hold that the 1967 Protocol to the UN Convention on the Status of Refugees applies to Haitian migrants interdicted on the high seas. It was also error to interpret the non-refoulement obligation to require high seas interdicts to receive the same hearing on their asylum claims as they would receive if they were present within the territory of the interdicting state (…)' (ibid, para. 82). The US did not recognize the competence of the Commission and its interpretation of the Declaration about US extraterritorial acts occurring outside its territory but within its jurisdiction on the high seas.

Use of force by state agents when detaining persons in overseas detention centres

The indefinite detention of persons outside the territory, in overseas detentions centres by the US within the inter-American *espace juridique* (post-9/11 detainees in Guantanamo Bay) but also beyond the inter-American *espace juridique* (Bagram airbase, Diego Garcia, etc.) amounts to an exercise of extraterritorial detention.

In the *Guantanamo detainees* case, the Commission adopted precautionary measures in 2002 in favour of detainees held by the US at Guantanamo Bay, Cuba (IACmHR 2002, p. 16; Burbano Herrera and Viljoen 2015, p. 182), thereby implying that they were under US jurisdiction. Approximately 254 detainees were at that moment being held in Guantanamo (IACmHR 2011a (extension)) following their capture in Afghanistan. The detainees were allegedly at risk of irreparable harm because the US refused to treat them as prisoners of war until a competent tribunal determined otherwise in accordance with the Third Geneva Convention (IACmHR 2002). According to the petitioners, the detainees had been held arbitrarily, incommunicado and for a prolonged period of time and had been interrogated without access to legal counsel. Because certain detainees were at risk of trial and possible death sentences before military commissions, the US had in their view failed to comply with established principles of international law (ibid).

The Commission requested the US to take the urgent measures necessary to have the legal status of the detainees determined by a competent tribunal. Without prejudging the possible application of international humanitarian law to the detainees, the Commission considered that precautionary measures were both appropriate and necessary in the circumstances, in order to ensure that the legal status of each of the detainees was clarified and that they would be afforded the legal protections commensurate with that status (IACmHR 2002). The Commission held that:

> (…) no person, under the authority and control of a state, regardless of his or her circumstances, is devoid of legal protection for his or her fundamental and non-derogable human rights.
>
> *(Ibid, p. 16)*

Subsequently, precautionary measures have also been issued in partially similar cases (IACmHR 2006 (detained Canadian with regard to prohibition of torture and right to integrity); IACmHR 2015a (detained Saudi in Guantánamo with regard to right to life and personal integrity due to detention conditions)).

The existing precautionary measures in Guantanamo cases have subsequently, on different occasions, been amplified, even beyond the inter-American *espace juridique.*

In 2003, the Commission, following an additional request for precautionary measures from Guantanamo detainees' representatives in connection with unnamed individuals alleged to have been detained in Guantanamo, but also at Bagram Air Force base in Afghanistan, the island of Diego Garcia and other similar US facilities, confirmed its earlier precautionary measures order and also requested the US for special information concerning allegations of ill-treatment of detainees, in particular regarding 'the location, status and treatment of individuals detained by the US in other facilities' (IACmHR 2003; further IACmHR 2004). Subsequently, the measures were amplified to take account of the alleged danger of rendition to third countries where the victim could be ill-treated (IACmHR 2005; also 2015b). On multiple occasions, the IACmHR has also called on the US to close Guantanamo (e.g. IACmHR 2012a; IACmHR 2015b).

In 2013, having been informed of US non-compliance with existing safeguards, the Commission requested information from the US government on the unnecessary and demeaning searches, the force-feeding of prisoners and the increasing segregation and isolation of prisoners, and mandated the US to extend the scope of safeguards to protect the life and integrity of the 166 remaining detainees (IACmHR 2013a).

Ameziane concerned an Algerian detainee held in 2008 at Guantanamo (IACmHR 2012b), who had been captured by the US military in Pakistan in 2002, detained at the Kandahar Airbase in Afghanistan for more than a month and later transferred to Guantanamo. While in Guantanamo, he was, among others, allegedly subjected to torture, cruel and degrading treatment and at risk of being transferred back to Algeria where he would be at risk of serious harm. The decisive element to establish the jurisdiction of the state over the apprehension of Ameziane was that the actions implied an exercise of physical power and control over him performed by US agents (ibid, paras. 31–32). The US exercised total and exclusive *de facto* control over this prison and the individuals detained there. As to the facts that took place in Guantanamo, the Commission indicated that the US had exercised its jurisdiction there (*de jure* and *de facto*) for more than a century (ibid, para. 33). As Guantanamo Bay fell under US jurisdiction, a precautionary measure directed to protect all prisoners detained in the Guantanamo Bay Detention Facility had been adopted by the Commission (ibid, para. 34; also: IACmHR 2002). In 2020, the IACmHR concluded that the US has violated the Declaration (IACmHR 2020, paras. 5 and 285).

Khaled El-Masri concerned the capture by Macedonian intelligence agents acting at the behest of the US Government, following which he was being held incommunicado in Macedonia for three weeks and subsequently transported (extraordinary rendition) to a prison in Afghanistan. With regard to El-Masri's apprehension, the IACmHR deferred its decision as to jurisdiction to the merits stage (IACmHR 2016, para. 25), but with regard to the alleged acts committed against Mr El-Masri during his transfer and detention at the Afghanistan 'Salt Pit' prison, the Commission held that the petitioner was under US jurisdiction due to the 'total and exclusive *de facto* control over the prison' in Afghanistan (IACmHR 2016, para. 25).

Extraterritorial environmental obligations

The Inter-American Court has not yet addressed extraterritorial obligations through its contentious jurisdiction. However, in its 2017 advisory opinion on the environment and human rights, the Court interpreted the concept of state obligations within Article 1(1) ACHR, in response to a request made by Colombia concerning state environmental obligations, particularly in relation to conduct outside the national territory of a state, or with effects beyond the national territory of a state (IACtHR 2017). The Court stated that the protection of human rights under the Convention includes situations beyond the territorial limits of the states, and links that concept, as the Commission has done, with the principle of universality and the jurisdiction clause (ibid, para. 78).

The Court referred to extraterritorial obligations, emphasizing that states' human rights obligations extend to all people, even those outside of a state's borders. According to Article 1(1) ACHR, states are obligated to respect and guarantee the rights therein to all persons subject to their jurisdiction. The Court clarified that the term 'jurisdiction' in the American Convention is broader than the territory of a state, holding that a person can bring a claim if they are within the state's territory or outside the border but under a state's authority or effective control, if the state's actions caused environmental damage, and that damage resulted in a violation of a human right. The Court also indicated that states must cooperate in good faith with other states, which involves notifying, consulting and negotiating with other states whenever the state is aware that an action planned within their territory or under their control or authority may generate significant transboundary environmental harm (ibid, para. 173 and paras. 181–210).

In order to explain the scope of extraterritorial obligations within Article 1 ACHR, just like the IACmHR had done earlier, the Court also referred to the rules of interpretation for treaties, the ordinary meaning of the word jurisdiction interpreted in good faith and taking into account the *travaux préparatoires* as well as the context, object and purpose of the Convention (ibid, paras. 40–42) and held that the concept of jurisdiction encompasses any situation in which a state exercises effective authority or control over an individual or individuals, either within or outside its territory. Consequently, the Court emphasised that states must respect and ensure the human rights of all persons subject to their jurisdiction, even if they are not within its territory:

> (…) the use of the word 'jurisdiction' in Article 1(1) of the American Convention signifies that the state obligation to respect and to ensure human rights applies to every person who is within the state's territory *or who is in any way subject to its authority, responsibility or control.*
>
> *(Ibid, para. 73)*

> (…) Accordingly, the margin of protection for the rights recognized in the American Convention was expanded insofar as the states Parties' *obligations are not restricted to the geographical space corresponding to their territory, but encompass those situations where, even outside a state's territory, a person is subject to its jurisdiction.* In other words, states may not only be found internationally responsible for acts or omissions attributed to them within their territory, *but also for those acts or omissions committed outside their territory, but under their jurisdiction* (emphasis added).
>
> *(Ibid, para. 77; also Minutes 1st session 1969, p. 145 and 147 and Minutes 2nd session 1969, pp. 156–157)*

It held that the Commission had also consistently given this interpretation to the *travaux préparatoires* of the Convention with regard to the word 'jurisdiction' in the Convention. In sum, the Court followed the interpretation already developed by the Commission's case law (IACtHR 2017, para. 75, referring particularly to: IACmHR, 2011c, para. 91; IACmHR 1999a, paras. 15–20; IACmHR 1999c, paras. 23–25; IACmHR 1999b, para. 37).

Likewise, the Court (IACtHR 2017, para. 79) referenced cases where the Commission had recognized extraterritorial jurisdiction generally through the actions of that state's agents abroad (i.e. IACmHR 1999c; IACmHR 1993), particularly cases relating to military interventions (IACmHR 1993, paras. 14–15 and 17; IACmHR 1999b, para. 37), military operations in international airspace (IACmHR 1999c) and on the territory of another state (IACmHR 1993;

IACmHR 2010, para. 98), as well as in military facilities outside a state's territory (IACmHR 2012b, para. 35). According to the Court:

> (...) most of these situations involve military actions or actions by state security forces that indicate "control", "power" or "authority" in the execution of the extraterritorial conduct.
> *(IACtHR 2017, para. 80)*

While the effective control test remains essential, the Court held that, with regard to cross-border damage, the exercise of jurisdiction occurs 'when the state of origin exercises effective control over the activities carried out that caused the damage and the resulting violation of human rights' in the foreign state. This basically implies that 'effective control' is no longer only something to be exercised over territory ('spatial jurisdiction') or over individual victims ('personal jurisdiction'), but also over the activities responsible for harm (ibid, para. 104(h); see Berkes 2018, para. 1). The effective control test is based on the factual, the causal nexus between conducts performed on the territory of the state of origin and a violation of rights and freedoms occurring abroad (ibid, para. 95 and paras. 101–102). A home state can eventually be held responsible for failing to exercise its obligation of 'due diligence' within its territory (Berkes 2018, para. 2).

However, the Court also emphasized that extraterritorial obligations and therefore the exercise of jurisdiction outside the territory of a state is an 'exceptional situation' that must be examined restrictively in each specific case, thereby referring to a number of cases decided by the European Court of Human Rights (i.e. *Al-Skeini, Ilaşcu, Catan, Chiragov, Banković*) (ibid, para. 88, 104(d)).

Specifically, in the context of environmental obligations, the Court indicated that states must ensure that their territory is not used in any way that may cause significant damage to the environment of other states or of areas outside their territorial limits. States have the obligation to prevent causing transboundary damage. Furthermore, states are obligated to adopt all necessary measures to avoid that activities – carried out on their territory or under their control – affect the rights of individuals within or outside their territory. Thus, to examine the possibility of extraterritorial exercise of jurisdiction in the context of compliance with environmental obligations, the obligations derived from the Convention must be analyzed in light of state obligations in that regard. In addition, the possible grounds for jurisdiction that arise from this systematic interpretation must be justified based on the particular circumstances of the specific case (IACtHR 2017, para. 81).

In that context, the Court held that state obligations include the obligation to take measures to prevent significant environmental harm, within and outside of their territories. The Court defined 'significant' as any harm that could result in a violation of the right to life and personal integrity. As preventative measures, states should regulate, supervise and monitor activities that could cause environmental harm, conduct environmental impact studies when there is a risk of harm, establish contingency plans and mitigate harm, if it has occurred despite the state's preventative actions. Furthermore, states have procedural obligations, which include guaranteeing access to information related to possible environmental harms, securing the right to public participation in decision-making processes about environmental impact and ensuring the right to access to justice to enforce state obligations regarding the environment (ibid, paras. 123–243).

Overall, the advisory opinion is very important because the Court broadened the scope of what extraterritorial jurisdiction implies, and it is for the first time that the Court explained its understanding of extraterritorial obligations, thus strengthening its jurisprudence in relation to the scope of states' human rights obligations.

Conclusions

The IACmHR has established that the Declaration and the Convention have extraterritorial application, notwithstanding that the latter contains a jurisdiction clause whereas the former does not (have an explicit clause), and the IACtHR seems to have endorsed this position. The IACmHR has emphasized that the responsibility of member states is not confined to actions inside their territories, but rather extends, in addition, to circumstances occurring in the territory of another state, in international airspace or on the high seas. States in the Americas are obligated to uphold the protected rights of any person subject to their jurisdiction.

In the IAHRS, the scope of extraterritorial obligations is linked to the universality principle and the jurisdiction clause. According to the supervisory bodies, human rights are inherent to all human beings, they are not based on their nationality or location. States can be held internationally liable for deeds or omissions that were attributable to them within their own territory, but also to those perpetrated outside their territory but within the sphere in which they have jurisdiction.

This chapter examined 16 situations in practice within the IAHRS on the issue of extraterritoriality (in the ambit of country reports, contentious decisions, precautionary measures issued by the Commission and an advisory opinion issued by the Court). In most matters the facts occurred during military interventions or operations in international airspace and in the territory of another state, as well as in detention facilities outside a state's territory. In those cases, civil and political rights were violated. Only three cases before the Commission were related to violations of the American Convention, while the remainder concerned violations of the American Declaration. Once, in the ambit of an advisory opinion on the international obligations in the framework of the environment, the IACtHR has been able to deal with the issue of extraterritorial obligations. In short, most cases concerning extraterritoriality have been dealt with by the IACmHR under the Declaration.

In order to establish extraterritorial jurisdiction and ultimately responsibility, a person must be under the 'effective control or authority' of the foreign state, whereby the 'personal jurisdiction model' has been adopted as an alternative to the 'spatial jurisdiction' of control over a foreign territory. Since the extraterritorial application of human rights has been connected by the IACmHR with the recognition of the principle of universality, the threshold for the extraterritorial application of the Declaration and Convention seems to be quite low.

The Commission also stressed that, when examining the scope of the Declaration or Convention, the 'authority and control test' is based on causality. It must more specifically be ascertained whether there was a causal link between the extraterritorial conduct of a state through the actions or omissions of its agents and/or persons who have acted under its orders or acquiescence and the alleged violation of the rights and freedoms of an individual.

In its Advisory Opinion, the Court has taken things a step further, as it has broadened what constitutes extraterritorial jurisdiction by recognizing a new extraterritorial jurisdictional link based on control over domestic activities with extraterritorial effect, thereby departing from the two existing criteria to establish extraterritorial jurisdiction. While the effective control test remains essential, the Court held that, with regard to cross-border damage, the exercise of jurisdiction occurs when the state of origin exercises effective control over the activities carried out that caused the damage and the resulting violation of human rights abroad. This basically implies that 'effective control' is no longer only something to be exercised over territory ('spatial jurisdiction'), nor over individual victims ('personal jurisdiction'), but can also be something only to be exercised over the activities responsible for harm. The effective control test is based on the factual-causal nexus between conducts performed on the territory of the state of origin and a violation of rights and freedoms occurring abroad.

This novel interpretation of what constitutes 'effective control' seems to imply that home states, when awarding an oil or mining exploitation concession on their territory or within their waters, will in the future not be able to argue anymore that such activities are wholly beyond their 'effective control', and they can thus eventually never be held responsible for subsequent environmental degradation in case of an environmental spillover effect towards neighboring countries.

Even where the Court has clearly held that extraterritorial obligations are 'exceptional', the new jurisdictional link has opened a clear pathway to future transnational human rights claims when a state is factual-causally linked to extraterritorial situations, without it having physical control over a territory or over persons, and where a home state has the knowledge about the risk of wrongful acts and is capable of providing protection as a result of its effective control over activities within its territory. One might for example think of a home state's responsibility for the extraterritorial human rights violations by one of its (transnational) companies.

In the ambit of the earlier-mentioned situations examined by the IAHRS case law, a very broad range of rights and freedoms has been given extraterritorial application, including: the rights to life; liberty and personal security; humane treatment; preservation of health and well-being; equality before the law; work; a passport; property; petition; residence and movement; juridical personality; religious freedom and worship; freedom of expression; protection of honor, personal reputation and private and family life; protection of mothers and children; right to family and protection thereof; assembly; protection from arbitrary arrest; fair trial/judicial protection; due process of law; and a healthy environment.

While most alleged violations have happened within the 'inter-American *espace juridique*', some cases relate to actions beyond the confines of the 'Inter-American legal space', implying that the inter-American monitoring bodies, and certainly the IACmHR, have adopted an expansive view – probably also in view of the case law of the European Court of Human Rights which is regularly referred to – thereby extending the scope *ratione loci* of inter-American instruments and its obligations beyond the American continent, although the latter instruments were originally adopted for this specific region.

References

American Convention on Human Rights, 22 November 1969.

American Declaration on the Rights and Duties of Man, 2 May 1948.

Berkes, A. (2018) 'A New Extraterritorial Jurisdictional Link Recognised by the IACtHR', 28 March 2018, www.ejiltalk.org [accessed 8 January 2021].

Buergenthal, T. and Norris, R. (eds). (1982–1993) *Human Rights: The Inter-American System*, Oceana, Dobbs Ferry.

Burbano Herrera, C. and Viljoen, F. (2015) 'Danger and Fear in Prison': Protecting the Most Vulnerable Persons in Africa and the America's by Regional Human Rights Bodies through Interim Measures', *NQHR* 33(2), 163–193.

Burbano Herrera, C. (2011) *Provisional Measures in the Case Law of the Inter-American Court of Human Rights, Antwerp*, Intersentia.

Cassel, D. (2004) 'The Extraterritorial Application of Inter-American Human Rights instruments' in Coomans, F. and Kamminga, M. (eds). *Extraterritorial Application of Human Rights Treaties*, Intersentia.

Cerna, C. (2004) 'The Extraterritorial Application of the Human Rights Instruments of the Inter-American System' in Coomans, F. and Kamminga, M. (eds). *Extraterritorial Application of Human Rights Treaties*, Intersentia.

Cerqueira, D. (2015) 'The Attribution of Extraterritorial Liability for the Acts of Private Parties in the Inter-American System: Contributions to the Debate on Corporations and Human Rights', *Aportes DPLF* 20, 18-21 (available at https://dplfblog.com).
Coomans, F. and Kamminga, M. (eds). (2004) *Extraterritorial Application of Human Rights Treaties*, Intersentia.
Haeck, Y. Ruiz O. and Burbano-Herrera C. (eds). (2015) *The Inter-American Court of Human Rights: Theory and Practice, Present and Future*, Intersentia.
Inter-American Commission on Human Rights (IACmHR) (1985a) *Chile Country Report.*
_______ (1985b) *Suriname Country Report.*
_______ (1987) *Disabled Peoples International v. US*, Case 9213, Admissibility Decision.
_______ (1993) *Jose Isabel Salas Galindo et al. v. US,* Case 10.573, Admissibility Report 31/93.
_______ (1996) *Disabled Peoples' International v. US,* Case 9213, Report to Conclude Case 3/96.
_______ (1997) *Haitian Centre for Human Rights et al. v. US,* Case 10.675, Merits Report 51/96.
_______ (1999a) *Victor Saldaño v. Argentina*, Inadmissibility Report 38/99.
_______ (1999b) *Coard v. US,* Case 10.951, Merits Report 109/99.
_______ (1999c) *Armando Alejandre Jr et al. v. Cuba,* Case 11.589, Admissibility Report 86/99.
_______ (2002) *Persons detained by the United States in Guantanamo Bay v. US*, Precautionary Measures 259/02.
_______ (2003) *Persons detained by the United States in Guantanamo Bay*, Precautionary measures.
_______ (2004) *Persons detained by the US in Guantanamo Bay*, Precautionary measures.
_______ (2005) *Persons detained by the United States in Guantanamo Bay*, Precautionary measures.
_______ (2005) *Hossein Alikhani v. US*, Case 4618/02, Admissibility Report 63/05.
_______ (2006) *Omar Khadr v. US*, Precautionary Measures 8/06.
_______ (2008) *Djamel Ameziane v. US*, Precautionary Measures.
_______ (2010) *Franklin Guillermo Aisalla Molina (Ecuador) v. Colombia,* Inter-state petition PI-02, Admissibility Report 112/10.
_______ (2011a) Resolution 2/11, *Regarding the Situation of Detainees at Guantanamo Bay*, United States MC 259-02.
_______ (2011b) *Danny Honorio Bastidas Meneses at al (Ecuador) v. Colombia*, Admissibility Report 153/11, Petition 189/03.
_______ (2011c) *Aisalla Molina v. Ecuador,* Case IP-02, Report No. 112/10.
_______ (2012a) *10 Years After Detentions in Guantanamo Began, the IACHR Repeats its Call to Close the Detention Center,* Press Release 3/12.
_______ (2012b) *Djamel Ameziane v. US*, Petition P-900-08, Admissibility Report 17/12.
_______ (2013a) *Detainees in the US Military Base in Guantanamo v. United States*, Extension Precautionary Measures 259/02.
_______ (2013b) *Franklin Guillermo Aisalla Molina (Ecuador) v. Colombia*, Inter-state petition PI-02, Report 96/131.
_______ (2015a) *Mustafa Adam Al-Hawsawi v. US*, Precautionary measure 422/14.
_______ (2015b) *Towards the closure of Guantánamo* OEA/Ser.L.
_______ (2016) *Khaled El-Masri v. US*, Petition 419-08, Admissibility Report 21/16.
_______ (2018) *Jose Isabel Salas Galindo v. US*, Case 10.573, Merits Report 121/18.
_______ (2020) *Djamel Ameziane v. US*, Petition 12.865, Merits Report 29/20.
Inter-American Court of Human Rights (IACtHR) (2017) Environment and Human Rights, Advisory Opinion OC-23/17.
Milanovic, M. (2011) *Extraterritorial Application of Human Rights Treaties, Law Principles, and Policy*, Oxford University Press.
Minutes of the 1st and 2nd session of Committee I on November 10, 1969, in Actas y Documentos of the Inter-American Specialized Conference on Human Rights, 1966, OAS, Washington DC.
Vienna Convention on the Law of Treaties, 22 May 1969.

9

Extraterritorial obligations in the European human rights system

Yves Haeck, Clara Burbano-Herrera and Hannah Ghulam Farag

Introduction

The conduct of state authorities may affect the human rights of individuals located outside their territory. In Europe the scope of extraterritorial obligations is closely tied to the jurisdiction clause in the European Convention on Human Rights (ECHR). States will be internationally responsible not only for human rights violations attributed to them within their own territory, but also for actions and omissions perpetrated outside their own territory but within their jurisdiction. This chapter explores the criteria developed by the European Court of Human Rights (ECtHR) and the former European Commission on Human Rights (ECmHR) to establish the international responsibility of states in the framework of extraterritorial obligations in specific cases and identifies the types of situations in which extraterritorial responsibility has been established. It will first deal with the provision related to extraterritorial jurisdiction and obligations. Subsequently, it will elaborate on the specific extraterritorial instances under which a state can be held responsible under the ECHR for acts of its agents outside its territory, as well as the extraterritorial obligations this entails. It will do so under two jurisdictional models used by the Court and ECommHR, namely the personal model and the spatial model. We will end with the concurrent jurisdiction in case of the spatial model and with some conclusions.

Extraterritorial obligations within the ECHR in a nutshell

The general international obligation of the ECHR states is enshrined in Article 1 ECHR. This clause defines the scope of application of the ECHR and the obligations of the Member States. The European Court links the extraterritorial application of human rights (explicitly or implicitly) with this so-called jurisdiction clause.

(Extra)territorial jurisdiction

The ECHR contains a so-called jurisdiction clause (on its history: Gondek 2009, pp. 84–92; Mallory 2020, pp. 15–23), which holds that every ECHR state is obliged to guarantee the rights

DOI: 10.4324/9781003090014-12

and freedoms in the ECHR to everyone within its own 'jurisdiction'. Article 1 ECHR reads as follows:

> The High Contracting Parties shall secure to everyone within their jurisdiction the rights and freedoms defined in Section I of this Convention.

This implies that the exercise of 'jurisdiction' of a Member State over an act or omission is a prerequisite – a threshold criterion – before a state can be held responsible under the ECHR (ECtHR 2004c, para. 311; Milanovic 2011, p. 19). State responsibility or attribution to a state only arises after it has been asserted that the matter complained of is within the jurisdiction of the Member State concerned (O'Boyle 2004, p. 131). So, the term 'jurisdiction' is an autonomous concept, distinct from the issue of attribution of responsibility for an internationally wrongful act, that is a violation of the Convention (ECtHR 2012a, para. 115; Karakaş and Bakırcı 2018, p. 132).

In Strasbourg case-law, jurisdiction under Article 1 ECHR is primarily a territorial matter, confined within state borders (ECtHR 2004a, para. 139).

In case of acts which have taken place outside the territory of a Member State but have led to civil proceedings in the state concerned, a jurisdictional link has been established (ECtHR 2003a, para. 54). This also counts as to the instigation of a criminal investigation or proceedings within that Member State concerning the death of a person outside that state (ECtHR 2019a, para. 188) or the ill-treatment or deprivation of liberty (ECtHR 2019b, para. 157). The existence of a 'jurisdictional link' was also established between the applicants and Belgium, i.e. the respondent state, failing to fulfil its positive, procedural obligation to cooperate following a European Arrest Warrant issued by Spain regarding a suspected ETA member living in Belgium allegedly implicated in the murder of the father of the applicants (*Romeo Castaño* 2019, paras. 38–42).

In exceptional circumstances, however, Member States may also be held responsible for extraterritorial acts (ECtHR 2001b, para. 67; ECtHR 2011b, para. 131), in light of the particular facts of the case. Over the years the Court has indeed found in a number of instances that states exercised jurisdiction extraterritoriality concerning acts of their authorities producing effects beyond their own territory (ECtHR 2011b, para. 133).

The Court, in *Al-Skeini*, i.e. the leading judgment on extraterritoriality, established a state's extraterritorial jurisdiction and therefore possible responsibility through the use of two models, i.e. (1) when an individual is located within a territory or area over which the state has effective control (*spatial jurisdiction*); (2) when an individual is subject to the authority or control of a state agent (*personal jurisdiction*) (Milanovic 2011, p. 127 and 173).

Overall, the case-law on extraterritorial jurisdiction has received a good deal of criticism. The most outspoken is judge Bonello, who held that it was 'a patch-work case-law at best', with 'case-by-case improvisations, more or less inspired, more or less insipid, cluttering the case-law with doctrines which are, at best, barely compatible and at worst blatantly contradictory'. He pleads for a 'functional test' to jurisdiction, whereby '[j]urisdiction arises from the mere fact of having assumed those obligations [under the ECHR] *and from having the capability to fulfil them* (or not to fulfil them)' and states that a state is effectively exercising 'jurisdiction' 'whenever it falls within its power to perform') (Bonello, Concurring Opinion in ECtHR 2011b, paras. 3–20). Judge Motoc speaks of the case-law as 'one of the most problematic in terms of its application' and with 'several contradictions in the manner in which the Court has interpreted it' (Motoc, Concurring Opinion in *Jaloud* 2015, para. 2; further criticism Hampson 2008, pp. 570–571; Mallory 2020, pp. 8–10). The ECHR states, however, prefer the Court to take a more cautious approach and give a more restrictive interpretation to Article 1 ECHR than it is proposing today (Karakaş and Bakırcı 2018, p. 113).

(Extra)territorial obligations

Once control and authority of ECHR state agents over an individual is established, and therefore jurisdiction, the state has the obligation to secure to that individual the rights and freedoms under the ECHR that are relevant to the situation of the individual concerned. In this sense, therefore, the rights can be 'divided and tailored' (ECtHR 2011b, para. 137; a position which is plainly in contradiction with ECtHR 2001b, para. 75). In *Al-Skeini*, for example, the UK had the obligation to guarantee the victims only those rights and freedoms which were relevant to their situation, i.e. the right to life (ECHR, art. 2).

When an individual is within a territory or area over which the state has effective overall control and is thus within the state's jurisdiction, the state has the obligation to refrain from actions in contravention of the ECHR or its positive obligations to guarantee the rights and freedoms under the ECHR (ECtHR 2004c, para. 322). This concerns the entire range of substantive rights set out in the ECHR and the additional protocols ratified by the respondent state (ECtHR 2001a, para. 77).

The existence of positive obligations in an extraterritorial setting was established for the first time in *Isaak*, where the Court held that Turkey had an obligation to protect the life of the victim (ECtHR 2008a, para. 119).

In what follows, we examine the personal and spatial model of jurisdiction in more detail.

State agent authority and control – personal model

There is extraterritorial jurisdiction in case a state exercises effective control over a person outside its national territory. Such an exercise of effective control over a person may occur in different ways.

Acts of diplomatic personnel abroad or acts of state agents on aircraft or ship

In specific situations, customary international law and international treaties have recognized the extraterritorial exercise of jurisdiction by states (ECtHR 2001b, para. 73). This includes cases involving the activities of diplomatic/consular agents abroad and on board of aircraft and vessels registered in, or flying the flag of a Member State.

Activities of diplomatic or consular agents abroad as exercise of extraterritorial jurisdiction

Activities of diplomatic/consular agents abroad, when they perform certain duties with regard to nationals who are domiciled or resident abroad (ECmHR 1965), amount to the exercise of extraterritorial jurisdiction, when they exercise authority over such nationals (ECtHR 2011b, para. 134) or their property and their acts or omissions thus affect such nationals or property (ECmHR 1977b)

The applicants were within the jurisdiction of a state when German consular staff in Casablanca and Tanger allegedly acted against a German couple, asking the Moroccan authorities to expel the applicant from the country (ECmHR 1965), where the British consul in Amman allegedly failed to provide assistance to a British woman, whose husband had abducted their daughter to Jordan, to restore her custody over her child (ECmHR 1977b), or where the Danish Ambassador in the then DDR requested the police to take a group of 18 East-Germans who had entered the Danish embassy in an attempt to leave their home country (ECmHR 1992).

However, persons simply entering an embassy of a Member State are, by the fact alone that the state exercises administrative control over the premises of its embassies, not brought within that state's jurisdiction. The applicants having submitted a visa application at the embassy of a Member State, are not within the jurisdiction of a state, as – unlike aforementioned case-law – it concerns non-nationals and the diplomatic agents did not exercise a *de facto* control over the applicants, which indeed had freely chosen one embassy above another one and were subsequently free to leave the premises without any hindrance. The Court deemed it irrelevant that the diplomatic agents had, as in the present case, merely a 'letter-box' role, or to ascertain who was responsible for taking the decisions, the Belgian authorities in the national territory or the diplomatic agents abroad (ECtHR 2020b, paras. 114 and 118–119).

Activities on board an aircraft and vessels of a Member State as exercise of jurisdiction

Activities of state agents on board an (air)craft and vessels registered in, or flying the flag of a Member State, are expressions of extraterritorial exercise of jurisdiction, in conformity with customary international law and treaty provisions (ECtHR 2001b, para. 73). The death of a sailor on a Lithuanian merchant vessel off the Brazilian coast did not absolve Lithuania from an obligation to carry out an effective investigation into this death, as the ship belonged to a Lithuanian company, was registered in Lithuania and sailed under a Lithuanian flag, and the relations between the crew and the captain, including those related to safety at work, were determined by Lithuanian law (ECtHR 2016b, para. 63).

Use of force by state agents operating outside state territory

When state agents operating outside the territory of a Member State use force against a person, such person(s) may be subject to the authority or control of the state and may therefore be brought under the jurisdiction of the state (ECtHR 2011b, para. 136).

Use of force by military in or immediately next to a military buffer zone

When a Greek-Cypriot man was kicked and beaten to death by private citizens and at least four Turkish soldiers or soldiers from the north during a demonstration in the UN buffer zone between the North and South of Cyprus, the deceased was deemed to be under the authority and/or effective control of the Member State (Turkey) through its agents, even though the acts complained of took place in the neutral buffer zone. Therefore, the matters complained of fell within the jurisdiction of Turkey (ECtHR 2006). When a petitioner near a Greek-Cypriot checkpoint was hit by a bullet fired cross-border by a Turkish soldier, although he was injured in territory over which Turkey did not exercise control, the opening of fire was the direct and immediate cause of those injuries, and consequently the applicant had to be regarded equally as within Turkish jurisdiction (ECtHR 2008b).

Use of force by police or military when arresting or abducting a person abroad

Following Öcalan's being handed over by the Kenyan authorities to the Turkish agents in the international zone of Nairobi airport and his subsequent arrest on the plane, the PKK (Kurdistan Workers Party) leader was under Turkish authority and control and therefore within Turkish jurisdiction (ECtHR 2003b, para. 91). Turkey was, with the approval of Kenya, exercising effective control over the applicant within Kenyan territory. In the case of a person who had been detained in Ukraine and handed over to or abducted abroad by Russian state agents – even if the latter were only presumed to be such agents; it also did not matter whether the latter were operating lawfully or unlawfully – jurisdiction had been established, as such person was subject to Russian authority or control allegedly exercised through its agents operating abroad (ECtHR 2019b, para. 161).

Use of force by military when arresting a person on/taking persons on board of naval vessels on the high seas

The sailors of a commercial vessel suspected of drugs smuggling, intercepted and boarded by the French navy on the Atlantic, were brought under French jurisdiction as from the subsequent taking of full, exclusive, uninterrupted, at least *de facto* control by the French military over the vessel and its crew, until the latter were taken off board in Brest (ECtHR 2010, paras. 66–67). Similarly, migrants trying to cross the Mediterranean who were taken on board ships of the Italian navy were under the continuous and exclusive *de jure* and *de facto* control of the Italian authorities, in the period between boarding the ships and their handing over to the Libyan authorities (ECtHR 2012b, paras. 81–82).

Use of force by military over persons held in detention centres abroad or killings during a military security operation abroad

Al-Skeini concerned the killing of six Iraqis in Basra by British soldiers in 2003, when the UK had the status of occupying power. Four persons died following gunfire during military security operations, one drowned after being shot and obliged to jump into a river and the last victim died while being tortured at a British military base. It was alleged by the victims' relatives that the British authorities had not conducted a decent investigation into the killings.

The Court noted that following the removal from power of the previous regime and until the accession of the interim Iraqi government at the end of June 2004, the UK (together with the US) assumed in Iraq the 'exercise of some of the public powers normally to be exercised by a sovereign government'. More specifically, the UK assumed authority and responsibility for the maintenance of security in south-east Iraq. In these exceptional circumstances, the UK, via its troops in security operations, exercised authority and control over persons killed during such security operations, so that a jurisdictional link was established between the UK and the persons killed (ECtHR 2011b, paras. 149–150).

Although *Al-Skeini* set the stage for further findings of extraterritorial jurisdiction in the Iraqi context, the Court did not fully overrule its decision in *Banković* (on this case, *infra*). While a personal model of jurisdiction was applied to the killing, this was done so exceptionally, because the UK 'exercised public powers' in Iraq. By focusing on the 'exercise of some of the public powers normally to be exercised by a sovereign government', the Court merely framed the case as an exception to *Banković* (Milanovic 2012, pp. 130–131; also Karakaş and Bakırcı 2018, p. 131 (holding this is 'a drawback')). A contrario, if the UK had not exercised such public powers, the personal jurisdiction model would not have been applicable. And Milanovic pursues: '[w]hile the ability to kill is "authority and control" over the individual if the state has public powers, killing is not authority and control if the state is merely firing missiles from an aircraft. Under this reasoning, drone operations (…) wherever would be just as excluded from the purview of human rights treaties as under Bankovic' (Milanovic 2012, p. 130). In our opinion, it remains unclear whether the present-day Court would now rule differently on extraterritorial jurisdiction for bombing without boots on the ground or without these vague 'public powers'. However, it could also be argued that this line of reasoning is justified. According to Besson, the jurisdiction threshold requires effective, overall and normative power and control, normative indicating that there are reasons for the action with a claim to legitimacy, not just mere coercion (Besson 2012, pp. 872–874). This criterion would manifest itself in the public powers the Court referred to in *Al-Skeini* (Besson 2012, p. 873).

With regard to the merits, namely that the UK allegedly failed to comply with its procedural obligation to investigate the killings, while logically finding a procedural violation of the right to life (ECHR, art. 2) (except for the last victim), the Court was pragmatic and sensible where holding that in circumstances such as in (post-conflict) Iraq at the time 'the procedural duty under Article 2 must be applied realistically, to take account of specific problems faced by investigators' (ECtHR 2011b, para. 168), herewith implying that the provision could not be applied in an identical manner as in a country in peacetime, given the difficult conditions *in situ*. So, the Court interpreted Article 2 flexibly, and did not impose unrealistic burdens on the UK, while eventually still finding a violation (ECtHR 2011b, paras. 169–177).

Two Iraqis suspected of involvement in the murders of British soldiers and detained by the British army in a UK-managed military detention centre in south-east Iraq in 2003 were deemed to be under UK jurisdiction until being handed over to the Iraqi authorities in 2008. The Court based itself on the total and exclusive *de facto* and later also *de jure* control of the UK over the detention centre and the detained Iraqi's there (ECtHR 2009b, paras. 86–89), although the *de facto* control was decisive (Karakaş and Bakırcı 2018, p. 128).

In the case of the internment of an Iraqi citizen in a British-run detention centre from October 2004 until December 2007, the UK exercised exclusive control over the facility and the detention was decided upon by a British soldier. Therefore, the Court concluded that the applicant was placed within the authority and control of the UK and the detention was ultimately attributable to the UK (*Al-Jedda* 2011, para. 85). Strasbourg was not persuaded by the argument that the detention should have been attributed to the UN, since the organization did not have effective control or ultimate authority over the acts of the troops in the Multinational Force (ECtHR 2011c, paras. 78–84).

In *Hassan*, an Iraqi citizen, between being captured somewhere in 2003 by British troops in the morning and his admission to a detention camp later that afternoon, was within the physical power and control of the UK soldiers and therefore fell within UK jurisdiction. In the ensuing period in a US-run detention camp, Hassan continued to fall under the authority and control of UK forces as he was admitted as a UK prisoner. Moreover, shortly after his admission, he was taken to a compound entirely controlled by UK forces. While under UK jurisdiction in accordance with the US-UK MOA concerning the detainees, the UK was responsible for the classification of its detainees and for the decision to release them. While certain operational aspects relating to Hassan's detention were transferred to US forces, in particular as to the escorting and guarding Hassan, the UK retained authority and control over all aspects of the detention relevant to the case. Hassan remained in the custody of armed military personnel and under the authority and control of the UK until his release from the bus that took him from the detention camp to the drop-off point, so that Hassan fell within the UK's jurisdiction from the moment of his capture by UK troops until his release (ECtHR 2014b, paras. 76–78).

Use of force by military over persons at a checkpoint abroad

In *Jaloud*, an Iraqi citizen died in 2003 when soldiers at a Dutch/Iraqi-manned checkpoint in south-east Iraq under the command and direct supervision of a Dutch officer had opened fire at the vehicle in which he was occupying the front-seat. The fact that the Dutch soldiers at the checkpoint functioned under the operational control of the UK did not absolve the Netherlands of its responsibilities under the Convention (ECtHR 2014a, para. 143). The Court emphasized especially that the Netherlands retained 'full control' over the Dutch soldiers, who had not been placed 'at the disposal' or 'under the exclusive direction or control' of any other state (ECtHR 2014a, paras. 143–151). The alleged victim was deemed to be under the jurisdiction of the Netherlands, since the Netherlands exercised its jurisdiction within the limits of the Stability Force in Iraq Mission and for the purpose of asserting authority and control over persons passing through the checkpoint (ECtHR 2014a, paras. 152–153). The control over the checkpoint was clearly enough for jurisdiction to materialize (Mallory 2020, p. 181), and effective control over the related territory was therefore not necessary to have jurisdiction (Karakaş and Bakırcı 2018, p. 132). This seems to be corroborated in a separate opinion, which speaks of authority and control over persons passing through the checkpoint (concurring opinion Spielmann and Raimondi in ECtHR 2014a).

Foreign individuals exercising state authority with its agreement

The Court has recognized the exercise of extraterritorial jurisdiction by a Member State when the Member State, through the consent, invitation or acquiescence of the local government of that territory, exercises all or some of the public powers normally to be exercised by that government (ECtHR 2001b, para. 71; ECtHR 2011b, para. 135). Therefore, where, in conformity with custom, an international treaty or another agreement, the authorities of the Member State carry out executive or judicial functions on the territory of another state, the Member State may be responsible for violations thereby incurred, as long as the acts in question are attributable to it rather than to the territorial state (ECtHR 2011b, para. 135; ECtHR 2014b, para. 74). In *Drozd and Janousek*, two convicted criminals alleging that an Andorran court, composed of judges appointed by Spain and France, was incompatible with the right to a fair trial, did not fall under French or Spanish jurisdiction. The judges did not act as French or Spanish judges, the court was independent from both countries, which did not interfere with the proceedings (ECtHR 1992, para. 96). When an arrest warrant containing an irregularity is issued by an ECHR state, the requesting state is responsible under the ECHR for the detention in the other state, even if it was executed by the other state in compliance with its international obligations, as long as the requested state could not have detected this irregularity (ECtHR 2009a, para. 52).

Effective control over an area – spatial model

There is extraterritorial jurisdiction in case a state exercises effective control over a territory outside its national territory, either through a military occupation or through a subordinate or separatist local administration (ECtHR 2012a, para. 106; ECtHR 2016a, para. 98). This assessment will primarily depend on military involvement, i.e., the strength of the state's military presence in the area (ECtHR 1996, para. 56), but other indicators, such as military, political and economic-financial support to a separatist or subordinate local administration may also be of relevance (ECtHR 2012a, para. 107). According to Mallory, the duration of time a state will need to have spent exerting such influence or support may appear to be the determining factor before the jurisdiction it exercises moves from the personal ground to the spatial ground (Mallory 2020, p. 191).

The Court now accepts that there can be extraterritorial jurisdiction within but also beyond the territory ('espace juridique') covered by the CoE states (ECtHR 2011b, paras. 138–142).

Initially, in *Banković*, where the applicants complained about a NATO (North Atlantic Treaty Organization) bombing of Serb radio and television premises in Belgrade in April 1999 and claimed that the 17 respondent NATO states had exercised effective, extraterritorial control through the bombing, which created a jurisdictional link with the applicants, the Court disagreed with this argument, stating that such an approach to jurisdiction would go too far (ECtHR 2001b, para. 75). The dropping of bombs from the air on persons outside an ECHR state's territory did not create a jurisdictional link in the sense of Article 1 ECHR. The Court also stressed that the ECHR operates in an essentially regional context and notably in the *espace juridique* of the contracting states, which Yugoslavia was not a part of (ECtHR 2001b, para. 80). The Court received heavy criticism for its inadmissibility decision (e.g. Altiparmak 2004, pp. 242–243; Leach 2005, p. 57; Loucaides 2006, pp. 398–399 (all criticizing the *espace juridique* criterion)). These statements set a sombre stage for extraterritorial human rights protection in non-Member States.

Subsequently, the Court rejected the notion of *espace juridique* in a number of cases on Turkish military operations in Iraq and Iran (ECtHR 2004b, paras. 73–81; ECtHR 2007, paras. 54–55), but especially in its ensuing *Al-Skeini* Grand Chamber case concerning British military security operations in Iraq. Ruling on the killing or fatally wounding of a number of Iraqi nationals in Southern Iraq in 2003, the Court retraced its steps in *Banković* by denying that jurisdiction can never exist outside of the territory of the CoE states. It first confirmed that where the territory of an ECHR state is occupied by the armed forces of another ECHR state, the occupying state should in principle be held accountable under the ECHR for human rights violations within the occupied territory, because to hold otherwise would be to deprive the population of that territory of the rights hitherto enjoyed and would result in a 'vacuum' of protection within the 'legal space of the Convention'. However, the Court thereafter said that the importance of establishing the occupying state's jurisdiction in such cases does not imply, *a contrario*, that jurisdiction can never exist outside the territory covered by the CoE states and underscored that it had not in its case-law applied any such restriction (ECtHR 2011b, para. 142; Milanovic 2012, p. 129).

Moreover, in *Issa*, the ECtHR held that it did not exclude that effective control could be exercised in a temporary manner (ECtHR 2004b, para. 74).

The application of the ECHR to military operations abroad has in turn led to certain unease with some ECHR states, and certainly within the UK, which is concerned about its military operations abroad, and in 2016 floated the proposal of entering an 'extraterritorial derogation' (Rooney 2016, pp. 656–663; pro: Milanovic 2016, p. 55 and Wallace 2019, p. 193; nuanced contra: Mallory 2020, pp. 134–136 and 203–204).

Military occupation

A Member State may exercise extraterritorial jurisdiction in case of a 'traditional' military occupation. The Court thereby refers to Article 42 of the Hague Convention (IV) respecting the Laws and Customs of War on Land (1907), which reads as follows: 'Territory is considered occupied when it is actually placed under the authority of the hostile army. The occupation extends only to the territory where such authority has been established and can be exercised'. However, the qualification as an 'occupying power' is not *per se* determinative to conclude whether certain facts fall within a state's extraterritorial jurisdiction (ECtHR 2014a, para. 142). There is no direct correlation between occupation and effective control of an area (Mallory 2020, p. 188).

In order to establish whether a state has effective control over an area, it seems that the strength of the military presence and extent to which a state supports a regime militarily, economically and politically play a role (ECtHR 2011b, para. 138), while the size of the occupying military forces also seems to play a role (*supra*) (also Mallory 2020, p. 190). Anyway, *Al-Skeini* (ECtHR 2011b, paras. 143–150) and subsequent cases (e.g. ECtHR 2014a; ECtHR 2014b) seem to demonstrate that the Court avoids the question of extraterritorial jurisdiction based on effective control over territory in *Al-Skeini*-like cases, approaching these cases from a perspective of individual personal jurisdiction instead. It has also been pointed out that, as individual personal jurisdiction had already been established in *Al-Skeini*, and that in its subsequent *Hassan* judgment, the Court itself indicated that factual info available (under 'Facts') in *Al-Skeini* simply tended to demonstrate that the UK was far from being in effective control of the area which it occupied, the Court had deemed an analysis of extraterritorial jurisdiction based on effective control over territory unnecessary (Guide 2019d, para. 54).

Unrecognized subordinate or separatist local administration

The acquiescence or connivance of the authorities of an ECHR state in the acts of private individuals which violate the ECHR rights of other individuals within its jurisdiction may engage the state's responsibility (ECtHR 2001a, para. 81), especially in the case of recognition by the state concerned of the acts of self-proclaimed authorities which are not recognized by the international community (ECtHR 2004c, para. 318). The responsibility of states has been examined with regard to such authorities in Northern Cyprus, Transdniestria and Nagorno-Karabakh.

The responsibility of Turkey has been examined as to facts which took place during its military intervention in the north of Cyprus in 1974 and the subsequent establishment of the Turkish Republic of Northern Cyprus (TRNC). On different occasions the Court has said that the alleged acts have taken place under the jurisdiction of Turkey.

In *Loizidou*, the Court held that the fact that the Greek-Cypriot applicant had lost control of her property in Northern Cyprus stemmed from the occupation of that part of Cyprus by Turkish troops and the establishment there of the TRNC, as well as the fact that she was prevented by Turkish troops from gaining access to her property (ECtHR 1995, paras. 63–64). It was not deemed necessary to determine whether Turkey actually exercised detailed control over the policies and actions of the authorities of the TRNC, as it was obvious from the large number of troops engaged in active duties that the Turkish army exercised effective overall control over the north of the island. Such control entailed its responsibility for the TRNC policies and actions. Consequently, persons affected by such policies or actions came within Turkish jurisdiction (ECtHR 1996, paras. 56–57). In *Cyprus v. Turkey*, it was confirmed that as Turkey had effective overall control over Northern Cyprus, its responsibility was not restricted to the acts of its own soldiers or officials, but was also engaged by virtue of the acts of the local administration which survived by virtue of Turkish military and other support (ECtHR 2001a, para. 77).

In turn, Russia has been examined as to its jurisdiction and eventually responsibility for various alleged ECHR violations taking place in the Moldavian Republic of Transdniestria (MRT), a breakaway territory within Moldova not recognized by the international community. In *Ilascu* a petition was lodged by a number of persons as to the imposition of the death penalty, ill-treatment following the arrest and detention and some other issues. The Court found that, in view of Russia's military and political support to setting up a separatist regime in Transdniestria (1991–1992) and the subsequent continued military, political and economic support to the separatist regime, Russia's responsibility was engaged with regard to the unlawful acts in which Russian state agents participated and those committed by the Transdniestrian separatists. The MRT remained under the effective authority, or at the very least under the decisive influence, of Russia, and survived by virtue of the Russian military, economic, financial and political support. Therefore, the applicants were within the jurisdiction of Russia (ECtHR 2004c, paras. 379–394). In the follow-up case of *Ivantoc*, which was lodged by two persons being kept in prison despite their detentions having been found in contravention of the ECHR in the previous judgment, the Court did not see any changes as to the Russian policy and collaboration with the MRT, nor did it see a Russian attempt to end the applicants' situation brought about by its agents. After the July 2004 *Ilascu*-judgment and at least until the applicants' release in June 2007, Russia had continued to enjoy a close relationship with the MRT, amounting to providing political, financial and economic support to the separatist regime. Besides, the Russian army was at the date of the applicants' release still stationed on Moldovan territory in breach of Russia's undertakings to withdraw completely and in breach of Moldovan legislation. Finally, Russia continued to do nothing to prevent the alleged violations after July 2004 nor to terminate the applicants' situation brought about by its agents. Consequently, the applicants continued to be within Russian jurisdiction until their release (ECtHR 2011a, paras. 116, and 118–120). In *Catan*, which concerned a petition concerning the closure of a number of schools by the local administration because the schools had continued using the Latin alphabet notwithstanding a prohibition, as well as harassment, the Court basing itself on the evidence presented and relying on its *Ilascu* and *Ivantoc* findings, held that during the period concerned (2002–2004) the separatist local administration enjoyed continued Russian military, economic and political support. Therefore, although there was no evidence that Russian state agents were involved in the actions against the schools, Russia exercised effective control over Transdniestria, and the alleged facts thus fell within Russian jurisdiction (ECtHR 2012a, paras. 116–123). In turn, Moldova's jurisdiction was limited to certain residual positive obligations (ibid, paras. 109–110 (see infra)). Since then, on multiple occasions, similar conclusions were reached in further cases (e.g. ECtHR 2016a, paras. 109–111; ECtHR 2020a, paras. 44 and 48).

Finally, Armenia has also been assessed as to acts which had taken place in the Nagorno-Karabach region in Azerbaijan. In *Chiragov* the petitioners held that they were unable to access their homes as a result of their displacement due to the conflict between Armenia and Azerbaijan during the first half of the 1990s. While Armenia said that it could not be held responsible for acts of the autonomous Nagorno-Karabach Republic (NKR), the Court held that on the basis of the evidence presented that firstly, as to military involvement, the Armenian military support had been/was decisive for the conquest of and continued control over the territories concerned, and the evidence showed that the Armenian armed forces and the NKR forces were highly integrated; secondly, there was clear political and legal integration, given the general political support given by Armenia to the NKR, the interchange of prominent politicians, the need for NKR residents to acquire Armenian passports for travel abroad, the adoption of Armenian legislation in the NKR, the presence of Armenian law-enforcement agents and the exercise of jurisdiction by Armenian courts in the NKR; and thirdly, as to finances, the Armenian financial support was substantial, to the extent that the NKR would not be able to subsist economically without this support (ECtHR 2015, paras. 172–185). The Court concluded that from the beginning of the conflict, Armenia had had a significant and decisive influence over the NKR, that the two entities are highly integrated in virtually all important matters. The NKR and its administration survived by virtue of the military, political, financial and other support given to it by Armenia which, consequently, exercised effective control over Nagorno-Karabakh and the surrounding territories. The matters at the basis of the application therefore came within the jurisdiction of Armenia (ibid, para. 186).

Concurrent jurisdiction in case of the spatial model of jurisdiction

Acts which have happened in an ECHR state confronted with a military occupation or a subordinate or separatist local administration, are, as a starting point, still presumed to have happened within the jurisdiction or competence of the ECHR state concerned. However, this presumption of jurisdiction or competence is rebuttable (ECtHR 2004a, para. 139).

The territorial jurisdiction may be limited where a state is prevented from exercising its authority in part of its territory as a result of military occupation by the armed forces of another state which effectively controls the territory concerned, acts of war or rebellion, or the acts of a foreign state supporting the installation of a separatist state within the territory of the state concerned. If such a situation is proven, the state's responsibility is limited to the positive obligations to take all the appropriate measures still within its power to take ('residual positive obligations'), i.e. to take the diplomatic, economic, judicial or other measures in accordance with international law to secure to the applicants the ECHR rights (ECtHR 2004c, paras. 312–313 and 331). It must endeavour, with all the legal and diplomatic means available to it *vis-à-vis* foreign states and international organizations, to continue to guarantee the ECHR rights (ibid, para. 333). While it is not for the Court to indicate which measures the authorities should take in order to comply with their obligations most effectively, it must verify that the measures taken were in casu appropriate and sufficient. When faced with a partial/total failure to act, the Court must determine to what extent a minimum effort was nevertheless possible and whether it should have been made, especially in Article 2 and 3 cases (ECtHR 2004c, para. 334; for criticism: Milanovic and Papic 2018).

Conclusions

In a globalizing/globalized world, extraterritorial acts by ECHR states may easily lead to extraterritorial human rights violations. In Europe the scope of extraterritorial obligations is closely tied to the ECHR's jurisdiction clause. States will be internationally responsible not only for human rights violations attributed to them within their own territory, but also for actions and omissions perpetrated outside their territory but within their jurisdiction. It is therefore interesting to explore to what extent the obligations incumbent on states under the ECHR extend beyond the national borders or territorial waters of its Members. Over the past decades, the Court has, through its case-law, gradually broadened the application and protection offered by the ECHR, be it not always in a clear and coherent way, but still beyond the confines of Europe.

The Court, in its leading *Al-Skeini* judgment on the issue of extraterritoriality, which was a unanimous decision of the Grand Chamber, has established a state's extraterritorial jurisdiction under Article 1 ECHR – jurisdiction being the threshold issue before issues of state responsibility – and therefore possible responsibility through the use of two models of jurisdiction, namely the 'spatial model' (when an individual is located within a territory or area over which the state has effective control) and the 'personal model' (when an individual is subject to the authority or control of a state agent).

Importantly, the Court has also underscored in the same judgment that jurisdiction can exist outside the territory ('espace juridique') covered by the CoE states, thereby setting aside its earlier *Bankovic* decision on this point (but which has in turn led to certain unease with some

ECHR states, and certainly within the UK, which – concerned about its military operations abroad – in 2016 suggested to enter an 'extraterritorial derogation').

During the past decade, the Court has been generous as to its understanding of extraterritorial jurisdiction. The Strasbourg case-law provides ample illustrations of extraterritorial situations which are dealt with under the 'personal jurisdiction model'. It concerns extraterritorial cases such as acts of diplomatic personnel abroad or acts of state agents on aircraft or ship as exercise of extraterritorial jurisdiction in accordance with principles international and Article 1 ECHR, the use of force in a regular, classic wartime scenario (e.g. Iraq) by state agents operating outside state territory as exercise of extraterritorial jurisdiction, such as force used by military personnel in or immediately next to a military buffer zone, by police or military when arresting or abducting a person abroad, by the military when arresting a person on/taking persons on board of naval vessels on the high seas, by the military over persons at a checkpoint or over persons held in detention centres abroad, or killings during a military security operations abroad, as well as where foreign individuals exercise state authority with the latter state's agreement. In contrast, bombing abroad does not amount to jurisdiction.

In turn Strasbourg cases handled under the 'spatial jurisdiction model' exclusively relate to situations where a subordinate, breakaway administration receives support from an ECHR Member State (Transdniestria, Nagorno Karabakh, North Cyprus). The sparing application by the Court of the 'spatial model' is due to the fact that the threshold to find that a Member State has effective control and therefore exercises jurisdiction over a region or territory is quite high.

Overall, it is to be expected in the mid and long term that the Strasbourg case law will further expand and broaden the extraterritorial application of the ECHR in the ambit of the 'personal jurisdiction model'. A range of upcoming cases concerning the conflict between Ukraine and Russia in East-Ukraine and the Crimea, extraterritorial assassination attempts or targeted killings through the use of drones beyond the borders of the ECHR states, an extraterritorial environmental case, and extraterritorial pullback migration cases in the Mediterranean, as well as surveillance cases will undoubtedly lead to further refinement of the Strasbourg case-law on extraterritorial jurisdiction and extraterritorial obligations.

Which indeed brings us to the key issue of extraterritorial state obligations under the ECHR. The state's jurisdiction, and its exercise, is closely tied up to its ECHR obligations. Member States are obliged to guarantee the protected rights. More specifically, where control and authority of state agents over an individual and therefore jurisdiction abroad have been established, the state has the extraterritorial obligation to secure to that individual the rights and freedoms under the ECHR which are relevant to the situation of the individual concerned. However, where effective control over an area has been established, therefore bringing that area and the persons there within the state's jurisdiction, the state has the extraterritorial obligation to refrain from actions which go against the full range of ECHR rights and must also comply with its positive obligation to guarantee those rights and freedoms.

While the Court's present-day case-law following *Al-Skeini* has shed light on a number of issues, its case-law remains very contextual and has attracted criticism in that regard, to the extent that next to, or even instead of the two existing jurisdictional models, i.e. the 'spatial model' and the 'personal model', some former ECtHR judges (e.g. Loucaides, already far earlier than Al-Skeini, in a Concurring Opinion in ECtHR 2004a; and Bonello in a Concurring Opinion in ECtHR 2011b), as well as certain legal doctrine (Gondek 2009, p. 375; Lawson 2011, p. 70; Mallory 2020, pp. 205–211), have been arguing in favour of a third, 'functional jurisdiction model' (while often proposing different variations but connected with a state's power). This model would grosso modo imply that a Member State must respect and protect

ECHR rights and freedoms of persons with regard to whom it is in a position to respect and protect, to the extent it is in a position to do so (see also Milanovic 2011 and Mallory 2020, pp. 206–211 (who advocate for a division between 'negative obligations' – which should automatically be falling under the jurisdiction of a Member State – and 'positive obligations' – which Milanovic restricts to areas where a Member State exercises effective control – while Mallory proposes a functional test of whether the action required was one within the power of the Member State).

Meanwhile, across the Atlantic, in its 2017 Advisory Opinion on Environment and Human Rights, the Inter-American Court of Human Rights has broadened what constitutes extraterritorial jurisdiction by recognizing a new extraterritorial 'functional jurisdiction model or link' based on control over domestic activities with extraterritorial effect (even where the Inter-American Court has said that extraterritorial obligations are 'exceptional'), thereby departing from the two existing criteria to establish extraterritorial jurisdiction. While the functional model has thus as such been given certain traction by the Inter-American Court, it remains to be seen whether the European Court will follow suit, especially in times where human rights are experiencing a certain backlash and the Court might be wary of losing chunks of its built-up legitimacy.

Whereas a functional approach would extend the scope of protection offered by the ECHR, implying that certain issues such as extraterritorial assassination attempts or targeted killings through the use of drones beyond the borders of the ECHR states, and extraterritorial pullback migration cases with the distanced assistance of ECHR states on the high seas, would be within the jurisdiction of the implementing state, and maybe even impact extraterritorial or cross-border environmental cases or actions of the Member States (transnational) companies abroad, this might ultimately also push back against the European human rights system, or even lead to withdrawals from the ECHR altogether.

References

Altiparmak, K. (2004) 'Bankovic: An Obstacle to the Application of the European Convention on Human Rights in Iraq?', *JCSL* 9(2), 213–251.

Besson, S. (2012) 'The Extraterritoriality of the European Convention on Human Rights: Why Human Rights Depend on Jurisdiction and What Jurisdiction Amounts to', *LJIL* 25(4), 857–884.

Coomans, F. and Kamminga, M. (eds). (2004) *Extraterritorial Application of Human Rights Treaties*, Intersentia.

European Commission on Human Rights (ECmHR) (1965) *X v. Germany*, Application no: 1611/62.

_______ (1977a) *Y v. Switzerland*, Application no: 7289/75.

_______ (1977b) *X v. UK*, Application no: 7547/76.

_______ (1992) *M v. Denmark*, Application no: 17392/90.

European Court of Human Rights (ECtHR) (1992) *Drozd and Janousek v. France and Spain*, Application no: 12747/87.

_______ (1995) *Loizidou v. Turkey*, Application no: 15318/89.

_______ (1996) *Loizidou v. Turkey*, Application no: 15318/89.

_______ (2001a) *Cyprus v. Turkey*, Application no: 25781/94.

_______ (2001b) *Banković and Others v. Belgium and Others*, Application no: 52207/99.

_______ (2003a) *Marković and Others v. Italy*, Application no: 1398/03.

_______ (2003b) *Öcalan v. Turkey*, Application no: 46221/99.

_______ (2004a) *Assanidze v. Georgia*, Application no: 71503/01.

_______ (2004b) *Issa and Others v. Turkey*, Application no: 31821/96.

_______ (2004c) *Ilaşcu and Others v. Moldova and Russia*, Application no: 48787/99.

_______ (2006) *Isaak and Others v. Turkey*, Application no: 44587/98.

_______ (2007) *Pad and Others v. Turkey*, Application no: 60167/00.

_______ (2008a) *Isaak and Others v. Turkey*, Application no: 44587/98.
_______ (2008b) *Andreou v. Turkey*, Application no: 45653/99.
_______ (2009a) *Stephens v. Malta (no. 1)*, Application no: 11956/07.
_______ (2009b) *Al-Saadoon and Mufdhi v. UK*, Application no: 61498/08.
_______ (2010) *Medvedyev. and Others v. France*, Application no: 3394/03.
_______ (2011a) *Ivanţoc and Others v. Moldova and Russia*, Application no: 23687/05.
_______ (2011b) *Al-Skeini and Others v. UK*, Application no: 55721/07.
_______ (2011c) *Al-Jedda v. UK*, Application no: 27021/08.
_______ (2012a) *Catan and Others v. Moldova and Russia*, Application no: 43370/04 and 2 others.
_______ (2012b) *Hirsi Jamaa and Others v. Italy*, Application no: 27765/09.
_______ (2014a) *Jaloud v. Netherlands*, Application no: 47708/08.
_______ (2014b) *Hassan v. UK*, Application no: 29750/09.
_______ (2015) *Chiragov and Others v. Armenia*, Application no: 13216/0.
_______ (2016a) *Mozer v. Moldova and Russia*, Application no: 11138/10.
_______ (2016b) *Bakanova v. Lithuania*, Application no: 11167/12.
_______ (2019a) *Güzelyurtlu and Others v. Cyprus and Turkey*, Application no: 36925/07.
_______ (2019b) *Razvozzhayev v. Russia and Ukraine and Udaltsov v. Russia*, Application no: 75734/12 and 2 others.
_______ (2019c) *Romeo Castaño v. Belgium*, Application no: 8351/17.
_______ (2019d) Guide on Article 1 of the European Convention on Human Rights Obligation to respect human rights – Concepts of "jurisdiction" and imputability.
_______ (2020a) *Cazac and Surchician Moldova and Russia* Application no: 22365/10.
_______ (2020b) *M.N. and Others v. Belgium*, Application no: 3599/18.

Gondek, M. (2009) *The Reach of Human Rights in Globalising World: Extraterritorial Application of Human Rights Treaties*, Intersentia.

Hampson, F. (2008) 'The Relationship between International Humanitarian Law and Human Rights Law from the Perspective of a Human Rights Treaty Body', *IRRC* 90(871), 549–572.

Inter-American Court of Human Rights (IACtHR) (2017) Advisory Opinion on Environment and Human Rights, OC-23/17.

Karakaş, I. and Bakırcı, H. (2018) 'Extraterritorial Application of the European Convention on Human Rights Evolution of the Court's Jurisprudence on the Notions of Extraterritorial Jurisdiction and State Responsibility' in Van Aken, A. and Motoc, I. (eds). *The European Convention on Human Rights and General International Law*, Oxford University Press.

Kempees, P. (2020) 'Hard Power' and the European Convention on Human Rights, Brill.

Lawson, R. (2011) 'Really out of Sight? Issues of Jurisdiction and Control in Situations of Armed Conflict under the ECHR' in Buyse, A. (ed). *Margins of Conflict: The ECHR and Transitions to and from Armed Conflict*, Intersentia.

Leach, P. (2005) 'The British military in Iraq - The Applicability of the "Espace Juridique" Doctrine under the European Convention on Human Rights', *Public Law* 3, 448–458.

Loucaides, L. (2006) 'Determining the Extra-Territorial effect of the European Convention', *EHRLR* 2(4), 391–407.

Mallory, C. (2020) Human Rights Imperialists. The Extraterritorial Application of the European Convention on Human Rights, Hart.

Milanovic, M. (2011) *Extraterritorial Application of Human Rights*, Oxford University Press.
_______ (2012) 'Al-Skeini and Al-Jedda in Strasbourg', *EJIL* 23(1), 121–139.
_______ (2016) 'Extraterritorial Derogations from Human Rights Treaties' in Armed Conflict' in Bhuta, N. (ed). *The Frontiers of Human Rights*, Oxford University Press.
_______ (2018) 'Jurisdiction and Responsibility: Trends in the Jurisprudence of the Strasbourg Court' in Van Aken, A. and Motoc, I. (eds). *The European Convention on Human Rights and General International Law*, Oxford University Press.

Milanovic, M. and Papic, T. (2018) 'The Applicability of the ECHR in Contested Territories', *ICLQ* 67(4), 779–800.

O'Boyle, M. (2004) 'The European Convention on Human Rights and Extraterritorial Jurisdiction: A Comment on "Life after Banković"' in Coomans, F. and Kamminga, M. (eds). *Extraterritorial Application of Human Rights Treaties*, Intersentia.

Rooney, J. (2016) 'Extraterritorial Derogation from the European Convention on Human Rights in the United Kingdom', *EHRLR* (6), 656–663.

Wallace, S. (2019) *The Application of the European Convention on Human Rights to Military Operations*, Cambridge University Press.

10

Enforcement of extraterritorial human rights obligations in the African human rights system

Anne Oloo and Wouter Vandenhole

Introduction

This chapter focuses on the enforcement of extraterritorial human rights obligations in the African Union by its human rights monitoring bodies. The main human rights instrument of the African Union is the African Charter on Human and Peoples' Rights (ACHPR, Charter or Banjul Charter), which was adopted in 1981 and entered into force in 1986. The Banjul Charter is monitored by the African Commission on Human and Peoples' Rights (ACmHPR or 'the Commission') and the African Court on Human and Peoples' Rights (ACtHPR or 'the Court'). The ACtHPR was only established in 1998 due to lack of support for a judicial enforcement mechanism of the Charter at the time of drafting (Plagis and Riemer 2020, p. 16). It then only became fully operational in 2008 due to the slow ratification of the Protocol establishing the Court (Ssenyonjo 2011, pp. 9–10). At the time of writing, only 30 out of 55 AU member states have accepted the Court's jurisdiction, and only 7 member states have made a declaration allowing individual complaints and NGOs direct access to the Court (African Union 2017). This explains the low number of judgments so far.

The 2014 Malabo Protocol creates an African Court of Justice and Human and Peoples' Rights, thereby merging the ACtHPR with the African Court of Justice, but has not yet entered into force. Another influential human rights instrument is the African Charter on the Rights and Welfare of the Child (ACRWC 1990), which is monitored by the African Committee of Experts on the Rights and Welfare of the Child (ACERWC or 'the Committee').

Our interpretative approach in this chapter can be explained as follows: we seek to identify whether, and if so, which unique African perspective has been adopted on extraterritorial human rights obligations. It is worth noting that unlike other international and regional human rights treaties, neither the ACHPR nor the ACRWC contain any reference to jurisdiction, let alone extraterritorial jurisdiction. Since the legal instruments in themselves neither exclude (through restrictive notions of jurisdiction) nor explicitly include extraterritorial obligations, we look primarily at the (teleological) interpretation given by the monitoring bodies. A comprehensive review of the Commission's, Court's and Committee's work has been undertaken. Since we did not have access to the *travaux préparatoires* – in fact, many documents on the preparatory work are generally inaccessible (Plagis and Riemer 2020, p. 8) – we have not been able to look into

DOI: 10.4324/9781003090014-13

the intentions of the drafters. In order to structure the analysis and to contextualise it within the global ETO discussion, we have sought to draft this chapter in analogy with the other chapters on regional enforcement in this Handbook.

In the first section, we look at the way human rights obligations are attributed to states other than the territorial state. In the second section, we examine the nature and scope of extraterritorial obligations under African human rights instruments. The third section zooms in on the division of responsibility for human rights violations between the territorial and one or more foreign states. The fourth section concludes and offers a forward-looking perspective.

Attribution of obligations (jurisdiction)

The most common concept for attributing human rights obligations is the notion of jurisdiction (see also Chapters 7, 8 and 9 in this Handbook). The starting point in much of human rights law is that jurisdiction is territorial: a state is duty-bound towards those who find themselves on the territory of a state. We refer to this state as the territorial state. At least three models of extraterritorial jurisdiction have been identified and employed by human rights monitoring bodies: the personal model, the spatial model, and the cause-and-effect model. These refer to control over persons, control over territory, or a merely causal relationship (see Chapter 9 in this Handbook; see also Vandenhole 2019).

The literature on extraterritorial jurisdiction in the African system has not reached a consensus, as some have argued for a strictly territorial approach, whereas others have suggested to follow the principles adopted by the European Court of Human Rights (ECtHR) (Pascale 2014, p. 646). This is partly because neither the ACHPR nor the ACRWC contain any reference to jurisdiction, let alone extraterritorial jurisdiction. Article 1 ACHPR simply states that the state parties must recognise and give effect to the rights in the Charter, without any limitation as to legal space or people concerned. In other words, the general obligation incumbent on states does not limit the scope of their obligations under the Charter to their territory, or the legal space of the African Union, for example. Lack of access to the (limited) *travaux préparatoires* also renders it impossible to determine whether this was a deliberate omission at the time of drafting and negotiations (1979–1981). Plagis and Riemer have identified four meta-narratives – sovereignty, African particularity, types of rights, and no expansive list of rights – to elucidate the content of the Charter. These four meta-narratives draw on the 'political and historical circumstances of the drafting process of the Charter' (Plagis and Riemer 2020, p. 6), but are to be distinguished from the 'drivers of context' (Plagis and Riemer 2020, p. 9). Since the already limited *travaux préparatoires* are moreover not easy to access, we will resort to these meta-narratives as a kind of secondary source to understand the intentions of the drafters.

The four meta-narratives do not lead to an unequivocal conclusion regarding the lack of explicit reference to jurisdiction. For instance, sovereignty neither implies nor precludes the deliberate exclusion of extraterritorial obligations, as it was predominantly geared towards independence from the former colonial powers, self-determination, and limited regional accountability and adjudication (Plagis and Riemer 2020, pp. 13–16). This leaves room for a teleological interpretation whereby obligations are not exclusively assigned to the territorial state. The meta-narrative of African particularities also leaves the door open to extraterritorial obligations. One of the intentions of the drafters was to draft a regional instrument that reflected 'an *African* understanding of human rights' (Plagis and Riemer 2020, p. 19). As a consequence, unlike other regional human rights instruments, the ACHPR imposes obligations not only on states individually but also collectively. This, for instance, applies to the right to economic, social, and cultural development (ACHPR, art. 22) and to the right to free disposal of wealth and natural resources, with Article 21(4) ACHPR calling on states to 'individually and collectively exercise the right to free disposal of their wealth and natural resources with a view to strengthening African Unity and solidarity'.

The next section examines the jurisprudence of the regional bodies to determine whether this potential extraterritorial application of the African human rights instruments has materialised and to identify which of the three models of extraterritorial jurisdiction it embodies. However, the dearth of case-law on extraterritorial human rights obligations in the African human rights system makes any strong conclusions premature.

Commission decisions

Early attempts to hold states responsible for extraterritorial violations of rights in the Charter were unsuccessful as they were brought against non-African states and were thus dismissed for lack of jurisdiction of the ACmHPR.[1] This shows the limitations of invoking extraterritorial obligations under a regional human rights instrument. Inevitably, these obligations will only apply to states that belong to the legal space of that regional instrument, in this case, the African Union. Moreover, only states that are party to a treaty are bound by it. Nonetheless, monitoring bodies could choose, even if only by way of obiter dictum, to also include in their analysis extraterritorial obligations of non-state parties.

The jurisprudence of the Commission is thus primarily embodied in three later cases involving African states and in the Commission's General Comment on the right to life:

- The *DRC Invasion* case (ACmHPR 2003b), involving accusations by the DRC of large-scale human rights violations (mass killing of civilians and Congolese military personnel, destruction of property, sexual violence) resulting from the armed activities of the three respondent states (Rwanda, Burundi and Uganda) within Congolese territory.
- The *Burundi Embargo* case (ACmHPR 2003a), involving the imposition of economic sanctions on Burundi by Tanzania, Kenya, Uganda, Rwanda, the DRC (then Zaire), and Zambia, preventing the importation of vital goods (e.g. fuel, school materials).
- The *Al-Assad* case (ACmHPR 2014), on the alleged extraordinary rendition of a Yemeni citizen from Tanzania to Djibouti, where he claimed to have been interrogated by US government agents at Camp Lemonnier.
- The General Comment on the Right to Life (African Commission on Human and Peoples' Rights 2015), which elaborates on the nature and scope of this right in the ACHPR, including issues of extraterritorial obligations. Like other human rights bodies, the Commission adopts and relies on General comments (see ACmHPR 2009b, paras. 209–210) to elaborate and give guidance on specific provisions of the Charter. It is empowered to do so vide Article 45(1)(b) of the Charter, which authorises the African Commission to 'formulate and lay down principles and rules aimed at solving legal problems relating to human and peoples' rights'.

In these cases and general comment, the Commission unequivocally recognised the extraterritorial jurisdiction of states under the personal and spatial model and offered less conclusive suggestions that it may accept principles akin to the cause-and-effect model.

The *DRC Invasion* and *Burundi Embargo* cases also shed light on state parties' views on the extraterritorial application of the ACHPR. Although they involved activities located outside the territories of the respondent states, none of the parties argued against extraterritorial application of the ACHPR. This suggests 'that the African states tend not to reject the principle for which a State Party has to comply with the obligations deriving from the ACHPR even in case of actions which take place or produce effects outside of the national territory' (Pascale 2014, p. 650). This lack of objection could be taken as tacit acceptance by state parties to imposition of extraterritorial human rights obligations under the Charter (Chenwi and Bulto 2018, p. 40).

Military presence and occupation (spatial model)

The *DRC invasion* case is the first instance in which the Commission recognised extraterritorial obligations stemming from military presence and occupation, thereby affirming (though not explicitly) the spatial model. This recognition was, however, perhaps surprisingly, primarily done in passing when, at the admissibility stage, the Commission 't[ook] note that the violations complained of are allegedly being perpetrated by the Respondent states in the territory of the Complainant State' (para. 63). The Commission repeated subsequently at the merits stage, as a matter of fact, 'that there cannot be peace and security "under the conditions created by the Respondent States in the eastern provinces of the Complainant State" (para. 66), which is qualified as occupation (para. 69). While not framed in terms of jurisdiction, this corresponds to the spatial model of extraterritorial jurisdiction. Military action (boots on the ground) and (in this case illegal) occupation of the territory of another state leads to the assignment of human rights obligations with regard to that extraterritorial conduct, given the effective control exercised over parts of the DRC territory (paras. 88 and 91).

As noted above, the three defendant states also did not seem to object to the Commission's jurisdiction. To the contrary, Rwanda and Uganda recognised and justified the presence of their troops in the DRC (paras. 22 and 24).

The *Al-Asad* case further affirmed the Commission's recognition of extraterritorial obligations when states are in effective control over parts of a territory. The Commission drew attention to the difference between the Articles 1 of the International Covenant on Civil and Political Rights (ICCPR) and of the Banjul Charter: 'the former expressly limits the application of the ICCPR to within the territory and jurisdiction of a state Party. The latter by contrast does not expressly limit the application of the Charter within the territory and jurisdiction of State Parties' (para. 134). The Commission further noted that, while the jurisdiction exercised by states is primarily territorial, 'circumstances may obtain in which a state assumes obligations beyond its territorial jurisdiction such as when a state assumes effective control of part of a territory of another state (spatial model of jurisdiction)[…]' (para. 134). In the present case, the Commission relied on the International Court of Justice's (ICJ) decision in the *Armed activities in the Congo case* to hold that occupation by a state of the territory of another state amounts to effective control and triggers the obligations of the occupying state under the charter (ACmHPR 2014, paras. 135, 136, and 139).

Control over individuals (personal model)

In *Al-Asad*, the Commission also explicitly endorsed the personal model, noting that 'circumstances may obtain in which a state assumes obligations beyond its territorial jurisdiction such as […] where the state exercises control or authority over an individual (personal model of jurisdiction)' (para. 134). The Commission emphasised a requirement to establish 'a sufficient connection between the alleged violation and the Respondent State' (para. 135), i.e. 'by proving that he or she was under the territorial jurisdiction or effective control or authority of the Respondent State when the alleged violation occurred' (para. 136). In the case at hand, the complainant failed to demonstrate that he had been 'within the territorial jurisdiction or indeed under the effective control or authority of the Republic of Djibouti' (para. 176), leading the Commission to declare this case inadmissible.

Cause-and-effect jurisdiction

While the previous cases centred on effective control over territory or individuals, the Commission also appears prepared to hold states in violation of the Charter where their actions or those of their authorities have effects outside their territory. While the defendant parties were absolved of any wrongdoing in the *Burundi Embargo* case, the Commission indicated that it would be ready to hold states responsible for acts committed extraterritorially if their actions were found 'disproportionate to the end sought to be achieved or are indiscriminate or lack monitoring mechanisms to ensure that the basic rights of individuals and groups are not jeopardised' (Chenwi and Bulto 2018, p. 38; 2003, para. 75). Thus, had the embargo been disproportionate, indiscriminate, and without monitoring and adjustment (paras. 75–76), the Commission may have held the respondent states responsible, even though they had control over neither Burundian territory nor individuals. This suggests that the Commission may accept that the states that had imposed the sanctions were duty-bearers with regard to the effects caused to the Burundian people, although this is not expressed explicitly.

In its *General comment No. 3 on the right to life (2015)*, the Commission again explicitly referenced the personal and spatial model of extraterritorial jurisdiction (as in ACmHPR 2014) by referencing notions of 'effective authority, power, or control over either the perpetrator or the victim (or the victim's rights)', and of 'effective control over the territory on which the victim's rights are affected, or whether the state engages in conduct which could reasonably be foreseen to result in an unlawful deprivation of life'. This last clause suggests that cause-and-effect may play a role in attributing extraterritorial jurisdiction. In the same vein, the Commission also made the bold claim that 'in any event, customary international law prohibits, without territorial limitation, arbitrary deprivation of life' (para. 14), which can be read as a recognition of another dimension of a cause-and-effect model.

Court

The ACtHPR has hitherto only opined on territorial jurisdiction. In *ACmHPR v. The Republic of Libya* (ACmHPR 2016b), it held that since the events had occurred in a territory under the authority of Libya, which was a party to the ACHPR, the instrument applied 'with respect to Libya and on its territory' (2016, paras 58–59). Although the Court noted this in the context of the examination of its own territorial jurisdiction to hear the case, it reflects (not surprisingly) that territorial jurisdiction of a state is taken for granted.

Committee

The ACERWC has attributed extraterritorial effect to Article 22 ACRWC on children and armed conflict. In its 2020 General Comment on children in situations of conflict (ACERWC 2020), it has stated that the said provision defines States Parties' obligations 'domestically and abroad' (para. 45). With respect to the obligation to ensure respect for international humanitarian law, it considers this obligation applicable not only to the domestic state, but also to 'other states and non-State partners operating in other states' (para. 52). The latter reflects the spatial model. Elsewhere in that same General Comment, it refers to control over territories (para. 70), which reaffirms the spatial model that the Committee seems to envisage.

In sum, whereas the case-law of the African human rights monitoring bodies on extraterritorial obligations is too limited to draw any firm conclusions, the Commission in particular has been willing to go beyond the spatial and personal model commonly found in the case-law of the ECtHR, and has aligned itself with the Human Rights Committee's and inter-American monitoring bodies in (albeit tentatively) applying also the cause-and-effect model of jurisdiction.

Nature and scope of extraterritorial obligations

Commission

The precise contours of extraterritorial obligations remain to be defined by the Commission. Most importantly, while the Commission has recognised that extraterritorial obligations stem from effective control over territory and individuals (and perhaps from cause-and-effect), it is yet to elucidate what effective control entails. This has led some to conclude that the expression 'effective control' in the African system is not used in the '(European)' technical-juridical meaning, perhaps to allow a broad extraterritorial applicability of the Charter (Pascale 2014, p. 648). In the *Al-Asad* case (ACmHPR 2014, para. 134), however, the Commission in outlining effective control situations, references European court decisions seemingly attaching the same meaning as their European counterparts. Defining effective control remains especially crucial when several states are implicated (such as in ACmHPR 2003b) and questions may arise regarding the respective level of control (and therefore perhaps of obligations and responsibility) of each of these states (see also Section 4 below).

The nature and scope of extraterritorial obligations derive from the general obligations incumbent on the state parties to the ACHPR, which are traditionally divided into four levels: the obligation to *respect, protect, promote,* and *fulfil* rights under the Charter (ACmHPR 2016a, para. 68). A violation of rights under the Charter entails a breach of any/of all the four obligations (ACmHPR 2018, para. 127). These four levels of obligations entail both negative and positive duties of the state (ACmHPR 2001, para. 44). The obligation to protect, promote, and fulfil rights constitutes positive duties, while the obligation to respect is a negative duty which also 'obligates states to refrain from measures that would unjustifiably curtail or prevent individuals from enjoying the rights and freedoms' (ACmHPR 2001, para. 45; ACmHPR 2018, para. 93).

The obligation to *respect* rights requires the state to refrain from interfering with the enjoyment of all rights. In both the *Burundi embargo* and *DRC invasion* cases, the respondent states were found to have certainly negative extraterritorial obligations, namely the obligation to respect the rights in the Charter. The respondent states were thus required to *refrain* from any action or omission that would nullify or interfere with the enjoyment of human rights in other (Complainant) states.

In the *DRC invasion case,* Burundi, Rwanda, and Uganda were found in violation of many provisions of the Banjul Charter including Article 2 on non-discrimination as the violations were directed at the victims as result of their national origin, the right to respect for life and integrity (Article 4), the right to dignity (art. 5), the right to freedom of movement (art. 12), the right to property (Article 14), the right to family life (Article 18), and the right use and dispose of wealth and natural resources (Article 21) (paras. 86–89). Additionally, the Commission found the killings, massacres, rapes, and mutilation committed by the three respondent states' armed forces to be in contravention of international humanitarian law (para. 79). The long list of violations found, across categories of civil, political, economic, social, cultural, and collective rights, suggests that the Commission assigns to them as occupying forces obligations with regard to the full range of rights (see in particular 2003b, para. 88). This is in line with the Commission's jurisprudence on the indivisibility and interrelatedness of all rights in the Charter (ACmHPR 2001, para. 44; ACmHPR 2003c, para. 80).

The complaint in the *Burundi Embargo* also involved an alleged breach of negative obligations. Burundi alleged that the imposition of the embargo prevented the importation of essential goods and school materials, and the exportation of tea and coffee, which 'are the country's only source of revenue'. They thus alleged that the respondent states violated the right to life (art. 4), right to education (art. 17(1)), and the right to economic, social, and cultural development (para. 3). Additionally, Burundi claimed that the embargo constituted an interference into its internal affairs thereby infringing on Articles 3(1), (2), and (3) of the OAU Charter. The Commission, though absolving the respondent states of any wrongdoing, showed that it would have found a violation of the Charter where a sanction was determined to be 'excessive, disproportionate, indiscriminate and seeks to achieve ends beyond the legitimate purpose' (ACmHPR 2003a, para. 79).

The obligation to *protect* rights entails the state protecting 'right holders against other subjects by legislation and provision of effective remedies' (ACmHPR ESCR Principles and Guidelines 2010, para. 46). The Commission has held that illegal acts by third parties even when not directly attributable to the state 'can constitute a cause of international responsibility of the state, not because it has itself committed the act in question, but because it has failed to exercise the conscientiousness required to prevent it from happening and for not having been able to take the appropriate measures to pay compensation for the prejudice suffered by the victims' (ACmHPR 2009a, para. 89). In *General comment No. 3 on the right to life*, the Commission thus further elucidates the scope of states' extraterritorial obligations to include the responsibility of the state to hold third parties domiciled in their jurisdiction accountable for any extraterritorial violations of the right to life (para. 18). Similarly, the Commission affirms in General Comment No. 4 on Torture (ACmHPR General Comment no. 4 2017, para. 27) that the obligation to provide an effective remedy and means of reparation extends to victims of torture regardless of where the torture and other ill treatment were committed and that state parties to the charter are 'obliged to prosecute or extradite alleged perpetrators of torture when they are present in any territory under their jurisdiction and to adopt the necessary legislation to make this possible'.

The obligations to *promote* and *fulfil* human rights require states to provide an environment in which individuals can exercise the rights through, for instance, 'promoting tolerance, raising awareness and building infrastructures' (ACmHPR 2001, paras. 45–47). In the *DRC invasion case*, the Commission also seemed to impute positive obligations to the occupying foreign states, by arguing that 'the general duty of states to individually or collectively *ensure* the exercise of the right to development' (emphasis added) had been violated (2003b, para. 95).

The jurisprudence of the Commission shows that not only does it assign the four-layer of obligations (to respect, protect, promote, and fulfil) to states Parties for their extraterritorial conduct but that states' extraterritorial obligations extend to the full range of rights under the Charter. The ECtHR has most clearly spelt out that the scope of obligations varies with the model of jurisdiction: under the personal model, the obligations are limited to the rights at stake, whereas under the spatial model, the full range of rights applies. The African Commission has clearly endorsed the latter approach.

Court

The ACtHPR has not yet had the opportunity to pronounce itself on the nature and scope of extraterritorial obligations. Plans to merge the ACtHPR with the Court of Justice of Human and Peoples' Rights may provide it with more occasions to develop its jurisprudence on the matter (Chenwi and Bulto 2018, p. 36). The merged court once in operation will have jurisdiction to try transboundary crimes such as trafficking in persons, drugs and hazardous wastes, terrorism, money laundering, illicit exploitation of natural resources, and mercenary (Malabo Protocol, art. 46C). Transboundary harmful conduct by states, such as transboundary pollution (ICJ 2008, para. 37), may trigger states' extraterritorial obligations (See Altwicker 2018; and Boyle 2012).

Committee

The ACERWC has argued that the extraterritorial positive obligation to ensure respect for international humanitarian law extends to 'both civil and political rights, and economic and social rights' (GC armed conflict, para. 52, footnote 16). For example, it considers the positive obligation to protect the right to health applicable in instances 'where children have been displaced to other states or territories where a state or receiving state has control' (GC armed conflict, para. 70).

Division of responsibility for violations

So far, the question of division of responsibility between the territorial state and foreign states, or between foreign states, has only arisen in cases before the Commission.

In the *DRC Invasion* case, Uganda argued, while referring to the joint case against itself, Rwanda, and Burundi, that '[t]here is never group responsibility for violations' (para. 30). The Commission did not take up that point. In the *Burundi Embargo* case though, which considered a complaint lodged against six states that had imposed an embargo, the Commission did not seem to reject group responsibility as a matter of principle. Of course, since it did not find a violation, there was also no need to clarify whether there was shared responsibility, nor the need to divide responsibility between the territorial state (Burundi) and the sanctioning states, or between the sanctioning states. More generally, the division of responsibility for violations of extraterritorial obligations remains an underdeveloped question (see Vandenhole 2015).

Conclusions

The relative paucity of cases pertaining to extraterritorial obligations in the African system makes premature any definitive conclusion regarding the adoption of a uniquely African perspective by its human rights enforcement bodies. This especially applies to the Court and the Committee, as only the Commission has repeatedly pronounced itself on extraterritorial obligations. These decisions have however had a far-reaching impact on the work of the Commission, informing its guidelines on counterterrorism (ACmHPR Principles and Guidelines on Counterterrorism 2015), ESC rights (ACmHPR ESCR Principles and Guidelines 2010), and its approach to protecting the right to life (ACmHPR General Comment no. 3 2015).

The jurisprudence of the Commission does not reveal a uniquely African perspective, so that the meta-narrative of African particularities does not seem to have much relevance for extraterritorial obligations. The models of extraterritoriality that it endorses are greatly aligned with the European approach, mirroring its terms (for instance, by adopting the concepts of personal and spatial model) and envisioning extraterritoriality as an exception to the default principle of territoriality. However, there are also suggestions that the Commission may be open to a cause-and-effect understanding of extraterritoriality, thus also potentially aligning with the approach of the Inter-American monitoring bodies and Human Rights Committee which have gone beyond the personal and spatial models used in the European approach. While not reflecting a uniquely African perspective, the latter takes it beyond the narrow European approach.

One avenue through which the African system could distinguish itself is by further developing the relationship between extraterritoriality and the collective duties found in the ACHPR, which are recognised as its distinguishing features and reflect the meta-narrative of African particularities. This would be consonant with the emphasis on these collective duties in the Commission's principles and guidelines (for instance, on counterterrorism). The *Maastricht Principles* distinguish between two types of extraterritorial obligations: extraterritorial obligations sensu stricto, as discussed above in this chapter, but also obligations of a global character. Obligations of a global character require 'action, separately and jointly through international cooperation, to realize human rights universally' (Principle 8, *Maastricht Principles* 580). The notion of collective duties in the provisions of the Charter can help to conceptually develop a notion of regional obligations in parallel to the notion of global obligations that can be found in the *Maastricht Principles*. Regional obligations could be said to require individual and collective action from African states to realise collective human rights regionally. Such regional obligations, for instance, with regard to the right to free disposal of their wealth and natural resources (ACHPR, Article 21), could help to strengthen protection against predatory exploitation of natural resources by state companies of other African states, or by companies that are incorporated in other African states. The regional obligation to ensure the exercise of the right to development would put all African states under an obligation to collectively ensure the right to development.

The lack of explicit jurisdiction clause in the ACHPR additionally provides an opportunity to move beyond existing approaches to extraterritoriality, as no territorial limit or definition of territoriality is set in stone. The willingness of states Parties to accept extraterritorial obligations bides well for the development of the doctrine of extraterritorial obligations in the African system. It is now up to the African monitoring bodies to fully exploit these possibilities in their case-law. Nonetheless, much of the interference on the African continent stems from non-African states or companies that are domiciled in non-African states. These issues can only be addressed under UN or other regional human rights treaties.

Note

1. These include ACmHPR 1988b; ACmHPR 1990b; ACmHPR 1988c; ACmHPR 1990a; ACmHPR 1988a.)

References

African Charter on Human and Peoples' Rights (1981) CAB/LEG/67/3 Rev. 5, 21 I.L.M. 58 (Banjul Charter).

African Commission on Human and People's Rights (ACmHPR) (1988a) *Centre for the Independence of Judges and Lawyers v. Yugoslavia*, Communication 3/88.

_______ (1988b) *Committee for the Defence of Political Prisoners v. Bahrain*, Communication 7/88.

_______ (1988c) *Iheanyichukwu A Ihebereme v. USA*, Communication 2/88.

_______ (1990a) *Georges Eugene v. USA*, Communication 37/90.

_______ (1990b) *Wesley Parish v. Indonesia*, Communication 38/90.

_______ (2001) *The Social and Economic Rights Action Centre and the Centre for Economic and Social Rights v. Nigeria*, Communication No. 155/96.

_______ (2003a) *Democratic Republic of Congo v. Burundi, Rwanda and Uganda,* Communication 227/99.

_______ (2003b) *Association pour la sauvegarde de la paix au Burundi v. Kenya, Uganda, Rwanda, Tanzania, Zaire (DRC), Zambia*, Communication 157/96.

_______ (2003c) *Purohit et al. v. Gambia*, Communication 241/2001.

_______ (2009a) *Association of Victims of Post Electoral Violence and Interights v. Cameroon*, Communication 272/2003.

_______ (2009b) *Sudan Human Rights Organisation & Centre on Housing Rights and Evictions (COHRE) v. Sudan*, Communication 279/03- 296/05.

_______ (2010) Principles and Guidelines on the Implementation of Economic, Social And Cultural Rights in the African Charter on Human and Peoples' Rights, available at https://www.achpr.org/public/Document/file/English/achpr_instr_guide_draft_esc_rights_eng.pdf.

_______ (2014) *Mohammed Abdullah Saleh Al-Asad v. the Republic of Djibouti,* Communication 383/10.

_______ (2015a) Principles and Guidelines on Human and Peoples' Rights While Countering Terrorism in Africa, available at https://www.achpr.org/legalinstruments/detail?id=9.

_______ (2015b) GC 3 on The African Charter On Human And Peoples' Rights: The Right To Life (Article 4), Adopted during Its 57th Ordinary Session.

_______ (2016a) *Organisation Mondiale Contre la Torture et Ligue de la Zone Afrique pour la Défense des Droits des Enfants et Elèves (pour le compte de Céline) v. DRC.*

_______ (2016b) *The African Commission on Human and Peoples' Rights v. Libya*, Communication 002/2013.

_______ (2017) GC 4 on the African Charter on Human and Peoples' Rights: The Right to Redress for Victims of Torture and Other Cruel, Inhuman or Degrading Punishment or Treatment (Article 5), Adopted at the 21st Extra-Ordinary Session, available at https://www.achpr.org/legalinstruments/detail?id=60.

_______ (2018) *Hossam Ezzat & Rania Enayet (represented by Egyptian Initiative for Personal Rights & INTERIGHTS) v. The Arab Republic of Egypt*, Communication 355/07.

African Committee of Experts on the Rights and Welfare of the Child (ACERWC) (2020) General Comment on Article 22 of the African Charter on the Rights and Welfare of the Child: Children in Situations of Conflict, available at https://www.pulp.up.ac.za/edocman/journals/AHRY_2020/Charissa_2020.pdf (19 July 2021).

African Union (2014) Protocol on Amendments to the Protocol on the Statute of the African Court of Justice and Human Right (Adopted June 2014, Not yet in Force) (Malabo Protocol), available at https://au.int/sites/default/files/treaties/36398-treaty-0045_-_protocol_on_amendments_to_the_protocol_on_the_statute_of_the_african_court_of_justice_and_human_rights_e.pdf. (19 July 2021)

_______ (2017) List of Countries Which Have Signed, Ratified/Acceded to the Protocol to the African Charter on Human and Peoples' Rights on the Establishment of an African Court on Human and Peoples' Rights, available at https://au.int/sites/default/files/treaties/36393-sl-protocol_to_the_african_charter_on_human_and_peoplesrights_on_the_estab.pdf (19 July 2021).

Altwicker, T. (2018), 'Transnationalizing Rights: International Human Rights Law in Cross-Border Contexts', *European Journal of International Law* 29(2), 581–606.

Boyle, A. (2012) 'Human Rights and the Environment: Where Next?', *European Journal of International Law* 23(3), 613–642.

Chenwi, L. and Bulto, T.S. (2018) 'Extraterritoriality in the African Regional Human Rights System from a Comparative Perspective' in Chenwi, L. and Bulto, T.S. (eds). *Extraterritorial Human Rights Obligations from an African Perspective*, Intersentia.

Giuseppe, P. (2014) 'Extraterritorial Applicability of the African Charter on Human and Peoples' Rights', *Diritti Umani e Diritto Internazionale* (3), 644–653.

International Court of Justice (ICJ) (2008) *Case Concerning Aerial Herbicide Spraying (Ecuador v. Colombia) (application by Ecuador). I.C.J. Reports* 2013, p. 278.

Maastricht Principles on Extraterritorial Obligations of States in the Area of Economic, Social and Cultural Rights.

Pascale, G. (2014), 'Extraterritorial Applicability of the African Charter on Human and Peoples' Rights', *Diritti umani e diritto internazionale* 3, 644–653.

Plagis, M.A. and Riemer, L. (2020) 'From Context to Content of Human Rights: The Drafting History of the African Charter on Human and Peoples' Rights and the Enigma of Article 7', *Journal of the History of International Law/Revue d'histoire Du Droit International*, December, 1–33.

Ssenyonjo, M. (2011) *The African Regional Human Rights System: 30 Years After the African Charter on Human and Peoples' Rights*, Martinus Nijhoff Publishers.

Tilmann, A. (2018) 'Transnationalizing Rights: International Human Rights Law in Cross-Border Contexts', *European Journal of International Law* 29(2), 581–606.

Vandenhole, W. (2015) 'Obligations and Responsibility in a Plural and Diverse Duty-Bearer Human Rights Regime' in Vandenhole, W. (ed). *Challenging Territoriality in Human Rights Law Building Blocks for a Plural and Diverse Duty-Bearer Regime*, Routledge.

_______ (2019) 'The "J" Word: Driver or Spoiler of Change in Human Rights Law?' in Allen, S., Costelloe, D., Fitzmaurice, M., Gragl, P. and Guntrip, E. (eds). *The Oxford Handbook of Jurisdiction in International Law*, Oxford University Press.

Part III

Migration and refugee protection

11

Extraterritorial human rights obligations in regard to refugees and migrants

Thomas Gammeltoft-Hansen[1]

Introduction

Extraterritorial human obligations (ETOs) have always played a particular role in regard to refugees and migrants. As individuals by definition outside their countries of origin, this naturally applies in regard to their home states, with whom jurisdiction based on nationality remains an essential link. But ETOs may also arise in regard to foreign states, whether in the context of prospective access, measures of expulsion or relocation to third states or global responsibilities to assist refugees more generally.[2] Within international refugee law, in particular, discussions about the cornerstone principle of *non-refoulement* have always been characterised by geographic boundary-drawing. As Atle Grahl-Madsen bluntly notes in his seminal commentary to the 1951 Refugee Convention:

> It must be remembered that the Refugee Convention to a certain extent is a result of the pressure by humanitarian interested persons on Governments, and that public opinion is apt to concern itself much more with the individual who has set foot on the nation's territory and thus is within the power of the national authorities, than with the people only seen as shadows or moving figures "at the other side of the fence." The latter have not materialized as human beings, and it is much easier to shed responsibility for a mass of unknown people than for the individual whose fate one has to decide.
>
> *(Grahl-Madsen 1963)*

Writing in 1963, Grahl-Madsen's concern was whether the *non-refoulement* principle applied to situations where refugees presented themselves at, but had not yet crossed, the physical border of a state (a question he, alongside other contemporary commentators, answered in the negative). He could not possibly have known how prescient his description would seem today. Since the mid-1980s, developed states have routinely attempted to stop unauthorised migrants and refugees in their tracks, applying ever more sophisticated forms of extraterritorial, or transnational, migration control and deterrence (Gammeltoft-Hansen 2011).[3] These policies are designed exactly to keep migrants and refugees in the 'shadows' and avoid triggering the human rights obligations of extraterritorially acting or sponsoring states.

DOI: 10.4324/9781003090014-15

For years, these practices went largely unchallenged. As international legal regimes without dedicated courts or supervisory bodies, interpretation of international migration and refugee law is principally left to domestic courts and governments themselves, many of which have shown a reluctance to apply foreigners' rights extraterritorially. During past decades, however, international human rights courts and bodies – and their growing jurisprudence in regard to extraterritorial obligations – have come to play an increasingly important role in this issue area. So much, in fact, that individual cases regarding *non-refoulement* are the single most prominent issue confronting UN human rights committees (Cali, Costello and Cunningham 2020). International human rights law, to paraphrase Dembour, has helped pull migrants and refugees out of the shadows and re-materialise as humans in the legal sense (Dembour 2015).

This chapter sets out by reviewing the 'human rights turn' in regard to transnational migration control (Section 2). It charts the early responses to transnational migration control based on international refugee law and the wider impact of growing human rights litigation on state practice and policy development. It secondly argues that, the historical importance of ETOs in this area notwithstanding, we may be seeing the beginning of a counter-progressive development, in which at least some international human rights institutions are facing increasing political pressure to take a more restrictive line in refugee and migrant cases (Section 3). This not only has implications for a number of currently pending and important cases concerning human rights responsibility related to transnational migration control, but it should also prompt practitioners and scholars looking to promote ETO protection of migrants and refugees to critically rethink existing approaches. To this end, the final part of the article outlines two different, largely complementary approaches to respectively *reframe* and *redirect* extraterritorial human claims in the context of transnational migration control (Section 4).

Human rights responses to transnational migration control

Migration control features among some of the earliest forms of transnational law enforcement. High seas interdiction policies were pioneered by the United States in the 1990s and quickly spread to other parts of the world (Ghezelbash 2018). The use of offshore detention facilities stretches back even further. Decades before the 'war on terror', the United States began detaining Haitian and other boat refugees at the Guantanamo base in Cuba (Dastyari 2015). The deployment of immigration officers at foreign airports began in the 1980s and quickly spread across European and other developed countries (Bigo 2002).

Enlisting private actors as part of transnational migration control similarly has a long history. In its modern incarnation, the concept of carrier sanctions emerged in the 1980s (Cruz 1995), but the imposition of fines on shipmasters for bringing in unlawful migrants or failing to perform pre-boarding screenings can be traced back as far as to the 18th century. Today, private actors perform a broad range of functions related to transnational migration management – from handling visa claims, to operating offshore detention centres (Gammeltoft-Hansen 2015).

The early onset of these practices similarly shaped the outlook of advocacy organisations and scholars in terms of how to respond to transnational migration control. Initially, legal arguments centred on the 1951 Refugee Convention itself (e.g. Vedsted-Hansen 1988; Goodwin-Gill 1994). Central debates revolved around the geographical scope of the *non-refoulement* principle and the implications of the non-penalisation principle. In some instances, this has led to evidently expansive interpretations. For example, Article 31 of the Refugee Convention prohibiting states from penalising refugees for irregularly entering their territory has been argued to equally encompass financial penalties imposed on airline companies in the context of carrier sanctions (Feller 1989).

The absence of a dedicated international court or other supranational supervisory mechanism in the field of migration and refugee law further meant that concrete legal challenges to transnational migration control were largely dependent on national avenues for adjudication. Domestic courts have, in several instances, played an important role in upholding refugee and migrant rights as part of transnational migration control.[4] Yet, national courts from key states implementing transnational migration control have so far been reluctant to extend protection under the Refugee Convention to situations involving extraterritorial action. Thus, despite broad scholarly consensus and UNHCR's support for the position that the *non-refoulement* principle enshrined in Article 33 of the Refugee Convention applies extraterritorially wherever a state exercises jurisdiction, higher courts in the United States, the United Kingdom and Australia have all adopted more restrictive interpretations.[5] Challenging the long-standing involvement of private actors in transnational migration control through domestic courts has proven equally difficult (Gammeltoft-Hansen 2017),[6] leaving long-standing and pervasive measures such as carrier sanctions virtually unchallenged from a rights-based perspective (Scholten and Minderhoud 2008).

Since the 1990s, however, the so-called 'human rights turn' in migration and refugee law scholarship has gradually changed this situation. Framing arguments against migration control through international human rights law provided refugee advocates access to an array of regional and international litigative avenues never entrusted to the international refugee and migration law regimes themselves. Consequently, several important cases relating to migrants and refugees have been heard before regional human rights courts and different UN human rights committees.

Specific human rights litigation has in several instances forced states to either abandon or substantially adjust both domestic and transnational migration control policies. This applies to, for instance, policies of excising coastal territory or designating so-called 'international zones'.[7] Similarly, the European Court of Human Rights has repeatedly challenged governments' use of 'safe third country' notions and time limits in asylum procedures.[8] International and regional human rights institutions have further played an important role in addressing interdiction policies involving maritime patrols in international or third country waters.[9] Last, but not least, governments' own interpretation of extraterritorial human rights obligations has been argued to pre-emptively block earlier proposals to outsource asylum processing (Garlick 2006).

During this period, the growing body of general ETO jurisprudence may further be seen to support similar shifts in interpretation within, for example, international refugee law. One of the most remarkable developments of international refugee law concerns the interpretation of the geographical scope of the *non-refoulement* principle. Unlike most other Articles in the Convention, no specific delimitation *ratione loci* is set for Article 33 of the 1951 Refugee Convention. Early commentaries on the convention have thus maintained a strictly territorial interpretation (as in the case of Grahl-Madsen cited above), while some later scholars have vice versa argued the principle to be geographically unlimited in its application (Lauterpacht and Bethlehem 2003). Today, however, the dominant interpretation reflects a jurisdictional *ratione loci* in line with general human rights law (Gammeltoft-Hansen 2011). Taking on a somewhat surrogate role across regimes, the European Court of Human Rights has similarly suggested that international refugee law, notably the principle of *non-refoulement*, must be observed when states exercise extraterritorial jurisdiction through migration control.[10]

A human rights retreat in regard to migrant and refugee rights?

As new and important cases are being brought forward to regional human rights courts and UN bodies, one could of course expect this dynamic to continue. Several factors, however, suggest that the position of migrant and refugee rights issues within the larger ambit of extraterritorial human rights obligations may be changing once again.

First, early claims concerning transnational migration control followed in the footsteps of broader ETO developments. In the *Hirsi* case, for example, litigators were able to rely on recent jurisprudence concerning other types of transnational law enforcement in order to establish Italy's jurisdiction over migrants and refugees brought onboard government vessels on the high seas.[11] In contrast, recent examples of transnational migration control are increasingly premised on shifting enforcement responsibilities to third state authorities and/or private actors – sometimes dubbed 'contactless control' (Moreno-Lax and Giuffré 2019) – specifically intended to eclipse any jurisdictional links to the sponsoring state. The current generation of transnational migration control schemes will thus require human rights judiciaries to break new ground in substantive terms as opposed to simply applying an evolutive approach to existing precedent related to ETOs and extraterritorial human rights jurisdiction. As argued elsewhere, principled arguments exist for holding sponsoring states responsible for, for example, their complicity in human rights violations committed by partner states (Gammeltoft-Hansen and Hathaway 2015). Yet, this form of responsibility has still to be applied as a matter of human rights case law. Doing so would set a much wider precedent across a variety of other issue areas.

Second, the call for human rights judiciaries to intervene comes at a time when many of these institutions face substantial political backlash, often specifically related to their progressive role in regard to migrant and refugee rights. As early as 2011, the Council of Europe member states noted in the Izmir Declaration, '[t]he Court is not an immigration Appeals Tribunal or a Court of fourth instance'. The statement was repeated in 2018 in the draft Copenhagen Declaration, along with proposals that the Court generally defer to domestic asylum and immigration procedures and 'where these are seen to operate fairly and with respect for human rights, avoid intervening except in the most exceptional circumstances'.[12] In 2017, the United States for the first time refused to attend a hearing before the Inter-American Commission on Human Rights concerning the US immigration ban policy. UN treaty bodies have faced similar criticism from governments, and even national human rights institutions, for their role in regard to *non-refoulement* cases.[13]

If and how this will impact the direction of human rights institutions when responding to transnational migration control remains to be seen. On the one hand, the politicised nature of this issue area may be exactly what drives judiciaries to dynamically develop interpretation in order to ensure the continued effectiveness of human rights in the face of new restrictive measures towards migrants and refugees (Wilde 2017; Gammeltoft-Hansen 2014). On the other hand, the general pushback against supranational human rights institutions may equally push judiciaries to become politically risk-averse, avoiding borderline cases at the admissibility stage and shying away from legal reasoning likely to establish wider precedents (Tan and Gammeltoft-Hansen 2020).

The most recent European case law concerning transnational migration control may indeed suggest a more restrictive trend among international courts. In the case of *MN and Others*, the Grand Chamber of the European Court of Human Rights refused the applicant's argument that a Syrian family's humanitarian visa application at the Belgian embassy in Beirut triggered the state's human rights law obligations, declaring the case inadmissible.[14] A similar case concerning the extension of humanitarian visas to Syrian refugees was rejected by the Court of Justice of the European Union in 2017 – notably ruling against the opinion of the Advocate-General.[15] The European Court of Human Rights further dismissed the applicants in *ND and NT v. Spain*, arguing that the prohibition against collective expulsions did not apply as the claimants had placed themselves in danger and entered illegally by climbing the fence between Morocco and the Spanish enclave of Melilla, as opposed to making use of supposed 'legal pathways' available to them.[16]

Just as migrant rights claims have been able to benefit from the wider ETO case law developments, a more restrictive turn in this issue area may ultimately come to impact ETO jurisprudence more generally. *MN and Others* is a case in point. While the Court acknowledged Belgium's exercise of public powers in taking a decision on the applicant's visa application, it deemed this to be insufficient to trigger extraterritorial jurisdiction (para. 122), thereby limiting the scope of the 'public powers' doctrine developed in *Al-Skeini and Other v. United Kingdom*. Secondly, the emphasis on the exceptional nature of extraterritorial jurisdiction appears to be particularly pointed in this judgment. The Grand Chamber does not simply insert the usual disclaimer that a state's jurisdictional competence for the purpose of Article 1 is 'primarily territorial' (para. 98). It also revives the old all-or-nothing approach set out in *Bankovic*, arguing that any extraterritorial exercise of jurisdiction is 'as a general rule, defined and limited by the sovereign territorial rights of the other relevant states' (para. 99). This appears to be the first time that the Court cites this particular passage from *Bankovic*, and it is bound to raise questions in relation to the Court's subsequent jurisprudence, which generally applies a less rigid understanding of the concept.

It is still too early to pass judgment on the general direction of international human rights courts and bodies based on these few European cases. Yet, these cases underscore that the trajectory of international human rights jurisprudence in this area is hardly unidirectional. In this context, it is worth reminding ourselves that the embrace of migrant rights by international human rights institutions was never a foregone conclusion. As Dembour argues in respect to the European human rights system, '[...]migrants were hardly a consideration in the newly created human rights scheme. The Convention was not meant to sustain their rights' (2015, p. 2). The jurisprudence establishing extraterritorial effect of Article 3 was initially developed not via migrant cases but in the context of extradition of a German citizen to the United States, where the Court found that the risk of the 'death-row phenomenon' would constitute inhuman and degrading treatment.[17] As Gammeltoft-Hansen and Madsen conclude, 'the discreet turn towards migration law in Strasbourg occurs rather late, and generally after the member states had started developing their own legislation in this area' (Gammeltoft-Hansen and Madsen 2021). As immigration legislations and practices are now developing in a more restrictive direction, the political pressure is equally mounting on human rights institutions to follow suit.

Forward-looking strategies for ETOs in the context of transnational migration control

If the current normative trajectory for ETO protection of migrants and refugees is less certain, transnational migration control policies are meanwhile developing in a manner that risks eclipsing accountability under international refugee and human rights law altogether. Drawing on different strands of recent scholarship and legal development, this final section thus outlines two different sets of approaches for future research and legal actions in this area.

Reframing ETOs in the context of migration control

Perhaps the most immediate response to the situation sketched out above is to critically engage with and seek to *reframe* dominant understandings of current ETO jurisprudence. In the context of migration control, extraterritorial jurisdiction for the purpose of human rights responsibility is generally assumed to arise whenever a state exercises effective control over either individuals or territory. Within the ETO literature, however, the exact contours of what constitutes 'effective control' varies according to interpretive outlook, and different variants, such as 'functional jurisdiction' (Moreno-Lax 2020; De Boer 2014; Gammeltoft-Hansen 2011), 'public powers jurisdiction' (Gammeltoft-Hansen and Hathaway 2015) and 'effective control over situations' (Altwicker 2018), have been advanced by individual scholars.

Even within these more expanded notions of jurisdiction, however, several recent instances of cooperative deterrence are likely to fall outside its scope. By design these schemes place the emphasis on control being carried out not just within the territory but also at the hands of the authorities of partner states, thereby hoping to insulate sponsoring states from any direct human rights responsibility. Other scholars have thus examined the possibility of applying the general law on state responsibility, including notions such as 'complicity', 'direction and control' and 'shared responsibility' to such instances of cooperative deterrence (Pijnenburg 2018; Tan 2017; Gammeltoft-Hansen and Hathaway 2015; den Heijer 2013). Yet, the thresholds for applying these forms of attribution and derived responsibility are often high and as a matter of practice much less established within human rights jurisprudence.

In a recent article, Moreno-Lax (2020) thus argues for a model of 'functional jurisdiction' in human rights law intended to overcome these obstacles. Like previous conceptions of 'functional jurisdiction' (e.g. Gammeltoft-Hansen 2011), it takes as a starting point the relationship between state authority and responsibility as fundamental and inseparable. The concept of jurisdiction, in this sense, 'has an essential role to play in arbitrating between duty, capability, and desirability of compliance by any specific state vis-à-vis any specific human rights holder' (Moreno-Lax 2020, p. 396). Although jurisdiction cannot simply be presumed beyond the state's territory, it nonetheless follows directly from a state's exercise of 'public powers', whether or not acting *ultra vires* (p. 413).[18]

Her argument is closely linked to a concrete pending case, *S.S. and Others v. Italy*, lodged by the Global Legal Action Network (GLAN) and concerning Libyan-Italian interdiction cooperation in the Mediterranean. This interdiction scheme was specifically designed to eclipse the precedent set in *Hirsi v. Italy*, placing the Libyan Coast Guard as opposed to Italian authorities in charge of effectuating interceptions. It is thus a key example of the kind of cooperative migration control detailed above, in which enforcement responsibilities are increasingly delegated to third state authorities. However, according to Moreno-Lax, a basis for extraterritorial jurisdiction can nonetheless be established based on a combination of three factors. Firstly, despite its more hands-off approach, Italy nonetheless had a decisive impact in regard to applicants by coordinating operations from its national Maritime Rescue Coordination Centre in Rome and directing intercepted migrants and refugees to be returned to Libya. Secondly, Italy maintained significant influence over the Libyan Coast Guard, having actively worked to revive its authority and (together with the EU) providing substantial material support, financing and capacity-building. Last, but not least, the plaintiffs in *S.S. v. Italy* argue that Italian authorities continued to exercise 'overall control' of the Libyan Coast Guard's operations, making the Libyan a 'subrogate Italian proxy for interdiction and pull-back at sea' (Moreno-Lax 2020, p. 412). She argues that these three elements, taken together, may suffice to establish Italy's jurisdiction in the functional sense.

A second response in this category involves taking a step back and re-examine other bases for extraterritorial human rights jurisdiction useful in the context of transnational migration. One track, long recognised within both human rights and other areas of international law, concerns extraterritorial effects jurisdiction (Gammeltoft-Hansen 2018; Kessing 2017). As a matter of human rights law, extraterritorial effects jurisdiction may come about as a result of actions taking place within a state's own territory, leading to human rights violations on the territory of another state. In contrast to other bases for extraterritorial jurisdiction, there is thus no requirement that the responsible state itself acts extraterritorially or exercises effective control over the individuals or territory in question.

Within international human rights law, extraterritorial effects jurisdiction has been applied in instances where either executive or legislative measures were argued to have 'direct and immediate' effects beyond their territory. In *Andreou,* for example, the European Court of Human Rights held that shooting down a demonstrator across the border inside the UN-controlled demilitarised zone in Cypris amounted to jurisdiction, noting that 'even though the applicant sustained her injuries in territory over which Turkey exercised no control, the opening of fire on the crowd from close range, which was the direct and immediate cause of those injuries, was such that the applicant must be regarded as within the jurisdiction of Turkey'.[19] The UN Human Rights Committee has similarly expressed its concern that, for example, domestically implemented surveillance programs or government measures, such as the issuing of a Fatwa, may violate the human rights of individuals in other territories.[20] The extraterritorial effects doctrine is moreover a well-established principle of public international law[21] and a central concept in, for example, international environmental law.

As Kessing (2017) points out, the extraterritorial effects doctrine remains comparatively less developed in international human rights law. Whether a 'direct and immediate' link can be established between European or other Global North states and human rights violations suffered by refugees and migrants as part of transnational migration control depends on the individual case. Yet, it is not inconceivable that human rights judiciaries or treaty bodies would find that a combination of funding, training and directing migration control performed by third state authorities would fall within the ambit of the extraterritorial effects jurisdiction; and the extraterritorial effects doctrine is thus something that merits further research and testing also within an ETO approach more generally.

Third and finally, some scholars have attempted to more fundamentally reframe existing ETO approaches to transnational migration control by appealing to the normative foundations or *telos* of human rights law. As Dupuy (1998) has argued, human rights can never be entirely reduced to positive international law but also, always remain a 'normative ideal' which invariably impacts interpretation. In a similar vein, Mann (2016) takes the entire phenomenon of transnational migration control to construct a theory of human rights based on the encounter between the 'universal boatperson' and state officials. According to Mann, '[h]uman rights aren't naturally given' but rather 'the result of active assertions of rights by persons who have no rights within existing states' (pp. 58–59). The principle of *non-refoulement* is thus essential not only to refugee law, but to help 'shed light on the moral and legal structure of the entire normative universe of human rights' (p. 10).

Transnational migration control in this sense serves as a kind of developer fluid for ETOs more generally. While Mann's universal boatperson formally remains outside of state authority and beyond the ordinary social-contractual obligations maintained by states, the very encounter nonetheless triggers a human rights dilemma for state authorities. The legal geography of this particular type of encounter allows us to see this more clearly as the sea 'opens a crack between the territorial jurisdictions established by sovereignty' (p. 25). Through an exegesis of major political crises surrounding boat migration since the Second World War, Mann shows that even the most disenfranchised are never without political agency, and that the very act of putting one's life at risk crossing the sea imposes an undeniable human rights claim upon the sovereign.

Contrary to the strategies reflected above, Mann's approach suggests that challenging transnational migration control from a strictly positive human rights law perspective is ultimately a rear-guard battle. Despite multiple cases of successful strategic litigation and pushing forward the law on extraterritorial jurisdiction, transnational migration control has continued unabated. For every new judgment, migration management is adapting and itself developing (Gammeltoft-Hansen 2014; Mann 2013). As Mann argues, Strasbourg has at best made border control in the Mediterranean more costly for European states. If there is any hope for overcoming this problematic dynamic, the human rights claims forwarded in regard to transnational migration control must dig deeper both inside and outside the court room.

Redirecting ETOs in the context of migration control

Following on from the above, a second set of strategies instead seek to promote accountability related to transnational migration control by *redirecting* human rights claims institutionally, across regimes as well as geographically.

Although recent case law suggests that key regional human rights courts have begun to approach migration cases more cautiously, the international landscape of human rights institutions is hardly uniform. As detailed above, not least the UN human rights committees have taken a more active role and generally remain more open to migration cases. *Non-refoulement* today constitutes the single most petitioned issue across all UN human rights committees, with the vast majority specifically concerning asylum claims rejected at the national level (Cali et al. 2020, p. 360). But the committees have also heard several cases specifically related to transnational migration control. In *JHA v. Spain*, for example, the Committee Against Torture found Spain to have exercised jurisdiction both during interception of migrants off the West African coast and 'throughout the identification and repatriation process' during which the applicants were detained at a fishing plant in Mauritania.[22] Although the individual decisions issued by these human rights bodies are not binding as a matter of international law, their quasi-judicial function has nonetheless been described as 'soft courts' (Cali et al. 2020) and in many cases leads national authorities to overturn or at least re-examine their decisions.

In their comparative analysis of the committee's migration jurisprudence, Cali, Costello and Cunningham further argue that several of the committees apply a decidedly more expansive interpretation of extraterritorial jurisdiction as compared to other international human rights institutions (2020, p. 363 ff.). This applies not only to the threshold criteria for establishing jurisdiction as a result of a state's own authorities acting abroad, but also in respect to, for example, effects-based jurisdiction mentioned above. The Committee on the Elimination of Discrimination against Women, for example, maintains that states remain 'responsible for all their actions affecting human rights, regardless of whether the affected persons are in their territories'.[23] In their joint general comment, the Committee on the Rights of the Child and the Committee on the Rights of Migrant Workers have similarly underscored that the *non-refoulement* principle applies everywhere a state exercises full or even partial jurisdiction, 'including in international waters or other transit zones where states put in place migration control mechanisms'.[24]

But human rights accountability in the context of transnational migration may also be pursued through other avenues, not directly linked to international human rights law. In recent years, a number of scholars have called attention to the possibility of establishing responsibility for migration control in relation to legal regimes and adjudicatory fora pertaining to a range of national, regional and international regimes. At the international and regional levels, this includes, for example, international criminal law (Kalpouzos 2020), EU public procurement law (Spijkerboer and Steyger 2019) and the law of the sea (Papastavridis 2020). At the domestic level, tort law, constitutional law and non-discrimination law have each been important regimes for establishing responsibility in cases involving, for example, privatisation or outsourcing of migration control (Tan and Gammeltoft-Hansen 2020).

While neither of these regimes is specifically geared towards migrants and refugees, they nonetheless provide a range of alternative inroads for thinking about and practically pursuing accountability in the context of transnational migration control. Pushing beyond the 'human rights turn' in this way may further side-step some of the current legal and political constraints facing current litigation in regard to transnational migration control before general human rights courts. Tort cases, for example, typically involve a lower standard of proof and may thus constitute a 'powerful means of providing redress for (human rights) wrongs' particular in cases concerning delegation of migration control responsibilities (Holly 2020).

One example of such an approach has been championed by Mann (2020). Drawing on broader work linking human rights and international criminal law (Engle et al. 2016), Mann explores to what extent border violence may be legally framed as crimes against humanity. According to Mann, the 'structural accountability deficit when it comes to irregular migrants' is 'hard-wired in international law' (ibid, p. 9). Recasting border violence as an issue of international criminal liability, however, represents an opportunity to partly overcome this deficit by shifting from an individual victims' approach to documenting the systematic and structural effects of transnational migration control. Concretely testing this argument, Mann was also one of the main authors of an Article 15 communication to the International Criminal Court related to Australia's forced relocation and detention of migrants and refugees in neighbouring states – Nauru and Papua New Guinea.[25] In 2019, a similar communication was filed addressing Italy and the European Union's cooperation with Libya since 2014.[26]

The turn to international crimes in human rights and refugee law is not without its critics, however. The focus on anti-impunity, Samuel Moyn argues, is self-validating in a way that invites 'political trials' for which legal argumentation ultimately tend to take a backseat (Moyn 2014). As Mann further concedes, 'trials for mass human rights violations, particularly at the ICC, have largely been ineffective' (Mann 2020, p. 719) – and indeed the Office of the Prosecutor has so far declined to open preliminary investigations into the above-mentioned complaints. Whether this threshold will be crossed in the future remains to be seen – current developments suggest a continued harshening of border control practices across Europe, Australia and the United States. Moreover, not only international but also domestic courts are currently being confronted with migration-related cases couched in the language of international crimes.[27] Similarly, although the Australian submission was rejected by the ICC, it helped bolster a subsequent class action suit linking international criminal law and torts (ibid, p. 49).

A third and related strategy involves geographically redirecting claims. So far, litigation efforts concerning transnational migration control has been almost exclusively focused on sponsoring states in the Global North. There may be both political and legal reasons to maintain such a focus (Gammeltoft-Hansen 2018). Yet, at a time where international cooperation on migration control is generally tipping towards stronger involvement of authorities in transit and origin states, it becomes all the more important to consider the role and responsibility of these states, as well as the legal remedies available within these jurisdictions. From an international law perspective, a holistic approach is the natural starting point in any case concerning cooperative deterrence whether concerning independent or shared responsibility. This does not imply that political power asymmetries and questions of relative authority should be ignored. Each state should be held accountable only to the extent of its legal responsibility for breach of refugee and human rights. In that sense, holding partner states responsible complements rather than excludes destination state responsibility (ibid).

Recent examples illustrate that domestic courts in partner states may sometimes be able to indirectly enforce refugee and migrant rights even in states with limited to no adherence to international refugee and human rights law. As Tan (2018) documents in a recent article, it was neither UN treaty bodies nor domestic courts in Australia that finally undid Australia's offshore processing centre on Manus Island. Rather, the Supreme Court of Papua New Guinea ruled that the detention of asylum seekers within the centre violated the right to personal liberty enshrined in the country's constitution.[28] Similarly, in March 2017 a Libyan appeals court formally suspended the Memorandum of Understanding signed between Libya and Italy and ordered a halt to all current cooperation on migration control between the two countries on the basis that Faiez Serraj, acting on behalf of the Government of National Accord, did not have authority to enter into an international agreement not approved by the House of Representatives.

Although the Libyan case was subsequently overturned by the Libyan Supreme Court, the role of domestic courts in major refugee hosting countries should not be underestimated (Abass and Ippolito 2014). For example, in a landmark judgment from 2017, the Kenyan High Court declared that the closure of the Dadaab camp and consequent expulsion of refugees was a violation of both the Kenyan Constitution and Kenya's international obligations, including the 1951 Refugee Convention and the 1969 Refugee Convention adopted by the Organisation of African Unity (OAU).[29] A holistic approach to establishing responsibility for refugee and human rights violations in the context of cooperative deterrence further opens up a range of regional avenues in transit and origin countries. At the normative level, this includes regional refugee instruments such as the 1969 OAU Refugee Convention and the 1984 Cartagena Declaration, both of which in their content and/or surrounding political tradition entail more refined approaches to international cooperation and responsibility-sharing. At the institutional level, refugee and migration issues may not only be pursued via regional human rights courts, such as the Inter-American System of Human Rights and the African Court on Human and Peoples' Rights, but also, and importantly, in the context of broader regional institutions and legal frameworks linked to, for example, economic cooperation, trade and free movement (Gammeltoft-Hansen 2018).

Conclusions

Although migration control remains one of the oldest forms of transnational law enforcement, the inclusion of migrant and refugee issues in extraterritorial human rights case law remains a somewhat latecomer within the wider ETO jurisprudence. As argued in this article, this timing sequence could be seen as an important factor for the progressive developments in regard to transnational migrant and refugee rights during the last two decades. It allowed migrant and refugee cases to benefit from precedents established in regard to other issues and the wider attention to extraterritorial rights, thereby helping to counter previous reluctance to apply national or international migration law extraterritorially among domestic courts. The importance of the 'human rights turn' in this regard can hardly be overstated – not only in terms of providing access to international litigation in an area of international law without a dedicated international court or supervisory committee, but also in shifting dominant interpretations within international refugee law itself.

However, a number of factors suggest that this relationship between the specific legal regimes related to migrants and refugees, on the one hand, and general human rights law, on the other hand, is currently changing. Practices of transnational migration control have been significantly developing in recent years, meaning that migration and refugee issues are moving from a trailing to a pole position when it comes to ETO litigation. Several of the cases currently pending raise new and difficult legal questions regarding the boundaries of extraterritorial jurisdiction and shared forms of responsibility, the adjudication of which will likely reverberate across other issue domains as well. Meanwhile, international human rights institutions have come under increasing political pressure, not least for their role in regard to migrant and refugee cases. Consequently, at least in the European context, we may be seeing the contours of a more cautious, or even regressive, approach to migrant and refugee rights.

While it is too early to draw more general conclusions in terms of the broader human rights response on this basis, this chapter nonetheless takes the opportunity to explore alternative pathways forward for progressively realising ETOs in regard to transnational migration control. These may be seen as a set of compensatory strategies, represented by different nascent or currently applied approaches championed by either academics or practicing lawyers (in some cases with a significant overlap between the two).

For the purpose of this chapter, these approaches have been divided into two overall groups. The first concerns efforts to *reframe* existing approaches to ETOs, essentially seeking to move or challenge the status quo of existing human rights jurisprudence. Examples within this category involve efforts to expand dominant understandings of extraterritorial jurisdiction and responsibility, for example, by drawing on seemingly outlier cases, or by exploring different bases for jurisdiction, such as the extraterritorial effects doctrine. But it also includes attempts to more fundamentally reconstruct human rights approaches to migrants and refugees that look to wider legal principles and historical cases.

A second group of approaches involves strategies to redirect accountability claims towards other legal regimes and institutional settings. As is already happening, this may include a greater emphasis on 'soft courts' (Cali et al. 2020) in the form of individual petitions to the different UN human rights committees. But it also entails exploring possibilities for pursuing human rights claims via other international legal regimes, such as international criminal law. Last, but not least, it may involve a geographic reorientation to examine litigation possibilities in and related to partner states in the Global South as exemplified by the Supreme Court of Papua New Guinea's ruling in regard to the Australian offshore processing facility on Manus Island.

While individual scholars may disagree regarding the relative potential of these different strategies from both a practical and doctrinal perspective, they are presented here as largely complementary. For the purpose of the present chapter, they represent an incomplete catalogue that highlights the growing diversity of approaches pursued by advocates and academics navigating and responding to the different impulses set out above. Just as international migration and refugee law has historically benefited from similar creativity and diversity of approaches within the broader field of human rights scholarship and practice, present developments in regard to migrants and refugees may perhaps equally inspire the wider field of ETOs.

Notes

1. Professor WSR in migration and refugee law. The present contribution draws in parts on two earlier publications: Gammeltoft-Hansen, T. (2018) 'International Cooperation on Migration Control: Towards a Research Agenda for Refugee Law', *European Journal of Migration and Law* 20(4), 373–395 and Tan, N.F. and Gammeltoft-Hansen, T. (2020) 'A Topographical Approach to Accountability for Human Rights Violations in Migration Control', *German Law Journal* 21(3), 335–354.

2. The preamble to the 1951 Convention Relating the Status of Refugees famously notes, 'the grant of asylum may place unduly heavy burdens on certain countries....a satisfactory solution of a problem of which the United Nations has recognized the international scope and nature cannot therefore be achieved without international co-operation' (para. 4).
3. The term 'transnational migration control' is used from here on as a broad signifier encompassing both situations where states carry out controls outside their territory through their own officials as well as practices involving private parties and/or third state authorities implementing controls.
4. See for instance England and Wales Court of Appeal (2003) *R. (European Roma Rights Centre and Others) v. Immigration Officer at Prague Airport,* QB 811 EWCA Civ. 666; High Court of Australia (HCA) (2010) *Plaintiff M61 and Plaintiff M69 v Commonwealth of Australia,* HCA 41. See more generally, Gammeltoft-Hansen 2014.
5. Supreme Court of the United States (1993) *Sale v. Haitian Center Council,* 509 US 155; United Kingdom House of Lords (2004) *Regina v. Immigration Officer at Prague Airport, Ex parte European Roma Rights Centre and Others,* UKHL 55 para. 68; HCA (2015) *CPCF v. Minister for Immigration and Border Protection,* HCA 1, para. 461; HCA (2002) *Minister for Immigration and Multicultural Affairs v. Khawar,* HCA 14, para. 42; HCA (2000) *Minister for Immigration and Multicultural Affairs v. Haji Ibrahim,* HCA 55, para. 137.
6. For a recent counterexample, however, see Papua New Guinea Supreme Court (2016) *Namah v. Pato (Minister for Foreign Affairs and Immigrations) and Ors,* PJSC 13.
7. European Court of Human Rights (ECtHR) (1996*) Amuur v. France,* Application no: 19776/92, Judgment.
8. See e.g. ECtHR (2000) *T.I. v. United Kingdom,* Application no: 43844/98; ECtHR (2011) *MSS v. Belgium and Greece,* Application no: 30696/09.
9. See e.g. ECtHR (2012) *Hirsi Jamaa and Others v. Italy,* Application no: 27765/09; ECtHR (2017) *ND and NT v. Spain,* Application numbers 8675/15 and 8697/15; UN Committee Against Torture (CAT) (2008) *J.H.A. v. Spain,* CAT/C/41/D/323/2007; Inter-American Commission of Human Rights (1997) *Haitian Center for Human Rights v. United States* ('US Interdiction of Haitians on the High Seas'), Case 10.675.
10. ECtHR (2012) *Hirsi Jamaa and Others v. Italy*, European Court of Human Rights, Application no: 27765/09, par. 134–135.
11. ECtHR (2010) *Medvedyev. and Others v. France,* Application no: 3394/03.
12. Paragraph 26. This paragraph was ultimately dropped from the final text but arguably still sends a clear signal as to where Member States would like to see the Court apply a wider margin of appreciation.
13. Charleswort, H. and Triggs, G. (2017) 'Australia and the Protection of Human Rights', Australian Institute for International Affairs Analysis, 29 May 2017; Ritzau (2016) 'Institut for menneskerettigheder bakker nævn op: FN's afgørelser kan ikke bare tages for gode varer', 23 March 2016.
14. ECtHR (2000) *MN and Others v. Belgium,* Application no: 3599/18.
15. Court of Justice of the EU (CJEU) (2017) *X and X v. Belgium,* Case C-638/16.
16. ECtHR (2020) *ND and NT v. Spain,* Application numbers 8675/15 and 8697/15.
17. ECtHR (1989) *Soering v. the United Kingdom,* Application no: 14038/88.
18. For a similar argument see Gammeltoft-Hansen and Hathaway 2015.
19. ECtHR (2008) *Georgia Andreou v. Turkey,* Application no: 45653/99, admissibility, p. 11.
20. Human Rights Committee (2014) *Concluding Observations, United States of America,* UN Doc. CCPR/C/USA/CO/4, 23 April 2014, para. 22. Human Rights Committee (1992) *Concluding observations, Islamic Republic of Iran,* UN Doc. CCPR/12/Add.1, Vol. 2, 1992, para. 256.
21. See for example, International Court of Justice (ICJ) (1949) *Corfu Channel Case,* ICJ Reports 1949; Trail Smelter Arbitral Tribunal (1942) *Trail Smelter Arbitral Decision* (*United States v. Canada*), Reports of International Arbitral Awards vol. 3.
22. CAT (2008) *JHA v. Spain,* UN doc CAT/C/41/D/323/2007. The case was, however, declared inadmissible as the complainant was not expressly authorized to act on behalf of the victims.
23. UN Committee on the Elimination of Discrimination Against Women (CEDAW) (2010) *General Recommendation No. 28 on the Core Obligations of States Parties under Article 2 of the Convention on the Elimination of All Forms of Discrimination against Women,* U.N. Doc. CEDAW/C/GC/28, para. 12.

24. UN Committee on the Protection of the Rights of All Migrant Workers and Members of Their Families (CMW) (2017) *Joint General Comment No. 3 (2017) of the Committee on the Protection of the Rights of All Migrant Workers and Members of Their Families and No. 22 (2017) of the Committee on the Rights of the Child on the General Principles regarding the Human Rights of Children in the context of International Migration*, U.N. Doc. CMW/C/GC/3- CRC/C/GC/22, para. 12.
25. Achiume, T.E. et al. (2017) '*The Situation in Nauru and Manus Island: Liability for crimes against humanity in the detention of refugees and asylum seekers*', Communiqué to the Office of the Prosecutor of the International Criminal Court Under Article 15 of the Rome Statute, https://www-cdn.law.stanford.edu/wp-content/uploads/2017/02/Communiqu%C3%A9-to-Office-Prosecutor-IntlCrimCt-Art15RomeStat-14Feb2017.pdf
26. Shatz, O. and Juan Branco, J. (2019) *EU Migration Policies in Central Mediterranean and Libya (2014-2019),* Communication to the Office of Prosecutor of the International Criminal Court Pursuant to the Article 15 of the Rome Statute, https://www.statewatch.org/news/2019/jun/eu-icc-case-EU-Migration-Policies.pdf.
27. Notable cases pending include United States Supreme Court (2019) *Hernandez v. Mesa*, case submitted 9 August 2019 concerning US-Mexico border control and multiple lawsuits concerning Rohingyan refugees and genocide claims (See further Pillai 2019).
28. Papua New Guinea Supreme Court (2016) *Namah v. Pato* (Minister for Foreign Affairs and Immigrations) and Ors, PJSC 13.
29. High Court of Kenya (2017) 'Constitutional Petition 227 of 2016', 9 February 2017, http://www.refworld.org/cases,KEN_HC,589c3c514.html [accessed 20 November 2020].

References

Abass, A., and Ippolito, F. (2016) 'Introduction–Regional Approaches to the Protection of Asylum Seekers: an International Legal Perspective', *Regional Approaches to the Protection of Asylum Seekers. Routledge*, 1-18.

Altwicker, T. (2018) 'Transnationalizing Rights: International Human Rights Law in Cross-Border Contexts'. *European Journal of International Law* 29.2 (2018): 581-606.

Bigo, D. (2002) 'Security and Immigration: Towards a Critique of the Governmentality of Unease', *Alternatives* 27, 63–92.

Cali, B., Costello, C. and Cunningham, S. (2020) 'Hard Protection through Soft Courts? Non-Refoulement before the United Nations Treaty Bodies', *German Law Journal* 21, 355–384.

Court of Justice of the EU (CJEU) (2017) *X and X v. Belgium*, Case C 638/16.

Charlesworth, H. and Triggs, G. (2017) 'Australia and the Protection of Human Rights', *Australian Institute for International Affairs* Analysis, 29 May 2017

Cruz, A. (1995) *Shifting Responsibility: Carriers' Liability in the Member States of the European Union and North America*, Trentham Books.

Dastyari, A. (2015) *United States Migrant Interdiction and the Detention of Refugees in Guantanamo Bay*, Cambridge University Press.

De Boer, T. (2014) 'Closing Legal Black Holes: The Role of Extraterritorial Jurisdiction in Refugee Rights Protection', *Journal of Refugee Studies* 28(1), 118–134.

Dembour, M.B. (2015) *When Humans Become Migrants: Study of the European Court of Human Rights with an Inter-American Counterpoint*, Oxford University Press.

den Heijer, M. (2013) 'Shared Responsibility Before the European Court of Human Rights', *Netherlands International Law Review* 60, 411–440.

Dupuy, P.M. (1998) 'International Law: Torn between Coexistence, Cooperation and Globalization. General Conclusions', *European Journal of International Law* 9(2), 278–286.

England and Wales Court of Appeal (2003) R. (European Roma Rights Centre and Others) v. Immigration Officer at Prague Airport, QB 811 EWCA Civ. 666.

Engle, K., Miller, Z. and Davis, D. M. eds. (2016) *Anti-impunity and the human rights agenda*. Cambridge University Press.

European Court of Human Rights (ECtHR) (1989) *Soering v. the United Kingdom*, Application no: 14038/88.

_______ (1996) *Amuur v. France*, Application no: 19776/92, Judgment.
_______ (2000) *MN and Others v. Belgium*, Application no: 3599/18.
_______ (2000) *T.I. v. United Kingdom*, Application no: 43844/98.
_______ (2008) *Georgia Andreou v. Turkey*, Application no: 45653/99.
_______ (2010) *Medvedyev. and Others v. France*, Application no: 3394/03.
_______ (2011) *MSS v. Belgium and Greece*, Application no: 30696/09.
_______ (2012) *Hirsi Jamaa and Others v. Italy*, Application no: 27765/09.
_______ (2017) *ND and NT v. Spain*, Application numbers 8675/15 and 8697/15.
_______ (2020) *ND and NT v. Spain*, Application numbers 8675/15 and 8697/15.

Feller, E. (1989) 'Carrier Sanctions and International Law', *International Journal of Refugee Law* 1(1), 48–66.

Gammeltoft-Hansen, T. (2011) *Access to Asylum: International Refugee Law and the Globalisation of Migration Control*, Cambridge University Press.

_______ (2014) 'The Role of International Refugee Law in Refugee Policy', *Journal of Refugee Studies* 27(4), 574–595.

_______ (2015) 'Private Security and the Migration Control Industry' in Abrahamsen, R. and Leander, A. (eds.). *Routledge Handbook of Private Security Studies*, Routledge.

_______ (2017) 'Private Actor Involvement in Migration Management' in Nollkaemper, A. and Plakokefalos, I. (eds.). *The Practice of Shared Responsibility in International Law*, Cambridge University Press.

_______ (2018) 'International Cooperation on Migration Control: Towards a Research Agenda for Refugee Law', *European Journal of Migration and Law* 20(4), 373–395.

Gammeltoft-Hansen, T. and Hathaway, J. C. (2015) 'Non-refoulement in a World of Cooperative Deterrence', *Columbia Journal of Transnational Law* 53(2), 235–284.

Gammeltoft-Hansen, T. and Madsen, M. R. (2021) *The Uneasy Marriage of Human Rights and Migration Law: The Case of Denmark, Nordiques*.

Gammeltoft-Hansen, T. and Tan, N. F. (2021) 'Extraterritorial Migration Control and Deterrence' in Costello, C., Foster, M. and McAdam, J. (eds.). *Oxford Handbook of International Refugee Law*, Oxford University Press.

Garlick, M. (2006) 'The EU Discussions on Extraterritorial Processing', *International Journal of Refugee Law* 18(3/4), 601–630.

Ghezelbash, D. (2018) *Refuge Lost: Asylum law in an interdependent world*, Cambridge University Press.

Goodwin-Gill, G. (1994) 'The Haitian Refoulement Case: A Comment', *International Journal of Refugee Law* 6(1), 103–109.

Grahl-Madsen, A. (1963 (republished 1997)) *Commentary on the Refugee Convention 1951 Articles 2-11, 13-37*, Division of International Protection of the United High Commissioner for Refugees.

High Court of Australia (HCA) (2000) *Minister for Immigration and Multicultural Affairs v. Haji Ibrahim*, HCA 55.
_______ (2002) *Minister for Immigration and Multicultural Affairs v. Khawar*, HCA 14.
_______ (2010) *Plaintiff M61 and Plaintiff M69 v. Commonwealth of Australia*, HCA 41.
_______ (2015) *CPCF v. Minister for Immigration and Border Protection*, HCA 1.

High Court of Kenya (2017) 'Constitutional Petition 227 of 2016', 9 February 2017, http://www.refworld.org/cases,KEN_HC,589c3c514.html [accessed.].

Holly, Gabrielle (2020) Challenges to Australia's Offshore Detention Regime and the Limits of Strategic Tort Litigation', *German Law Journal* 21(3), 549-570.

Human Rights Committee (1992) Concluding observations, Islamic Republic of Iran, UN Doc. CCPR/12/Add.1, vol. 2.

_______ (2014) *Concluding Observations, United States of America, UN Doc.* CCPR/C/USA/CO/4.

Inter-American Commission of Human Rights (1997) *Haitian Center for Human Rights v. United States ('US Interdiction of Haitians on the High Seas')*, Case 10.675.

International Court of Justice (ICJ) (1949) *Corfu Channel Case*, ICJ Reports 1949.

Kalpouzos, I. (2020) 'International Criminal Law and the Violence against Migrants', *German Law Journal* 21(3), 571-597.

Kessing, P. V. (2017) 'Transnational Operations Carried Out From a State's Own Territory: Armed Drones and the Extraterritorial Effect of International Human Rights Conventions' in Gammeltoft-Hansen, T. and Vedsted-Hansen, J. (eds.). *Human Rights and the Dark Side of Globalisation: Transnational Law Enforcement and Migration Control*, Routledge.

Lauterpacht, E. and Bethlehem, D. (2003) 'The Scope and Content of the Principle of *Non-Refoulement*: Opinion' in Feller, E., Türk, V. and Nicholson, F. (eds.), *Refugee Protection in International Law: UNHCR's Global Consultations on International Protection*, Cambridge University Press.

Mann, I. (2013) 'Dialectic of Transnationalism: Unauthorized Migration and Human Rights, 1993-2013.' *Harv. Int'l LJ* 54, 315.

Mann, I. (2016) *Humanity at Sea: Maritime Migration and the Foundation of International Law*, Cambridge University Press.

_______ (2020) 'The new impunity: Border violence as crime', *University of Pennsylvania Journal of International Law* 42.

Moreno-Lax, V. (2020). The Architecture of Functional Jurisdiction: Unpacking Contactless Control–On Public Powers, SS and Others v. Italy, and the "Operational Model". *German Law Journal*, 21(3), 385–416.

Moreno-Lax, V. and Giuffré, M. (2019) "The Rise of Consensual Containment: From 'Contactless Control' to 'Contactless Responsibility' for Forced Migration Flows." In Juss, S. (ed), *Research Handbook on International Refugee Law*, Edward Elgar, 20.

Moyn, S. (2016) 'Anti-Impunity as Deflection of Argument' in Engle, K., Miller, Z. and Davis, D. M. (eds.). *Anti-impunity and the Human Rights Agenda*. Cambridge University Press, pp. 68–94.

Papastavridis, E. (2020) 'The European Convention of Human Rights and Migration at Sea: Reading the "Jurisdictional Threshold" of the Convention Under the Law of the Sea Paradigm', *German Law Journal* 21(3), 417–435.

Papua New Guinea Supreme Court (2016) Namah v. Pato (Minister for Foreign Affairs and Immigrations) and Ors, PJSC 13.

Pijnenburg, A. (2018) 'From Italian Pushbacks to Libyan Pullbacks: Is Hirsi 2.0 in the Making in Strasbourg?', *European Journal of Migration and Law* 20(4), 396–426.

Ritzau (2016) 'Institut for menneskerettigheder bakker nævn op: FN's afgørelser kan ikke bare tages for gode varer', 23 March 2016.

Scholten, S. and Minderhoud, P. (2008) 'Regulating Immigration Control: Carrier Sanctions in the Netherlands', *European Journal of Migration and Law* 10, 123–147.

Spijkerboer, T. and Steyger, E. (2019) 'European External Migration Funds and Public Procurement Law', *European Papers* 4(2), 493–521.

Supreme Court of the United States (1993) *Sale v. Haitian Center Council*, 509 US 155.

Supreme Court of the United States (2019) *Hernandez v. Mesa*, case submitted 9 August 2019.

Tan, N. F. (2017) 'State Responsibility and Migration Control: Australia's International Deterrence Model' in Gammeltoft-Hansen, T. and Vedsted-Hansen, J. (eds.). *Human Rights and the Dark Side of Globalisation: Transnational Law Enforcement and Migration Control*, Routledge.

_______ (2018) 'The Manus Island Regional Processing Centre: A Legal Taxonomy', *European Journal of Migration and Law* 20(4), 427-451.

Tan, N. F. and Gammeltoft-Hansen, T. (2020) 'A Topographical Approach to Accountability for Human Rights Violations in Migration Control', *German Law Journal* 21(3), 335–354.

Trail Smelter Arbitral Tribunal (1942) Trail Smelter Arbitral Decision (United States v. Canada), *Reports of International Arbitral Awards* vol. 3.

UN Committee Against Torture (CAT) (2008) *J.H.A. v. Spain*, CAT/C/41/D/323/2007.

UN Committee on the Elimination of Discrimination Against Women (CEDAW) (2010) General Recommendation No. 28 on the Core Obligations of States Parties under Article 2 of the Convention on the Elimination of All Forms of Discrimination against Women, U.N. Doc. CEDAW/C/GC/28.

UN Committee on the Protection of the Rights of All Migrant Workers and Members of Their Families (CMW) (2017) *Joint General Comment no.* 3 of the Committee on the Protection of the Rights of All Migrant Workers and Members of Their Families and no. *22 (2017)* of the Committee on the Rights of the Child on the General Principles regarding the Human Rights of Children in the context of International Migration, U.N. Doc. CMW/C/GC/3- CRC/C/GC/22.

United Kingdom House of Lords (2004) *Regina v.* Immigration Officer at Prague Airport, Ex parte European Roma Rights Centre and Others, UKHL 55.

Vedsted-Hansen, J. (1988) 'Transporters' Responsibilities under the Chicago Convention on International Civil Aviation' in Kjærum, M. (ed.). *The Role of Airline Companies in the Asylum Procedure*, Danish Refugee Council.

Wilde, R. (2017) 'The Unintended Consequences of Expanding Migrant Rights Protections'. *American Journal of International Law* 111, 487–491.

12

The establishment of ETOs in the context of externalised migration control

Kristof Gombeer and Stefaan Smis

Affluent states increasingly seek to control migration beyond their borders. One means of doing this has been to relegate migration administration to third states. To illustrate, Australia places asylum seekers offshore, while the EU-Turkey agreement has served to limit the number of Syrian refugees able to access other parts of Europe. In addition, states have set up cooperative arrangements with transit states with problematic human rights records, such as Libya. These practices raise the question whether states remain responsible under human rights law for protecting migrants whose stakes are governed by the third countries with which they cooperate. The first part of this chapter describes the concepts of externalisation and outsourcing of migration control and provides illustrations from state practice. The second part analyses to which extent migration control beyond the border can trigger the applicability of human rights instruments. It is shown how the notion of 'human rights jurisdiction' may be further developed so as to accommodate for human rights checks on these emerging practices in the field of migration control.

The transformation of migration control

Externalisation

Today's prevailing view is that states have an 'undeniable sovereign right to control aliens' entry into and residence in their territory' (European Court of Human Rights (ECtHR) *Amuur v. France,* para. 41). Destination countries, however, do not wish to fully close off their borders as they rely on the movement of goods, services and labour to sustain their wealth (Jones 2016, pp. 165–166). Solutions to this dilemma have been sought within three different spaces: at the border, inside the border and before the border. More border checks impede the movement of goods and people, while fewer checks are said to diminish security. States have therefore tried to make administration and control *at* the border 'smarter' (Longo 2018, p. 141), or to manipulate the legal borders of parts of their territory to exclude migrants from judicial protection (see also Maillet in this volume). Techniques of control have also been pushed inward from the linear state border. Since administrations cannot fully filter unwanted movements at the border, they increasingly submit people under surveillance *within* their territory, ultimately resulting in

DOI: 10.4324/9781003090014-16

detention and deportation. Affluent countries such as Australia, the USA and the member states of the EU increasingly attempt to control migratory movements *before* people reach their territories. The third space where today's migration control takes shape, is the one *beyond* the border: 'externalisation' seeks to prevent having to deal with control measures at and inside the border in the first place. The latest development, 'outsourcing', occurs when states rely heavily on third parties to realise such externalisation.

Externalisation rests on the belief that efficient control entails 'going beyond the place and time of the entry point' and 'locating where the migrant is in his or her process of moving towards an assumed destination point' to then stem that flow through the most effective method (Casas-Cortes and Cobarrubias 2019, p. 200). For example, the imposition of visa restrictions has proven an effective method to remotely control migrant mobility (Weber and Pickering 2011, p. 95). Since the second half of the twentieth century, visas have become a tool for targeting specific nationalities in general and refugee-producing countries in particular (FitzGerald 2019, pp. 59–60, 164–166 and 221–222; Moreno-Lax 2017, pp. 81–116). Absent legal pathways, migrants have been funnelled into using clandestine methods and routes towards the territories of destination states. Western states initially responded to this by pushing back migrants *at* or *before* they reach their territory. Yet, these methods of externalisation have been increasingly curtailed by ETOs (*infra* part 2). Outsourcing has therefore emerged as a 'hands-off' variant of externalisation based on the idea that affluent countries thereby might avoid legal responsibilities, including ETOs, towards migrants (Gammeltoft-Hansen and Hathaway 2015, p. 243; FitzGerald 2019). With outsourcing, destination countries have started to rely more and more on third states as the locus and executors of migration control measures.

Outsourcing

Outsourcing to third states can achieve migration control in three main ways. Firstly, outsourcing efforts may target (would-be) migrants directly by *limiting their ability to enter or stay in transit countries*. Third state entry control is usually employed to make the neighbours of affluent countries less attractive as a transit state. Third countries may be nudged to adopt legislation which enhances their control over inward movements of third country nationals, for instance, by emulating strict visa regimes. The outsourcing state may, for example, also finance deportations programmes of transit countries to dissuade the latter as transit options. Secondly, destination states may seek to *outsource the provision of international protection* such as asylum to third states. This is usually done by labelling the latter as 'safe countries' to which migrants can be returned. Third countries may be pushed to adopt legislation which enhances them as a 'safe' third country by reforming its asylum laws and refugee reception capacities and conditions. A variation of this outsourcing method consists of deviating migrants to the territory of third countries when migrants are *en route* to the destination state but are intercepted before they reach the latter's territory. Thirdly, outsourcing efforts may target the stakes of migrants by *limiting their ability to exit third countries* towards the ultimate destination countries. Third state exit control aims at containing migrants within the borders of the third state. To this end, the outsourcing state usually encourages the third state to adopt stricter anti-smuggling laws and to enhance its operational capacities to prevent migrants from leaving the latter's territory.

Outsourcing states themselves can be involved to varying degrees and use different means to galvanise cooperation. States may, for instance, use diplomatic sticks and carrots to incentivise states to take on migration control functions. They may provide direct financial incentives or directly provide equipment, assets and training. States may also deploy liaison officers, joint enforcement operations, the use of intergovernmental agencies and direct migration control in the territory of the cooperating state (Gammeltoft-Hansen and Hathaway 2015, pp. 250–256). In these instances, it is the state agents of the destination state itself that assert authority and/or control over migrants, often – even though consent is needed from the cooperating third state – acting on a legal basis provided by the laws of the destination state. This can be thought of as *externalisation* but does not constitute *outsourcing* per se. Compare this, for instance, with the deployment of British immigration officers at the Eurostar terminal in Brussels. The authority and control over the stakes of the traveller here is not asserted by the cooperating third state (Belgium) but by the externalising state (United Kingdom). Techniques of outsourcing, however, attempt to *shift the direct authority and control over the stakes of the migrant to the third state.*

When destination states are themselves strongly operationally involved in control beyond their border, the fact that they exercise authority or control over the person of the migrant usually suffices to trigger the applicability of human rights law. However, it is when states seek *a deeper hands-off approach by relying heavily on the conduct of third states* that establishing relations of duty for human rights purposes becomes more complicated. Before turning to the legal challenges for establishing ETOs in the context of externalisation and outsourcing of migration control, the next section provides examples of outsourcing in state practice. The section also points to human rights issues that may arise in the wake of such outsourcing efforts.

State practice

Australia

In a move to externalise and outsource responsibilities for migration control, Australia has initiated and funded both bilateral and regional initiatives with neighbouring countries. Central to its multilateral efforts is the Bali Process, established in 2002, whose role has mostly been limited to facilitating cooperation in addressing irregular migration (Kneebone 2014, pp. 599–606). Australia has also been able to rely on bilateral cooperation to outsource migration control areas far beyond its territory (Larking 2017). It has sought cooperation with countries of origin such as Sri Lanka and with countries of transit such as Malaysia. It has moreover concluded deals with countries such as Cambodia and the US with a view to resettle or exchange refugees, but these have been largely unsuccessful. Central to Australia's outsourcing efforts, however, has been its cooperation with Indonesia, Nauru and Papua New Guinea (PNG).

Efforts to outsource migration control to Indonesia have focused on legislative reform and on the prevention and disruption of unauthorised departures to Australia. This resulted first in the establishment of the Regional Cooperation Model in 2000 through which Australia encouraged and almost entirely financed the use of migrant detention. Australia has further provided financial and technical assistance, training of border and immigration officials, equipment, assets such as patrol vessels to enhance Indonesia's capacity to perform exit controls. Australia has moreover invested in Indonesia's entry control by influencing Indonesia to adopt stricter visa policies vis-à-vis refugee producing countries (Mussi and Feith Tan 2015, pp. 97–98).

Cooperation with PNG and Nauru has predominantly revolved around containment by outsourcing the status determination of migrants and their detention. In response to the *M/V Tampa* incident, Australia supplemented its novel maritime interception programme ('Operation Relex') and excision of certain islands for migration purposes, with a mechanism to fully outsource status determination procedures to PNG and Nauru. Under what became known as the 'Pacific Solution', Australia concluded Memorandums of Understanding with both countries in 2001. It renewed them – after a brief interruption – again in 2012 and in 2013. The gist of this outsourcing mechanism is that Nauru and PNG host one or more so-called Regional

Processing Centres, while Australia incurs their cost, including that of the additionally required infrastructure and services. Migrants eligible for international protection by PNG and Nauru are either 'settled' there or – with the assistance of Australia – in third countries. They are not resettled to Australia. This re-routing continued under subsequent administrations under 'Operation Sovereign Borders' (Phillips 2017).

Europe

European states have organised the outsourcing of migration control both as a matter of EU policy and at the level of the individual EU Member States engaging in bilateral relations with third states.

The EU has stressed the 'efficient management of migration flows at all their stages' in cooperation with countries of origin and transit since the 1999 summit in Tampere (European Council 1999). While in 2000 the Cotonou development agreement between the EU and the group of African, Caribbean and Pacific states made migration the subject of *dialogue* for both sides, the 2002 summit went a step further by *conditioning* closer relations between the Union and third countries on the latter's cooperation in 'combatting illegal immigration' (European Council 2002). In 2005, the European Council adopted the 'Global Approach to Migration' which prioritised cooperation with third countries in Africa and the Mediterranean, in particular Morocco, Algeria and Libya (European Council 2005). In 2011, this programme was renewed under the 'Global Approach to Migration and Mobility' (European Commission 2011). In 2015, the EU adopted a 'European Agenda on Migration' which continued on the path of stemming unauthorised migration via cooperation with third countries. Later that year, the Summit of Valletta reaffirmed the EU's focus on addressing the root causes of migration and stemming irregular migration through cooperation. An 'EU Emergency Trust Fund for Africa' was created to form the financial backbone of the scheme.

While some efforts at the level of the EU are genuinely directed at development, they are increasingly dominated by a logic of stemming onward movement of migrants. EU initiatives have tried to enhance the containment and buffer function of third countries through several techniques. Firstly, there is the export of EU modelled legislation, one of the EU's traditional modi operandi. New anti-smuggling laws temper the ability of clandestine movement (e.g. Niger's 2015 Law against Illicit Smuggling of Migrants), while improved laws on asylum, reception conditions and readmission attempt to enhance transit countries as bona fide safe countries for forcibly displaced migrants or as countries from which return can be organised (e.g. Morocco's revision of Immigration Law 02/03). The EU has also trained the local administrations (border guards, police, judges, asylum workers) to enhance the capacity to function as asylum states and to step-up the level of enforcement capacity. Europe moreover financially invested in third countries' buffer roles by providing surveillance and patrolling equipment, setting up information campaigns discouraging onward movement and funding information and reception centres (European Commission 2011, pp. 15–16). The EU's outsourcing targets have been situated increasingly further down the migration routes, to for instance the Sahel region (e.g. 'capacity-building mission' EUCAP Sahel Niger). For example, Niger on its own has received several hundred million euros to curb transit migration towards Libya and Algeria, in addition to the €609 million in earmarked development aid between 2016 and 2020 (Tubiana et al. 2018, p. 22). Combined, these strategies of outsourcing turn third countries in concentric buffer layers against onward movement towards Europe.

The second leg of European outsourcing efforts has rested on bilateral relations between individual European states on the one hand and third countries predominantly situated in the

MENA and Sahel region on the other hand. Three examples are illustrative of the evolution of externalisation to outsourcing.

Spain has since the early 2000s developed cooperation with countries such as Morocco, Mauritania and Senegal to stem migration towards its land and sea borders. A central element to these exit control efforts has been the setting up of joint patrols to interrupt maritime departures within the territorial waters of third states. In 2004, for example, Spain launched a mission with the Moroccan Gendarmerie whereby Spanish Civil Guards joined on Moroccan patrol vessels. In 2006, Spain established a similar mechanism with Mauretania in which it moreover supplied Mauretania with patrol boats and trained its border control agents. In addition to operational involvement and support aimed at exit control, Spain has since the beginning invested heavily in linking development funding to migration control. For example, since 2006 Mauretania and Senegal have respectively received €88.6 and €34.9 million in aid destined for border control (Gonzalez Garcia 2020).

Italy has a long history of collaboration on migration control with Libya, the first formalised cooperation dating back to an agreement in 2000 addressing irregular migration among other things. Since then, Italian-Libyan cooperation has been governed by both formal and informal agreements. The agreements have come with large financial transfers, political support and the provision of equipment and patrol vessels in exchange for tighter Libyan exit control. These bilateral deals arranged for the joint patrolling of the waters off the Libyan coast with migrants intercepted being returned to Libya. With the removal of Gaddafi and the condemnation by the European Court of Human Rights of push-back operations by the Italian coast guard, cooperation was on a low but still alive: even amidst the civil war in 2011 did Italy seek cooperation with the National Transitional Council. Cooperation was fully revitalised through a 2012 Memorandum of Understanding, focussing on the exchange of liaison officers, readmission, training for the Libyan police, the recovery of detention centres, readmission from Libyan detention centres and the use of Italian drones to provide early detection of unauthorised maritime departures. This support was supplemented at the European level by an EU Border Assistance Mission to develop a Libyan border control strategy. In addition, EUNAVFOR MED *Sophia* (now operation *IRINI*) was transformed into a training and technical assistance mission in 2016. Italian outsourcing efforts – backed-up with EU support – have turned Libya in an effective actor preventing migrants from embarking upon journeys towards Europe (Spagnolo 2019; Campesi 2018; Mussi and Feith Tan 2015).

Given the strained relation between Greece and Turkey, cooperation with the latter has mainly come from the EU level. Given the increasing pressure on the EU's external border in Greece, a deal was struck in 2016 between the EU Member States on the one hand and Turkey on the other: visa liberalisation, the speeding up of the disbursement of 3 billion Euros under the 'Facility for Refugees in Turkey' and the re-energising of the process of accession of Turkey to the EU in return for Turkey's commitment to 'prevent new sea or land routes for illegal migration opening up from Turkey to the EU' and to take back 'all new irregular migrants crossing from Turkey into the Greek islands' (EU-Turkey Statement 2016).

Externalisation, outsourcing and the establishment of ETOs

By externalisating and outsourcing migration control, affluent states undeniably have an impact on the enjoyment of human rights by (would be) migrants. Australia's outsourcing efforts have shown to negatively impact the human rights of the migrants targeted through exit control, entry control and containment. In addition to issues of refoulement and the right to leave in light of Australian maritime pushbacks, the conditions of Australian-backed detention in countries such as Indonesia, PNG and Nauru have been denounced. This has not only been pointed out by NGOs, but by multiple states as well (Human Rights Council (hereafter 'HRC') 2015a, paras. 22–24; HRC 2015b, paras. 63 and 68; Human Rights Watch 2013; Papua New Guinea Supreme Court 2016); Achiume et al. 2017). Australia has, however, been dismissive of this critique, arguing that it has been respecting the human rights of those 'claiming protection within Australia's jurisdiction' and of the 'transferees' in its cooperation with third countries. What is more, Australia prides itself that through cooperation with third countries, it has been able to 'deter' people from undertaking 'dangerous sea journeys', thereby saving lives (Human Rights Council 2015, paras. 125–127). European cooperation with third countries has impacted the enjoyment of human rights of migrants in its wake as well. All along the south-north migration routes, migrants are increasingly prevented from exercising their right to leave, thereby exposing them to violence from law enforcement, militias and – as a result of tougher anti-smuggling laws – more ruthless methods employed by smugglers. Perhaps the most egregious case is that migrants re-displaced in places such as Libya are thereby becoming exposed to practices of torture, trafficking and enslavement (Moreno-Lax 2020a). Like Australia, Europe too has increasingly justified cooperation – despite the clear human rights impact – with third countries as contributing to the 'saving of lives' by for instance preventing them undertaking 'dangerous journeys' at sea (European Commission 2017).

A question that arises is to which extent the application of human rights norms and accompanying state obligations is triggered vis-à-vis these externalisation and outsourcing practices in the first place. For human rights purposes, the responsibility of states can arise in mainly two ways. Firstly, as a primary duty-bearer under the human rights instruments it is bound by (via the triggering of the so-called 'human rights jurisdiction' of the state), and secondly, as a duty-bearer of a secondary order when another state is identified as the primary duty-bearer, but the outsourcing state can still be held responsible due to its relation to the violations committed by the former. This is, for instance, the case when a state aids and assists the primary duty-bearer in the commission of the human rights violation (see also Erdem Türkelli in this volume). While this section of the chapter as such does not look at the complementary role that the law on state responsibility may provide in this regard, certain features of ancillary responsibility are referred to when discussing the modalities of human rights jurisdiction. The primary goal of the remainder of this contribution is to identify the extent to which externalisation and outsourcing practices can be captured under notion of 'human rights jurisdiction'.

The problem of 'jurisdiction' for human rights purposes

Human rights treaties necessarily have to define *whose* rights the state has to protect. While some human rights instruments such as, for example, the ICCPR, CRC, ACHR and ECHR contain written provisions delineating their scope of application (referring either to 'territory', 'jurisdiction' or a combination thereof as the relevant benchmarks for their applicability) other human rights instruments, however, do not.

International and regional courts and human rights bodies have developed an extensive practice of interpreting the conditions for the extraterritorial application of these instruments (see also Pribytkova; Haeck, Burbano Herrera and Ghulam Farag in this volume). Meanwhile, scholars have attempted to find a coherent way to look at the rich material generated in practice. Some authors define 'jurisdiction', 'authority', 'public powers' or 'political power' over a person's stakes as the normative linchpin of primary duty (Besson 2012; Raible 2020). Others have emphasised the exercise of 'physical' or 'effective' control or 'actual power' over a person's situation (Milanovic 2011). Still others have argued that 'affecting' the enjoyment of rights or 'the ability' to do so is what establishes relations of duty and thus the triggers applicability of human rights instruments (Shany 2013).

Turning to the issue of externalisation and outsourcing of migration control, justifications for establishing 'human rights jurisdiction' that rest on actual authority or control have only proven useful when state agents are themselves directly involved in the stakes of (would-be) migrants in a legislative, executive or judicial capacity. With regard to pushbacks by coast guard vessels at sea, for example, the European Court of Human Rights (hereafter 'ECtHR') deemed the European Convention applicable by virtue of both the *de jure* and *de facto* control over the migrants intercepted at sea. As a result, Italy was under the non-refoulement principle prohibited from returning the migrants concerned to Libya (ECtHR, *Hirsi Jamaa v. Italy*; see also Inter-American Court of Human Rights (hereafter 'IACtHR') 2018, para. 122).

Yet, even when state agents are directly involved, problems of attribution may undermine the establishment of jurisdiction for human rights purposes. Ship-rider techniques during patrolling, for example, or instances where civil servants of the outsourcing state not only train third country officials but also make decisions about applications by migrants, constitute more complicated cases: even though the agents of the outsourcing state exercise control and/or authority over migrants, this conduct may be considered as attributable to the neighbouring state.

Moreover, assertions of power over the migrant's situation abroad for the purposes of triggering human rights jurisdiction have not been recognised consistently: while in the past physically removing individuals from diplomatic premises (control) or the non-issuing of passports to nationals in embassies abroad (authority) were deemed sufficient to trigger 'jurisdiction' for human rights purposes (European Commission on Human Rights (hereafter 'ECmHR'), *M v. Denmark* and Human Rights Committee (hereafter 'HRCee'), *Lichtensztejn v Uruguay* respectively), the European Court of Human Rights recently ruled that the processing of a humanitarian visa request submitted by Syrians in Belgian consular premises in Beirut did not suffice to fall 'within the jurisdiction' of Belgium for the purposes of the Convention. As a result, the applicants concerned could not complain that the non-granting of a visa by Belgium would expose them to the risk of torture and ill-treatment in Syria (ECtHR *M.N. and others v. Belgium*; on ETOs arising in diplomatic premises; see also Wilde in this volume).

The classic models of authority and control over persons will especially be of no avail in the context of outsourcing, i.e. in situations no state agents of the outsourcing state are involved and where migration is not stemmed but for the conduct of the cooperating third state and the resulting power that they have over the stakes of migrants concerned. Two jurisprudential developments may nonetheless provide an avenue for establishing 'human rights jurisdiction' in those scenarios: when control over a situation can be established by virtue of a subordinate foreign administration (the proxy model) and when a state has the ability to affect the rights of the persons concerned (the effects model). The remainder of this section explores how these models could ensure that not only externalisation involving state agents of the destination state, but also involving projections of power over migrants' ability to move through third states (outsourcing) may end up within the scope of human rights instruments.

Outsourcing and the proxy model

When a state exercises power over an area abroad by using a subordinate local administration, this can serve as a basis for establishing human rights jurisdiction. Under the proxy model, a human rights treaty can apply when a state exercises overall control over an area by financing, equipping and politically and militarily supporting administrations or *de facto* regimes abroad. This doctrine has its roots in the Northern Cyprus and Transdniestria case law of the Strasbourg

Court. In both contexts, the fact of control over the foreign area was enabled through the presence of troops on the ground (ECtHR *Loizidou (preliminary objections),* para. 63; ECtHR *Ilascu,* paras. 380 and 383). Financial and political support constitute further indicators to determine whether a foreign administration resorts 'under the effective authority, or at the very least under the decisive influence' of the state concerned (ECtHR *Ilascu,* para. 392). The sharing of military expertise and equipment can be of relevance too (ECtHR *Chiragov,* para. 180). The adoption of legislation by the proxy regime modelled on that of the influencing state is one of the other pieces to take into account when assessing the influence of one over the other (ECtHR *Chiragov,* para. 182). Importantly, it is not necessary for the state concerned to exercise detailed control over the policies and actions of the proxy administration (ECtHR *Loizidou,* para. 56). Interestingly, this distinguishes primary relations of duty under the proxy model from state responsibility arising from 'direction and control' pursuant to Article 17 ARSIWA. In sum, even though the individualised acts based on policies of the proxy administration are not as such imputable to the state concerned, the latter is nonetheless responsible for it by virtue of its *overall control* established by the presence of troops and influence gained through logistical, financial, economic and political means.

Under a strict reading of the law as it stands, it is not certain whether outsourcing efforts in a third state could trigger human rights jurisdiction under the proxy model, unless the outsourcing states become heavily involved on the ground. For instance, if the United States authorities would push for Mexican legislation emulating American immigration and border control standards, deploy US border guards for training and support at the border with Guatemala and pay for deportation flights for people detained at that border, this may still not meet the threshold of the proxy-model. Similarly, suppose the Libyan Coast Guard intercepts vessels or the Nigerien police confiscates vehicles used by smugglers, while Europe provided training, assets and model statutes to couch the whole enterprise in a legislative framework: this may still be not enough. After all, in all the judgments of the Strasbourg Court embracing the proxy model, the respondent states were always: 1) strongly military involved on the ground, 2) creating overall control over the foreign territory, while 3) the local administration – often a 'puppet regime' – survived by virtue of the support from the respondent state.

Nonetheless, an argument that can be developed and that lies within the reach of adjudicative bodies to embrace is that the proxy model does not necessarily have to aim at plain control over a foreign territory but may instead be applied to functionally limited areas of governmental activity. One such functional area of government activity could be migration control. Just as the exercise of authority (ECmHR *X and Y v Switzerland*; HRC *Gueye*) or control (HRC *Saldias de Lopez*) abroad can be functionally limited (whether exercised *de jure* or *de facto*), foreign subordinate administrations might be targeted as proxies for limited purposes.

A case in point would be the Libyan GNA after the removal of Gaddafi and the way it has been sustained not only to create stability in parts of Libya, but also to function as a tool for stemming migration towards the EU. As pointed out by *inter alia* Giuffré and Moreno-Lax (2019, pp. 105–106), Moreno-Lax (2020b) and Pijnenburg (2020, p. 326), both Italy and the EU have been heavily involved in Libyan exit control by the combined use of the Italian MRCC's coordination, intelligence sharing, the training of Libyan border guards, the provision of equipment and large assets such as patrol vessels and the deployment of an Italian vessel and staff in the port of Tripoli for technical support. If proxy control need neither cover an entire area nor a multiplicity of areas of governmental activity, Italy's efforts suffice to constitute functionally limited human rights jurisdiction by proxy. The same is true for Australia's outsourcing of processing to Nauru and PNG where asylum seekers their refugee status was to be determined by the local administration but with heavy financial, logistical and technical support from Australia.

What these novel interpretations of the above-mentioned scholars do is increasingly isolate 'decisive influence' as a new autonomous basis for the triggering of primary duty, emancipating it from the context in which the proxy model came into existence: control over foreign territory through the use of puppet regimes. The challenge, then, lies in being able to establish *decisive influence over a functionally limited area of governmental activity* as a sufficient justification for the extraterritorial applicability of human rights law. It is a route taken by the Human Rights Committee in its observations with regard to Australian practices when it considered that 'significant levels of control and influence exercised by the state party over the operation of the offshore regional processing centres, including over their establishment, funding and service provided therein, amount to such effective control' (Human Rights Committee (hereafter 'HRCee') 2017, para. 35). It is to be seen whether human rights courts and other bodies will follow suit.

It should be noted that as the level of practical involvement on the ground of the outsourcing state becomes thus high, it can be qualified as an instance of *externalisation* through the use of state agents and resources, rather than an instance of *outsourcing* which is about leaving migration administration primarily up to the apparatus of foreign governments as is the case with for instance Turkey. Lower levels of involvement, on the other hand, may not suffice to trigger the outsourcing state to become an additional primary duty-bearer as the third state remains the one with actual political power over the stakes of the (would-be) migrants. This does not have to obstruct that the outsourcing state may incur legal responsibilities for human rights purposes of a secondary order, for instance, under the state responsibility rules on complicity. Contrary to the threshold of the proxy model which requires decisive influence, it suffices under Article 16 ARSIWA that a state's conduct merely contributed to the commission of human rights violations in order to entail the assisting state's responsibility for that aid. Different from responsibility as a result of human rights jurisdiction, however, aid and assistance would not entail the responsibility of the outsourcing state for the human rights violations themselves, but only for act of giving aid and assistance to the cooperating third state.

Outsourcing and the effects model

According to the *effects model*, the applicability of a human rights instrument can be triggered when state conduct has an effect on the enjoyment of rights even when the person whose rights are affected is situated abroad and the state lacks authority or control over the stakes of the person concerned. Purely causal models for establishing human rights jurisdiction are *in an early stage of development* in legal practice. *Drozd and Janousek* (ECtHR 1992, para. 91) and *Munaf* (HRCee 2009, paras. 7.5 and 14) are often cited as precedents recognising the effects model. While they did indeed employ the language of 'effects', they in fact did not established anything along the lines of cause-and-effect doctrine for establishing human rights jurisdiction. Strasbourg cases which could potentially be conceived of as instantiations of the effects model, such as *Pad* (ECtHR 2007, paras. 6 and 54) and *Kovačić* (ECtHR 2004, p. 52(c)) can also rather be categorised under the control model (physical control over persons established through the firing from a helicopter) and authority model (legislative authority over banking services of banks operational abroad), respectively. An affirmative judicial opinion has, however, come from the Inter-American Court of Human Rights, opining that effective control over a domestic source causing extraterritorial harm impacting the human rights of persons abroad suffices to trigger human rights jurisdiction (IACtHR 2017, paras. 101–102 and 104).

The state of the art of the case law aside, *theoretically* the effects model differs from models emphasising authority or control in that the latter are supposed to involve *effecting* the stakes of a person (in casu the power to determine the status or control the movement of (would-be) migrants), while the former only involves the *affecting or the ability to affect* the stakes of a person (cf. Raible 2020, pp. 106–113). Practically, a continuum may exist between effecting and affecting the stakes of individuals. Both Lawson and Shany, for instance, require state conduct as a cause to be *sufficiently close and tangible* to its effects in order to bring about the primary duty of states (Lawson 2004, p. 104 ('direct and immediate link'); Shany 2013, p. 69 ('direct, significant, and foreseeable')). Per these views, relations of duty should evaporate as causal chains stretch out too far. Other commentators, however, have argued to follow through further along the causal chain (Salomon 2013, pp. 280-282; Vandenhole 2007, pp. 87-88). Principle 9 of the *Maastricht Principles*, for instance, suggests that a state incurs obligations in situations over which state acts or omissions bring about *foreseeable* effects on the enjoyment of economic, social and cultural rights, whether within or outside its territory. It requires these effects neither to be *direct (or 'immediate')* nor to be *significant* (cf. Lawson and Shany). As models for triggering human rights obligations seek to explain their relation to notions of justice, they may not only climb down the causal chain but also introduce temporal aspects of causation as relevant to the establishment of duty; for instance, by introducing past wrongs and their continuing effects (Achiume 2019; Miller 2007, Chapter 6).

The implications for bringing the outsourcing of migration control within the ambit of the human rights instruments are complicated along these lines. When techniques of migration control end up in direct and reasonably foreseeable human rights abuses, this may entail the 'human rights jurisdiction' of the outsourcing state and thus trigger the applicability of the human rights instrument at hand. The direct affecting of the EU-Turkey deal of exit options of vulnerable migrants at variance with the right to leave may be a case in point. Incentivising transit states to enhance their state apparatus and legislation, as we saw with, for instance, Niger and Morocco, and the human rights abuses that might arise as a result, may however be too remote. Much will depend on how far judicial and monitoring bodies are willing to go down the causal chain for establishing human rights jurisdiction. This would indeed require relaxing the combined qualifying criteria of directness, significance and foreseeability of the connection between the power projected by the outsourcing state and the actual power exercised by the third state over the migrant.

Conclusion

Territorial migration control ordinarily does not pose any problems in terms of the applicability of human rights law: being subjected to the authority and control of state officials in airports, harbours or land crossing points suffices to engage the state not to return persons away where this would prejudice their human rights. The link between the efforts of affluent states to control migration outside their borders and the negative impact this has on the rights of (would-be) migrants is less straightforward but undeniable nonetheless. However, while human rights courts and bodies have been able to call out states on the human rights implications of a first wave of externalisation methods, a second generation of such externalisation efforts has arisen in response to this judicial oversight: western destination states more frequently and intensely rely on the involvement of third states to stem migratory movements towards their territories. The first generation of externalisation was relatively easy to accommodate under the concept of human rights jurisdiction by virtue of the externalising states' use of state agents to assert authority and/or control over the stakes of migrants. The second generation of outsourcing, however, precisely seeks to avoid these assertions of authority and control over the person of the migrant to function as a catalyst for relations of duty to arise.

More than the first generation of externalisation of migration control, outsourcing challenges the classic vocabulary available to human rights lawyers. It should encourage them to explore and develop understandings of 'human rights jurisdiction' or other concepts for that matter which are able to capture the actual relations of power which continue to inform (enhance even) the control of affluent states over the mobility of people. This contribution depicted two promising avenues in this regard: the proxy model and the effects model. It is in the zones between *effecting* and *affecting*, between *control* and *influence*, between *direct* and *indirect*, between *present* and *past* assertions of power that concepts await further research. Through carefully crafting piecemeal changes in these models' margins, lawyers may convince adjudicators to take these models beyond the contexts in which they were conceived and to adapt them to projections of state power in the context of migration control. Absent progressive developments in legal practice, advocates may still seek to rely on ancillary forms of state responsibility for outsourcing practices of states. The challenge there lies not so much with meeting the conditions for establishing complicity under the rules on state responsibility but in finding out to which extent affected migrants may seek standing before the relevant courts and bodies absent finding themselves 'within the human rights jurisdiction' of the potential respondent states.

References

Achiume, E.T. (2019) 'Migration as Decolonization', *Stanford Law Review* 71(6), 1509–1574.

Achiume, E.T. et al. (2017) *'The Situation in Nauru and Manus Island: Liability for Crimes Against Humanity in the Detention of Refugees and Asylum Seekers', Communiqué to the Office of the Prosecutor of the ICC.*

Besson, S. (2012) 'The Extraterritoriality of the European Convention on Human Rights: Why Human Rights Depend on Jurisdiction and What Jurisdiction Amounts to', *Leiden Journal of International Law* 25(4), 857–884.

Campesi, G. (2018) 'Italy and the Militarisation of Euro-Mediterranean Border Control Policies' in Burroughs, E. and Williams, K. (eds.). *Contemporary Boat Migration: Data, Geopolitics, and Discourses*, Rowman & Littlefield.

Casas-Cortes, M. and Cobarrubias, S. (2019) 'Genealogies of Contention in Concentric Circles: Remote Migration Control and its Eurocentric Geographical Imaginaries' in Mitchell, K. et al. (eds.). *Handbook on Critical Geographies on Migration*, Elgar.

European Commission (EC) (2011) Communication from the Commission to the European Parliament, the Council, the European Economic and Social Committee and the Committee of the Regions – The Global Approach to Migration and Mobility, 18 November 2011, COM(2011) 743 final.

_______ (2015) Communication from the Commission to the European Parliament, the Council, the European Economic and Social Committee and the Committee of the Regions: A European Agenda on Migration, 13 May 2015, COM(2015) 240 final 8–9.

_______ (2017) 'Migration on the Central Mediterranean route: Managing flows, saving lives', Joint Communication to the European Parliament, the European Council and the Council, 25 January 2017.

European Commission of Human Rights (ECmHR) (1977), *X and Y v Switzerland* (App. No. 7289/75).

_______ (1992), *M. v Denmark* (App. No. 17392/90).

European Council (2016), EU-Turkey statement, 18 March 2016, press release.

_______ (2002), Presidency Conclusions of the Seville European Council of 21–22 June 2002.

_______ (1999), Presidency Conclusions of the Tampere European Council of 15–16 October 1999.

European Court of Human Rights (ECtHR) (1992), *Drozd and Janousek v France and Spain* (App. No. 1274/87).

_______ (1995), *Loizidou v. Turkey (preliminary objections)* (App. No. 15318/89).

_______ (1996), *Loizidou v. Turkey* (App. No. 15318/89).

_______ (2004), *Ilaşcu and Others v. Moldova and Russia* (App. No. 48787/99).

_______ (2004), *Kovačić and Others v. Slovenia* (App. Nos. 44574/98 and others).

_______ (2007), *Pad and Others v. Turkey* (App. No. 60167/00).

_______ (2012), *Hirsi Jamaa and Others v. Italy* (App. No. 27765/09).

_______ (2015), *Chiragov and Others v. Armenia* (App. No. 13216/05).

_______ (2020), *M.N. and Others v. Belgium* (App. No. 3599/18).

FitzGerald, D.S. (2019) *Refuge Beyond Reach: How Rich Democracies Repel Asylum Seekers*, Oxford University Press.

Gammeltoft-Hansen, T. and Hathaway, J. (2015) 'Non-Refoulement in a World of Cooperative Deterrence', *Columbia Journal of Transnational Law* 53(2), 235–284.

Giuffré, M. and Moreno-Lax, V. (2019) 'The Rise of Consensual Containment: From Contactless Control to Contactless Responsibility for Migratory Flows' in Juss, S.S. (ed.). *Research Handbook on International Refugee Law*, Elgar.

Gonzalez Garcia, I. (2020) 'Immigration in Spain: Migratory Routes, Cooperation with Third Countries and Human Rights in Return Procedures' in Ippolito, F. et al. (eds.). *Bilateral Relations in the Mediterranean. Prospects for Migration Issues*, Elgar.

Human Rights Committee (HR Cee) (1983), *Lichtensztejn v Uruguay* (Comm. No. 77/1980).

_______ (1984), *Saldias de Lopez v. Uruguay* (Comm. No. 52/1979).

_______ (1989), *Gueye and Others v. France* (Comm. No. 196/1985).

_______ (2009), *Munaf v. Romania* (Comm. No. 1539/2006).

_______ (2017) Concluding observations on the sixth periodic report of Australia, CCPR/C/AUS/CO/6, 1 December 2017.

Human Rights Council (HRC) (2015a) UPR Summary prepared by the OHCHR – Australia A/HRC/WG.6/23/AUS/3.

_______ (2015b), UPR Compilation prepared by the OHCHR – Australia A/HRC/WG.6/23/AUS/2.

_______ (2015c), National report of Australia submitted in the context of the Universal Periodic Review, A/HRC/WG.6/23/AUS/1.

Human Rights Watch (2013) Barely surviving. Detention, Abuse, and Neglect of Migrant Children in Indonesia.

Inter-American Court of Human Rights (IACtHR) (2017), *Advisory Opinion 23/17.*

IACtHR (2018), *Advisory Opinion 25/18.*

Jones, R. (2016) *Violent borders. Refugees and the right to move*, Verso.

Kneebone, S. (2014) 'The Bali Process and Global Refugee Policy in the Asia-Pacific Region', *Journal of Refugee Studies* 27(4), 596–618.

Larking, E. (2017) 'Controlling Irregular Migration in the Asia-Pacific: Is Australia Acting against its Own Interests?', *Asia & Pacific Policy Studies* 4(1), 85–103.

Lawson, R. (2004) 'Life after Banković: On the Extraterritorial Application of the European Convention on Human Rights' in Coomans, F. and Kamminga, M.T. (eds.). *Extraterritorial Application of Human Rights Treaties*, Intersentia.

Longo, M. (2018) *The Politics of Borders. Sovereignty, Security, and the Citizen after 9/11*, Cambridge University Press.

Milanovic, M. (2011) *Extraterritorial Application of Human Rights Treaties: Law, Principles, and Policy*, Oxford University Press.

Miller, D. (2007) *National Responsibility and Global Justice*, Oxford University Press.

Moreno-Lax, V. (2017) *Accessing Asylum in Europe. Extraterritorial Border Controls and Refugee Rights under EU Law*, Oxford University Press.

Moreno-Lax, V. (2020a) *EU External Migration Policy and the Protection of Human Rights, European Parliament's subcommittee on Human Right.*

_______ (2020b) 'The Architecture of Functional Jurisdiction: Unpacking Contactless Control', *German Law Review* 21(3), 385–416.

Mussi, F. and Tan, N.F. (2015) 'Comparing Cooperation on Migration Control: Italy-Libya and Australia-Indonesia', *Irish Yearbook of International Law* 10, 87–108.

Papua New Guinea Supreme Court (2016), *Belden Norman Namah and Others v PNG* (SC1497).

Phillips, J. (2017) 'A Comparison of Coalition and Labor Government Asylum Policies in Australia since 2001', *Research Paper Series*, Parliament of Australia, February 2017.

Pijnenburg, A. (2020) 'Containment Instead of Refoulement: Shifting State Responsibility in the Age of Cooperative Migration Control?', *Human Rights Law Review* 20(2), 306–332.

Raible, L. (2020) *Human Rights Unbound: A Theory of Extraterritoriality*, Oxford University Press.

Salomon, M.E. (2013) 'Deprivation, Causation and the Law of International Cooperation' in Langford, M. et al. (eds.). *Global Justice, State Duties*, Cambridge University Press.

Shany, Y. (2013) 'Taking Universality Seriously: Functional Approach to Extraterritoriality in International Human Rights Law', *Law & Ethics of Human Rights* 7(1), 47–71.

Spagnolo, A. (2019) 'The Conclusion of Bilateral Agreements and Technical Arrangements for the Management of Migration Flows: An Overview of Italian Practice', *Italian Yearbook of International Law* 28(1), 209–230.

Tubiana, S. et al. (2018) *Multilateral Damage: The Impact of EU Migration Policies on Central Saharan Routes*, Clingendael.

Vandenhole, W. (2007) 'Third State Obligations under the ICESCR: A Case Study of EU Sugar Policy', *Nordic Journal of International Law* 76, 73–100.

Weber, L. and Pickering, S. (2011) *Globalization and Borders. Death at the Global Frontier*, Palgrave MacMillan.

13

Climate change displacement and socio-economic rights of the child under the African human rights system

The relevance of ETOs

Ademola Oluborode Jegede

Introduction

Climate change poses challenges to the populations of the world. Underlying the phenomenon is the increasing concentration of greenhouse gases resulting from anthropogenic activities which are pushing the climate beyond the level that is considered safe for livelihood (Intergovernmental Panel on Climate Change (IPCC) 2018; United Nations General Assembly (UNGA) 1988). This development has resulted in an increased warming of the earth surface which negatively affects societies and their populations (UN 2020; IPCC 2018). While climate change has several adverse effects on populations, displacement and its associated plight as consequence are significant for children in Africa. Importantly, how extraterritorial conduct or omissions associated with climate change can result in displacement of children in Africa merits scrutiny. Generally, extraterritorial obligations (ETOs) are a burgeoning topic in international human rights law (Vandenhole 2020; Bulto 2011). Hence, the extraterritorial link of climate change with displacement of children as both a challenge and driver of possible measures to address it in Africa is not as clear.

For instance, without a reference to displacement or ETOs, the UN Human Rights Council (UNHRC) Resolution 26/33 (UNHRC 2014), linking climate change to human rights, mentions only in passing that children are vulnerable to climate change. The subsequent report of the Office of the High Commissioner for Human Rights (OHCHR) connects climate change and the enjoyment of the rights of the child under the Convention on the Rights of the Child (CRC 1989) and highlights measures including 'extraterritorial jurisdiction' as a recommendation (OHCHR 2017, paras. 29 and 62(c)). Nevertheless, the basis for the application of such measures in the context of displacement of children in Africa is not articulated. Reports by Mbaye (2020), BBC (2019) and writings of other authors such as Boko *et al.* (2008) establish that states in Africa are more vulnerable to climate change. Also, the Committee on the Rights

 DOI: 10.4324/9781003090014-17

of the Child, the treaty monitoring body for the Convention on the Rights of the Child (CRC 1989), identifies climate change as a threat to children's health and urges states parties to put children's health concerns at the centre of their climate change adaptation and mitigation strategies (CRC Committee, General Comment no. 15), but this is done without any comments on extraterritoriality.

The extraterritorial nature of climate change is evident in its global nature (UNGA 1988) and climate pillar instruments such as the United Nations Framework Convention on Climate Change (UNFCCC 1992), and Kyoto Protocol (2005), and the Paris Agreement (2015) that recognise the global threat of climate change. For instance, the Paris Agreement (2015) draws no jurisdictional boundary in its call upon states to respect, promote and consider their respective human rights obligations towards the protection of the rights of the child and intergenerational equity when taking actions to address climate change. The nature of ETOs required of states in socio-economic and cultural rights context has been carefully expounded in the *Maastricht Principles* on Extraterritorial Obligations of States in the Area of Economic, Social and Cultural Rights (Maastricht ETO Principles 2011), and the authoritative writings including De Schutter *et al.* (2012). But, there is a rare scrutiny on the causal link of displacement of children to extraterritorial acts underlying climate change and its implication for their socio-economic rights in Africa.

Mutua (2000) defines the African human rights system by its normative instruments and jurisprudence. These normative instruments and jurisprudence reflect the efforts by Africa to respond to its own challenges by offering solutions to Africa's problems. Consequently, the children rights protection regime exists within the system, but the form of legal protection available to children in the context of displacement linked to climate extraterritorial conduct or omission requires an interrogation. For instance, there is the African Charter on the Rights and Welfare of the Child (ACRWC 1990) which prescribes a range of socio-economic rights for children. The treaty monitoring body of the instrument, the African Committee of Experts on the Rights and Welfare of Children (CERWC), nonetheless, has neither any jurisprudence nor major work on climate-induced displacement of children. Relevant activities around climate change have no specific focus on displacement. For instance, only a call for general awareness of the general impact of climate change is urged in a 2020 press statement where the CERWC reiterates that children are the most vulnerable to bear the brunt of the impacts of climate change in Africa (AU Press 2020). Resolution 153 (African Commission on Human and Peoples' Rights (ACHPR) 2009a) in relation to climate change in Africa is also not supported or informed by detailed analysis and bears nothing on extraterritorial link of climate change and displacement. A novel regional convention called the African Union Convention for the Protection and Assistance of Internally Displaced Persons in Africa (Kampala Convention 2009) recognises that climate change may occasion displacement in its Article 5(4); however, what this normative environment entails for the plight of climate-displaced children is neither specified in the instrument nor explained in the jurisprudence of the African Commission on Human and People's Rights (the African Commission), which is the treaty monitoring body for the African Charter on Human and Peoples (African Charter) (OAU 1986).

Against this backdrop, this chapter articulates the extraterritorial link of climate change to displacement and the socio-economic rights of children in Africa. It then explores how ETOs may be deployed under the African human rights system in response to the challenge. Some caveats are, however, necessary at the onset. First, the major focus of the chapter is not on the right to asylum-seeking or refugee status which may or may not be the legal consequence of displacement. Displacement generally happens within a territory. Second, in dealing with displacement caused by climate change, it is acknowledged that even if differentially, scenarios causing climate change may occur within and outside Africa. These scenarios include population dynamics (Bongaarts and

O'Neill 2018), historic fossil-based economic development path (IBRD and World Bank 2010), and the unsustainable consumption or 'way of life' of the North (Paris Agreement 2015, preamble; Mckibben 2003). However, in discussing displacement of children linked to climate change in Africa, emphasis is placed on the failure of states within and outside Africa to regulate the conduct or omission of non-state actors responsible for extractive activities and climate change response measures which may result in displacement of children abroad. Third, the focus on children is due to their vulnerability and dependent circumstance which, as shall manifest, may negatively impact their socio-economic rights. Lastly, while the plights of displaced children are certain, the contribution is exploratory in the sense that there is no present jurisprudence of the African human rights system on children's rights that either draws a linkage to climate change or specifically mandates the extraterritorial application of its instruments on the protection of children.

The plight of climate-induced displacement of children and extraterritoriality

The World Bank (2018) estimates that 140 million people will be internally displaced by slow-onset climate change impacts by 2050. Of the 79.5 million displaced, the UNHCR (2019, p. 2) in its global report on forced displacement shows that 30–34 million are children. Due to circumstances including war and natural disasters, evidence exists that displaced children can cross national borders within Africa. Hence UNICEF (2018) highlights that 1/4 immigrants in Africa is a child, a development more than twice the global average. Of the African countries, South Africa and Nigeria host some of the largest child migrant populations in Africa (UNICEF 2018). Generally, the situations facing children substantiate unique challenges of displacement either at home or abroad. This is due to their vulnerability, reliance on adults and decreased ability to protect themselves from danger and to make decisions (Pfefferbaum et al. 2016). Displaced children lose the security, shelter, comfort, traditions and familiarity of a place and family which they have usually enjoyed. Where unaccompanied and separated from their parents, they are exposed to starvation and abuse in forms including trafficking, exploitation and violence (UNICEF 2018). This is not surprising in that displacement disrupts their access to necessities including food, water and sanitation, health and education (UNICEF 2018; UNICEF 2003). The plight of displaced children is not any different even where they are in the company of a displaced family. Loss of land and income that are associated with displacement often render parents and/or extended families incapable of providing for the necessities of children. When displaced outside their states, they need asylum protection and access to basic amenities that are often lacking in a foreign land (UNICEF 2018; UNICEF 2003).

Whether the displacement of children may result from effects of climate change linked to extraterritorial activities is the focus of this section. Extraterritoriality connotes the activities by a state outside its territorial borders (Kanalan 2018; Colangelo 2014). It contrasts generally with the traditional notion of human rights that regulates the relationship between the state and individuals within the territory of the states (Kanalan 2018). In the context of this paper, extraterritoriality encompasses the conduct or omission of a state linked to climate change within or beyond its territory that has effects of displacement on children. It raises a significant issue as to whether a state in Africa or beyond can be responsible for the climate-induced displacement of children and its threat to their socio-economic rights in another African state. This section demonstrates that this is possible in two ways: through the conduct or omission of an African state or its non-state actor in and outside its territory in Africa; and through the conduct or omission of foreign non-state actors from non-African states (developed states) in their territories and in Africa.

Conduct or omission of an African state or its non-state actor

Emissions that are generated in African states and projects associated with alternative energy sources are significant to climate change, and arguably the displacement of children in Africa. To be sure, Africa accounts for only 2–3 per cent of the world's carbon dioxide emissions from energy and industrial sources; hence, it contributes least to climate change (UN 2006). This development is changing, though. In a new study featuring data compiled from two satellites, Japan's Greenhouse Gases Observing Satellite (GOSAT) and NASA'S Orbiting Carbon Observatory (OCO-2), Palmer *et al.* (2019) found that Africa's tropical lands released about close to 6 billion tonnes of CO_2 in 2016. ACHPR (2019) and earlier writing of Gorte & Sheikh (2010) explain that other carbon emission sources such as mining, construction and logging are a substantial driver of climate change in Africa. These findings are supported in more recent works. For instance, Burck *et al.* (2019) find that although Morocco has significantly increased the share of renewables over the past five years, its GHG emissions per capita are still high. The Mineral Council of South Africa (2019) and the Carbon Relief (2018) respectively account that due to its principal reliance on coal for energy, South Africa is adjudged as the world's 14th largest emitter of greenhouse gases (GHGs). Nigeria's CO_2 emissions has increased through 1999–2018 period to end at 110.7 million tonnes in 2018 (World Data Atlas 2018a), while within the same period, there was an increase which ended at 2.9 million tonnes in 2018 in Democratic Republic of the Congo (World Data Atlas 2018b). Despite a noticeable decline in Egypt, at current level of 217.44 million tonnes, carbon emissions remain high (Y Charts 2020). The impact of these activities may not be directly responsible for the immediate state of the climate and displacement, nevertheless, it is beyond territorial boundaries of these states and will contribute its own share to the worsening of the climate everywhere including Africa. These emissions are linked to global warming which generate climatic problems, including heat waves, flooding, pollution and a rise in sea level, drought, flooding (Toulmin 2009) which by implication can trigger the displacement of populations including children in Africa.

Also, the pursuit of climate response measures by states in Africa such as alternative and renewable energy sources has extraterritorial implications for the displacement of populations including children. It occurs where a state-owned company in one African state embarks on climate response activities in another state which leads to expropriation of land belonging to families and thereby occasion the displacement of children belonging to such communities. To illustrate, a company based in South Africa, Sasol has projects in Mozambique that are allegedly linked with temporary or permanent loss of access to land and location of cultural significance such as graves, damage to public and private property, permanent physical and economic displacement of families including children (Globeleq 2015). STEG International Services, which is a subsidiary of the Tunisian State-Owned Company of Electricity and Gas (STEG), implements projects in other states in Africa including Sierra Leone, Tanzania, Rwanda and Democratic Republic of Congo (Concord Times 2020). Evidence from Rwanda shows that the activities of STEG have the potential for displacing populations including children (REG 2019). The fact that the activities of businesses can be conducted in this manner points at a lack of exercise of legislative control by the states in which the parent businesses are established in Africa.

Conduct or omission of foreign-owned businesses of the North in Africa

Climate-induced displacement of children linked to extraterritorial acts can arise from the failure of developed states to control effectively the conduct or omission of their private companies operating in states in Africa. In particular, the activities of companies of the North in the extractive sector during the mining process, as shown by reports, contribute greatly to the release of greenhouse gases such as carbon dioxide and methane which aggravate climate change (Bruckner et al. 2014). As reported by the UN Environment (2019), such extraction activities have been responsible for 18 per cent of resource-related climate change. The negative implication of this development on water resources, food security, biodiversity, human health and infrastructure triggers displacement of populations including children.

The lack of appropriate control by developed states can incentivise widespread expropriation of land for climate response projects by companies and thereby drive the displacement of children along with their families. There are examples on the foregoing activities in different parts of Africa. For instance, Nigeria has a range of western oil companies, such as Mobil, Texaco, Agip, Chevron, Exxon and Royal Dutch/Shell that hold oil production licences in the Niger Delta, one of the biggest wetlands in the world. Of all these companies, Shell Nigeria, a subsidiary of Royal Dutch/Shell, was the first to discover oil in Ogoniland, Niger Delta area (Hennchen 2015). Persistent oil and gas flaring in Ogoniland does not only contribute to climate change as it means the releases of carbon dioxide underlying global warming into the atmosphere (Bruckner et al. 2014, p. 522; UN 2006). Its associated effects including the pollution of the ecosystem and devastation of the land, water and air cause displacement of populations and importantly children in Ogoni land (UNHRC 2018).

The implementation of the project that aimed to address climate change by promoting alternative energy also causes displacement of children. For instance, the involvement of London-based Central African Mining and Exploration Company (CAMEC) in a large bio-ethanol project, called Procan, plays a significant role in the dispossession and displacement of populations including children in Central and Southern Africa (Vermeulen and Cotula 2010). Overall, the conduct or omission of state-owned corporations by Africa in other African states and the conduct or omission of foreign companies of the North in Africa may result in the displacement which involves children in Africa. The next section considers the likely implications of this displacement for broader socio-economic rights of children in Africa.

Extraterritorial climate displacement as a violation of socio-economic rights of children

Although not yet applied extraterritorially, the instruments in the African human rights system seek to protect the socio-economic rights of children through the provisions of the ACRWC (1990), the African Charter (OAU 1986), and the Kampala Convention (2009), the latter being relevant in the context of climate change and displacement. The provisions of these instruments are instructive on socio-economic rights linkage to displacement and are further illuminated by the decisions of treaty monitoring bodies at the African regional level, notably, the CERWC and the African Commission. Both monitoring bodies apply international human rights instruments under the United Nations, through Article 60 of the African Charter (OAU 1986) and Article 46 of the ACERW (1990) which empowers them respectively to draw inspirations from international human rights instruments. The treaty monitoring bodies within the African human rights system has handled matters of significance to socio-economic rights, foreign non-state actors and displacement of children. In *Institute for Human Rights and Development and Others v. Democratic Republic of Congo* (ACHPR 2016, *Kilwa* case), the African Commission noted that the displacement of populations including children and the destruction of the socio-economic infrastructure such as the schools, hospital and other structures can be linked to activities of foreign-owned companies operating in Africa. Hence, it condemned the atrocious involvement of corporations (particularly Anvil mining, Australia) in the violations of rights and gave clear directions as to the minimum obligation on companies not to actively violate or support the violation of human rights in Africa. Understandably, it is difficult to find a violation of extraterritorial obligations as neither Australia (Developed state) nor Anvil mining (non-state actor) is party to the African Charter or other instruments in the African human rights system.

Also, the decision of CERWC in *Michelo Hansungule and others (on behalf of Children in Northern Uganda) v. the Government of Uganda* (*Children of Northern Uganda* case) (ACHPR 2013) is instructive on the general effects of displacement on children's rights. In that case, the CERWC establishes the link between massive displacement and gross violations of human rights including children's rights (ACHPR 2013, paras. 2, 3 and 7). In doing so, it found their displacement a violation of Article 1(1) of the ACRWC (ACHPR 2013, para. 37) which requires states in Africa to adopt legislative and other measures for the recognition rights, freedoms and duties enshrined in the instrument (ACHPR 2013, para. 37).

Arguably, climate-induced displacement of children can infringe a range of socio-economic rights of children. Rights of children are indivisibly linked, but activities of actors underlying climatic problems trigger several distressing events that separate them from friends and family members. Even when families stay together, the difficulties they face in establishing a degree of security and community solidarity affects them and pose a general threat to Article 18 of the ACRWC (1990) on the right to children to parental care and protection. Such activities also have implications on the right to health, the right to education and culture, the right to water and the right to food of children in Africa.

All said, the extraterritorial link of climate change to displacement infringes a range of socio-economic rights of the child, namely, the right to health, the right to education and culture, the right to water and the right to food of children in Africa. It remains to be seen the extraterritorial potentials within the African human rights system that may apply to respond to climate-induced displacement and its impact on socio-economic rights of children in Africa.

Potentials for extraterritorial response to climate-induced displacement of children

Generally, the protection of human rights is territorial (Kanalan 2018), but recent writings argue the possibility of extraterritorial application of economic and social cultural rights guaranteed in key UN human rights instruments (Vandenhole 2020; Skogly 2013; Coomans 2011) and their relevance to the children's rights protection regime (Vandenhole 2020; Vandenhole 2009). For instance, Coomans (2011) explains that the International Covenant on Economic, Social and Cultural Rights (ICESCR) has extraterritorial dimension in that its treaty monitoring body, the CESCR Committee, calls upon states to seek foreign assistance in fulfilling socio-economic responsibilities (CESCR General Comment no. 22, paras. 50–52). Using UN General Comment no. 19 on public budgeting resources to fully realise the CRC (CRC Committee General Comment no. 19) as an example, Vandenhole (2020, p. 227) clarifies that the interpretation of the Committee on the Rights of the Child regarding extraterritorial application of the CRC is in line with that of the CESCR.

Triggers for the application of extraterritorial fulfilment of human rights include the causation of human rights harm (Skogly 2013), and historical responsibility (Vandenhole 2020; Vandenhole and Benedek 2013). The latter point is in fact instructive as it is the basis for the principle of common but differentiated responsibility which is entrenched in Articles 3(1) and 4(1) of the UNFCCC (1992), Article 10 of the Kyoto Protocol (2005) and Article 2(2) of the Paris Agreement (2015) to ensure fairness and equity between the North and South in the global response to climate change (Wang and Gao 2018). It also agrees with the 'polluters pay principle', which traces responsibility to address environmental change to those who are responsible for its cause (Luppi, Parisi and Rajagopalan 2012; Rio Declaration 1992, principle 16). Addressing causation linked to activities of North is problematic, although attribution science is developing and making it possible to address causation challenges by linking a company's conduct to climate harm. This is done by establishing: (a) the association between greenhouse gas emissions and meteorological change; and (b) the relationship between meteorological change and societal impacts (McCormick et al. 2018). Hence, it may be possible to be able to link a company's conduct with a particular climate harm even if only partially (McCormick et al. 2018).

At the African regional level, the possibilities of extraterritorial application of key instruments have also been subject of scholarship. With respect to the African Charter, Viljoen (2008, p. 107) notes that accountability is possible where 'an extraterritorial incident or even in cases where the state has *de facto* control over that incident or event'. On the same instrument, Bulto (2011, p. 523) argues that there is 'no textual basis to limit the spatial reach of socio-economic rights such as the right to water or correlative state obligations to a state's territorial jurisdiction'. In a number of his writings, Jegede (2017; 2016) argues that key African regional human rights instruments including the Kampala Convention may apply extraterritorially in the context of climate-induced displacement of indigenous peoples. Regarding obligations of states towards children, General Comment no. 5 of the CERWC (2018) generally discusses the obligations of states in Africa in strengthening the protection of the rights of the child. Using the instruments that constitute children rights regime under the AU as a basis of analysis, this section argues that extraterritorial responsibility for climate-induced displacement of children is possible on two grounds: extraterritorial application of obligations among states in Africa; and obligations applicable to developed states outside Africa.

Extraterritorial obligations among states towards children in Africa

According to the General Comment no. 5 of the CERWC (2018, para. 3.5), the core and universally accepted obligations to 'respect', 'protect', 'promote' and 'fulfil' children's rights apply to the implementation of the ACRWC as a whole. These obligations agree with the Kampala Convention (2009, preamble), and the African Charter (1986) as discernible from the jurisprudence of the African Commission in the *Ogoniland* case (para. 45). It is also supported by the provisions of *Maastricht Principles* (2011, p. 3) on extraterritorial obligations of states representing international expert opinion that clarifies states obligations under international human rights law. The principles are applicable as part of the children's rights regime in Africa by virtue of Article 61 of the African Charter (1986) and Article 46 of the ACERWC (1990) which allow the monitoring bodies of these respective instruments to draw inspiration from international human rights law.

That the provisions of AU human rights instruments are applicable extraterritorially among states in Africa is not farfetched. Article 1 of the ACRWC (1990), which speaks to obligations of states, is not territorial in nature. Rather, it calls upon states to recognise all the rights and duties entrenched in the instrument and takes needful measures to ensure its realisation. Besides, the extraterritorial application of these instruments to climate-induced displacement of children is in the best interest of the child in Africa. Article 4(1) of the ACRWC (1990) establishes that 'in all actions undertaken by any person or authority, the best interests of the child shall be the primary consideration'. It is in the best interest of the child to require actors responsible for climate-induced displacement to contribute towards its solution whether they are based within or outside the territory of its occurrence. This reasoning is consistent with General Comment no. 5 of the

CERWC (2018, para. 4.2) which dismisses the idea that there can be any conditions that could thin the scope, reach or standard of the application of the principle of the best interest of the child. Interestingly, General Comment no. 5 of the CERWC (2018, para. 4.2) also requires 'private actors, including parents, institutions, business entities and various non-state actors engaged with children's rights and services' to adopt the principle of the best interest of the child in all endeavours. Hence, considering that private and non-state actors are involved in activities triggering the climate change scenarios that drive displacement of children, it is legally plausible to construe that extraterritorial obligations exist among states in Africa to 'respect', 'protect', 'promote' and 'fulfil' rights as a response to climate-induced displacement of children in Africa.

The obligation to 'respect' connotes that states should not interfere in the enjoyment of rights of collective groups (ACHPR 2001, para. 45). The *Maastricht Principles* (2011, Principles 29–35), De Schutter *et al* (2012, pp. 1126–1133) indicate that the extraterritorial obligation to 'respect' requires states to refrain from direct conduct which may hinder the realisation of rights outside their territories. Articles 3(1)(a), (d) & 4(1) of the Kampala Convention (2009) reflect obligations to 'respect' children rights in the context of displacement where it requires state parties to 'refrain from, prohibit and prevent arbitrary displacement of populations'. In the situation of climate-induced displacement and children, the extraterritorial application of the obligation to 'respect' signifies that no state in Africa should, through its agents, be involved in climate response projects in a manner that brings about the displacement of children in another African state. It demands that where involvement in such projects is inevitable, the best interest of the child should be a consideration.

The obligation to 'protect', according to the African Commission, requires states to adopt measures such as legislation and to provide effective remedies for the protection of rights holders 'against political, economic and social interferences' and to control non-state actors so that their operations do not hamper rights (ACHPR 2001, para. 46). This position resonates with the *Maastricht Principles* (2011) which require states to ensure through appropriate legislation that their non-state actors do not hinder rights abroad. Where states cannot regulate their conduct, they should at the very least influence the conduct of non-state actors and cooperate to ensure that rights are not impeded extraterritorially by non-state actors. To children at risk of climate-induced displacement, this means states should put in place a mix of laws and regulations so that their rights are not impeded due to climate change but protected. Also, it means that states should seek to apply existing legislation and regulation in such a manner that children imperilled by climate-induced displacement are offered adequate assistance.

The obligation to 'fulfil' requires states to mobilise 'its machinery towards the actual realisation of the rights' (ACHPR 2001, para. 47). It includes the provision of 'basic needs such as food or resources that can be used for food'. The *Maastricht Principles* specify that the extraterritorial implication of the obligation to 'fulfil' involves cooperation, request and response to international assistance. In relation to obligation to cooperate, Article 8(3)(d) tasks the AU to cooperate with African states and other actors for protecting and assisting displaced persons. The General Comment no. 5 of the CERWC (2018, para. 7.2) calls upon states to cooperate with AU structures, as well as with national and international partners, to discourage practices that are incompatible with the ACERWC. Arguably, this cooperation can be in form of relaxing asylum-seeking rules and expediting the asylum-seeking applications where children are involved. For instance, one would expect an African state whose non-state actor is known for activities responsible for displacement of children in another state in Africa to be obliged to accept asylum-seeking applications involving children from states where their corporations operate. Doing so is not based on moral guilt but on the best interest of children to enable children, and by implication, their care givers settle quickly, and access resources required for the welfare and upbringing in foreign African states.

The obligation to *fulfil* also involves assistance. Article 20 (2)(a) of the ACRWC (1990) urges state parties to provide material support and assistance. Along similar lines, Article 3(2)(d) of the Kampala Convention (2009) urges state parties to make available, as far as possible, the necessary funds and seek international support for protecting displaced persons in Africa. Article 9(2)(b) of the same instrument reinforces that the assistance includes the provision of food, water, shelter and medical care for their necessary protection. Also, at least states from which corporations whose climate-related activities occasion displacement originate should be willing to assist in making these essential provisions possible. Where unable to provide, they should lead or support the request for international assistance either within or outside Africa. In line with this obligation, states in Africa can seek assistance from one another in responding to climate-induced displacement of children in Africa. Also, based on the vulnerability of children, assistance that addresses pressing needs such as food shelter and water should be a matter of priority.

The obligation to 'promote' the enjoyment of all human rights entails that state parties should ensure 'that individuals are able to exercise their rights, for example, by promoting tolerance, raising awareness, and even building infrastructures' (ACHPR 2001, para. 46). Its extraterritorial connotation is explained by the *Maastricht Principles* (2011) to include the observance of principles such as informed participation (Principle 7), and impact assessment (Principle 14). This obligation is evident in the provisions of Articles 10(2) and 10(3) of the Kampala Convention (2009) that aim at promoting consultation and participation of displayed persons in decision-making and the socio-economic and environmental impact assessment of projects related to development. While these provisions generally relate to displaced persons, it applies to the specific circumstance of children confronted by climate-induced displacement. Its application requires that states with actors operating in other states in Africa should ensure that such actors engage children in participation, assess climate-related projects in terms of their potential impacts of children and embark on programmes and activities that strengthen and do not undermine the best interest of children. Doing so may help in averting displacement and its harmful consequences on the socio-economic rights of children in Africa.

Role of developed states towards climate-displaced children in Africa

There are provisions in the children's rights protection regime of Africa that justify a proposition that developed states, in particular, those whose non-state actors are at the heart of climate-related displacement, have a role to play for extraterritorial conduct or omission underlying the climate-induced displacement of children. Article 20 (2)(a) of the ACRWC (1990) urges state parties to provide material support and assistance but does not foreclose assistance from states outside Africa. Also, Article 8(3)(b) of the Kampala Convention (1990), which requires the AU to 'co-ordinate mobilisation of international resources for the assistance and protection' for displaced persons, can be applied to mobilise funds in support of children displaced by climate change. To fulfil the role, emphasis is placed in Article 8(3)(c) of the Kampala Convention on 'collaboration with international organisations and humanitarian agencies, civil society organisations and other relevant actors' to support concerned state parties. The fact that these provisions highlight the relevance of 'international organisations and humanitarian agencies, civil society organisations and other actors', without limiting this to Africa, suggests that states in Africa can reach for international support beyond Africa for children displaced due to climate change.

Where the above provisions in the children rights regime of the African human rights system are activated, developed countries in the North, even if not state parties to the instruments, should be obligated to support displaced children outside the accountability framework of the African human rights system. One reason is that the operations of foreign companies can be linked to displacement and violations of rights as seen in the *Kilwa* case. Another reason in support of such an expectation is that attribution science can help in linking causation of displacement of children with climate-related activities of companies from the North. Yet another reason is the necessity for 'colonial justice' which, according to Wilde (2020, p. 58), speaks to 'the environmentally harmful basis on which the economically privileged parts of the world attained this privilege'. The latter resonates loudly with Africa's tragic historical experience of colonialism and marginal contribution of the continent to the present state of the climate. Besides, within the pillar instruments on climate change, there are grounds to expect that the request and response to such assistance extend to developed states outside Africa. Developed states under the climate change related instruments, in particular, Article 4(1)(b) of the UNFCCC (1992) and Article 9 of the Paris Agreement (2015) have greater commitment to provide different forms of assistance, including the promotion, facilitation and provision of finances and appropriate technology, practices and processes to address the adverse effect of climate change in developing states, including Africa.

In the context of Africa and reference to children displaced by climate change, international organisations and humanitarian agencies should be willing to facilitate how children so displaced may be helped to settle down and access amenities in their newly found places or states, and thereby ensure that their socio-economic rights are not denied. This reasoning is supported by the *Maastricht Principles* (2011), which recognise the role of international assistance and cooperation of organisations and humanitarian agencies, civil society organisations and other actors (De Schutter *et al* 2012, p. 1104). Hence, regarding climate-induced displacement of children, states can request the AU as an entity to use its platforms of engagement to mobilise international resources for the assistance and resources required to address the climate-related displacement of children in Africa. States in Africa can also assist one another to take care for children migrants displaced by climate change to ensure that their socio-economic rights are protected.

Conclusion

Displacement linked to climate affects all mankind but its impact on children in Africa is peculiar due to their vulnerability and the risk which it poses to a range of their socio-economic rights. This chapter interrogates whether extraterritorial link of climate change to displacement of children exists, and if so, how it affects their socio-economic rights as well as the manner through which ETOs can be deployed as a response to its effect on socio-economic rights of children in Africa. As has been demonstrated, on the one hand, climate change is linked to displacement of children through the conduct or omission of an African state or its actors in and outside its territory in Africa. On the other hand, it is connected by means of the conduct or omission of actors from the developed North in their territories and in states within Africa. The failure of a state to address the extraterritorial reach of activities underlying climate change and actions relating to climate change response may have implications on the right to property, the right to health, the right to education and culture, the right to water and the right to food of children in Africa. To adequately respond to this risk to key socio-economic rights, states in Africa can among themselves apply obligations to 'respect', 'protect', 'promote' and 'fulfil' rights as a response to climate-induced displacement of children in Africa. Also, there are provisions dealing with international cooperation and assistance in key human rights instruments of the African human rights system that support the position that developed states have a role to play in response to the implications of extraterritorial conduct or omission underlying the climate-induced displacement of children in Africa.

References

African Charter on the Rights and Welfare of the Child (ACERW) (2018) GC 5 on State Party Obligations under the African Charter on the Rights and Welfare of the Child (Article 1) and Systems Strengthening for Child Protection.

African Charter on the Rights and Welfare of the Child (ACRWC) (1990) OAU Doc. CAB/LEG/24.9/49.

African (Banjul) Charter on Human and Peoples' Rights (1982) OAU Doc. CAB/LEG/67/3 rev. 5, 21 I.L.M. 58.

African Commission on Human and Peoples' Rights (ACHPR) (1995) Free Legal Assistance Group and Others v. Zaire, AHRLR 74.

_______ (2001) *Social and Economic Rights Action Centre (SERAC) & Another v. Nigeria*, AHRLR 60.

_______ (2009a) Resolution on climate change and human rights and the need to study its impact in Africa, ACHPR/Res153(XLVI)09.

_______ (2009b) *Sudan Human Rights Organization & Centre for Housing Rights and Evictions v. Sudan*, Communication 279/03 and 296/05.

_______ (2012) Resolution 231 on the right to adequate housing and protection from forced evictions, adopted at the 52nd ordinary session of the held in Yamoussoukro, Côte d'Ivoire.

_______ (2013) *Michelo Hansungule and others (on behalf of Children in Northern Uganda) v. the Government of Uganda*, Communication 1/2005.

_______ (2015) *The Nubian Community in Kenya vs The Republic of Kenya*, Communication 317/2006.

_______ (2016) *Institute for Human Rights and Development and Others v. Democratic Republic of Congo*, Communication 393/10.

_______ (2019) 'Background Study on the Operations of the Extractive Industries Sector in Africa and its Impacts on the Realisation of Human and Peoples' Rights under the African Charter on Human and Peoples' Rights', https://www.achpr.org/public/Document/file/English/Background%20Study%20on%20the%20Operations%20of%20the%20Extractive%20Industries%20Sector%20in%20Africa_ENG.pdf [accessed 8 October 2020].

African Committee of Experts on the Rights and Welfare of the Child (2014) *Centre for Human Rights and Rencontre Africaine pour la Défense des Droits de l'Homme v. Senegal*, Communication 003/12.

African Union (2009) Convention for the Protection and Assistance of Internally Displaced Persons in Africa, 'Kampala Convention'.

AU Press (2020) '*Press Statement on the Occasion of the 33rd Assembly of the Heads of State and Government of the African Union*', Addis Ababa Ethiopia.

BBC (2019) 'How Africa will be Affected by Climate Change', https://www.bbc.com/news/world-africa-50726701 [accessed 8 October 2020].

Boko, M.I. et al. (2007) 'Africa' in Parry, M.L. et al. (eds). *Climate Change, Impacts, Adaptation and Vulnerability, Contribution of Working Group II to the Fourth Assessment Report of the Intergovernmental Panel on Climate Change*, Cambridge University Press.

Bongaarts, J. and O'Neill, B. (2018) 'Global Warming Policy: Is Population Left Out in the Cold?', *Science* 361(6403), 650–652.

Bruckner, T. et al. (2014) 'Energy Systems' in Edenhofer, O.R. et al. (eds.). *Climate Change 2014: Mitigation of Climate Change. Contribution of Working Group III to the Fifth Assessment Report of the Intergovernmental Panel on Climate Change*, Cambridge University Press.

Bulto, T.S. (2011) 'Towards Rights-Duties Congruence: Extraterritorial Application of the Human Right to Water in the African Human Rights System', *Netherlands Quarterly Human Rights* 29(4), 491–523.

Burck, J. et al. (2019) 'Climate Change Performance Index: Results', https://germanwatch.org/sites/germanwatch.org/files/CCPI2019_Results.pdf [accessed 8 October 2020].

Colangelo, A.J. (2014) 'What is Extraterritorial Jurisdiction?', *Cornell Law Review* 99, 1303–1352.

Committee on Economic, Social, and Cultural Rights (CESCR) (2016) GC 22 on the right to sexual and reproductive health (article 12 of the International Covenant on Economic, Social and Cultural Rights), UN Doc E/C.12/GC/22.

Committee on the Rights of the Child (CRC Committee) (2013) GC 15 on the right of the child to the enjoyment of the highest attainable standard of health, CRC/C/GC/15.

_______ (2016) GC 19 on public budgeting for the realization of children's rights (art. 4), CRC/C/GC/19.

Convention on the Rights of the Child (1989) *U.N.T.S.* vol. 1577.

Concord Times (2020) 'Sierra Leone's Electricity Development Partner Appointed Energy Minister in Tunisia', http://slconcordtimes.com/sierra-leones-electricity-development-partner-appointed-energy-minister-in-tunisia/ [accessed 8 October 2020].

De Schutter, O. et al. (2012) 'Commentary to the *Maastricht Principles* on Extraterritorial Obligations of States in the Area of Economic Social and Cultural Rights', *Human Rights Quarterly* 34(4), 1084–1169.

ETO Consortium, '*Maastricht Principles* on Extraterritorial Obligations of States in the Area of Economic, Social and Cultural Rights', https://www.etoconsortium.org/nc/en/main-navigation/library/maastricht-principles/?tx_drblob_pi1%5BdownloadUid%5D=23 [accessed 8 October 2020].

Globeleq (2015) 'Sasol Natural Gas Project Resettlement Planning and Implementation Programme Addendum 15 – Mozambique Gas to Power Plant (MGtP) Interim Report', Globeleq

Gorte, R.W. and Sheikh, P.A. (2010) *Deforestation and climate change*, CRS Report for Congress.

Greenpeace (2010) 'Left in the Dust: AREVA's Radioactive Legacy in the Desert Towns of Niger', https://www.sortirdunucleaire.org/IMG/pdf/greenpeace-2010-left_in_the_dust-areva_s_radioactive_legacy_in_the_desert_towns_of_niger.pdf [accessed 8 October 2020].

Hennchen, E. (2015) 'Royal Dutch Shell in Nigeria: Where Do Responsibilities End?', *Journal of Business Ethics* 129(1), 1–25.

IBRD and World Bank World Development Report (2010) *Development and climate change*, World Bank.

Intergovernmental Panel on Climate Change (IPCC) (2014) *Climate Change 2014: Impacts, Adaptation, and Vulnerability. Summary for Policymakers. Contribution of Working Group II to the Fifth Assessment Report of the Intergovernmental Panel on Climate Change*, IPCC.

_______ (2018) 'Summary for Policymakers' in Masson-Delmotte, V. et al. (eds). *Global Warming of 1.5°C. An IPCC Special Report on the Impacts of Global Warming of 1.5°C Above Pre-Industrial Levels and related Global Greenhouse Gas Emission Pathways, in the context of Strengthening the Global Response to the Threat of Climate Change, Sustainable Development, and Efforts to eradicate Poverty*, Cambridge University Press.

International Covenant on Economic, Social and Cultural Rights (ICESCR)

Jegede, A.O. (2016) 'Rights Away from Home: Climate-Induced Displacement of Indigenous Peoples and the Extraterritorial Application of the Kampala Convention', *African Human Rights Law Journal* 16(1), 58–82.

Jegede, A.O. (2017) 'The Protection of Indigenous Peoples' Lands by Domestic Legislation on Climate Change Response Measures: Exploring Potentials in the Regional Human Rights System of Africa', *International Journal on Minority and Group Rights* 24(1), 24–56.

Kanalan, I. (2018) 'Extraterritorial State Obligations Beyond the Concept of Jurisdiction', *German Law Journal* 19(1), 44–63.

Luppi, B., Parisi, F. and Rajagopalan S. (2012) 'The Rise and Fall of the Polluter-pays Principle in Developing Countries', *International Review of Law and Economics* 32(1), 135-144.

Mbaye, A.A. (2020) 'Confronting the Challenges of Climate Change on Africa's Coastal Areas', https://www.brookings.edu/blog/africa-in-focus/2020/01/16/confronting-the-challenges-of-climate-change-on-africas-coastal-areas/ [accessed 8 October 2020].

McCormick, S. et al. (2018) 'Strategies in and Outcomes of Climate Change Litigation in the United States', *Nature Climate Change* 8, 829–833.

Mckibben, B. (2003) *The End of Nature: Humanity, Climate Change and the Natural World,* Random House Trade Books.

Mineral Council South Africa (2019) *Facts and Figures Pocketbook*, Mineral Council South Africa.

Mutua, M. (2000) 'The African Human Rights System: A Critical Evaluation', https://digitalcommons.law.buffalo.edu/other_scholarship/16/ [21 July 2021].

Palmer, P.I. et al. (2019) 'Net Carbon Emissions from African Biosphere dominate Pan-tropical Atmospheric CO2 Signal', *Nature Communication* 10, 1–9.

Paris Agreement under the United Nations Framework Convention on Climate Change (2015) adopted 30 Nov.- 11 Dec. 2015 at the 21st Sess., Conference of the Parties, FCCC/CP/2015/L.9/Rev.1

Pfefferbaum, B. et al. (2016) 'Effects of Displacement in Children Exposed to Disasters', *Current Psychiatry Reports* 18(8), 71.

REG (2019) 'Plant Design, Supply, and Installation of Low Voltage and Medium Voltage Lines and Service Connections in the Huye, Nyamagabe, Nyanza, Kamonyi and Ruhango Districts, Southern Province of Rwanda contract agreement N° 11.07.023/1256/19/EDCL-MD/FG/cm', https://www.reg.rw/fileadmin/user_upload/ESMP__STEG_IS_Project_Southern_province.pdf [accessed 8 October 2020].

Skogly, S. (2013) 'Causality and Extraterritorial Human Rights Obligations' in Langford, M. et al. (eds). *Global Justice, State Duties: the Extraterritorial Scope of Economic, Social and Cultural Rights in International Law*, Cambridge University Press.

The Carbon Brief Profile (2018) 'South Africa', https://www.carbonbrief.org/the-carbon-brief-profile-south-africa [accessed 8 October 2020].

Toulmin, C. (2009) *Climate Change in Africa*, Zed Books.United Nations (UN) (1991) GC 4 on the right to adequate housing, art. 11(1) of the Covenant, 6th session.

UN (1997) GC 7 on the right to adequate housing, art .11(1) of the Covenant: Forced evictions 16th session.

UN (1998) Kyoto Protocol to the United Nations Framework Convention on Climate Change.

UN (2020) 'Climate change', https://www.un.org/en/sections/issues-depth/climate-change [accessed 8 October 2020].

United Nations Framework Convention on Climate Change (UNFCCC) (n.d.) 'The impact of climate change on the rights of the child', https://www.ohchr.org/EN/Issues/HRAndClimateChange/Pages/RightsChild.aspx [accessed 8 October 2020].

United Nations International Children's Emergency Fund (UNICEF) (2003) 'Displaced children', https://www.unicef.org/emergencies/index_displacedchildren.html [accessed 8 October 2020].

_______ (2016) 'Collecting water is often a colossal waste of time for women and girls', https://www.unicef.org/press-releases/unicef-collecting-water-often-colossal-waste-time-women-and-girls [accessed 8 October 2020].

_______ (2018) 'Around 30 million children displaced by conflict need protection now and sustainable solutions over the long term', https://www.unicef.org/press-releases/around-30-million-children-displaced-conflict-need-protection-now-and-sustainable [accessed 8 October 2020].

United Nations Office of the High Commissioner for Human Rights (UNHCR) (2018) 'Summary of Stakeholders' submissions on Nigeria. Report of the Office of the United Nations High Commissioner for Human Rights', https://digitallibrary.un.org/record/1643075/files/A_HRC_WG-6_31_NGA_3-EN.pdf. [accessed 8 October 2020].

_______ (2019) 'Global Trends Forced Displacement in 2019', https://www.unhcr.org/5ee200e37.pdf [accessed 8 October 2020].

United Nations General Assembly (1988) Protection of global climate for present and future generations of mankind, 70th plenary meeting, UNGA Res 43/53.

United Nations High Commissioner for Human Rights (2018) Summary of Stakeholders' submissions on Nigeria, A/HRC/WG.6/31/NGA/3 24.

United Nations Human Rights Council (2014) Resolution 26 L/33 – Human rights and climate change, A/HRC/26/L.33.

Vandenhole, W. (2009) 'Economic, Social and Cultural Rights in the CRC: Is there a Legal Obligation to Cooperate Internationally for Development?', *International Journal of Children's Rights* 17, 23–63.

_______ (2020) 'Towards a Division of Labour for Sustainable Development: Extraterritorial Human Rights Obligations' in Kaltenborn, M., Krajewski, M. and Kulin, H. (eds.). *Sustainable Development Goals and Human Rights, Interdisciplinary Studies in Human Rights*, Springer Cham.

Vandenhole, W. and Benedek, W. (2013) 'Extraterritorial Human Rights Obligations and the North-South Divide' in Langford, M. et al. (eds.). *Global Justice, State Duties: The Extraterritorial scope of Economic, Social and Cultural Rights in International Law*, Cambridge University Press.

Vermeulen, S. and Cotula, L. (2010) 'Over the Heads of Local People: Consultation, Consent, and Recompense in Large-Scale Land Deals for Biofuels Projects in Africa', *Journal of Peasant Studies* 37(4), 899–916.

Viljoen, F. (2008) 'Communications under the African Charter: Procedure and Admissibility' in Evans, M. and Murray, R. (eds.). *The African Charter on Human and Peoples' Rights: The System in Practice 1986–2006*, 2nd ed., Cambridge University Press.

Wang, T. and Gao, X. (2018) 'Reflection and Operationalization of the Common but Differentiated Responsibilities and Respective Capabilities Principle in the Transparency Framework under the International Climate Change Regime', *Advances in Climate Change Research* 9, 253–263.

Wilde, R. (2020) 'Pursuing Global Socio-Economic, Colonial and Environmental Justice through Economic Redistribution: The Potential Significance of Human Rights Treaty Obligations' in Bander, C. et al. (eds.). *Research Handbook on International Law and Social Rights*, Edward Elgar.

World Bank (2018) *Groundswell: Preparing for Internal Climate Migration*, The World Bank.

World Data Atlas (2018a) 'Nigeria - CO2 emissions', https://knoema.com/atlas/Nigeria/CO2-emissions [accessed 8 October 2020].

World Data Atlas (2018b) 'Democratic Republic of the Congo - CO2 emissions', https://knoema.com/atlas/Democratic-Republic-of-the-Congo/CO2-emissions [accessed 8 October 2020].

Y Charts (2020) 'Egypt. Carbon Dioxide Emissions', https://ycharts.com/indicators/egypt_carbon_dioxide_emissions [accessed 8 October 2020].

14

Diplomatic asylum and extraterritorial *non-refoulement*

The foundational and enduring contribution of Latin America to extraterritorial human rights obligations

*Ralph Wilde**

Introduction

Diplomatic asylum—a state offering refuge in its diplomatic premises in a foreign state to an individual requiring protection from that foreign state, as happened with Julian Assange in the Ecuadorean Embassy in London—is a practice long associated with Latin American States (Vieira 1961; Planas-Suárez 1953). Although not usually thought of in this way, it can and should be viewed as an extraterritorial form of human rights protection. Whether and to what extent obligations to provide such protection exist are contested, including, notably, in Europe At the same time, it is often the European region that is commonly understood to have led jurisprudential developments here, via the case law under the European Convention on Human Rights (ECHR). The present chapter challenges this narrative. The Latin American region, through its much earlier normative commitment to providing diplomatic asylum, should be regarded as having paved the way for the concept of extraterritorial human rights protection. This set a precedent that would, much later, become understood in terms of an obligation to provide such protection in international human rights law, including European human rights law. Moreover, the most recent, contrasting developments in Inter-American and European human rights jurisprudence regimes suggests that the former is now advocating a more protective approach on this subject whereas the latter is potentially pulling back from certain protections.

Linking 'diplomatic asylum' to human rights law

Diplomatic asylum involves, in effect, the operation of the concept of *non-refoulement*—the idea that a state does not transfer an individual from its control, to the space (usually) of another state, when there is a risk of human rights abuse in that space. An obligation to this effect (with important variations) exists expressly in the Refugee and Torture Conventions, and has been read into other human rights treaties.

 DOI: 10.4324/9781003090014-18

As this concept is being invoked by a state in its embassy in a foreign country, it is necessarily extraterritorial as far as that state is concerned. Contrary to what is sometimes suggested, diplomatic premises are not somehow discrete territorial enclaves of the foreign states involved. Thus situations like that of Julian Assange in the Ecuadorean Embassy operate in the arena of *extraterritorial* human rights protections.

European and Latin American contributions to international human rights jurisprudence

As far as extraterritorial protections operating in international human rights law is concerned, the story told by the predominantly European, Europe-based commentators is that this is a relatively recent area of normative development (e.g. Milanovic 2011, pp. 1, 4–5; Wallace 2019, p. 1). The relevant jurisprudential authority crystallized long after the adoption of the early, foundational international instruments, notably through decisions under the ECHR mostly from the 1990s onwards with the main decisions about northern Cyprus.

This story disregards important decisions of the Organization of American States (OAS), such as the 1999 *Coard* decision about the US invasion of Grenada. It also overlooks decisions by the UN Human Rights Committee about situations in Latin America, such as the 1981 *Lopez Burgos* and *Celiberti de Casariego* decisions ('Views'), concerning the kidnapping of individuals by Uruguay in Argentina and Brazil (UN Human Rights Committee 1981a; 1981b).

But more fundamentally, such an account is only possible by adopting a siloed view of the subject-matter coverage of international law, whereby human rights protections only exist in international human rights law.

This exclusive focus paves the way for the following view, again amongst Europe-based international lawyers. It is the 'European' region (defined broadly—the Council of Europe (CoE)) that made the most significant, and well-developed, contribution to the protection of human rights in international law (e.g. Harris et al. 2018, pp. 35–36; Milanovic 2011, p. 4). This is because of the relative significance accorded to the jurisprudence of the CoE Human Rights mechanisms compared to the jurisprudence of other equivalent mechanisms, including the OAS bodies. This significance is not simply a matter of comparing the position within each regime. It is also because of a common assumption that the general approach taken in decisions made under one regime is potentially transferrable to other regimes with similar norms. Through such transference, the European regime contributed to international human rights law jurisprudence generally (e.g. Harris et al. 2018, p. 36; Heyns and Killander 2013, p. 688; Bantekas and Oette 2020, pp. 243–244, 249). In consequence, there has been a process of universalization from the particular—globalizing from the European region.

Such a narrative has purchase in Europe partly because it feeds into and reflects broader European tropes about European civilizational exceptionalism, and the bringing of these exceptional European standards to other parts of the world via their transfer to other regional normative systems and/or the globally-applicable normative system. This fits into one narrative associated with the broader theory and practice of colonialism and post-colonialism, both generally and in how these practices relate to international law. According to this narrative, in the colonial era, European notions of statehood, sovereignty and territorial title were universalized via colonial subjugation in a particular fashion. Certain non-Europeans were regarded to lack what Europeans possessed, paving the way for European domination. Specifically, their societies were conceptualized by Europeans as lacking statehood, and so, in consequence, lacking sovereignty and title to their land. Such land was therefore *terra nullius* and could be acquired by Europeans. At the same time, the international legal concept of a racist standard of civilization—which Europeans met, and certain non-Europeans fell below—used as the alibi for the non-application of the foregoing entitlements to such non-Europeans, was deployed as the basis for what Europeans would and should (legally, in certain international law arrangements of trusteeship) bring to such non-Europeans—the 'civilizing mission'.

There is much to challenge in the narrative of the exceptional contribution of European human rights law, notably through a greater appreciation of the other regimes of international human rights law. But there is a more fundamental challenge. If the focus moves out from 'human rights law' to international law generally, and the Latin American practice of diplomatic asylum is viewed as a species of extraterritorial human rights protection, things look different. Such a standpoint reveals the Latin American region grappling with the subject of extraterritorial human rights protections much earlier than the relatively recent sagas under the European human rights system.

It is perhaps fitting, then, that the most complete treatment of the subject of extraterritorial *non-refoulement* by an international human rights body to date is that provided by the Inter-American Court of Human Rights (IACtHR), in its 2018 Advisory Opinion on Asylum (I-A Asylum AO). The Opinion was requested by Ecuador, prompted by the Assange situation. In it, the Court addressed the subject holistically and, in terms of the legal regimes potentially in play, broadly. It reflected on the Latin American practice and associated treaties on diplomatic asylum (covered further below), the question of whether the right to 'asylum' in the Inter-American Declaration and Convention on Human Rights applied to extraterritorial diplomatic premises (it did not) and whether the separate but related obligation of *non-refoulement* in the Inter-American human rights instruments applied in such places (it did—covered further below). The Court drew widely on the jurisprudence from other international human rights regimes, including the ECHR regime, in its analysis.

The broad-ranging and comparative nature of this analysis is in contrast to the narrower and more parochial approach taken in, and some of the external characterizations of, the three main decisions on extraterritorial *non-refoulement* applying the ECHR.

European story of groundbreaking European decisions on extraterritorial *non-refoulement* obligations

In 2012, the *Hirsi* decision of the European Court of Human Rights (ECtHR) held that the *non-refoulement*-type obligation in the ECHR, and the separate provision prohibiting the collective expulsion of aliens in ECHR Protocol 4 Article 4, apply extraterritorially—in this instance to Italian maritime push-backs of migrants outside Italian territorial waters—and that these obligations were violated. A common reaction amongst human rights lawyers was to view this as a landmark affirmation of the extraterritorial application of *non-refoulement* protection (e.g. Giuffré 2016, p. 272; Kim 2017, p. 49); and/or the prohibition of the collective expulsion of aliens (e.g. Costello 2012, p. 323). The response by them, and by ECHR-contracting states, NGOs concerned with human rights in general and refugees in particular, European institutions with an interest in the subject etc., was then to try to explore, *de novo*, some of the dilemmas and challenges the operation of such protection throws up.

Such dilemmas and challenges were also raised in another case, *Al-Saadoon*. This concerned UK troops in Iraq handing individuals over to the Iraqi criminal justice system when there was a risk of the use of the death penalty. It related to the situation after the 2003 war in and subsequent occupation of Iraq. Certain authority had been transferred from the occupiers to

Iraqi representatives. The continued UK military presence was subject to the agreement of those representatives. The case went through the English courts, applying the ECHR standards indirectly via the domestic law Human Rights Act (HRA). It ended up in Strasbourg, and two years before *Hirsi*, in 2010, the Court found that a *non-refoulement*-type obligation was in operation and had been violated.

Eight years before that, in 2004, the Court of Appeal of England and Wales, applying the HRA, considered individuals claiming refuge in the UK consulate in Melbourne in the *B & Others* case. It held that a *non-refoulement*-type obligation under the ECHR could potentially apply (the Court is somewhat ambiguous on whether it did, with a confused reasoning that shifts between permissive and obligatory normative concepts) but on the facts the relevant test was not met and so there was no violation (the ultimate finding of no violation seems to imply that an obligation was regarded to be applicable) (see paras. 88–89, 93–94, 96–97).

The dilemmas and challenges raised in the context of these cases, especially, because of the findings of a violation, and the decisions being made at Strasbourg, in *Al-Saadoon* and *Hirsi,* included the following: How can states discharge a *non-refoulement*-type obligation when they are acting extraterritorially, not within their own sovereign territories? What about the profoundly different circumstances that prevail, basis for their presence and other obligations they bear? Are they supposed to hold onto people until the human rights situation in the place where the individual would be transferred to improves? What if the nature of their presence extraterritorially is temporary? Should they somehow prolong this, in order to ensure protection? Alternatively, should they transfer the individuals to some third location, including, possibly, their own territories, to ensure protection there? In either case—prolonging the extraterritorial presence, or transferring the individual to a third location—what if these options are not practicable and/or are, indeed, objectionable, for example if they are opposed by the foreign state in whose territory the states are acting (where applicable)?

In *Al-Saadoon*, the UK government submitted that the continuance of the UK military presence in Iraq depended on agreement to this by the Iraqi authorities. And a factor in that agreement was whether or not the UK would hand over the suspects in question to those authorities (paras. 56, 66). Put differently, the UK's ability to continue to detain the suspects, rather than hand them over to the local authorities, was dependent on Iraqi agreement, and this would not be forthcoming. Thus there was no realistic prospect of the UK obtaining Iraqi consent enabling it to retain custody, whether indefinitely, or even just until after their trial had been conducted and the question of whether the death penalty would be applied was determined. The UK also submitted that Iraq would not agree to the UK transferring the individuals to the UK for trial there. The ECtHR found that there had been a moment when the Iraqi side was reluctant to try the suspects, and that this provided an:

> ...opportunity to seek the consent of the Iraqi government to an alternative arrangement involving, for example, the applicants being tried by a United Kingdom court, either in Iraq or in the United Kingdom. It does not appear that any such solution was ever sought.
>
> *(para. 141)*

A further, related, ultimately determinative issue was whether the UK could have obtained an assurance from Iraq that it would not seek the death penalty in the trial of the suspects. This could have paved the way for a transfer compatible with the *non-refoulement*-type obligation (para. 142). The ECtHR held that certain opportunities to obtain such an assurance were not taken by the UK, and in the absence of an assurance, the transfer was a breach of the *non-refoulement*-type obligation (paras. 142–143).

The extraterritorial form of *non-refoulement* protection implicates the paradoxical nature of that type of protection, and the challenges it creates, in a particular fashion. The extraterritorial state provides protection from things it may ultimately have no control over (the situation the individual will face when they are outside the control of that state—in the *Al-Saadoon* case, the use of the death penalty by Iraq). This is, of course, the case with protection from *non-refoulement* in the *territorial* context. But the two contexts are materially different. Territorially, the state might be in a better position to offer a sustainable temporary home to the individual affected, if the situation elsewhere giving rise to the need for protection does not improve. In the context of transfers from a state's territory, those states, including the UK, routinely seek assurances of the kind that was not obtained from Iraq. But if such efforts do not bear fruit, or the assurance is unreliable, the individual can remain in the state's territory. However challenging this might be, the challenges are of a different order if the issue involves a state providing protective care extraterritorially. In *Al-Saadoon* the ECtHR held that the UK had not explored fully the opportunities to obtain assurances from Iraq. Assuming this is correct: what if the UK had fully explored such opportunities, and no assurances could be obtained? Then the matter would turn to the foregoing challenges about the UK retaining protective custody of the individuals or somehow conducting a trial itself in Iraq or transferring the individuals to the UK for this. As indicated, the UK and the ECtHR disagreed on the nature of these potential impediments. But impediments of this kind would not present themselves in the first place were the individuals already in UK territory.

The idea that *Al-Saadoon* and then *Hirsi* established a requirement of *non-refoulement* protection extraterritorially in human rights law, and, in doing so, raised a novel set of dilemmas and challenges, even a matter of the European system of human rights protection, flies in the face not only of the *B* decision of 2004, but also the 1992 European Commission on Human Rights decision in *M v Denmark*. There, the Commission held that certain acts of the Danish ambassador in the Danish embassy in the DDR could have given rise to responsibility. These acts were: not allowing the applicant to seek refuge; requesting the applicant leave the embassy; and inviting the DDR police into the embassy—the police asked the applicant to leave with them, which he did. However, what happened to the applicant when he was arrested by DDR authorities outside the embassy (trial, conviction and 33 associated days in detention, for offences relating to entering and refusing to leave the embassy) did not reach the severity to cross the threshold for a transfer-related responsibility on the part of Denmark. Although not entirely clear, the Commission seemed to be using the threshold to determine whether the obligation was in operation, rather than whether the obligation, in operation, was violated. But the implication was that had the threshold been met, an obligation would exist, arising out of what happened to the applicant at the hands of DDR authorities, because of the unwillingness to offer protection from this in the embassy. Although not put in these terms, this operates as, in effect, a transfer-related obligation—an obligation of *non-refoulement* (and was characterized as such by the ECt. HR in *Al-Saadoon* (para. 139)).

Perhaps because there was no finding that the threshold for the operation of responsibility was not met, and it was only a Commission decision, this did not register within the collective consciousness. It fell largely to the wayside, along with certain other, even earlier, general non-transfer-related extraterritoriality decisions such as *Hess* in 1975, in the wake of the juggernaut narrative on extraterritoriality at Strasbourg that everything started with the main cases about northern Cyprus. As far as the *B* case having similarly already established the existence of an extraterritorial *non-refoulement*-type obligation, this may have been ignored in part because it was a domestic court decision, and, as with *M*, there was no ultimate finding of a violation.

More fundamentally, *M* and *B* could be distinguished because of the particular diplomatic context in which the *non-refoulement* obligation operated—i.e. *because* they were, in effect, forms of *diplomatic asylum* in human rights law and characterized as such. Although the *M* decision does not reference diplomatic asylum, in *Al-Saadoon* the Court, when discussing the concept, invokes *M*, seemingly to affirm that the finding of the possibility of an obligation in that decision was relevant to the concept (para. 139). In *B*, the finding that a *non-refoulement*-type obligation could exist is characterized as an obligation 'applying to diplomatic asylum' (para. 88). As it seems to root this in an extension of what was originally held in *M*, there is an implicit characterization, as in *Al-Saadoon*, of that decision as one concerned with diplomatic asylum (see para. 80 et seq.).

The English courts in the *Al-Saadoon* litigation considered the situation through the prism of a *non-refoulement*-type obligation classified in some sense as connected to the concept of diplomatic asylum as it had been understood in *M*. However, at Strasbourg, the Court departed from this, preferring to understand the obligation as conceptualized autonomously from diplomatic asylum and the *M* approach thereto (paras. 139–140). The later *Hirsi* decision of that Court does not even bother with any of this. There is no mention of any connection to principles developed in the context of diplomatic asylum. Nor does the Court discuss the potential relevance of the *M* and *B* decisions (or *Al-Saadoon*, other than on an unrelated issue (in para. 129)) (diplomatic asylum is discussed in the concurring opinion of Judge Pinto de Albuquerque).

The choice not to see all these cases as essentially concerned with the same thing—extraterritorial *non-refoulement*—and to avoid conceptualizing the obligation in a holistic, connected fashion, enables *Al-Saadoon* and then *Hirsi* to be understood not only as novel when it comes to ECHR-based jurisprudence (not following on from *M* and *B*). But also, more broadly, because they are most definitely *not* to be linked to diplomatic asylum, they can be understood as entirely disconnected from the earlier Latin American jurisprudence on that particular form of extraterritorial *non-refoulement*-type protection.

Even the findings that are characterized as forming an ECHR-basis for providing diplomatic asylum—*M* (not in the *M* decision itself) and *B*—this characterization does not pave the way for an acknowledgment of the link between the findings and the earlier Latin American practice. The only mention of that practice is a reference to it in a longer quotation from an article by Susanne Riveles (Riveles) in *B* (para. 87).

Disregarding the relevance of the Latin American precedent

It is no surprise, then, that the decisions and associated commentary on extraterritorial *non-refoulement* under the ECHR typically address the dilemmas and challenges this concept throws up as if they have not for most of the last century been played out in the Latin American region in its practice and associated treaties on diplomatic asylum. This practice and associated treaties are commonly understood in terms of a potential right on the part of the state to grant diplomatic asylum, not an obligation to do so (see e.g. Caracas Convention, Art. II; IA Asylum A-O, para. 87). Nonetheless, the practice and treaties involved approaches to address some of the dilemmas raised by the provision of protection extraterritorially which are relevant to circumstances where such provision is obligatory as a matter of human rights law.

This is illustrated by the 1954 OAS Caracas Convention on Diplomatic Asylum. That treaty addresses one of the aforementioned dilemmas, that extraterritorial facilities like embassies or military bases cannot serve anything other than very short-term havens, yet the extraterritorial state cannot control whether and when the host-state circumstances necessitating refuge will improve. It enables safe passage to ports of exit to be accorded by the territorial state (articles V, XI, XII). This creates a potential bridge between *extraterritorial* protection in a foreign embassy, and *territorial* protection by that same state (or a foreign state) which has greater potential to be sustained for longer if needed.

Had the situation at issue in *Al-Saadoon* not been treated as novel, but, rather, involving dilemmas concerning extraterritorial protection from *non-refoulement* that have come up from time to time and therefore require forward planning, things might have been different. Some sort of equivalent work-around mechanism, along the lines of the approaches reviewed by the ECtHR, might have been given greater priority, at the right time, than the court held had been the case. And/or such a mechanism might have had greater likelihood of being acceptable to Iraq than the UK claimed was the case.

The doctrine of misplaced European exceptionalism enables European lawyers and judges to heroically act as norm pioneers and problem-solvers. It also enables those European states who resist the development of extraterritorial *non-refoulement* protection in human rights law as unrealistic and problematic to avoid having to reckon with how Latin American states faced up to the dilemmas and challenges involved and attempted to craft solutions such as in the Caracas Convention. And how they somehow managed to do this so long ago, when international human rights law even as a territorial proposition was only just being established.

To understand further how these links end up being ignored, it can be helpful to look more into the concept of diplomatic asylum in international law. And, within this, to consider how the leading scholar globally of diplomatic law, Eileen Denza, treats the significance of the Latin American treaties and associated practice (Denza 2011; 2016).

Diplomatic law

The provision of diplomatic asylum implicates international diplomatic law, in particular the law of diplomatic immunities and privileges (Denza 2016). A key relevant norm is that the diplomatic premises of a foreign state are inviolable vis-à-vis the authorities of the host state (e.g. VCDR Art. 22, VCCR Art. 31). This and other immunities enable states to interact and operate in each other's territory without interference. The offer of diplomatic asylum exploits this to provide individuals protection from the authorities of the host state. International lawyers tend to suggest that this is unlawful in diplomatic law terms (Denza 2011). It is an abuse of the entitlement to inviolability of diplomatic/consular premises, and/or, more specifically, a violation of the stipulations in that area of law (e.g. the obligation to respect the laws of the host state, and not interfere in the internal affairs of that state—VCDR, Art. 41.1; VCCR, Art. 55.1). The Latin American treaties providing for a right to grant diplomatic protection in certain circumstances are regarded to be a compatible treaty-based derogation from this default position in diplomatic law, insofar as the right is exercised in the territory of another party to the treaty. Thus, the right to grant diplomatic asylum on this basis is kept within the Latin American region.

More significantly for wider purposes, Eileen Denza suggests that states generally have a 'limited and temporary' right in customary international law, left intact by diplomatic law, to provide protection 'as a matter of humanitarian protection' in diplomatic premises 'at least where there is immediate danger to the life or safety' of the individual concerned or 'where … there is no prospect of his or her being given a fair trial on any charges by the authorities of the territorial State' (Denza 2011, pp. 1426–1431, 1433–1434; Denza 2016, p. 115; Roberts and Denza 2016, Section 13.24).

Has the Latin American practice of providing diplomatic asylum, and the various treaties on the topic adopted by states in the region providing for a right to do this, played some role in the formation of this broader customary international law right? Judge Alvarez, in his Dissenting

Opinion in the 1950 *Asylum* decision of the ICJ, characterized these treaties as 'American International Law'. Did this American International Law universalize to the global in the context of a right to provide diplomatic asylum? Just as European human rights jurisprudence has, it is claimed, universalized to the global in the context of human rights law generally?

A preliminary question is whether the practice and treaties in Latin America have constituted customary international law for the region. The predominant view of experts does not seem to have shifted from that articulated by Judge Alvarez in his dissent, viz:

> ...there is no customary American international law of asylum properly speaking; the existence of such a law would suppose that the action taken by the Latin States of the New World was uniform, which is not at all the case: governments change their attitude according to circumstances and political convenience.
>
> *(Asylum, dissent of Judge Alvarez, 295)*

Denza writes:

> It has often been claimed that under certain conditions a state has a 'right' to grant asylum within its embassies abroad to fugitives and even that the individual fugitive has a 'right' to asylum if he has taken shelter in a foreign embassy. But the existence of such 'rights' is not generally accepted as a matter of customary international law. Within Latin America there exists an extensive network of treaties which for the states parties do create a right of granting diplomatic asylum. But it has not been shown that these treaties have created even a regional rule of customary international law and in other parts of the world there has been no disposition to accept the existence of any customary rule of international law.
>
> *(Denza 2011, 1426)*

This position on the lack of regional custom was affirmed by the IACtHR in the 2018 Advisory Opinion (IACtHR 2018, paras. 157–162).

Neither Judge Alvarez nor the IACtHR were concerned with the existence of a global norm of customary international law as well as a regional one. Denza, however, was, and in her writings follows her above-quoted rejection of a Latin American regional norm with an assertion that her 'limited and temporary' right exists as a matter of global custom (id., 1429). On the one hand, then, the Latin American practice and treaty-making on the subject has had no customary international law significance even to Latin American states, let alone on a global level. On the other hand, somehow at the same time as this extensive regional practice and treaty-making, but entirely disconnected from it, a global norm of customary international law has been in operation/has emerged on the subject.

What, then, is the evidence for the existence of this global norm? In her articulation of the norm, Denza offers citations to two dicta—one for each of her two elements of the test (the imminent threat to life/of injury, and the risk that there will be no fair trial)—of the International Court of Justice in the *Asylum* case (Denza 2011, p. 1426, 1429, citing *Asylum*, 282–284). This case was *about two Latin American states* (Columbia and Peru) *and the application of a regional treaty on diplomatic asylum to those states*. Assuming that Denza is correct about the meaning of these dicta on their own terms (a matter that is beyond the scope of this chapter), more fundamentally what is striking is that she is using the dicta as the sole authority for a proposition for a rule of custom that is somehow disconnected from the Latin American practice and treaty-making on the subject, *even though the case the dicta is derived from is about such practice and treaty-making.*

Why did Denza root her assertion of the existence of a customary rule on diplomatic asylum solely on dicta from a case about Latin American practice and treaty-making, but then articulate this rule as entirely disconnected and separate from the potential norm-generating significance of Latin American practice and treaty-making? This seems to at once acknowledge the latter significance—Denza needs something to underpin her assertion of the existence of a general norm—but then simultaneously disregard it.

Ultimately, regional exceptionalism is deployed to block the potential contribution to the development of the global normative regime. This is despite the idea that for a customary international law rule to exist, there needs to have been the relevant practice (linked to *opinio juris*), and the fact that the region has been the most prominent generator of this practice. Such an approach neatly complements and reinforces, while being based on a reversal of the underlying logic of, the exceptional narrative about the European contribution to the protection of human rights in international law. The Latin American practice of providing extraterritorial protection from *non-refoulement* stayed in the region when it came to any normative significance beyond the region. And this was the case even when an equivalent norm entitling states to provide such protection was regarded to be in existence at a global level, the generation and/or sustaining of which one might have expected the regional practice to have had had some bearing on.

The European affirmation that there is an *obligation* to provide such protection from *refoulement* extraterritorially as a matter of human rights treaty law can potentially effect a global shift. This shift can be viewed as a novel regional contribution to the general subject of extraterritorial protection from *refoulement because* of the dismissal that Latin American practice has global implications when it came to the supposedly already-existing norm of customary international law.

Moreover, the Latin American treaties cannot have a transferrable effect in the same fashion as European human rights jurisprudence because they are not part of a broader jurisprudential regime. Thus, ironically, because the Latin American region was so historically innovative in relation to this arena of protection—developing it *before* human rights-specific treaty law existed—the right to provide it (although not the obligation to do so) existed for the region in treaties that, unlike the later treaties that were the basis for the European developments, did not have the potential to be jurisprudentially linked to a global normative regime.

When human rights treaty law then came along, there was not the same pressing need to explore the possibility of developing extraterritorial human rights obligations that might operate in diplomatic premises. There were *already treaties on the topic,* albeit only covering a right to provide asylum, not an obligation to do so. European 'innovation' came partly, then, because, unlike in Latin America, there was a complete absence of normative standards in this area (Denza's mysterious customary entitlement notwithstanding). In Latin America, individuals may not have had a right to, effectively, protection from extraterritorial *non-refoulement* in diplomatic premises. But states were sometimes willing to give them such protection, and, crucially, arrangements were in place enabling them to do this without breaching diplomatic law. The latter was presumably not unconnected to the former. Whenever protection was forthcoming, the need for assistance from regional or international human rights bodies was reduced. And states wishing to provide protection did not need to risk violating their obligations to host states. Indeed, it is notable that the main contribution from within Latin American human rights jurisprudence to the topic came only when a Latin American state faced a situation outside the operation of the regional diplomatic asylum treaties—Ecuador in the UK. In this context, the state required normative guidance as to its position as a matter of the obligations it had in human rights law—an area of law which is not limited, as those treaties are, to situations arising in the context of its relations with certain other Latin American states.

Europeans only got to 'innovate' human rights law, then, because Latin American innovation on the underlying issue—extraterritorial human right protection—had already happened decades earlier, and addressed the matter, to a certain extent (the provision of protection was discretionary) before human rights treaty law even existed. If Denza's account is correct, European states seemingly chose to forego aligning in some way with this approach as the basis for a customary international law rule (even as supposedly such a rule did exist/emerge for them, on some other basis). And as a matter of a treaty-based equivalent, things would have to wait until much later. And when this came, it was through the very different, relatively precarious jurisprudential route of innovations in the interpretation of ambiguous treaty provisions by courts, rather than, as in Latin America, with states choosing to adopt specific treaties addressing the situation. Moreover, this happened on the basis of a big leap from a seeming absence of even being entitled to provide protection (Denza's customary right notwithstanding) to now having an *obligation* to do so. The abrupt nature of how this came about, and the consequent treatment of the challenges it raises as novel, are in sharp contrast with how the position in Latin America shifted more gradually from arrangements that provided a right to provide protection in asylum terms (the diplomatic asylum treaties) to the IACtHR's 2018 affirmation of an obligation to provide protection in *non-refoulement* terms.

Indeed, this abrupt shift for ECHR contracting states seems also to have led to a backlash by some such states, which, in turn, seems to have been accommodated in the 2020 *MN* decision by the ECtHR. In that decision, the Court seemed to pull back on the scope of the extraterritorial application of the *non-refoulement* obligation as it might operate in diplomatic premises from what had seemingly been affirmed at Strasbourg in the *M* case and the English courts in the *B* case. In doing this it adopted the arguments made in submissions to it by not only Belgium, the respondent state, but also 11 other European intervening states (ECtHR 2020, para. 86).

MN concerned Syrian would-be asylum seekers in the Belgian embassy in Lebanon who asked for a visa to travel to Belgium to claim asylum there. They argued that a denial of this visa would amount to *refoulement*. And that Belgium's obligations to protect them from this were applicable *inter alia* because they were in operation within the Belgian embassy, on the basis of the control exercised by the Belgian authorities over the embassy generally and/or as far as their treatment there (in denying the visa) was concerned. The Court rejected this, seeming to hold, in effect, that an obligation of *non-refoulement* cannot be in operation in diplomatic premises simply by virtue of the control exercised by the state over such premises through its operation of them (ECtHR 2020, para. 119). Also relevant was the absence of '*de facto* control' exercised by diplomatic agents over the individuals—they entered and could leave the embassy of their own free will (ibid, para 118).

The IACtHR's Advisory Opinion two years earlier, by contrast, affirms the operation of the *non-refoulement* obligation in diplomatic premises on a seemingly more general basis (IACtHR 2018, paras. 188, 192, 194). It does not stipulate that the control exercised by the state over such premises is insufficient to trigger the obligation. Nor is the existence or otherwise of '*de facto*' control by agents in such contexts invoked as a relevant factor. Just as the Latin American region had adopted a right to provide diplomatic protection earlier than other states, including in Europe, now it has potentially affirmed an obligation to provide a protection from *non-refoulement* in a broader set of circumstances in diplomatic premises than seems to be the position as a matter of the most recent European human rights law-based decision.

Diplomatic law has its origins in an exclusively state-centric period of international law. It reflects policy considerations relating only to the rights of states, and the correlative, and reciprocal, obligations of states to those other states, not also other forms of obligations owed to individuals. It would be odd to conceive a right to asylum for an individual/an obligation to confer asylum to an individual from within the logic of an exclusively state-centric conception of rights and obligations. Hence diplomatic asylum in the Latin American treaties being a state entitlement, not an obligation. But when that right is exercised, human rights protection is forthcoming. This can be understood, then, as a limited form of human rights protection, covering the same activity by the state that human rights law conceptualizes as an arena of obligation rather than discretion. Human rights protection has been provided pursuant to these treaties. And, as indicated, the likelihood that states will be willing to do this is enhanced by the way the treaties render such provision permissible as far as the legal relationship between the providing state and the host state is concerned.

It is important to appreciate, then, as the IACtHR did in its Advisory Opinion, that what are effectively human rights protections might exist in both diplomatic/general international law and human rights law. Moreover, rejecting the intersection between these two areas of law also enables states to miss the link between the developments in the latter, which have affirmed an extraterritorial obligation of *non-refoulement*—and the situations covered by the former—diplomatic premises. Instead, the former coverage can be treated as if it is the only operative legal regime, with such situations therefore untouched by any requirements in human rights law. In turn, the provision of protection in diplomatic premises can then be framed as an abuse of diplomatic privileges. No account is given to the idea that the state involved might be using its privileges to enable it to discharge its human rights obligations. Or, put differently, that it is the very existence of the diplomatic law privileges, for example, concerning inviolability, that created the background conditions that put the state in a position to offer protection, which needs, therefore, to be provided precisely because of this capacity to do so.

The Latin American identity of Ecuador foregrounds the significance of the tradition of states in that region for doing what that state did in London. At the same time, it may have been this very identity that enabled the situation to be viewed as entirely disconnected from the developments on extraterritorial human rights obligations in European human rights law generally, and such obligations of *non-refoulement* in particular. *B* had seemingly established the existence of the latter-type obligation in 2004, eight years before Assange entered the Ecuadorean embassy, as applicable to the UK in its diplomatic premises (although *B* was only a domestic court decision, there was no ultimate finding of violation, and things would seemingly take a different turn in Strasbourg in the *MN* decision of 2020).

Now that the shoe was on the other foot, and Ecuador was in the same position *vis-à-vis* the UK that the UK had been *vis-à-vis* Australia, the potential transferability of the normative position in human rights law that had been held to apply to the UK in *B* was not invoked. Here, then, suddenly the aforementioned grand project of universalizing European norms on human rights ground to a halt. This suggests a project operating only when such norms transfer over to non-European others (here, Ecuador) without any secondary, blow-back implications for European states (here, the UK, as the host state that cannot have Assange transferred to its custody). Again, colonial echoes are evident. In the colonial era, European colonial powers saw themselves as bringing standards of civilization to non-civilized societies. But, paradoxically, whereas these standards were somehow understood to derive from European societies, they were not understood to apply to the relations between Europeans and colonial peoples. Such relations were characterized by mass murder, other atrocities, enslavement and the plunder of land and resources.

As will be explained, this link to colonial-era double standards extends over to the wider issue at stake on this topic: resistance to the extraterritorial application of human rights as far as the UK and certain other European states are concerned.

Broader issues at stake—what is sauce for the goose is sauce for the gander

The insistence on two entirely mutually exclusive categories of diplomacy on the one hand, and human rights protection, on the other—of diplomatic law, on the one hand, and human rights law, on the other—in the case of Assange in the Ecuadorean Embassy was tied up in a broader UK policy initiative. This is the state's ongoing campaign, supported by certain other states, to challenge the scope of the two key areas of human rights law that are implicated in this issue: *non-refoulement* in general—territorial and extraterritorial—and the extraterritorial application of human rights law in general. (Cf. the role of the UK and other European states as intervenors in the *WM* case.) The stakes are, thus, high.

This links things back to the context of *Al-Saadoon*. The UK was present in Iraq alongside the US because the two states had invaded, removed the government of, militarily occupied, and sought to transform the social, economic, legal and political system in, the country. Whereas the ostensible reason put forward for this related to weapons of mass destruction, the enterprise was commonly understood, and, indeed, even partly justified as such by the leaders of the states involved, as being concerned with removing a human-rights-abusing autocratic government and replacing it with a human-rights-protecting democratic regime. Yet, when the issue arose of these two states being subject to human rights law standards themselves in the way they engaged in this enterprise, this was dismissed by them. The US has a longstanding position that human rights treaty obligations do not apply extraterritorially. When the UK position on the issue generally had to be addressed in the *Al-Skeini* litigation, the state similarly refuted applicability on a range of grounds, challenging this all the way through protracted litigation in domestic courts and on to Strasbourg. An equivalent resistant standpoint and its litigation consequences were then repeated when it came to *non-refoulement*-type obligation in particular in the *Al-Saadoon* litigation.

A further feature of colonial ideology and practice was the way that this was based on orientalist, racist notions of civilizational difference. Whereas these may have had legitimate purchase on various delusional tropes self-identity when it came to Europeans, they had had no legitimacy when it came to the position of the societies subject to European colonial domination. These notions enabled Europeans to overlook/downgrade the merit of the 'civilizations' they were subjugating. Again, the stakes were high, because this process was necessary not only to justify the subjugation, but also to undergird the very societal self-esteem of European societies and individuals themselves, via ideas of civilizational superiority.

In *Al-Saadoon*, this issue came to the fore because it implicated the human rights issue where Europeans are typically the most globally-sanctimonious—the death penalty. The extraterritorial application of the *non-refoulement*-type obligation was implicated in the case only because the UK was bound by an international human rights law obligation prohibiting this, and Iraq was not. It was the very existence of divergent applicable human rights law standards that gave rise to the UK's obligation. The UK was caught between the rock of refuting the application of human rights standards to itself when it comes to its relations with people in other parts of the world, and the hard place of its commitment to promoting the application of such standards for such people against their own governments. A European state sees two cardinal principles of European colonial doctrine, and their modern manifestation in European human rights promotion, come up against each other. The effect of the position the UK took in the *Al-Saadoon* litigation was to choose the former over the latter.

The tables were then turned when it came to the situation in the Ecuadorean embassy in London. There the UK risked being itself in the role of the host state that seemingly has a lower commitment to human rights compared to the extraterritorial state—the reverse of the position it claimed for itself in Iraq. A non-European state was applying a higher standard of human rights protection than the European host state seemed to accept for itself when it faced the same situation in a different non-European context. Moreover, this standard was derived from norms understood partly to have been developed *outside Europe*. For this to be acceptable, Europeans would have had to accept that their position as a beacon of progressive human rights protection for the world was on shaky foundations.

In offering protection to Assange, then, Ecuador also intervened within a hugely contested debate amongst European states on extraterritoriality, and *non-refoulement*, and the intersection of the two, by example, a commitment to protections in this area which the UK itself if faced by a similar situation would wish to challenge (and did challenge, as respondent in the *B* and *Al-Saadoon* cases, and as a third party intervenor with ten other European states in the *MN* case). The problem for the UK, then, was that Ecuador was not only preventing the UK from doing what it wanted to do with Julian Assange. Also, Ecuador was acting in a way that suggests commitment to an obligation *for itself* which the UK and certain other European states would seek to refute *for themselves* in equivalent circumstances. Put differently, the UK's rejection of the legality of Ecuador's action, if grounded in a bypassing of any consideration of the potential relevance of human rights law, corresponds to the position it would want for itself as far as the extraterritorial application of human rights law is concerned. For the UK not to be bound by human rights law extraterritorially, or, at least, for the scope of extraterritorial applicability to be highly attenuated, excluding, for example, a *non-refoulement* element, necessarily requires a general position to be taken on human rights law which renders Ecuador's actions lacking in legal foundation. The position Ecuador took was transgressive, then, not only on the specific matter of what should happen to Assange. Also, it challenged the UK position on the very notion that states should have protective obligations in such contexts. And this was something which was, if anything, more of a concern to the UK as the potential *bearer* of such obligations in other contexts—i.e., playing the role performed by Ecuador—than being the host state in whose territory such obligations being applicable to other states would cause problems. Indeed, an economically privileged and militarily powerful state like the UK is much more used to being in the situation of acting outside its borders, and having to respond to human rights challenges arising out of this (as in Iraq), than dealing with the human rights implications in its own territory of the actions of other states.

That such a situation arose is due to the fact that the Assange situation occurred outside Latin America. A Latin American state sought to implement a Latin American approach to human rights protection outside its region. And it came up against a position seemingly rooted not only in a rejection of diplomatic asylum as a universal doctrine as a matter of general international law (or a Denza-esque definition of this as very limited, and inapplicable to the situation), but also skeptical of and resistant to the general project of extraterritorial human rights obligations within which an equivalent obligation of extraterritorial *non-refoulement* applied to diplomatic premises could be, and indeed had already been, situated.

Conclusions

The Assange-Ecuador embassy saga implicated a much bigger set of issues, with important historical resonances, than simply what was at stake for Assange and all the matters implicated in his situation. It is a reminder that the extraterritorial protection of human rights in international law has its historical origins in the Latin/South American region, not, as Europeans tell themselves, in Europe. As the ECHR system seemed to catch up with the more longstanding Latin American normative developments concerning protection from *non-refoulement* extraterritorially generally, it was a Latin American state which, through its own example, affirmed a commitment to these developments (albeit a commitment that did not survive a change of government in that state) at the very time when they were under threat in Europe. With the Strasbourg Court then seeming to give into pressure and deciding to rein in the potential operation of an extraterritorial *non-refoulement* obligation in diplomatic premises in the *MN* decision of 2020, it is the 2018 Advisory Opinion of the IACtHR that provides the most robust affirmation of the operation of such an obligation to date.

Just, then, as Latin America was the historical site of norm entrepreneurism on this subject, so too much later it was, aptly, a Latin American state acting in Europe, and then the IACtHR sending out a message from San José, that served, in effect, to push back on the backlash against these norms as they had been adopted in the European system.

Note

* My warm thanks to Nabila Roukhamieh-McKinna, doctoral student at UCL Laws, for excellent research assistance, and the two anonymous reviewers, and the Editors of this volume, for their valuable feedback. This chapter was accepted for publication on the basis of double-blind peer review.

References

Bantekas, I. and Oette, L. (2020) *International Human Rights Law and Practice* (3rd Ed.), Cambridge University Press.

Caracas Convention on Diplomatic Asylum (1954) (Organization of American States [OAS]) 1438 UNTS 104, UN Reg No I-24377.

Costello, C. (2012) 'Courting Access to Asylum in Europe: Recent Supranational Jurisprudence Explored', *Human Rights Law Review* 12(2), 287–339.

Denza, E. (2011) 'Diplomatic Asylum', in Zimmermann, A. (ed.), *The 1951 Convention Relating to the Status of Refugees and its 1967 Protocol – A Commentary*, Oxford University Press.

Denza, E. (2016) *Diplomatic Law: A Commentary on the Vienna Convention on Diplomatic Relations* (4th Ed.), Clarendon.

England and Wales Court of Appeal (ECWA) (2004) *R. (on the application of B) v Secretary of State for Foreign and Commonwealth Affairs*, [2004] EWCA Civ 1344CA (Civ Div) (18 October 2004).

European Commission of Human Rights (ECmHR) (1975) *Hess v. United Kingdom*, DR 2, 72 Application No. 6231/73.

European Commission on Human Rights (1992) *M. v. Denmark*, Application No. 17392/90.

European Court of Human Rights (ECtHR) (2010) *Al-Saadoon and Mufdhi v United Kingdom*, Application No. 61498/08.

_______ (2012) *Hirsi Jamaa and Others v Italy* Application No. 27765/09, Judgment (Grand Chamber).

_______ (2020) *M.N. and Others v Belgium*, Application No: Judgment, 5 March 2020

Giuffré, M. (2016) 'Access to Asylum at Sea? Non-refoulement and a Comprehensive Approach to Extraterritorial Human Rights Obligations' in Moreno-Lax, V. and Papastavridis, E. (eds.) *Boat Refugees' and Migrants at Sea: A Comprehensive Approach Integrating Maritime Security with Human Rights*, Brill.

Guerrero, R. and Palacios, H. (1979). *El derecho de asilo*, Editorial Kelly.

Harris, D. J. et al. (2018) *Harris, O'Boyle & Warbrick: Law of the European Convention on Human Rights* (4th Ed.) Oxford University Press.

Heyns, C. and Killander, M. (2013) 'Universality and the Growth of Regional Systems,' in Shelton, D. (ed.), *The Oxford Handbook of International Human Rights Law*, Oxford University Press.

Inter-American Commission on Human Rights (IACmHR) (1999) *Coard v US*, Report No.109/99, OEA/Ser.L./V/II.85, doc. 9 rev. (1999) Case 10.951 (29 September 1999).

Inter-American Court of Human Rights (IACtHR) (2018) 'Advisory Opinion OC-25/18 The Institution of Asylum and its Recognition as a Human Right in the Inter-American System of Protection'.

International Court of Justice (ICJ) (1950) 1950 *Asylum Case*, ICJ Reports 266.

Kim, S. (2017) 'Non-refoulement and Extraterritorial Jurisdiction: State Sovereignty and Migration Controls at Sea in the European Context', *Leiden Journal of International Law* 30, 49

Milanovic, M. (2011) *Extraterritorial Application of Human Rights Treaties: Law, Principles and Policy*, Oxford University Press.

Planas-Suárez, S. (1953) *El Asilo Diplomático*, Imprenta López.

Roberts, I. and Denza, E. (2016) *Satow's Diplomatic Practice* (7th Ed.), Oxford University Press. (the relevant section is described as 'with Eileen Denza')

UN Human Rights Committee (1981a) *Lopez Burgos v Uruguay*, UN Doc. A/36/40 Communication No. R.12/52, Supp. No. 40.

UN Human Rights Committee (1981b) *Lilian Celiberti de Casariego v Uruguay*, UN Doc. CCPR/C/13/D/56/1979 Communication No. 56/1979.

Vieira, M. A. (1961) *Derecho de asilo diplomático: asilo político*, Biblioteca de Publicaciones Oficiales de la Facultad de Derecho y Ciencias Sociales de la Universidad de la Republica, seccion III-CXVIII.

Vienna Convention on Consular Relations (1963) 596 UNTS 261, 24 April 1963.

Vienna Convention on Diplomatic Relations (1961) 500 UNTS 95, 18 April 1961.

Wallace, S. (2019) *The Application of the European Convention on Human Rights to Military Operations*, Cambridge University Press.

Part IV

Financial assistance and sanctions

15

Human rights-based approaches to development assistance and policies

Lilian Chenwi

Introduction

Development assistance (also referred to as foreign aid or international cooperation for development) is a global or extraterritorial activity that is crucial in promoting human rights and development. It is of particular importance to poor or low-income countries in stimulating social and economic development (Kieh 2014, p. 261; Sengupta 2002, p. 1424). It is also 'a crucial countercyclical flow in times of crisis' with 'the potential to be a transformative force to support and guide a sustainable recovery in developing countries' (Organisation for Economic Cooperation and Development (OECD) 2020, p. 8; see also United Nations (UN) 2020, p. 58). The international community continues to experience global crises that not only threaten human rights and development but also necessitate transnational and collaborative action in addressing them. The COVID-19 crisis, for example, has negatively impacted the global economy, human rights and development, and has brought to the fore the need to intensify and rethink approaches to international cooperation and assistance and to adopt responses that are human rights-based (Guterres 2020a; Guterres 2020b). Development assistance has been useful in funding/building health and social protection systems and funding medical research, which are crucial to national responses to the COVID-19 crisis (OECD 2020, p. 8; UN 2020, p. 31). Hence, development assistance 'could play a crucial role in tackling the immediate impacts of the coronavirus crisis and supporting a recovery centred on human rights, gender equality and a just transition' (Van de Poel 2020).

There is a common understanding that development cooperation and assistance should further the realisation of human rights and that the international human rights (IHRs) framework is necessary for realising development (OHCHR 2006, pp. 7–14 and 35). Though many core UN human rights treaties contain references to international cooperation and assistance, which is code for development assistance/foreign aid, in realising human rights, development assistance activities exist that are contrary to human rights standards, resulting in hindrances to the realisation of rights and promotion of well-being of individuals in the receiving state (see Chenwi 2018, pp. 99 and 112–130, highlighting examples where rights violations have been linked to projects for which development assistance has been provided to African states; Sengupta 2002, pp. 1432–1433 on failures of development assistance/aid; Committee on Economic, Social and Cultural Rights (CESCR) 2014a, para. 12 raising concerns over China's economic and technical assistance

DOI: 10.4324/9781003090014-20

projects that 'have reportedly resulted in rights violations in the receiving countries; and Herre and Backes' chapter in this book explaining how financialisation in the context of development cooperation impacts the enjoyment of human rights). It should be noted that there have also been critical voices on development aid undermining sovereignty of recipient states (see Brown 2013 for detailed discussion of sovereignty questions in the context of aid) or it being neo-colonial, facilitating foreign/external influence/control and perpetuating forms of economic exploitation (see for example Langan 2018, pp. 61–88). In addition to sovereignty being 'the very basis upon which aid relations are conducted', recognition of sovereign rights of recipient states forms 'the base from which recipients are able to contest the terms of aid relationships' (Brown 2013, pp. 263 and 274). Hence, while internationally recognised human rights impose limits on state sovereignty, donor states have a duty to respect the sovereignty of territorial/recipient states (De Schutter et al. 2012, pp. 1142 and 1146). Also, IHRL, as seen from the discussion on human rights-based approach (HRBA) in this chapter, provides guiding principles that are useful, if applied effectively, in addressing unequal power relations and risks of conditionalities/neo-colonialism in the context of development assistance while furthering rights realisation and development.

Over the past decade, the need to apply a HRBA in the context of development assistance has surfaced constantly, as the approach 'entails the promotion of legal rights and legal capacity building within the context of (international) development activities' (Broberg and Sano 2018, p. 664). The COVID-19 crisis, as stated above, has reinforced this need. A HRBA has its basis in the recognition of the interdependence and mutually reinforcing dynamic between human rights and development. There is no one HRBA, as approaches to integrating human rights in development assistance vary; but at the core of a HRBA is the need to ensure compliance with IHRL standards and principles when engaging in development assistance. Consequently, the IHRs framework (which extraterritorial obligations (ETOs) are part of) should be applied in developing, implementing, assessing and evaluating development assistance policies and practices. Hence, donor and recipient states' obligations to respect, protect and fulfil human rights in their activities implies that they have a duty to adopt a HRBA, as it not only facilitates mainstreaming of human rights principles but also compliance with their human rights obligations when engaging in development assistance activities. A HRBA is thus relevant to operationalising ETOs in practice. The duty to adopt a HRBA is reinforced through the increasing emphasis by treaty bodies, among others, in the context of implementation of states' obligations. A HRBA has also received support from international development cooperation actors (including UN agencies) and domestic actors such as non-governmental organisations (NGOs) active in developing countries (ibid, pp. 664 and 665).

This chapter explains development assistance and its legal basis, the nature and scope of states' ETOs in the context of development assistance, highlighting donor states' ETOs to respect, protect and fulfil rights when engaging in development assistance, including their obligation to offer assistance. As ETOs of donor states do not leave recipient/territorial states off the hook (that is, they too have IHRs obligations to comply with), the chapter also briefly highlights recipient states' obligations, specifically their obligation to seek assistance. The chapter then considers the relationship between human rights and development assistance, with specific focus on what a HRBA to development assistance entails.

Development assistance

There is no single internationally agreed definition of what development assistance constitutes (UN Economic and Social Council (ECOSOC) 2008, p. 4). Various bodies and writers have defined the term, with promotion of social and economic development and human rights among its constituent elements. Minoiu and Reddy (2009, p. 7) define development assistance as 'aid expended in a manner that is anticipated to promote development, whether achieved through economic growth or other means', which is distinguishable from non-development aid (the latter defined as 'aid of all other kinds'). Skogly (2006, p. 192) defines it in simple terms as 'a direct transfer of public funds from one state to another state'. OECD Development Assistance Committee (DAC), using the terminology official development assistance (ODA), defines it as 'government aid that promotes and specifically targets the economic development and welfare of developing countries' (OECD 2019).

Development assistance could be bilateral ('from official (government) sources directly to official sources in the recipient country') or multilateral ('core contributions from official (government) sources to multilateral agencies where it is then used to fund the multilateral agencies' own programmes') and is bi/multi where a government contracts a multilateral agency to provide a project on its behalf in a recipient country (OECD, cited in Chenwi 2018, p. 89). The main objective of development assistance is the promotion of development and welfare of the recipient country. Development assistance flows comprise, *inter alia*, 'programme and project assistance, humanitarian assistance, debt relief, costs of education provided to developing country nationals in the donor country, administrative costs of ODA programmes, subsidies to NGOs, and programmes to raise development awareness in donor countries' (ECOSOC 2008, p. 5). Loans 'must be deemed concessional' to qualify as development assistance (ibid). Hence, development assistance measures are not limited to economic or technical assistance.

Development assistance model has largely been North-South cooperation. However, with the ever-increasing global crises, it is more and more becoming universal and multidirectional. The COVID-19 crisis, for instance, has seen the North-South cooperation model, though still important, 'continuously losing significance as the predominant cooperation model in developing regions', with South-South cooperation receiving a visible push and stimulating creative solutions (Izmestiev and Klingebiel 2020). Also, other forms of cooperation such as '"South-North cooperation" (for example, China's support to Italy) and "East-North cooperation" (for example, Russia sending medical material to the United States)' have become increasingly prominent (ibid).

The Sustainable Development Goals 2015 (SDGs) – the Declaration and Goal 17 – confirm the international target for ODA by developed states to developing countries as a minimum of 0.7 per cent, and to least developed countries as 0.15 to 0.20 per cent, of the developed state's gross national income (UN 2015). Though the SDGs are not per se legally binding, they reflect state commitments. The mutually reinforcing dynamic between human rights and development (explained below) implies that IHRL ensures the monitoring and accountability mechanisms for their enforcement.

The legal basis of development assistance is the reference in various international human rights and development documents/frameworks to a duty of international cooperation and assistance or the need to increase development assistance to poorer countries, especially as a tool to promote development and facilitate enhanced human rights implementation (see Skogly's chapter in this book elaborating on this duty). While it remains contentious whether the obligation to cooperate is an enforceable binding legal obligation, the obligation is increasingly widely accepted and has been consistently reaffirmed by UN bodies and experts. The acceptance of the existence of a binding legal obligation in relation to development assistance is necessary in order to ensure that such assistance does not 'rests upon charity' (De Mesquita et al. 2010, p. 112) and is in line with relevant state obligations such as ETOs.

Extraterritorial obligations in development assistance

Consideration of ETOs in the context of development assistance is crucial because development agencies have traditionally viewed recipient states as the 'sole duty-bearers of human rights obligations in their countries', with donor agencies having the discretion to require compliance with human rights by the recipient countries (Khalfan 2012, p. 397). However, IHRs standards have given rise to extraterritorial human rights obligations of donor states in the context of development assistance. Furthermore, as seen below, states' ETOs have implications for the way development assistance is undertaken, including priority setting in development policy.

It is important to note at the outset that ETOs of donor states does not leave recipient/territorial states off the hook, as they too have IHRs obligations to comply with, which are of a territorial nature. Recipient states have territorial obligations to respect, protect and fulfil rights, including an *obligation to seek appropriate international assistance* in situations where they have inadequate national resources to ensure realisation of human rights, *to receive appropriate assistance* and *to make effective use of such assistance when provided* (*Maastricht Principles* on Extraterritorial Obligations of States in the area of Economic, Social and Cultural Rights 2011 (*Maastricht Principles*), Principle 34; CRC Committee, General Comment no. 4, para. 43 and General Comment no. 5, paras. 60–61; CESCR 2015c, para. 40 and 2015a, para. 28; CESCR 2007, para. 5). In relation to the duty to make effective use of assistance when received, the recipient state is obliged to put in place a sustainable institutional framework on its use; failing which, the state would be in breach of its obligation to take steps to use the maximum amount of its resources towards the progressive realisation of rights. The state must also ensure compliance with human rights principles and priorities in the use of development assistance. For example, development assistance must be allocated to priority sectors and be used for the progressive realisation of rights (CESCR 2009b, paras. 16 and 29). States are also required to 'enhance the transparency of the receipt, management and spending of official development funds' that they receive (CESCR 2015b, para. 11).

Regarding ETOs, donor states are required, in their development assistance activities, to comply with their obligations to respect, protect and fulfil rights under applicable human rights treaties. Though the extent of the latter obligation remains contentious, treaty bodies such as the CESCR have elaborated on the extraterritorial dimensions of these obligations (see, for example: CESCR, General Comment no. 24, paras 29–37). The *Maastricht Principles* also elaborate on these obligations. It should be noted that the extraterritorial application of these obligations does not imply that 'each state is responsible for ensuring the human rights of every person in the world' (De Schutter et al. 2012, p. 1090).

Extraterritorial obligation to respect requires that states refrain from conduct, including in the context of international cooperation, which directly or indirectly interferes with enjoyment of rights by persons outside their territories, and 'not obstruct another state from complying with its [human rights] obligations' (*Maastricht Principles*, Principles 19–21; CESCR, General Comment no. 24, para. 29; CESCR, General Comment no. 19, para. 53; CESCR, General Comment no. 15, para. 31). Therefore, in the context of development assistance, the extraterritorial obligation to respect requires that a state's action should respect, and not impair, rights enjoyment in other states (Skogly 2006, p. 68). A state should also ensure that any change in its funding policies in the course of development assistance provision does not result in retrogression in rights enjoyment in the receiving state and that it has taken all necessary efforts to prevent or limit the extent of any retrogression (De Mesquita et al. 2010, p. 116). Failing which, it would amount to a breach of the state's obligation to respect access to rights in other states.

Extraterritorial obligation to protect requires that states take necessary measures, including through international cooperation, to prevent and redress rights infringements that occur outside their territories as a result of the activities of entities that they are in a position to regulate or influence, and to ensure effective remedy for those affected, 'especially in cases where the remedies available to victims before the domestic courts of the state where the harm occurs are unavailable or ineffective' (*Maastricht Principles*, Principles 23–27; CESCR, General Comment no. 24, para. 30; CESCR 2013a, para. 6). In the context of development assistance, the extraterritorial obligation to protect requires the donor state to, as far as possible, protect against the implementers of a project funded through its development assistance violating rights in the recipient state. The donor state should therefore exercise oversight over the implementation of the project as part of fulfilling its extraterritorial obligation to protect. Oversight does not however imply implementation of a solely donor-driven approach to development assistance or detrimental tied aid practices, as recipient countries should not be prevented from taking responsibility for their own development in utilising the aid.

The *extraterritorial obligation to fulfil* requires that states contribute to creating an international enabling environment for rights fulfilment, including in matters relating to development cooperation (*Maastricht Principles*, Principles 28–29; CESCR, General Comment no. 24, para. 37). Further, if in a position to assist, states have an obligation to *provide (offer) appropriate international assistance*, 'consider [a request to assist or cooperate] in good faith, and respond in a manner consistent with their obligations to fulfil … rights extraterritorially' (*Maastricht Principles*, Principles 33 and 35; also see De Mesquita et al. 2010, p. 113).

Though the legally binding nature of the *obligation to provide assistance* in the context of development assistance has been questioned (Vandenhole 2007, p. 97), the obligation is recognised and confirmed in international instruments and by various bodies. International standards on international cooperation and assistance explicitly refer to an obligation on states to 'take' steps/actions 'individually and through international assistance and co-operation' towards rights realisation (see Skogly's chapter in this book). The Optional Protocol to the CRC on the Involvement of Children in Armed Conflict 2000 (OPAC) (art. 7), for instance, explicitly recognises the obligation of states that are 'in a position to do so', to 'provide' assistance – 'including … technical cooperation and financial assistance'. The Committee on the Rights of the Child (CRC Committee) (General Comment no. 5, para. 7) has also recognised that the obligations on states parties include an obligation 'to contribute, through international cooperation, to global implementation' of children's rights. Similarly, the CESCR (General Comment no. 3, para. 14) has recognised states' duty to offer assistance, stating that it will not be possible to realise economic, social and cultural rights to the fullest extent in many countries if states that are capable of taking part in an active programme of international assistance and cooperation do not do so. The UN requires rich countries to ensure that a large part of the financial resources they provide to developing countries be in the form of ODA, which should be progressively increased (UN General Assembly, Resolution 262 (XXV), para. 43). As stated above, developed states have an obligation to allocate a minimum of 0.7 per cent (to developing states), and 0.15 to 0.20 per cent (to least developed states), of their gross national income for development assistance. Accordingly, various UN bodies have raised concerns over states' non-compliance with the minimum target and urged states to comply (see for example: CRC Committee, General Comment no. 5, para. 61; CESCR 2014b, para. 18, 2015d, para. 36 and 2013b, para. 9). In line with principles and priorities in cooperation, states that offer assistance have an obligation to, *inter alia*: prioritise realisation of the rights of vulnerable, disadvantaged and marginalised groups, prioritise core obligations for the realisation of minimum essential levels of rights, move expeditiously and effectively towards full realisation of rights, observe IHRs standards and avoid retrogressive steps unless they can be reasonably justified (*Maastricht Principles*, Principle 32; also see De Schutter et al. 2012, pp. 1154–1157 for examples of general comments by the CESCR accentuating these obligations).

The extraterritorial obligation to fulfil thus requires that 'states' extraterritorial activities … positively improve human rights situations of individuals in third states' (Skogly 2006, p. 71).

In the context of development assistance, therefore, states should ensure that their activities contribute to rights fulfilment and the principles and priorities in cooperation stated above should be taken into consideration in the development and implementation of their development assistance policies and programmes.

Using the right to health as an example to illustrate the extraterritorial obligations to respect, protect and fulfil in the context of international assistance, a state must ensure that its actions '*respect* the right to health in other countries', '*protect* against third parties undermining the right to health in other countries' and, subject to available resources, *fulfil* the right to health through, for instance, facilitating 'access to essential health facilities and services in other countries' (De Mesquita et al. 2010, p. 116). Also, in the course of development assistance provision, a state should not 'withdraw critical right-to-health aid without first giving the recipient reasonable notice and opportunity to make alternative arrangements'; otherwise, this would amount to procedural unfairness, in breach of its extraterritorial obligation to *respect* access to health (ibid).

The ETOs to respect, protect and fulfil rights thus provide a framework for development of policymaking and implementation. They also provide a means to monitor the performance of donor states regarding the integration of human rights with development, including in the context of development assistance, required under a HRBA. One of the key components of a HRBA to development assistance is 'actual status of human rights in the setting where development assistance is to be provided' in relation to, *inter alia*, 'duty-bearers' commitment to respect, protect and fulfil human rights' (Broberg and Sano 2018, p. 669). Hence, integration of human rights into analysis of development policies and their implementation can be facilitated through a matrix of donor policies and programmes vis-à-vis state obligations to respect, protect and fulfil rights (see UNDP 2015, p. 12 where this is further illustrated). ETOs can thus be operationalised in practice through a HRBA.

A human rights-based approach to development assistance

The link and importantly the interdependence between human rights and development, plus state commitments to comply with human rights and correlating obligations in the context of development (including development assistance), have been recognised in various international documents including the DRD and SDGs, and by various UN agencies/bodies (OHCHR 2008; UNDP 2007; UN 2015, paras. 3, 8, 10 and 19). About 90 per cent of the SDG targets are linked to IHRs (Smith 2020, pp. 405 and 417–419). Treaty bodies have urged states to mainstream human rights into implementation and monitoring of the 2030 Agenda and SDGs (see for example: Committee on the Rights of Persons with Disabilities (CRPD Committee), 2019c, para. 67, and 2019a, para. 60). This is crucial considering that donor states are focused on the SDGs (Smith 2020, p. 414). The relationship is also evident in the discussion on ETOs in the preceding section.

Despite the relationship between development and human rights, earlier approaches to development did not place human rights at the centre of development. The approaches either reinforced inequality, existing power structures and failed to achieve sustainable outcomes, as beneficiaries were viewed as objects/passive recipients and not partners in development (the charity approach), or donors determined the needs of the beneficiaries which ended up being supply-based, with the donor 'dumping whatever surplus it had on developing countries' (needs-based approach) (Bokulić and Taneja 2009, pp. 10–11). Hence, 'traditional approaches to development assistance … focused largely on needs of the poor and the provision of specific commodities and services to meet those needs' (Ussar 2011, p. 7). The non-placement of human rights at the centre of development, it can be argued, implied that (sufficient) attention was not given to ETOs of donor states with human rights conditionalities often placed on recipient states and not donor states. The challenges with these earlier approaches and the increasing recognition of the congruence between human rights and development has given rise to the need for both donor and recipient countries to pursue development policies and their implementation within a human rights framework. Hence, human rights conditionality in aid, for instance, should not be placed only on recipients but also on donor countries themselves.

A HRBA to development seeks to place human rights principles at the core of development policies and practices 'in order to support a conceptual shift from development based on externally devised, charity-focused aid provided to passive recipients to looking at development as a process that empowers people through an inclusive and participatory approach' (Ussar 2011, p. 4). 'Human rights provide a means of empowering all people to make decisions about their own lives rather than being the passive objects of choices made on their behalf' (UNDP 2015, p. 1). An inclusive and participatory approach to development assistance is crucial considering concerns over lack of, or insufficient, participation of vulnerable groups in the planning, design, implementation, monitoring and evaluation of international cooperation projects, including efforts aimed at achieving the 2030 Agenda for sustainable development (see for example: CRPD Committee 2019b, paras. 57–58 and 2019e, paras. 61–62).

Previous understandings of what the HRBA to development entailed differed among UN agencies, resulting in the need to adopt a common understanding of the concept and its implication for development cooperation and assistance policies and programmes (OHCHR 2006, p. 35). In 2003, a Statement of Common Understanding on a HRBA to development cooperation and development programming by UN agencies was adopted (ibid, pp. 35–37). As recognised in the Statement, the main objective of development policies and programmes should be fulfilment of human rights guaranteed in IHRs instruments; and IHRs standards and principles 'should guide all development cooperation and programming in all sectors in all phases of the programming process' (ibid, pp. 15–16 and 35–36; see also OECD 2007, p. 11). This implies that ETOs of donor states cannot be ignored in the development and implementation of development assistance policies, as they have been recognised under, *inter alia*, IHRL. Considering their relevance in development assistance, there is therefore the need to clarify ETOs in the context of development aid and strengthen their legal base.

Approaches to integrating human rights into development activities and definitions of HRBA to development vary. The OHCHR (2006, p. 15) defines HRBA to development as 'a conceptual framework for the process of human development that is normatively based on international human rights standards and operationally directed to promoting and protecting human rights'. In simple terms, a HRBA 'is a way (or a "method") of implementing human rights in a development context' (Broberg and Sano 2018, p. 665) or 'a commitment to systematically integrate human rights norms, standards or principles in all aspects and areas of development cooperation' (D'Hollander et al. 2014, p. 238). A narrow definition, focussing on poverty (excluding the rights of the relatively well-off) and emphasising resources and regulation is provided by Gauri and Gloppen (2012, p. 486), defining 'HRBAs as principles that justify demands against privileged actors made by the poor or those speaking on their behalf, for using national and international resources and rules to protect the crucial human interests of the globally or locally disadvantaged' (see also pp. 488–502 where they distinguish and elaborate on types of HRBAs, which includes, *inter alia*, '"Global compliance approaches" rooted in and pressuring for compliance with international and regional treaties' and '"Programming approaches" focusing on policies and principles of donors and executive agencies'; the approaches have implications for ETOs, as they imply pressuring for compliance with ETOs recognised under applicable treaties and evaluating donors' development assistance policies' compliance with ETOs).

The 'multifaceted and intersectoral nature' of the HRBA to development implies 'that human rights values, standards and principles come to bear at different times (together or independently) during the programming exercise' and there is 'subsequent need for alignment of development assistance' (UNDP 2015, p. 9). The 2003 Statement of Common Understanding identifies and elaborates on the following principles that should guide development polices: 'universality and inalienability; indivisibility; interdependence and interrelatedness; non-discrimination and equality; participation and inclusion; accountability and the rule of law' (OHCHR 2006, p. 36). The HRBA therefore 'has significant implications for the manner in which development priorities and objectives are identified and country programme outcomes formulated' (ibid, p. 28; see also UNDP 2015, p. 1). Treaty bodies have thus urged states to adopt development policies that are in line with human rights treaties, with measurable and tangible targets and indicators (see for example, CRPD Committee 2019a, para. 60).

Operationalisation of the HRBA involves various modalities and institutional mechanisms. An 'intersectoral perspective' is needed, with the approach being applied in all phases of development, including during planning, implementation and evaluation of results (UNDP 2015, p. 9; World Bank and OECD 2016, p. 54). 'Contextual analysis, insights about institutional constraints and sensitivities are all important dimensions that must also be taken into account' (Broberg and Sano 2018, p. 676). Approaches to its application might thus vary depending on the context. In addition to context, a 'donor's human rights policies' and the parameters of its 'mandates, capacity, or comparative advantage in the field' influences its approach to integrating human rights into development activities (World Bank and OECD 2016, p. 52).

Despite the varied approaches to integrating human rights in development assistance, there are common characteristics for operationalising a HRBA to development assistance. These common characteristics include, among others: 'employment of the concept of human rights' (that is, not viewing development assistance as charity 'but as part of efforts to fulfil rights'); linking rights to corresponding obligations; focussing on capacity building, enabling duty bearers to respond to claims from recipients, ensuring minimum core rights are fulfilled, facilitating access to services for rights-holders and ensuring their free participation in decisions that affect their livelihood; and addressing marginalisation and vulnerability to discrimination (Broberg and Sano 2018, pp. 667–669). Corresponding IHRs obligations include ETOs, as explained above. In short, rights-holders and corresponding duty-bearers have to be identified in specific development assistance contexts, and their capacities to claim their rights and fulfil their duties, respectively, has to be promoted (Ussar 2011, pp. 4 and 8; World Bank and OECD 2016, p. 53). In addition to taking remedial measures and ensuring accessible mechanisms for violation of rights in the recipient state, a HRBA requires that a donor state undertakes 'systematic and independent human rights impact assessment prior to making funding decisions' and establish 'an effective monitoring mechanism to regularly assess the human rights impact of its policies and projects in the receiving countries' (CESCR 2014a, para. 12). However, mainstreaming human rights in all development aid or all areas of development work might be challenging in some communities or contexts (for example, in rural communities' context where, as argued by some scholars, a HRBA is 'less effective because literacy is lower than average, and the state is less present'), necessitating strategic and 'targeted interventions on the part of governments, donors, and civil society actors' that are adapted according to the sector, the rights-holders and the duty-bearers (Gauri and Gloppen 2012, p. 487; Broberg and Sano 2018, pp. 673 and 676).

There is emerging state practice on integration of a HRBA into development assistance, as various states and other development actors have integrated human rights in their mandates through adoption of a HRBA to development assistance, particularly at the level of policy commitments. World Bank and OECD (2016) highlight some examples of successfully integrating human rights in development assistance. They include the Swedish International Development Cooperation Agency (SIDA)'s mainstreaming of 'child rights in all aid interventions as part of a long-term, sustainable development cooperation strategy, while also engaging in targeted interventions with a more immediate impact' (ibid, p. 67). SIDA 'uses the acronym P.L.A.N.E.T. as a way of organizing and remembering what to consider when applying a HRBA to development cooperation', in terms of which it considers, *inter alia*: 'participation; links to human rights in legal instruments at the national, regional, and international levels, such as the CRC and the African Charter on the rights and welfare of the child; accountability; non-discrimination; empowerment; and transparency' (ibid). Sweden's Kenya programme is also seen as a 'longstanding example of mainstreaming human rights in a bilateral country program' with success (see ibid, pp. 64–66, explaining the programme). Norway has also 'introduced human rights as a crosscutting issue to be mainstreamed across all parts of Norway's Development Cooperation' (ibid, p. 63). In operationalising its HRBA, Norway has given special attention to 'participation, accountability, and non-discrimination' (ibid). Following 'reported difficulties' in implementation of crosscutting issues of 'gender, anticorruption, and climate/the environment', Norway formulated a new standard, requiring 'that all grants be assessed from the "do no harm" principle and that risk factors that might have a negative impact on human rights be mitigated' (ibid, pp. 63–64). This approach accords with ETOs, which includes a duty on states to prevent, or avoid causing, harm (*Maastricht Principles*, Principles 13 and 14).

Generally, the HRBA has been adopted, to varying degrees, by, for example, UN bodies and specialised agencies, European Union (EU), OECD/DAC, bilateral agencies (with policies and programmes that apply a HRBA to development found in, for example, Australia, Austria, Canada, Germany, Netherlands, New Zealand, Norway, Ireland, Sweden, Switzerland, UK and USA), international financial institutions (IFIs) and NGOs that are engaged in development assistance activities (Broberg and Sano 2018, p. 667; Gauri and Gloppen 2012, p. 492; Ussar 2011, p. 4; World Bank and OECD 2016, pp. 92–120; see also D'Hollander et al. 2014, pp. 86–234 and 237 for case studies of applying a HRBA). However, some IFIs' ability to address human rights considerations in their environmental and social policies is constrained by provisions in their constitutive legal instruments (see World Bank and OECD 2016, pp. 113–118 elaborating on this). Nonetheless, the support for SDGs by donors and banks implies a recognition that development policy priorities be set on human rights grounds.

A HRBA to development has thus gained general acceptance, with UN treaty bodies calling on states to adopt a HRBA to their development cooperation and assistance policies and programmes (see for example: CRC Committee, General Comment no. 5, paras. 61 and 64 and General Comment no. 3, para. 41; CESCR 2015d, para. 36 and 2014a, para. 12; CRPD Committee 2017, paras. 66–67 and 2019d, para. 63). They have also called on organisations or institutions like the World Bank Group, the International Monetary Fund and World Trade Organization to ensure that their activities related to international cooperation and economic development are in accordance with IHRL (see for example: CRC Committee, General Comment no. 5, para. 64).

It is evident from various writings that have considered how the HRBA works in practice that it has value, for example, its usefulness in improving aid effectiveness and facilitating operationalisation of IHRs obligations, including ETOs (for a discussion of its values, see for example: OHCHR 2006, p. 16; Gauri and Gloppen 2012, p. 486; World Bank and OECD 2016, pp. 26–50; Sengupta 2002, p. 1434; Broberg and Sano 2018, pp. 672–674 and 677). However, it also has challenges such as its unsuitability for all development aid interventions, but which can be mitigated if a strategic approach to its implementation is adopted, taking context into consideration and without ruling out the possibility of using other suitable methods to complement the approach (for a discussion of its challenges and how they can be mitigated, see for example: Broberg and Sano 2018, pp. 673–674; World Bank and OECD 2016, pp. 54 and 121–137).

Conclusion

Development assistance is a global or extraterritorial activity that several development agencies or states are involved in. This chapter has established that states (particularly developing or poorer states) have an obligation to seek development assistance should they lack the ability to realise rights, and states that are able to do so (particularly developed or richer states) have a duty to offer such assistance. There are, however, debates as to whether the latter is of an enforceable binding nature. Notwithstanding, IHRL standards establish ETOs to respect, protect and fulfil rights in the provision of development assistance. Furthermore, the adoption of a HRBA in development assistance has been emphasised, which requires, *inter alia*, compliance with IHRL obligations, including ETOs. A HRBA requires that states and development agencies that are engaged in development assistance, as well as civil society actors involved in the process, ensure a process of development where human rights are realised and in a way that not only establishes the specific entitlements in a non-discriminatory manner but also ensures accountability, including extraterritorial responsibility, for the non-achievement or violation of the entitlements. The HRBA has the potential to enrich development assistance policies and their implementation and is important in addressing challenges with previous approaches to development and ensuring that development assistance activities promote human rights and sustainable development. The approach also provides a framework for consideration of ETOs in the context of development assistance and directs states on how to abide more operationally with their ETOs in the context of development aid.

References

Bokulić, S. and Taneja, P. (eds). (2009) 'Human Rights-Based Approaches to Development Education: A Toolkit for Activists in New EU Member States', Minority Rights International, https://minorityrights.org/publications/human-rights-based-approaches-to-development-education-a-toolkit-for-activists-in-new-eu-member-states-november-2009/ [accessed 12 August 2020].

Broberg, M. and Sano, H-O. (2018) 'Strengths and Weaknesses in a Human Rights-Based Approach to International Development: An analysis of a Rights-Based Approach to Development Assistance Based on Practical Experiences', *The International Journal of Human Right* 22(5), 664–680.

Brown, W. (2013) 'Sovereignty Matters: Africa, Donors, and the Aid Relationship', *African Affairs* 112(447), 262–282.

Chenwi, L. (2018) 'Extraterritorial Human Rights Obligations in the Context of Development Assistance to African States' in Chenwi, L. and Bulto, T. S. (eds.). *Extraterritorial Human Rights Obligations from an African Perspective*, Intersentia.

Committee on Economic, Social and Cultural Rights (CESCR) (1990) GC 3 on the Nature of States Parties' Obligations, E/1991/23.

_______ (2003) GC 15 on the Right to Water, E/C.12/2002/11.

_______ (2007) 'An Evaluation of the Obligation to Take Steps to the "Maximum of Available Resources" under an Optional Protocol to the Covenant', E/C.12/2007/1.

_______ (2008) GC 19 on the Right to Social Security, E/C.12/GC/19.

_______ (2009a) 'Guidelines on Treaty-Specific Documents to be Submitted by States Parties under Articles 16 and 17 of the International Covenant on Economic, Social and Cultural Rights', E/C.12/2008/2.

_______ (2009b) Concluding Observations on the Combined Second to Fourth Periodic Reports of the Democratic Republic of the Congo, E/C.12/COD/CO/4.

_______ (2011) 'Statement on the Obligations of States Parties Regarding the Corporate Sector and Economic, Social and Cultural Rights', E/C.12/2011/1.

_______ (2013a) Concluding Observations on the Fifth Periodic Report of Norway, E/C.12/NOR/CO/5.

_______ (2013b) Concluding Observations concerning the Fourth Periodic Report of Belgium, E/C.12/BEL/CO/4.

_______ (2014a) Concluding Observations on the Second Periodic Report of China, including Hong Kong, China, and Macao, China, E/C.12/CHN/CO/2.

_______ (2014b) Concluding Observations on the Sixth Periodic Report of Finland, E/C.12/FIN/CO/6.

_______ (2015a) Concluding Observations on the Combined Initial and Second Periodic Reports of Thailand, E/C.12/THA/CO/1-2.

_______ (2015b) Concluding Observations on the Combined Second and Third Periodic Reports of Tajikistan, E/C.12/TJK/CO/2-3.

_______ (2015c) Concluding Observations on the Initial Report of Uganda, E/C.12/UGA/CO/1.

_______ (2015d) Concluding Observations on the Third Periodic Report of Ireland, E/C.12/IRL/CO/3.

Committee on the Rights of the Child (CRC Committee) (2003a) GC 3 on HIV/AIDS and the Rights of the Child, CRC/GC/2003/3.

_______ (2003b) GC 4 on Adolescent Health and Development in the Context of the Convention on the Rights of the Child, CRC/GC/2003/4.

_______ (2003c) GC 5 on General Measures of Implementation of the Convention on the Rights of the Child, CRC/GC/2003/5.

Committee on the Rights of Persons with Disabilities (CRPD Committee) (2017) Concluding Observations on the Initial Report of the United Kingdom of Great Britain and Northern Ireland, CRPD/C/GBR/CO/1.

_______ (2019a) Concluding Observations on the Combined Second and Third Periodic Reports of Australia, CRPD/C/AUS/CO/2-3.

_______ (2019b) Concluding Observations on the Combined Second and Third Periodic Reports of Ecuador, CRPD/C/ECU/CO/2-3.

_______ (2019c) Concluding Observations on the Initial Report of India, CRPD/C/IND/CO/1.

_______ (2019d) Concluding Observations on the Initial Report of Kuwait, CRPD/C/KWT/CO/1.

_______ (2019e) Concluding Observations on the Initial Report of Myanmar, CRPD/C/MMR/CO/1.

De Mesquita, J.B., Hunt, P. and Khosla, R. (2010) 'The Human Rights Responsibility of International Assistance and Cooperation in Health' in Gibney, M. and Skogly, S. (eds.). *Universal Human Rights and Extraterritorial Obligations*, University of Pennsylvania Press.

De Schutter, O. et al. (2012) 'Commentary to the *Maastricht Principles* on Extraterritorial Obligations of States in the Area of Economic, Social and Cultural Rights', *Human Rights Quarterly* 43, 1084–1169.

D'Hollander, D., Marx, A. and Wouters, J. (2014) 'Integrating Human Rights into Development Cooperation: A Comparative Assessment of Strategies and Practices of Donors', *Leuven Centre for Global Governance Studies, Paper No. 15.*

Gauri, V. and Gloppen, S. (2012) 'Human Rights Based Approaches to Development: Concepts, Evidence, and Policy', *Polity* 44(4), 485–503.

Guterres, A. (2020a) 'COVID-19: We Will Come Through This Together', https://www.un.org/en/coronavirus/covid-19-we-will-come-through-together [accessed 3 July 2020].

_______ (2020b) 'We are all in this Together: Human Rights and COVID-19 Response and Recovery', https://www.un.org/en/un-coronavirus-communications-team/we-are-all-together-human-rights-and-covid-19-response-and [accessed 4 July 2020].

Izmestiev, A. and Klingebiel, S. (2020) 'International (Development) Cooperation in a Post COVID-19 World: A New Way of Interaction or Super-Accelerator?', https://devpolicy.org/international-development-cooperation-in-a-post-covid-19-world-a-new-way-of-interaction-or-super-accelerator-20200501-1/ [accessed 4 July 2020].

Khalfan, A. (2012) 'Development Cooperation and Extraterritorial Obligations' in Langford, M. and Russell, A. (eds.). *The Right to Water Theory, Practice and Prospects*, Cambridge University Press.

Kieh, G.K. (2014) 'Official Development Assistance in Africa' in Murithi, T. (ed.). *Handbook of Africa's International Relations*, Routledge.

Langan, M. (2018) *Neo-Colonialism and the Poverty of 'Development' in Africa*, Palgrave Mamillan.

Minoiu, C. and Reddy, S. G. (2009) 'Development Aid and Economic Growth: A Positive Long Run Relation', *IMF (International Monetary Fund) Working Paper WP/09/118.*

Office of the United Nations High Commissioner for Human Rights (OHCHR) (2006) 'Frequently Asked Questions on a Human Rights-Based Approach to Development Cooperation', United Nations HR/PUB/06/8.

OHCHR (2008) 'Claiming the Millennium Development Goals: A Human Rights Approach', United Nations.

Organisation for Economic Cooperation and Development (OECD) (2007) 'Action-Oriented Policy Paper on Human Rights and Development', DCD/DAC(2007)15, https://www.oecd.org/dac/accountable-effective-institutions/Action-oriented_Policy_Paper_on_HR_and_Development.pdf [accessed 30 August 2020].

_______ (2019) 'Official Development Assistance (ODA)', https://www.oecd.org/dac/financing-sustainable-development/development-finance-standards/official-development-assistance.htm [accessed 3 July 2020].

_______ (2020) 'Six Decades of ODA: Insights and Outlook in the COVID-19 Crisis' in Development Cooperation Profiles, https://doi.org/10.1787/2dcf1367-en [accessed 3 July 2020].

Sengupta, A. (2002) 'Official Development Assistance: The Human Rights Approach', *Economic and Political Weekly* 37(15), 1424–1436.

Skogly, S.I. (2006) *Beyond National Borders: States' Human Rights Obligations in International Cooperation*, Intersentia.

Smith, K.M. (2020) *International Human Rights Law*, 9th Ed., Oxford University Press.

United Nations (UN) (2015) 'Transforming our World: The 2030 Agenda for Sustainable Development', A/RES/70/1.

_______ (2018) 'Financing for Development: Progress and Prospects. Report of the Inter Agency Task Force on Financing for Development', https://developmentfinance.un.org/sites/developmentfinance.un.org/files/Report_IATF_2018.pdf [accessed 11 August 2020].

_______ (2020) 'The Sustainable Development Goals Report 2020', https://unstats.un.org/sdgs/report/2020/The-Sustainable-Development-Goals-Report-2020.pdf [accessed 9 October 2020].

United Nations Development Programme (UNDP) (2007) 'Human Rights and the Millennium Development Goal: Making the Link. UNDP Oslo Governance Centre', https://www.undp.org/content/dam/aplaws/publication/en/publications/poverty-reduction/poverty-website/human-rights-and-the-millennium-development-goals/Human%20Rights%20and%20the%20MDGs.pdf [accessed 3 August 2020].

_______ (2015) 'A Human Rights-Based Approach to Development Programming in UNDP: Adding the Missing Link', https://www.undp.org/content/undp/en/home/librarypage/democratic-governance/human_rights/a-human-rights-based-approach-to-development-programming-in-undp.html [accessed 15 August 2020].

United Nations Economic and Social Council (ECOSOC) (2008) 'Background Study for the Development Cooperation Forum: Trends in South–South and Triangular Development Cooperation', http://www.un.org/en/ecosoc/docs/pdfs/south-south_cooperation.pdf [accessed 3 July 2020].

_______ (2018) 'Trends and Progress in International Development Cooperation. Report of the Secretary-General', E/2018/55.

United Nations General Assembly (1970) Resolution 262(XXV) on International Development Strategy for the Second United Nations Development Decade, A/Res/25/2626.

Ussar, M. (2011) 'The Human Rights-based Approach: A More Effective Framework for International Development Policies in New EU Member States. Minority Rights Group.

International Policy Paper', https://www.civicspace.eu/upload/library/the-human-rights-basedapproach-5d629a64619cc.pdf [accessed 15 August 2020].

Van de Poel, J. (2020) 'Covid-19 and Official Development Assistance: Current Issues and Challenges', Eurodad Briefing Paper, https://www.eurodad.org/covid19_oda_challenges [accessed 22 August 2020].

Vandenhole, W. (2007) 'EU and Development, Extraterritorial Obligations under the International Covenant on Economic, Social and Cultural Rights' in Salomon, M., Tostensen, A. and Vandenhole, W. (eds). *Casting the Net Wider: Human Rights, Development and New Duty Bearers*, Intersentia.

World Bank and Organisation for Economic Cooperation and Development (2016) *Integrating Human Rights into Development: Donor Approaches, Experiences and Challenges* 3rd edn., World Bank.

16

Financialization of development cooperation

ETO responses

Roman Herre and Stephan Backes

Introduction

Today's finance industry is inherently global and beyond borders – in the European Union, the free movement of finance capital between its Member States even received the rank of one of the four 'fundamental freedoms' (to the extent that all restrictions on capital movement are prohibited since the entry into force of the Treaty of Maastricht, in 1994). For finance industry, national states and jurisdictions today only have an economic strategic value for the construction of investment and finance chains and webs by playing off territorial regulations on taxes, investments, or transparency against each other. This characteristic makes the case for an ETO approach and increases the relevance of extraterritorial human rights obligations (ETOs) in human rights work today. After a short historic overview of the process of financialization (1920 to today), this chapter applies an ETO lens on two different aspects of financialization: its impact on substantive human rights and related (extraterritorial) obligations, as well as its impact on procedural human rights and related (extraterritorial) obligations. The chapter draws on evidence from cases the human rights organization FIAN has been working on in recent years. Special focus will be given to the role of public development cooperation and its financialization process. The final section will provide some insights and reflections on the responses from affected communities and the human rights scene, like 'follow the money' and 'investment chain mapping' initiatives.

A short history of financialization

Once upon a time, there were regulations...

The deregulation of finance and the reduction of controls over international movements of capital are closely linked to the end of the so-called Bretton Woods monetary system in the 1970s. This system had been put in place after the Wall Street Crash in 1929, which was followed by the banking crisis and the Great Depression. Among other things, the Glass-Steagall Act (1932) in the US and similar laws in Europe limited the possibility of banks to use state or private money, i.e., peoples' savings, for their own speculative activities and separated commercial and investment banks.

 DOI: 10.4324/9781003090014-21

It created a period of relative financial stability, which lasted up to the 1970s. At that time, the USA started to take a number of measures that dismantled this system and reduced control over international movements of capital. In 1971, the USA ended the gold standard – the international convertibility of the US dollar to gold (i.e., a material and limited resource). A number of new laws followed, repealing the separation of commercial and investment banks, and opening the doors for new ways of financial speculation. Most notably in the US, the Garn–St. Germain Depository Institutions Act of 1982 by the Reagan administration, and especially the Gramm–Leach–Bliley Act of 1999 repealed the separation between commercial and investment banks. The end of fixed convertibility of the US dollar to gold also led to the emergence of new financial centres and the re-shaping of the entire global financial architecture. In the national jurisdictions of the Global South, neoliberal deregulations were implemented dominantly by the Structural Adjustment Programs of the International Monetary Fund and the World Bank (so-called Washington Consensus).

The deregulation of financial markets was a response to a crisis of accumulation of capital, i.e., difficulties of business actors, especially banks, to generate ever-increasing surplus/profits from their investments. In order to respond to such crisis, it was necessary to allow for the creation of more finance capital, and of new possibilities for those who owned this money to 'invest' it, including in and by development cooperation, as we will show below.

The financial crisis of 2007–2008, which caused a broad global economic crisis, was the result of financialization and has contributed to further deepening it. The crisis was triggered by speculation in the housing and real estate markets, in particular in the USA and Europe. With rising real estate prices, banks gave mortgage loans to non-creditworthy (subprime) customers and then sold these as securities on financial markets, passing on the risk to a number of actors that participated in this speculation. When the bubble burst and real estate prices fell, several banks and other financial players faced bankruptcy. However, this did not compel governments to address the underlying issues, but rather increased the power of finance capital. First, several governments bailed out banks and other financial actors – as well as their shareholders – in order to end the contagion in financial markets. Second, the decrease of real estate prices (and the prices of other 'assets', such as agricultural commodities) in the aftermath of the crash, led financial actors to look for new areas of investment and speculation, such as farmland – with substantive implications on human rights as underpinned by the vast body of literature coined under the phrase 'land grabbing' (Hall 2015; Borras 2020).

From financing development to development finance

This whole development also implicated a shift in the area of development cooperation. In a bit more than ten years, finance industry has gained considerable importance in development cooperation. Interestingly, the main development cooperation actors themselves do not reject such criticism by civil society organizations (CSOs), but use different names for it. Donors, development banks, and implementing organizations talk about development finance, financial inclusion, leveraging public development aid, blended finance, 'maximizing finance for development' or 'finance for all' (World Bank 2018 and 2008).

Data show that this development took off especially from the financial crisis onwards (cf. Figure 16.2). This then has been reinforced by the narrative heavily advocated for within the Sustainable Development Goals (SDGs) frame: the need of massive private finance to reach these sustainable development goals. Thus, finance industry – the 'bad guys' of the financial crisis – in a somehow miraculous way turned from problem to solution.

A variety of indicators demonstrate the structural significance of financialization of development cooperation, as the example of Germany underlines (Herre 2020). Four indicators will be highlighted below: the role of funds and fund management companies, the funding of financial intermediaries, the increase of market-based funding of official development assistance (hereafter: ODA), and the impressive growth of development banks (or Development Finance Institutions, DFIs).

Development cooperation itself started establishing outsourced fund-management companies, to set up and manage investment funds and assets with (sub-)objectives related to development policy: through the International Finance Corporation (IFC), the World Bank founded in 2009 the IFC Asset Management Corporation (IFC-AMC). At the end of 2018, this corporation managed 13 funds with a book value of $10.1 billion (IFC-AMC 2019). The EU set up the European Development Finance Institutions (EDFI) Management Company (ElectriFI and AgriFI), and the Dutch FMO set up FMO Investment Management, which as of December 2019 managed four funds with assets of approximately $600 million.

Even without institutionally outsourced investment companies, fund investments by development cooperation are expanding rapidly. The German KfW development bank, which is actually mandated for financial cooperation with state institutions in developing and emerging countries, currently has investments in 43 investment funds with a book value of €1.6 billion. Some of these funds were set up by KfW itself (KfW, n.d.).

A substantive share of DFIs' investments flows to the finance sector typically summarized as financial intermediaries. In 2019, IFC invested 40 percent of its portfolio – $17.8 billion – in the finance sector (IFC 2019). The German DFI *Deutsche Investitions-und Entwicklungsgesellschaft* (DEG) already facilitates 57 percent of its business through financial intermediaries (DEG 2021). In addition, the number and volume of finance provided through Offshore Finance Centres has risen significantly in recent years. In 2017 alone, DEG held shares of companies in these financial centres – or secrecy jurisdictions (see section 4.6) – worth €372 million; from 2008 to 2017, its shareholdings in companies in the Cayman Islands and Mauritius alone rose from €50 million to €263 million (Deutscher Bundestag 2018).

Another indicator is the market-based funding of ODA. Governments committed and recommitted to contribute 0.7 percent of the national GDP to development cooperation. The commitment is measured by ODA quota. Research on the German ODA quota shows that especially since the global financial crisis, a substantive part of Germany's ODA has been delivered by loans that have been only channelled by state actors: a good ten years ago, German development cooperation used negligible funding borrowed from private market to pass on to so-called development countries. In the meantime, this funding has literally shot through the roof. The market-based funding of development cooperation in Germany has increased 18 times within 10 years to €3.6 billion and now accounts for a significant share of the state development funding ODA (Figure 16.1).

Finally, DFIs, that provide finance for the private sector, have seen impressive growth rates of an average annual rate around 10 percent over the last 10–20 years: 'Since 2002, total annual commitments by all DFIs have grown from $10 billion to around $70 billion in 2014 – an increase of 600 percent' (Savoy et al. 2016, p. V). In comparison, the overall ODA volumes have only grown slowly in the same period, i.e., some 20–30 percent between 2002 and 2014 (Ahmad et al. 2020). The same is true for the European DFIs organized under the EDFI. From 2005 to 2018, their portfolio of committed investments had grown from €10.9 billion to €46 billion (EDFI 2016 and 2019). Those indicators illustrate the substantive approximation of development cooperation to global finance industry – and its logic – with implications for human rights.

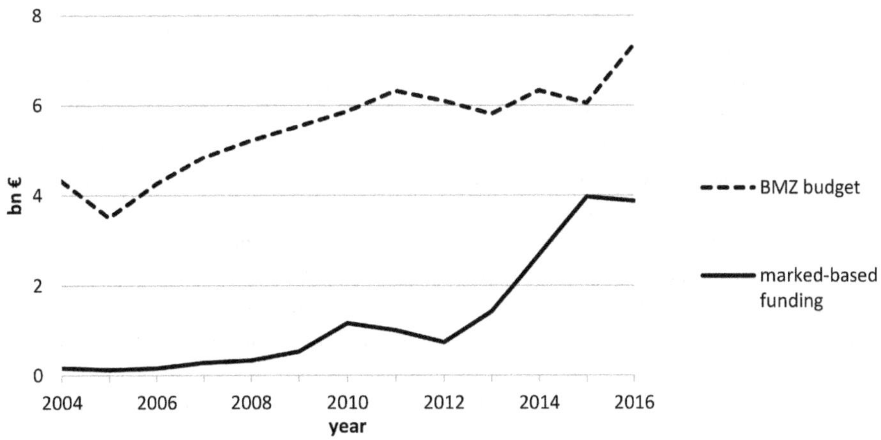

Figure 16.1 Increase in market-based development funding in Germany compared to the BMZ budget 2006–2016.

Source: Own calculation, based on BMZ annual report format 'Source of funds'.

How financialization impacts the enjoyment of human rights

Today's finance industry penetrates almost all aspects of life – health, culture, or food, to name some (Seufert et al. 2020). It thus exerts substantive influence on the enjoyment of a broad array of human rights. The interaction of financial actors with multiple states and their jurisdictions/regulations, highlighted again and again by leaked information like the Panama Papers or the recent FinCEN Files, today is a central part of their profit-making strategy (for e.g., aggressive tax evasion by creative bookkeeping between two or more states/jurisdictions). Financialization is therefore an important area for ETO analysis. While it is clear that development finance is a rather small actor in the world of finance, the complex web of specific responsibilities and accountabilities is slightly reduced as it directly addresses state actors as duty-bearers. Moreover, the obligation to respect human rights beyond borders in the context of development cooperation is more or less accepted by states – often addressed under the term 'do no harm' (see ETO Principle 13 (ETOP 13): 'Obligation to avoid causing harm').

We focus on rather emblematic cases to illustrate how financialization comes along with increasing exploitation and dispossession of communities, people, and their livelihoods, above all land and natural resources – and impunity of international (financial) actors involved. As a starting point for such a strategic approach, the following section will apply an ETO lens to two different – but closely interwoven – human rights aspects of financialization: its impact on substantive as well as procedural human rights in the context of development cooperation.

How financialization impacts substantive human rights & obligations

Development finance and the right to food

Zambian peasant communities are struggling to defend their livelihoods against the financial investor Agrivision Africa. The investor is based in Mauritius and owned by the World Bank's IFC, the Norwegian Development Finance Institution (Norfund), and the South Africa-based investment company Zeder. The overall plan of Agrivision Africa is to aggregate 100,000 hectares of land in Zambia and its neighbouring countries. By the end of 2019, Agrivision acquired at least 7 farms in Zambia amounting to 19,219 hectares (Zeder 2020).

In Mkushi Province, Agrivision expanded its industrial farming to an area that has, for many years, been cultivated for food production by the local community, Ngambwa. Through the expansion, this community has lost most of its agricultural land and has been threatened several times with eviction by the private security forces of the company. A community member complains: 'Now they come and take the land [...]. Where shall we cultivate our food now? We want our children to have to eat!' (interview conducted by the authors in 2016). In May 2017, the UN Special Rapporteur on the Right to Food visited the community. She concluded in her report 'that the people ate barely once a day, that sometimes they were forced to make soup from local green plants to feed their families and children, and that they were under the constant threat of eviction [...]' and demanded that the authorities 'take all measures necessary to guarantee the affected families' right to food, including their access to land' (Human Rights Council 2018, p. 9).

In August 2011, the Africa Agriculture Trade and Investment Fund (AATIF) invested $10 million in Agrivision Africa. The AATIF is a public-private financing structure based in Luxembourg and established by the German *Ministry for Economic Cooperation and Development* (BMZ and its financial assistance branch, KfW Development Bank) in cooperation with *Deutsche Bank AG* (DB). The Fund's stated mission 'is to realize the potential of Africa's agricultural production, manufacturing, service provision and trade for the benefit of the poor' (AATIF 2012, p. 8). Major shareholders include BMZ, KfW, DB, European Commission, the Austrian development bank OeEB, and unknown private investors. By March 2019, the fund disbursed $300 million, which generated $52 million interest income on the loans and fees in Luxembourg (FIAN Germany 2020a).

This case illustrates a broad array of ETO-related violations of the right to food in Zambia. The ownership structures link ETOs to many donor countries: the executive directors of the World Bank are representatives of member states (ETO Principle 11 also highlights state responsibility when acting jointly with other states), and Norfund is fully owned by the Norwegian Ministry of Foreign Affairs. The investment of AATIF is another ETO component, which has been inquired by FIAN Germany for multiple years. Germany (through BMZ with KfW, the latter chairs the AATIF board) accepted some responsibility related to the case. They have taken up critique, including commissioning a 'beacon identification exercise' in 2017. However, response to the critique had substantive limitations from an ETO perspective: it focused on property rights (with all its own issues related to the land law in Zambia), thus excluding a human rights analysis based on the right to food of the local population. Moreover, it was not understood as an obligation based on the International Covenant on Economic, Social, and Cultural Rights (ICESCR) and related to the affected people in Ngambwa, but rather as an act to deal with critique inside Germany, including from parliament.

Financial inclusion and the right to land

Public development institutions also support and promote microcredits and the broader concept of so-called 'financial inclusion' as a strategy to empower poor people and trigger development impacts. However, research shows that microcredits can have serious adverse impacts on the right to land of rural communities. This can be observed in Cambodia, where a booming and poorly regulated microfinance industry has put thousands of, mainly female, borrowers at risk of losing their land, which forms the basis of their economic and cultural life. In Cambodia, land titles are routinely collected as a collateral for the microcredits, and there is evidence that

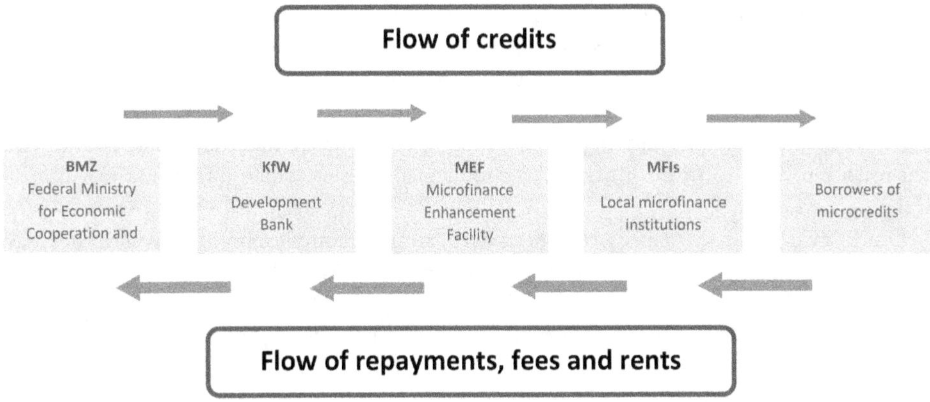

Figure 16.2 Financial flows between actors in the case of the Microfinance-Fund MEF, helping to unpack obligations.

aggressive debt collection practices by microfinance lenders result in stress sales or coerced land sales to repay loans. The loss of land is a massive problem for the local people: 'We are living on the land, we do everything on the land. We are not able to live in the sky', as one affected puts it (LICADHO 2019).

Local civil society has warned repeatedly that the economic crisis caused by the Covid-19 pandemic in 2020 could result in a wave of land dispossessions, particularly affecting women. In April 2020 for instance, 135 communities, labour unions, and human rights NGOs, called on the Cambodian government and microfinance institutions (without avail) to suspend all loan repayments and return land titles collected as collateral to the landowners. European and German development banks are major financiers of the microcredit sector in Cambodia. One example and financing vehicle is the Microfinance Enhancement Facility (MEF), an investment fund established in Luxembourg (Figure 16.2). Cambodia is one of the key countries of the fund. MEF is mostly financed by international donors including banks like IFC, KfW, and OeEB but also BMZ and SIDA (MEF 2020). In ten years, MEF generated an income from interest on loans and fees of $350 million (FIAN Germany 2020b).

Despite multiple demands, European and German development banks have also so far not taken any substantive action to prevent this dispossession crisis. The question arises then to what extent Germany violates its ETOs related to access to and the right to land as enshrined under the ICESCR and the United Nations Declaration on the Rights of Peasants and Other People Working in Rural Areas (UNDROP) and specified in the UN Voluntary Guidelines on the Responsible Governance of Tenure of Land, Fisheries, and Forests in the Context of National Food Security. As Germany is in a position to control and regulate MEF (e.g., KfW is chairing the MEF board of directors), it could, among others, prohibit the use of land as a collateral for the MFI they fund.

Blended finance and the right to water

The water sector provides for the basic needs of the population and was until recently a mostly publicly run sector. Comparable to the health sector, privatization efforts increased during the last two decades. Especially since the adoption of the SDGs, debates around the financial needs for a sustainable water sector have proliferated, generating products and vehicles for financial investments in the sector. One of them is a blended finance approach in development cooperation. This can have substantive implications on the right to water (CESCR 2003; UN General Assembly 2010 and 2018). Through the integration of private, rent seeking finance, commercial interests become immanent, triggering human rights issues (Eurodad 2018). First, the complex governance of blended finance risks eroding local ownership, decision-making, and accountability; and second, it risks diverting attention from water and sanitation services that reach especially most marginalized to commercial interest, which might lead to violations of the right to water.

Under such blended finance constructs, states are in a complex position where they have not only an obligation to respect the right to water (ETO Principle 20), but also to protect by ensuring that the involvement of private (investment) actors does not impede on the right to water (ETO Principles 24 to 26), as well as to fulfil by prioritizing the rights of marginalized groups (ETO Principle 32). The questions arise then, how this complex state role is institutionally anchored in a blended finance instrument, and how such a role conflicts with the economic aims of the common finance vehicle?

Financialization and its implications for procedural human rights & obligations

Within the scope of solely publicly led development cooperation, a state's accountability can be easily established in the case of extraterritorial human rights violations resulting from the implementation of specific development cooperation measures or policies.

Yet, as seen above, in many cases of (public) policies – be it in development cooperation or others – the huge variety of actors involved adds a serious set of obscure layers, when it comes to identifying actors to be held accountable or liable for human rights violations. Clapp (2014) describes that amplified financialization of the global food politics leads to an increasing two-fold 'distancing': first, the rising number of various types of actors involved in global food chains and, second, the transformation of food as a common good into 'highly complex agricultural commodity derivatives that are difficult to understand for all but seasoned financial traders'. This means that financialization undoubtedly also brings about 'distancing accountability' (Michéle, Fyfe and Slot-Tang 2017).

What share of human rights obligations and – in case of violations – responsibility has each of the actors involved in complex investment webs? In the context of financialization, projects or policies count a manifold set of actors involved in different ways, whose respective (share of) responsibility is difficult to identify. It is therefore key to examine the relationships between interconnected corporations, finance flows, and the degree of control that states exercise over them.

Transparency and accountability vis-à-vis finance intermediaries

Most DFIs adopted similar financing instruments and mechanisms, as highlighted, involving a diverse set of financial actors commonly following comparable schemes. In order to expose related transparency and accountability issues, we will illustrate this with examples from Germany and its development finance.

As seen above, the DEG today facilitates well over half of their investments via financial intermediaries. Regularly, requests for information on environmental, social, and human rights impacts are turned down with reference to banking secrecy.

One of these investments goes in the specialized bank Latin American Agribusiness Development Corporation (LAAD). DEG holds 9 percent of the bank's shares and frequently gives loans to the bank harboured in Curacao. LAAD is a specialized bank that 'finances and develops private agribusiness projects in Latin America and the Caribbean'. In its annual reports, LAAD does not list the investments they make; it just highlights countrywide investment volumes. In its 2015 report, LAAD explains that it invested 'US$13.4 million to 11 projects in the cattle industry, 3 in the Chaco region' in Paraguay (LAAD 2016, p. 6). The Paraguayan Chaco has undergone a massive eco-destruction and deforestation in the last few years, especially due to cattle ranching, triggering many, sometimes violent, land conflicts with local indigenous groups as well as small-scale food producers. Moreover, land concentration is extremely high and an issue of concern for the CESCR. In its 2008 concluding observations, the Committee 'notes with concern the concentration of land ownership in the hands of a very small proportion of the population' (CESCR 2008, p. 3). Overall, such investments have a high human rights risk.

In this context, the German parliament asked the Government in a written request about the human rights implications of these investments for development. The government explained it had no further information beyond the annual report (Deutscher Bundestag 2019). This raises substantive concerns about the German government's capability to adequately address its extraterritorial human rights obligations in such investment constructs, not to speak about the parliament – as the government-controlling body – that is left without information. An interesting side note: due to public pressure, DEG introduced a transparency guideline that in case of investments include land over 5,000 hectares, environmental and social action plans will be published. In the case of LAAD, research revealed that one investment in the Chaco is a farm holding 13,500 hectares of land. Due to indirect funding via LAAD, the guideline will not be triggered however.

Such cases are examples of a 'distancing accountability' strategy, that – by intention or not – erode extraterritorial obligations with regard to human rights principles of transparency and accountability (ETO Principle 2 and 32 c). Moreover, domestic non-juridical accountability mechanisms (in our example the German parliament) are severely hindered in their monitoring role (see ETO Principle 40).

ETO responses to financialization

This section looks into possible avenues to approach financialization in ETO work. We propose to distinguish between tools and strategies that help identifying duty-bearers through 'lines of obligations' in the complex and opaque webs of development finance, and the ones that help holding a state identified this way accountable to the respective obligation. Some of them are already more systematically applied by academics, NGOs, and affected communities. In practice, a combination of different tools and strategies may be the best option for applying ETOs.

Unpacking 'lines of obligations'

Piercing the corporate veil

Holding states accountable, in contexts of development finance through shareholding and financing of private companies, will require deconstructing complex holding structures that obscure specific and distinct obligations. Corporations often have limited liability and consequently, as such, are difficult to be held accountable for adverse human rights impacts of their actions. Courts make moves in order to hold natural persons accountable, be it the corporation's director(s) and/or shareholders. Affected communities and supporting CSOs regularly face obstacles when it comes to identifying who the decision makers within a project, an activity or a company are. Yet, the shareholders of a given company are not always exclusively natural persons but also other types of private actors. The Feronia case (Figure 16.3) illustrates how the holding and shareholding structure of the private palm oil company Feronia controlling over 110,000 hectares of land in the Democratic Republic of Congo (DRC) unveils: (a) the shareholding of many public development banks in different countries, and (b) that they indeed are – through African Agriculture Fund and CDC Group – majority owners of the company. Thus, the respective states through their development banks are not only in a strong position to

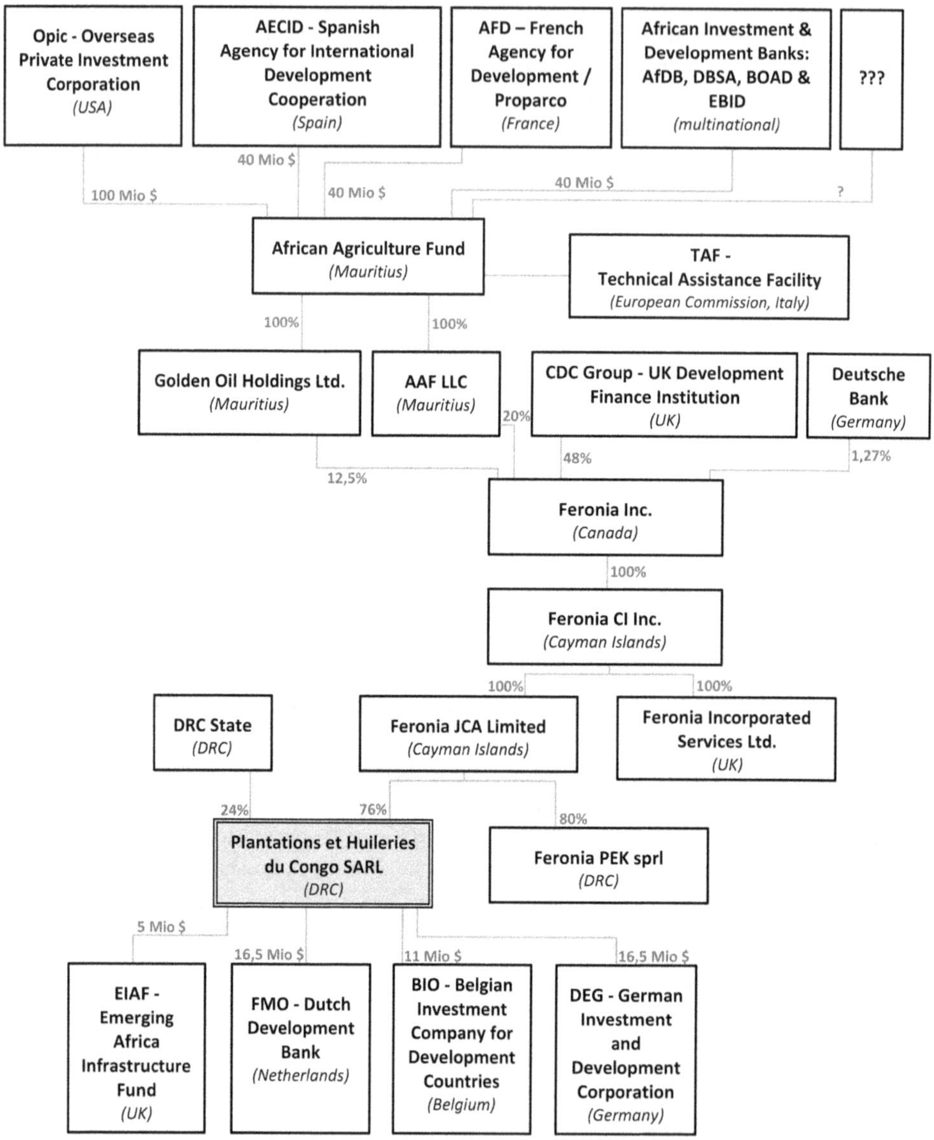

Figure 16.3 Feronia's investment web: Shareholding and financing structure.

Source: Authors' own elaboration. The data gathered in 2016 is from different sources and years. Thus, the figure does not reflect the precise current situation. However, this does not impede the purpose of the figure, which is to illustrate the complexity of the investment webs surrounding development finance.

regulate the company (ETO Principle 24), but they must also respect human rights in a context of 'direct interference' (ETO Principle 20).

Investment chain mapping: 'follow the money'

From an ETO perspective, mapping of investment chains is producing an explicit and distinct chain of obligation. This mapping can be very complex and time-consuming. Often, information about the various actors can be difficult to find – sometimes by design. This means that specialized research is often needed to get access to trade and financial databases to unravel the complex web of backers of harmful investment projects. As a result, a systematic web of investors, financiers, and buyers behind projects unveils lines of obligations that often lead to other states than the one where a project is physically implemented. Such research can identify, *inter alia*: i) shareholders of companies or entities involved at all levels of a project; ii) loans, bonds, and other debt instruments that provide funding throughout an investment chain; iii) international financial institutions, such as the World Bank Group, contributing funding to a project; iv) buyers of products, suppliers of raw materials or providers of equipment essential to the operations of a project.

In a second step, points of leverage can be analyzed and, subsequently, advocacy strategies be developed to support communities in defending their rights.

The Feronia case (Figure 16.3) exposes the lack of transparency and accountability with development finance. As it can be seen, the enterprise operating in the DRC belongs to Feronia Inc. which was domiciled in Canada at that time. A wide set of public DFIs as well as banks and holdings from different countries funded Feronia Inc., for its palm oil activities in DRC leading to land conflict. Holding and financing structures lead to at least eight public development finance institutions of seven different countries. Public DFIs should uphold their extraterritorial human rights obligations, and states are also obliged to protect human rights from the interference of private actors they are in a position to regulate (ETO Principle 24).

Institutional Conflict of Interest

Institutional Conflict of Interest (ICOI) can be a relevant tool/approach for applying ETOs in the context of development cooperation. 'Institutional conflicts of interest arise when an institution's own financial interests or those of its senior officials pose risks of undue influence on decisions involving the institution's primary interests' (Lo and Field 2009).

Let us look at the German development bank DEG. Its statutes define that profit seeking should be only a secondary aspect of the banks conduct: 'The company pursues exclusively and directly charitable purposes' (§2(1)) and '[the] company is selflessly active; it does not pursue primarily self-economic purposes' (§2(7)) (DEG 2017; *authors' own translation*). An ICOI can arise, when for example an investment's environmental and social risk mitigation increases to such an extent that the whole project is at risk to fail. Therefore, the development mandate and the aim to generate profits and growth may come into conflict. Here are two examples that indicate the relevance of ICOI, a structural one and a case-related one: in case of conflict between profit (or substantial losses) and social and environmental impacts.

- The growth of DEG has been massive in the last years. The investment volume grew from EUR 343 million in 1999 to EUR 1,866 million in 2018 – a staggering 540 percent growth in 20 years. This growth is based on retained profits out of development projects. Being largely tax exempted through its 'charitable' status is of help.

- In 2011, DEG invested USD 25 million in the dam construction project Barro Blanco in Panama. The impact on land and environment, especially land rights of indigenous people, generated many years of protest and local opposition. In February 2015, the national environmental agency (*Autoridad National de Ambiente, ANAM*) temporarily suspended the dam construction. As a longer construction stop would implicate substantive financial losses, DEG together with other lenders pressured the government to proceed with the dam project. In their letter to the Panama Minister of External Affairs, they argue:

  As lenders of the Barro Blanco Project, but more importantly, as lenders to projects in Panama in general, we fear that actions such as the one taken against GINESA may weigh upon future investment decisions, and harm the flow of long-term investments in Panama. We ask the relevant authorities, including ANAM, to take prompt actions in search of reaching a favourable agreement by all stakeholders involved in the Barro Blanco Project (DEG, FMO and EICE 2015).

The letter has been interpreted as blackmail by powerful development banks. While it is impossible to detail the impact of this letter, it is a fact that quickly afterwards, in May 2015, the project was resumed. With massive growth of development banks and funds, ICOI related to financial interests – or 'rent seeking pressure' – is undoubtedly on the rise. Attributing ICOI to a specific entity or units inside a development bank/fund could be an additional avenue for affected communities and supporting organization to identify actors that can be held accountable for specific acts or omissions. Where COI-policies are in place, it should be checked if they have adequate scope for human rights related ICOI.

Pathways for holding states to account

The role of donor embassies

ETOs include 'institutional obligations' (Pribytkova 2021) to create efficient accountability mechanisms to hold violators responsible, and to ensure an effective remedy for victims. This is of special relevance when accountability and remedies in the state, where violations occur, are unavailable or inefficient.

As has been illustrated in the cases above, especially the Zambia cases, financialization makes donor involvement in specific cases opaquer. We use the example of German embassies. On the one hand, German embassies sometimes do not have knowledge about funding activities mandated by Germany's official development assistance, especially when financial intermediaries and regional funding vehicles are deployed by ODA. On the other one, embassies are hesitant to pro-actively monitor complaints about human rights violations. This can be related to different reasons: first, embassies explain that a clear mandate for such conduct is missing; second, they argue that they do not have capacities and/or thematic competence to deal with specific human rights issues (for example applying the *UN Voluntary Guidelines on the Responsible Governance of Tenure of Land, Fisheries and Forests in the Context of National Food Security* to assess land conflicts); third, assessing human rights conduct of companies that are supported by development cooperation can create a conflict of interest between the embassies and their capital-based foreign ministries they are subordinated to, when it comes to support economic actors from their home country.

One way forward could include proposals and demands for formalized institutional arrangements in embassies that are responsive to human rights risks and indications of violations (ETO Principle 36). German embassies for example explain that a directive ('*Weisung*') from the capital to actively monitor human rights violations that are linked to German actors could be an appropriate step to mandate embassies. Moreover, it would be key that mechanisms exist to inform embassies if indirect funding via financial intermediaries occurs in the country where the embassy is based.

A role for of the Optional Protocol to the ICESCR?

The Optional Protocol to the International Covenant on Economic, Social and Cultural Rights (OP-ICESCR) allows people whose economic, social, and cultural rights have been violated to bring a complaint (communication) to the international level, i.e., to the CESCR. To do so, two prerequisites need to be met: first, the concerned state must be a Party to the OP-ICESCR (OP-ICESCR, art. 1.2) and, second, available domestic remedies must have been exhausted (OP-ICESCR, art. 3.1). Can the OP-ICESCR also be a tool for alleged victims to submit a communication to the CESCR if the violating state is another state as the one they are living in? At first sight, the OP-ICESCR seems to be silent on this issue. Yet, in its article 2, the OP-ICESCR stipulates that '[communications] may be submitted by or on behalf of individuals or groups of individuals, under the jurisdiction of a State Party, claiming to be victims of a violation of any of the economic, social and cultural rights set forth in the Covenant by that State Party' (OP-ICESCR, art. 2; authors' emphasis). As Coomans argues, the mention of the term 'jurisdiction' is interesting as 'there was no reason to include a jurisdictional limitation clause in the Protocol because the ICESCR does not use that term' (Coomans 2011, p. 5). The *Maastricht Principles* thus explain how jurisdiction should also be considered extraterritorially (ETO Principle 9). In the case of public development banks or development funds, state entities are in a position to 'exercise authority or effective control', including in supervision board positions, and thus clearly part of the states' jurisdiction. Furthermore, Scheinin argues the use of the word 'jurisdiction' should be 'read as referring to the admissibility conditions that require a sufficient factual link', so also extraterritorially (Scheinin 2012, p. 228).

The International Court of Justice (ICJ 2004, paras. 111–113) took the view that, next to the International Covenant on Civil and Political Rights (ICCPR) and the Convention on the Rights of the Child (CRC), the ICESCR is applicable extraterritorially 'in respect to acts committed by a state in the exercise of its jurisdiction outside its territory' (Courtis and Rossi 2016, p. 50). In addition, the inquiry procedure (OP-ICESCR, art. 11) applies to acts and omissions of a State Party leading to violations of rights of individuals outside this state's territory, and may create the possibility to develop the jurisprudence about a state's extraterritorial obligations, regarding foreign operations of private companies domiciled under its jurisdiction, and that this state is in a position to regulate. Sullivan (2016) has significantly detailed the strong potential in this regard. Using the OP-ICESCR provisions to establish the infringement of a state's extraterritorial obligations would definitely advance the jurisprudence – and help affected communities to use a further avenue to get redress for the harm done (see also example, section 4.6). An important obstacle remains the fact that up to now, only 24 out of the 171 state Parties to the ICESCR have become parties to the OP-ICESCR.[1]

Parallel reporting to the ICESCR

The reporting procedure under the ICESCR has already been used by civil society to raise ETOs. In its 2018 parallel report complementing the 6th Report of the Federal Republic of Germany on the ICESCR, German civil society brought to the attention of the UN Committee the cases highlighted above (AATIF and LAAD), including their financial opaqueness. Civil society, under the German *Forum Menschenrechte* (Forum Menschenrechte 2018), recommended that the Committee calls on the state Party to:

- Commission independent HRIAs prior to its development financing and financing by state-owned banks. Areas with high human rights risks like large-scale agribusiness, large-scale mining, and infrastructure projects should have priority. All reports should be published;
- Fully disclose loans and investments of state-owned banks and actors with a public mandate such as DEG, KfW Entwicklungsbank, and AATIF before the project's start;
- Publish project information, environmental, social, and HRIA as well as plans of action and monitoring reports on all funded projects of all branches of the KfW Group;
- Give embassies a formal directive and resources to monitor the impact of those investments on the enjoyment of ESCR;
- Establish an independent complaint mechanism for the whole KfW Group following the example of the independent complaint mechanisms of the World Bank, the European Investment Bank (EIB), or the DEG.

The distinct use of ETOs in such reporting mechanisms could be an important pillar to further the practical application of ETOs, not only by academics and civil society but also by states.

Conclusion

Compared to the dominant financial actors like asset management companies or pension funds, the financial volume of development cooperation (e.g., DFIs, development funds) is 'relatively' small; yet, the volume of activities of 450 public development banks worldwide amounts to USD 2 trillion per year (Finance in Common 2020). Additionally, these development actors have become increasingly intertwined with, and are often part of, the finance industry.

Tackling those developments with a human rights lens requires some financial expertise. This is not frequently found in the human rights field, especially among local communities and human rights organizations dealing with development cooperation. Alliances with finance experts from academia and civil society can provide strategic help.

On the other side, the topic of financialization has 'arrived' in UN Treaty Bodies, periodic state reviews, and Special Procedures (cf., e.g., 'Guideline no. 12: Ensure the regulation of businesses in a manner consistent with state obligations and address the financialization of housing', Human Rights Council (2017)). However, the link between financialization and development cooperation is a somehow orphan issue – also because of the high opaqueness of public and publicly mandated development finance. Moreover, governments frequently dodge assigned ETOs with their own lack of knowledge of actors and impacts on the ground when making use of financial intermediaries.

This highlights the urgent need for Governments to implement ambitious and effective disclosure laws, obliging them to pierce the corporate veil, i.e., making it possible for people whose rights have been infringed to get a full picture of the private actors and their 'backstage' financiers – as all of them have a certain, but distinct responsibility when it comes to human rights abuses. In the case of development finance where private actors are involved, this will prevent states from claiming to have no responsibility. Other possible pillars of such a strategic approach include, *inter alia*, but not exclusively: 1) to unpack the lines of obligations through actions aiming at piercing the corporate veil and making in-depth analyses of investment webs (investment chain mapping, 'follow-the-money', and the use of institutional conflict of interest), and 2) to hold states accountable through different ways (be it the role of donor embassies, exploring promising avenues through the OP-ICESCR and/or parallel reporting to the ICESCR, and other UN treaty bodies). The true test then for ETOs in development cooperation should be: can a state be effectively held accountable (including remediation) for human rights violations related to its development finance?

In the field of development cooperation, a timid ETO approach can be observed at state level – such as the 'do no harm' one in Germany. But states are still more than reluctant to fully accept – and spell out – their obligations extraterritorially, despite important advancement of ETOs within different treaty bodies in the last decade. However, the wide array of cases and examples in the field of development cooperation can be used in order to further ETOs and formulate concrete answers – including feasible ways of accountability – in case of human rights violations through development cooperation.

Note

1. Situation on 22 October 2020.

References

AATIF (2012) 'Increasing income. Improving food security', AATIF Annual Report 2012.

Ahmad, Y., Bosch, E., Carey, E. and Mc Donnell, I. (2020) 'Six decades of ODA: Insights and outlook in the COVID-19 crisis', OECD Library, https://www.oecd-ilibrary.org/sites/5e331623-en/index.html?itemId=/content/component/5e331623-en [accessed 19 October 2020].

Borras, S., Mills, E., Seufert, P., Backes, S., Fyfe, D., Herre, R. and Michéle, L. (2020) 'Transnational Land Investment Web: Land Grabs, TNCs, and the Challenge of Global Governance', *Globalizations* 17(4), 608–628.

Committee on Economic, Social and Cultural Rights (CESCR) (2003) GC 15 on the right to water (arts. 11 and 12 of the Covenant), E/C.12/2002/11.

_______ (2008) Concluding Observations of the Committee on Economic, Social and Cultural Rights. Paraguay, E/C.12/PRY/CO/3.

Clapp, F. (2014) 'Financialization, Distance and Global Food Politics', *The Journal of Peasant Studies* 41(5), 797–814.

Coomans, F. (2011) 'The Extraterritorial Scope of the International Covenant on Economic, Social and Cultural Rights in the Work of the United Nations Committee on Economic, Social and Cultural Rights', *Human Rights Law Review* 11(1), 1–35.

Courtis, C. and Rossi, J. (2016) 'Individual Complaints Procedure' in Langford, M., Porter, B., Brown, R. and Rossi, J. (eds) *The Optional Protocol to the International Covenant on Economic, Social and Cultural Rights: A Commentary*, Pretoria University Law Press (PULP), 37–75.

DEG (2021) Annual Report 2020, p.20. At: https://www.deginvest.de/DEG-Documents-in-English/Download-Center/DEG_JAB_2020_EN.pdf

DEG, FMO and EICE (2015) 'Undated letter from DEG, FMO and EICE of 2015 to the Vice-President and Minister of External Affairs of Panama'.

Deutscher Bundestag (2018) *Antwort der Bundesregierung auf die Kleine Anfrage Beteiligung der DEG-Deutsche Investitions- und Entwicklungsgesellschaft an Unternehmen, Zweckgesellschaften und Fonds in Offshore-Finanzplätzen*, Drucksache 19/1508

_______ (2019) *Antwort der Bundesregierung auf die Kleine Anfrage KfW-Auslandsgeschäfte im Agrarbereich*, Drucksache 19/7868.

Eurodad (2018) 'Blended finance and the water sector – four risks to consider', Eurodad.

European Development Finance Institutions (2016) *Investing to Increase Growth, Boost Jobs and Fight Poverty*, EDFI.

_______ (2019) 'Facts and figures', EDFI, https://www.edfi.eu/members/facts-figures/ [accessed 19 October 2020]. FIAN Germany (2020a) *Finanzeckdaten AATIF*, unpublished.

FIAN Germany (2020b) *MEF Finanzierungsfluss und Einkommen*, unpublished.

Finance in Common (2020) 'What are public development banks?', https://financeincommon.org/why-finance-in-common [accessed 22 October 2020].

Forum Menschenrechte (2018) 'Implementation of ICESCR in Germany: Parallel Report of Forum Menschenrechte (Extraterritorial Obligations) complementing the 6th Report of the Federal Republic of Germany on the International Covenant on Economic, Social and Cultural Rights (ICESCR)', Berlin, https://tbinternet.ohchr.org/Treaties/CESCR/Shared%20Documents/DEU/INT_CESCR_CSS_DEU_32158_E.docx [accessed 22 October 2020].

Hall, R., Edelman, M., Borras, S., Scoones, I., White, B. and Wolford, W. (2015) 'Resistance, Acquiescence or Incorporation? An Introduction to Land Grabbing and Political Reactions "from below"', *Journal of Peasant Studies* 42, 3–4.

Herre, R. (2020) 'Keine Hilfe ohne Rendite! Einblicke in die zunehmende Finanzialisierung der Entwicklungszusammenarbeit', *Weltwirtschaft und Internationale Zusammenarbeit* 23, 99-114.

Human Rights Council (2017) 'Report of the Special Rapporteur on adequate housing as a component of the right to an adequate standard of living, and on the right to non-discrimination in this context', A/HRC/34/51.

Human Rights Council (2018) 'Report of the Special Rapporteur on the right to food on her mission to Zambia', A/HRC/37/61/Add.1.

IFC (2019) *Investing for Impact. Annual Report 2019*, Washington (DC).

IFC-AMC (2019) at: https://www.ifcamc.org/sites/amc/files/IF3509_AMC_Annual_Review_2018%2014_LR_SPREADS.pdf

International Court of Justice (ICJ) (2004) 'Advisory opinion on the legal consequences of the construction of a wall in the occupied Palestinian territory', 9 July 2004.

KfW (n.d.), 'KfW Development Bank', https://www.kfw-entwicklungsbank.de/International-financing/KfW-Entwicklungsbank/ [accessed 18 September 2020].

Latin American Agribusiness Development Corporation (LAAD) (2016) 'Annual Report 2015', LAAD.

LICADHO (2019) 'Vicious cycle of Dept, Video Interview', https://www.licadho-cambodia.org/video.php?perm=82 [accessed 8 October 2020].

Lo, B. and Field, M. (eds). (2009) *Conflict of Interest in Medical Research, Education, and Practice*, The National Academies Press.

MEF (2020) 'Quarterly Factsheet March 2020', Microfinance Enhancement Facility, https://www.mef-fund.com/downloads/factsheets/2020/Innpact_Factsheet_March.pdf [accessed 24 September 2020].

Michéle, L., Fyfe, D. and Slot-Tang, Y. (eds). (2017) *For Human Rights beyond Borders. How to Hold States Accountable for Extraterritorial Violations*. Handbook, FIAN International.

Pribytkova, E. (2021) 'Extraterritorial Obligations in the United Nations System: U.N. Treaty Bodies' in Erdem Türkelli, G., Gibney, M., Krajewski, M. and Vandenhole, W. (eds). *Routledge Research Handbook on Extraterritorial Human Rights Obligations*, Routledge.

Savoy, C., Carter, P. and Lemma, P. (2016) *Centre for Strategic & International Studies (2016) Development Finance Institutions Come of Age*, Center for Strategic & International Studies.

Scheinin, M. (2012) 'Just Another Word? Jurisdiction in the Roadmaps of State Responsibility and Human Rights' in Langford, M., Vandenhole, W., Scheinin, M. and van Genungten, W. (eds). *Global Justice, State Duties: The Extraterritorial Scope of Economic, Social, and Cultural Rights in International Law*, Cambridge University Press.

Seufert, P., Herre, R., Monsalve, S. and Guttal, S. (eds). (2020) *Rogue Capitalism and the Financialization of Territories and Nature*, FIAN International, Transnational Institute & Focus on the Global South.

Sullivan, D. (2016) 'The Inquiry Procedure' in Langford, M., Porter, B., Brown, R. and Rossi, J. (eds). *The Optional Protocol to the International Covenant on Economic, Social and Cultural Rights: A Commentary*, Pretoria University Law Press.

UN General Assembly (2010) 'The human right to water and sanitation. Resolution adopted by the General Assembly on 28 July 2010', A/RES/64/292.

World Bank (2008) 'Finance for all? Policies and pitfalls in expanding access', A World Bank Policy Research Report.

_______ (2018) 'Maximizing Finance for Development (MFD)', https://www.worldbank.org/en/about/partners/maximizing-finance-for-development [accessed 18 September 2020].

Zeder Investments Limited (2020) 'Annual Report 2020', http://www.zeder.co.za/Zeder-Annual-Report-2020.pdf [accessed 19 October 2020].

17

Extraterritorial human rights obligations and sovereign debt

Emma Luce Scali

Introduction

Today, sovereign financing is central to the realisation of human rights. States need to raise and allocate resources 'to create, implement and sustain the network of institutions (such as courts, legislative bodies, national human rights institutions), policies and programmes (such as general plans of basic education or training programmes for security forces), services (free legal aid, primary health care), infrastructure (appropriate detention facilities, schools, recreational spaces), personnel (administrative and technical staff), procedure and systems (fair trials, birth registration, immunization against infectious diseases), etc., that are necessary to fulfil the[ir] broad range of human rights obligations' (Office of the United Nations High Commissioner for Human Rights (OHCHR) 2017, p. 18). Furthermore, governments across the world appear under increasing pressures to step in and level off – often by recourse to public resources – the structural imbalances and recurring manifold crises of financialised global capitalism. Especially since the 1970s, however, sovereign financing has evolved into a predominantly debt- and market-based practice, with an evident transnational dimension (Megliani in Bantekas et al. 2018; Frieda in Lastra et al. 2014). States (nowadays, also many advanced economies) increasingly rely on debt, global financial markets and international institutions to fund their sovereign functions, including the realisation of human rights, a trend that has been worryingly intensified by the COVID-19 pandemic (United Nations General Assembly (UNGA) 2020; International Monetary Fund (IMF) 2020; Scali 2020), and which ultimately points to a form of 'public poverty' linked, among other things, to the growing privatisation of global wealth (United Nations Human Rights council (HRC) 2020, paras. 14–15; IMF 2018; HRC 2016a). In such interconnected scenery, economic, monetary and fiscal decisions – increasingly governed by supranational legal regimes (Lastra 2015) – and their human rights consequences, naturally transcend territorial boundaries, eliciting consideration of the relevance for the sovereign financing-related conduct of state and non-state actors of extraterritorial human rights obligations (hereinafter, ETOs). Since their notion is more thoroughly discussed by Gibney at the outset of this volume, it seems sufficient to recall here that ETOs identify the human rights obligations owed by states to individuals located outside their territory (the latter comprising land, sea and airspace, as defined by borders), or on territory not subject to any particular state; and they can arise in relation to: *a)* extraterritorial

DOI: 10.4324/9781003090014-22

conduct, or *b)* territorial conduct with extraterritorial human rights effects – i.e., an act/omission performed either directly outside or inside a state's territory, but which has implications for the human rights of individuals located outside it.

After briefly introducing sovereign debt as a human rights issue and the relevant international law (Section 2), this chapter will review the notion of ETOs, its reliance on the (unsettled) concept of jurisdiction and the main jurisdictional models so far developed by monitoring bodies (Section 3), before discussing their applicability, and some of the possible limitations, in relation to sovereign debt (Section 4).

Sovereign debt, human rights and international law

Sovereign debt identifies the sum of the existing (contractual and non-contractual) obligations (including, but not limited, to financial obligations) owed by a state (and by all entities for whose debts the state is ultimately responsible) to one or more (in the case of multilateral lending) creditor(s). The latter include other states and public institutions (e.g., central banks), international financial institutions (e.g., the IMF or the World Bank), as well as private financial institutions and bondholders (e.g., commercial or investment banks, insurance companies, pension or hedge funds and retail investors). Sovereign debt instruments vary greatly in their nature and governing law (HRC 2012; Paulus 2014). However, especially since the Latin American debt crisis of the 1980s (which marked a steep decline in syndicated lending) sovereign bonds have resumed as a major global source of sovereign financing. Although, as it has been noted, every financing method presents its own specific risks, '[t]he speculative nature of short-term bond investment, backed by technological advances, subjects many [...] countries to the risk of arbitrary and irrational choices by a multitude of different investors', and 'may involve submitting the sovereignty of a country to the forces of private financial speculation' (Megliani in Bantekas et al. 2018, pp. 78–79; see also IMF 2002).

However, as recently reaffirmed, among others, also by the Independent Expert on the effects of foreign debt and other related international financial obligations of states on the full enjoyment of all human rights, particularly economic, social and cultural rights (hereinafter, Independent Expert on debt and human rights), debt is not 'per se a human rights problem, even less a violation' (HRC 2020, para. 20), but 'depending on a variety of factors, such as responsible lending and borrowing, the loan terms and conditions, prudent use of loans and proper debt management, debt financing can contribute to countries' economic development and the establishment of conditions for the realization of human rights' (HRC 2011, p. 3). However, unsustainable debt burdens (on definitions of sustainability that also take human rights obligations into account, see HRC 2018b, p. 13; HRC 2012, p. 18) and the costs associated with their servicing, can reduce the number of resources available, especially to poorer countries, for the realisation of human rights (Lumina in Bantekas et al. 2018), hinder the achievement of development goals, and pose a more general threat to economic, social and political stability and to democratic regimes. Recent debt trends are particularly alarming in this regard. As noted by the Independent Expert on debt and human rights in relation to the effects of the COVID-19 pandemic on the debt situation of developing countries, 'since the 1990s, and especially since the 2008 global financial crisis, some countries, including low-income countries [...] have shifted to riskier debt, [...] [they] have to accept increasing debt payment burden, thus less fiscal space, and exposing themselves more to external shocks like exchange rate and interest rate volatilities. [...] Moreover, external debt with short terms to maturity has been on the rise since 2010, [...] a very dangerous trend, resulting in greater vulnerability to rollover and solvency risk and thus potentially affecting resources available for the progressive realization of economic, social and cultural rights' (HRC 2020, pp. 8–9).

In addition to excessive debt levels, the harmful consequences on a wide range of human rights and on specific individuals and groups (OHCHR 2013) of the (neoliberal) policy conditions generally attached to loans, emergency assistance and debt relief – typically including: *a)* fiscal measures directed at reducing public (above all social) expenditure; *b)* (often regressive) structural reforms of labour markets, the public administration and the pension, social security, healthcare and education systems; and *c)* the privatisation of public assets (CoE Commissioner for Human Rights 2013) – have been extensively documented (e.g., HRC 2019; HRC 2018a; Tamamović 2015; Ortiz et al. 2015) and conceded by the IMF itself (Ostry et al. 2016; IMF 2013). Remarkably, the Independent Expert on debt and human rights has recently upheld that 'given the direct causal link between austerity and human rights violations, the latter being foreseeable consequences of the former', there is 'a solid legal basis to make the case for a prima facie inconsistency between the imposition of austerity policies in times of recession and the enjoyment of human rights' (HRC 2019, paras. 75 and 79).

As is well known, sovereign financing and debt remain largely unregulated under international law (Esposito et al. 2013). Especially since the wave of debt crises set in motion by the 2008 global financial crisis, however, various UN agencies, special procedure mandate holders and treaty monitoring bodies have attempted to fill this normative gap by extrapolating 'guiding principles' from existing international human rights law (hereinafter, IHRL) to direct and assess lending, borrowing and state budgeting practices against international human rights obligations (with the disputed expression 'IHRL' I refer, for the present purposes, to the core UN international human rights instruments and their protocols, as well as the European Convention on Human Rights/ECHR, the American Convention on Human Rights/ACHR and the African Charter on Human and Peoples' Rights/ACHPR). Besides the guidance provided in specific statements or General Comments (GC) – e.g., the Committee on the Rights of the Child (CRC) 2016 GC 19 on budgeting for children's rights, or the Committee on Economic Social and Cultural Rights (CESCR) 2016 statement on public debt and 2012 Letter on austerity measures – these attempts have resulted in the elaboration of the UN Guiding Principles on foreign debt and human rights (2011), the UNCTAD Principles on responsible sovereign borrowing and lending (2012), the Basic Principles on sovereign restructuring processes (2015) and the Guiding Principles on human rights impact assessments of economic reforms (2018b). Among other things, these reaffirm that states have the obligations to respect, protect and fulfil human rights whenever they act, individually or collectively, including as members of international organisations. This entails that they are obliged, at all times and also at times of economic crisis, to adopt economic policies and manage their fiscal affairs – including 'any and all of their activities concerning their lending and borrowing decisions [and] those of international or national public or private institutions to which they belong or in which they have an interest' (HRC 2012, pp. 11–12) – to ensure that these respect, protect and fulfil all human rights without discrimination (HRC 2018b, Principles 3 and 6–8). As more extensively maintained by the CESCR in its 2016 Statement on public debt, states retain their human rights obligations also when making decisions in their capacity as members of international financial institutions. Thus, they would be 'acting in violation of their obligations if they were to delegate powers to IMF or to other agencies and allowed such powers to be exercised without ensuring that they do not infringe on human rights', or 'if they were to exercise their voting rights within such agencies without taking human rights into account' (para. 9). Nor would states be absolved of their international responsibility were they, in that capacity, to act in full accordance with the rules of the organisation (Art. 58(2) of the 2011 Draft articles on the responsibility of international organisations).

With regard to both public and private creditors, the principles (in a rather summary way) affirm that they have an obligation to respect human rights (HRC 2012, p. 12), and consequently 'should ensure that the terms of their transactions and [...] proposals for reform policies and conditionalities for financial support do not undermine the borrower [...] state's ability to respect, protect and fulfil its human rights obligations' (HRC 2018b, Principles 15–16). In particular, since they 'share responsibility' with debtors for sovereign debt burdens and for preventing and resolving unsustainable debt situations (HRC 2018b, para. 12.9; HRC 2012, p. 14), creditors have an obligation to perform due diligence on the creditworthiness of the borrower, and to make sure that the loan will be used for a public purpose; that it will not increase the borrower's external debt stock to an unsustainable level; that it will not finance activities/projects that (would foreseeably) violate human rights in the borrower state (HRC 2012, pp. 14–15). To this aim, creditors (and debtors) are under an obligation to conduct an independent, credible, participatory and transparent human rights impact assessment (HRC 2018b, Principles 3 and 15; HRC 2012, pp. 15–16). Furthermore, they 'should not exert undue influence on other [debtor] states so that [these remain] able to [... use] their policy space in accordance with their human rights obligations'. Nor should they 'compel borrowing/receiving states to compromise satisfying their international human rights obligations' (HRC 2018b, Principles 14–15; HRC 2012, p. 19).

With regard to ETOs (only tangentially addressed) the principles assert, without expounding on the details, that '[b]ilateral lenders [i.e. creditor states] and other public donors, including Government-guaranteed financial institutions or private institutions extending loans with government guarantees have extraterritorial human rights obligations governing their decisions in the context of economic reform measures of the concerned [debtor] states' (HRC 2018b, para. 15.4). They also affirm that, as part of their duty of international assistance and cooperation (ICESCR, art. 1(2); CESCR 1990, para. 14; see more extensively Chenwi in this volume), 'states have an obligation to respect and to protect the enjoyment of human rights of people outside their borders', which 'involves avoiding conduct that would foreseeably impair the enjoyment of human rights by persons living beyond their borders' (HRC 2018b, Principle 13) and ensuring 'that their activities, and those of their residents and corporations, do not violate the human rights of people abroad' (HRC 2012, p. 13).

As these instruments explicitly admit, they do not aim to create new international rights and obligations, but rather to identify existing IHRL standards applicable to sovereign debt and related policies (HRC 2012) and, importantly, to persuade and influence states and other subjects to carry out their borrowing/lending activities in accordance with their human rights obligations. Perhaps also because of their non-legally binding (nonetheless, authoritative) nature (it is debated whether especially some of the UNCTAD Principles reflect customary international law, Esposito et al. 2013), these instruments appear to make at times broad statements, not fully substantiated by existing practice, although they do so with legitimate and laudable promotional intents. Unfortunately, they have so far received rather limited attention by states and (especially judicial) monitoring bodies (Bradlow 2016).

Extraterritorial human rights obligations

From a legal perspective, the existence and scope of ETOs are essentially a matter of interpretation of existing IHRL (Milanovic 2011). In this regard, reference to territoriality for delimiting the applicability of IHRL is to an extent a 'misnomer' (ibid., p. 61), since both in the text of most human rights treaties (e.g., ICCPR, art. 2(1); CRC, art. 2(1); ECHR, art. 1; and ACHR, art. 1(1)) and in the interpretative practice (including its more 'progressive' instances) of (especially judicial) monitoring bodies (see also Pribytkova, and Burbano Herrera and Haeck in this volume), the scope of IHRL obligations is decoupled from formal title over territory alone, and premised on states' exercise of *jurisdiction*. I will call this 'IHRL jurisdiction' to differentiate it from the notion of jurisdiction more generally existing in public international law or 'PIL jurisdiction', which identifies the authority of each state, based in and limited by international law, to prescribe, adjudicate and enforce its own domestic law in respect of natural and legal persons, property or events located within or, exceptionally – generally, in the presence of some personal or functional connecting factor – outside its territory (on such distinction, see i.a. Milanovic 2011; den Heijer et al. in Langford 2012). A reference to the notion of IHRL jurisdiction is also contained in the *Maastricht Principles* on the Extraterritorial Obligations of states in the area of Economic, Social and Cultural Rights (2011, Principle 9). The *exercise of IHRL jurisdiction by a state* represents a 'threshold criterion' and 'necessary condition' (European Court of Human Rights (ECtHR) 2011, para. 130; IACtHR 2017, para. 72) for that state to have human rights obligations towards individuals outside (and ultimately also inside, e.g., ECtHR 2004, para. 312) its territory, and thus to incur potential responsibility for any conduct attributable to it which violates an IHRL norm. In other words, states have ETOs whenever they exercise extraterritorially their IHRL jurisdiction.

As of today, monitoring bodies have acknowledged the extraterritorial exercise of IHRL jurisdiction in:

1 Cases where *a state exercises, lawfully or unlawfully, its PIL jurisdiction (as legal authority, through the exercise of legislative/judicial/enforcement powers) or PIL jurisdiction on behalf of another state, over persons, property or events located outside its territorial boundaries, with or without necessarily exercising effective physical control over an area or over individuals* ('*de jure* control' or 'public powers' model). In effect, there seems to be a presumption, at least in part of the jurisprudence of the ECtHR and the CCPR – dealing with state conduct that Milanovic (2011) broadly termed 'extraterritorial law enforcement', such as in absentia trials of a person located in another country (ECtHR 2006), extraterritorial trials by courts of one state sitting in another (ECtHR 2006a), the issuance of passports by consular authorities (CCPR 1990), or rescue/police operations on the high seas (ECtHR 2012) – as well as in a very recent judgment of the German Constitutional Court (2020, but see, *contra*, e.g., UK Investigatory Powers Tribunal 2016) that when a state is lawfully/unlawfully exercising extraterritorially elements of its governmental authority, its IHRL jurisdiction is also triggered, so that that state is under an obligation to secure all the relevant rights to the specific individuals involved by such exercise. With regard to the ECtHR in particular, this jurisdictional model can be deemed to cover also the scenarios of 'state agent authority' *sub* para. 134 a) and b) in *Al-Skeini* (ECtHR 2011; these cases amount, in effect, to exercises of PIL enforcement jurisdiction) and, more recently, it has been quite loosely applied to assert states' extraterritorial IHRL jurisdiction with regard to procedural obligations under Article 2 ECtHR (ECtHR 2014 and 2015).
2 Cases where a state exercises, lawfully or unlawfully, directly (e.g., through its armed forces) or through a subordinate local administration, *de facto* effective overall control of an area outside its own territory ('spatial' model, generally applied in cases of military occupation/interventions on a foreign territory) (i.a. ECtHR 1996 and 2001a; CCPR 1998; CESCR 1998; CAT 2004; CRC 2002; ICJ 2004 and 2005). The threshold of 'overall control' required by the courts has generally been high, demanding some physical presence (not always consistently defined and of varied duration) of the controlling state over the area in question. However, in more recent case law, the ECtHR has submitted that, besides having 'primarily

[...] reference to the strength of the state's military presence in the area', '[i]n determining whether effective control exists, [...] [o]ther indicators may also be relevant, such as the extent to which [a state's] military, economic and political support for the local subordinate administration provides it with influence and control over the region' (ECtHR 2011, para. 139) (so called 'decisive influence' test, see ECtHR 2004; ICJ 2007; Bantekas et al. 2020).

3 Cases where a state exercises, through its agents, physical control and authority over persons located outside its territorial boundaries ('personal' model, generally applied to instances of extraterritorial arrest, detention, abduction and extradition; see also ECtHR 2008 with regard to the possibility that the acquiescence/connivance of state authorities in the acts of private individuals may engage a contracting state's responsibility under the personal model). As the ECtHR has clarified, '[w]hat is decisive in such cases is the exercise of physical power and control over the person in question', not solely 'over the buildings, aircraft or ship in which the individuals were held' (ECtHR 2011, para. 136). Direct physical contact is not always necessary, as long as control is indeed effective ('contactless control' test, ECtHR 2009; Moreno-Lax 2020). The personal model has been endorsed also by the CCPR (e.g., 2004) and the IACmHR (e.g., 2012).

4 Cases where state conduct, or conduct originating or taking place in whole or in part in a state's territory and over which that state has control, has direct and reasonably foreseeable extraterritorial effects on the human rights of individuals outside its territory ('cause-and-effect' model). This broader (and not uncontested) jurisdictional model has been recently affirmed by the CCPR (2019, para. 63: 'a State party has an obligation to respect and ensure the rights under article 6 [ICCPR] of [...] all persons over whose enjoyment of the right to life it exercises power or effective control. This includes persons located outside any territory effectively controlled by the State whose right to life is nonetheless affected by its military or other activities in a direct and reasonably foreseeable manner'; but see the comments of the US, Canada, France, Germany, Austria, Norway and the Netherlands to this GC's draft version. More recently, see also CCPR 2020). It has also been affirmed – importantly, this being a judicial body – by the IACtHR (2017, para. 104(h): 'when transboundary harm or damage occurs, a person is under the jurisdiction of the State of origin [of such harm], if there is a causal link between the action that occurred within its territory and the negative impact on the human rights of persons outside its territory. The exercise of jurisdiction arises when the State of origin exercises effective control over the activities that caused the damage and the consequent human rights violation'). The existence of ETOs based on a 'cause-and-effect' model of IHRL jurisdiction has been, on the contrary, expressly rejected by the ECtHR (2001, para. 75, but see ECtHR 2008) and espoused, instead, by the CESCR (2017, para. 28) which upheld that '[e]xtraterritorial obligations arise when a State party may influence situations located outside its territory, consistent with the limits imposed by international law, by controlling the activities of corporations domiciled in its territory and/or under its jurisdiction, and thus may contribute to the effective enjoyment of economic, social and cultural rights outside its national territory'.

It must be noted that, in order for this jurisdictional test to be triggered, it is not enough for the relevant conduct to have 'kinetic' effects on human rights extraterritorially, but: *1)* such effects must be a direct/necessary and reasonably foreseeable consequence of that conduct (causal link), and *2)* the latter must be attributable to the state (in the case of the CCPR), or it must be alternatively proved (in the case of the IACtHR) that the state had effective control (not further specified in the IACtHR's advisory opinion) over the territorial activity (including of private actors, e.g., corporations) that originated the alleged extraterritorial human rights violation (attribution). This last model clearly opens the door to affirming state ETOs in cases where state conduct, or the conduct of a non-state actor over which a state has control is directly linked to a reasonably foreseeable extraterritorial human rights violation, regardless of any spatial or personal control. Although neither the CCPR nor the IACtHR have further elaborated on principles to establish such causal link in practice, causation is generally assessed (the burden of proof resting with the victim/applicant) by recourse to: *a)* a 'but for' (sine qua non) test, according to which causation is only established if the act/omission of a state is a 'but for', necessary cause of the human rights violation (where a state's act/omission is one among multiple factual causes, a causal link will be established only if that state's contribution was a 'principal cause'); *b)* a 'foreseeability' test, requiring that the wrongful human rights impact that eventually materialises could have been reasonably foreseen by a person of normal prudence when the relevant act/omission was carried out (this standard generally depends on the knowledge/information available to a state at the relevant time); and *c)* a 'remoteness' test, requiring a certain 'proximity' or significance of the conduct in question to the human rights violation, especially in cases where multiple successive causes may disrupt the chain of causation rendering the damage too 'remote' (Skogly in Langford et al. 2012; Plakokefalos 2015; Chauhan 2019).

ETOs and sovereign debt

Clearly, the first and last jurisdictional models could more aptly apply to debt relationships, which generally do not entail physical control over territory or individuals. Nonetheless, the required exercise of IHRL jurisdiction for the affirmation of ETOs poses some limitations to the applicability of the notion in the sovereign debt context (the following list of issues is not exhaustive).

Issue 1. States as main ETOs-bearers.

A first point to be noted is that, as interpreted so far, the concept of ETOs refers to the human rights obligations owed by *states* to individuals *abroad*, and thus is not particularly apt to clarify the contents/scope of non-state actors' human rights obligations (Gibney in Langford et al. 2012, such as international organisations (e.g., the EU or the IMF) or private creditors, who do not possess any territory nor exercise jurisdiction as interpreted by international bodies, and yet in the sovereign debt context are often significantly able to affect the enjoyment of human rights. Furthermore, even with regard to state actors, the notion of ETOs is suitable to apply to *creditor states*, particularly in the context of financial assistance and debt relief initiatives, as their conduct can have negative effects on the human rights of people located abroad, presumably in the territory of a debtor state. Instead, *debtor states'* ETOs may come into play, for instance, should one of them unilaterally repudiate its odious, illegitimate or illegal debt (Bantekas et al. 2018), and such decision have negative consequences on the human rights of individuals abroad (e.g., on the right to property of small bondholders who might, in specific cases, lose their savings, as it was the case, for instance, with the 2012 restructuring of the Greek debt, see ECtHR 2016).

Issue 2. Attribution of conduct in the case of complex multilateral debt-related activities and involvement of the territorial state.

For ETOs to be affirmed based on the jurisdictional models summarised above, attribution of conduct to a state is a necessary (though not a sufficient) condition: it is a conduct of the state or, in the case of the IACtHR 'cause-and-effect' model, a (at least partly) territorial conduct over which that state has effective control, that *de facto* creates the conditions for affirming the extraterritorial exercise by that state of its IHRL jurisdiction, further based on the additional elements of *de jure*/physical control or ability to influence the enjoyment of human rights abroad. Especially in the context of multilateral debt, the direct attribution of conduct having negative human rights effects – e.g., the adoption of austerity measures, which tends to involve: *a)* multiple actors (including international organisations, private actors and the, at least formally, consenting territorial state); *b)* complex decision-making processes; and *c)* instruments, such as Memoranda of Understanding, characterised by a certain 'opacity' in terms of the role, relative bargaining power and legitimacy of the actors involved (Ioannidis 2014; Costamagna 2012) – to specific (creditor) states for the purposes of any of the jurisdictional models summarised above, may prove arduous (for a significant attempt, however, see De Schutter et al. 2015). The relevant acts/omissions may be more easily formally attributable to the territorial state or to an international organisation (the involvement of the territorial state may be also – although not necessarily successfully – raised by creditor states and international organisations as a legal defence against their international responsibility).

A similar issue may arise when considering other debt- or financial assistance-related decisions, especially of supranational actors, with negative human rights impacts, e.g., the Eurogroup decision – after the June 2015 announcement by Greece of a referendum on the bailout terms then put forward by its international creditors – not to grant the requested one-month extension of Greece's Master Financial Assistance Facility (MFAFA). This decision led the country to default on its €1.6 billion repayment to the IMF due on the 30 June 2015 (on those same days, the Eurogroup was also discussing the forthcoming expiry of Greece's European Financial Stability Facility (EFSF) financial assistance and issued a statement, for the first time in history breaking the Eurogroup conventional unanimity rule, as Greece was arbitrarily excluded from the meeting; Eurogroup 2015). Similarly, on 28 June 2015 (i.e., a few days before the Greek referendum, which eventually took place on 5 July 2015), 'taking note of [Greece's] decision on [the] Greek referendum', the ECB decided 'to maintain the ceiling to the provision of emergency liquidity assistance (ELA) to Greek banks' (European Central Bank 2015), in other words, not to provide further financial support despite being clear at the time that funds were leaving the country and bank reserves running low (more than €7 billion-worth deposits left Greek banks in less than a week, as a 'mini-bank run' took place). This decision forced, on 29 June 2015, the Greek authorities to impose a bank closure and capital controls, capping money withdrawals at €60 per day, in order to avoid financial panic. The everyday life scenes that directly followed these announcements were sadly familiar: queues at ATMs, car lines at petrol stations, supermarkets reporting unusual volumes of sales, as people were making stocks of basic goods in fear of the worst (e.g., The Guardian 2015; Financial Times 2015). The Independent Expert on debt and human rights has noted how some observers perceived the ECB decision to reduce emergency credit to Greek banks shortly before the referendum 'as an attempt to influence the outcome of the democratic decision-making process in Greece' (HRC 2015, p. 2) and to (coercively) induce the Greek people to accept financial assistance under the proposed terms. In this case as well, a 'direct' causal link between the Eurogroup/ECB decisions and a potential interference with the human rights of people in Greece could be established, and yet issues of attribution in particular (perhaps more easily surmountable in the case of the Eurogroup, this being an informal body actually composed of the Ministers of Finance of the Euro Area member states) for the purposes of ETOs, persist.

Attribution may be less of an issue, instead, for the purposes of acknowledging the existence of creditor states' ETOs in the case of bilateral debt-related agreements (and conditionality).

Tangentially, it must be noted that attribution problems may arise as well with regard to the question of international responsibility (on responsibility scenarios linked to ETOs and their own potential limitations, see Erdem Türkelli in this Research Handbook). In this respect, existing grounds for state responsibility and for the responsibility of international organisations in connection with the act of a third state, in particular, may perhaps better assist attempts to hold state and non-state creditors accountable for their debt-related activities that have negative human rights effects abroad, and thus certainly merit further consideration (see arts. 16–18 of the 2001 Draft Articles on the Responsibility of States for Internationally Wrongful Acts, and arts. 58–63 of the 2011 Draft Articles on the Responsibility of International Organisations; the latter in particular include the case of IOs' aid and assistance to the internationally wrongful conduct of a state – remarkably, an hypothesis recently explored by the Independent Expert on debt and human rights in relation to the debt-related conduct of IFIs (HRC 2019) – as well as the cases of potential direction or control, or coercion by an IO).

Issue 3. Qualification of a debt-related state act as an exercise of its PIL jurisdiction for the purposes of the applicability of the first model.

As per the first model, IHRL jurisdiction may be affirmed where a state exercises, lawfully or unlawfully, its own legal authority/PIL jurisdiction over persons, property or events located outside its territorial boundaries, without necessarily exercising effective physical control over individuals ('*de jure* control' model). A difficulty that could arise in such instances would concern the qualification of the debt-related conduct of a state as an exercise of its PIL jurisdiction, in order potentially to affirm IHRL jurisdiction and thus the existence of ETOs.

For instance, does the exercise of creditor states' adjudicative and enforcement powers in relation to (foreign) debt contracts constitute an exercise of PIL jurisdiction triggering the adjudicating state's IHRL jurisdiction and ETOs? Although we may suppose that, if so, a state would be in theory under an IHRL obligation to secure to the specific individuals involved all the relevant rights, litigation in these cases is generally promoted by private actors (not seldom also vulture funds) against a (debtor) state, and thus would hardly fit that specific model in practice. Likewise, does the provision by means of domestic legislation of debt-related financial assistance to a foreign state with attached harsh conditionality, or the domestic regulation of debt-related financial activities with extraterritorial effects, amount to an extraterritorial exercise of state PIL jurisdiction in the above-mentioned sense (for a non-debt related example in this sense, see Coomans et al. 2012)?

Issue 4. Necessity and proximity of harm for the applicability of the fourth model.

The 'cause-and-effect' model of IHRL jurisdiction clearly opens the way to affirm ETOs on the part of all the actors potentially involved in sovereign debt relationships in a much broader range of situations. However, in the sovereign debt context, both because of the frequent involvement of multiple actors, including the territorial state, as mentioned, and because of the not necessarily strict causal connection between a specific (foreign state) debt-related conduct and human rights violations, it might be difficult (though not impossible) to prove that a creditor state's conduct, or conduct over which it has control, has been the necessary and principal cause of harm and is not too remotely connected with a human rights violation abroad. It must be noted, however, that in some cases – for instance, with regard to conditionality, as mentioned in

Section 2 – the human rights impact of certain acts/omissions have been now extensively and persuasively documented (HRC 2019 and 2016b), and thus may be easier to prove.

Nonetheless, even assuming that, as convincingly argued by the Independent Expert on debt and human rights, a 'direct causal link between austerity and human rights violations' can be asserted, 'the latter being foreseeable consequences of the former' (HRC 2019, para. 75), issues of attribution (point 2 above) may persist.

Conclusions

From a legal perspective, the exercise by a state of IHRL jurisdiction, referred to by most IHRL instruments and as currently interpreted by monitoring bodies, represents a threshold criterion to affirm the existence of a state's ETOs towards individuals outside (and, as mentioned, ultimately also inside) its territory. With regard to sovereign debt in particular, the '*de jure* control' or 'public powers', and the 'cause-and-effect' models of IHRL jurisdiction – the latter more recently adopted by the CCPR and the IACtHR, and endorsed i.a. by the CESCR, and opening the way to the recognition of (creditor) states' ETOs whenever their conduct or conduct originating or taking place in whole or in part in their territory, and over which they have effective control, has direct and reasonably foreseeable effects on the human rights of individuals abroad – certainly bear important consequences for sovereign financing and debt. Nonetheless, the affirmation of ETOs and more generally the applicability of the concept in the realm of sovereign debt remains potentially limited, i.a. because of some of the peculiarities of contemporary debt relationships that this contribution has attempted to explore.

References

Bantekas, I. and Lumina, C. (eds). (2018) *Sovereign Debt and Human Rights*, Oxford University Press.

Bantekas, I. and Oette, L. (2020) *International Human Rights Law and Practice*, Oxford University Press.

Bradlow, D. (2016) 'Can Parallel Lines Ever Meet? The Strange Case of the International Standards on Sovereign Debt and Business and Human Rights', *Yale Journal of International Law* 41, 201–239.

Chauhan, A. (2019) 'A Causal Model for the Extraterritorial Application of Human Rights Treaties', *The Oxford University Undergraduate Law Journal, Issue VIII*, 107–135.

Coomans, F. and Künnemann, R. (eds). (2012) *Cases and Concepts on Extraterritorial Obligations in the Area of Economic, Social and Cultural Rights*, Intersentia.

Costamagna, F. (2012) 'Saving Europe "Under Strict Conditionality": A Threat for EU Social Dimension?', *LPF Working Paper* 7/12, 1–24

Council of Europe (CoE) Commissioner for Human Rights (2013) 'Safeguarding Human Rights in Times of Economic Crisis'.

De Schutter, O. and Salomon, M.E. (2015) 'Economic Policy Conditionality, Socio-Economic Rights and International Legal Responsibility: The Case of Greece 2010-2015', Legal brief prepared for the Special Committee of the Hellenic Parliament on the Audit of the Greek Debt (Debt Truth Committee).

Draft Articles on the Responsibility of International Organizations (2011).

Draft Articles on the Responsibility of States for Internationally Wrongful Acts (2001).

Espósito, C., Li, Y. and Bohoslavsky, J.P. (2013) *Sovereign Financing and International Law: The UNCTAD Principles on Responsible Sovereign Lending and Borrowing*, Oxford University Press.

Eurogroup (2015) 'Ministerial statement of 27th June 2015', No. 534/15.

European Central Bank (ECB) (2015) 'ELA to Greek banks maintained at its current level', Press release June 28.

European Court of Human Rights (ECtHR) (1996) *Loizidou v. Turkey*, Application no: 15318/89, Judgment.

_______ (2001) *Banković and Others v. Belgium and Others*, Application no: 52207/99, Admissibility Decision.

_______ (2001a) *Cyprus v. Turkey,* Application no: 25781/94, Judgment.
_______ (2004) *Ilaşcu and Others v. Moldova and Russia,* Application no: 48787/99, Judgment.
_______ (2006) *Sedjovic v. Italy,* Application no: 56581/00, Judgment.
_______ (2006a) *Martin v. United Kingdom,* Application no: 40426/98, Judgment.
_______ (2008) *Andreou v. Turkey,* Application no: 45653/99, Admissibility Decision.
_______ (2009) *Women on Waves and Others v. Portugal,* Application no: 31276/05, Judgment.
_______ (2011) *Al-Skeini and Others v. United Kingdom,* Application no: 55721/07, Judgment.
_______ (2012) *Hirsi Jamaa and Others v. Italy,* Application no: 27765/09, Judgment.
_______ (2014) *Jaloud v. The Netherlands,* Application no: 47708/08, Judgment.
_______ (2015) *Pisari v. The Republic of Moldova and Russia, Application no:* 42139/12, Judgment.
_______ (2016) *Mamatas and Others v. Greece,* Application nos: 63066/14, 64297/14 and 66106/14, Judgment.

Financial Times (2015) 'Greek banks given one-day reprieve as depositors pull out €1.6bn'.

German Constitutional Court (2020) *Gesetz über den Bundesnachrichtendienst,* Judgment on the German Act on the Federal Intelligence Service, 1 BvR 2835/17.

Inter-American Commission on Human Rights (IACmHR) (2012) *Djamel Ameziane v. United States,* Admissibility Report no: 17/12.

Inter-American Court of Human Rights (IACtHR) (2017) *The Environment and Human Rights,* Advisory Opinion OC-23/17.

International Court of Justice (ICJ) (2004) *Legal Consequences of the Construction of a Wall in the Occupied Palestinian Territory,* Advisory Opinion.
_______ (2005) *Armed Activities on the Territory of the Congo (Congo v. Uganda),* Judgment.
_______ (2007) Application of the Convention on the Prevention and Punishment of Genocide (Bosnia and Herzegovina v. Serbia and *Montenegro*), Judgment.

International Monetary Fund (IMF) (2002) 'Assessing sustainability'.
_______ (2013) 'Greece: Ex Post Evaluation of Exceptional Access under the 2010 Stand-By Arrangement', IMF Country Report no. 13/156.
_______ (2018) 'Fiscal Monitor: Managing Public Wealth', October 2018.
_______ (2020) 'World Economic Outlook, April 2020: The Great Lockdown'.

Ioannidis, M. (2014) 'EU Financial Assistance Conditionality after "Two Pack"', *Heidelberg Journal of International Law* 74(1), 61–104.

Langford, M., Vandenhole, W., Scheinin, M. and van Genugten, W. (eds). (2012) 'Global Justice', *State Duties: The Extraterritorial Scope of Economic, Social and Cultural Rights in International Law,* Cambridge University Press.

Lastra, R.M. (2015) *International Financial and Monetary Law,* Oxford University Press.

Lastra, R.M. and Buchheit, L. (eds). (2014) *Sovereign Debt Management,* Oxford University Press.

Maastricht Principles on Extraterritorial Obligations of States in the area of Economic, Social and Cultural Rights (2011).

Milanovic, M. (2011) *Extraterritorial Application of Human Rights Treaties: Law, Principles, and Policy,* Oxford University Press.

Moreno-Lax, V. (2020) 'The Architecture of Functional Jurisdiction: Unpacking Contactless Control – On Public Powers, *S.S. and Others v. Italy,* and the "Operational Model"', *German Law Journal* 21(3), 385–416.

Office of the High Commissioner for Human Rights (OHCHR) (2013) 'Report on austerity measures and economic and social rights'.
_______ (2017) 'Realizing Human Rights through Government Budgets', United Nations.

Ortiz, I., Cummins, M., Capaldo, J. and Karunanethy, K. (2015) 'The Decade of Adjustment: A Review of Austerity Trends 2010–2020 in 187 Countries', International Labour Organization.

Ostry, J.D., Loungani, P. and Furceri, D. (2016) 'Neoliberalism: Oversold?', *Finance and Development* 53(2), 38–41.

Paulus, C.G. (2014) 'Debt', *Max Planck Encyclopedia of Public International Law.*

Plakokefalos, I. (2015) 'Causation in the Law of State Responsibility and the Problem of Overdetermination: In Search of Clarity', *European journal of International Law* 26(2), 471–492.

Scali, E.L. (2020) 'Sovereign Financing during the COVID-19 Pandemic: The Debt Implications of Italy's Socio-Economic Measures for 2020 and the Response of the European Union' in Acconci, P. and Baroncini, E. (eds). *Gli effetti della pandemia Covid-19 su commercio, investimenti e strumenti finanziari*, Editoriale Scientifica.

Tamamović, A.I. (2015) 'The impact of the crisis on fundamental rights across Member States of the EU: Comparative analysis', Study for the LIBE Committee, European Union.

The Guardian (2015) 'Greek crisis: episodes of despair and drama as moment of truth nears'.

UK Investigatory Powers Tribunal (2016) *Human Rights Watch Inc. and Others v. The Secretary of State for the Foreign Commonwealth Office and Others*, [2016] UKIPTrib 15_165-CH.

UN Committee Against torture (CAT) (2004) Conclusions and Recommendation: United Kingdom of Great Britain and Northern Ireland, CAT/C/CR/33/3.

UN Committee on Economic, Social and Cultural Rights (CESCR) (1990) GC 3 on the nature of States Parties' obligations (Art. 2, Para. 1, of the Covenant), E/1991/23.

_______ (1998) Concluding Observations: Israel, E/C.12/1/Add.27.

_______ (2012) Letter dated 16 May 2012 addressed by the Chairperson of the Committee on Economic, Social and Cultural Rights to States Parties to the International Covenant on Economic, Social and Cultural Rights.

_______ (2016) Public debt, austerity measures and the International Covenant on Economic, Social and Cultural Rights, E/C.12/2016/1.

_______ (2017) GC 24 on State obligations under the International Covenant on Economic, Social and Cultural Rights in the context of business activities, E/C.12/GC/24.

UN Committee on the Rights of the Child (CRC) (2002) Concluding Observations: Israel, CRC/C/15/Add.195.

_______ (2016) GC19 on public budgeting for the realization of children's rights (Art. 4), CRC/C/GC/19.

UN Conference on Trade and Development (UNCTAD) (2012) Principles on Promoting Responsible Sovereign Lending and Borrowing.

UN General Assembly (UNGA) (2015) 'Basic Principles on Sovereign Debt Restructuring Processes', A/RES/69/319.

_______ (2020) 'Addressing, from a human rights perspective, the debt-related problems of developing countries caused by the coronavirus disease (COVID-19) pandemic', Report of the Independent Expert on the effects of foreign debt and other related international financial obligations of States on the full enjoyment of all human rights, particularly economic, social and cultural rights, Yuefen Li, A/75/164.

UN Human Rights Committee (CCPR) (1990) *Liechtensztejn v. Uruguay*, CCPR/C/OP/2.

_______ (1998) Concluding Observations: Israel, CCPR/C/79/Add.93.

_______ (2004) GC 31 on the nature of the general legal obligations imposed on States Parties to the Covenant, CPR/C/21/Rev.1/Add. 13.

_______ (2019) GC 36 on Article 6: Right to life, CPR/C/GC/36.

_______ (2020) *A.S. and others v. Italy*, CCPR/C/130/D/3042/2017.

UN Human Rights Council (HRC) (2011) 'Guiding principles on foreign debt and human rights', Report of the Independent Expert on the effects of foreign debt and other related international financial obligations of States on the full enjoyment of human rights, particularly economic, social and cultural rights, Cephas Lumina, A/HRC/20/23.

_______ (2015) 'End-of-Mission Statement. Visit to the European Institutions'.

_______ (2016a) 'Report of the Independent Expert on the effects of foreign debt and other related international financial obligations of States on the full enjoyment of human rights, particularly economic, social and cultural rights', A/HRC/31/60 (on inequality and debt crises).

_______ (2016b) 'Report of the Independent Expert on the effects of foreign debt and other related international financial obligations of States on the full enjoyment of all human rights, particularly economic, social and cultural rights', A/HRC/34/57.

_______ (2018a) 'Extreme poverty and human rights', Report of the Special Rapporteur on extreme poverty and human rights, A/73/396 (on privatization and human rights).

_______ (2018b) 'Guiding Principles on human rights impact assessments of economic reforms', Report of the Independent Expert on the effect of foreign debt and other related international financial obligations of states on the full enjoyment of human rights, particularly economic, social and cultural rights, A/HRC/40/57.

_______ (2019) 'Report of the Independent Expert on the effects of foreign debt and other related international financial obligations of States on the full enjoyment of all human rights', Responsibility for complicity of international financial institutions in human rights violations in the context of retrogressive economic reforms, A/74/178.

_______ (2020) 'Private debt and human rights', Report of the Independent Expert on the effects of foreign debt and other related international financial obligations of States on the full enjoyment of human rights, particularly economic, social and cultural rights, A/HRC/43/45.

18

Extraterritorial human rights obligations in the context of economic sanctions

Joseph Schechla

Introduction

Economic sanctions are a time-honoured feature of international relations governed by international law (IL). While various tools and iterations of economic sanctions are optional and discretionary in nature, they have been used as much for enforcing IL as they have been means of unilateral punitive action that may contravene international agreements, including human rights treaties and principles. Thus, economic sanctions can be a double-edged sword and, therefore, the subject of much-deserved critical inquiry to determine not only their effectiveness, but also their legality and legitimacy in practice, because of their human rights and other IL consequences.

This chapter explores sanctions and sanction regimes under human rights law. In particular, it presents the relevant human rights norms to be applied not only as states undergoing sanctions (i.e., the domestic and individual dimensions of human rights obligations), but particularly also as states and other parties carrying out sanctions (collective and extraterritorial dimensions of human rights obligations).

Definitions and scope

Generally, a sanction in IL is a penalty or punishment for disobeying a law or other established norm. The purpose of sanctions can be synonymous with terms such as threat, deterrent, penalty, disciplinary action/punishment, penalization, coercively corrective measure, retribution and may take the form of an embargo, a ban, prohibition, boycott, barrier, restriction or tariff.

More specifically, economic sanctions considered here are measures taken by a state, or states, and/or their corresponding organs to coerce another state to conform to an international agreement or norm of conduct, typically in the form of restrictions on trade, access to finance or other goods and services.

The purposes and degrees of economic sanctions may vary in their application, whether as a tool of political pressure, as an alternative to exacting enforcement or judicial action, or other coercive measure. The scope of economic sanctions also may range widely from international, as exercised by the UN Security Council (SC) or General Assembly (GA), as in the case of boycott,

DOI: 10.4324/9781003090014-23

divestment and sanction (BDS) applied against the practice of apartheid in southern Africa. Alternatively, the actual source, scope and practice of economic sanctions could be regional, imposed by a regional organization of states, another groups of states or unilaterally.

Economic sanctions can also be used by central or local spheres of government and their corresponding organs (Schechla 2015) in the fields of trade, finance or public procurement, or could even be applied in civil initiatives with cross-border implications, as in the case of popular BDS movements against illegal situations, including systematic human rights violations. Economic sanctions could be applied against a particular state (or states), or even against subnational regions or groups within an affected state's jurisdiction or territory of effective control, as practiced by occupying Powers in administered territories in the case of India's internet blackout, movement restrictions and trade sanctions applied in Kashmir, or Israel's various closures, revenue seizures, travel bans and blockades in occupied Palestine.

Within the realm of economic sanction, two types are most common: financial sanctions and trade sanctions. *Financial sanctions* involve monetary issues and transactions. More specifically, financial sanctions could take the form of blocking government assets held abroad; limiting access to financial markets; and restricting loans and credits, international money transfers, the sale and trade of property abroad; and/or freezing development aid (SFOFEA, 1998). *Trade sanctions* restrict imports and exports to and from the target country. These restrictions can be comprehensive, as was the case with sanctions against Iraq (1990–2003), or selective, restricting only certain commodities connected with a more-specific trade dispute.

Financial and trade sanctions may overlap significantly, especially in the case of comprehensive sanctions. For example, where foreign assets may be frozen and access to new funds blocked, governments would be unable to pay for imports, thus affecting trade, including imports of goods essential for the enjoyment of the human rights to health and/or adequate food. Coinciding, too, may be other types such as travel sanctions; military sanctions, affecting military activities and trade in matériel;[1] diplomatic sanctions; and cultural sanctions, encompassing artistic, education and athletic exchanges. These may form ancillaries or subcategories of economic sanctions when applied simultaneously with trade and financial sanctions.

Legality and legitimacy of economic sanctions

The United Nations Security Council

The SC holds the UN Charter-based mandate and 'primary responsibility for the maintenance of international peace and security' (UN Charter (UNC), art. 24). Within its authority, the SC has several remedial measures at its disposal, in addition to the binding authority of its resolutions, to call on UN Members and other states to take effective measures, either individually or jointly, to bring an end to an illegal situation, including by the imposition of sanctions. As of 2021, the SC maintains 14 sanctions regimes, while all but 2 of them coincide with other overt diplomatic initiatives, including direct negotiations (UNDPPA 2021).

The basis for UN sanctions under IL derives from Chapter VII of the UNC. Its Article 41 covers enforcement measures not involving armed force. The SC may decide which measures are to be taken to give effect to its decisions, and it may call upon the Members of the UN to apply such measures.

Although it does not explicitly refer to 'sanctions', Article 41 contains an illustrative list of specific sanctioning measures, namely 'complete or partial interruption of economic relations and of rail, sea, air, postal, telegraphic, radio, and other means of communication, and the severance of diplomatic relations'. The same article allows for other non-sanction measures, such as establishing a remedial compensation fund, such as the UN Compensation Commission following Iraq's invasion of Kuwait, which effectively was funded by an economic sanction (seizure) of Iraq's oil revenues.

The SC sanctions regimes have become well institutionalized, diversified and targeted through more than 55 years of operation. In doing so, the SC has grounded effective measures in the domestic, individual, collective and extraterritorial obligations of states under IL, IHL, criminal law and peremptory norms, including the duty of non-recognition of a situation created by the illegal use of force or other serious breaches of *jus cogens* (Crawford et al. 2010; Dawidowicz 2010; ILC 2019, pp. 141–207; Kohen 2011; Meng 1982; Milano 2009; Talmon 2005; Tomuschat and Thouvenin 2005).

States and their constituent organs bear positive extraterritorial obligations to 'bring an end to illegal situations' under IL, including 'to ensure respect' for IHL (G4, art. 1), uphold *erga omnes* obligations and under IHRL treaties. The ICJ, in its 2004 Advisory Opinion on the construction of a wall in the occupied Palestinian territory, reiterated that the illegal situation has resulted in 'an obligation not to render aid or assistance in maintaining the situation created by such construction'. The ICJ reminded that, in the context of war and occupation, The Hague Convention and the four Geneva Conventions 'incorporate obligations essentially of an *erga omnes* character' (ICJ 2004). The ETO duty of non-recognition, non-cooperation or non-transaction with parties to the illegal situation is self-executing, in the sense that such *erga omnes* requirements are axiomatic and do not require specific SC resolutions for states to exercise this extraterritorial obligation (Crawford et al. 2010; ILC 2019). In such a case, the sanctions imposed in response to a breach of peremptory norms would not be optional and discretionary. However, the SC is specially mandated to articulate, operationalize and monitor these obligations as the UN body with 'primary responsibility for the maintenance of international peace and security' (UNC, art. 24). Nonetheless, neither is the SC the *sole* organ with that responsibility, nor are its actions and inactions in maintaining universal standards in the conduct of sanctions immune to the test of institutional and legal integrity.

The UN sanctions regimes involve countermeasures that generally seek at least one of five purposeful objectives: conflict resolution, democratization, nonproliferation, counterterrorism and the protection of civilians (including human rights). The SC has evolved to apply targeted sanctions, rather than comprehensive sanctions, the latter of which had proved to cause adverse humanitarian impacts.

Amid the proliferation of sanction regimes, the UN Secretary-General saw the need in 1995 to assess the potential impact of sanctions before they are imposed, and to enhance arrangements for the provision of humanitarian assistance to vulnerable groups (A/RES/50/60-S/RES/1995/1). In the following year, a major UN study found that:

> humanitarian exemptions tend to be ambiguous and are interpreted arbitrarily and inconsistently. Delays, confusion and the denial of requests to import essential humanitarian goods cause resource shortages…these effects…inevitably fall most heavily on the poor (A/51/306; IASCWG, 2000).

A subsequent study for the UN Office for the Coordination of Humanitarian Affairs (OCHA) also found that the review procedures established under the various SC sanctions committees 'remain cumbersome and aid agencies still encounter difficulties in obtaining approval for exempted supplies… [and] neglect larger problems of commercial and governmental violations in the form of black-marketing, illicit trade, and corruption' (Minear et al. 1998).

Other sanctioning authorities

The SC is not the only actor in the field of international relations ostensibly to uphold universal human rights. The European Commission (EC) and the High Representative of the Union for Foreign Affairs and Security Policy have issued a joint proposal for an EU policy on restrictive measures against serious human rights violations and abuses worldwide committed by entities and persons (EU press release 2020). The new horizontal EU Global Human Rights Sanctions Regime provides for such measures as asset freezes, with EC oversight of travel bans. However, the new policy would not replace geographic sanctions regimes, some of which already address human rights violations and abuses, peace, security, and support democracy and international law. They target persons and entities whose actions endanger these values, and intend to reduce as much as possible any adverse consequences on civilian populations.

It is notable that communities, through their local authorities, may act conscientiously on their *erga omnes* obligations as organs of the legally bound state, by taking it upon themselves to impose restrictive economic measures within their power that seek to prevent, mitigate or remedy human rights abuses perpetrated extraterritorially. Such actions are typically grounded in international law arguments, moral indignation and/or national interest. These actions often take the form of boycott or 'selective-procurement resolutions', implementing the self-executing duty of non-recognition, non-cooperation or non-transaction with parties to illegal situations, even when their central government organs fail to do so (Schechla 2015). To wit, a local authorities' forum in Canoas RS, Brazil in 2012 declared that '…Brazilian local governments…commit to responsible investment by avoiding contracting with parties that support or benefit from occupation, or violate related prohibitions under international law' (LAF 2012). In December 2014, another gathering of local governments reiterated their pledge to fulfil that same *erga omnes* obligation: 'Local governments…commit to responsible investment by not contracting with parties and not twinning with cities that support or benefit from occupation, or violate related prohibitions under international law' (FAMSI 2014).

The proliferation of such examples, including the citizens' boycott, divestment and sanctions initiatives, promise to form a critical mass or movement that raises the grassroots call to the 'primarily responsible' parties (states and IOs) to apply effective measures to enforce the IL that they are supposed to uphold.

Unilateral sanction regimes

Nothing in the UNC can be read as authorizing unilateral coercive measures, including economic sanctions. Such measures are incompatible with general principles of IL and may violate the prohibition of interference in the internal affairs of other states and violate their sovereignty when they fail the human rights and IL tests outlined here (Beaucillon 2016; Emmenegger 2016; Jazairy 2017; Jennings and Watts 2008; de Zayas 2018). For example, the GA has condemned the US embargo against Cuba (A/RES/73/8). In this reaffirmation of the existing law on unilateral sanctions, it has explicitly cited US legislation, namely the 1996 'Helms-Burton Act', whose extraterritorial consequences 'affect the sovereignty of other States, the legitimate interests of entities or persons under their jurisdiction and the freedom of trade and navigation' (ibid, preamble). Also, in 2018, the UN Human Rights Council (UNHRC) overwhelmingly condemned unilateral coercive measures, recalling that economic sanctions demonstrably cause death, aggravate economic crises, disrupt the production and distribution of food and medicine, constitute a push factor generating emigration and lead to violations of human rights (A/HRC/

RES/37/21). UNHRC adopted similar resolutions in 2019 (A/HRC/RES/40/3), as well as in 2020 (A/HRC/RES/43/15).

Prima facie, unilateral sanctions are incompatible with ETOs under IL and potentially harmful to the human rights of the affected persons in the target country/ies. The Vienna Declaration and Programme of Action, cautions states 'to refrain from any unilateral measures... that create obstacles to trade relations among states and impedes the full realization of the human rights set forth in the Universal Declaration of Human Rights (UDHR) and international human rights instruments, in particular the rights of everyone to a standard of living adequate for their health and well-being, including food and medical care, housing and the necessary social services... [and] affirms that food should not be used as a tool for political pressure' (A/CONF.157/23). Application of unilateral sanctions may also invoke ETOs to avoid an adverse impact on the enjoyment of human rights in third countries, which are not targeted directly, but are prevented by the operation of the (extraterritorial) foreign law from engaging in economic relations with the target country.

Extraterritorial obligations

States bear the principal duty to maintain: (1) international peace and security, (2) progressive (i.e., sustainable) development and (3) human rights 'in larger freedom' (UNC, arts. 1 and 55–56; A/59/2005). Extraterritorial obligations also invoke this indivisible bundle of simultaneous duties in the context of sanction regimes. Notably, the International Covenant on Economic, Social and Cultural Rights (ICESCR) has no territorial or jurisdictional limitations on the scope of its application (Sepulveda and Courtis 2009; Milanovic 2011). Whereas the International Covenant on Civil and Political Rights (ICCPR, art. 2.1) sets out the obligation of states parties to respect and ensure the rights of all individuals within its territory and subject to its jurisdiction, the equivalent provision in Article 2.1 of ICESCR avoids any reference to 'jurisdiction' or 'territory'. Moreover, ICESCR imposes an explicit obligation upon all states parties to take steps, individually and through international assistance and cooperation, with a view to achieving the full and progressive realization of the guaranteed economic, social and cultural human rights (ESCHRs) on a progressive basis (ICESCR, arts. 11(2), 15(4) and 23). This means that states parties assume certain obligations of an external or international nature, setting forth certain extraterritorial obligations to individuals in other states parties within the scope of their conduct (CESCR, General Comment no. 8 and General Comment no. 14; Coomans 2011; De Schutter 2008; Gondek 2009; Jazairy 2017).

In addition, an argument can be made that such position would be consonant with the rule of customary IL that prohibits a state from allowing its territory to be used to cause damage on the territory of another state, a requirement that has gained particular relevance in international environmental law (CESCR, General Comment no. 24) and may be considered relevant also to the field of protection of human rights (Bartels 2014; De Schutter et al. 2012; Vennemann 2006).

The issue of extraterritorial obligations raises the question whether states, or international organizations (IOs) implementing the sanctions, are subject to extraterritorial obligations under human rights instruments in relation to the application and effects of the sanctions they impose (Jazairy 2017). Other authors have addressed the need to prevent a violation of primary (human rights) norms in the case of economic sanctions (Bartels 2014; Beaucillon 2016; Cosnard 1995; Emmenegger 2016; Minear et al. 1998, Rathbone et al. 2013), while little jurisprudence exists from adjudication of a breach of human rights in the course of imposing economic sanctions (Beaulieu 2008; ECtHR 2014; Lamrani 2013; Sachs and Weisbrot 2019; Wintour 2020). (For discussion of the attribution of extraterritorial responsibility, see Erdem Türkelli in this volume.)

The *Maastricht Principles* on Extraterritorial Obligations of States in the area of Economic, Social and Cultural Rights (MP) channel the relevant IL guidance that applies to dilemmas of extraterritorial behaviour of states and IOs across the spectrum of indivisible and interdependent human rights, despite the ESCHR-specific title. With specific reference to ETOs in the context of sanction regimes, 'Sanctions and equivalent measures' (para. 22) advises that:

> States must refrain from adopting measures, such as embargoes or other economic sanctions, which would result in nullifying or impairing the enjoyment of economic, social and cultural rights. Where sanctions are undertaken to fulfil other international legal obligations, states must ensure that human rights obligations are fully respected in the design, implementation and termination of any sanction regime. States must refrain in all circumstances from embargoes and equivalent measures on goods and services essential to meet core obligations.

This may be seen as providing needed specificity to Principle III. Obligations to respect (MP, paras. 19–21; De Schutter et al. 2012, p. 1131); however, the same guidance relates to the obligations also to protect (MP, IV, paras. 23–26) and fulfil (MP,V, paras. 28–29), as well as general obligations to engage in international cooperation (MP, paras. 27 and 30). While para. 22 aligns with ARSIWA (para. 50), it also exemplifies the *preventive* dimension of human rights application in the acts related to *refraining* from harm and the *design* of economic sanction measures. Corresponding guidance related to the *remedial* dimensions of human rights application is addressed also under VI. Accountability and Remedies (MP, paras. 36–41).

As already noted with specific regard to ESCHRs, ICESCR is a binding normative instrument that readily provides for the extraterritorial dimensions of state obligations, having no territorial or jurisdictional limitations on the scope of its application. The relationship between economic sanctions and a participating state's obligations to respect and protect economic, social and cultural human rights (ESCHR) rose on the agenda of the UN Committee on Economic, Social and Cultural Rights (CESCR) in the 1990s, resulting in the adoption of a General Comment (GC) on the obligations of states party to ICESCR in the context of sanctions (CESCR, General Comment no. 8). The GC noted the increasing frequency of economic sanctions imposed internationally, regionally and unilaterally. Without calling into question the necessity for sanctions in appropriate cases in accordance with Chapter VII of the Charter or other applicable IL, the GC sought to give specificity to the above-cited provisions of the UNC related to human rights (arts. 1, 55 and 56) and, particularly, rights under ICESCR.

CESCR has observed through its periodic reviews of states parties that economic sanctions 'often cause significant disruption in the distribution of food, pharmaceuticals and sanitation supplies, jeopardize the quality of food and the availability of clean drinking water, severely interfere with the functioning of basic health and education systems, and undermine the right to work' (CESCR, General Comment no. 8, para. 3). As in other crisis situations, the Committee also has warned of accompanying hazards and unintended consequences such as the reinforcement of the power of oppressive élites, the almost-invariable emergence of a black market and the generation of huge windfall profits for the privileged classes that manage it, enhancement of the control of governing parties over the population at large and restriction of opportunities to seek asylum or to manifest political opposition. While these phenomena may be political in origin and nature, CESCR focused on their impact on ESCHR (ibid).

While SC-imposed sanctions include certain humanitarian exemptions, those do not address, for example, the impediments to access primary education, nor provide for repairs and maintenance to vital infrastructures essential to ensure the enjoyment of clean water, sanitation, adequate housing, health care, social security, protection of the family, decent work, participation in culture or other ESCHRs, especially for at-risk groups. Despite numerous UN studies and assessments, CESCR found it apparent that 'in most, if not all, cases, those consequences have either not been taken into account at all or not given the serious consideration they deserve' (ibid, para. 6).

With regard to the common and simultaneous individual, collective, domestic and extraterritorial human rights obligations of states, CESCR has stated: 'Just as the international community insists that any targeted State must respect the civil and political rights of its citizens, so too must that State and the international community itself do everything possible to protect at least the core content of the economic, social and cultural rights of the affected peoples of that State' (ibid, para. 7). This comment aligns with ICESCR obliging states parties to 'take steps, individually and through international assistance and cooperation, especially economic and technical, to the maximum of its available resources, with a view to achieving progressively the full realization of the rights recognized in the present Covenant by all appropriate means….' (ICESCR, art. 2.1).

This obligation, as with IHRL generally, applies under all circumstances—including states of emergency, conflict, occupation and war—and, while economic sanctions must not prevent the duty-bound state or sub-national authorities from meeting their core ESCHR obligations, nor must any responsible party impede the over-riding implementation principles of applying the maximum available resources or progressive realization of ESCHR. While achieving that formula under sanctions may prove difficult, both the imposition of economic sanctions and responses to them must ensure that duty-bearers avoid harm to the civilian population, including collective punishment prohibited under IHL (G4, arts. 33, 53 and 68) and/or violation of non-derogable human rights (ICCPR, arts. 4–6).

Subsequent GCs have given specificity to ETOs under ICESCR related to sanctions. Notably, GC14 on the right to health advises that states parties 'should refrain at all times from imposing embargoes or similar measures restricting the supply of another State with adequate medicines and medical equipment. Restrictions on such goods should never be used as an instrument of political and economic pressure' (CESCR, General Comment no. 14, para. 41). GC24 provides guidance for imposing sanctions on business operations that violate covenanted human rights (CESCR, General Comment no. 24, paras. 15, 50, 53–54).

CESCR also urges states parties to prioritize vulnerable groups when imposing sanctions on states that are not parties to ICESCR, given the status of the ESCHR of vulnerable groups as part of general IL, as evidenced, for example, by the near-universal ratification of the Convention on the Rights of the Child (CRC) and the customary-law status of UDHR. In this context, the reader should note, however, that the United States, the world's leader at imposing unilateral sanctions, remains the only permanent SC member that remains outside ICESCR and the only UN Member state that has not yet ratified CRC.

Under human rights treaties, two sets of obligations flow from these considerations: one set lies with the sanction-affected state, whereas sanctions in no way nullify or diminish the relevant obligations of that state party. Rather, they take on greater practical importance in times of hardship such as those under sanctions. Those obligations call for the affected state to assess its fulfilment of individual and domestic Covenant obligations to apply 'the maximum of its available resources' for the greatest possible respect, protection and fulfilment of ESCHRs of each individual living within its jurisdiction and territory of effective control. That means that, while sanctions inevitably diminish the affected state's capacity to fund or support some of the necessary measures, it still remains under an obligation to eliminate discrimination in the enjoyment of ESCHRs and to take all possible measures, including cooperation with the international community to minimize the negative impact upon the human rights of vulnerable social groups.

Another set of obligations relates to the party or parties responsible for imposing, implementing and maintaining the sanctions, whether it be the international community, an international or regional organization, or a state, a group of states and/or, by extension, any of their organs. CESCR has identified three conclusions that logically follow from ESCHRs in the context of economic sanctions:

1 ESCHRs must be taken fully into account when designing an appropriate sanctions regime. Without endorsing any particular measures, CESCR notes proposals within the UN System to create a mechanism for anticipating and tracking the impacts of sanctions throughout the period they are in force, the elaboration of a more-transparent set of agreed principles and procedures respecting human rights, widening the range of exempt goods and services, authorizing technical agencies to determine necessary exemptions, better resourcing sanctions committees to ensure respect, protection and fulfilment of ESCHRs, more precise targeting of the vulnerabilities of those whose behaviour the international community wishes to change, and introducing greater overall flexibility.
2 The Committee interpreted that, when an external party assumes even partial responsibility for the situation within a country (under Chapter VII, or otherwise), it also unavoidably assumes a responsibility to do all within its power to respect, protect and fulfil the affected population's ESCHR. Although CESCR does not elaborate further, this logically means that any state, state organ or multilateral party formed of ICESCR states parties, or whose economic sanctions extend to an ICESCR state party, that state, organ or multilateral party likewise assumes all obligations arising from ICESCR in the affected territory.
3 CESCR also invoked the over-riding ICESCR implementation principle and obligation 'to take steps, individually and through international assistance and cooperation, especially economic and technical', in order to prevent and/or remedy any disproportionate suffering experienced by vulnerable groups within the sanctioned country (Minear et al. 1998).

Amid a paucity of cases asserting ETOs in the context of sanctions, the ICJ did issue a 2018 judgment, in which Iran argued that, by the re-imposition of unilateral sanctions lifted by Executive Order 13716 of 16 January 2016, the USA was strangling the country 'through naked economic aggression' (Simons and Cowell 2018) and, thus, was violating the Treaty of Amity signed in 1955. The ICJ issued an interim order to the United States to lift sanctions linked to humanitarian goods and civil aviation imposed against Iran.[2] The USA responded by withdrawing from the Treaty of Amity (Wong and Sanger 2018), while 11 US senators urged the US Administration to temporarily ease unilateral sanctions on Iran and Venezuela (USIP 2020), followed by a similar joint letter of 34 Congresspersons and 14 endorsing organizations reiterated the humanitarian call to ease sanctions (CotUS 2020). Despite these and other pleas by human rights organizations and even the urging of allied states (Wintour 2020), the US Administration reportedly did not respond (Borger 2020; Calderon 2020).

However, the ICJ interim order was equivocal and did not explicitly assert the ETOs of the sanctioning state. At some future date, the ICJ still may demonstrate the integrity to affirm such a finding in a contentious case or an advisory opinion requested by the GA under Article 96 of the UNC, or even in an opinion expressed as an *obiter dictum*.

Smarter sanctions

The now defunct UN Sub-Commission on prevention of Discrimination and Protection of Minorities interrogated the continuing dilemmas and human rights consequences of economic sanctions. A dedicated study concluded with a preliminary six-prong test to determine whether economic sanctions be 'smart', (E/CN.4/Sub.2/2000/33, pp. 11-12), namely that:

1 **They should always be limited in time**: sanctions should be subject to periodic (annual) review and evaluation before extension;
2 **They must not affect the innocent population, especially the most vulnerable**: implementing the humanitarian law prohibition against collective punishment;
3 **They must not aggravate imbalances in income distribution**: minimizing discrimination and exacerbation of prior violations;
4 **They must not generate illegal and unethical business practices**. Benchmark questions to evaluate sanctions include:

   (i) *Are the sanctions imposed for valid reasons?* Sanctions under the United Nations system must be imposed only when there is a threat of, or actual breach of, international peace and security. While unilateral sanctions are, *prima facie*, incompatible with this criterion, sanctions should not be imposed for invalid political reasons and should not arise from, or produce an economic benefit for one state or group of states at the expense of the sanctioned state or other states.
   (ii) *Do the sanctions target the relevant parties?* Sanctions should not target civilians who are not involved with the threat to peace or international security, nor should they target, or result in *collateral damage* to 'third party' states or peoples.
   (iii) *Do the sanctions target the relevant goods or objects?* Sanctions should not interfere with the free flow of humanitarian goods or target goods required to ensure the basic subsistence of the civilian population, nor impede essential medical provisions or educational materials of any kind. The target must have a reasonable relationship to the threat of or actual breach of peace and international security.
   (iv) *Are the sanctions reasonably time-limited?* Legal sanctions may become illegal when they have been applied for too long without meaningful results. Sanctions that continue for too long can have a negative effect long after the wrongdoing ceases.

5 **They should be effective**: sanctions must be reasonably capable of achieving the desired result in terms of threat or actual breach of international peace and security. Sanctions that are targeted in ways that would not affect the wrongdoing, may be viewed as ineffective. Poorly enforced sanctions can result in continuing and escalating abuses of human rights, as exemplified in the case of Libya (Sautter 2020).
6 **They should not violate the 'principles of humanity and the dictates of the public conscience'**: while this final test may appear ambiguous or subjective, it relates to codified IL such as the Martens Clause (eighth preambular paragraph, re-stated in the Geneva Conventions of 1949, arts. 63-68, 142 and 158 and Additional Protocol I thereto, art.1, para. 2) mandates that all situations arising from war be governed by principles of law of civilized nations, principles of humanity and the dictates of the public conscience. The Hague Regulations further provide: 'No general penalty, pecuniary or otherwise, shall be inflicted upon the population on account of the acts of individuals for which they cannot be regarded as jointly and severally responsible' (art. 50).

To meet these criteria, the impact of sanctions on the enjoyment of human rights by the affected populations should be regularly evaluated from the perspective of all parties' ETOs. That exercise, related to one above, would clarify whether or not the desired results are being attained within a reasonable time period. If not, the measures should be revised or suspended. Otherwise, the sanctions may not only lose their presumed legitimacy, but may also become counterproductive. Added to these criteria are the other applicable public international law regimes, not least of which are international criminal law and IHL, with its necessity and proportionality requirements.

Conclusion

While the law of international responsibility constitutes an element of law and order and a foundation of international legality, it is difficult to imagine the existence of IL without the rules of responsibility (Doussis and Economides 2007, pp. 19–20). Both the strength of the theory of ETOs and the dearth of jurisprudence rather should form incentives for further inquiry and litigation.

Moreover, the inquiry into ETOs as they apply to the practice of economic sanctions opens several possibilities to expand the understanding and application of ETOs more generally. Examples from this review indicates not only the relevance of ETOs to the indivisibility of all human rights, including civil and political rights that may be eroded with the accompanying hazards and unintended consequences of sanctions. The further development of ETOs in the context of economic sanctions also arises from their application in relation to other IL regimes, especially trade and investment, peremptory norms and *jus cogens*, as well as IHL (e.g., prohibition against collective punishment and enabling the fulfilment of core IHL obligations), with consequences also for refugee law provisions for protection and assistance for those affected.

The evolving practice of economic sanctions calls for more legal research, monitoring, evaluation and analysis of ETOs shared among international organizations, implementing agencies, regional bodies, all states and their constituent organs. That inquiry extends also commonly, but differentially to Special Procedures, business enterprises, nongovernmental institutions, National Human Rights Institutions and civil society organizations. Each is potentially concerned with the way that economic sanctions are applied.

The purpose of critically reviewing the practice of economic sanctions is not to give aid or comfort to violators, nor is it to undermine the legitimate interests of the international community in enforcing IL in pursuit of conflict resolution, democratization, nonproliferation, counterterrorism, bringing an end to an illegal situation or upholding human rights, including the protection of civilians. The higher purpose is to insist upon and contribute to ensuring that lawlessness of one kind not give way to lawlessness of another. Rather, their task is to be guardians of respect for, protection and fulfilment of human rights that any collective or unilateral action such as economic sanctions be sufficiently legitimate insofar as they remain consistent with participating states' ETOs.

Notes

1. This term, in English usage, refers to military supplies only.
2. The Court ruled that the US lift sanctions on 'the importation and purchase of goods required for humanitarian needs, such as (i) medicines and medical devices; and (ii) foodstuffs and agricultural commodities; as well as goods and services required for the safety of civil aviation, such as (iii) spare parts, equipment and associated services (including warranty, maintenance, repair services and safety-related inspections) necessary for civil aircraft, such as (iii) spare parts, equipment and associated services (including warranty, maintenance, repair services and safety-related inspections) necessary for civil aircraft' paras. 70, 90 and 98; and 'The Court further considers that restrictions on the importation and purchase of goods required for humanitarian needs, such as foodstuffs and medicines, including

life- saving medicines, treatment for chronic disease or preventive care, and medical equipment may have a serious detrimental impact on the health and lives of individuals on the territory of Iran'. para. 91. 'The Court considers that the United States, in accordance with its obligations under the 1955 Treaty, must remove, by means of its choosing, any impediments arising from the measures announced on 8 May 2018 to the free exportation to the territory of Iran of goods required for humanitarian needs…' para. 98. Alleged Violations of the 1955 Treaty of Amity, Economic Relations, and Consular Rights (*Islamic Republic of Iran v. United States of America*), Request for the Indication of Provisional Measures, Order of 3 October 2018, available at: https://www.icj-cij.org/files/case-related/175/175-20181003-ORD-01-00-EN.pdf.

References

Bartels, L. (2014) 'The EU's Human Rights Obligations in Relation to Policies with Extraterritorial Effects', *European Journal of International Law* 25.

Beaucillon, C. (2016) 'Practice Makes Perfect, Eventually? Unilateral State Sanctions and the Extraterritorial Effects of National Legislation' in Ronzitti, N. (ed). *Coercive Diplomacy, Sanctions and International Law*, Brill/Nijhoff.

Beaulieu, C. (2008) *Extraterritorial Laws: Why They Are Not Really Working and How They Can Be Strengthened*, ECPAT International.

Borger, J. (2020) 'US ignores calls to suspend Venezuela and Iran sanctions amid coronavirus pandemic', *The Guardian*, 31 March 2020, available at: https://www.theguardian.com/world/2020/mar/31/us-ignores-global-appeals-suspend-sanctions-coronavirus-pandemic-iran-venezuela [accessed 29 November 2020].

Calderon, M. (2020) 'U.S. sanctions deadly in Iran, Venezuela', Committee on U.S.-Latin American Relations (CUSLAR)', 13 May 2020, available at: https://cuslar.org/2020/05/13/u-s-sanctions-deadly-in-iran-venezuela/ [accessed 29 November 2020].

Congress of the United States (CotUS) (2020) 'Letter to The Honorable Michael Pompeo and The Honorable Steven Mnuchin', 31 March 2020, available at: https://huffman.house.gov/imo/media/doc/Iran%20Sanctions%20Relief%20Letter_Final.pdf [accessed 29 November 2020].

Coomans, F. (2011) 'The Extraterritorial Scope of the International Covenant on Economic, Social and Cultural Rights in the Work of the United Nations Committee on Economic, Social and Cultural Rights', *Human Rights Law Review* 11.

Cosnard, M. (1995) 'Les lois Helms-Burton et d'Amato-Kennedy, interdiction de commercer avec et d'investir dans certains pays', *Annuaire français de droit international* 42.

Crawford, J., Pellet, A. and Olleson, S. (eds). (2010) *The Law of International Responsibility*, Oxford University Press.

Dawidowicz, M. (2010) 'The Obligation of Non-recognition of an Unlawful Situation' in Crawford, J., Pellet, A. and Olleson, S. (eds). *The Law of International Responsibility*, Oxford University Press.

De Schutter, O. (2008) 'A human rights approach to trade and investment policies', available at www.iatp.org/sites/default/files/451_2_104504.pdf [accessed 29 November 2020].

De Schutter, O. et al. (2012) 'Commentary to the *Maastricht Principles* on Extraterritorial Obligations of States in the Area of Economic, Social and Cultural Rights', *Human Rights Quarterly* 34.

De Zayas, A.M. (2018) 'Report of the Independent Expert on the promotion of a democratic and equitable international order on his mission to the Bolivarian Republic of Venezuela and Ecuador', A/HRC/39/47/Add.1, available at: https://undocs.org/A/HRC/39/47/ADD.1.

Doussis, E. and Economides, C. (2007) *State Responsibility for Internationally Wrongful Acts*, Sederis.

Emmenegger, S. (2016) 'Extraterritorial Economic Sanctions and Their Foundation in International Law', *Arizona Journal of International & Comparative Law* 33.

European Court of Human Rights (ECtHR) (2014) *Jaloud v. The Netherlands*, Application no. 47708/08, Judgment.

Gondek, M. (2009) *The Reach of Human Rights in a Globalising World: Extraterritorial Application of Human Rights Treaties*, Intersentia.

Inter-Agency Standing Committee Working Group (IASCWG) (2000) 'Background paper on economic sanctions and human rights', XLI Meeting, 18–19 May 2000, available at: https://interagencystandingcommittee.org/system/files/legacy_files/WG41_7.pdf [accessed 29 November 2020].

International Conference of Seville in Support of Palestinian Rights (2014) 'Organized by Fondo Andaluz de Municipios para la Solidaridad Internacional (FAMSI), United Cities and Local Government (UCLG) and the UN Committee on the Exercise of the Inalienable Rights of the Palestinian People (CEIRPP), "Olive Declaration"', 2–3 December 2014, available at: http://www.hlrn.org/img/documents/olivedeclaration.pdf [accessed 29 November 2020].

International Court of Justice (ICJ) (2004) 'Legal consequences of the construction of a wall in the occupied Palestinian territory', Advisory Opinion, available at: https://www.icj-cij.org/en/case/131/advisory-opinions [accessed 29 November 2020].

Jazairy, I. (2017) 'Report of the Special Rapporteur on the negative impact of unilateral coercive measures on the enjoyment of human rights', A/HRC/36/44, available at: https://undocs.org/en/A/HRC/36/44 [accessed 29 November 2020].

Jennings, R. and Watts, A. (eds). (2008) *Oppenheim's International Law* (9th Ed.), Oxford University Press.

Kohen, M. (2011) 'La contribución de América Latina al desarrollo progresivo del Derecho Internacional en materia territorial', *Anuario de derecho internacional* XVII, 57–78, available at: http://dadun.unav.edu/bitstream/10171/22094/1/ADI_XVII_2001_04.pdf [accessed 29 November 2020].

Lamrani, S. (2013) *The Economic War against Cuba: A Historical and Legal Perspective on the U.S. Blockade*, Monthly Review Press.

Local Authorities Forum (LAF) (2012) 'Free Palestine Statement', Canoas RS, Brazil, 27 November 2012, article 6, available at: http://www.hlrn.org/img/documents/final%20statement%20LAF.pdf [accessed 29 November 2020].

Meng, W. (1982) 'Stimson Doctrine' in Bernhardt, R. (ed). *Encyclopedia of Public International Law* (IV).

Milano, E. (2009) 'The doctrine(s) of non-recognition: theoretical underpinnings and policy implications in dealing with *de facto* regimes', conference paper, 2nd ESIL Research Forum, 'The Power of International Law in Times of European Integration', available at: https://esil-sedi.eu/wp-content/uploads/2018/04/Agora-3-Milano.pdf [accessed 29 November 2020].

Milanovic, M. (2011) *Extraterritorial Application of Human Rights Treaties*, Oxford University Press.

Minear, L, Cortright, D., Wagler, J., Lopez, G.A. and Weiss, T.G. (1998) 'Toward More Humane and Effective Sanctions Management: Enhancing the Capacity of the United Nations System', *Occasional Paper #31*, The Thomas J. Watson Jr. Institute for International Studies Brown University, available at: https://sanctionsandsecurity.nd.edu/assets/110294/toward_more_humane_.pdf [accessed 29 November 2020].

Rathbone, M., Jeydel, P. and Lentz, A. (2013) 'Sanctions, Sanctions Everywhere: Forging a Path through Complex Transnational Sanctions Laws', *Georgetown Journal of International Law* 44, 1055–1126.

Sachs, J. and Weisbrot, M. (2019) 'Economic sanctions as collective punishment: The case of Venezuela', Center for Economic and Policy Research, available at: https://cepr.net/images/stories/reports/venezuela-sanctions-2019-04.pdf [accessed 29 November 2020].

Sautter, G. (2020) '(Libya Sanctions Committee Chair, Germany) on the situation in Libya -Security Council Media Stakeout', available at: https://media.un.org/en/asset/k14/k14f1yr05t [accessed 29 November 2020].

Schechla, J. (2015) 'Extraterritorial human rights obligations of local government', *Local Authorities in support of Palestinian rights*, available at: https://www.stopthewall.org/local-authorities-support-palestinian-rights [accessed 29 November 2020].

Sepulveda, M. and Courtis, C. (2009) 'Are Extra-territorial Obligations Reviewable under the Optional Protocol to the ICESCR?', *Nordic Journal of Human Rights* 27.

Simons, M. and Cowell, A. (2018) 'UN court orders US to lift some Iran sanctions', *SFGATE*/Hearst Newspapers, 3 October 2018, available at: https://www.sfgate.com/news/article/UN-court-orders-US-to-lift-some-Iran-sanctions-13279399.php [accessed 29 November 2020].

Swiss Federal Office for Foreign Economic Affairs (SFOFEA) (1998) 'Interlaken Expert Seminars I and II on Targeting United Nations Financial Sanctions', 17–19 March 1998, available at: https://www.seco.admin.ch/dam/seco/de/dokumente/Aussenwirtschaft/Wirtschaftsbeziehungen/Exportkontrollen/Sanktionen/Smart%20Sanctions%20%E2%80%93%20Gezielte%20Sanktionen/Report%20on%20the%20Expert%20Seminar%20on%20Targeting%20UN%20Financial%20Sanctions,%2017.%20-%2019.03.1998%20(Interlaken).pdf.download.pdf/Report%20on%20the%20Expert%20Seminar%20on%20Targeting%20UN%20Financial%20Sanctions,%2017.%20-%2019.03.1998%20(Interlaken).pdf and 29–31 March 1999, available at: https://www.seco.admin.ch/dam/seco/de/dokumente/Aussenwirtschaft/Wirtschaftsbeziehungen/Exportkontrollen/Sanktionen/Smart%20Sanctions%20%E2%80%93%20Gezielte%20Sanktionen/Report%20on%20the%202nd%20Interlaken%20Seminar%20on%20Targeting%20UN%20Financial%20Sanctions%2029-31%20March,%201999%20(Interlaken).pdf.download.pdf/Report%20on%20the%202nd%20Interlaken%20Seminar%20on%20Targeting%20UN%20Financial%20Sanctions%2029-31%20March,%201999%20(Interlaken).pdf [accessed 29 November 2020].

Talmon, S. (2005) 'The Duty Not to 'Recognize as Lawful' a Situation Created by the Illegal Use of Force or Other Serious Breaches of a Jus Cogens Obligation: An Obligation without Real Substance?' in Tomuschat, C. and Thouvenin, J. M. (eds). *The Fundamental Rules of the International Legal Order. Jus Cogens and Obligations Erga Omnes*, Martinus Nijhoff [accessed 29 November 2020].

United Nations Department of Political and Peacebuilding Affairs (UNDPPA) (2021) Subsidiary Organs of the United Nations Security Council, Fact Sheet, available at: https://www.un.org/securitycouncil/sites/www.un.org.securitycouncil/files/subsidiary_organs_factsheets.pdf [accessed 30 August 2021].

United Nations, International Law Commission (ILC) (2019). Report of the International Law Commission, Seventy-first session (29 April–7 June and 8 July–9 August 2019), A/74/10, avalable at: https://undocs.org/en/A/74/10 [accessed 29 November 2020].

United Nations Sub-Commission on the Promotion and Protection of Minorities (2000), 'The adverse consequences of economic sanctions on the enjoyment of human rights,' Working paper prepared by Mr. Marc Bossuyt, E/CN.4/Sub.2/2000/33, available at: https://undocs.org/E/CN.4/Sub.2/2000/33 [accessed 29 November 2020].

United States Institute of Peace (USIP) (2020) 'Senators urge Trump to ease Iran sanctions', *Iran Primer*, 27 March 2020, available at https://iranprimer.usip.org/blog/2020/mar/27/senators-urge-trump-admin-ease-iran-sanctions [accessed 29 November 2020].

Vennemann, N. (2006) 'Application of International Human Rights Conventions to Transboundary State Acts' in Bratspies, R.M. and Miller, R.A. (eds). *Transboundary Harm in International Law, Lessons from the Trail Smelter Arbitration*, Cambridge University Press.

von Sponeck, H.C. (2006) *A Different Kind of War: The UN Sanctions Regime in Iraq*, Berghahn Books.

Wintour, P. (2020). 'UK presses US to ease Iran sanctions to help fight coronavirus', *The Guardian*, 18 March 2020, available at: https://www.theguardian.com/world/2020/mar/18/uk-presses-us-to-ease-iran-sanctions-to-help-fight-coronavirus [accessed 29 November 2020].

Wong, E. and Sanger, D.E. (2018) 'U.S. withdraws from 1955 Treaty normalizing relations with Iran', *The New York Times*, 3 October 2018, available at: https://www.nytimes.com/2018/10/03/world/middleeast/us-withdraws-treaty-iran.html [accessed 29 November 2020].

Part V

Finance, investment and trade

19

Extraterritorial human rights obligations and international financial institutions

Stéphanie de Moerloose, Gamze Erdem Türkelli and Joshua Curtis

Introduction

International Financial Institutions (IFIs) are international institutions that provide public financing for development policies, projects, programmes or macroeconomic policy. IFIs comprise global and regional multilateral development banks (MDBs) such as the World Bank Group (WBG),[1] the European Investment Bank, the European Bank for Reconstruction and Development (EBRD), the African Development Bank (AfDB), the Asian Development Bank (ADB) and the Inter-American Development Bank (IADB). The development financing also includes so-called development finance institutions (DFIs) of developed states that work principally but not exclusively on a bilateral basis, where a state is either the sole or majority shareholder. In addition, macroeconomic policy institutions such as the International Monetary Fund (IMF) are considered to fall under the umbrella.

The various positive and negative effects on human rights resulting from the policies and practices of IFIs have been deliberated since the 1990s within academia, United Nations (UN) human rights mechanisms and beyond, most often in the context of economic, social and cultural rights and increasingly through the lens of extraterritorial human rights obligations. This debate has been enriched by human rights scholars' and practitioners' increasing engagement with global finance (Dowell-Jones and Kinley 2011; Nolan 2016), sovereign debt (Bohoslavsky and Letnar Cernic 2014; Bantekas and Lumina 2018), austerity policies (Krajewski 2014; Salomon 2015; Warwick 2018) and numerous other aspects of IFI conditionality and structural adjustment (Kentikelenis et al. 2016; Stubbs and Kentikelenis 2018). Of note, an initial legal-doctrinal focus on the relationship between IFIs and human rights has been productively complemented over time with the integration of broader, contextually driven political economy and governance perspectives (Salomon 2007; von Bogdandy et al. 2010; Evans 2011; De Schutter 2012; Augenstein 2014). This is especially welcome given the centrality of IFIs to the global economic order and its governance, which increasingly determines the prospects for human rights realisation in every state. The dominance of economic norms over human rights norms is a recurrent and key theme in this, now extensive, body of work, as is the manner in which international law is (ab)used to constrain the effectiveness and development of the latter set of norms in favour of enhanced protection, enforcement and incentivisation of the former set.

DOI: 10.4324/9781003090014-25

Conceptually, human rights obligations beyond borders (for the sake of brevity, Extraterritorial Obligations (ETOs)) related to IFIs may be defined along two main axes. The first axis is state obligations as members and owners (shareholders) of IFIs. The second axis centres on the human rights obligations of IFIs themselves. This chapter first takes stock of ETOs of states when they are members and shareholders of IFIs and then moves on to explore the human rights obligations of IFIs directly under international law. Subsequently, the chapter looks into the question of human rights accountability of IFIs, both internally and externally. Finally, the chapter draws general conclusions and takes a forward-looking perspective and assesses the normative development of ETOs related to IFIs under international law.

States as members and shareholders of IFIs

The basic principle that states retain the full range of their human rights obligations as members of international organisations (IOs), including IFIs, has been reiterated in various General Comments (GCs) of UN treaty bodies. The UN Committee on Economic, Social and Cultural Rights (CESCR) in its GC 3 on the nature of states parties' obligations notes that under international law 'international cooperation for development and thus, for the realization of economic, social and cultural [(ESC)] rights is an obligation of all states. It is particularly incumbent upon those states which are in a position to assist others in this regard' (1990b, para. 14). CESCR has underscored that states have obligations of international assistance and cooperation for the realisation of ESC rights, particularly with respect to development projects and debt relief (CESCR 1990a, para. 8; CESCR 1990b, para. 14). CESCR's statement on the COVID-19 pandemic and ESC rights underscores that states 'should … use their voting powers in [IFIs] to alleviate the financial burden of developing countries in combating the pandemic, with measures such as granting these countries different mechanisms of debt relief' (CESCR 2020, para. 21).

Substantive rights such as rights to health, to water, to work, to just and favourable working conditions and to social security should be 'taken into account' when states 'influence the lending policies, credit agreements and international measures' of IFIs, particularly referring to the WBG and the IMF (CESCR 2000, para. 39; 2002, para. 36; 2005, para. 30; 2008, para. 58; 2016, para. 71). Even more strongly, CESCR's GC 23 on the Right to Just and Favourable Working Conditions holds that states as members of IFIs 'should ensure that the policies and practices of international and regional financial institutions, in particular those concerning structural and/or fiscal adjustment, promote and do not interfere with the right' (2016, para. 71). CESCR's concluding observations have also called on developed countries to ensure that the actions of IFIs of which they are members and shareholders do conform to ESC rights obligations (Khalfan 2017). State duties to uphold ESC rights also hold when the IFIs of which they are members are architects of structural adjustment and austerity policies to be implemented in third states (CESCR 2002, para. 36). Similarly, Principle 15 of the *Maastricht Principles* on Extra-Territorial Obligations of States (The *Maastricht Principles*) underscores that states remain 'responsible for [their] own conduct in relation to [their] human rights obligations within [their] territory and extra-territorially' as members of IOs. In line with CESCR's relevant GCs, when states 'transfer[.] competences to, or participate[.] in, an [IO]', they 'must take all reasonable steps to ensure that the relevant organisation acts consistently with' its human rights obligations. Similarly, Principle 10 of the UN Guiding Principles on Business and Human Rights (UNGPs) notes that member states of IFIs (and other multilateral institutions working on business-related areas) should '[s]eek to ensure that [they] neither restrain the ability of their member states to meet their duty to protect nor hinder business enterprises from respecting human rights; [and] [e]ncourage [them], within their respective mandates and capacities, to promote business respect for human rights and, where requested, to help States meet their duty to protect against human rights abuse by business enterprises, including through technical assistance, capacity-building and awareness-raising' (UN HRC 2011).

The relative weight of different state members in the decision-making structures of IFIs and thus their ability to 'ensure' the respect for, protection of and fulfilment of human rights obligations when they participate in IFIs or confer competences to them, differ wildly. Yet, the conceptual legal debates on the attribution and distribution of human rights obligations to states as members of IOs and IFIs have not distinguished between states or argued for differentiated obligations on the basis of how they impact decision-making processes within these institutions, including shareholding, voting and ownership structures. Comparable to the position of multinational companies that can exercise their leverage in their supply chains in order to incentivise the observance of human rights, certain member states of IFIs have the possibility – by virtue of their voting or economic power – to wield greater influence within these institutions and could deploy such influence to promote respect for and protection of human rights by IFIs.

Much of the work on state obligations with respect to human rights beyond borders when they participate in IFIs and the obligations of IFIs themselves has focused on conceptualising what Tan terms 'rights compliance – refraining from interfering directly or indirectly with the right in question or preventing third party interference with such a right' (Tan 2008, p. 84). The legal questions around attribution and distribution of duties and thus of responsibility for violations among states as members/shareholders of IFIs and IFIs themselves have thus taken place in the context of legal responsibility. That process has been particularly influenced by the International Law Commission's Articles on State Responsibility for Internationally Wrongful Acts (ARSIWA) and Articles on the Responsibility of International Organisations (ARIO). Accordingly, IOs as international legal persons, including IFIs, bear direct responsibility under international law for the breaches of their international legal obligations. Consequently, the legal responsibility of member states for the breaches resulting from IO acts or omissions is treated as the exception to this rule (Ryangaert and Buchanan 2011). There are, nonetheless, arguments suggesting that responsibility of IFIs and their member states may be jointly invoked depending on the specific mandate and relationship between the member state and the IFI in question (Sarooshi 2005). Joint responsibility may entail the responsibility of the IFI for its operations while member states may retain responsibility for their involvement in the decision-making processes leading to internationally wrongful acts. It stands to reason, thus, that greater the influence a state wields and the greater its contribution to an organisation's decision-making, the greater the responsibility it should incur as a result of any wrongdoing stemming from the organisation's operations based on those decisions. In addition, states members may be responsible for the acts of IFIs if the acts fall under the powers conferred to the IFI (Sarooshi 2005).

Human rights obligations and IFIs

There is a long-lasting discussion as to whether IFIs themselves are obligated or should be obligated to comply with human rights. The debate has seen two contradictory main arguments. The first supports the obligation of IFIs to comply with and implement human rights, and the second refutes this obligation, generally based on an argument around the protection of the recipient state's sovereignty. According to the first argument, IFIs should comply with hard international law, which is legally binding for recipient states and also applies to IFIs themselves as they are IOs (Bradlow 1996). Recalling the ICJ: 'international organizations are subjects of international law and, as such, are bound by any obligation incumbent upon them under general rules of international law' (ICJ 1980, p. 73 para. 37). As IOs, IFIs are therefore generally recognised as also bound by norms of customary international law (Bradlow 2001; Dann 2013). A distinct case should be made of the WBG institutions, which, as specialised agencies of the United Nations, should be recognised as bound by human rights law as well (United Nations 1947; Dann 2013).

Some scholars have suggested that IFIs bear direct human rights duties under international law based on their mandates, constituent agreements and relevant international law principles (Van Genugten et al. 2003; De Schutter et al. 2012). According to Skogly (2003), IFIs bear direct obligations to respect human rights. In addition to obligations to respect, IFIs have an obligation to protect human rights in the domain of their activities and operations that is auxiliary to state obligations (Bradlow 1996). IFIs may also play a role in promoting the realisation of human rights in their member states when they finance projects and policy interventions (Bradlow 1996; McInerney-Lankford 2010). *Maastricht Principle* 16 notes that states' obligations as members and shareholders of IFIs do not prejudice the existence of IO obligations under 'general international law and international agreements to which they are parties'. This view is also supported by proponents of the human rights-based approach to development adopted by many development institutions (UN Practitioners' Portal on Human Rights Based Approaches to Programming). Also, as long as member states entrust IFIs with the power to create policies that respect hard and soft international law, the principle of specialty is respected (ICJ 1996, p. 226 para. 25; Dupuy and Kerbrat 2016). Echoing McBeth, IFIs should be assigned 'independent legal obligations' as they autonomously carry out various delegated functions without these functions being 'the direct result of collective State action' (McBeth 2009, p. 67).

The second argument is a direct rebuttal of the positions exposed above, as it questions the legitimacy of the implementation of human rights by IFIs, principally because it forces the recipient state to take certain measures in exchange for financing, often through the insertion of conditionality. This position has often been shared by recipient states' government and by IFIs' senior staff. This argument rests on the principle of the sovereign equality of states recognised in Article 2 of the UN Charter and in several international UN declarations, which prohibits intervention in foreign states' political affairs (Res. 2131 (XX) 1965; Res. 2625 (XXV) 1970; Res. 36/103 1981; Dann 2013; Woods 2001; Babb and Carruthers 2008). The Charters of most MDBs share this principle, prohibiting intervention in the recipient states' political affairs, through the so-called political prohibition (Killinger 2003; Shihata 1988–1989 and 1992; Naudé Fourie 2009; McInerney-Lankford 2010). This very principle supports a number of movements calling for, *inter alia*, the eradication of conditionality and the restructuring of IFI governance (CNN 2010; Woods 2006).

Contradicting this argument, some proponents of the recognition of direct human rights obligations by IFIs have called for a restriction of the use of the principle of sovereignty, especially when it is claimed in order to shield recipient governments from their international human rights obligations (Henkin 1999). Furthermore, sovereignty also gives the donor states the right to choose how to manage their own resources. In that sense, donor states may demand resources to be used in compliance with human rights (Dann 2013; Mosley et al. 1995). There is thus an obligation to respect the sovereignty of both parties, which can possibly be in conflict. In any case, the respect of a recipient state's sovereignty in a domain underpinned by power asymmetries is a particularly important but delicate exercise (Anghie 2000; Pahuja 2011; Escobar 1995). Indeed, recipient states are generally minority voters and IFIs are often effectively dominated by donor states. The discontent among emerging economic powers with this situation has led to the creation of the New Development Bank in 2014 and the Asian Infrastructure Investment Bank in 2015, which are controlled by these emerging economies (Dann and Dollmaier 2021), but these actors are also governed by similar structures, including political prohibitions in their constitutive legal documents. Finally, in addition to sovereignty, it is important to also take into account the recipient state's context for the implementation of human rights obligations within IFI activities. Although they may themselves be bound by human rights obligations and treaties, such implementation may be rendered problematic by different circumstances such as internal conflicts of interests, insuperable economic barriers, corrupt political power structures, conflicts or cultural dynamics, such as informal alternatives to formal institutions (Channell 2006, pp. 138–139).

Over the last three decades, CESCR has been addressing IFIs directly with respect to their substantive human rights obligations in its GCs under the rubric of the obligations of 'actors other than states parties' or 'non-state actors'. At a very basic level, CESCR's GCs 14, 18 and 23 note that 'the World Bank, regional development banks, the International Monetary Fund' should 'cooperate effectively with States parties in the implementation of [the rights to health, to work and to just and favourable conditions of work]' (CESCR 2002, para. 64; 2005, para. 53; 2016, para. 76). The CESCR underscores that IFIs, in particular the WBG and the IMF, should take into account and/or 'pay greater attention to the protection of' the rights to health, to water and to work in lending policies, credit and other agreements as well as structural adjustment programmes (ibid). Cognisant of the negative impact that structural adjustment programmes have in terms of the loss of public employment, the CESCR (2005) notes more strongly that 'particular efforts should be made to ensure that the right to work is protected in all structural adjustment programmes' (para. 53). In addition, the 'enjoyment of the right to social security, particularly by disadvantaged and marginalized individuals and groups, [should be] promoted and not compromised' in the work of IFIs (CESCR 2008, para. 83).

The UN Committee on the Rights of the Child (CRC Committee) (2013) also notes that '[IOs] should have standards and procedures to assess the risk of harm to children in conjunction with new projects and to take measures to mitigate risks of such harm' and 'put in place procedures and mechanisms to identify, address and remedy violations of children's rights in accordance with existing international standards, including when they are committed by or result from activities of businesses linked to or funded by them' (para. 48).

Most recently, the Guiding principles on human rights impacts assessments of economic policy reforms has underscored that IFIs 'should not exert undue external influence … so that [states] are able to take steps to design and implement economic programmes by using their policy space in accordance with their human rights obligations' (Principle 14, footnote omitted) and 'should ensure that the terms of their transactions and their proposals for reform policies and conditionalities for financial support do not undermine the borrower/recipient State's ability to respect, protect and fulfil its human rights obligations' (Bohoslavsky 2020, pp. 1416–1417).

Accountability

Internal accountability

Generally, IFIs do not consider their activities to be directly bound by international human rights law, as explained above (Killinger 2003). However, pressure from states and NGOs has pushed IFIs to self-regulate their activities regarding human rights and sustainable development obligations (Park 2005; Houghton 2019). This has been done through conditionality, both regarding the selection of the project and then regarding its implementation. Generally, IFIs have no implementation mandate: the recipient state carries out the project and reports to the IFIs, which may provide support and shall supervise the project's implementation. Thus, the conditionality, enclosed in the contractual documents, defines what the recipient state needs to do or abstain from doing, in order to obtain the scheduled disbursements. This type of conditionality generally originates from the IFIs' environmental and social safeguards, the substantive instruments that integrate some human rights and other sustainable development-related concerns in IFIs, especially in MDBs. They describe the recipient state's obligations regarding environmental and social matters and can be stricter than national laws.

The safeguards vary in each IFIs, but some topics are commonly covered throughout the MDBs. Each has provisions on at least certain aspects of biodiversity and natural resources; pollution; community health, safety and security; occupational health and safety; climate change; cultural resources and heritage; indigenous peoples; land acquisition, resettlement or gender (Himberg 2015; Mbengue and de Moerloose 2017). However, these topics are dealt with differently, which marks a disparity between MDBs on the extent to which they adhere to human rights standards. For instance, the United Nations adopted the Convention on The Rights of Persons with Disabilities in 2006. However, how disability is taken into account varies amongst MDBs: the WB does include disability, the IFC expressly mentions 'physical or mental disability' to determine an individual's vulnerability, the AfDB specifically includes the 'physically handicapped' as vulnerable, while the ADB safeguards do not include disability (IFC 2012, Performance Standard 1 n18; World Bank 2017, i.a. ESS 10, para. 20; AfDB Group 2013, Operational Safeguard 1). Another example is the MDBs' list of prohibited activities. Only the AfDB prohibits investments in precious stones, pearls and gold, only the IADB bans non-compliance with workers' rights at work, only the EBRD's list does not include child labour, while the WB has no exclusion list (AfDB Group 2013, Policy Statement n5, p. 18; IADB Exclusion list; EBRD 2008). Of course, the safeguards apply in a project together with the recipient state's normative framework. By using local courts, affected populations can demand their rights be respected as recognised in the recipient state, but the courts generally cannot take the safeguards into account. It is important to note that there seems to be a process of harmonisation of safeguards across IFIs, often on the basis of the IFC's safeguards, the IFC Performance Standards (de Moerloose 2020). IFC's Performance Standards and Exclusion List are equally influential in the realm of bilateral development financing for the private sector through DFIs that are often majority or wholly owned by donor states as seen in the example of the Harmonized Environmental and Social Standards and Exclusion List of European Development Finance Institutions (EDFI) (EDFI 2020). Likewise, the Equator Principles, a framework for the management of environmental and social risks adopted by 113 financial institutions, such as BNP Paribas or JPMorgan Chase & Co., in 37 countries to date, incorporate the IFC Performance Standards (Equator Principles 2020). The latter are therefore very influential, as, in addition to being a basis on which other IFIs harmonise, they are shared by financial institutions worldwide.

The procedural instruments for the integration of certain human rights and sustainable development concerns are the internal accountability mechanisms (IAM). Indeed, the implementation of the environmental and social safeguard can be reviewed by these IAMs, mostly in MDBs (Mbengue and de Moerloose 2018). In 1993, the WB became the first MDB to create an IAM, the Inspection Panel. All the other MDBs followed over the next years. IAMs have diverse proceedings and competences, and operate with different sets of environmental and social safeguards. However, broadly, they function in similar ways. Taking the WB as an example, after receiving a request by a party affected by a project, the Inspection Panel can review the compliance of the WB with its environmental and social safeguards with respect to the design, appraisal, implementation or supervision of a project (Bridgeman and Hunter 2008; Brunori 2019). A report may then be issued by the Inspection Panel. It is important to note that, generally, IAMs only statute on the noncompliance with the safeguards by the MDB and not by the recipient state. Furthermore, they cannot determine the consequence of a violation of the safeguards and have to transmit their findings to the Banks' respective authorities for their final decision. They have been qualified as 'quasi-judicial mechanism', as their competence and effectiveness for the redress of affected people's harm is limited (Tignino 2016).

External Accountability

External accountability of IFIs and their member states to human rights duty-bearers has been difficult to achieve. Yet, as Tan notes, focusing on internal accountability of IFIs without ensuring external accountability has the risk of reinforcing global power imbalances, by entrenching 'the normative authority of these institutions over countries in the Global South' but not delivering justice to rights-holder who find their rights violated (Tan 2019).

Accountability for ETOs in the context of IFIs may concern the activities and decisions of states as IFI members and shareholders. Khalfan (2017) argues that representatives voting on behalf of a single state or multiple states in IFIs would be 'responsible' (as in the ordinary sense of having responsibilities) to these states for their votes. Similarly, Barros (2019) finds that states as members of IFIs may and do maintain legislative supervision of their involvement in IFIs and what that involvement means in terms of their human rights obligations but that such supervisory practice is not exercised by all member states. Answerability to legislative or executive bodies of a state on behalf of which a representative is acting is not, as Alvarez underscores, the same as 'these institutions (or their executive boards or distinct major contributors to their respective budgets) [being] accountable to the poor or indigenous peoples affected by … infrastructure projects or the macroeconomic conditions imposed under … structural adjustment loans' (2016, p. 15). Additionally, external accountability also falls apart in the context of accountability of IFI member states (with strong decision-making power and influence) to rights-holders in third states. It is argued, for instance, based on ARIO, that votes cast by State representatives for or against individual policies or programmes cannot give rise to legal responsibility (Crawford 2014).

The central aspect of external accountability is direct accountability of IFIs to rights-holders. Yet, the 'broad (and often unlimited) immunities' that IFIs, in particular MDBs have enjoyed at the domestic level, 'have shielded the institutions from the reach of external accountability mechanisms' (Erdem Türkelli 2020, p. 258). The latest developments in the field with respect to direct external accountability of IFIs reflect the ongoing struggle to clarify the parameters of such accountability and the transformation of the law with respect to limiting IFI immunity. In 2015, a group of fishing communities and farmers from India sued the IFC in the United States District Court for the District of Columbia. The petitioners live near a coal-fired power plant, constructed with a $450 million loan from the IFC to an Indian company. According to the complaint, the plant had polluted the air, landand water, destroyed the communities' livelihood and affected their health. The District Court held that the IFC enjoyed absolute immunity from suit. However, in Jam v. the IFC, the Supreme Court of the United States (SCOTUS) then held that IFC, as an IO, did not have absolute immunity from suit under US law given that some of its activities were commercial (SCOTUS 2019). The former Independent Expert on Debt and Human Rights also noted in his 2019 report that IFIs may be attributed legal responsibility for violations of human rights on the basis of complicity for imposing retrogressive economic measures, particularly in the context of austerity. The report underscores: 'There can be no legal justification for international financial institutions not to facilitate civil and political rights violations and to remain complicit in the imposition of economic, social and cultural rights violations' (UNGA 2019, para. 86). Still, on remand, the District Court upheld the immunity of IFC, deeming its nexus to the United States insufficient (Dias 2020).

Conclusions and future directions

The gaps in human rights protection and accountability to rights-holders in the context of IFI macroeconomic or development policies or programmes and investment projects supported by IFIs require strengthening human rights beyond borders, both of states as members of IFIs and of IFIs as entities in their own right.

The differences between IFI member states in terms of their capabilities to influence the decision-making processes within IFIs of course arise from the differences in financial contributions and ownership. In addition, because any member state responsibility for IFI acts and omissions is viewed as exceptional, even major shareholding states with outsized influence within an institution are, as international law currently stands, not legally responsible for human rights violations resulting from IFI acts or omissions. The same states are also the home states of business enterprises that operate in host recipient countries backed by development financing that de-risks their investments. Power structures in the global economy determine to what extent and how states are able to impact the enjoyment of human rights, whether that is through IFI membership or through housing major multinational companies. Many recipient states where rights-holders impacted by IFI projects, programmes and policies are located are disadvantaged both in terms of how they are situated in the global economy generally and their positioning within IFIs. As the UN Secretary General António Guterres pointed out during his 2020 Mandela lecture, former colonised states, particularly in Africa, experience double exclusion as they are 'at greater risk of getting locked into the production of raw materials and low-tech goods' and are disadvantaged in terms of voting power and representation on the boards of international organisations, including Bretton Woods institutions (McVeigh 2020). Going forward, there is a need to address structural power dynamics underlying the global economy. This may mean that States' human rights obligations when they are members or 'owners' of IFIs need to be conceptualised as obligations shared by all states but differentiated by the measure of power accorded to each of those states in the globalised market economy as well as the historical underpinnings of these power structures. This may also demand for a reform of voting power in the IFIs, to remedy the power asymmetries.

'[IFI] decisions and performance are still often only measured against their own self-regulatory norms, which fall short of providing comprehensive rights protections to persons affected by such decisions and performance' (Erdem Türkelli 2020, p. 259). There are several policy measures that could provide for a better protection of human rights within IFI work. First, problems of noncompliance are often linked to the institutional organisation of the IFIs, particularly MDBs. In the case of the WB, the contradictory incentives for the staff include an accent on economic results versus compliance with environmental and social safeguards. The issues of noncompliance resulting from such organisational structures and incentives can only be reversed by institutional measures, which would demand that the Bank favours social and environmental sustainability and the respect of human rights above the pressures to commit and disburse funds. Secondly, it is important to also take into account the recipient state's context for the protection of rights within IFI activities: if the internal circumstances are not suitable for the protection of human rights, an investment project should be modified, postponed or dropped. Thirdly, problems of noncompliance are also linked to the fragmentation of environmental and social safeguards amongst IFIs. Safeguards are not yet harmonised despite a trend towards convergence. There are also clear difficulties for recipient states to implement conditionalities with which they are not familiar. Therefore, safeguards should be harmonised across IFIs and aligned with human rights in order to provide both legitimacy and a predictable framework (de Moerloose 2020, pp. 203–210). Fourthly, external accountability of IFIs and their more powerful member states to rights-holders, particularly in third states, should be strengthened by balancing the scales through enhanced due diligence obligations incumbent on these actors. The Guiding principles on human rights impacts assessments of economic policy reforms proposed by the former UN Independent Expert on Debt and Human Rights rightly places the 'burden of proof' on creditors (both states and IFIs) to 'demonstrate that their proposed economic reform measures will realize, and not undermine, States' human rights obligations'. According to the Guiding Principles, IFIs have 'a duty to carry out human rights impact assessments to evaluate and address any foreseeable effects of their economic policies on human rights' to be undertaken in consultation with rights-holders and made public 'in adequate formats' (Principle 13) (Bohoslavsky 2020, p. 1405).

The question of the immunity of IFIs also requires urgent reform to enable respect for and protection of human rights standards. Indeed, the terrible consequences for local population in the Jam v. IFC case cited above are hardly unique. Reading the findings of the IAMs suffices to show the detrimental impact that IFIs investments can have on local populations (Jokubauskaite 2018). Limiting the immunities of IFIs to allow for external oversight of their activities is a relevant response to the lack of accountability to rights-holders that characterises their operational landscape (Erdem Türkelli 2020). Because courts seem unwilling or unable to move past the immunity, the IFIs should modify their charters to restrict their immunity in case of human rights violations, or at least in case of violation of their own safeguards that amount to human rights violations. This is, in fine, the responsibility of Members states and would be a clear signal from IFIs that they are willing to 'do no harm' and also change internal incentives. A coherent and legally solid structural change would consist in both harmonising the safeguards by aligning them with human rights as well as limiting their immunity. Furthermore, the application of external accountability to all IFIs together with a human rights-based harmonisation would alleviate fears that more rigid safeguards adopted by a given IFI would allow another less rigorous IFI to attract clients and lead to an even more harmful outcome in terms of human rights (Erdem Türkelli 2020). Finally, when IFIs interact with rights-holders, their activities and policies are intertwined with multiple layers of other private actors such as financial intermediaries and business enterprises and conducted through private law arrangements (CESCR 2017; Bhatt 2020; Erdem Türkelli 2020). Without an adequate human rights legal regime that assigns human rights duties (beyond borders) to private actors in addition to states and IFIs, attempts at accountability of IFIs and their member states to rights-holders will always fall short of delivering their promise.

Note

1. Regarding the WBG, the chapter concentrates on three of its institutions: the International Bank for Reconstruction and Development, the International Development Association – both hereinafter collectively referred to as the World Bank or WB – and the International Finance Corporation (IFC).

References

African Development Bank Group (AfDB) (2013) Integrated Safeguards System, available at https://www.afdb.org/fileadmin/uploads/afdb/Documents/Policy-Documents/December_2013_-_AfDB'S_Integrated_Safeguards_System__-_Policy_Statement_and_Operational_Safeguards.pdf. (accessed 16 July 2021).

Alvarez, J.E. (2016) 'International Organizations and the Rule of Law', *New Zealand Journal of Public International Law* 14(1), 3–46.

Anghie, A. (2000) 'Time Present and Time Past', *New York University Journal of International Law and Politics* 32, 243–290.

Asian Development Bank (ADB) (2009) Safeguard Policy Statement, available at http://www.adb.org/sites/default/files/institutional-document/32056/safeguard-policy-statement-june2009.pdf (accessed 16 July 2021).

Augenstein, D. (2014) 'The Crisis of International Human Rights Law in the Global Market Economy', *Netherlands Yearbook of International Law* 44, 41.

Babb, S. and Carruthers, B. (2008) 'Conditionality: Forms, Function, and History', *Annual Review of Law and Social Science* 4, 13–29.

Bantekas, I. and Lumina, C. (eds.). (2018) *Sovereign Debt and Human Rights*, Oxford University Press.

Barros A.S. (2019) *Governance as Responsibility: Member States as Human Rights Protectors in International Financial Institutions*, Cambridge University Press.

Bhatt, K. (2020) *Concessionaires, Financiers and Communities: Implementing Indigenous Peoples' Rights to Land in Transnational Development Projects*, Cambridge University Press.

Bohoslavsky, J.P. (2020) 'Guiding Principles on Human Rights Impacts Assessments of Economic Policy Reforms', *The International Journal of Human Rights* 24(9), 1400–1428.

Bohoslavsky, J.P. and Letnar Cernic, J. (eds.). (2014) *Making Sovereign Financing and Human Rights Work*, Hart.

Bradlow, D.D. (1996) 'The World Bank, the IMF, and Human Rights', *Transnational Law and Contemporary Problems* 6(1), 47–90.

Bradlow, D.D. (2001) 'International Law and the Operations of International Financial Institutions' in Bradlow, D.D. and Hunter, D.B. (eds.). *International Financial Institutions and International Law*, Kluwer Law International.

Bridgeman, N.L. and Hunter, D.B. (2008) 'Narrowing the Accountability Gap: Toward a New Foreign Investor Accountability Mechanism', *Georgetown International Environmental Law Review* 20(2), 187–236.

Brunori, M. (2019) 'Protecting Access to Land for Indigenous and Non-Indigenous Communities: A New Page for the World Bank?', *Leiden Journal of International Law* 32(2), 1–16.

Channell, W. (2006) 'Lessons Not Learned about Legal Reform' in Carothers, T. (ed.). *Promoting the Rule of Law Abroad, in Search of Knowledge*, Carnegie Endowment for International Peace.

CNN (2010) 'BRIC leaders: IMF, World Bank has "legitimacy deficits"', 16 April 2010, http://edition.cnn.com/2010/BUSINESS/04/15/bric.summit.brazil/index.html. (accessed 16 July 2021).

Crawford, J. (2014) *State Responsibility*, Cambridge University Press.

Dann, P. (2013) *The Law of Development Cooperation, A Comparative Analysis of the World Bank, the EU and Germany*, Cambridge University Press.

Dann, P. and Dollmaier, T. (2021) 'Multilateral Development Banks' in De Feyter, K. et al. (eds.). *Encyclopedia of Law and Development*, Edward Elgar.

de Moerloose, S. (2020) *World Bank Environmental and Social Conditionality as a Vector of Sustainable Development*, Schulthess Verlag.

De Schutter, O. (2012) 'The Role of Human Rights in Shaping International Regulatory Regimes', *Social Research* 79(4), 785.

De Schutter, O. et al. (2012) 'Commentary to the *Maastricht Principles* on Extraterritorial Obligations of States in the Area of Economic, Social and Cultural Rights', *Human Rights Quarterly* 34(4), 1084–1169.

Dias, S. (2020) 'Jam v. IFC before the D.C. District Court: Forget the Floodgates, there won't even be a Trickle', EJIL: Talk! –Blog of the European Journal of International Law, 1 April 2020, https://www.ejiltalk.org/jam-v-ifc-before-the-d-c-district-court-forget-the-floodgates-there-wont-even-be-a-trickle/ [accessed 16 July 2021].

Dowell-Jones, M. and Kinley, D. (2011) 'Minding the Gap: Global Finance and Human Rights', *Ethics and International Affairs* 25(2), 183.

Dupuy, P.-M. and Kerbrat, Y. (2016) *Droit International Public*, 13th Ed., Dalloz.

Equator Principles, 'The Equator Principles', available at http://equator-principles.com/about (accessed 16 July 2021).

Erdem Türkelli, G. (2020) 'The Best of Both Worlds or the Worst of Both Worlds? Multilateral Development Banks, Immunities and Accountability to Rights-Holders', *Hague Journal on the Rule of Law* 12, 251–281.

Escobar, A. (1995) *Encountering Development, The Making and Unmaking of the Third World*, Princeton University Press.

European Bank for Reconstruction and Development (EBRD) (2008) 'Environmental and Social Exclusion List', available at http://www.ebrd.com/downloads/about/sustainability/Environmental_and_Social_Exclusion_and_Referral_Lists_15092008.pdf. (accessed 16 July 2021)

_______ (2014) 'Environmental and Social Policy', available at http://www.ebrd.com/downloads/research/policies/esp-final.pdf. (accessed 16 July 2021)

European Development Finance Institutions (2020) 'Policy', available at https://www.edfi.eu/policy/ (accessed 16 July 2021).

Evans, T. (2011) *Human Rights in the Global Political Economy: Critical Processes,* Lynne Rienner.

Henkin, L. (1999) 'That "S" Word: Sovereignty, And Globalization, And Human Rights, Et Cetera', *Fordham Law Review* 68, 1–14.

Himberg, H. (May 2015), 'Comparative Review of Multilateral Development Bank Safeguard Systems, Main Report and Annexes', available at https://consultations.worldbank.org/sites/default/files/consultation-template/review-and-update-world-bank-safeguard-policies/en/related/mdb_safeguard_comparison_main_report_and_annexes_may_2015.pdf. (accessed 16 July 2021)

Houghton, R. (2019) 'Looking at the World Bank's Safeguard Reform Through the Lens of Deliberative Democracy', *Leiden Journal of International Law* 32(2), 1–18.

Inter-American Development Bank (IADB) (n.d.) 'List of Excluded Activities for Non-Sovereign-Guaranteed (NSG) Operations', available at https://idbinvest.org/en/download/6392 (accessed 16 July 2021).

_______ (n.d.) 'Operational Policies', available at https://www.iadb.org/en/about-us/operational-policies.(accessed 16 July 2021)

International Finance Corporation (IFC) (2012) 'Performance Standards on Environmental and Social Sustainability', available at https://www.ifc.org/wps/wcm/connect/Topics_Ext_Content/IFC_External_Corporate_Site/Sustainability-At-IFC/Policies-Standards/Performance-Standards (accessed 16 July 2021).

International Court of Justice (ICJ) (1980) Interpretation of the Agreement of 25 March 1951 between the WHO and Egypt, Advisory Opinion.

_______ (1996) Legality of the Use by a State of Nuclear Weapon in Armed Conflict, Advisory Opinion.

Jokubauskaite, G. (2018) 'Tied affectedness? Grassroots resistance and the World Bank', *Third World Thematics: A TWQ Journal* 3(5–6), 703–724.

Kentikelenis, A. et al. (2016) 'IMF Conditionality and Development Policy Space, 1985-2014', *Review of International Political Economy* 23(4), 543.

Khalfan, A (2017) 'Development Cooperation and Extraterritorial Obligations' in Langford, M. and Russell, A. (eds). *The Human Right to Water: Theory, Practice and Prospects*, Cambridge University Press.

Killinger, S. (2003) *The World Bank's Non-Political Mandate*, Heymann.

Krajewski, M. (2014) 'Human Rights and Austerity Programmes' in Cottier. T. et al. (eds.). *The Rule of Law in Monetary Affairs: World Trade Forum*, Cambridge University Press.

Mbengue, M.M. and de Moerloose, S. (2017) 'Multilateral Development Banks and Sustainable Development: On Emulation, Fragmentation and a Common Law of Sustainable Development', *Law and Development Review* 10(2), 389–424.

_______ (2018) 'A Managerial Approach for the Coherent Development of Sustainable Development Law: The Kenya Electricity Expansion Project before the World Bank and the European Investment Bank's International Accountability Mechanisms', *Revista Jurídica Piélagus* 17(2), 83–99.

McBeth, A. (2009) *International Economic Actors and Human Rights*, Routledge.

McInerney-Lankford, S. (2010) 'International Financial Institutions and Human Rights: Select Perspectives on Legal Obligations' in Bradlow, D.D. and Hunter, D.B. (eds.). *International Financial Institutions and International Law*, Kluwer Law International.

McVeigh, K. (2020) 'UN chief slams 'myths, delusions and falsehoods' around inequality', *The Guardian*, 18 July 2020, https://www.theguardian.com/global-development/2020/jul/18/un-chief-slams-myths-delusions-and-falsehoods-around-inequality (accessed 14 December 2020).

Mosley, P. et al. (1995) *Aid and Power, the World Bank and Policy-based Lending, Volume 1, Analysis and policy proposals*, 2nd Ed., Routledge.

Naudé Fourie, A. (2009) *The World Bank Inspection Panel and Quasi-Judicial Oversight, in Search of the 'Judicial Spirit' in Public International Law*, Eleven International Publishing.

Nolan, A. (ed.). (2016) *Economic and Social Rights after the Global Financial Crisis*, Cambridge University Press.

Pahuja, S. (2011) *Decolonising International Law: Development, Economic Growth and the Politics of Universality*, Cambridge University Press.

Park, S. (2005), 'Norm Diffusion within International Organizations: A Case Study of the World Bank', *Journal of International Relations and Development* 8(2), 111–141.

Ryangaert, C. and Buchanan, H. (2011) 'Member State Responsibility for the Acts of International Organizations', *Utrecht Law Review* 7(1), 131–146.

Salomon, M. (2007) 'International Economic Governance and Human Rights Accountability' in Salomon, M. et al. (eds.). *Casting the Net Wider: Human Rights, Development and New Duty-Bearers*, Intersentia.

_______ (2015) 'Of Austerity, Human Rights and International institutions', *European Human Rights Journal* 21(4), 521.

Sarooshi, D. (2005) *International Organizations and their Exercise of Sovereign Powers*, Oxford University Press.

Shihata, I.F.I. (1988-1989) 'The World Bank and Human Rights: An Analysis of the Legal Issues and the Record of Achievements', *Denver Journal of International Law and Policy* 17(39), 39–66.

Shihata, I.F.I. (1992) 'Human Rights, Development, and International Financial Institutions', *American University International Law Review* (1), 27–36.

Skogly, S. I. (2003) *The Human Rights Obligations of the World Bank and the International Monetary Fund*, Cavendish Publishing.

Stubbs, T. and Kentikelenis, A. (2018) 'Conditionality and Debt Relief: An Overview' in Bantekas, I. and Lumina, C. (eds). *Sovereign Debt and Human Rights*, Oxford University Press.

Supreme Court of the United States (SCOTUS) (2019) *Budha Ismail Jam et al. v. International Finance Corp.*, 586 U.S.

Tan, C. (2008) "Mandating Rights and Limiting Mission Creep: Holding the World Bank and the International Monetary Fund Accountable for Human Rights Violations", *Human Rights and International Legal Discourse* 2(1), 79-116.

_______ (2019) 'Human Rights and the Bretton Woods Institutions: Moving Beyond Institutional Remedies' in Bretton Woods Project, *Bretton Woods at 75: a series of critical essays*, Bretton Woods Project.

Tignino, M. (2016) 'Quasi-Judicial Bodies' in Brolmann, C. and Radl, Y. (eds.). *Research Handbook on the Theory and Practice of International Lawmaking*, Edward Elgar.

United Nations General Assembly (UNGA) (1947) Agreement between the United Nations and the International Bank for Reconstruction and Development, 16 U.N.T.S 346.

_______ (1965) "Declaration on the Inadmissibility of Intervention in the Domestic Affairs of States and the Protection of Their Independence and Sovereignty" United Nations, Res. 2131 (XX), U.N. Doc. A/RES/2131.

_______ (1970) *Declaration on Principles of International Law concerning Friendly Relations and Co-operation among States in accordance with the Charter of the United Nations*, Res. 2625 (XXV), U.N. Doc. A/RES/2625.

_______ (1981) *Declaration on the Inadmissibility of Intervention and Interference in the Internal Affairs of States*, Res. 36/103, U.N. Doc. A/RES/36/103.

_______ (2019) Report of the Independent Expert on the effects of foreign debt and other related international financial obligations of States on the full enjoyment of all human rights, particularly economic, social and cultural rights: Responsibility for complicity of IFIs in human rights violations in the context of retrogressive economic reforms, A/74/178.

UN Committee on Economic, Social and Cultural Rights (CESCR) (1990a) GC 2 on International technical assistance measures (Art. 22 of the Covenant), E/1990/23.

_______ (1990b) GC 3 on the Nature of States Parties' Obligations (Art. 2, Para. 1, of the Covenant), E/1991/23.

_______ (2000) GC 14 on the right to the highest attainable standard of health, E/C.12/2000/4.

_______ (2002) GC 15 The Right to water, E/C.12/2002/11.

_______ (2005) GC 18 The Right to Work, E/C.12/GC/18.

_______ (2006) *Convention on The Rights of Persons with Disabilities*, UN Doc. A/RES/61/611.

_______ (2017) GC 24 on State obligations under the International Covenant on Economic, Social and Cultural Rights in the context of business activities, E/C.12/GC/24.

_______ (2020) Statement on the coronavirus disease (COVID-19) pandemic and economic, social and cultural rights, E/C.12/2020/1.

UN Committee on the Rights of the Child (CRC Committee) (2013) GC 16 on State obligations regarding the impact of the business sector on children's rights, CRC/C/GC/16.

UN Human Rights Council (2011) UN Guiding Principles on Business and Human Rights (UNGPs) Implementing the United Nations "Protect, Respect and Remedy" Framework.

United Nations (UN) (1945) Charter of the United Nations and Statute of the International Court of Justice (24 November 1945).

United Nations Practitioners' Portal on Human Rights Based Approaches to Programming (n.d.) 'HRBA Portal, The Human Rights Based Approach to Development Cooperation: Towards a Common Understanding Among UN Agencies', available at https://hrbaportal.undg.org. (accessed 16 July 2021)

van Genugten, W. et al. (2003) *World Bank, IMF and Human Rights*, Wolf Legal Publishers, 2003.

von Bogdandy, A. et al. (eds). (2010) *The Exercise of Public Authority by International Institutions: Advancing International Institutional Law*, Springer.

Warwick, B. (2018) 'Debt, Austerity and the Structural Responses of Social Rights' in Bantekas, I. and Lumina, C. (eds). *Sovereign Debt and Human Rights*, Oxford University Press.

Woods, N. (2001) 'Making the IMF and the World Bank more accountable', *International Affairs* 77(1), 83–100.

_______ (2006) *The Globalizers: The IMF, the World Bank, and Their Borrowers*, Cornell University Press.

World Bank (2017) 'Environmental and Social Framework', available at https://www.worldbank.org/en/projects-operations/environmental-and-social-framework

20

Home-state regulation of corporations

Daniel Augenstein

Introduction

Home-state regulation of corporations refers to legislation, adjudication, and other regulatory measures aimed at preventing and redressing business-related human rights violations in the host state of corporate investment (Zerk 2006, pp. 145–197). In the most common model, the home state imposes on corporate actors and activities within its territorial jurisdiction regulatory (due diligence) requirements that apply throughout the corporate group and the global supply/value chain. The business and human rights debate about home-state regulation centres on two interrelated issues: first, the extent to which international law imposes obligations on states to prevent and redress business-related human rights violations for the benefit of individuals located outside their territory (international extraterritorial obligations); and second, the extent to which states could and should use domestic law to regulate the extraterritorial human rights impacts of business enterprises (domestic regulation with extraterritorial effect).

The UN Guiding Principles on Business and Human Rights (UNGPs), endorsed by the Human Rights Council in 2011, encourage states to regulate business actors and activities with extraterritorial effect. Yet, they did not clearly recognise corresponding state obligations to prevent and redress business-related human rights violations outside their territory:

> At present states are not generally required under international human rights law to regulate the extraterritorial activities of business domiciled within their territory and/or jurisdiction. Nor are they generally prohibited from doing so, provided there is a recognised jurisdictional basis. Within these parameters, some human rights treaty bodies recommend that home state take steps to prevent abuse by business enterprises within their jurisdiction.
>
> *(HRC 2011, Principle 2)*

The chapter traces a gradual convergence between the regulatory models that underpin these different (international & domestic) domains of legal ordering one decade after the endorsement of the UNGPs. It is argued that the location of business actors and activities within the state's territorial jurisdiction not only justifies domestic regulation with extraterritorial effect but also grounds international obligations to prevent and redress extraterritorial corporate

DOI: 10.4324/9781003090014-26

human rights abuse. This convergence suggests the emergence of a new legal consensus on business and human rights, according to which states' regulation of the global human rights impacts of business enterprises are anchored in international legal obligations toward foreign victims of business-related human rights violations.

Section 2 discusses doctrinal developments in international law galvanised by the *Maastricht Principles* on Extraterritorial Obligations of States in the Area of Economic, Social, and Cultural Rights (*Maastricht Principles*) that link states' extraterritorial human rights obligations to authority, power, or control they may exercise over business actors and activities within their territorial jurisdiction. Section 3 discusses states' increasing use of domestic law to impose legal due diligence requirements on these business actors and activities that reach out into the global supply/value chain. While most existing examples of home-state regulation fall short of the requirements for extraterritorial human rights protection laid down in the *Maastricht Principles*, they are evidence of a growing recognition among states that corporate respect for human rights should be brought under the purview of (international) human rights law.

Home-state regulation in international law

International extraterritorial obligations: A restrictive approach

The extent to which states are permitted and/or required to regulate the human rights impacts of business enterprises for the benefit of individuals located outside their territory depends on the relationship between territory and jurisdiction in international law. Jurisdiction circumscribes the scale and scope of international human rights obligations by predicating them upon a sufficiently concrete normative relation of authority, power, or control between the state *qua* duty-bearer and the individual rights-holder (Besson 2012). At the most general level, two countervailing principles inform the relationship between jurisdiction and extraterritorial human rights obligations (den Heijer and Lawson 2013; Augenstein and Kinley 2013). On the one hand, a state's exercise of jurisdiction to protect human rights outside its borders should not unduly interfere with the sovereign rights that third states wield over their territory and people therein. This explains why the scope of extraterritorial human rights obligations is commonly delimited by states' jurisdictional competence, determined on the basis of a recognised basis of jurisdiction in public international law (the territoriality principle; the nationality principle; etc.). On the other hand, a state should not be permitted to circumvent its international human rights obligations by exceeding its jurisdictional competences in public international law. This explains why the decisive criterion for allocating human rights obligations to states is not the international lawfulness of the extraterritorial exercise of state powers but a jurisdictional relationship of authority, power, or control between the state and an individual located outside its borders (European Court of Human Rights (ECtHR) 2011; Inter-American Commission on Human Rights (IACHR) 1999).[1]

While the text of international human rights treaties does not suggest that states' human rights obligations should be confined to individuals within their borders, concerns with state sovereignty have nevertheless tended international courts towards a 'primarily territorial' interpretation of human rights jurisdiction (International Court of Justice (ICJ) 2004, para 109). In *Al Skeini* – one of the leading cases on the extraterritorial application of the European Convention – the European Court of Human Rights considered that 'jurisdiction is presumed to be exercised normally throughout the state's territory. Conversely, acts of the contracting states performed, or producing effects, outside their territories can constitute an exercise of jurisdiction within the meaning of Article 1 ECHR only in exceptional circumstances (ECtHR 2011, para 131). Similarly, the Inter-American Court of Human Rights noted in a more recent *Advisory Opinion on the Environment and Human Rights* that whereas jurisdiction was not confined to territory, the conditions under which extraterritorial state conduct qualifies as an exercise of jurisdiction within the meaning of Article 1 IACHR required a restrictive interpretation (IACtHR 2017, para 81).

The two constellations of extraterritorial jurisdiction recognised by the ECtHR in *Al Skeini* – acts 'performed' and 'producing effects' outside the state's territory – correspond to a more commonly used distinction between extraterritorial state conduct and the extraterritorial effects of states' domestic laws and policies. As traditionally framed in the case-law, neither constellation easily lends itself to establishing home-state obligations to prevent and redress business-related human rights violations for the benefit of individuals located outside its borders. Establishing extraterritorial jurisdiction through acts 'performed' outside the state's territory requires state agents to exercise authority, power, or control over persons and/or an area located on the territory of another state (ECtHR 2011, paras 134–138). Accordingly, traditional variations of the 'control over persons' test (such as the detention or abduction of individuals) and the 'control over an area' test (such as military occupation) are premised on the physical presence of home-state agents on foreign soil. In the standard case of home-state regulation, by contrast, the extraterritorial human rights violation is committed by a non-state actor operating in the host state of corporate investment.

The best-known examples of 'extraterritorial effects' cases concern the extradition or deportation of an individual to a country where she faces substantial risks of serious human rights violations (*non-refoulement*). The protection of *non-refoulement* extends to threats to human rights caused by private (non-state) actors abroad (ECtHR 2016). In *Rantsev,* the ECtHR furthermore recognised that states can be under an obligation to regulate private actors on their own territory in order to prevent and redress human rights violations committed outside their borders (ECtHR 2010). Nevertheless, both in *non-refoulement* cases and in the *Rantsev* scenario, the necessary jurisdictional link is established through the victim's initial presence on (home) state's territory. In the standard case of home-state regulation, by contrast, a constituent part of the parent – or controlling – company will be domiciled within the state's territorial jurisdiction while the victim is permanently located on the territory of the host state of corporate investment.

There is some case-law to suggest that the European Court of Human Rights is prepared to recognise extraterritorial human rights obligations absent effective control over a foreign person/area (ECtHR 2015) and to dispense with the requirement that the applicant in extraterritorial effects cases must be located on the state's territory (ECtHR 2012). Moreover, foreign victims seeking to vindicate their human rights through private litigation in the domestic courts of the home state can come under that state's international human rights jurisdiction (ECtHR 2006). However, this case-law has not yet translated into a robust and coherent approach to international extraterritorial obligations to prevent and redress business-related human rights violations.

With power comes responsibility

A guiding assumption behind the restrictive approach to international extraterritorial obligations is that perpetrators and victims of business-related human rights violations will reside in the same territorial space and will therefore be subject to the authority, power, or control of a single state. This state-sovereigntist approach not only belittles the 'governance gaps' created by, and the transnational human rights impacts of, global supply and value chains (HRC 2008), but it also fails to respond to a core concern in the business and human rights domain, namely human rights obligations of the home state of the parent – or controlling – company of 'multinational' corporations to prevent and redress human rights violations committed in the host state of corporate investment (Augenstein 2018).

The *Maastricht Principles* – a set of non-legally binding principles adopted by a group of human rights experts in 2011 – address this concern by supplementing international extraterritorial obligations with 'obligations relating to the acts and omissions of a state, within or beyond its territory, that have effects on the enjoyment of human rights outside that state's territory' (Principle 8a). This considerably broadens the scope of extraterritorial state obligations to prevent business-related human rights violations:

> All states must take necessary measures to ensure that non-state actors which they are in a position to regulate, as set out in Principle 25, such as private individuals and organisations, and transnational corporations and other business enterprises, do not nullify or impair the enjoyment of economic, social and cultural rights. These include administrative, legislative, investigative, adjudicatory and other measures.
>
> *(Principle 24)*

Pursuant to Principle 25, circumstances under which a home state is in a position to regulate corporate actors and activities abroad include 'where the corporation, or its parent or controlling company, has its centre of activity, is registered or domiciled, or has its main place of business or substantial business activities, in the state concerned'. International extraterritorial obligations also include obligations to redress business-related human rights violations across state borders by ensuring that foreign victims have 'a prompt, accessible and effective remedy before an independent authority, including, where necessary, recourse to a judicial authority' (Principle 37).

The *Maastricht Principles* find support in various 'transnational', 'functional', and 'diagonal' approaches to extraterritorial human rights protection discussed in the literature (Altwicker 2018; Shany 2013; Knox 2010; Skogly and Gibney 2002). They build upon, and are further corroborated by, the interpretation of international extraterritorial obligations endorsed by the UN Treaty Bodies. Alongside general comments on extraterritorial state obligations concerning business activities that impact on the right to water, the right to work, and the right to social security, the Committee on Economic, Social, and Cultural Rights (CESCR) published in 2011 a statement on human rights and the corporate sector in which it called upon states to 'take steps to prevent human rights contraventions abroad by corporations which have their main seat under their jurisdiction, without infringing the sovereignty or diminishing the obligations of the host states under the Covenant' (CESCR 2011, para 5).

In its 2017 General Comment on State Obligations under the International Covenant on Economic, Social, and Cultural Rights in the Context of Business Activities, CESCR considered that:

> Extraterritorial obligations arise when a state party may influence situations located outside its territory, consistent with the limits imposed by international law, by controlling the activities of corporations domiciled in its territory and/or jurisdiction, and thus may contribute to the effective enjoyment of economic, social and cultural rights outside its national territory.
>
> *(CESCR 2017, para 28)*

Specifically concerning the extraterritorial obligation to protect, the Committee noted that 'corporations domiciled in the territory and/or jurisdiction of states parties should be required to act with due diligence to identify, prevent and address abuses to Covenant rights by subsidiaries and business partners, wherever they may be located' (CESCR 2017, para 33). Regarding redress, states are duty-bound to remove legal and practical barriers to access to justice and effective remedies faced by victims of transnational corporate abuses, including 'by establishing parent company or group liability regimes' (CESCR 2017, para 44).

The other UN Treaty Bodies have expressed similar views. In a 2017 Communication concerning Canada's responsibility for human rights violations involving Canadian building companies in the occupied Palestinian territories, the Human Rights Committee noted that 'there are situations where a state party has an obligation to ensure that rights under the [International Covenant on Civil and Political Rights] are not impaired by extraterritorial activities conducted by enterprises under its jurisdiction' (HRC 2017, para 6.5). According to the Concurring Opinion of two Committee Members, the necessary jurisdictional link between the state and third-country victims could be established on the basis of: '(a) the effective capacity of the state to regulate the activities of the businesses concerned and (b) the actual knowledge that the state had of those activities and their necessary and foreseeable consequences in terms of violations of human rights recognised in the Covenant' (HRC 2017, Concurring Opinion of Committee Members Olivier de Frouville and Yadh Ben Achour, para 10).

One important doctrinal justification behind this more robust approach to international extraterritorial obligations is the prohibition in customary international law, initially recognised in the context of transboundary pollution, for a state to use or permit the use of its territory such that it causes injury to another state or persons therein. In the *Corfu Channel Case*, the International Court of Justice derived from 'every state's obligation not to allow knowingly its territory to be used for acts contrary to the rights of other states' due diligence obligations to prevent such harmful acts from occurring or continuing (ICJ 1949, pp. 4, 22). In its *Advisory Opinion on the Environment and Human Rights*, the Inter-American Court of Human Rights linked states' due diligence obligations to prevent transboundary environmental harm to the human rights entitlements of third-country victims. According to the Court, the required jurisdictional link (Article 1 IACHR) could be established in virtue of a 'causal relationship' between the polluting activities within the state's borders and extraterritorial human rights violations, provided the state exercised 'effective control' over the relevant activities and was in a position to prevent the harm from occurring:

> In cases of transboundary damage, the exercise of jurisdiction by a state of origin is based on the understanding that it is the state in whose territory or under whose jurisdiction the activities were carried out that has the effective control over them and is in a position to prevent them from causing transboundary harm that impacts the enjoyment of human rights of persons outside its territory. The potential victims of the negative consequences of such activities are under the jurisdiction of the state of origin for the purposes of the possible responsibility of that state for failing to comply with its obligation to prevent transboundary damage.
>
> *(IACtHR 2017, paras 102, 103)*

The IACtHR's recognition of international extraterritorial obligations resonates with functional approaches to extraterritorial human rights protection considered under the ECHR and the EU Charter of Fundamental Rights (Moreno-Lax 2020; Moreno-Lax and Costello 2014). In his concurring opinion to *Al Skeini*, Judge Bonello envisaged a 'functional' approach to extraterritorial jurisdiction that should transcend the state-based territoriality/extraterritoriality divide:

> Jurisdiction means no less and no more than 'authority over' and 'control of'. In relation to Convention obligations, jurisdiction is neither territorial nor extraterritorial: it ought to

> be functional … The duties assumed through ratifying the Convention go hand in hand with a duty to perform and observe them. Jurisdiction arises from the mere fact of having assumed those obligations and from having the capacity to fulfil them (or not to fulfil them.
>
> *(ECtHR 2011, Concurring Opinion of Judge Bonello, paras 12, 13)*

In a similar vein, the General Court of the European Union held in *Front Polisario* that EU institutions must protect foreign victims against the harmful human rights impacts of international trade agreements. According to the Court, the EU Charter of Fundamental Rights imposes extraterritorial obligations to 'examine, carefully and impartially, all the relevant facts in order to ensure that the production of goods for export is not conducted to the detriment of the population of the territory concerned, or entails infringements of fundamental rights' (EGC 2012, para 228).[2]

Towards an international business and human rights treaty

International extraterritorial obligations are also at the heart of the draft international business and human rights treaty currently under negotiation. In June 2014, the UN Human Rights Council adopted Resolution 26/9 that established an open-ended intergovernmental working group on transnational corporations and other business enterprises with respect to human rights (OEIGWG), with a mandate to 'elaborate an international legally binding instrument to regulate, in international human rights law, the activities of transnational corporations and other business enterprises' (HRC 2014). In August 2020, the OEIGWG Chairmanship published a second revised draft (OEIGWG 2020). The revised draft treaty text clearly references the UNGPs' notion of corporate human rights due diligence, while also consolidating states' international extraterritorial human rights obligations to prevent and redress business-related human rights violations.

Regarding prevention, Article 6(1) of the 2020 draft provides that 'states parties shall regulate effectively the activities of all business enterprises within their territory or jurisdiction' or 'otherwise under their control' to ensure that these business enterprises 'respect all internationally recognised human rights and prevent and mitigate human rights abuses throughout their operations'. To comply with their international extraterritorial obligations, 'states parties shall require business enterprises to undertake human rights due diligence' concerning their own business activities and their business relationships with third parties (Article 6(2)). Regarding redress, Article 7(1) requires states parties to endow their domestic courts and non-judicial remedy mechanisms 'with the necessary jurisdiction … to enable victims' access to adequate, timely and effective remedy'. This includes 'legal and other measures to necessary to ensure that [states'] domestic jurisdiction provides for effective, proportionate, and dissuasive criminal and/or administrative sanctions' (Article 8(4)); and civil jurisdiction of domestic courts over tort claims brought by victims against business enterprises not domiciled in the forum state (Article 9). As an exception to the otherwise applicable *lex loci delicti* rule, Article 11 provides that, upon request of the victim, the applicable law in 'all matters of substance regarding human rights law' is that of the domestic (home state) court where the proceedings are brought.

If adopted, the international business and human rights treaty would further consolidate states' international extraterritorial obligations to prevent and redress business-related human rights violations, as envisaged by the *Maastricht Principles* (de Schutter 2015). To comply with their duty to protect, states must enact domestic legislation that imposes human rights due diligence requirements on business enterprises across their global supply/value chain; and ensure that their domestic jurisdiction provides for effective civil remedies and administrative and criminal sanctions for the benefit of foreign victims of business-related human rights violations. Different from earlier attempts to regulate the human rights impacts of global business enterprises in international law (UN Sub-Commission on Human Rights 2003), the draft treaty duly recognises that 'the primary obligation to respect, protect, fulfil and promote human rights ... lies with the state' (OEIGWG 2020, Preamble), while also placing existing examples of unilateral domestic regulation with extraterritorial effect on a secure multilateral footing.

Home-state regulation in domestic law

Home-state regulation and the UNGPs

Apart from forming an integral part of states' international extraterritorial obligations as envisaged by the *Maastricht Principles*, domestic regulation with extraterritorial effect also plays an important role in the implementation of the UN Guiding Principles on Business and Human Rights. The UNGPs are organised around three pillars: the state duty to protect human rights against violations by third parties, including business enterprises; the corporate responsibility to respect human rights, meaning to act with due diligence to avoid infringing the rights of others; and greater access to remedies, both judicial and non-judicial, for victims of business-related violations (HRC 2011).

As part of their responsibility to respect, business enterprises should carry out human rights due diligence (HRDD) to identify, prevent, mitigate, and account for how they address adverse human rights impacts they cause or contribute to through their own activities or which are directly linked to their operations, products, and services. As part of their duty to protect, states have to assume a proactive role in incentivising and, where necessary, requiring corporate respect for human rights through appropriate policies, legislation, adjudication, and enforcement. Home-state regulation of HRDD can thus contribute to a 'hardening' of the soft-law requirements bound up with the corporate responsibility to respect human rights (Nolan 2018; Macchi and Bright 2020). To close governance gaps at the global level, such regulation should include instruments with extraterritorial effect that reach out to corporate conduct abroad. Accordingly, the UN Working Group on Business and Human Rights tasked with overseeing states' implementation of the UNGPs, including through the development of National Action Plans (NAPs), has called upon governments to ensure that 'measures outlined in the NAP take full advantage of the leverage home states have in order to effectively prevent, address, and redress extraterritorial impacts of corporations domiciled within their territory and/or jurisdiction' (UNWG 2016, p. 19).

Neither the concept of home-state regulation nor the distinction between (nationality-based) direct extraterritorial jurisdiction and (territory-based) domestic measures with extraterritorial implications is new (Muchlinski 2007, pp. 125–140; Zerk 2010). Specifically in regulatory areas with a strong market nexus such as competition/antitrust, anti-bribery, and corruption, states rather commonly make use of domestic legislation to govern corporate conduct across territorial borders. Once the epistemic bias against 'extraterritoriality' is dispersed, the question becomes less whether states regulate corporations with extraterritorial effect than whether they do so to promote and protect human rights. In particular the earlier business and human rights NAPs show little evidence of states taking seriously the importance of extraterritorial regulation – an omission which, *contra* the UNGPs, risks to re-entrench the old dichotomy between mandatory international human rights norms and voluntary corporate social responsibility.

Meanwhile, states in Europe and elsewhere have enacted or consider enacting home-state regulation that renders legally binding (selective elements of) the UNGPs' HRDD requirements.

Existing examples range from attempts to enhance corporate transparency through disclosure and reporting to the imposition of substantive due diligence obligations on business enterprises to protect human rights and the environment. While soft/voluntary measures incentivising corporate respect for human rights still dominate the regulatory landscape, states have made use of administrative, civil (corporate & tort), and criminal law to monitor and enforce HRDD within corporate groups and throughout the global supply/value chain. To date, most enacted examples of home-state regulation are either sector-specific (e.g., preventing trade in conflict minerals and illegally harvested timber) or tailored to certain groups of rights holders (e.g., protecting children and victims of modern slavery).

Transparency legislation

Transparency legislation aims to promote corporate respect for human rights by imposing on business enterprises reporting and disclosure requirements concerning non-financial information about their global supply/value chains. Enhancing transparency should help investors and consumers to evaluate the human rights and environmental record of large companies and create market incentives for these companies to develop a more responsible and sustainable approach to business. The EU Non-Financial Reporting Directive, for example, considers that 'disclosure of non-financial information is vital for managing change towards a sustainable global economy by combining long-term profitability with social justice and environmental protection'. In line with the approach suggested by the UNGPs, reporting should cover 'the principal risks related to those matters linked to the undertaking's operations including, where relevant and proportionate, its business relationships, products or services which are likely to cause adverse impacts in those areas; and how the undertaking manages those risks' (Article 1(1)). The Directive allows for significant discretion as to what 'relevant and proportionate' information should be disclosed, and EU member states' implementation has tended to focus on risks to shareholders rather than risks to victims of business-related human rights and environmental harm (European Commission 2020, p. 166).

The California Transparency in Supply Chains Act (2010), the UK Modern Slavery Act (2015) and the Australian Modern Slavery Act (2018) aim to prevent forced labour in global supply chains by requiring companies to report on actions taken to eradicate slavery and human trafficking. According to Section 54 of the UK Modern Slavery Act, companies of a certain size which, wherever incorporated, carry out (part of their) business in the United Kingdom have to prepare an annual slavery and human trafficking statement. This statement 'may' include information about its policies and due diligence processes in relation to slavery and human trafficking throughout the supply chain. Alternatively, companies may simply declare that they have not taken steps to develop and implement HRDD policies and processes ('comply or explain'). The more recent Australian Modern Slavery Act lays down mandatory reporting requirements, including a company assessment of the effectiveness of measures taken to identify and address risks of modern slavery. A 2019 Norwegian legislative proposal on supply chain transparency moreover couples the monitoring of corporate reporting requirements with 'a right to information about fundamental human rights and working conditions in businesses and supply chains' – non-compliance with which attracts penalties (Norway Ethics Information Committee 2019, p. 36).

Transparency legislation was among the first attempts to ensure corporate respect for human rights by imposing on business actors and activities within the state's territorial jurisdiction reporting requirements that cover their global supply/value chain. Yet, on its own, transparency legislation does meet the requirements of the state duty to protect in international human rights law. Neither does it impose due diligence obligations on business enterprises, nor does it secure remedies to victims of business-related human rights violations. Moreover, existing examples of transparency legislation have proven of limited use in monitoring corporate respect for human rights and promoting HRDD policies and processes within companies (European Commission 2020; Alliance for Corporate Transparency 2019). A main challenge in this regard has been the poor quality of company responses (Mares 2018). Without sufficiently concrete and dedicated information, investors and consumers cannot use their purchasing power to reward companies for taking a proactive approach to human rights, nor can governments assess the effectiveness of their legislation. To play a meaningful part in the monitoring and enforcement of the corporate responsibility to respect human rights, transparency legislation needs to prescribe mandatory reporting requirements, based on concrete and tangible internationally recognised standards and indicators (Alliance for Corporate Transparency 2019; UK Government 2019).

Market-based due diligence legislation

Due diligence legislation combines corporate reporting with global supply/value chain due diligence requirements imposed on business actors and activities within the state's territorial jurisdiction. Apart from the business entity's place of incorporation ('parent-based' due diligence legislation), the necessary jurisdictional link can also be established in virtue of products and services placed on the state's domestic market ('market-based' due diligence legislation). On the former model, a business enterprise domiciled within the state's jurisdiction is legally required to exercise HRDD throughout its global supply chain. On the latter model, market access by business enterprises is conditional upon compliance with certain product and process (due diligence) standards protecting human rights and/or the environment abroad. Both models can be combined, for example, by imposing parent-based due diligence obligations on companies with substantial business activities within the state's territorial jurisdiction.

The first European Union 'market-based' instrument to impose mandatory due diligence obligations with extraterritorial effect was the EU Timber Regulation (EUTR), which aims to reduce illegal logging worldwide by prohibiting operators in Europe to place illegally harvested timber and timber products on the European market. Next to a requirement for traders of timber (products) to keep records of their suppliers and customers, EUTR obliges operators to develop a due diligence system to identify, assess, and mitigate the risk of illegally lodged timber (products) being sold in the European Union. EU Member States must apply 'effective, proportionate and dissuasive' penalties in case of non-compliance (Article 19), which may include fines and trading suspensions. A similar regulatory model underpins the 2012 Australian Illegal Logging Prohibition Act and – in the area of conflict minerals – the 2010 US Dodd-Frank Wall Street Consumer Protection Act and the new EU Conflict Minerals Regulation. The latter advances beyond EUTR in two regards: first, it requires EU importers of minerals and metals to incorporate their supply chain policy into agreements with suppliers, thus rendering the Regulation's due diligence standards legally binding between the contracting parties wherever located; and second, it requires EU importers of minerals and metals to establish or provide for an internal grievance mechanism that should function as an 'early-warning risk-awareness system' (Article 4).

In May 2019, the Dutch Senate adopted a Child Labour Due Diligence Law that imposes due diligence (*gepaste zorgvuldigheid*) obligations to prevent child labour in the supply chain on business enterprises selling goods and providing services to Dutch end-users. The Act, which has not yet entered into force, applies to all business enterprises (whether domiciled in the Netherlands or abroad) that supply goods and services to consumers in the Netherlands. Companies have to issue a statement that they conduct due diligence to prevent child labour in their supply chain (Article 4). This entails investigating reasonable suspicions of, and drawing up and implementing an action plan to address, child labour in their supply chain. The due diligence statements must be submitted to a supervisory authority that publishes them in a publically available online registry. Business enterprises providing goods and services to Dutch end-users can also discharge their due diligence obligations by sourcing from (lower-tier) companies that have issued a due diligence statement. In either case, due diligence is construed as a one-off exercise, which in the longer term limits the effectiveness of the legislation. The Act provides for public monitoring and enforcement that combines administrative and criminal sanctions, but does not include civil remedies for victims of child labour.

Market-based due diligence legislation conditions market-access by business enterprises upon compliance with substantive due diligence requirements that reach out into the global supply/value chain. While this addresses some of the shortcomings of transparency legislation in ensuring corporate respect for human rights, existing examples of home-state regulation in this area do not fully implement the UNGPs (Macchi and Bright 2020), nor do they satisfy the requirements of the state duty to protect in international human rights law. Confining the scope of market-based due diligence legislation to particular sectors and/or groups of rights holders contravenes the universality and indivisibility of human rights. Most existing examples of 'market-based' due diligence legislation moreover lack a dedicated human rights focus, which considerably limits their capacity to mainstream HRDD into corporate practice (McCorquodale et al. 2017). Finally, as the main concern of market-based due diligence legislation lies with the protection of domestic consumers, it does not include civil remedies for victims of business-related human rights violations inside or outside the state's territorial jurisdiction.

Parent-based due diligence legislation

To date, the only general parent-based due diligence law that covers human rights and environmental impacts and that also includes civil remedies is the 2017 French Duty of Vigilance Law. The law imposes 'vigilance' obligations on large companies with a registered office in France, including subsidiaries of foreign companies. These due diligence obligations extend to all (directly or indirectly) controlled companies as well as to activities of subcontractors and suppliers within established commercial relationships. At the heart of the law is a threefold obligation to enact, implement, and disclose a *plan de vigilance* that must contain reasonable due diligence measures to identify risks and prevent serious harm to human rights, fundamental freedoms, the health and safety of individuals, and the environment. In case of non-compliance, interested parties including civil society organisations can serve a notice to companies and subsequently seek an injunction backed up by periodic penalty payments. This mechanism has been used in a number of instances, with court decisions still pending (Brabant and Savourey 2020). In addition, the Duty of Vigilance Law creates a civil liability regime that enables (foreign) victims to sue the parent/controlling company in France for human rights and environmental damages in its global supply chain. As the civil liability mechanism has not yet been used, it remains unclear whether the substantive provisions of the law would apply in cases where the damage occurs outside France.[3]

The German National Action Plan, released in 2016, set the goal of at least 50% of German companies with more than 500 employees having implemented human rights due diligence by 2020 (German Federal Foreign Office 2016). As government monitoring of the NAP's implementation suggested that the 50% benchmark would not be met, the Federal Ministry for Labour and Social Affairs and the Federal Ministry for Economic Cooperation and Development drafted the cornerstones of a general value chain due diligence law. The German Supply

Chain Due Diligence Act adopted in June 2021 bears the mark of protracted political negotiations and falls behind the standards set in earlier proposals and drafts (Initiative Lieferkettengesetz.de 2021). The law's due human rights and environmental due diligence obligations are principally limited to direct suppliers, with HREDD further down the supply chain only being required where a company fraudulently circumvents the direct supplier or obtains substantiated knowledge of potential human rights abuses by indirect suppliers. While NGOs and trade unions are empowered to represent victims in civil proceedings before German courts, the law does not explicitly provide for civil liability for harm incurred through violations of corporate due diligence obligations.

The enactment of parent-based due diligence legislation has also been announced or is being considered in various other European countries and in the European Union. In March 2021, a coalition of Dutch political parties proposed a new Bill for Responsible and Sustainable International Business Conduct which, different from the earlier Dutch Child Labour Due Diligence Law, would impose cross-sectoral human rights and environmental due diligence obligations across the global value chain; and would provide for civil remedies in addition to administrative and criminal sanctions (MVO Platform 2021). The 2019 Norwegian legislative proposal on a supply chain transparency envisages imposing on 'larger enterprises' substantive due diligence obligations to 'identify, prevent and mitigate possible adverse impacts on fundamental human rights and decent work and account for how they address any adverse impacts' (Norway Ethics Information Committee 2019, p. 57). A popular initiative in Switzerland to make human rights and environmental supply chain due diligence mandatory for Swiss-based companies by amending the Swiss constitution (Swiss Responsible Business Initiative 2015) was narrowly rejected in a public referendum in late November 2020. The original proposal would have enabled foreign victims of human rights and environmental harm to seek civil redress in Switzerland, with a company's exercise of adequate due diligence serving as a defence against liability. The compromise reached in June 2020 between the Swiss Council of States and the Swiss National Council, which now renders into effect, only contains sector-specific due diligence requirements (child labour and conflict minerals) and no civil liability mechanism.

Following the publication of a major due diligence study (European Commission 2020) and increasing calls by all groups of relevant stakeholders for a Europe-wide HRDD legislation, the European Parliament's Committee on Legal Affairs tabled a motion for a European Parliament Resolution recommending a European Directive on Corporate Due Diligence and Corporate Accountability, which the Parliament adopted in a landslide vote in March 2021 (European Parliament 2021). If enacted, the directive would provide for the most comprehensive regulation of corporate due diligence and corporate accountability, in line with the UNGPs (Augenstein and Macchi 2021). The EP Resolution envisages EU Member States to require business enterprises domiciled in the European Union and/or placing products in the internal market to exercise human rights and environmental due diligence throughout their global value chains. It would further require Member States to impose tort liability on business enterprises for human rights and environmental harm, with the exercise of due diligence serving as a defence. To ensure that the Directive's HRDD requirements also apply in transnational tort litigations for damages that occurred outside the European Union, Member States are to denomiate these requirements as overriding mandatory provisions of the forum.[4] A European Commission legislative initiative that was initially expected for summer 2021 has been delayed as the EP Resolution did not pass the Commission's regulatory scrutiny board.

Existing examples of parent-based legislation only impose due diligence obligations on large or larger companies and restrict their reach into the global value chain (Krajewski 2020, pp. 10–11). The German Supply Chain Due Diligence Act unduly discriminates between direct (first-tier) and indirect suppliers. The French Duty of Vigilance Law exonerates small and medium-sized enterprises and limits supply chain due diligence to 'established business relationships' – whereas the UNGPs cover all adverse human rights impacts 'which may be directly linked to [the business enterprise's] operations, products or services by its business relationships' (HRC 2011, Principle 17a). Such priori restrictions of the scope and scale of parent-based due diligence legislation is also incompatible with states' international extraterritorial obligations, which as interpreted by the *Maastricht Principles* only require 'a reasonable link between the state concerned and the conduct it seeks to regulate, including where the relevant aspects of a non-state actor's activities are carried out in that state's territory' (Principle 25(d)). To comply with their duty to protect, states should ensure that due diligence obligations apply to all business actors and activities within their territorial jurisdiction and extend across the entire supply/value chain. A company's size and its operational remoteness from the human rights harm should be accounted for by proportionality and/or reasonableness criteria built into the due diligence requirements. The French law is currently the only example of states' implementation of their international extraterritorial obligation to redress business-related human rights violations that includes a civil remedy mechanism – this notwithstanding that civil redress is a core ingredient of the human right to remedy and remains a major concern in the effective implementation of the UNGPs (HRC 2016).

Conclusion

The chapter set out by distinguishing two legal issues pertinent to the home-state regulation of corporations. First, the extent to which international law imposes obligations on states to prevent and redress business-related human rights violations for the benefit of individuals located outside their territory; and second, the extent to which states could and should use domestic law to regulate the extraterritorial human rights impacts of business enterprises. While both issues remain subject to considerable political debate, the chapter argued that states' increasing use of domestic regulation with extraterritorial effect goes hand-in-hand with the incremental recognition of international extraterritorial obligations to prevent and redress business-related human rights violations. The chapter interpreted these developments in terms of a gradual convergence between the regulatory models that underpin both domains of legal ordering. It was argued that this convergence is evidence of a growing recognition among states that corporate respect for human rights should be brought under the purview of international human rights law – such that states' domestic regulation of the global human rights impacts of business enterprises becomes anchored in international legal obligations towards foreign victims of business-related human rights violations. As envisaged by the *Maastricht Principles*, international extraterritorial obligations thus not only reinforce the primary obligation of states to respect, protect, and fulfil human rights in international law but may also contribute to a more effective implementation of the UNGPs through domestic regulation with extraterritorial effect that addresses existing shortcomings of home-state regulation.

Notes

1. The terminology used by international courts and treaty bodies is not uniform and does not yield an unequivocal distinction between authority, power, and control. It appears useful to distinguish between effective control as *de facto* power and control as *de jure* authority, which recognises the difference between the facticity of coercion and the normative command to act in accordance with the law.
2. The judgment was quashed on appeal for lack of standing of the applicants under Article 263 TFEU.

3. As an exception to the otherwise applicable *lex loci delicti* rule; see Article 4 Regulation (EC) No 864/2007 of the European Parliament and of the Council of 11 July 2007 on the law applicable to non-contractual obligations.
4. Two annexes to the Committee on Legal Affairs' proposal that envisaged a more comprehensive reform of EU private international law to address barriers to access to justice encountered by third-country victims of human rights and environmental harm were not included in the final resolution. A more comprehensive reform of EU private international law envisaged in two Annexes to the Committee of Legal Affairs'initial proposal.

Bibliography

Alliance for Corporate Transparency (2019) Research Report 2019: An analysis of the sustainability reports of 1000 companies pursuant to the EU Non-Financial Reporting Directive, available at: https://www.allianceforcorporatetransparency.org/ [accessed 28 July 2021].

Altwicker, T. (2018) 'Transnationalising Rights: International Human Rights Law in Cross-Border Contexts' *European Journal of International Law* 29(2), 581–606.

Augenstein, D. (2018) 'Torture as Tort? Transnational Tort Litigation for Corporate-Related Human Rights Violations and the Human Right to Remedy' *Human Rights Law Review* 18(3), 593–612.

Augenstein, D. and Kinley, D (2013) 'When Human Rights "Responsibilities" become "Duties": The Extraterritorial Obligations of States that bind Corporations' in Deva, S. and Bilchitz, D. (eds.) *Obligations of Business: Beyond the Corporate Responsibility to Respect?*, Cambridge University Press, 271–294.

Augenstein, D. and Macchi, C. (2021), *The Role of Human Rights and Environmental Due Diligence Legislation in Protecting Women Migrant Workers in Global Food Supply Chains*, available at: https://papers.ssrn.com/sol3/papers.cfm?abstract_id=3847676 [accessed 28 July 2021].

Besson, S. (2012) 'The Extraterritoriality of the European Convention on Human Rights: Why Human Rights Depend on Jurisdiction and What Jurisdiction Amounts to' *Leiden Journal of International Law* 25(4), 857–884.

Brabant, S. and Savourey, E. (2020) 'All Eyes on France – French Vigilance Law First Enforcement Cases (1/2)' *Cambridge Law Blog*.

Committee on Economic, Social and Cultural Rights (2011) Statement on the Obligations of States Parties Regarding the Corporate Sector and Economic, Social and Cultural Rights, E/C.12/2011/1.

Committee on Economic, Social and Cultural Rights (2017), GC 24 on State Obligations under the International Covenant on Economic, Social and Cultural Rights in the Context of Business Activities, E/C.12/GC/24.

de Schutter (2015) 'Towards a New Treaty on Business and Human Rights' *Business and Human Rights Journal* 1, 41–67.

den Heijer, M. and Lawson, R. (2013) 'Extraterritorial Human Rights and the Concept of Jurisdiction', in Langford M., Vandenhole W., Scheinin, M. and van Genugten, W. (eds.) *Global Justice, State Duties*, Cambridge University Press, 153–191.

ETO Consortium (2011) *Maastricht Principles* on Extraterritorial Obligations of States in the Area of Economic, Social and Cultural Rights.

European Commission (2020) Study on Due Diligence Requirements through the Supply Chain, Final Report, available at: https://op.europa.eu/en/publication-detail/-/publication/8ba0a8fd-4c83-11ea-b8b7-01aa75ed71a1/language-en [accessed 28 July 2021].

European Court of Human Rights (2006) *Markovic and Others v. Italy*, Application No: 1398/03, Judgment (Merits).

_______ (2010) *Rantsev v. Cyprus & Russia*, Application No: 25965/04, Judgment (Merits).

_______ (2011) *Al-Skeini and Others v. United Kingdom*, Application No: 66721/07, Judgment (Merits).

_______ (2012) *Nada v. Switzerland*, Application No: 10593/08, Judgment (Merits)

_______ (2015) *Sargsyan v. Azerbaijan*, Application No: 40167/06, Judgment (Merits).

_______ (2016) *J.K. and Others v. Sweden*, Application No: 59166/12, Judgment (Merits).

European Parliament (2021) Resolution of 10 March 2021 with Recommendations to the Commission on Corporate Due Diligence and Corporate Accountability (2020/2129(INL), A9-0018/2021.

German Federal Foreign Office (2010) National Action Plan: Implementing the UN Guiding Principles on Business and Human Rights 2016-2020, available at: https://www.auswaertiges-amt.de/de/aussenpolitik/themen/aussenwirtschaft/wirtschaft-und-menschenrechte/-/227580 [accessed 28 July 2021].

General Court of the European Union (2012) Case T-512/12 *Front Polisario*, ECLI:EU:T:2015:953.

Human Rights Committee (2017) Basem Ahmed Issa Yassin et al. v. Canada, Communication No. 2285/2013, CCPR/c/120/D/2285/2013.

Human Rights Council (2008) Protect, Respect and Remedy: A Framework for Business and Human Rights, A/HRC/8/5.

_______ (2011) Guiding Principles on Business and Human Rights: Implementing the United Nations' 'Protect, Respect and Remedy' Framework, A/HRC/17/31.

_______ (2014) Elaboration of an International Legally Binding Instrument on Transnational Corporations and Other Business Enterprises with Respect to Human Rights, A/HRC/Res. 26/9.

_______ (2016) Improving Accountability and Access to Remedy for Victims of Business-related Human Rights Abuse, A/HRC/32/19.

Initiative Lieferkettengesetz.de (2021), What the new Supply Chain Act delivers – and what it doesn't, available at: https://lieferkettengesetz.de/pressemitteilung/german-parliament-passes-supply-chain-law/ [accessed 28 July 2021].

Inter-American Commission of Human Rights (1999), *Coard v. United States*, Report No. 109/99.

Inter-American Court of Human Rights (2017) Advisory Opinion OC-23/17 requested by the Republic of Colombia: The Environment and Human Rights, Series A No. 23.

International Court of Justice (1949) *Corfu Channel Case (United Kingdom v. Albania)*, ICJ Rep 4.

_______ (2004) Legal Consequences of the Construction of a Wall in the Occupied Palestinian Territory, *ICJ Rep* 136.

Knox, J. (2010) 'Diagonal Environmental Rights', in Gibney M. and Skogly S. (eds.) *Universal Human Rights and Extraterritorial Obligations*, University of Pennsylvania Press, 82–103.

Krajewski, M. (2020) 'Human Rights Due Diligence Legislation – Options for the EU' *Policy Briefing for the European Parliament's Subcommittee on Human Rights*, PE 603.495.

Macchi, C. and Bright, C. (2020) 'Hardening Soft Law: The Implementation of Human Rights Due Diligence Requirements in Domestic Legislation', in Buscemi, M., Lazzerini, N. and Magi, L. (eds.) *Legal Sources in Business and Human Rights – Evolving Dynamics in International and European Law*, Brill Publishers, 218–247.

Mares, R. (2018) 'Corporate Transparency Laws: A Hollow Victory?' *Netherlands Quarterly of Human Rights* 36(3), 189–213.

McCorquodale, R., Smit, L., Neely, S. and Brooks, R. (2017) 'Human Rights Due Diligence in Law and Practice: Good Practices and Challenges for Business Enterprises' *Business and Human Rights Journal* 2, 195–224.

Moreno-Lax, V. (2020) 'The Architecture of Functional Jurisdiction: Unpacking Contactless Control – On Public Powers, *S.S. and Others v. Italy*, and the "Operational Model"' *German Law Journal* 21, 385–416.

Moreno-Lax, V. and Costello C. (2014) 'The Extraterritorial Application of the EU Charter of Fundamental Rights: From Territoriality to Facticity, The Effectiveness Model', in Peers, S. et al. (eds.) *Commentary on the EU Charter of Fundamental Rights*, Oxford University Press, 1657–1683.

Muchlinski, P. (2007) *Multinational Enterprises and the Law*, 2nd edn, Oxford University Press.

MVO Platform (2021), Translation of the Bill for Responsible and Sustainable International Business Conduct, available at: https://www.mvoplatform.nl/en/translation-of-the-bill-for-responsible-and-sustainable-international-business-conduct/ [accessed 28 July 2021].

Nolan, J. (2018) 'Hardening Soft Law: Are the emerging corporate social disclosure and due diligence laws capable of generating substantive compliance with human rights norms? *Revista de Direito Internacional* 15(2), 65–83.

Norwegian Ethics Information Committee (2019) Supply Chain Transparency: Proposal for an Act regulating Enterprises' transparency about supply chains, duty to know and due diligence, available at: https://www.regjeringen.no/en/dokumenter/supply-chain-transparency/id2680057/ [accessed 28 July 2021].

OEIGWG Chairmanship (2020) Second Revised Draft: Legally Binding Instrument to Regulate, in International Human Rights Law, the Activities of Transnational Corporations and Other Business Enterprises.

Shany, Y. (2013) 'Taking Universality Seriously: A Functional Approach to Extraterritoriality in International Human Rights Law' *The Law and Ethics of Human Rights* 7(1), 47–71.

Skogly, S. and Gibney, M. (2002) 'Transnational Human Rights Obligations' *Human Rights Quarterly* 24, 781–798.

Swiss Coalition for Corporate Justice (2015) 'The Initiative Text with Explanations', available at: https://corporatejustice.ch/about-the-initiative/ [accessed 28 July 2021].

UK Government (2019) 'Independent Review of the Modern Slavery Act: Final Report', available at: https://www.gov.uk/government/publications/independent-review-of-the-modern-slavery-act-final-report [accessed 28 July 2021].

UN Sub-Commission on the Promotion and Protection of Human Rights (2003) Draft Norms on the Responsibilities of Transnational Corporations and Other Business Enterprises with Regard to Human Rights, E/CN.4/Sub.2/2003/12.

UN Working Group on Business and Human Rights (2016) 'Guidance on National Action Plans on Business and Human Rights'.

Zerk, J. (2006) *Multinationals and Corporate Social Responsibility*, Cambridge University Press.

_______ (2010) 'Extraterritorial Jurisdiction: Lessons for the Business and Human Rights Sphere from Six Regulatory Areas' *Corporate Social Responsibility Initiative Working Paper No. 59*, John F. Kennedy School of Government, Harvard University.

21

International tax transparency and Least Developed Countries

Rod Michelmore

Introduction

The 46 Least Developed Countries are home to over 1 billion people, most of whom live in poverty. The severe structural handicaps of these countries are such that their governments are the least likely to be able to mobilise the domestic tax revenues required to realise minimum essential socioeconomic rights. The large scale of cross-border tax evasion by high-net-worth individuals (HNWIs) and aggressive tax avoidance by multinational enterprises (MNEs) in many Least Developed Countries raises urgent international human rights law considerations concerning the deficit of international cooperation to detect the widespread misuse of the international financial system – that drains the revenues of those governments with primary responsibility for fulfilling the rights of most people living in extreme poverty.

This interface between international tax law and international human rights law has generated a growing body of literature (International Bar Association 2013; Beckett 2018; Alston and Reisch 2019). In particular, the magnitude of offshore revenue leakage from developing countries has prompted analysis across a wide range of international tax law issues, including: inequitable allocation of taxing rights between developed and developing countries; asymmetrical bilateral treaties that subvert domestic taxation; and most notably inadequate international cooperation to methodically identify concealed cross-border tax evasion and aggressive tax avoidance from developing countries.

The failure of global economic policymakers and standard setting bodies to adequately address the impact of offshore financial secrecy on the administration and enforcement of revenue laws in developed and developing countries has prompted the most extensive critical examination. Calls for reform have included: international conventions (Norwegian Government Commission 2009, p. 13; Etter-Phoya et al. 2019), global registries (Independent Commission for the Reform of International Corporate Taxation 2019, p. 13; Zucman 2015, p. 92) and even the outlawing of tax havens (de Zayas 2016, p. 27). Notwithstanding mounting concerns regarding the negative impacts of offshore financial secrecy, the outcomes of past UN Financing for Development Conferences hold out little prospect of forging an international political coalition for innovative *across-the-board* international tax transparency reform.

This chapter takes a more nuanced approach towards the international transparency standards that regulate offshore financial secrecy, by focussing on their impact on the Least Developed

DOI: 10.4324/9781003090014-27

Countries. It examines the opportunities for international human rights law and the 2030 Agenda for Sustainable Development (*2030 Agenda*) to bring about reform of international tax transparency standards that have marginalised the Least Developed Countries in crucial areas such as the automatic exchange of tax-related information. Specifically, it considers their scope to advance a human rights-based approach towards unchecked financial flows from low-income countries, within a bifurcated framework of international tax transparency cooperation.

With three quarters of Least Developed Countries in sub-Saharan Africa (referred to here as Africa), it is projected that the region will be home to 90% of the world's poorest people by the end of the decade (Kharas et al, 2018). Yet, Africa currently loses more in illicit financial flows (IFFs) than it receives in overseas aid – making it a net creditor to the world (United Nations Economic Commission for Africa (UNECA) 2015, p. 2). Despite estimates of IFFs from Africa ranging from US$50–80 billion annually (Global Forum on Transparency and Exchange of Information for Tax Purposes 2020, p. 7); the one-size-fits-all approach of the international transparency standards that regulate cross-border financial flows has largely overlooked the structural handicaps and urgent needs of Africa's Least Developed Countries, none of which automatically receive tax-related information.

Cross-border tax evasion and aggressive tax avoidance (*tax-related IFFs*) from Least Developed Countries are more likely to go unchallenged when transparency standards allow such misuse of the international financial system to remain concealed. This may lead to foreseeable human rights violations for those who rely upon Least Developed Country governments to fulfil core socioeconomic rights. Those violations can, *inter alia*, be indirectly attributed to states that exercise authority and control over the global standards that determine whether core offshore financial information on non-residents, and corporate reporting information on MNEs in each jurisdiction where they do business, is actually made available to the Least Developed Countries to administer and enforce their revenue laws (*core transparency information*).

The political commitments that launched the developmental concept of IFFs in 2015 offer a singular practical opportunity to address the harms that unchecked international financial flows can cause to those in the poorest countries. The Third International Conference on Financing for Development in Addis Ababa stressed the urgent need to address IFFs from developing countries; resolving that future international tax cooperation should fully take into account the different needs and capacities of all countries – in particular Least Developed Countries (United Nations 2015, para. 24). Later that year the 2030 Agenda in New York resolved at the highest political level to significantly reduce IFFs (United Nations General Assembly (UNGA) 2015, SDG 16.4).

Yet, global policy actions on IFFs continue to lag behind political rhetoric to address misuse of the international financial system (United Nations 2020, p. 38). The resulting schism between international tax law and international human rights law can be explained by various political, economic and ideological factors. A crucial technical barrier to their congruence has been the challenge of defining and measuring cross-border tax evasion and aggressive tax avoidance. Delimiting these cross-border practices that illicitly drain public revenues is critical to linking the international tax transparency standards that allow unchecked financial flows from the Least Developed Countries, to the manifest human rights violations of their peoples.

International development forums, specifically the 2030 Agenda, provide a political framework to address this longstanding quandary. The UN General Assembly in settling the parameters to measure tax-related IFFs will enable such misuse of the international financial system to be juxtaposed with Sustainable Development Goals (SDGs) in key areas like education, health and housing. This opens the way to establishing a correlation between the regulatory standards that determine how international capital engages with systemically disadvantaged low-income countries, and their abilities to realise minimum essential socioeconomic rights.

Extraterritorial obligations of states

International human rights law jurisprudence has conventionally focused on the conduct of states towards their own peoples. However, it is increasingly recognised that when states conduct themselves in a way that has foreseeable effects on human rights in other jurisdictions, they must ensure they respect and protect those rights. In certain situations, these extraterritorial obligations (*ETOs*) may require states to fulfil the rights of those living beyond their borders.

Economic globalisation has contributed to a states of affairs in which impairment of socioeconomic rights in other territories is more likely to be caused by 'externalities' from national laws, policies and practices – than the conduct of state organs that are physically present on foreign soil (Askin 2019). The idea of invoking socioeconomic human rights obligations against states other than the territorial state emerged around the turn of the millennium, and has gained transformative momentum since then (Peters 2018, p. 302). However, such progressive interpretations of international human rights law aren't universally accepted within the academy, and it has proven difficult to put these ideas into practice.

The conventional pathways used to entrench ETOs involving civil and political human rights are generally not available for clarifying state duties regarding socioeconomic rights. Moreover, governments in most advanced economies have been unwilling to recognise legally binding socioeconomic ETOs, given their potential to require the redistribution of states' resources. That said, the globalisation process has fundamentally shifted the human rights focus from 'government' to 'governance' – diversifying the number and range of actors that could be regarded as impacting the enjoyment of human rights in other territories (Vandenhole and Benedek 2013, p. 332).

This chapter examines the scope for integrating emerging legal doctrines concerning the extraterritorial application of socioeconomic rights into the international standards that determine whether Least Developed Countries receive core transparency information from the global network of over 80 jurisdictions seeking to attract internationally mobile capital (*offshore states*). The salient international human rights law obligations of states in this all-important aspect of global economic governance are rooted in the International Covenant on Economic Social and Cultural Rights (United Nations 1966).

In considering *how* international law determines the way that states act, it is important to distinguish the law of jurisdiction in general international law, which is about 'entitlements to act'; from the law of state responsibility, which is about 'obligations incurred when a state does act' (Higgins 1995, p. 146). In that sense, it may be argued that in certain circumstances the international human rights law obligations of states can operate as a check on the exercise of their otherwise sovereign powers to regulate those under their effective control.

The legal ramifications of the international human rights law obligations undertaken by states have been distilled into the *Maastricht Principles* on Extraterritorial Obligations of States in the Area of Economic, Social and Cultural Rights – which offer a progressive interpretation of the diverse jurisprudence in this nascent area of international law. The *Maastricht Principles*' approach towards jurisdiction stipulates that a state has obligations to respect, protect and fulfil socioeconomic rights in situations over which: it exercises authority or effective control; its acts or omissions bring about foreseeable effects on socioeconomic rights in other jurisdictions; or where a state, acting separately or jointly, is in a position to exercise decisive influence or to take measures to realise such rights (De Schutter et al. 2012, Principle 9).

State responsibility for preventing adverse human rights impacts from concealed tax-related IFFs from the Least Developed Countries can be assessed individually and collectively. The extraterritorial obligation to protect requires offshore states to take the necessary steps at a national level to prevent infringements of socioeconomic rights due to activities of private actors under their effective control (CESCR 2017, p. 30). However, the breadth of the global network of offshore states implicated in the concealment of international financial flows from the Least Developed Countries is such that overarching global tax transparency standards that reflect the needs and capacities of systemically disadvantaged low-income countries are necessary. As such, this chapter focuses on the obligations of international cooperation and assistance of states in a position to assist with the implementation of a human rights-based approach towards international tax transparency.

Article 2(1) of the Covenant sets out the expectation that states will take collective action to help fulfil the socioeconomic rights of persons outside their territories – by creating an international environment that enables the fulfilment of socioeconomic rights (CESCR 2017, pp. 36–37). The *Maastricht Principles* stipulate states must take all reasonable steps to ensure that organisations in which they participate act consistently with their state obligations (De Schutter et al. 2012, Principle 15). By virtue of the Organisation for Economic Cooperation and Development's (OECD) role as the *de facto* global tax standard setting body, its members are expected to take the steps necessary to prevent the adverse human rights impacts of tax-related IFFs that are attributable to Least Developed Countries not receiving the core transparency information needed to administer and enforce their revenue laws.

The practical implications of states' duties in this regard are laid out in the *Maastricht Principles*, which assert that in matters concerning the establishment of global regulatory standards, the extraterritorial obligations of states include the requirement to elaborate international tax standards in a manner consistent with their human rights obligations (De Schutter et al. 2012, Principle 17). The Committee on Economic, Social and Cultural Rights in calling for deeper international tax cooperation has acknowledged that providing excessive bank secrecy may affect the abilities of states where economic activities take place, to meet their obligation to mobilise the maximum available resources to implement socioeconomic rights (CESCR 2017). This human impact is particularly evident in the poorest countries with limited administrative capacities and meagre tax bases that increase their reliance upon taxation from HNWIs and MNEs.

Given that the primary duty-bearer of human rights obligations is the territorial state, the question arises whether ETOs are triggered when that state is unwilling or unable to meet its obligations; or whether ETOs are complementary (Askin 2019, p. 39)? In the case of the extraterritorial obligation to fulfil, it has been considered that they only arise when the territorial state is unwilling or unable to meet its obligations (Vandenhole and Benedek 2013, p. 335). The remainder of this chapter makes evident why it is that the Least Developed Countries are currently unable to detect concealed tax-related IFFs that drain their public revenues. This avoidable situation contributes to the most systemically disadvantaged low-income countries being unable to meet their obligations to fulfil core socioeconomic rights.

A systemic analysis of the standards that underpin existing international tax transparency frameworks demonstrates how they have marginalised Least Developed Countries, thereby allowing tax-related illicit financial outflows to remain concealed in a way that foreseeably effects socioeconomic rights. Relatedly, it shows that OECD nations are in fact in a position to exercise decisive influence or take measures to realise those rights – by implementing the type of international cooperation needed for the timely and methodical detection of tax-related IFFs from low-income countries unable to meet their human rights obligations.

International support for the Least Developed Countries

The designation 'Least Developed Country' was established by the UN General Assembly in 1971 to provide special international support to low-income countries with 'severe structural handicaps to economic growth and development' (UNGA 1971). Thus far the principal support for Least Developed Countries has been duty-free and quota-free access to global markets, with supplemental development assistance as a stopgap measure before integration into the world economy. However, the generic structural transformation predicted by international trade theory has not materialised; with only five low-income countries graduating from Least Developed Country status over the last 50 years.

The most salient problems for the Least Developed Countries include a shortage of sustainable investment, deficiency of capital stock and scarce public revenues; with the external harms caused by tax havens, farm subsidies and immigration restrictions far outweighing the benefits of existing support measures (Gay 2018). Amongst their varied international support requirements, of particular importance are the needs for global governance mechanisms to address secrecy jurisdictions, dedicated global tax transparency assistance and dedicated assistance to improve domestic resource mobilisation capacity (Gay 2018). Yet, international assistance in these areas has been in short supply; with only 0.16% of total aid from OECD nations to African countries applied to domestic resource mobilisation programs in 2017 (OECD 2017c).

In his final report as Special Rapporteur on Extreme Poverty and Human Rights, Philip Alston described the persistence of global poverty as a 'political choice' (Alston 2020, p. 1). This dynamic has been particularly evident in the global responses to largely poverty-driven issues, such as infant mortality in low-income countries. Currently 1 in 14 children born in these countries die before their 5th birthday, from diseases that are largely preventable and treatable through simple and affordable interventions (World Health Organization 2019).

Such egregious human rights violations that are attributable to the want of basic healthcare require offshore states to address the ease with which tax-related IFFs can be concealed from the Least Developed Countries. Yet, two countervailing narratives impinge upon the political resolve to take decisive action to address such misuse of the international financial system. Accounts of dramatic progress towards poverty eradication in Africa driven by economic growth (Beegle and Christiaensen 2019) have been reinforced by the purported imperative for liberalised capital flows to hasten economic growth (International Monetary Fund 2019). Indeed in Africa, even human rights-based approaches to development have tended to premise the realisation of socioeconomic rights on the creation of economic growth (Vandenhole 2018, p. 657).

The narrative of progress towards poverty eradication is tied to the World Bank's international poverty line (*IPL*), which has been used to rationalise globalisation policies such as international capital mobility for developing countries. Yet, the IPL (currently $1.90 per day) sets the bar so low as to all but guarantee the appearance of victory over global poverty. The standard of living established by the IPL is well below any reasonable conception of a life with dignity – and in the view of the Special Rapporteur is a world apart from the one set by human rights law (Alston 2020, p. 5).

With the impending arrival of SDG data on IFFs, a more robust poverty metric is needed to evaluate the human impact of international standards that sustain unchecked financial flows from the poorest countries. A promising alternative is the 'rights-based poverty line' that combines outcome indicators with the principle of country-specific poverty lines. For instance, this human rights-based benchmark reveals that a line 4.2 times higher than the IPL is required to achieve an infant mortality threshold of no more than 20/1000 lives (Woodward 2010, pp. 38–39).

International tax transparency and the Least Developed Countries

The financial globalisation project has made tax information sharing between states crucial to the administration and enforcement of revenue laws. HNWIs and MNEs can evade or avoid domestic taxes easily, unless limited by concerted multilateral efforts (Neubig 2018, p. 1137). The two principal methods for tax information exchange between states are: exchange of information on request (*EOIR*) where a specific application for information is made of a foreign tax authority; and the complementary post-Global Financial Crisis frameworks for automatic continuing exchange of prescribed information.

The former is facilitated through arrangements based on: the OECD Model Tax Convention on Income and on Capital (OECD 2017b, art. 26); the UN Model Double Taxation Convention Between Developed and Developing Countries (United Nations Department of Economic and Social Affairs (UNDESA) 2017 art. 26); and the OECD Model Agreement on Exchange of Information on Tax Matters (OECD 2002). The latter methods were designed by the OECD pursuant to a 2013 G20 mandate, and comprise the 2014 Standard for Automatic Exchange of Financial Account Information in Tax Matters (OECD 2017d); and Action 13 of the 2015 Final Report of the OECD/G20 Base Erosion and Profit Shifting Project (OECD 2015b). Albeit international tax cooperation has now been streamlined by the Multilateral Convention on Mutual Administrative Assistance in Tax Matters (OECD and the Council of Europe 2011, p. 5), automatic tax information sharing remains contingent upon some form of bipartite agreement between the competent authorities of individual states.

The EOIR standard has been the mainstay of international tax cooperation for most states since the 1960s. However, it has two significant limitations for under-resourced Least Developed Country revenue authorities: the specific information requested must be detailed on the basis of a clearly defined suspicion; and it requires them to reach bipartite agreements with the global network of offshore states. Revenue authorities in low-income countries generally lack the specific information required to initiate large-scale EOIR applications with multiple jurisdictions. To methodically detect tax-related IFFs Least Developed Countries require automatic tax information exchange with offshore states. Indeed, the automatic exchange process is said to enhance the 'means of production' of the information needed to combat cross-border tax evasion and avoidance (Ates 2020, p. 4).

The OECD's Global Forum on Transparency and Exchange of Information for Tax Purposes (*Global Forum*) requires participating states to ensure information on legal and beneficial ownership of relevant entities is *available* to their authorities (OECD 2016). However, they are not obliged to maintain ownership registers. The fact that under-resourced Least Developed Country revenue authorities are still obliged to submit an EOIR application to ascertain the beneficial ownership of offshore companies, trusts and foundations in most offshore states is a further serious obstacle to the methodical detection of illicit cross-border tax practices.

The OECD's 2014 standard for automatic exchange of information (AEOI) on the offshore wealth of non-residents requires reporting across three dimensions. It encompasses different types of investment income and capital; includes individuals and interposed legal entities; and applies to banks and financial institutions such as brokers and insurers (OECD 2017d, p. 12). The OECD's 2015 country-by-country reporting (CbC Reporting) standard requires MNEs with group incomes over €750 million to provide relevant governments with prescribed information in each tax jurisdiction where they do business. That information includes the amount of revenue, profit before income tax and income tax paid and accrued; and the number of employees, stated capital, retained earnings and tangible assets in each tax jurisdiction (OECD 2015b, p. 9).

Yet, before a Least Developed Country can sign a Multilateral Competent Authority Agreement (*MCAA*) to receive AEOI or CbC Reporting (under either a bilateral or multilateral treaty), it must prove compliance with extensive legal and administrative standards. It must also overcome the administrative burden of gathering, organising and sharing information for reciprocal exchange with authorities in offshore states. Minimum legal standards include domestic legislation with strong sanctions for breach of confidentiality obligations under tax treaties, whilst minimum administrative practices include security screening, revised employment contracts and ongoing training, together with strict infrastructure standards (OECD 2012, pp. 29–30).

These exacting standards do not reflect the needs and capacities of the Least Developed Countries. Typically, low-income countries have approximately one-tenth of revenue staffing of high-income countries (United Nations 2020, p. 40). The OECD's Global Forum has acknowledged developing countries face significant resource and political challenges in implementing its standards. Their resource challenges include a lack of human resources to translate standards into domestic laws; limited institutional capacity to handle exchanged data; inadequate finances for administrative and information technology infrastructures; and inadequate finances to collect domestic information for other jurisdictions (OECD 2017a), whilst the political challenges for developing countries include balancing the costs of implementing OECD mandated standards with domestic spending priorities; and taking on those with entrenched financial interests in the status quo (OECD 2017a).

Should a Least Developed Country government overcome these challenges, they face an additional legal hurdle before opening transparency pathways with the global network of offshore states. Automatic exchange relationships are only activated amongst jurisdictions that individually choose each other (OECD 2017d, p. 221). Should a Least Developed Country implement the prescribed laws and administrative practices, the MCAA does not come into effect until such time as a co-signatory notifies the Coordinating Body Secretariat that it intends to exchange information with that jurisdiction. Should the jurisdiction in which an ultimate parent entity resides decide not to activate an exchange relationship with that country, then it will not receive CbC information from the applicable foreign tax authority (Ates 2020, p. 18).

Even supposing a Least Developed Country were to surmount these regulatory barriers to securing automatic tax transparency, its authorities would face significant limitations in how they would be allowed to use the exchanged information. For instance, Section 5(2) of the Country-by-Country MCAA stipulates a CbC Report shall not be used as a 'substitute for a detailed transfer pricing analysis of individual transactions and prices based on a full functional analysis and a full comparability analysis' (OECD 2015a, p. 19). The independent BEPS Monitoring Group has described the OECD's continued insistence on a full functional analysis as inappropriate for developing countries that generally lack the technical capacity to apply such detailed investigations (BEPS Monitoring Group 2020, p. 3).

Consequently, the governments of the majority of people in extreme poverty lack the international cooperation needed to administer and enforce their revenue laws against those who transfer taxable income, capital and the proceeds of trade offshore. The international human rights obligations of OECD nations require them to take the necessary steps to bridge the gulf between their transparency standards and the legal and administrative capacities of the Least Developed Countries. The following section considers how the developmental concept of IFFs might support a differentiated approach towards tax information sharing.

The developmental concept of illicit financial flows

The developmental concept of illicit financial flows runs counter to the longstanding practice of rich nations prescribing the regulatory terms on which international capital holders engage with poor countries. Whilst not yet a legal term of art, IFFs have become a salient consideration for global economic policymakers and standard setting bodies. Although the OECD's lexicon of international transparency standards does not yet reference IFFs – the concept figures prominently in the Paris-based organisation's policy documents that deal with the imperative for domestic resource mobilisation in poor countries (OECD 2018).

The global agenda to address illicit financial flows was launched by African countries. Spurred by a determination to ensure accelerated and sustained development relying as much as possible upon domestic resources, the 2011 Conference of African Ministers of Finance, Planning and Economic Development issued the UN with a mandate to establish a High-Level Panel on Illicit Financial Flows from Africa. The High-Level Panel's core finding was that IFFs from Africa were large and increasing, with large commercial corporations the main culprits (UNECA 2015, p. 64). The policy implications of those findings were that urgent and coordinated action was needed to address the development impacts of tax losses and the opportunity costs of lost savings and investment in various sectors of African economies.

At the heart of the IFF concept is the universal recognition that taxation is the primary source of funding available to realise the SDGs. However, the High-Level Panel's findings also focused attention on the wider economic benefits African countries could have obtained, had international tax transparency standards sufficiently assimilated low-income countries. Instead, the systemic prioritisation of foreign investment over the mobilisation of domestic investment in poor countries has undercut a key economic benefit of international tax cooperation that should have been available to the private sector in Africa's Least Developed Countries.

Notably the global target to significantly reduce IFFs by 2030 (*SDG 16.4*) encompasses both illicit *outflows* and *inflows*. As such, it encompasses financial flows out of Least Developed Countries and financial flows into offshore states. The concept's core elements are that they must be: illicit in nature; cross national borders; and involve flows instead of stocks (United Nations Confernece on Trade and Development 2018). Given that illicit cross-border tax practices by MNEs make up the bulk of IFFs from developing countries, global policymakers have faced considerable conceptual, legal and practical challenges in determining whether this developmental concept should be extended from cross-border tax evasion, to include aggressive cross-border tax avoidance by MNEs.

The task of examining the conceptual and measurement challenges of IFFs has been assigned to SDG 16.4's joint custodians – the UN Office on Drugs and Crime and the UN Conference on Trade and Development (UNGA 2019). The joint custodians issued a Conceptual Framework for the Statistical Measurement of IFFs in October 2020 that distinguished four main categories of IFFs. Relevant for the purposes of this chapter is the category of "illicit tax and commercial IFFs" which they divided into two components: illegal tax and commercial IFFs; and flows generated from legal economic activities through aggressive tax avoidance. This broad-based approach to strategic cross-border tax planning by MNEs could have significant implications for addressing the human rights impacts of concealed tax-related IFFs from low-income countries.

The opportunity to bring those MNE cross-border practices that exist in a grey area between tax evasion and purportedly legal tax avoidance, under the developmental rubric of illicit financial flows, signals an important synergy between the 2030 Agenda's political processes and the creation of an international environment that enables the fulfilment of socioeconomic rights in the Least Developed Countries – by ensuring they receive the core transparency information needed to administer and enforce their revenue laws. Currently, the 2030 Agenda's system of Voluntary National Reviews does not provide a robust process for monitoring global targets such as SDG 16.4. That said, there is scope to be address this limitation by repositioning its

High-level Political Forum more firmly into the UN General Assembly machinery, as was the case with the Human Rights Council (Adams 2019, p. 36).

A human rights-based approach towards international tax transparency

In extolling the purported benefits of the EOIR framework, the OECD's Global Forum recently used the 'Butterfly Effect' metaphor to claim that in the fight against IFFs small changes can make big differences to African states seeking to improve domestic resource mobilisation (Manatta 2020). Notwithstanding that Edward Lorenz's notion that the flap of a butterfly's wings in Brazil might set off a tornado in Texas speaks to the unpredictability of chaos theory, it seems most unlikely that the limited benefits of EOIR will address the wide-ranging systemic misuse of the international financial system that drains the public revenues of the Least Developed Countries. Whilst it remains unclear precisely what the international human rights law obligation of international cooperation and assistance entails (Askin 2019, p. 37), this solemn state responsibility cannot be said to be met by *small* steps towards the multilateral action needed to detect tax-related IFFs from the Least Developed Countries.

To date, international support for Least Developed Countries has largely neglected their manifest need for assistance to address the human rights impacts of unchecked international financial flows. As of the end of 2019, the OECD's AEOI and CbC Reporting reforms had failed to make any automatic tax-related information available to the 46 Least Developed Countries (United Nations 2020, p. 44). Albeit there have been stop gap measures such as Tax Inspectors Without Borders program that operates with a global roster of 50 tax audit experts (OECD and UNDP 2019); such initiatives clearly lack the resources (and the legal frameworks) to deal with the scale of tax-related IFFs from Africa.

The limited progress towards an inclusive system of international tax cooperation that makes its benefits are available to all countries has led to increasing misgivings regarding the role of the *de facto* global tax standard setting body. Most notably, in March 2020, the UN General Assembly launched the *High-level Panel on International Financial Accountability, Transparency and Integrity for Achieving the 2030 Agenda*, tasked with identifying gaps, impediments and vulnerabilities in the design and implementation of international institutional and legal financial transparency frameworks (Presidents of the UN General Assembly and the Economic and Social Council 2020). The FACTI Panel issued a final report in February 2021 in which they concluded IFFs were a systemic problem requiring a systemic solution, making 14 Recommendations including *inter alia* a call to end asymmetries in relation to information shared for tax purposes so that all countries can receive information (UN FACTI Panel 2021).

Although tackling cross-border tax avoidance is now received international development policy (Beegle and Christiaensen 2019, p. 1), the practical question of *how* to deal with such practices from poor countries persists. The 2030 Agenda provides an important segue into operationalising the ETOs of states in a position to assist with the fiscal scrutiny of international financial flows from systemically disadvantaged low-income countries – whose transparency needs are different to those of OECD nations.

By way of illustration, the OECD's CbC Reporting standards imposed a €750 million group income threshold, below which there are no automatic disclosure requirements for MNEs. This group income threshold captures the bulk of cross-border trade, but it excludes the vast majority of MNEs. Whilst the impacts of the OECD setting such a high-income level are limited for its members with small corporate tax bases, that is not the case for Least Developed Countries which tend to rely heavily upon corporate income tax from foreign investors. Should such a country eventually manage to activate a CbC Reporting relationship with a corporate tax haven, it is likely to apply to only a limited number of MNEs.

Such incompatibilities, together with the gulf in the legal and administrative capacities of revenue authorities in Least Developed Countries and OECD nations, necessitate a differentiated system of international tax transparency. That said, reform to prevent the adverse human rights impact of tax-related IFFs from Least Developed Countries must balance the imperative for urgent action in countries facing intensifying extreme poverty, with the ideological commitment of OECD nations to financial privacy and confidentiality for non-residents.

The extensive interest in initiatives such as Tax Inspectors Without Borders that seek to bridge capacity gaps in developing countries provides an auspicious precedent for reform in this crucial area of global economic governance. The widely acknowledged legal and administrative deficits of Least Developed Country revenue authorities in subjecting international financial flows to methodical fiscal scrutiny justify expanding the scale of technical assistance made available to these systemically disadvantaged low-income countries in the short-to-medium term.

Having regard to the foregoing, this chapter concludes by outlining one possible reform pathway that builds on the type of reporting requirements established by the OECD's Financial Action Task Force (FATF 2012). A differentiated transparency framework would integrate jurisdictions that exceed a specified annual volume of cross-border financial services to non-residents. It would require law, accounting and corporate service professionals in those jurisdictions to collate prescribed information from clients connected to international financial transfers from Least Developed Countries that exceed a prescribed value.

That prescribed information, together with AEOI and CbC Reporting information, would then be analysed by a global panel of independent tax experts under the auspices of a jointly funded UN/OECD secretariat. The panel's objective would be to identify international financial flows by persons and entities in respect of whom there is prima facie evidence of cross-border tax practices involving illegal tax and commercial IFFs or IFFs from aggressive tax avoidance (as set out in the Conceptual Framework) with the objective of concealing revenues and reducing tax burdens through evading controls and regulations. The details of any prima facie tax-related IFFs identified by the panel would then be transmitted through a global transparency register.

This type of differentiated approach towards producing the information needed to combat cross-border tax evasion and aggressive tax avoidance from the Least Developed Countries would maintain existing offshore confidentiality standards for residents of the majority of countries, and would impact approximately 1% of global trade. To be sure, a human rights-based approach towards international tax cooperation would require the renegotiation of bilateral and multilateral agreements, and the amendment of ancillary national laws.

Whilst such reform would raise sovereignty issues, it is noted that the OECD was able to overcome similar issues when it implemented its 2014–2015 automatic tax transparency reforms. Moreover, it could be argued that offshore states' ETOs to protect require them to implement differentiated global tax transparency standards designed to prevent infringements by private actors of the socioeconomic rights of those living in systemically disadvantaged low-income countries.

Conclusion

Implementing international transparency standards that can accommodate the needs and capacities of the Least Developed Countries is first and foremost a political process, not a technical one. The leading standards for tax information exchange between states have been shaped by the OECD's ideological commitment to liberalised capital flows as a prerequisite for the economic growth required for national development. Yet, under existing global frameworks, when economic growth has occurred in Africa, it has generally not led to significant poverty reduction. Indeed, using the very low standard of the World Bank's IPL, and assuming a return to pre-Global Financial Crisis growth levels, it is estimated that the eradication of poverty will take at least 100 years (Woodward 2015).

Since the launch of the financial globalisation project in Africa in the 1980s, progress towards securing core transparency information for the countries least likely to fulfil their human rights obligations has been piecemeal, at best. However, the universal human rights obligations undertaken half a century ago in the wake of the last great global upheaval could provide a legal basis on which to challenge the enduring failure of global economic policymakers to implement the international tax cooperation needed to address the haemorrhaging of public revenues from Africa's poorest countries. At the same time, there is now a novel political setting in which to evaluate the human impacts of international tax standards that are conducive to the continuing concealment of tax-related IFFs from low-income countries with severe structural handicaps.

Over 30 years have now passed since renowned African novelist Chinua Achebe accepted an invitation to attend the OECD headquarters in Chateau de la Muette to listen to Western bankers and economists preach the virtues of structural adjustment and market discipline in Africa. They urged Achebe and other invited Africans to trust in their expertise, and most of all to be patient. He was left in no doubt regarding the self-assurance of these experts – they were 'the masters of our world, savouring the benefits of their success' (Achebe 2009, p. 40). Yet, when the time eventually came for Achebe to respond to their insistence on African forbearance, he demanded of the illuminati of neoliberalism – 'would you recommend a similar remedy to your own people, and your own governments' (Achebe 2009, p. 42).

References

Achebe, C. (2009) *Africa's Tarnished Name,* Penguin Random House.

Adams, B. (2019) *Democratic Global Governance: If It Doesn't Challenge Power It Isn't Democratic. Reshaping Governance for Sustainability*, Global Civil Society Report.

Alston, P. (2020) *The Parlous State of Poverty Eradication: Report of the Special Rapporteur on Extreme Poverty and Human Rights*, Human Rights Council.

Alston, P. and Reisch, N. (2019) *Tax, Inequality and Human Rights*, Oxford, Oxford University Press.

Askin, E. (2019) 'Economic and Social Rights, Extraterritorial Application' in Wolfrum, R. and Ruiz Fabri, H. (eds). *Max Planck Encyclopedias of International Law*, Oxford Public International Law.

Ates, L. (2020) 'Tax Information Production, Sharing, Use and Publication' *FACTI Panel Background Paper*, UNDESA.

Beckett, P. (2018) *Tax Havens and International Human Rights*, Routledge.

Beegle, K. and Christiaensen, L. (2019) *Accelerating Poverty Reduction in Africa*, World Bank.

BEPS Monitoring Group (2020) Submission to the Inclusive Framework on BEPS on the Public Consultation Document: Review of Country by Country Reporting.

Committee on Economic, Social and Cultural Rights (CESCR) (2017) General Comment 24 on State Obligations Under the Internaitonal Covenant on Economic, Social and Cultural Rights in the Context of Business Activities, E/C.12/GC/24.

De Schutter, O. et al. (2012) 'Commentary to the *Maastricht Principles* on Extraterritorial Obligations of States in the Area of Economic, Social and Cultural Rights', *Human Rights Quarterly* 34, 1084–1069.

De Zayas, A.-M. (2016) *Promotion of a Democratic and Equitable International Order. Promotion and Protection of Human Rights: Human Rights Questions, Including Alternative Approaches for Improving the Effective Enjoyment of Human Rights and Fundamental Freedoms*, UN General Assembly.

Etter-Phoya, R., Lima, S. and Meinzer, M. (2019) *Corporate Income Taxation in the Digital Age: Africa in the Corporate Tax Haven Index 2019*, Tax Justice Network.

Financial Action Task Force (FATF) (2012-2018) International Standards on Combating Money Laundering and the Financing of Terrorism & Proliferation, FATF.

Gay, D. (2018) 'International Support for Least Developed Countries: A Different Way', https://www.un.org/ldcportal/international-support-for-the-least-developed-countries-a-different-way/ [Accessed 21.9.21].

Global Forum on Transparency and Exchange of Informaiton for Tax Purposes (2020) *Tax Transparency in Africa 2020: Africa Initiative Progress Report 2019*, OECD.

Higgins, R. (1995) *Problems and Process: International Law and How We Use It*, Clarendon.

Independent Commission for the Reform of International Corporate Taxation (2019) A Roadmap for a Global Asset Registry: Measuring and Tackling Inequality; Curbing Tax Avoidance, Tax Evasion, Corruption and Illicit Financial Flows.

International Bar Association (2013) *Tax abuses, Poverty and Human Rights*, Cambrian Printers.

International Monetary Fund (2019) *Regional Economic Outlook Sub-Saharan Africa: Navigating Uncertainty*, IMF.

Kharas, H. and Hamel, K. (2018) 'The Start of a New Poverty Narrative', https://brookings.edu/blog/future-development/2018/06/19/the-start-of-a-new-poverty-narrative/ (Accessed 21.9.21).

Manatta, Z. (2020) 'Exchange of Tax Information: A Butterfly Effect on Domestic Resource Mobilisation', *Development Matters*, http://oecd-development-matters.org (Accessed 21.9.21).

Neubig, T. (2018) Global Tax Administration Initiatives Addressing Tax Evasion and Avoidance, *Tax Notes International*.

Norwegian Government Commission (2009) *Tax Havens and Development: Status, Analyses and Measures*, Department of Government Publications.

Organisation for Economic Co-operation and Development (OECD) (2002) *Model Agreement on Exchange of Information in Tax Matters*, OECD Publishing.

OECD (2012) *Keeping it Safe: The OECD Guide on the Protection of Confidentiality of Information Exchanged for Tax Purposes*, OECD Publishing.

_______ (2015a) *Action 13: Country-by-Country Reporting Implementation Package*, OECD Publishing.

_______ (2015b) *Transfer Pricing Documentation and Country-by-Country Reporting Action 13: 2015 Final Report OECD G20 Base Erosion and Profit Shifting Project*, OECD Publishing.

_______ (2016) *Global Forum on Transparency and Exchange of Information for Tax Purposes: 2016 Terms of Reference to Monitor and Review Progress Towards Transparency and Exchange of Information on Request for Tax Purposes*, OECD Publishing.

_______ (2017a) *'The Global Forum's Plan of Action for Developing Countries Participation in AEOI' in Global Forum (ed). Global Forum on transparency and exchange of informaiton for tax purposes*, OECD Publishing.

_______ (2017b) *Model Tax Convention on Income and on Capital: Condensed Version*, OECD Publishing.

_______ (2017c) Revenue Statistics in Africa, OECD Publishing.

_______ (2017d) *Standard for Automatic Exchange of Financial Account Information in Tax Matters*, Second Edition ed., OECD Publishing.

_______ (2018) *Illicit Financial Flows: The Economy of Illicit Trade in West Africa*, OECD Development Centre.

OECD and Council of Europe (2011) *The Multilateral Convention on Mutual Administrative Assistance in Tax Matters: Amended by the 2010 Protocol*, OECD Publishing.

OECD and UNDP (2019) *Tax Inspectors Without Borders Annual Report 2019*. OECD/UNDP.

Peters, A. (2018) 'Global Constitutionalism: The Social Dimension' in Suami, T., Peters, A. and Vanoverbeke, D. (eds). *Global Constitutionalism from European and East Asian Perspectives*, Cambridge University Press.

Presidents of the General Assembly and the Economic and Social Council (2020) *Terms of Reference High-Level Panel on International Financial Accountability, Transparency and Integrity for Achieving the 2030 Agenda*, United Nations.

UN Conference on Trade and Development (UNCTAD) (2018) Report of the Second Expert Meeting on the Statistical Measurement of Illicit Financial Flows.

UNCTAD and UNODC (2020) Conceptual Framework for the Statistical Measurement of Illicit Financial Flows; Vienna; United Nations.

UN High Level Panel on International Financial Accountability, Transparency and Integrity for Achieving the 2030 Agenda (2021) Financial Integrity for Sustainable Development; United Nations.

United Nations Department of Economic and Social Affairs (UNDESA) (2017) *United Nations Model Double Taxation Convention Between Developed and Developing Countries: 2017 Update*, United Nations.

_______ (2018) *Metadata Indicator SDG 16.4.1*, UN Statistics Division.

United Nations Economic Commission for Africa (UNECA) (2015) *Illicit Financial Flows: Report of the High Level Panel on Illicit Financial Flows From Africa. Addis Baba*, United Nations.

United Nations General Assembly (UNGA) (1971) 'Identification of the least developed among the developing countries', Resolution adopted by the General Assembly on 18 November 1971, A/RES/26/2768.

_______ (2015) 'Transforming our world: The 2030 agenda for sustainable development', Resolution adopted by the General Assembly, A/RES/70/1.

_______ (2019) Report of the Secretary General: International Financial System and Development Macroeconomic Policy Questions, United Nations.

UN High Level Panel on International Financial Accountability, Transparency and Integrity for Advancing the 2030 Agenda (UN FACTI Panel) (2021) *Financing for Sustainable Development*, United Nations.

United Nations (UN) (1966) International Covenant on Economic, Social and Cultural Rights. *Adopted and Opened for Signature, Ratification and Accession by General Assembly Resolution 2200A* (XXI).

_______ (2015) *Addis Ababa Action Agenda of the Third Conference on Financing for Development*, UNDESA.

_______ (2020) Inter-Agency Task Force on Financing for Sustainable Development: 2020 Financing for Sustainable Development Report.

Vandenhole, W. (2018) 'De-Growth and Sustainable Development: Rethinking Human Rights Law and Poverty Alleviation', *Law and Development Review* 11, 647–675.

Vandenhole, W. and Benedek, W. (2013) 'Extraterritorial Human Rights Obligations and the North-South Divide' in Langford, M., Vandenhole, W., Scheinin, M. and Van Genugten, W. (eds). *Global Justice, State Duties: The Extraterritorial Scope of Economic, Social and Cultural Rights in International Law*, Cambridge University Press.

Woodward, D. (2010) *How Poor is 'Poor'? Towards a Rights-Based Poverty Line*, New Economics Foundation.

_______ (2015) 'Incrementum ad Absurdum: Global Growth, Inequality and Poverty Eradication in a Carbon-Constrained World', *World Social and Economic Review of Contemporary Policy Issues* 4.

World Health Organisation (2019) World Health Statistics 2019: Monitoring Health for the Sustainable Development Goals.

Zucman, G. (2015) *The Hidden Wealth of Nations: The Scourge of Tax Havens*, University of Chicago Press.

22

Corruption, human rights and extraterritorial obligations

Khulekani Moyo

Introduction

Corruption is one of the greatest evils in the fight to eradicate poverty and in ensuring a dignified living for all people. Corruption has long been recognised as a potentially serious problem in every polity and an impediment to economic development especially in less developed countries (Krever 2007). Corruption impedes the fight against poverty as it increases the cost-of-service delivery through theft and misallocation of resources meant for the provision of public goods. Much of the literature on the causes and consequences of corruption, however, often focus on the demand side – the officials who accept corrupt payments in exchange for favour and influence (Krever 2007). Slowly, however, the impetus has begun to shift towards focusing on the supply side of corruption. Some powerful multinational corporations (MNCs) based in the global north are more often than not identified as common culprits of supply-side corruption and in the process giving corruption a transnational character calling for global solutions (Krever 2007).

Corruption is also closely linked to severe loss of potential public revenue due to illicit financial flows. According to the High-Level Panel on Illicit Financial Flows from Africa, the continent loses over 88.6 billion dollars annually due to illicit financial flows (United Nations Conference on Trade and Development (UNCTAD) 2020). It is not surprising then that Sustainable Development Goals (SDGs) include targets such as the reduction of corruption and bribery in all their forms (UN 2015). The realisation of the SDGs is to a considerable extent predicated on transparency, participation, accountability – values that are important for an anti-corruption drive.

There is little doubt that corruption is one of the biggest obstacles for an effective implementation of economic, social and cultural rights as well as civil and political rights. Corruption is an impediment not only for the realisation of human rights but also for development in general. The diversion and siphoning off of public resources as a result of endemic corruption impacts heavily on the marginalised members of the community and denudes them of their dignity. At the very least, corruption compromises a state's capacity to deliver public services, particularly socio-economic goods such as water, housing, sanitation, healthcare and education.

DOI: 10.4324/9781003090014-28

Increasingly, there is a realisation in the interconnected nature of the world. Whether it is the coronavirus pandemic or terrorist attacks, events occurring in one part of the world have impact on the other corner of the globe. In addressing such impacts, coordinated global responses are required for any meaningful impact.

The incidence of corruption, given its transnational character, has the capacity to engage state responsibility under international law where a state fails to prevent or regulate actors from its territory from engaging in corrupt activities which have deleterious acts on the enjoyment of human rights abroad. The Committee on Economic, Social and Cultural Rights (CESCR 2017, para. 28) has explained that:

> Extraterritorial obligations arise when a state party may influence situations located outside its territory, consistent with the limits imposed by international law, by controlling the activities of corporations domiciled in its territory and/or under its jurisdiction, and thus may contribute to the effective enjoyment of economic, social and cultural rights outside its national territory.

The CESCR in its General Comment no. 24 (2017, para. 20) has further noted that 'Corruption constitutes one of the major obstacles to the effective promotion and protection of human rights, particularly as regards the activities of businesses'. The *Maastricht Principles* on Extraterritorial Obligations of states in the Area of Economic, Social and Cultural Rights (*Maastricht Principles* 2011) are particularly illuminating by their clarification that a state has obligations not only to desist from infringing on the human rights of those beyond its territorial limits, but also to regulate individuals and entities within its jurisdiction from perpetrating acts of corruption and bribery abroad. According to the *Maastricht Principles*, the extraterritorial obligation to respect requires states to refrain from interfering directly or indirectly with the enjoyment of rights by persons outside their territories (Principle 29). It is also noteworthy that under international law, a state may incur responsibility for human rights violations when any entity, such as a business enterprise, which they have obligations to regulate engage in acts or omissions resulting in human rights violations abroad. This obligation is also addressed in the *Maastricht Principles*. An extraterritorial obligation to protect requires states to take steps to prevent and redress infringements of rights that occur outside their territories due to the activities of business entities over which they can exercise control (Principle 30). The obligation to protect with respect to extraterritorial obligations thus enjoins a duty on the state to regulate the conduct of non-state actors, over which a state has regulatory authority.

Corruption is a particularly insidious phenomenon, which stifles economic development, has devastating effects on the most vulnerable members of society, both in developing and developed nations. As noted by Cleveland et al. (2009), there is a universal disdain for corruption that transcends borders, cultures and ideology and this has provided a global impetus and vigour to curb the corruption plague. It is against this background that both practice and scholarship have increasingly courted a human rights-based approach in the fight against the scourge of corruption (Peters 2018). Anti-corruption and anti-bribery are among issues that states have recognised a regulatory role with respect to extraterritorial acts of their natural and legal persons. States have adopted domestic legislation designating bribery and corruption abroad as offences. In addition, states have adopted a number of international and regional anti-corruption conventions to address the scourge of corruption. This chapter explores the developments on ETOs in the anti-corruption/anti-bribery field. It also engages with human rights ETOs around anti-corruption and links them with debates on the fulfilment of state human rights obligations. This chapter is divided into four parts. The first part defines corruption, followed by a discussion of international law's response to corruption, highlighting the extraterritorial dimension of the response against corruption. The United States' (US) domestic legislation is also discussed given its importance in the development and growth of the international, regional and comparative legal regimes aimed at addressing corruption. The third part evaluates the legal question on whether corruption should be regarded as human rights violations. This part thus examines how re-framing corruption as a rights violation has important normative implications and could improve enforcement measures against acts of corruption and bribery at both national and international levels. In that regards, the part seeks to address whether corruption can and should be conceptualised as a violation of human rights engaging state responsibility where individuals or groups living are denied access to public goods they are entitled to as a result of corruption and acts of bribery by using social and economic rights to illustrate on how corruption can violate human rights, followed by the conclusion.

Definition of corruption

The most common definition of corruption is by Transparency International, which defines corruption as the abuse of entrusted power for private gain (Moyo 2017). The United Nations (UN) and African Union (AU) conventions adopted to address corruption and related issues do not provide a precise definition of corruption, but rather stipulate a range of corrupt practices that must be criminalised under national laws. The UN Convention Against Corruption (2003), for instance, criminalises corrupt practices such as bribery, money laundering, abuse of power, embezzlement and trading in influence. Similarly, the AU Convention on Preventing and Combating Corruption (2003) criminalises a wide range of acts, including domestic and foreign bribery, illicit enrichment, money laundering and concealment of property. The common denominator of such corrupt practices is that they consist of inducing undue advantage from public officials and private entities for personal gain. The Southern African Development Community Protocol against Corruption (2001) defines corruption as 'includ[ing] bribery or any other behaviour in relation to persons entrusted with responsibilities in the public and private sectors which violates their duties as public officials, private employees, independent agents or other relationships of that kind and aimed at obtaining undue advantage of any kind for themselves or others' (art. 1).

Corruption may happen on the level of day-to-day administration and public service referred to as petty corruption or at the high level of political office referred to as grand corruption (Shah and Schacter 2004). Corrupt practices include bribery, nepotism, theft and other abuses of public power for private benefit (Ünver and Koyuncu 2016). Corruption, by its nature, uses state resources and institutions to purloin, embezzle or enrich those in public office at the expense of the state's wealth and its citizens' welfare.

The literature generally emphasises corruption in the public sector, even though the private sector is a prominent player in the corruption stakes (United Nations Economic Commission for Africa (UNECA) 2015). The narrow notion of understanding corruption as the 'abuse of public office for private gain' should be challenged. Such an understanding of corruption neglects the corrupt tendencies that are rampant in the private sphere. Corruption can and does occur between firms and individuals or between actors in the private sector and the public sector, for example, through state capture, where private entities 'capture' state institutions for their own benefit (UNECA 2015). It is imperative to understand the importance and implications of viewing corruption as a broader phenomenon where non-state actors share a significant responsibility for engaging and aiding corruption as captured in the SADC Protocol's definition of corruption.

Corruption and human rights – the gap

Although corrupt conduct undoubtedly impedes the realisation of human rights, international and regional human rights instruments make no direct mention of corruption. Furthermore, the human rights treaty monitoring bodies have failed to bring conceptual clarity to the question of how corruption can potentially be construed as a human rights violation. Thus, as a language for describing the harms caused by corruption, international human rights law lacks explicit legal provisions or helpful guidance by treaty monitoring bodies. Moreover, the state-centred character of human rights law reduces its usefulness with respect to corruption, an insidious practice that often takes place at the intersection of the public and private sectors (Rose 2016). Fundamentally, the state-centric nature of human rights law limits its capacity to address such conduct as corruption is not limited to public actors but also permeates the private sector. The relationship between corruption and human rights is addressed in the part below. The next section discusses some of the international law responses to the corruption phenomenon, as well as the importance of an extraterritorial approach to addressing this scourge.

International law's response to corruption

Apart from being the target of transnational norms, corruption and other undesirable transnational activities such as human trafficking have been increasingly subject to national norms of municipal regulation with extraterritorial effect. This has resulted in the extraterritorial application and enforcement of national laws to subjects acting beyond the borders of a given country. The increasing international and national recognition of rights that protect interests closely related to poverty such as the rights to adequate healthcare, sufficient and safe water and sanitation, education, housing and food has begun to change the landscape in the fight against corruption. The period from the early 1990s saw the adoption of global and regional treaties aimed at addressing and curbing the scourge of corruption. Their emergence in the 1990s, in turn, was a reaction to the globalisation of corruption itself, an acknowledgement that corruption had acquired transboundary elements.

Consequently, there is a growing tendency to criminalise and prosecute corruption in its various manifestations such as bribery, both internationally and domestically. What is discernible is the shift from where corruption beyond the borders of a nation state was not regulated at all (before 1977), through one where only the United States (US) formally prohibited foreign bribery (1977–1998), to the current state of affairs where a considerable number of international, regional and national normative standards have been adopted to address corruption. This section discusses some of the international norms, albeit briefly, that aim to address corruption in its extraterritorial manifestations. Given its importance in driving the impetus in the adoption of international norms, the US' Foreign Corrupt Practices Act of 1977 (FCPA 1977), although national legislation, is the subject of this discussion given its importance in the emergence and development of international, regional and domestic anti-corruption norms.

Foreign Corrupt Practices Act

The adoption of the first comprehensive set of domestic norms on transnational bribery goes back to 1977, when the US adopted the FCPA. In that regard, the US was the first country to prohibit payments to foreign government officials to secure a business advantage (Searle Civil Justice Institute 2012). Investigations by the US Congress in the mid-70s revealed that many US corporations were making payments to foreign government officials to obtain business.

Simultaneous investigations surrounding the Watergate scandal revealed that many US firms maintained slush funds to bribe foreign and domestic political officials. These revelations led the US Congress to adopt the FCPA, making the US the global pioneer to enact a law that criminalises acts of corruption in transnational business transactions (Searle Civil Justice Institute 2012).

The FCPA's anti-corruption provisions are thus implicated when engaging in transnational business. The FCPA (1977) criminalises the provision of anything of value to a foreign official for the purposes of securing any improper business advantage. The FCPA thus exclusively focuses on the supply side of the corruption transaction (FCPA 1977, para. 78dd-1(a)). Furthermore, the FCPA only addresses public corruption in the context of international business, and proscribes corrupt acts that are provided to foreign public officials. Significantly, the FCPA is unique because of its jurisdictional provisions that provide a state with extraterritorial enforcement jurisdiction to reach a wide range of domestic and foreign subjects. One may argue that such a broad construction of jurisdiction is desirable from the perspective of stamping out foreign corrupt practices as a global evil whose transnational tentacles require the exercise of extraterritorial jurisdiction.

There is little doubt that the internationalisation of the anti-corruption effort is key to bolstering anti-corruption efforts (Krever 2007). The FCPA provided the impetus and raised the public profile of corruption, both domestically in the US and internationally, thereby paving the way for the adoption of international, regional and domestic norms meant to curb corruption. The FCPA has thus been responsible for increasing political pressure to pursue multilateral conventions on corruption and the increased international awareness has also encouraged many developing countries to join the bandwagon in addressing the demand side of bribery (Krever 2007). Ultimately, the FCPA became the model for similar international initiatives such as the Organisation for Economic Cooperation and Development's Convention on Combating Bribery of Foreign Public Officials in International Business Transactions (OECD Convention), which is discussed below.

Inter-American Convention Against Corruption

Another particularly watershed international development was the decision of the Organization of American States (OAS) to address corruption and bribery. The OAS' Inter-American Convention Against Corruption, adopted in March 1996 (IACA), was the first binding international legal instrument to establish a comprehensive legal framework aimed at preventing and combating corruption. The IACA, which has been ratified by 34 states from the Americas, has particular significance in that it marked the beginning of an international legal regime to combat corruption by criminalising domestic and transnational bribery. The OAS' adoption of IACA thus ranks among the first efforts, outside of the US, to codify extraterritorial efforts to fight corruption.

The IACA (art. 11.1) emphasises as one of its purposes to 'promote, facilitate and regulate co-operation among States Parties to ensure the effectiveness of measures and actions to prevent, detect, punish and eradicate corruption in the performance of public functions and acts of corruption'. A particularly noteworthy feature of the IACA is that amongst the proscribed conduct, it includes corrupt activities of both public officials and foreign public officials, and such a provision empowers member states to exercise both prescriptive and enforcement extraterritorial jurisdiction to prevent and curb corruption. In that regard, the IACAC has an extraterritorial dimension and makes active bribery of a foreign public official an offence (art. VIII). The IACAC extends criminal jurisdiction based on territoriality and nationality principles (art.V). Importantly, state parties are required to extend jurisdiction to offences committed by their nationals or residents, even if they were not committed inside their territory (art. 5, para. 2), thereby magnifying the extraterritorial character of the IACA is addressing transnational corruption.

OECD Convention

The process of moving from a unilateral American legislative initiative to an international anti-corruption movement spanned more than 20 years. Another important international development relating to corruption was the adoption of the OECD Convention in 1997. The OECD Convention's primary objective goal was to eliminate the unfair competitive advantages obtained by corporations paying bribes in foreign markets. The OECD Convention was thus seen as a landmark in combating international corruption by requiring legislative convergence on the addressing transnational corruption. Its significance is that it was the first international attempt by the major capital-exporting countries to curb the 'supply side' of corruption, that is, the willingness of MNCs from the global north to bribe foreign public officials (Kaczmarek and Newman 2011). To achieve this goal, the OECD enjoins its member states to enact legal and policy measures to prevent, detect, investigate, prosecute and sanction corruption of foreign public officials. In that regard, the OECD member states pledged to enact domestic legislation with extraterritorial effect in order to effectively regulate corporations domiciled in their jurisdictions when such corporations engaged in business activities abroad. Proponents of the OECD Convention suggest that it marks a revolution in the fight against corruption and is a significant component of the international legal regime to address transnational corruption in its various dimensions (Kaczmarek and Newman 2011).

At the core of the OECD Convention is Article 1, which elaborates the key elements constituting the offence of bribery of foreign public officials. Article 3 of the Convention states that member countries should criminalise the bribery of foreign public officials, stating that:

> The bribery of a foreign public official shall be punishable by effective, proportionate and dissuasive criminal penalties. The range of penalties shall be comparable to that applicable to the bribery of the Party's own public officials and shall, in the case of natural persons, include deprivation of liberty sufficient to enable effective mutual legal assistance and extradition.

Additionally, Article 2 permits the exercise of extraterritorial jurisdiction by enjoining that every state party shall establish the liability of legal persons who bribe a foreign public official in accordance with national legal principles of each member state. Article 2 is thus important in its explicit authorisation of state parties to exercise both prescriptive and enforcement extraterritorial jurisdiction to prevent and punish corrupt acts occurring beyond a state's shores.

UN Convention Against Corruption

The key global anti-corruption instrument, the UN Convention Against Corruption (UNCAC), adopted in 2003, went beyond previous international agreements on corruption. It enjoins state parties to criminalise not only basic forms of corruption such as bribery and embezzlement of public funds but also trading in influence and concealment and laundering of the proceeds of corruption. Significantly, the high number of signatories and ratifications (187 currently) reflects the broad international consensus on the UNCAC. The UNCAC focuses on three major areas, namely prevention, criminalisation and enforcement against corruption and its various manifestations. The UNCAC requires states to introduce effective policies and institutional arrangements for the prevention of corruption, including the introduction of a specific anti-corruption body, codes of conduct and policies promoting good governance, the rule of law, transparency and accountability (UNCAC 2003).

The UNCAC (art. 5.4) enjoins states to collaborate with each other, and with relevant international and regional organisations, in promoting and developing the measures to prevent and combat corruption. Significantly, each state party is enjoined, within its domestic legal system, to identify, trace freeze, seize or confiscate proceeds of corruption (art. 31). Chapter IV of the UNCAC is exclusively devoted to international cooperation, setting forth detailed guidelines relating to extraditions, investigations, prosecutions and judicial legal proceedings. Article 42 UNCAC permits state parties to exercise jurisdiction over corruption on the basis of the normal principles of jurisdiction, namely nationality, territoriality and protection of state interests. Article 42 also contains a savings clause, which allows states to exercise other types of jurisdiction, provided that they are in keeping with international law. In that regard, Article 42 of the UNCAC is significant for its permissive approach to the exercise of jurisdiction to curb corruption, including the exercise of extraterritorial jurisdiction.

Council of Europe's Criminal Law and Civil Law Conventions on Corruption

The Council of Europe (CoE)'s Criminal Law Convention (Criminal Law Convention), adopted in 1999, covers both active and passive bribery (art. 2) of domestic and foreign public officials as well as a long list of other national and international bureaucrats (arts. 4–11). A pioneering feature of the Criminal Law Convention is that it extends criminal responsibility for bribery to the private sector, which is absent in some of the international anti-corruption instruments such as the OECD Convention. This reflects recognition of the need to emasculate any differences in the rules applicable to the private and public sector, which becomes especially important in view of the transfer of public functions to the private sector as a result of privatisation and public/private partnerships.

Article 17 of the Criminal Law Convention, which provides for jurisdiction, establishes a series of criteria under which state parties can exercise enforcement jurisdiction over the criminal offences enumerated in Articles 2–14 of the Convention. Article 17 also provides for the principle of territoriality as a ground for the exercise of jurisdiction. What is clear is that it does not require that a corruption offence as a whole be committed exclusively on the territory of a state to enable it to exercise enforcement jurisdiction. If only parts of the offence were committed on its territory, a state may still exercise enforcement jurisdiction. In that regard, Article 17 permits the expansion of the principle of territoriality to encompass an extraterritorial dimension. Article 17 also sets out the principle of nationality as a ground for the exercise of jurisdiction. The nationality theory is also based upon the state sovereignty and provides that nationals of a state are obliged to comply with the domestic law even when they are outside its territory. It follows that if a national commits an offence abroad, then the state party is entitled to exercise jurisdiction in accordance with Article 17. Article 17 also provides for the exercise of jurisdiction based on the protection of the protection of the state or its interests. Article 17 is thus important to the extent that it provides a leeway for the state to exercise extraterritorial jurisdiction to investigate and punish acts of corruption, which is a significant provision to make the treaty more effective. Significantly, Article 25 enjoins states parties to cooperate with each other to the widest extent possible for the purposes of investigations and proceedings concerning criminal offences established in accordance with the Convention.

The CoE adopted the Civil Law Convention on Corruption in 1999 (Civil Law Convention). The Civil Law Convention provides for common international legal rules in the field of civil law and corruption (Council of Europe 1999). Importantly, the Civil Law Convention enjoins state parties to provide, in their domestic law, effective remedies for persons who have suffered damage as a result of acts of corruption, including the possibility of obtaining compensation for damage. The Civil Law Convention (art. 13) further provides for international cooperation by state parties in civil cases of corruption, including in obtaining evidence abroad, jurisdiction, recognition and enforcement of foreign judgments, thereby clothing the instrument with extraterritorial dimensions. In terms of Article 13, which provides for international cooperation, one of the guiding principles in the fight against corruption is an undertaking to develop international cooperation in all areas of the fight against corruption. This again provides the Civil Law Convention with an extraterritorial dimension in the fight against corruption and its various manifestations.

The African Union Convention on Preventing and Combating Convention

In 2003, the then-Organisation of African Unity, now the African Union, adopted the Convention on Preventing and Combating Corruption (AU Corruption Convention). The AU Corruption Convention also adds to a burgeoning series of international efforts to combat corruption through international law. The adoption of such international instruments is no doubt an acknowledgement of corruption and bribery's impacts on human welfare and the importance of a collective approach to address the scourge. Foremost among the AU Corruption Convention's objectives is promoting development by preventing, detecting and punishing acts of corruption on the African continent (art. 2).

The AU Corruption Convention mandates three essential steps: (1) prevention, (2) criminalisation and (3) international cooperation (art. 4–24) in addressing the domestic and international dimensions of corruption. The coverage of the AU Corruption Convention extends to public officials and to 'any other person', including members of the private sector (arts. 4 and 11) – an important provision to ensure that private sector corruption is also addressed. The AU Corruption Convention follows typical jurisdictional grounds for investigation and prosecution: the place of commission of the offence, the nationality and residence of the offender and the presence of the offender in a given territory (art. 13(1)(a)–(c).) Significantly, the AU Corruption Convention subjects anyone who commits an act of corruption or its various manifestations such as bribery anywhere to the jurisdiction of the state party if the offence affects the state's vital interests (art. 13(a)–(d)). This clearly clothes member states with extraterritorial prescriptive and enforcement jurisdiction in the fight against corruption.

The international cooperation provisions in the AU Corruption Convention include extradition, tracing, seizure and confiscation of proceeds of corruption and mutual legal assistance (arts. 16–18). Most importantly, the AU Corruption Convention highlights the importance of eradicating corruption in development aid (art. 19(4)). It is, however, noteworthy that global instruments such as the UNCAC discussed above avoid taking a concrete position on the relationship between corruption and human rights. Such a pattern is also observable in the OECD Corruption Convention and other regional instruments discussed above where corruption and bribery are considered as crimes that undermine good governance and transparency and must be prevented, detected, punished and eradicated. In that regard, these instruments frame corruption as a means by which public goods that are fundamental for the realisation of human rights are negatively impacted by corruption but without explicitly characterising corruption as a direct human rights violation. The next section engages on the issue of whether corruption could be regarded as a human rights violation, in the process highlighting the significance of national and extraterritorial measures anchored in human rights to address the corruption scourge.

Closing the gap

A growing number of legal scholars and activists are pushing for a human rights approach to addressing corruption (Rose 2016). Some scholars have sought to base their arguments in existing international human rights instruments. Others have advocated for a human right to a corruption-free society (Boersma 2011). One proposal is that the fight against corruption could be advanced by framing it under a 'freedom from corruption' banner (Murray and Spalding 2015, p. 4). This would add a new and powerful dimension to the fight against corruption. Some scholars have argued that corruption could qualify as a crime against humanity (Kofeke-Kale 2000).

As discussed further below, the thrust of the argument to infuse human rights in the fight against corruption is that corruption has identifiable victims of human rights violations. The victim-oriented approach stemming from a human rights-based approach in the fight against corruption would complement the existing approaches to curb corruption. It is important to note that all human rights are endangered where corruption is endemic, and thus an approach predicated on human rights should be part of the arsenal in the fight against corruption (Ramasastry 2015). Despite the recognition that corruption undermines human rights values and norms, efforts to combat corruption in many countries do not include a human-rights perspective – even though many of them have constitutions that contain bills or declarations of rights.

A critical legal question when drawing a nexus between corruption and human rights is whether corrupt acts could and should be regarded as human rights violations. The traditional approach is to view corruption as impacting the realisation of human rights but not itself constituting a human rights violation (Ramasastry 2015). However, attention is quickly shifting to cast a spotlight on the groups and individuals whose lives are negatively affected by rampant corruption.

The turn towards a human rights approach to corruption, which began in the late 1990s, appears to be motivated by a need to focus greater attention to the victims rather than solely on the perpetrators of such corrupt acts (Kofele-Kale 2015; Boersma 2012). The perpetrators of corruption are often the targets of international and regional treaties as well as domestic criminal laws that address corruption. Some commentators see human rights law as empowering for victims, though they have not elaborated on exactly how (Peters 2018). Others consider a human rights approach to be imperative given the inadequacies of anti-corruption norms and criminal law treaties in curbing corruption (Hatchard 2010). In that regard, a human rights lens provides a valuable normative framework to address corruption. The added value of elevating an issue to the level of a human right is that it establishes a universal norm that becomes more difficult to disregard. This approach also emphasises the duties of states, and in some cases non-state actors, as well as the rights of those negatively impacted by corruption. In that regard, the human rights framework helps to give a voice to those who otherwise are unable to assert their rights.

Acknowledging and deploying a human-rights lens in the fight against corruption would significantly strengthen the impetus to adopt preventative actions aimed at eradicating the scourge of corruption (Peters 2018). The human rights approach can explicitly highlight the deleterious effects of corruption, for example, the rights of persons denied access to safe drinking water, affordable housing and adequate healthcare due to misuse of public funds through corrupt activities. A human rights approach is also likely to engage state duties in the fight against corruption, and the possibility of engaging state responsibility for failing to protect the rights of those exposed to the damaging effects of corruption.

An illustration on how corruption can violate social and economic rights

It is noteworthy that corruption, by its nature, can impede the enjoyment of a very wide range of human rights, from civil, political, economic, social and cultural rights, to the rights of children, migrant workers and the disabled. It follows that, depending on the circumstances of a case, civil, political, economic, social and cultural rights can be violated by acts of corruption.

Under the ICESCR (art. 2), the obligation imposed on states is to 'take steps…to the maximum of its available resources, with a view to achieving progressively the full realisation of the rights recognised in the present Covenant by all appropriate means'. The human rights set out in the covenants, as well as the human rights contained in other international and regional instruments, as elaborated by the relevant treaty bodies, give rise to three kinds of duties, namely the duties to respect, protect and fulfil the protected rights.

The focus of this section is to illustrate the impact of corruption on the rights protected under the ICESCR because most, if not all, of the rights set forth in this instrument are commonly affected by all forms of corruption, be it petty or grand corruption. Considering the ICESCR is also important in that the instrument is the core international legal document on economic, social and cultural rights and affords protection to the most extensive range of these rights. These include the right to work, trade union rights, right to social security, rights to food, water, housing, the right to health and the right to education. The ICESCR therefore represents an important global instrument for evaluating the impact of corruption on the realisation of human rights.

Treaty monitoring bodies, courts and other tribunals have elaborated on the specific duties generated by human rights in the context of socio-economic rights as entailing the duties to respect, protect, promote and fulfil human rights (CESCR 2000; CESCR 2001; CESCR 2002). The duty to respect is essentially a negative obligation commanding the state to refrain from infringements that impede the enjoyment of rights. The duty to respect thus enjoins the state to desist from embarking on any measure that interferes with the individuals or groups' enjoyment of their rights (Chirwa 2004). The state is therefore required to refrain from obstructing or hindering the enjoyment of rights by adopting privatisation, trade or commercialisation policies that negatively interfere with the enjoyment of socio-economic rights (Moyo 2018).

The duty to protect primarily refers to protection from dangers emanating from third parties whose effect is to interfere with the enjoyment of human rights. While the duty to respect requires the state to abstain from deprivation of rights, the duty to protect enjoins the state to act positively to regulate, prevent and remedy rights breaches by non-state actors (Chirwa 2004). The duty to protect thus primarily imposes a positive obligation on the state to adopt the appropriate measures to protect rights holders from having their enjoyment of rights infringed by non-state actors.

The duty to fulfil requires the state to adopt appropriate legislative and other measures to ensure the full realisation of the right in question. The positive duty to fulfil is key to the enjoyment of socio-economic rights. The duties imposed by socio-economic rights enunciated above may become difficult to comply with in a climate characterised by corruption. A corrupt act may potentially violate each of these dimensions of state duties socio-economic rights impose on states.

Peters (2018), for instance, has argued that socio-economic rights comprise the element of 'affordability' such as the affordability of essential medicine as a component of the human right to fulfil the right to health, the fact that corruption in procurement processes may make medicines more expensive could be seen as a human rights violation. In such a case, there is a clear and direct nexus between corruption and the violation of the right to health. This is particularly the case where a state fails to put in place effective anti-corruption measures or fails to investigate, prosecute or punish those implicated in acts of corruption.

The duty to protect against human rights violations by third parties is important in the fight against corruption. Failure by the state to adopt effective anti-corruption measures may incur state responsibility under the state's domestic and international human rights obligations, particularly under the ICESCR. The duty to protect under human rights law does not only require the state to protect those within its jurisdiction from the human rights violating actions of third parties. The state is also bound to prevent human rights risks in which public officials may be involved (Ebert and Sijniensky 2015), particularly where such public officials are involved in corrupt acts that are linked to the denial of the rights to certain sectors of the population.

A state taking seriously its duty to protect would strengthen its legislative, regulatory and other measures aimed at curbing corruption. In an environment plagued with rampant corruption, this would include the establishment of an effective and appropriately resourced anti-corruption body. Related anti-corruption measures would include the enactment of codes of conduct for public officials in the execution of their public duties, strengthening of public procurement laws and regulations to curb malfeasance, and the adoption of norms and establishment of institutions to curb money laundering. The UN CESCR (2000) has emphasised the importance of states adopting effective measures to curb corruption. Within the context of the state's duty to fulfil, the UN CESCR, for instance, has identified misallocation of public resources resulting in the non-enjoyment of the right to health by individuals and groups, thereby impeding their enjoyment of that right (UN 2000). Where financial resources budgeted for the provision of healthcare services are corruptly misappropriated by government officials and thus resulting in the denial of healthcare services, the state might be held to be violating its duty to fulfil the right to adequate healthcare services (Peters 2018).

Conclusion

There is little doubt that corruption is one of the biggest obstacles for an effective implementation of economic, social and cultural rights as well as civil and political rights. Corruption is an impediment not only for the realisation of human rights but also for development in general. The diversion and siphoning off of public resources as a result of endemic corruption impacts heavily on the marginalised members of the community and denudes them of their dignity.

Anti-corruption and anti-bribery are among issues that states have recognised a regulatory role with respect to extraterritorial acts of their natural and legal persons. States have adopted domestic legislation designating bribery and corruption abroad as offences. In addition, states have adopted a number of international and regional anti-corruption conventions to address the scourge of corruption. This chapter explored the developments on ETOs in the anti-corruption/anti-bribery field. It also engages with human rights ETOs around anti-corruption and links them with debates on the fulfilment of state human rights obligations.

This chapter has demonstrated that corruption is not only an insidious phenomenon which stifles economic development but also a human rights violation with identifiable victims. The *Maastricht Principles* are particularly noteworthy in plugging the regulatory gap by clarifying of states' obligations not only to desist from infringing on human rights of individuals and groups abroad but also to regulate individuals and entities within their jurisdiction from perpetrating acts of corruption and bribery abroad. Importantly, the extraterritorial obligation to respect human rights, according to the *Maastricht Principles*, requires states to refrain from interfering directly or indirectly with the enjoyment of human rights by persons outside their territories. In the same vein, an extraterritorial obligation to protect human rights requires states to take steps to prevent and redress infringements of human rights that occur outside their territories due to the activities of individual and entities over which they can exercise control.

Acknowledging and deploying a human rights lens in the fight against corruption would significantly strengthen the impetus to adopt preventative actions aimed at eradicating the scourge of corruption. The human rights approach can explicitly highlight the deleterious effects of corruption, for example, the rights of persons denied access to safe drinking water, affordable housing and adequate healthcare due to misuse of public funds through corrupt activities. A human rights approach is also likely to engage state duties in the fight against corruption, and the possibility of engaging state responsibility, including their extraterritorial obligations, for failing to protect the rights of those exposed to the damaging effects of corruption. Thus, reframing corruption as a rights violation has important normative and utilitarian implications, and could improve enforcement at both national and international levels.

References

African Union (2003) Convention on Preventing and Combating Corruption, 43 I.L.M. 1.

African Union/United Nations Economic Commission for Africa (UNECA) (2015) Report of the High Level Panel on Illicit Financial Flows from Africa.

Boersma, M. (2012) *Corruption: A Violation of Human Rights and a Crime under International Law?*, Intersentia.

Chirwa, D.M. (2004) 'Water Privatisation and Socio-Economic Rights in South Africa', *Law, Democracy and Development* 4, 188–189.

Cleveland, M et al. (2009) 'Sixth Annual Ethical Dimensions In Business: Reflections From The Business Academic Community', *Journal of Business Ethics* 90, 199–244.

Ebert, F.C. and Sijniensky, R.I. (2015) 'Preventing Violations of the Right to Life in the European and the Inter-American Human Rights Systems: From the Osman Test to a Coherent Doctrine on Risk Prevention?', *Human Rights Law Review* 15, 343–368.

Foreign Corrupt Practices Act (FCPA) (1977) as amended, 15 U.S.C.

Hatchard, J. (2010) 'Adopting a Human Rights Approach Towards Combating Corruption' in Boersma, M. and Hans Nelen, H. (eds). *Corruption and Human Rights: Interdisciplinary Perspectives*, Intersentia.

Inter-American Convention Against Corruption (1996) 35 I.L.M. 724, available at http:/www.oas.org/juridico/english/Treaties/b-58.html.

Kaczmarek, S.C. and Newman, A.L. (2011) 'The Long Arm of the Law: Extraterritoriality and the National Implementation of Foreign Bribery Legislation', *International Organization* 65, 745–770.

Kofele-Kale, N. (2015) 'The Right to a Corruption-Free Society as an Individual and Collective Human Right: Elevating Official Corruption to a Crime under International Law', *International Lawyer* 34, 149–178.

Krever, T. (2007) 'Curbing Corruption - The Efficacy of the Foreign Corrupt Practice Act, 33 North', *Carolina Journal of International Law & Commercial Regulation* 33, 83–102.

Lippitt, A.H. (2013) 'An Empirical Analysis Of The Foreign Corrupt Practices Act', *Virginia Law Review* 99, 1893–1930.

Moyo, K. (2017) 'An Analysis of the Impact of Corruption on the Realisation of the Right to Development' *South African Journal on Human Rights* 33, 193–213.

_______ (2018) 'Taming the Leviathan: An Analysis of the Extraterritorial Application of the Right to Water under the African system for the Protection of Human Rights' in Chenwi, L. and Bulto, T. (eds). *Justice Beyond Borders: The Extraterritorial Reach of African Human Rights Instruments*, Intersentia.

Murray, M. and Spalding, A. (2015) 'Freedom From corruption as a Human Right', 4 Brookings Institution, available at http://www.brookings.edu/research/papers/2015/01/27-freedom-corruption-human-right-murray-spalding.

Organisation for Economic Cooperation and Development (OECD) (1999) Convention on Combating Bribery of Foreign Public Officials in International Business Transactions.

Peters, A. (2018) 'Corruption as a Violation of International Human Rights', *The European Journal of International Law* 29, 1251–1287.

Ramasastry, A. (2015) 'Is There a Right to Be Free from Corruption?', *University of California Davis Law Review* 49(2), 703–739.

Raoul Wallenberg Institute (2017) 'Anti-Corruption And Human Rights - How to Become Mutually Reinforcing?' (13-14 November 2017) <https://rwi.lu.se/app/uploads/2018/02/Anti-Corruption-and-Human-Rights-RWI.pdf> [accessed 24 January 2021].

Rose, C. (2016) 'The Limitations of a Human Rights Approach to Corruption', *International and Comparative Law Quarterly* 65, 405–438.

Searle Civil Justice Institute (2012) Preliminary Policy Report on the Foreign Corrupt Practices Act: An Empirical Examination Of Enforcement Trends, available at https://masonlec.org/site/rte_uploads/files/FINAL%20FCPA%20REPORT%20PDF.pdf.

Shah, A. and Schacter, M. (2004) 'Combating Corruption: Look Before you Leap', *Finance and Development, available at* https://www.imf.org/external/pubs/ft/fandd/2004/12/pdf/shah.pdf [accessed 24 January 2021].

United Nations Committee on Economic, Social and Cultural Rights (CESCR) (1999) GC 12 on the Right to Adequate Food, UN Doc E/C.12/1999/5.

_______ (2000) GC 14 on the Right to the Highest Attainable Standard of Health, UN Doc E/C.12/2000/4.

_______ (2000) GC 14 on the Right to the Highest Attainable Standard of Health, UN Doc E/C.12/2000/4.

_______ (2002) GC 15 on the Right to Water, UN Doc E/C.12/2002/11.

United Nations Conference on Trade and Development (UNCTAD) (2020) Economic Development in Africa Report: Tackling Illicit Financial Flows for Sustainable Development in Africa.

United Nations Economic Commission for Africa (UNECA) (2016) Measuring Corruption in Africa: The International Dimension Matters - African Governance Report IV.

United Nations General Assembly (2003) United Nations Convention Against Corruption (UNCAC), U.N. GAOR, 58th Sess., U.N. Doc. A/RES/58/4.

_______ (2015) Transforming our world: the 2030 Agenda for Sustainable Development, A/RES/70/1.

Ünver, M. and Koyuncu, J.C. (2016) 'The Impact of Poverty on Corruption', *Journal of Economics Library* 3, 632–642.

23

Obligations of international assistance and cooperation in the context of investment law

Tara Van Ho[1]

Introduction

This Chapter considers states' obligations to provide international assistance and cooperation (IAC) for the protection and realisation of human rights in the context of international investment law (IIL). It focuses on the obligations arising from Article 2(1) of the International Covenant on Economic, Social, and Cultural Rights (ICESCR) (1966). This is only one potential avenue for establishing extraterritorial human rights obligations in the context of IIL, but it is one that has not yet been seriously considered. As this Chapter concludes, a more structured and fully developed understanding of what Article 2(1) requires of states has the potential to upend current approaches to the relationship between IIL and international human rights law (IHRL).

IIL provides substantive protections to foreign investors, primarily businesses, when they undertake commercial investments outside their state of nationality (their 'home state') (Yilmaz Vastardis 2018).[2] There is neither a universal investment treaty nor a coherent body of interpretation and application of IIL. Its protections derive from bilateral and multilateral international investment agreements (IIAs), domestic investment laws, and direct contracts between an investor and a state. Conflicts between IIL and IHRL remain rare (see Coleman, Cordes and Johnson 2020) but, as is explained in Section 3, IIL can effectively constrain states' ability to respect, protect, and fulfil their IHRL obligations. This Chapter considers states' IAC obligations to address IIL impacts. Because this is the first sustained examination of the responsibility of IAC in the context of IIL, it focuses only IIAs as the treaties, unlike a state's contracts or national laws, require and invite the involvement of more than one state.

To date, scholarship has considered how ICESCR's IAC obligations might inform the analysis of particular issues within IIL. As such, scholars have narrowly focused on the obligations of investors' home states when developing and negotiating IIAs (*Maastricht Principles* 2013; De Schutter 2011; Davitti 2019, pp. 207–216) and when providing financial support to investors operating overseas (Krajewski 2013; Ruggie 2011, Principle 4), or to protect human rights by ensuring accountability for national investors that operate abroad (Sornarajah 2015, p. 320). This Chapter starts from a different position, centring the demands of IAC and asking about their implications for IIL. By looking at what is broadly required of states with regard to IAC (Section 2) before outlining the impact IIL has on IHRL (Section 3), I set a foundation to assess

DOI: 10.4324/9781003090014-29

the responsibility of negotiating states (Section 4). I am also able to reveal IAC obligations on third-party states in the context of IIL (Section 4). In this, I break novel ground. I conclude (Section 5) that the recognition of third-party obligations for IAC in the context of IIL has the potential to alter the existing relationship between IIL and IHRL, and raises further questions for scholars and practitioners.

Defining international assistance and cooperation obligations

ICESCR Article 2(1) requires states parties to 'take steps, individually and through international assistance and cooperation, especially economic and technical, to the maximum of [their] available resources' to realise the rights in the Covenant. It is complemented by three other articles in ICESCR. States recognise in Article 15 that international cooperation in the scientific and cultural fields can facilitate realisation of the Covenant and in Article 23 that they must undertake 'international action for the achievement' of the Covenant's obligations, including providing technical assistance and establishing fora for international cooperation. States uniquely agree to provide IAC, including technical assistance around issues of nutrition and agrarian reform, in Article 11. The commitment in Article 2(1), however, clarifies that the obligation to IAC does not operate in isolation but attaches to each right and to conduct that influences realisation of the Covenant as a whole.

Historically, the phrasing of Article 2(1) raised questions as to whether states merely must seek IAC when they need it, or if they are also required to provide IAC as well (Karimova 2014; Skogly 2006; Sepúlveda 2006). As I explain in this section, the UN Committee on Economic, Social, and Cultural Rights (CESCR) has now clarified that states carry obligations to provide IAC when they have the capacity to do so. For the purpose of this Chapter, I accept the jurisprudence of CESCR is, at the least, a highly persuasive interpretation of ICESCR representative of the 'teaching of the most highly qualified publicists of the various nations' (ICJ Statute 1946, art. 38(1)(d)) who have been entrusted by states parties to oversee compliance with the treaty and clarify the content of substantive commitments (Optional Protocol to ICESCR 2009). Their interpretation should be disregarded only with good reason and when displaced by a more persuasive interpretation.

CESCR 'has given little detailed direction as to the content of the obligation' to IAC (Salomon 2013, p. 279), and there remains limited scholarship examining the demands of IAC (cf., Sepúlveda 2006; Karimova 2014; *Maastricht Principles* 2013). Primarily, as is seen below, the focus thus far has been on framing the responsibility rather than elaborating specific obligations. Pulling together what does exist on IAC, as I do here, provides an important foundation for understanding states' obligations in the context of IIL. I examine how the framing of IAC obligations before identifying specific obligations pertinent to IIL.

Framing the obligations

CESCR has recognised that all states carry IAC obligations (e.g., CESCR 2000a, paras. 43–45), but, as noted above, the question has long been whether states who can provide IAC must do so (Karimova 2014; Skogly 2006; Sepúlveda 2006). To answer this, CESCR and noted scholars have framed IAC in two significant ways. First, they placed the IAC obligations in the context of the 'respect, protect, and fulfil' framework (CESCR 2017; Eide 1999; Skogly 2006; Sepúlveda 2006; De Schutter 2011; Vandenhole and Benedek 2012; *Maastricht Principles* 2013). That each human right entails three distinct state obligations—respect, protect, and fulfil—is now widely accepted (e.g., CESCR 2000a, para. 33; Human Rights Committee 2004, paras. 6–7; Mégret

2017, p. 130). States must respect human rights by refraining from interfering in their realisation, protect by preventing third-party actors from harming rights, and fulfil by adopting legislative, judicial, administrative, and educative measures aimed at ensuring the highest realisation of the right as is possible in light of financial and other practical constraints (Eide 1999, para. 130). Linking IAC to the tripartite obligations provides an interpretation of IAC consistent with other substantive obligations in ICESCR, clarifies when, how, and why responsibilities arise in areas that CESCR has not yet addressed or addressed fully, and allows states to distinguish between obligations of immediate effect—generally obligations of outcome to 'respect' human rights—and obligations of conduct aimed at the progressive realisation of rights in the Covenant, generally to 'protect' and 'fulfil'.

Second, the responsibility to provide IAC has been linked to states' *capacity* to give it (e.g., CESCR 2020, para. 35). CESCR has indicated 'that it is particularly incumbent on states parties and other actors *in a position to assist*, to provide' IAC in order to ensure all states parties can meet minimum core obligations (ibid, para. 45). It has repeated its exhortation that those 'in a position to assist' must do so in other General Comments and in state reports (CESCR 2016, para. 66; 2008, paras. 55–56; 2013, para. 32; 2018, paras. 20–21). CESCR's approach is buttressed by the *Maastricht Principles* on the Extraterritorial Obligations of States in the Area of Economic, Social, and Cultural Rights (2013, Principle 31)—developed by leading experts and relied upon by CESCR (2017, fn 71) and UN special procedure holders (e.g., Dandan 2016, paras. 30–36; Lumina 2014, paras. 37–41)—which indicate that obligations should be 'commensurate with' the state's 'economic, technical and technological capacities, available resources, and influence in decision-making processes'.

The focus on a state's capacity to provide is often presented as imposing obligations on 'developed states' to provide assistance and cooperation to 'developing states', but as Skogly (2006) has pointed out, this is inaccurate. The obligation applies equally to all states and is often an obligation of conduct rather than outcome. Developing states can use leverage, individually or collectively, to influence the international community, even where they lack the power to directly provide IAC (Vandenhole and Benedek 2012, p. 341). And, since 'capacity' includes various types of knowledge and resource, there are times when developing states' capacity and technical knowledge will be greater than developed states or international organisations who have never faced the constraints they do. For example, several developing states with experience in public health crises have thus far weathered the COVID-19 pandemic with less technology but better results than many developed states (e.g., Makoni 2020). Given their experience, the former category can assist other states in planning and assessing COVID-19 responses, and would have a responsibility to do so to the extent they can.

Identifying relevant IAC obligations for IIL

As noted above, CESCR has not fully addressed states' IAC obligations in the context of IIL. It has, however, identified some relevant obligations. In the context of IAC, the respect obligation requires states to refrain from any direct or indirect action that would interfere with the full realisation of rights in another territory (CESCR 2017, para. 29). When operating abroad, states and their state-owned enterprises should apply their domestic standards when those standards provide greater respect for human rights than the host state's laws and regulations (CESCR 2016, para. 69). States must not impose 'burdensome conditionalities' as part of their official development assistance programmes or adopt 'measures which are not guided by the needs of developing countries' (Sepúlveda 2006, pp. 281–282). Finally, states should be cognisant of how their trade and investment agreements impact human rights extraterritorially and ensure those agreements do not negatively impact economic, social, and cultural rights (CESCR 2017, para. 29; 2016, para. 72).

The duty to protect requires, *inter alia*, responding to the extraterritorial impacts of third-party actors (CESCR 2000a, para. 39; 2017, para. 30; 2020, para. 84). Primarily, states are to adopt legislation and other measures aimed at 'prevent[ing] and redress[ing] infringements of Covenant rights that occur outside their territory due to the activities of business entities over which they can exercise control' (CESCR 2020, para. 84; 2016, para. 70). Claire Methven O'Brien (2018, pp. 60–61) has argued that this obligation has been prematurely pronounced, a minority position amongst scholars (e.g., McCorquodale and Simons 2007; Seck 2011; De Schutter 2016; Davitti 2016). Methven O'Brien utilises jurisprudence from the European Court of Human Rights, with some insights from the International Court of Justice, to argue businesses' home states do not have jurisdiction over the victims of its business nationals operating abroad. As such, she submits that states do not owe any obligations to those harmed by the overseas operations of their corporate nationals. But, Methven O'Brien's objection is misplaced when considering states' IAC obligations. IAC is not tied to states' jurisdiction but to their capacity to provide assistance (e.g., CESCR 2020, para. 45). As is explained below, IIAs do not affect the relationship between a business and its home state, and as such home states are often in a greater position to regulate a business's extraterritorial impacts than the host state. That capacity is the metric by which to measure the state obligation, and that capacity suggests that in many cases there is an IAC obligation to regulate business nationals' extraterritorial impacts.

Finally, to 'fulfil', states should 'promote an enabling environment' that facilitates the advancement of economic, social, and cultural rights (CESCR 2020, para. 77). This includes ensuring their overseas development assistance takes account of human rights (CESCR 2017, para. 24; Eide 1999, para. 130; Sepúlveda 2006, p. 285) and that the international organisations they are members of respect, protect, and fulfil human rights (CESCR 2001, para. 31). CESCR has repeatedly stressed the importance of States Parties to the International Monetary Fund, the World Bank, and regional development banks monitoring and influencing the organisations' policies for the protection of human rights (e.g. CESCR 2000b, para. 126; 2001, para. 394; 2016, paras. 71–72; *Maastricht Principles* 2013, p. 10). This is recognised as an obligation of effort relative to the influence of the state (ibid). Less influential states may fulfil their obligations by raising points for debate and forming alliances in order to influence policy and practices (Vandenhole and Benedek 2012, p. 341).

Despite the limited development of IAC to date, as is seen below, what exists provides an important foundation for considering IAC in IIL. It is now necessary to consider how IIL harms, or threatens to harm, human rights so as to identify ways in which states' IAC obligations are triggered.

The impact of IIL on IHRL

Disputes arising from IIAs are generally decided by *ad hoc*[3] investor-state dispute settlement ('ISDS') panels appointed by the state and the complaining foreign investor (Yilmaz Vastardis 2020a; Sornarajah 2015, pp. 139–140). The World Bank has been the primary advocate of ISDS, based largely on a theoretical belief in its ability to facilitate foreign direct investment, and 'is the only [international organization] that has ever recommended governments provide access to investor-state arbitration in their domestic investment laws' (Berge and St John 2020, p. 5; see also Sattorova 2018). States sometimes condition the provision of IAC on a recipient state receiving guidance from the World Bank, and the Bank's guidance has encouraged states, particularly developing states, to adopt ISDS (ibid). Yet, ISDS tribunals rarely engage with IHRL in any significant manner, providing only '[s]uperficial acknowledgments of human rights law … unlikely to produce harmonized obligations' (Coleman, Cordes and Johnson 2020, p. 294). Decisions cannot be appealed, can be annulled only in rare circumstances, and are enforceable in the defending state and in up to 185 other states or territories (ICSID Convention 1966; New York Convention 1958). As Yilmaz Vastardis (2018, p. 280; also, 2020) has rightly argued, the current ISDS 'prioritises institutions of justice for foreign investors over the improvement of local institutions that could provide justice for members across society, including', but not limited to, foreign investors (see also Arcuri 2020).

This section cannot exhaustively examine the threats IIL poses to IHRL (see Davitti 2019; Wandahl Mouyal 2018), but highlights three dominant issues that affect states' ability and willingness to protect human rights: (1) the inconsistency of ISDS tribunal decisions; (2) the failure to recognise investors' responsibilities for human rights; and (3) the significant costs of ISDS. Collectively, these facets incentivise states to prioritise IIL at the expense of human rights (Bonnitcha 2011, p. 128; Van Ho 2016).

ISDS panels operate without binding precedent or *jurisprudence constante* (e.g. Schneiderman 2010). After Argentina placed caps on water and energy tariffs in furtherance of the human rights to water and an adequate standard of living during its 2001 financial crisis, various ISDS panels disagreed on pretty much everything: whether Argentina was in a position to invoke the defence of necessity; when the crisis started and ended; and why the state was or was not justified in its response, including the relevance of its IHRL obligations (e.g. ICSID 2007b; 2007a; 2010; 2008b; 2016; Zarra 2018, pp. 151–154). These are not the only cases with different outcomes arising from the same underlying facts and IIL protections merely because the claimants and tribunals differed (e.g. ICSID 2012; 2017). Nor are they alone in creating what might best be called IIL's *jurisprudence incohérente*,[4] which makes it difficult for states to know when or how they can protect human rights (e.g. Bonnitcha 2011; Zarra 2018, pp. 140–141). The limited means of challenging ISDS decisions makes the *jurisprudence incohérente* an embedded and pernicious feature in IIL.

ISDS panels have generally ignored investor responsibilities for human rights, even when human rights are a salient aspect of the business's operations. For example, the tribunal in *Biwater Gauff v. Tanzania* (2008, para. 149–152) found the investor underestimated the work necessary to operate Dar es Salaam's privatised water services. After the water services declined and the investment was, according to the Tribunal, rendered valueless by the investor's conduct, the state seized the company's assets. Nowhere—other than in a recitation of an *amici curiae* submission (ibid, paras. 356–391)—did the tribunal consider either the state's IHRL obligations or the investors' human rights responsibilities relevant. Instead, it found the state breached IIL but owed no reparations because of the value of the investment. The tribunal could justify finding the state breached IIL by ignoring the state and investors' human rights responsibilities instead of analysing whether the state owed an IHRL obligation to intervene in the investor's obligation. This approach effectively limits the actions states like Tanzania can take against investors to protect human rights.

This danger was repeated in *Urbaser v. Argentina* (2016), where the tribunal considered the first state counterclaim to assert that an investor was liable for breaching human rights standards by failing to fulfil promised reforms and investments in a water concession (ibid, para. 1128). But, the tribunal determined that the investor owed no positive IHRL obligations despite the inherent impact of its operations on human rights. Instead, the tribunal found the state should have included specific human rights obligations in its domestic laws or investment contracts (ibid, para. 1206 *et seq*). The case was heralded for recognising that states *could* bring human rights counterclaims in theory (Guntrip 2017; Nica 2018; also see Fahner and

Happold 2019). Yet, in practice, the substantive treatment of IHRL meant that the Argentinian government could not recoup losses caused by the company's conduct. When considering whether the Argentine government owed a responsibility to renegotiate the concession agreement, the company's previous impact on human rights played no part in the tribunal's assessment.

IIL would not be so dangerous if it were not so costly. Regardless of the outcome of the case, between 2011–2016, states paid an average of US $5.6 million to defend ISDS claims (Pelc 2017, p. 566). At one point, the claims against Argentina for its handling of the 2001 financial crisis amounted to around US $80 billion (Lavopa 2015, p. 2) while financially strapped Venezuela has been ordered to pay US $8 billion in a single case (ICSI 2019). Scholars recognise that the cost and *jurisprudence incohérente* of IIL can render states unwilling or unable to adopt necessary regulation that harms investors' interests (e.g., Sim 2018; Davitti 2019; Van Ho 2016; Wandahl Mouyal 2018; Meshel 2015; Choudhury 2009). Tribunals have never considered how these types of awards impact the state's ability to meet its IHRL obligations, particularly their obligation to use the maximum of their available resources to fulfil economic, social, and cultural rights. Yet, the costs undermine states' ability to realise their IHRL obligations.

Advocates of IIL have claimed that there is no conflict with IHRL because the principle of systemic integration allows for an integration of the two fields (e.g., Balcerzak 2017). Such claims fail to explain why this theoretical commitment rarely translates into practice. Others have argued that judicialising ISDS would alleviate the underlying problems (e.g., Svoboda 2020), but without any evidence that a standing court would adequately address IHRL. Still others have suggested better drafting of IIAs (Muchlinski 2016), even though the *jurisprudence incohérente* and limited means of challenging problematic decisions mean clauses may be interpreted or applied inconsistently even with better drafting. These proposals, as Ho (2020) has asserted, are often presented by IIL apologists 'with a pragmatic aura' that allows them to 'refus[e] to engage with the critics on the systemic failings of ISDS' while offering 'peripheral modifications'. Radical reform is needed instead (Ho 2020). States, and the field of IHRL, need to consider how this radical reform can be realised, and applying the demands of IAC to IIL can help in this regard.

Identifying obligations in the context of investment law

Because scholarship to date has focused on addressing specific problems within IIL, rather than considering more fully the demands of IAC in this context, scholars have developed only a few applications of IAC to state conduct in IIL. Literature has focused on the responsibility of the negotiating parties, who would appear to have the greatest capacity to influence the realisation of IHRL. That premise should be questioned by future scholars in light of the role the World Bank has played in promoting ISDS (Berge and St John 2020). In this section, I set aside the direct responsibility of the World Bank (but see, CESCR 1990; van Genugten 2015) to focus, first, on known responsibilities of negotiating states. I then make the novel argument that third-party states also have IAC obligations in the context of IIL.

Respect and protect obligations on negotiating parties

Thus far, two specific IAC obligations have been identified in the context of IIL: (1) their responsibility to undertake human rights impact assessments (HRIAs); and (2) their responsibility in how they negotiate the IIA. This section briefly delineates both expectations.

Human rights impact assessments

The adoption of IIAs entails a balancing of priorities as some individuals, businesses, and investors may benefit from increased foreign investment or opportunities to invest abroad while others are harmed by these developments (De Schutter 2011, Principle 6.1). While states must generally determine for themselves the appropriate balance between interests, CESCR has established a clear and general expectation on states to ensure their investment and trade agreements respect and protect human rights (CESCR 2008, para. 57; CESCR 2017, para. 13; Sepúlveda 2006, p. 282; Eide 1999, para. 130). This expectation was echoed in the UN Guiding Principles on Business and Human Rights (Ruggie 2011, Principle 9) and by other experts (e.g., de Zayas 2015, para. 4; Tauli-Corpuz 2016, para. 93(b); Krajewski 2017, p. 6; Kube 2019, pp. 241–287). Both negotiating states are expected to undertake HRIAs, which must account for general impacts but also for how the IIAs will affect conditions and rights in practice (De Schutter 2011, Principles 2.6 and 5–6). Where the HRIA reveals a negative impact, states are to 'take corrective measures' in the development or implementation of the IIA (Eide 1999, para. 130). The jurisprudence, however, has remained vague: states are to ensure IIAs do not harm human rights. *How* states are to do this has often been left unaddressed.

To assist states in realising their obligations, De Schutter (2011), in his mandate as UN Special Rapporteur on the right to food, promulgated UN Guiding Principles (UNGPs) on how to conduct HRIAs before concluding IIAs. Unfortunately, the guidance remains general and vague. The UNGPs do not mandate a methodology but call for states to explicitly reference the normative content of their human rights obligations, incorporate indicators, and engage in public consultations over the appropriate balance to be struck within the IIA (ibid, Principles 5–6 and 11). States must be cognisant of how these trade-offs will impact various communities, ensuring they 'never result in a deprivation of the ability of people to enjoy the essential content of their human rights', develop solutions so that 'losses and gains are shared across groups, rather than concentrated on one group', and ensure any trade-offs 'comport with the principles of equity and non-discrimination' (ibid, Principles 6 and 11). Finally, the IIA must not lead to retrogressive measures, which would undermine the progressive realisation of rights within ICESCR (ibid, Principle 11).

Despite the support for HRIAs from CESCR and other experts, and De Schutter's work in identifying a process for this, most states have ignored this obligation (see Dommen 2020, p. 307). It appears the EU has taken the most consistent approach to integrating HRIAs into their broader sustainability impacts, alongside labour and environmental concerns (European Commission 2017, p. 4). The EU claims that these impact assessments are 'a key tool for the conduct of sound, evidence-based and transparent trade negotiations' (ibid). Unfortunately, research indicates that even recent sustainability impact assessments by the EU fail the standards in the UNGPs (Lawrence, Van Ho and Yilmaz Vastardis 2020). The obligation to conduct HRIAs is intended to capture the full range of risks that IIAs can pose for IHRL. Yet, with limited guidance and practice, this obligation has, thus far, done little to advance or protect IHRL.

Negotiating IIAs

While striking the appropriate balance is primarily an obligation of the host state, negotiating partners are expected to respect this process and refrain from coercive measures that might require a different set of priorities (De Schutter 2011; Davitti 2019). Implicit in CESCR's call for states to ensure their IIAs respect human rights is a responsibility to negotiate a treaty that protects human rights both at home and in their negotiating partners' territory. De Schutter (2011) and Davitti (2019) make this explicit, asserting that states' IAC obligations should affect their conduct in the negotiation of treaties. De Schutter (2011) takes a minimalist approach, finding that states must refrain from using their 'economic leverage or other means of influence' to insist on clauses that impede compliance with human rights. This means states must forego economic opportunities they would normally have due to their relative power in order to respect human rights on the territory of another state.

Davitti (2019, pp. 207–216) pushes further. As CESCR (2017, para. 27) has, Davitti argues that customary international law in the context of due diligence obliges home states to ensure their territory is not used to harm human rights in another territory. Given the role of IIL in protecting corporations from accountability, Davitti's approach would oblige home states to negotiate IIAs in a way that accounts for and guards against specific human rights risks that arise from their business nationals operating on the territory of (an)other state(s). This requires concretising the risks posed by a state's nationals through an HRIA and negotiating not only for adequate regulatory space for states but also clear duties on investors to respect human rights. In this, Davitti rebukes Methven O'Brien's proposition, discussed in Section 2, above. Davitti's position suggests a responsibility on states to not only balance their own economic and policy interests—as De Schutter did—but to negotiate against their business interests if needed to protect human rights in a negotiating partner's territory. Neither De Schutter nor Davitti elaborate on what their approach would mean in practice, or how responsibility for specific impacts might be attributed between the parties.

Building on Davitti's argument, one might argue that if states must negotiate against their own interests to conclude human rights compliant IIAs, they should not negotiate IIAs at all. A more nuanced approach might be appropriate. There may be legitimate reasons for establishing investment protections, so long as they comply with IHRL. States have begun to develop clauses aimed at doing this, but such efforts remain limited. Several IIAs explicitly protect states' regulatory space, although these clauses are sometimes limited to environmental, public health, or labour issues without explicitly including human rights (e.g., Sri Lanka and China 1986, art. 11; Botswana and Ghana 2003, art. 5(3); Lawrence, Van Ho and Yilmaz Vastardis 2020, pp. 12 and 15–16). States commonly commit to not weakening their labour or environmental protections, but, again, this rarely includes language for human rights more broadly (e.g., United States 2012, art. 12; Japan and Colombia 2011, art. 21). States have also committed to 'encourag[ing] enterprises … to incorporate internationally recognized standards of corporate social responsibility in their practices and internal policies' (e.g., Canada and Burkina Faso 2015, art. 16), but in almost all cases they stop short of placing direct obligations on investors. In a rare exception, Morocco and Nigeria (2016, art. 18) included an explicit obligation on investors to 'uphold' and not 'circumvent' human rights, and to act in accordance with ILO core labour standards. That treaty has not yet entered into force, and there is an ongoing debate about whether it is desirable to recognise investor obligations within IIAs or if a better path is to develop those obligations in domestic law in a way that would impact the interpretation of rights and obligations in IIL (e.g., Ho 2019; Perrone 2019; Krajewski 2020). The SADC Model Bilateral Investment Treaty Template (2012, arts. 5.2 and 15) and the Draft Pan-African Investment Code (2016, arts. 8, 10(2), and 19–24) also include clauses that could be used to hold businesses accountable, including minimum standards for human rights.

Relying on better drafting may provide limited benefits for IHRL. As noted above, evolutionary and expansive interpretations of treaties by ISDS panels, their *jurisprudence incohérente* makes this approach inherently fragile. Additional and alternative developments may be needed to protect human rights.

Obligations on third-party states

While the negotiating parties may have the most immediate power, third-party states can have significant direct and indirect influence on the drafting of IIAs. If the obligation provides that IAC is tied to a state's capacity, there needs to be greater consideration of what constitutes power and how it should operate so as to protect IHRL in IIL. If Yilmaz Vastardis's position (2018; 2020a) is correct and ISDS itself undermines IHRL by privileging foreign investors and depriving developing states of resources needed for the development of local systems of justice, then power and capacity sits with those who protect and promote the ISDS regime. As mentioned above, states sometimes condition IAC on accepting guidance from the World Bank, and the World Bank in turn encourages states to adopt ISDS. The state conditioning its aid exercises significant power, both in relation to the receiving state and in the choice of the World Bank to provide policy advice. The conditioning states may therefore have IAC obligations. Under Yilmaz Vastardis' approach, these states should work to dismantle the ISDS system, develop local systems of justice capable of providing equal access to justice.

Even if one were to shy away from such a radical position, the conditioning states still seem to have an obligation to ensure the World Bank's guidance respects (and perhaps protects and fulfils) human rights within receiving states. This could be done in a few ways. First, they could have an obligation to ensure the receiving state is exposed to alternative, critical guidance on ISDS, giving the state an opportunity to develop their own policy priorities. The conditioning state should monitor and assess the Bank's guidance in light of the concerns set out in Section 3, above. Such oversight aligns well with the existing expectation on states to ensure that international organisations to which they are a party respect human rights. If the World Bank is committed to promoting ISDS regardless of the needs of a developing state, then requiring engagement with the World Bank may constitute a burdensome conditionality in breach of the conditioning state's ICESCR obligation. States with lesser power would also have an IAC obligation to use the leverage they do have, and to work with other states, to ensure IIL better respects human rights both by engaging the World Bank to influence its guidance and raising pertinent issues or advocating for change in other, relevant international fora such as the UN Conference on Trade and Development and the International Centre on the Settlement of Investment Dispute, both of which have a role in assessing or promoting IIL.

Moving beyond the issue of the World Bank's role, one could argue that various third-party states have different types of capacity and can influence the development of IIL. Developing or middle-income states that have suffered from ISDS decisions that restrict their ability to regulate for human rights—like Argentina—have learned valuable lessons about the balance between IIL and IHRL. These states may not be providing IAC in other ways, or they may not be conditioning their official development assistance on World Bank guidance, but they have gained important insights and technical competency that may not be shared by others states or the World Bank. Akin to states with greater success in combatting COVID-19 sharing their expertise and experience, states that have gained competency on the balance between IHRL and IIL have an obligation to provide guidance to others. Such leadership could manifest in the drafting of model treaty clauses that better protect regulatory space or that limit the level of compensation that can be awarded. As is common with the protect and fulfil obligations, the obligations of leadership generally and of drafting clauses specifically would appear to be obligations of conduct rather than outcome. States must exercise good faith in an effort to better protect human rights in light of ongoing developments within IIL. The possibilities for the exercise of these obligations should be examined more fully than what has occurred before, or than what the constraints of this Chapter allows. Recognising this broader leadership role clarifies that IAC imposes obligations both within the negotiation of IIAs but throughout the training, conditions, and international leadership surrounding the development of IIL so that IIL learns how to respect, protect, and fulfil IHRL.

It is significant to recognise that non-negotiating states have IAC obligations. This has the potential to transform the scholarship and practice on IHRL and IIL by expanding the range of duty-holders and the understanding of competency to lead in this area. For example, acknowledging that states that have been the subject of ISDS decisions affecting their IHRL obligations have a particular competency moves the conversation from one that centres the financial power and responsibility of developed states to one that centres the technical and experiential knowledge of other states. These states have IAC obligations to pass on their lessons and assume leadership within the IHRL-IIL discussion. It also prioritises state experience over the World Bank's ideological commitment to ISDS. 'Capacity' within the context of IIL has thus far been so narrowly drawn that these obligations and opportunities have been missed.

Conclusion

This Chapter has focused on the ICESCR obligation to provide IAC in the context of IIL. This area is under-developed, and merely identifying CESCR's relevant jurisprudence and the full remit of obligations on states negotiating IIAs provides a significant contribution to the literature on IHRL and IIL. I do that in this Chapter before going further. By recognising that CESCR identifies IAC obligations on the basis of capacity to influence change, and that some obligations are of conduct rather than outcome, I am able to establish that third-party states also have IAC obligations in the context of IIL. I explore some of the implications of this, recognising first that those states who condition assistance on World Bank guidance owe obligations to ensure that guidance complies with IHRL. Additionally, I note that capacity can exist in other ways, including technical expertise developed by losing past ISDS cases. Such technical expertise creates an obligation on states that may not otherwise be providing IAC in the context of IIL to provide guidance and to assume a leadership position in debates over the construct and operation of IIAs and ISDS. This has the radical potential to reorder whose experiences and knowledge is valued in discussing the intersection of IIL and IHRL.

The recognition that capacity extends beyond the negotiating states is significant. Rather than looking for small inroads into IIL, this Chapter suggests that centring IAC obligations opens up a stream of new questions. Future scholarship should consider how IAC obligations in ICESCR, and other treaties, might add to the analysis provided here. It should also consider how states' leadership in IIL should manifest, such as whether states must include or advocate for specific (types of) clauses, and at what point would states have an IAC obligation to work to dismantle ISDS. One set of questions this Chapter points to but did not examine relate to the obligations on states to *accept* IAC. If there is an obligation on states in need of IAC to accept it, one could argue that states developing IIAs must accept guidance from those who have learned from past ISDS decisions. This could give states significant influence over another state's policy choices, and scholars should examine how that relates to challenges, or builds upon, the existing obligation to accept help from states that condition assistance on World Bank guidance. If one accepts that such an obligation exists, are there any corresponding obligation on those states that currently condition assistance on World Bank guidance? This Chapter could not answer these questions, but it provides the foundation for analysing them in the future.

Notes

1. With appreciation to Sebastián Mantilla Blanco for influencing the direction this chapter took, and to Paolo Vargiu, Jessica Lawrence, and Jennifer Sellin who commented on earlier versions.
2. Investment law does not have a single or consistent test for corporate nationality. See, Yilmaz Vastardis 2020b.
3. Investment scholars often distinguish between tribunals convened under the International Centre for the Settlement of Investment Disputes ('ICSID'), which has a standing list of arbitrators, and those convened elsewhere, describing only the latter as *ad hoc*. This glosses over the fact that even within ICSID each panel is convened for the purpose of a single case or set of cases. There are no standing arbitration panels within ICSID.
4. Paolo Vargiu helped me coin this term for the purpose of this Chapter, conveying the inherent (and perhaps intended) chaotic nature of IIL jurisprudence, which sits in opposition to *jurisprudence constante*.

References

Arcuri, A. (2020) 'The Great Asymmetry and the Rule of Law in International Investment Arbitration' in Sachs, L., Johnson, L. and Coleman, J. (eds). *Yearbook on International Investment Law & Policy 2018*, Oxford University Press.

Balcerzak, F. (2017) *Investor-State Arbitration and Human Rights*, Brill.

Berge, T. L., and St John, T. (2020) 'Asymmetric diffusion: World Bank's 'Best Practice' and the Spread of Arbitration in National Investment Laws', *Review of International Political Economy*, DOI: 10.1080/09692290.2020.1719429.

Bonnitcha, J. (2011) 'Outline of a Normative Framework for Evaluating Interpretations of Investment Treaty Protections' in Brown, C. and Miles, K. (eds.). *Evolution in Investment Treaty Law and Arbitration*, Cambridge University Press.

Botswana and Ghana (2003) Agreement for the Promotion and Protection of Investments, available at https://investmentpolicy.unctad.org/international-investment-agreements/treaties/bilateral-investment-treaties/637/botswana—ghana-bit-2003- [accessed 29 December 2020].

Canada and Burkina Faso (2017) Agreement for the Promotion and Protection of Investments, 2015, available at https://investmentpolicy.unctad.org/international-investment-agreements/treaties/bilateral-investment-treaties/3557/burkina-faso—canada-bit-2015- [accessed 29 December 2020].

Choudhury, B. (2009) 'Democratic Implications Arising from the Intersection of Investment Arbitration and Human Rights', *Alberta Law Review* 46.

Coleman, J., Cordes, K.Y. and Johnson, L. (2020) 'Human Rights Law and the Investment Treaty Regime' in Deva, S. and Birchall, D. Research *Handbook on Human Rights and Business*, Edward Elgar Publishing.

Committee on Economic, Social and Cultural Rights (CESCR) (1966) International Covenant on Economic, Social and Cultural Rights, 993 U.N.T.S. 3.

_______ (1990) GC 2 on International Technical Assistance Measures (Art. 22), U.N. Doc. E/1990/23.

_______ (2000a) GC 14 on the Right to the Highest Attainable Standard of Health (Art. 12), U.N. Doc. E/C.12/2000/4.

_______ (2000b) Concluding Observations: Italy, U.N. Doc. E/2000/22.

_______ (2001) Concluding Observations: Germany, U.N. Doc. E/C.12/1/Add.68.

_______ (2008) GC 19 on the Right to Social Security (art. 9), U.N. Doc. E/C.12/GC/19.

_______ (2013) Concluding Observations on the Third Periodic report of Japan, U.N. Doc. E/C.12/JPN/CO/3.

_______ (2016) GC 23 on the right to just and favourable conditions of work (article 7 of the International Covenant on Economic, Social and Cultural Rights), U.N. Doc. E/C.12/GC/23.

_______ (2017) GC 24 on State Obligations under the International Covenant on Economic, Social, and Cultural Rights in the Context of Business Activities, U.N. Doc. E/C.12/GC24.

_______ (2018) Concluding Observations on the Sixth Periodic Report of Germany, U.N. Doc. E/C.12./DEU/CO/6.

_______ (2020) GC 25 on Science and Economic, Social and Cultural Rights, U.N. Doc. E/C.12/GC/25.

Dandan, V. (2016) 'Human Rights and International Solidarity: Report to the General Assembly', U.N. Doc. A/71/280.

Davitti, D. (2016) 'Refining the Protect, Respect and Remedy Framework for Business and Human Rights and its Guiding Principles', *Human Rights Law Review* 16(1).

_______ (2019) *Investment and Human Rights in Armed Conflict: Charting an Elusive Intersection*, Hart Publishing.

De Schutter, O. (2011) Report of the Special Rapporteur on the Right to Food, U.N. Doc. A/HRC/19/59/Add.5.

_______ (2016) 'Towards a New Treaty on Business and Human Rights', *Business and Human Rights Journal* 1(1).

De Zayas, A. (2015) Report of the Independent Expert on the Promotion of a Democratic and Equitable International Order, U.N. Doc. A/HRC/30/44.

Dommen, C. (2020) 'Human Rights Impact Assessment: Trade Agreements and Indigenous Rights' in Borrows, J. and Schwartz, R. (eds). *Indigenous Peoples and International Trade*, Cambridge University Press.

Draft Pan-African Investment Code (2016) available at https://au.int/en/documents/20161231/pan-african-investment-code-paic [accessed 4 January 2020].

Eide, A. (1999) The right to adequate food and to be free from hunger. Updated study on the right to food, U.N. Doc. A/CN.4/SUB.2/1999/12.

European Commission (2017) 'Sustainability Impact Assessment (SIA) in support of an Investment Agreement between the European Union and the People's Republic of China: Final Report', available at https://trade.ec.europa.eu/doclib/docs/2018/may/tradoc_156862.pdf [accessed 29 December 2020].

Fahner, J.H., and Happold, M. (2019) 'The Human Rights Defence in International Investment Arbitration: Exploring the Limits of Systemic Integration', *International and Comparative Law Quarterly* 68(3), 741–759.

Guntrip, E. (2017) '*Urbaser v. Argentina*: The Origins of a Host State Human Rights Counterclaim in ICSID Arbitration?', *EJIL Talk!*, 10 February 2017, https://www.ejiltalk.org/urbaser-v-argentina-the-origins-of-a-host-state-human-rights-counterclaim-in-icsid-arbitration/ [accessed 29 December 2020].

Ho, J. (2019) 'The Creation of Elusive Investor Responsibility', *AJIL Unbound* 113, 10–15.

_______ (2020) 'Hegemony 101 in International Investment Law', *AfronomicsLaw* 9 September 2020, available at https://www.afronomicslaw.org/2020/09/09/hegemony-101-in-international-investment-law/ [accessed 22 September 2020].

Human Rights Committee (2004) GC 31 on the Nature of the Legal Obligations Imposed on States Parties to the Covenant, U.N. Doc. CCPR/C/21/Rev.1/Add.13.

International Centre for Settlement of Investment Disputes (ICSID) (2007a) *Enron Corporation and Ponderosa Assets, L.P. v. Argentina*, ICSID Case no. ARB/01/3, Award.

_______ (2007b) *LG&E Energy Corp., LG&E Capital Corp. and LG&E International, Inc. v. Argentina,* ICSID Case No. ARB/02/01.

_______ (2008a) *Biwater Gauff (Tanzania) Ltd. v. Tanzania*, ICSID Case No. ARB/05/22, Award.

_______ (2008b) *Continental Casualty Company v. Argentina*, ICSID Case No. ARB/03/9, Award.

_______ (2010) *Suez, Sociedad General de Aguas de Barcelona SA and Vivendi Universal S.A. v. Argentina*, ICSID Case No. ARB/03/19, Decision on Liability ('*Suez and Vivendi v. Argentina*').

_______ (2012) *Occidental Petroleum Corporation and Occidental Exploration and Production Company v. Ecuador*, ICSID Case No. ARB/06/11, Award.

_______ (2016) *Urbaser S.A. and Consorcio de Aguas Bilbao Bizkaia, Bilbao Biskaia Ur Partzuergo*, ICSID Case. No. ARB/07/26, Award.

_______ (2017) *Burlington Resource Inc. v. Ecuador*, ICSID Case No. ARB/08/5, Decision on Reconsideration and Award.

_______ (2019) *ConocoPhillips Petrozuata B.V. et al. v. Venezuela*, ICSID Case No. ARB/07/30, Award.

International Convention on the on the Settlement of Investment Disputes between States and Nationals of Foreign States (ICSID Convention) (1966).

Japan and Colombia (2011) Agreement for the Liberalization, Promotion and Protection of Investment, available at https://investmentpolicy.unctad.org/international-investment-agreements/countries/105/japan [accessed 29 December 2020].

Karimova, T. (2014) 'The Nature and Meaning of "International Assistance and Cooperation" under the International Covenant on Economic, Social and Cultural Rights' in Riedel, E., Giacca, G. and Golay, C. (eds). *Economic, Social and Cultural Rights in International Law*, Oxford University Press.

Krajewski, M. (2013) 'Investment Guarantees and International Obligations to Reduce Poverty: a Human Rights Perspective' in Nadakuvukaren Schefer, K. (ed). *Poverty and the International Economic Legal System: Duties to the World's Poor*, Cambridge University Press.

_______ (2017) 'Ensuring the Primacy of Human Rights in Trade and Investment Policies: Model Clauses for a UN Treaty on Transnational Corporations, Other Business and Human Rights', CIDSE, https://www.cidse.org/2017/03/03/ensuring-the-primacy-of-human-rights-in-trade-and-investment-policies/ [accessed 18 September 2020].

_______ (2020) 'A Nightmare or a Noble Dream? Establishing Investor Obligations through Treaty-Making and Treaty-Application', *Business and Human Rights Journal* 5(1), 105–129.

Kube, V. (2019) *EU Human Rights, International Investment Law and Participation*, Springer.

Lavopa, F. (2015) 'Crisis, Emergency Measures and the Failure of the ISDS System: The Case of Argentina', *Investment Policy Brief* 2.

Lawrence, J., Van Ho, T., and Yilmaz Vastardis, A. (2020) 'EU-China Comprehensive Agreement on Investment: A Scoping Study', Heinrich Böll Stiftung, https://www.boell.de/en/2020/12/09/eu-china-comprehensive-agreement-investment-scoping-study [accessed 22 December 2020].

Lumina, C. (2014) The Negative Impact of the Non-Repatriation of Funds of Illicit Origin on the Enjoyment of Human Rights, U.N. Doc. A/HRC/25/52.

Maastricht Principles on Extraterritorial Obligations of States in the Area of Economic, Social and Cultural Rights (2013) available at https://www.etoconsortium.org/nc/en/main-navigation/library/maastricht-principles/?tx_drblob_pi1%5BdownloadUid%5D=23 [accessed 18 September 2020].

Makoni, M. (2020) 'COVID-19 in Africa: Half a Year Later', *The Lancet* 20(10), available at https://doi.org/10.1016/S1473-3099(20)30708-8.

McCorquodale, R. and Simons, P. (2007) 'Responsibility Beyond Borders: State Responsibility for Extraterritorial Violations by Corporations of International Human Rights Law', *Modern Law Review* 70(4), 598–625.

Mégret, F. (2017) 'Nature of Obligations' in Moeckli, D., Shah, S. and Sivakumaran, S. (eds). *International Human Rights Law*, 3rd ed., Oxford University Press.

Meshel, T. (2015) 'Human Rights in Investor-State Arbitration: The Human Right to Water and Beyond', *Journal of International Dispute Settlement* 6(2), 277–307.

Methven O'Brien, C. (2018) 'The Home State Duty to Regulate the Human Rights Impacts of TNCs Abroad: A Rebuttal', *Business and Human Rights Journal* 3(1), 47–73.

Morocco and Nigeria (2006) Reciprocal Investment Promotion and Protection Agreement, available at https://investmentpolicy.unctad.org/international-investment-agreements/countries/142/morocco [accessed 29 December 2020].

Muchlinski, P. (2016) 'Negotiating New Generation International Investment Agreements' in Hindelang, S., and Krajewski, M. (eds). *Shifting Paradigms in International Investment Law: More Balanced, Less Isolated, Increasingly Diversified*, Oxford University Press.

New York Convention on the Recognition and Enforcement of Foreign Arbitral Awards (1958).

Nica, A. (2018) 'David Aven v. Costa Rica: An Aftershock of Urbaser v. Argentina?', *Kluwer Arbitration Blog*, 12 December 2018, http://arbitrationblog.kluwerarbitration.com/2018/12/12/david-aven-v-costa-rica-an-aftershock-of-urbaser-v-argentina/ [accessed 29 December 2020].

Optional Protocol to the International Covenant on Economic, Social, and Cultural Rights (2008) U.N. Doc. A/63/435.

Pelc, K. (2017) 'What Explains the Low Success Rate of Investor-State Disputes', *International Organization* 71(3), 559–583.

Perrone, N.M. (2019) 'The "Invisible" Local Communities: Foreign Investor Obligations, Inclusiveness and the International Investment Regime', *AJIL Unbound* 113, 16–21.

Ruggie, J. (2011) 'UN Guiding Principles on Business and Human Rights, U.N. Doc. A/HRC/17/31.

SADC Model Bilateral Investment Treaty Template (2012) available at https://www.iisd.org/itn/wp-content/uploads/2012/10/SADC-Model-BIT-Template-Final.pdf [accessed 29 December 2020].

Salomon, M. (2013) 'Deprivation, Causation and the Law of International Cooperation' in Langford, M. et al. (eds). *Global Justice, State Duties: The Extraterritorial Scope of Economic, Social and Cultural Rights*, Cambridge University Press.

Sattorova, M. (2018) *The Impact of Investment Treaty Law on Host States: Enabling Good Governance?*, Hart Publishing.

Schneiderman, D. (2010) 'Judicial Politics and International Investment Arbitration: Seeking an Explanation for Conflicting Outcomes', *Northwestern Journal of International Law & Business* 30(2), 383–416.

Seck, S. (2011) 'Conceptualizing the Home State Duty to Protect Human Rights,' in Buhmann, K., Roseberry, L. and Mette, M. (eds). *Corporate Social and Human Rights Responsibilities*, Palgrave Macmillan.

Sepúlveda, M. (2006) 'Obligations of "International Assistance and Cooperation" in an Optional Protocol to the International Covenant on Economic, Social and Cultural Rights', *24 Netherlands Quarterly of Human Rights* 24(2), 271–303.

Sim, C. (2018) 'Strategies for Addressing Human Rights Violations in Investment Arbitration: Substantive Principles and Procedural Solutions', *Human Rights & International Legal Discourse* 12(2), 153–189.

Skogly, S. (2006) *Beyond National Borders: States' Human Rights Obligations in International Cooperation*, Intersentia.

Sornarajah, M., (2015) *Resistance and Change in the International Law on Foreign Investment*, Cambridge University Press.

Sri Lanka and China (1986) Reciprocal Promotion and Protection of Investment.

Statute of the International Court of Justice (ICJ Statute) (1946) 1 UNTS 16, Annex.

Svoboda, O. (2020) 'EU Reform Agenda in Defence of the Judicialization of International Economic Law', *European Foreign Affairs Review* 25(2), 177–196.

Tauli-Corpuz, V. (2016) Report of the Special Rapporteur on the Rights of Indigenous Peoples, U.N. Doc. A/HRC/33/42.

United States (2012) '2012 US Model Bilateral Investment Treaty', https://ustr.gov/sites/default/files/BIT%20text%20for%20ACIEP%20Meeting.pdf [accessed 10 January 2020].

van Genugten, W. (2015), *The World Bank Group, the IMF and Human Rights: A Contextualized Way Forward*, Intersentia.

Van Ho, T. (2016) 'Is it Already too Late for Colombia's Land Restitution Process?', *International Human Rights Law Review* 5(1), 60–85.

Vandenhole, W. and Benedek, W. (2012) 'Extraterritorial Human Rights Obligations and the North-South Divide' in Langford, M. et al. (eds). *Global Justice, State Duties: the Extraterritorial Scope of Economic, Social and Cultural Rights*, Cambridge University Press.

Wandahl Mouyal, M. (2018) *International Investment Law and the Right to Regulate: A Human Rights Perspective*, Routledge.

Yilmaz Vastardis, A. (2018) 'Justice Bubbles for the Privileged: A Critique of the Investor-State Dispute Settlement Proposals for the EU's Investment Agreements', *London Review of International Law* 6(2), 279–297.

_______ (2020a) 'Investment Treaty Arbitration as Justice Bubbles' in Schultz, T. and Ortino, F. (eds). *Oxford Handbook of International Arbitration*, Oxford University Press.

_______ (2020b) *The Nationality of Corporate Investors under International Investment Law*, Hart Publishing.

Zarra, G. (2018) 'The Issue of Incoherence in Investment Arbitration', *Chinese Journal of International Law* 17(1), 137–185.

24

Access to medicines and the TRIPS agreement

Recognising extraterritorial human rights obligations

Jennifer Sellin

Introduction

Access to medicines is a human rights issue. Human rights provide the tools for advancing global health by converting moral imperatives into legal entitlements. A total of 171 states worldwide are party to the 1966 International Covenant on Economic, Social and Cultural Rights (ICESCR), which recognises the right of everyone to the enjoyment of the highest attainable standard of physical and mental health (ICESCR, art. 12) and the benefits of scientific progress and its applications (ICESCR, art. 15(1)b). Today the use of medicines is an essential and indispensable part of the treatment of diseases and ill health, and as such a key element of the right to health. States, therefore, have human rights obligations to safeguard the availability and (economic) accessibility of safe, quality medicines, vaccines and other health technologies, such as diagnostic tools and medical equipment. The impact of intellectual property rights (IPRs) in that regard has been an issue of (academic) debate for over two decades (Committee on Economic, Social and Cultural Rights (CESCR) 2020, paras. 58–62; 't Hoen 2016; Sellin 2014; Forman 2011; Matthews 2010; Hestermeyer 2007; CESCR 2006, para. 35; United Nations Commission on Human Rights 2001).

The current biomedical research and development (R&D) model incentivises innovation by rewarding inventors with a time-limited market monopoly for producing, using and selling their end product. These monopoly rewards, enforced through IPRs, effectively prevent competition and enable the owner to largely set the price and production terms of its product. IP is argued to stimulate innovation by allowing medicines developers to recoup their investments in R&D. These same incentives, however, tend to draw medicines to the market for 'profitable' diseases, characterised as affecting large and/or wealthy populations with certainty.

With 164 members the World Trade Organisation's (WTO) adoption of the Agreement on Trade-Related Aspects of Intellectual Property Rights (TRIPS) has significantly influenced the international IP regime and the current biomedical R&D model as it provides minimum standards for the protection of intellectual property (IP). TRIPS demands that patent

DOI: 10.4324/9781003090014-30

protection must be available for any inventions that meet the conditions (novelty, inventiveness and capability of industrial application), including for biomedical and pharmaceutical products and processes, giving the patent-holder a monopoly position for at least 20 years. Although the 2001 Doha Declaration on the TRIPS Agreement and Public Health asserted that TRIPS 'can and should be interpreted and implemented in a manner supportive of WTO members' right to protect public health and, in particular, to promote access to medicines for all' (WTO Ministerial Conference 2001, para. 4), tension continues to arise between the international legal regime for the protection of IP and states' human rights obligation to secure access to affordable medicines.

Even though international (human rights) law places the primary responsibility on the state for realising access to medicines for its population within its territory, it is increasingly acknowledged that health is a global and shared responsibility. This chapter starts from the basis that states have human rights obligations beyond a state's national borders, so-called extraterritorial human rights obligations (ETOs) to respect, protect and fulfil access to medicines and examines how these should be applied in the context of states' existing TRIPS obligations. It aims to demonstrate that ETOs can act as an important facilitator to achieve universal access to affordable medicines and other health technologies.

Recognising ETOs for access to medicines

Health, as well as access to medicines, is a global and shared responsibility (CESCR 2000, para. 5; United Nations General Assembly (UN GA) 2015, SDG3; UN Special Rapporteur on the Right to Health 2013, para. 6; Tobin 2011, p. 325; Ooms and Hammonds 2010, p. 32). The Sustainable Development Goals (SDGs) represent an international commitment towards ensuring access to safe, effective, quality and affordable essential medicines and vaccines for all (UN GA 2015, SDG 3.8). However, a 2016 report of the Lancet Commission on Essential Medicines Policies finds that essential medicines pose a central challenge to the sustainable development agenda. Five core challenges are identified: financing, affordability, quality and safety, appropriate use and developing missing essential medicines (Wirtz et al. 2016, pp. 406–408).

States have human rights obligations to ensure that everyone can enjoy access to medicines, most notably under the ICESCR. The CESCR clarifies that medicines should be sufficiently available, economically and physically accessible on a non-discriminatory basis, culturally acceptable and scientifically and medically appropriate and of good quality (CESCR 2000, para. 12; CESCR 2016, paras. 12–21). That requires, amongst others, positive state measures to enable and assist individuals to enjoy access to medicines (i.e. a duty to facilitate), as well as a duty to provide access to medicines when individuals are unable, for reasons beyond their control, to secure these themselves by the means at their disposal (CESCR 2000, para. 37). However, these obligations are qualified in that the Covenant acknowledges the constraints due to limited resources. As such the obligation is one of progressive realisation to the extent of a state's maximum available resources (ICESCR, art. 2(1)).

Moreover, *essential* medicines are part of the core content of the right to health (CESCR 2000, para. 43(d); CESCR 2016, para. 49(f)), which refers to the right's minimum essential levels without which it would be devoid of any meaning or relevance, and thus establishes a core obligation for state parties to provide such essential medicines (CESCR 1990, para. 10; CESCR 2000, para. 43; CESCR 2016, para. 49). Additionally, the right to benefit from science establishes a core obligation to ensure access to those applications/innovations that are critical to the enjoyment of the right to health (CESCR 2020, para. 52). Such core obligations translate into prioritised state obligations under the Covenant (Forman et al. 2016).

According to the WHO, essential medicines are those that satisfy the priority healthcare needs of the population. They are selected with due regard to public health relevance, evidence on efficacy and safety and comparative cost-effectiveness.

> Essential medicines are intended to be available within the context of functioning health systems at all times in adequate amounts, in the appropriate dosage forms, with assured quality and adequate information, and at a price the individual and the community can afford.
>
> *(www.who.int)*

For low- and middle-income countries (LMICs), which struggle with (severe) resource constraints and have limited or no local pharmaceutical manufacturing capacity, that can be particularly difficult. Unsurprisingly therefore, the CESCR has repeatedly recognised the essential role of international assistance and cooperation (IAC) for the full realisation of the Covenant's rights (CESCR 1990, paras. 13–14; CESCR 2000, para. 38; CESCR 2006, para. 36; CESCR 2016, para. 50; CESCR 2020, para. 77), emphasising in particular the duties of those states and other actors 'in a position to assist' to 'enable developing countries to fulfil their core obligations' (CESCR 2000, para. 45).

The legal basis for such an obligation of IAC is found in Article 2(1) ICESCR, which commands each state party to take steps towards the progressive realisation of the Covenant's rights, *including through international assistance and cooperation*, that is, read together with Articles 55–56 of the UN Charter and in light of the ICESCR's object and purpose. As such, it is now recognised that states have health-related ETOs that exist alongside (and separate to) a state's domestic human rights obligations (Yamin 2010; Bueno de Mesquita et al. 2010). Yet, some disagreement and ambiguity remain as to the nature, scope and application of such obligations (Saul 2014, pp. 138–140; Tobin 2011, p. 368). The *Maastricht Principles* on Extraterritorial Obligations of States in the Area of Economic, Social and Cultural Rights (the *Maastricht Principles* on ETOs) aim to fill this gap (etoconsortium.org). Although formally non-binding, they are instructive as an interpretive tool and build on the CESCR's interpretation. Moreover, they have increasingly been referred to and used by international human rights bodies (CESCR 2017, footnote 71; UN Special Rapporteur on the Right to Water and Sanitation 2014, para. 70; UN Independent Expert on Foreign Debt 2014, paras. 37–41).

In general terms, states have ETOs to respect, that is, to refrain from interfering with the enjoyment of economic, social and cultural (ESC) rights in other countries (*Maastricht Principles* on ETOs, paras. 19 et seq.); to protect, that is, to prevent third parties from violating ESC rights in other states, as long as they are able to influence these third parties by way of legal or political means (*Maastricht Principles* on ETOs, paras. 23 et seq.); and to fulfil, that is, to act separately and jointly through international cooperation to facilitate and provide where necessary ESC rights in other states (*Maastricht Principles* on ETOs, paras. 28 et seq.; CESCR 2000, para. 39).

ETOs encompass 'obligations relating to the acts and omissions of a state [...] that have effects on the enjoyment of human rights outside that state's territory' (*Maastricht Principles* on ETOs, para. 8(a)). In today's globalised and interdependent world, state conduct can, and regularly does, affect individuals' access to (essential) health technologies both within and beyond a country's borders. For example, especially during the early stages of the COVID-19 pandemic, many countries responded to acute shortages of personal protective equipment (PPE), medicines and other medical equipment by imposing export restrictions to bolster domestic supplies. As a result, especially LMICs were left with few options to secure essential medical supplies in their fight against the pandemic. Another concern is that of 'vaccine nationalism', where governments have entered into pre-purchase agreements with COVID-19 vaccine developers to secure doses for their own population ahead of other countries, which has made the first developed vaccine(s) mainly available to rich countries, leaving vulnerable populations in LMICs behind.

The next section examines how international IP regimes, particularly the TRIPS Agreement, may impede access to medicines and negatively impact states' ability to comply with their human rights obligations.

Access to medicines & the TRIPS agreement

There are many reasons why patients lack adequate access to medicines. The problem is particularly prevalent in LMICs, disproportionately affecting the world's poor and marginalised. It is impossible to address all of these here, which is why this chapter focuses on two central issues as also indicated by the 2016 Lancet Commission report: affordability and missing essential medicines (Wirtz et al. 2016, pp. 406–408).

First, medicine pricing may significantly impact the (economic) accessibility of (essential) medicines. Especially in countries without a well-organised, well-functioning healthcare system where the majority of patients have to pay for their healthcare privately, the cost of medicines can easily become too burdensome. Most LMICs, having limited (financial) resources, struggle to facilitate and, if necessary, provide medicines to their population as this places a considerable burden on their healthcare budgets. That affordability poses a key challenge for access is well-recognised (Wirtz 2016, p. 421 et seq.; United Nations Secretary General's (UN SG's) High-Level Panel on Access to Medicines 2016, p. 15; 't Hoen 2016, p. 114).

The issue hit a high point at the height of the HIV/AIDS pandemic in the 1990s when antiretroviral medicines (ARVs) were first introduced but at a price of over US$10,000 per patient per year (p.p.p.y) that meant they were inaccessible to the majority of patients who needed them. These ARVs, as most new medicines are, were protected by IPRs such as patents. Patents are time-bound monopoly rights that grant the patent-holder the exclusive right to make, use and sell the patented invention. In the early 2000s, pharmaceutical companies, mostly from India, started offering generic versions of ARVs at significantly lower prices. Generic medicines are non-patented medicines that are equivalent to an existing approved brand name and patented medicine. They work in the same way and provide the same clinical benefits as the patented medicine. As such, the CESCR recommends that safe and effective generic medicines should be prioritised over expensive brand name products so as to make effective use of limited resources (UN CESCR 2020, para. 70). Due to concerns over access to low-cost medicines, India's 1970 Patents Act did not grant product patents for medicines, allowing it to develop a booming generic pharmaceutical industry. Yet, with the establishment of the WTO in 1995, India was now automatically bound by the TRIPS Agreement, although it did not have to grant and enforce patents for medicines until the end of TRIPS' transition period for developing countries in 2005. While implementing TRIPS' standards, India also purposefully used the flexibility in TRIPS to balance public health interests with IP protection, for example, through its introduction of Section 3(d) to prevent so-called 'evergreening', that is, the extension of patent protection for 'new inventions' that are essentially slight modifications of already existing medicines. To this day, India is seen as the 'pharmacy of the developing world' (Lee 2015, pp. 108–114). Generic competition has brought prices for standard HIV treatment down by 99% to around US$100 p.p.p.y. However, India's patent law has long been a target for the multinational pharmaceutical industry backed by the US and EU among others (MSF Access Campaign, n.d.).

A second issue that disproportionately affects access in LMICs is that of missing essential medicines or the unavailability of treatments options for so-called neglected and poverty-related diseases. Neglected diseases are those diseases that affect almost exclusively poor people in LMICs and for which health interventions and R&D are inadequate to the need (UN SG High-Level Panel on Access to Medicines 2016, p. 13; 't Hoen 2016, pp. 121–122). Examples include neglected tropical diseases such as Chagas disease and Leishmaniasis, but also multi-drug resistant tuberculosis (MDR-TB). For example, each year 500,000 people develop MDR-TB, with only 1/9 cases being successfully treated (www.stoptb.org). Even though TB is one of the top infectious diseases worldwide, most advances in treatment still come from recycling medicines first developed in the 1940s–1960s. In nearly 50 years, only few new medicines have been approved for treating MDR-TB and access to these has remained extremely limited. Investment in TB research continues to fall short of what is estimated to be required (Frick 2016).

The privatisation of science that has been prevalent during the last decades, especially in the biomedical and pharmaceutical field, has significantly impacted the manner in which science is conducted, facilitated and promoted and the role of the state in that regard. Economic globalisation, the increase and strengthening of global institutions such as the WTO and the growth of large and powerful multinational corporations have all played a role. Private corporations dominate the pharmaceutical sector and are major actors in pharmaceutical and biomedical R&D and innovation. As a result, the majority of private health-related R&D is profit-driven and invested in medicines and treatments with substantial guaranteed returns. However, extensive R&D targeted at diseases overwhelmingly prevalent in LMICs is missing. IPRs play a crucial role in that process. Moreover, significant disparities among states are increasing with respect to the availability of resources, capabilities and infrastructure necessary to engage in biomedical and pharmaceutical innovation and production, and thus widening the divide between the most and least scientifically and technologically developed states.

IPRs can, therefore, negatively impact the short- and long-term availability and accessibility of (essential) medicines. Especially in LMICs unsuitably high standards of IP protection are problematic because they ignore developing countries' specific local needs, technological abilities and public health conditions (Yu 2018, p. 9). However, most states are not free to design and implement a national IP regime that suits their needs best, since they are members of the WTO and therefore automatically bound by the TRIPS Agreement. As such TRIPS has widespread membership throughout the world, and, as opposed to previous conventions dealing with IP, is the first international instrument to set out minimum standards of IP protection and subject to the WTO dispute settlement mechanism.

Article 27 introduced one of the major achievements of the TRIPS Agreement, namely the extension of patent protection to *all fields* of technology. As a result, members can no longer exclude medicines or other health technologies from patent protection. Articles 28 and 33 TRIPS oblige members to grant patent-holders a set of exclusive rights (i.e. to prevent third parties from making, using, offering for sale, selling or importing for these purposes the patented product without consent) for a minimum period of 20 years. The monopolies created through patent protection can result in unduly expensive medicines and as such interfere with individuals' access to affordable medicines. Moreover, IP protection can create distortions in the funding of biomedical and pharmaceutical R&D with an undue focus on profit-making, rather than addressing the public health needs of the world's most poor and marginalised (CESCR 2020, paras. 60–61). As such, the TRIPS' minimum standards have a very real effect on (developing) members' ability to comply with their human rights obligations to ensure that (essential) medicines and health technologies are adequately available, accessible and affordable (UN SG's High-Level Panel on Access to Medicines 2016, p. 17).

At the same time, TRIPS also provides for flexibility as its object and purpose is not limited to the protection of IPRs only, but recognises the need to find a balance between IP protection and access, and between the needs of highly developed and developing and least developed countries (TRIPS, preamble and arts. 7 and 8; Seuba 2016, pp. 479–480). That was confirmed by the 2001 Doha Declaration on the TRIPS Agreement and Public Health which asserts that TRIPS 'can and should be interpreted and implemented in a manner supportive of WTO members' right to protect public health and, in particular, to promote access to medicines for all' (WTO Ministerial Conference 2002, para. 4). For example, TRIPS leaves members free to determine the appropriate method of implementation within their national legal systems as long as TRIPS' minimum standards are guaranteed (TRIPS, art. 1). Many of its provisions allow for a degree of interpretative flexibility, such as the term 'novelty' and 'inventive step' found in Article 27 TRIPS. These can be interpreted and implemented in a manner conducive to public health as, for example, India has done with its introduction of Section 3(d) to the Patents Act. Furthermore, TRIPS allows for some concrete tools to strike a fair balance between IP protection and access, such as the regulatory review exception and compulsory licensing (TRIPS, arts. 30–31). Originally, TRIPS limited the use of compulsory licensing to 'predominantly for the domestic market' (TRIPS, art. 31(f)) making it difficult for countries without local manufacturing capacity to import low-cost medicines and as such seriously undermining the usefulness of compulsory licensing for LMICs. The Doha Declaration promised to find a solution to this problem in its Paragraph 6. After tough negotiations, the WTO Decision of 30 August 2003 established a process to allow compulsory licensing for export on a case-by-case basis (WTO General Council 2003). This was followed by an amendment to the TRIPS Agreement in 2005 that took effect 23 January 2017 (TRIPS, art. 31*bis*).

Besides, in recognition of their special needs and economic, financial and administrative constraints, least-developed WTO members are exempted from implementing the substantive obligations for protection and enforcement of IPRs contained in the TRIPS Agreement until 2021. For pharmaceutical products specifically, least-developed members have until 2033 or when a particular country ceases to be in the least-developed category. These extensions have been granted through the TRIPS Council (TRIPS, art. 66.1), the body responsible for monitoring the operation of the TRIPS Agreement (TRIPS, art. 68).

The interface between TRIPS and the right to health has been comprehensively addressed in the context of access to medicines and will not be repeated here ('t Hoen 2016; Sellin 2014; Hestermeyer 2007). However, a brief mention should be made of the right to benefit from science, which according to the CESCR is a significant mediator between the right to health and IP protection (CESCR 2020, para. 69). The right to benefit from science has a complex relationship with IP protection regimes (UN CESCR, 2020, para. 60). Namely, on the one hand, IP protection is commonly justified because it is supposed to create incentives to innovate, while on the other hand, IP protection can also negatively affect the advancement of science and access to its benefits. A further complicating dimension is the link between IPRs and the right to the protection of the moral and material interests resulting from any scientific, literary or artistic production of which s/he is the author as found in Article 15(1)c ICESCR. However, contrary to human rights, which are derived from the inherent dignity and worth of all persons, IPRs are legal entitlements of a temporary nature that can be revoked, licenced or assigned to someone else. They primarily protect business and corporate interests and investments. They are tools by which states seek, among other things, to provide incentives for inventiveness and creativity and encourage the dissemination of innovations (CESCR 2006, paras. 1–2). IPRs should, therefore, not be equated with the right to benefit from the protection of the moral and material interests of the author (CESCR 2006, paras. 3 and 7). 'Ultimately, [IP] is a social product and has a social function. States parties thus have a duty to prevent unreasonable high costs for access to essential medicines' (CESCR 2006, para. 35; CESCR 2020, para. 62). That means striking an adequate balance between IP protection and the availability and (economic) accessibility of scientific knowledge and its benefits/applications (CESCR 2020, para. 62).

Consequently, TRIPS indirectly interferes with the rights to health and benefit from science where it undermines individuals' access to medicines. Not only do states have domestic human rights obligations to secure access to safe, quality, affordable medicines, for example, by making full use of the TRIPS flexibilities, but they also have ETOs to do so. What such ETOs could entail will be further examined in the next section.

Identifying ETOs for access to medicines

This section will attempt to demonstrate the value and importance of health-related ETOs to facilitate and contribute to achieving universal access to medicines, by providing an illustration of the nature and type of states' ETOs to safeguard access to affordable (essential) medicines in the context of states' TRIPS obligations. These examples are by no means an exhaustive analysis of states' ETOs in this context, but aim to demonstrate that it is neither impossible nor unworkable to identify a range of different, relatively specific types of ETOs for access to medicines. Even though the following examples are presented as separate obligations, there may be a degree of overlap between them in practice.

ETOs related to TRIPS

- WTO members should not engage in any conduct in the WTO that nullifies or impairs individuals' access to medicines in any (other) state, or a state's ability to comply with their access to medicines obligations. States should desist from actions or omissions that nullify or impair the enjoyment of access to medicines outside their territories (*Maastricht Principles* on ETOs, para. 20), as well as impairs the ability of another state to comply with its access to medicines obligations (*Maastricht Principles* on ETOs, para. 21). Specifically, as members of international organisations, states must take all reasonable steps to ensure that the organisation acts consistently with the human rights obligations of that state (*Maastricht Principles* on ETOs, para. 15).

For example, WTO members should not oppose requests from least-developed members to the TRIPS Council, which is open to all WTO members, to extend the transition period for TRIPS allowing them to forego the protection and enforcement of IPRs until their economies are stronger. In October 2020, Chad, on behalf of the LDC group, submitted such a request pointing to the difficulties that LDCs continue to face in reaching their development goals, which have been further aggravated by the COVID-19 pandemic. Unlike the previous extensions, the present request does not set a specific date for all LDCs for the termination of the transition period. Rather, it proposes establishing the extension for as long as a member remains a LDC and following graduation for a defined period of 12 years (WTO TRIPS Council 2020a).

- (Developed) states should not engage in conduct that impairs the ability of WTO members to make full use of the TRIPS flexibilities. States should elaborate, interpret and apply international agreements in a manner consistent with their human rights obligations (*Maastricht Principles* on ETOs, para. 17). According to the CESCR that requires that 'the right to health is given due attention in international agreements' (CESCR 2000, para. 39), meaning that states parties should take steps to ensure that their bilateral, regional or international agreements dealing with IP do not impede access to medicines and incorporate to the fullest extent any safeguard and flexibilities

to secure this (CESCR 2016, para. 51). States parties should identify any potential conflicts between the ICESCR and IP agreements and, in case a conflict is found, refrain from entering into such treaties (CESCR 2017, para. 13), as well as review their existing IP agreements, such as TRIPS, to ensure that they are consistent with their right to health obligations, and amend them as necessary (CESCR 2016, para. 51). For example, the TRIPS Agreement was formally amended in 2017 to allow members producing generic medicines under compulsory licence to export such medicines to LDCs that lack manufacturing capacity (TRIPS, art. 31*bis*). Effectively the provision was already in place since the 2003 WTO decision. Unfortunately, it has not proven to be a very effective tool for LMICs without manufacturing capacity to secure cheap generic medicines and is widely criticised for its complexity ('t Hoen 2016, pp. 45–46).

- *WTO members should initiate, promote and assist in adopting and implementing processes, and, where necessary reforms, that enhance systemic coherence between the TRIPS regime and international human rights law.* The problems surrounding access to medicines clearly illustrate the tension that exists between (national and international) IP regimes and international human rights. Although the TRIPS Agreement is not strictly incompatible with the ICESCR (Tobin 2011, pp. 357–358), the object and purpose of both treaties differ. The underlying values of the international trade regime and the international human rights regime are distinct, both have different starting points and principal characteristics. There is a lack of explicit human rights references in the WTO Agreement, TRIPS, WTO jurisprudence and even the Doha Declaration on TRIPS and Public Health. The WTO adjudicative bodies can clarify and apply WTO law but are not competent to give direct effect to international human rights law and formally interpret and enforce human rights treaties. However, there is scope to invoke human rights arguments in WTO jurisprudence (Seuba 2016, pp. 481–482; McBeth 2010, p. 163).

States parties to the ICESCR have a duty to 'prevent unreasonable high costs for access to essential medicines' (CESCR 2006, para. 35; CESCR 2020, para. 62). That means striking an adequate balance between IP protection and the availability and (economic) accessibility of (essential) medicines (CESCR 2020, para. 62). In achieving this balance, private or corporate interests should not be unduly favoured over the public interest. Thus, IP protection must not impede a state's ability to comply with their core obligations in relation to the rights to food, education and health (CESCR 2006, para. 35). In the context of their TRIPS obligations, WTO members should therefore initiate, promote and assist in adopting and implementing policies that safeguard that the TRIPS Council and WTO adjudicatory bodies interpret and apply WTO law in conformity with WTO members' human rights obligations. For example, in October 2020, India and South Africa submitted a request to the TRIPS Council to waive certain provisions of the TRIPS Agreement in light of the exceptional circumstances of the COVID-19 pandemic. The communication recognises that 'it is important for WTO Members to work together' to ensure that IPRs 'do not create barriers to the timely access to affordable medical products including vaccines and medicines or to scaling-up of research, development, manufacturing and supply of medical products essential to combat COVID-19'. The proposed waiver should continue until widespread vaccination is in place globally (WTO TRIPS Council 2020b).

ETOs related to TRIPS+ agreements

- *(Developed) states should not pressure LMICs to accept TRIPS+ standards.* Through the conclusion of free trade and/or investment agreements, high-income countries (HICs) in particular demand more extensive protections for IPRs than strictly required by TRIPS, and therefore named TRIPS+ (Yu 2018, pp. 7–10; 't Hoen 2016, pp. 85–86). Such agreements, among others, limit opposition to patent applications, prohibit national regulatory authorities from approving generic medicines until patents have expired, maintain data exclusivity and thereby delay the approval of generic medicines and limit the grounds for compulsory licensing. The negative impact of TRIPS+ agreements on access to affordable medicines is well-documented (UN SG's High-Level Panel on Access to Medicines 2016, pp. 24–26; Wirtz 2016, pp. 424–425). This is, moreover, exacerbated by the most-favoured-nation treatment principle, which, as a cornerstone of the WTO, requires that when granting a favour to one state that should also apply to all other WTO members (TRIPS, art. 4). The result is a development of ever-increasing standards of IP protection and fragmentation of the international regulatory system forcing LMICs to spread their scarce resources and personnel over a multitude of fora and negotiations (Yu 2018, p. 11). Consequently, such TRIPS+ arrangements indirectly interfere with the right to health, as they create a real and foreseeable risk of undermining access to affordable medicines in LMICs. Powerful (developed) states should, therefore, not encourage, or place undue pressure on LMICs to accept such TRIPS+ standards (UN Special Rapporteur in the field of Cultural Rights 2015, para. 104; UN Special Rapporteur on the Right to Health 2011, para. 90).

- *States should subject TRIPS+ agreements to human rights impact assessments.* States must conduct prior assessment of the potential extraterritorial impacts of their practices on the enjoyment of access to medicines (*Maastricht Principles* on ETOs, para. 14). The effect of TRIPS+ arrangements is exacerbated by the lack of any due diligence undertaken to assess, and if necessary, prevent, any harmful impact of TRIPS+ agreements on access to medicines. One policy tool regularly put forward to remedy this is human rights (or right to health) impact assessments (MacNaughton and Forman 2015, pp. 124 and 127). Such impact assessments allow policymakers and civil society actors to prevent or mitigate any negative impacts of a trade/investment agreement under negotiation on the right to health within or beyond their national territory. They measure the potential impact of the agreement under negotiation on the capacity of states to meet their (extra)territorial access to medicines obligations, as well as individuals' capacity to enjoy their rights.

Additional ETOs

- *(Developed) states should, to the extent possible, ensure that the pharmaceutical industry linked to their sphere of control or whose conduct they can influence, does not engage in conduct that impairs the ability of states to realise access to affordable medicines.* States must take necessary measures to ensure that non-state actors, which they are in a position to regulate, as well as in a position to influence, do not nullify or impair the enjoyment of access to medicines (*Maastricht Principles* on ETOs, paras. 24 and 26). Private pharmaceutical corporations are key players in the process of biomedical and pharmaceutical R&D, innovation and manufacturing, as well as key beneficiaries of IP regimes as they (generally) are the patent-holders of existing or new medicines. Their conduct can therefore significantly impact individuals' access to affordable (essential) medicines, both within and outside a state's borders.

Health emergencies, such as the COVID-19 pandemic, epitomise the need for (scientific and technical) international cooperation and regulation of private actors to ensure that vaccines, therapeutics and diagnostics are developed, if not yet existing, and thereafter made equitably available and accessible. As the CESCR highlights, in a pandemic 'sharing the best scientific knowledge and its applications, especially in the medical field, becomes crucial to mitigate the impact of the disease, and to expedite the discovery of effective treatments and vaccines' (CESCR 2020, para. 82).

The pricing of pandemic health products together with global manufacturing capacity are key determinants of their global availability and accessibility. Difficult allocation and rationing decisions can be eased through price reductions and increasing production capacity, including through non-exclusive licencing. Especially if governments have spent enormous amounts of public financing on R&D for new pandemic health technologies, they should leverage their positions as financiers to, for example, set the pricing terms of the end product, or require pharmaceutical and biomedical companies to voluntarily licence their IPRs on a non-exclusive and global basis. For example, in the context of the COVID-19 pandemic, the WHO launched the COVID-19 Technology Access Pool at the end of May 2020 on the initiative of Costa Rica. The proposed voluntary pool aims to collect patent rights, regulatory test data and other information that could be shared for developing medicines, vaccines and diagnostics to combat COVID-19 (www.who.int). The pharmaceutical industry, however, has opposed the effort (Silverman 2020).

In conclusion, all these examples of ETOs, in essence, come down to a general obligation for states to *create an international enabling environment conducive to the universal fulfilment of the right of everyone to have access to (essential) medicines* (*Maastricht Principles* on ETOs, para. 29; Tobin 2011, p. 344). In the words of the CESCR, states must, therefore, 'recognise the essential role of international cooperation' to fully realise the right to health (CESCR 2000, para. 38) and 'take steps through legislation and policies, including diplomatic and foreign relations, to promote an enabling global environment for the advancement of science and the enjoyment of the benefits of its applications' (CESCR 2020, para. 77).

Concluding remarks

Access to medicines is a global and shared responsibility. However, state conduct can and does affect individuals' access to (essential) medicines and health technologies both within and beyond a country's borders. International IP regimes such as the TRIPS Agreement may have such an effect. The monopolies created through patent protection can result in expensive medicines unduly restricting individuals' (economic) access to such patent protected products. Moreover, IP protection can create distortions in the funding of biomedical and pharmaceutical R&D with an undue focus on profit-making, rather than addressing the public health needs of the world's most poor and marginalised. In such cases, TRIPS indirectly interferes with the rights to health and benefit from science as it undermines individuals' access to medicines and negatively impacts (developing) members' ability to realise access to safe, quality and affordable (essential) medicines and health technologies.

In light of the rights to health and benefit from science, states have a range of different domestic and extraterritorial human rights obligations to respect, protect and fulfil access to medicines. Consequently, this chapter examined how such ETOs should be applied in the context of states' TRIPS obligations. The list of ETOs provided is intended as an illustration of the nature and type of states' ETOs in this context, but is by no means an exhaustive analysis. It demonstrates that it is neither impossible nor unworkable to identify a range of different, relatively specific types of ETOs for access to medicines. Moreover, it strengthens the importance and value of ETOs as a facilitator to achieve universal access to medicines for all. Now is the time to deepen and extend the analysis of the nature, scope and practical application of ETOs in relation to international IP regimes and in that context also focus on other areas of IP protection (copyright, indigenous knowledge, etc.) beyond access to medicines. Moreover, issues of accountability, remedies and enforcement mechanisms remain to be addressed.

References

Bueno de Mesquita, J. et al. (2010) 'The Human Rights Responsibility of International Assistance and Cooperation in Health' in Gibney, M. and Skogly, S. (eds). *Universal Human Rights and Extraterritorial Obligations*, University of Pennsylvania Press.

Committee on Economic, Social and Cultural Rights (CESCR) (1990) GC 3 on the Nature of States Parties Obligations, E/1991/23, E/C.12/1990/8, annex III.

_______ (2000) GC 14 on the Right to the Highest Attainable Standard of Health, E/C.12/2000/4.

_______ (2006) GC 17 on the Right of Everyone to Benefit from the Protection of the Moral and Material Interests Resulting from any Scientific, Literary or Artistic Production of which He or She is the Author, E/C.12/GC/17.

_______ (2016) GC 22 on the Right to Sexual and Reproductive Health, E/C.12/GC/22.

_______ (2017) GC 24 on State Obligations under the International Covenant on Economic, Social and Cultural Rights in the Context of Business Activities, E/C.12/GC/24.

_______ (2020) GC 25 on Science and Economic, Social and Cultural Rights, E/C.12/GC/25.

etoconsortium.org (n.d.) *Maastricht Principles* on Extraterritorial Human Rights Obligations of States in the Area of Economic, Social and Cultural Rights, available at https://www.etoconsortium.org/nc/en/main-navigation/library/maastricht-principles/?tx_drblob_pi1%5BdownloadUid%5D=23 [accessed 26 November 2020].

Forman L. (2011) 'An Elementary Consideration of Humanity? Linking Trade-Related Intellectual Property Rights to the Human Right to Health in International Law', *The Journal of World Intellectual Property*, 14(2), 155–175.

Forman, L. et al. (2016) 'Conceptualising Minimum Core Obligations under the Right to Health: How Should we Define and Implement the "Morality of the Depths"', *The Journal of Human Rights* 20(4), 531–548.

Frick M. et al. (2016) 'Falling Short of the Rights to Health and Scientific Progress: Inadequate TB Drug Research and Access', *Health and Human Rights Journal* 18(1), 9–23.

Hestermeyer, H. (2007) *Human Rights and the WTO. The Case of Patents and Access to Medicines*, Oxford University Press.

Lee, J-H. (2015) *A Human Rights Framework for Intellectual Property, Innovation and Access to Medicines*, Routledge.

MacNaughton, G. and Forman, L. (2015) 'Human Rights and Health Impact Assessments of Trade-Related Intellectual Property Rights: A Comparative Study of Experiences in Thailand and Peru', *Journal of Human Rights* 14(1), 124–148.

Matthews, D. (2010) 'Intellectual Property Rights, Human Rights and the Right to Health' in Grosheide, W. (ed). *Intellectual Property Rights and Human Rights: A Paradox*, Edward Elgar.

McBeth, A. (2010) 'Human Rights in Economic Globalisation' in Joseph, S. and McBeth, A. (eds). *Research Handbook on International Human Rights Law*, Edward Elgar.

MSF Access Campaign (n.d.) 'Affordable Medicines from India under Attack: What's at Stake', https://msfaccess.org/spotlight-pharmacy-developing-world [accessed 26 November 2020].

Ooms, G. and Hammonds, R. (2010) 'Taking Up Daniels' Challenge: The Case for Global Health Justice', *Health and Human Rights Journal* 12(1), 29–46.

Saul, B., Kinley, D. and Mowbray, J. (2014) *The International Covenant on Economic, Social and Cultural Rights. Commentary, Cases and Materials*, Oxford University Press.

Sellin, J. (2014) *Access to Medicines. The Interface between Patents and Human Rights. Does One Size Fit All?*, Intersentia.

Seuba, X. (2016) 'Human Rights and Intellectual Property' in Yusuf, A.A. and Correa, C.M. (eds). *Intellectual Property and International Trade. The TRIPS Agreement*, Kluwer Law International.

Silverman, E. (2020) Pharma Leaders Shoot Down WHO Voluntary Pool for Patent Rights on COVID-19 Products, STAT, available at https://www.statnews.com/pharmalot/2020/05/28/who-voluntary-pool-patents-pfizer/ [accessed 26 November 2020].

STOPTB (n.d.) 'Factsheets & Information Brochures', http://www.stoptb.org/resources/factsheets/ [accessed 26 November 2020].

't Hoen, E. (2016) 'Private Patents and Public Health. Changing Intellectual Property Rules for Access to Medicines', *Health Action International*, available at http://accesstomedicines.org/resources [accessed 26 November 2020].

Tobin, J. (2011) *The Right to Health in International Law*, Oxford University Press.

UN Special Rapporteur in the field of Cultural Rights (2015) Report of the Special Rapporteur in the Field of Cultural Rights, F. Shaheed, A/70/279.

UN Special Rapporteur on the Right to Health (2011) Report of the Special Rapporteur on the Right of Everyone to the Enjoyment of the Highest Attainable Standard of Physical and Mental Health, A. Grover. Addendum, Mission to Guatemala, A/HRC/17/25/Add.2.

_______ (2013) Report of the Special Rapporteur on the Right of Everyone to the Enjoyment of the Highest Attainable Standard of Physical and Mental Health on Access to Medicines, A. Grover, A/HRC/23/42.

_______ (2016) Report of the Special Rapporteur on the Right of Everyone to the Enjoyment of the Highest Attainable Standard of Physical and Mental Health, D. Puras, A/71/304.

UN Special Rapporteur on the Right to Water and Sanitation (2014) Report of the Special Rapporteur on the Human Rights to Safe Drinking Water and Sanitation, C. de Albuquerque, A/HRC/27/55.

United Nations (UN) (2014) Independent Expert on Foreign Debt: Final Report of the Independent Export on the Effects on Foreign Debt and other Related International Financial Obligations of States on the Full Enjoyment of All Human Rights, particularly Economic, Social and Cultural Rights, C. Lumina, A/HRC/25/52.

United Nations Commission on Human Rights (UN CionHR) (2001) Economic, Social and Cultural Rights. Globalisation and Its Impact on the Full Enjoyment of Human Rights. Progress Report Submitted by J. Oloka-Onyango and Deepika Udagama in Accordance with Sub-Commission Resolution 1999/8 and Commission on Human Rights Decision 2000/102, E/CN.4/2001/10.

United Nations General Assembly (UN GA) (2015) Transforming Our World: The 2030 Agenda for Sustainable Development, UNGA Res 70/1.

United Nations Secretary General's (UNSG's) High-Level Panel on Access to Medicines (2016) 'Promoting Innovation and Access to Health Technologies', Secretariat hosted by the United Nations Development Programme, available at http://www.unsgaccessmeds.org/final-report [accessed 26 November 2020].

Wirtz, V.J., Hogerzeil, H.V. and Gray, A. et al. (2016) 'The Lancet Commission on Essential Medicines Policies: Essential Medicines for Universal Health Coverage', *Lancet* 389, 403–476.

World Trade Organisation (WTO) (2001) Ministerial Conference: Doha Declaration on the TRIPS Agreement and Public Health. Adopted at the Doha Ministerial Conference, Fourth Session, WT/MIN(01)/DEC/2.

WTO General Council (2003) Implementation of Paragraph 6 of the Doha Declaration on the TRIPS Agreement and Public Health, WT/L/540.

WTO TRIPS Council (2020a) Extension of the Transition Period under TRIPS Article 66.1 for Least Developed Country Members. Communication from Chad on Behalf of the LDC Group, IP/C/W/668.

_______ (2020b) Waiver from Certain Provisions of the TRIPS Agreement for the Prevention, Containment and Treatment of COVID-19. Communication from India and South Africa, IP/C/W/669.

WHO (n.d.) 'COVID-19 Technology Access Pool', https://www.who.int/emergencies/diseases/novel-coronavirus-2019/global-research-on-novel-coronavirus-2019-ncov/covid-19-technology-access-pool [accessed 26 November 2020].

_______ (n.d.) 'Essential Medicines', https://www.who.int/topics/essential_medicines/en/ [accessed 26 November 2020].

Yamin, A.E. (2010) 'Our Place in the World: Conceptualising Obligations Beyond Borders in Human Rights-Based Approaches to Health', *Health and Human Rights Journal* 12(1), 3–14.

Yu, P.K. (2018) 'Realigning TRIPS-Plus Negotiations with UN Sustainable Development Goals', *Texas A&M University, School of Law. Legal Studies Research Paper Series* 18(40), 1–19.

Part VI

Peace and security

25

Extraordinary rendition

A classic example of the USA avoiding ETOs as seen from Europe

Elspeth Guild

Introduction

A number of European states participated in the US-led War on Terror that followed the attacks in the US on 11 September 2001. Among the activities that the US carried out as part of that 'War' was a Central Intelligence Agency (CIA) led programme of kidnapping, transport, interrogation and torture of persons suspected of having links with terrorism (mainly Al Qaeda). This programme was initiated by a covert action Memorandum of Notification signed by (then) President George W. Bush which authorised the director of the CIA 'to undertake operations designed to capture and detain persons who pose a continuing, serious threat of violence or death to US persons or interests or who are planning terrorist activities'. The programme ended when (then) President Obama signed Executive Order 13491 in January 2009 formally curtailing it. These CIA operations became known as the extraordinary rendition programme.

The programme has had a momentous impact on human rights. First, that a foremost liberal democracy, the USA, would disregard its international human rights commitments (in particular the UN Convention against Torture, Inhuman or Degrading Treatment or Punishment 1984) was a shock to the whole UN human rights system. The prohibition on torture was and continues to be considered by eminent jurists as a *jus cogens* obligation *erga omnes*, the highest level of prohibited state action. That the USA should disregard it was a very serious blow to the whole system. Secondly, the USA's example opened the way for other states also to disregard their international human rights obligation to prevent torture. It is towards this second aspect of the challenge which the CIA extraordinary rendition programme presented to the international community that this chapter is focused on. The fact that a US agency was requesting assistance in the 'War on Terror' was undoubtedly an important factor that led numerous European states to throw caution to the wind and become embroiled in the programme. It is not likely that a similar flexibility would be shown by those same states to a similar request should it have been made by the Russian Federation. However, the utter lack of care by state authorities regarding the practices which were being carried out on their territory was monstrous. Not surprisingly, as evidence of the programme began to leak to the press and the involvement of European states as well, damage limitation became a key priority. The judicial venue which became central to the search for remedies by the victims was the European Court of Human Rights. The European

DOI: 10.4324/9781003090014-32

Convention on Human Rights (of which the European Court of Human Rights (ECtHR) is the court charged with determining complaints) is the founding convention of the Council of Europe which is composed of 47 states in Europe. No state can be a member of the Council of Europe without ratifying the ECHR and accepting the jurisdiction of the ECtHR to hear both state and individual complaints against it. However, even at the time of writing, states that have been formally condemned by the European Court of Human Rights for their involvement continue to deny that the events ever took place.

The extraordinary rendition programme was highly secretive, complex and expensive. These negative characteristics, however, were offset by one key advantage – avoiding the jurisdiction of the US courts. The CIA had a problem with US law in at least three ways. Firstly, kidnapping (taking charge of a person without a duly issued warrant) by the competent authorities is a crime. Secondly, detaining people without due process of law is a crime. Thirdly, torturing people is a crime. The solution that the CIA came up with was to seek to avoid the jurisdiction of the US courts by carrying out these crimes in other countries, beyond the reach of the US courts. The possibility that the criminal justice systems of the countries where the criminal activities took place would investigate and charge those responsible was a risk. But as the US Senate documents, which evidence the programme, reveal (see below), the CIA was confident that bribery to local officials would be sufficient to diminish that risk.

As can be seen from the evidence, European states were very sensitive to publicity about their actions hosting black sites. A New York Times article implicating a European state (Poland) was sufficient to cause the authorities of that state to terminate its involvement immediately (Feinstein Report 2014). Enthusiastic participation by European states rapidly shifted to absolute denial of involvement. Yet, parts of European states still shield CIA agents from the legal consequences of their actions such as the Italian central authorities which continue to refuse to transmit the international arrest warrants for 23 named individuals (all CIA officers) who are alleged to have been at the centre of the kidnapping of Mr Nasr (one of the victims of the programme). The warrants were issued after extensive judicial consideration by the competent Italian courts. One of the constant findings of the European Court of Human Rights in the extraordinary rendition cases is a failure by the implicated states to carry out an effective investigation into the events and the prosecution of those responsible. This would seem to confirm the CIA's view that they could buy their way out of local scrutiny.

State authorities are uniquely well-placed to hide their tracks. This is particularly so when those tracks lead to very serious charges of human rights abuses. It is exactly this wall of silence by the states that participated in the CIA's programme which has made accountability so difficult. Not only have state authorities denied that the programme was ever hosted on their territory, notwithstanding overwhelming evidence to the contrary, but they have also colluded with US authorities to ensure that those investigating the allegations do not have access to the victims. This extends to refusing assistance to the European Court of Human Rights to have access to detainees at the US military base and detention centre in Cuba, Guantanamo Bay. The willingness of a number of European states to assist the CIA's extraordinary rendition programme has, nonetheless, had numerous unintended consequences and serious political ramifications for the leaders who took the decisions to participate. Little of this, however, has been the result of serious inquiries by the relevant governments or parliaments and even less sparked by legal proceedings at the national level (Bigo, Carrera, Guild and Radescu 2015, pp. 34–46). The heavy lifting in terms of determining the facts and law has primarily fallen on the UN Human Rights Treaty Bodies and the European Court of Human Rights.

While the US judiciary has been outspoken about the nature of detention in the US military installation in Guantanamo Bay (US Supreme Court 2004), it has been silent on compensation for persons tortured by CIA operatives in various black sites around the world (Reed 2014, p. 131; Johnnston 2007, p. 357). This has resulted in a displacement of responsibility from the principal state which authorised the programme of kidnapping and torture to other states which were complicit in the actions because of their political determination to support the USA in its fight against terrorism (Geyer 2007, pp. 1–15). In the first instance, the struggle for redress was driven by the need to establish the facts. A number of international non-governmental organisations have been outstanding in achieving what seemed likely to be impossible at the start – tracing the lines of responsibility for human rights abuses. Among the most impressive has been the Bureau of Investigative Journalism. The Justice Initiative of the Open Society Foundations, Amnesty International and Human Rights Watch have all been meticulous and exceptionally persistent in their work on the subject. Yet, the mechanisms through which redress has been sought and provided have been primarily international and supranational. Two exceptions stand out. Firstly, Canada: a Commission of Inquiry was established to determine the facts relating to the transport and torture of Maher Arar (a Canadian citizen) in Syria. The report issued in 2006 confirmed that Canadian intelligence had been responsible for the harm caused to him as a result of the exchange of information about him between Canadian and US intelligence services. The Canadian Government offered Mr Arar Can$10.5 million in damages. Secondly, Omar Khadr, a Canadian child who was detained for 10 years at the US military installation at Guantanamo Bay on terrorism charges until he was transferred to Canada for further imprisonment until 2015 when he was released. The Canadian Supreme Court found that Khadr's human rights have been violated during his detention in Guantanamo Bay and that the Canadian authorities were complicit (Khadr was also offered CAN$10.5 million in compensation). Secondly, the US Senate Select Committee on Intelligence produced an outstanding study on the CIA's detention and interrogation programme, commonly called the Feinstein Report after the chair of the Committee which produced it (Feinstein 2014). The full report is still confidential, but the Executive Summary and Findings and Conclusions were released and published, running to more than 500 pages (Guild 2018, pp. 10–29; Guild and Bigo 2018, p. 210). This is a particularly rich source of information about the programme which only became available in December 2014.

The programme

The CIA extraordinary rendition programme developed from the end of 2001, commencing from the Memorandum of Notification signed by (then) President George W. Bush on 17 September that year. From the European perspective, the European Court of Human Rights described the programme as follows: 'On an unspecified date following 11 September 2001 the CIA established a programme in the Counterterrorist Center ("CTC") to detain and interrogate terrorists at sites abroad. In further documents the US authorities referred to it as "the CTC program" but, subsequently, it was also called "the High-Value Detainee Program" ("the HVD Program") or the "Rendition Detention Interrogation Program" ("the RDI Program")' (ECtHR 2018b). The programme ended in 2009. At the start, it was fairly rudimentary as the Agiza and Alzery cases indicate (see below) – mainly involving asking allies to identify people who might be engaged in Al Qaeda related activities and on receiving information about identities and whereabouts to turn up with planes and colleagues and kidnap the individuals taking them to a country willing to detain and torture them. In the early cases, the victims were taken to Syria (Arar), Egypt (CAT 2005; Alzery – where both had been resident and from which both feared persecution) and Afghanistan (ECtHR 2012). The US controlled bases in Afghanistan would appear regularly throughout the whole period of the programme. The CIA prisoners were categorised into two groups: the High-Value Detainees (HVD, 17 in number) and the lower level detainees. The Justice Initiative has found that at least 136 persons were subject to rendition or secretly detained by the CIA and at least 54 governments participated in the CIA programme.

The Memorandum of Notification did not refer to interrogations or interrogation techniques, these would be dealt with later, but it gave the CIA authority to capture and detain people at will, without the objective of a criminal investigation and charges. By November 2001, the CIA determined that it would need to detain its victims outside the USA in order to avoid US oversight of detention facilities (Feinstein Report 2014, p 12.). So, the chase was on to find willing partners for the programme. Further, as one of the objectives of the programme was to obtain intelligence – to extract it from the detainees, the issue of interrogation arose. Until October 2001, CIA policy followed the US Department of the Army Field Manual 'Intelligence Interrogation'. CIA policy was not to participate in the use of force, mental or physical torture, extremely demeaning indignities or exposure to inhumane treatment etc. But on 26 November 2001, the CIA's General Counsel proposed a defence for CIA officers against charges of carrying out torture: that the torture was necessary to prevent imminent, significant, physical harm to persons, where there is no other available means to prevent the harm (Feinstein Report 2014, p. 12). In January 2002, the US authorities argued that the Geneva conventions relative to the treatment of Prisoners of War 1949 did not apply to their detainees, thus excluding the competence of the International Committee of the Red Cross. One particular detainee, Abu Zubaydah, was the first on which the enhanced interrogation techniques (EITs) were developed and used. According to the European Court of Human Rights, by August 2002 the US Justice Department had given a legal opinion to the CIA setting out the following ten EITs which could be used on detainees:

1 The attention grasp consists of grasping the detainee with both hands, with one hand on each side of the collar opening, in a controlled and quick motion. In the same motion as the grasp, the detainee is drawn toward the interrogator.
2 During the walling technique, the detainee is pulled forward and then quickly and firmly pushed into a flexible false wall so that his shoulder blades hit the wall. His head and neck are supported with a rolled towel to prevent whiplash.
3 The facial hold is used to hold the detainee's head immobile. The interrogator places an open palm on either side of the detainee's face and the interrogator's fingertips are kept well away from the detainee's eyes.
4 With the facial or insult slap, the fingers are slightly spread apart. The interrogator's hand makes contact with the area between the tip of the detainee's chin and the bottom of the corresponding earlobe.
5 In cramped confinement, the detainee is placed in a confined space, typically a small or large box, which is usually dark. Confinement in the smaller space lasts no more than 2 hours and in the larger space it can last up to 18 hours.
6 Insects placed in a confinement box involve placing a harmless insect in the box with the detainee.
7 During wall standing, the detainee may stand about 4–5 feet from a wall with his feet spread approximately to his shoulder width. His arms are stretched out in front of him and his fingers rest on the wall to support all of his body weight. The detainee is not allowed to reposition his hands or feet.
8 The application of stress positions may include having the detainee sit on the floor with his legs extended straight out in front of him with his arms raised above his head or kneeling on the floor while leaning back at a 45-degree angle.

9 Sleep deprivation will not exceed 11 days at a time.
10 The application of the waterboard technique involves binding the detainee to a bench with his feet elevated above his head. The detainee's head is immobilised, and an interrogator places a cloth over the detainee's mouth and nose while pouring water onto the cloth in a controlled manner. Airflow is restricted for 20 to 40 seconds and the technique produces the sensation of drowning and suffocation (ECtHR 2014). The constant case law of the European Court of Human Rights has found such measures, singly and together, breaches of Article 3 ECHR (the prohibition on torture) (ECtHR 1979–80).

As mentioned above, it is apparent that the CIA was fairly confident that the ten EITs would be crimes if committed in the USA. Thus, it needed to use the territory of other states for these purposes. The CIA is not an agency of a state bound by the ECHR, so the territory of the 47 Council of Europe states was an option. The actions of its agents would only be subject to the ECHR standards when carried out in a state bound by the convention, such as in the case of Nasr (see below). The CIA began a search for venues where it could carry out the EITs on its victims. These came to be known as black sites. In the Feinstein Report, each site is allocated a colour, providing a bizarre rainbow image of torture centres (Feinstein Report 2014).

The venues

By early 2002, a black site known as Cats Eye had been established in Bangkok, Thailand, but it had to be closed on short notice (presumably at the behest of the Thai authorities) and the victims moved elsewhere. The USA was not an option (see above). US military bases abroad seemed like an option but other than the base in Guantanamo Bay where the CIA negotiated with the US military to have its own 'private' area for detention and interrogation, the US military did not appear willing to participate (Feinstein Report 2014). It is not entirely clear what relationship the CIA black sites in Afghanistan had with the US military.

For European states, the venue where the CIA found partners was within NATO. One key criterion for the CIA was to avoid publicity and any form of parliamentary or other oversight. This requirement was met, it appears, by military intelligence organisations in a number of Central and Eastern European states, which, as one investigator put it (Marty 2007, p. 36), had come through democratisation unscathed by any form of parliamentary oversight. From 2002 onwards, it seems that CIA black sites were being prepared to receive victims in Lithuania, Poland, Romania and Thailand, though they opened and closed at different times and as a result of various pressures, internal and external (Feinstein Report 2014). The first to be closed was the one in Thailand which apparently resulted in victims being moved to Poland. As the programme developed and the EITs were signed off, the CIA took control of the interrogation but needed places where they could carry out the torture. As mentioned above, one NGO identified 54 governments which assisted the CIA in its extraordinary rendition programme. That complicity varied substantially. In the case of Sweden and the countries condemned by the ECtHR, the assistance was explicit and intense including hosting black sites, in others it was logistical and somewhat easier to hide. Even among European states which hosted black sites, there are variations of complicity at least as identified by the European Court of Human Rights. While the ECtHR is highly critical of Poland which hosted a site when the most extreme use of the EITs were being practiced by the CIA, it reserved slightly less criticism for Romania where the site was established later and the conditions were less horrific (ECtHR 2014; ECtHR 2018b).

The quest for accountability

Extraordinary rendition before the UN treaty bodies

Chronologically, the cases of Agiza and Alzery against Sweden regarding their rendition to US and Egyptian authorities in Sweden and transfer to Egypt were the first European ones to be dealt with by international Treaty Bodies (Agiza by the UN Committee against Torture and Alzery by the UN Human Rights Committee), both of which found violations of their relevant convention (International Covenant on Civil and Political Rights 1966 and UN Convention against Torture and Other Cruel, Inhuman or Degrading Treatment or Punishment 1984). Agiza was an Egyptian national who applied for asylum in Sweden in 2000 on account of his treatment in Egypt. His asylum application was rejected on 18 December 2001 without the possibility of any appeal with suspensive effect because of the national security ground on which the decision was taken. On the same day, according to a Swedish television broadcast of 10 May 2004 entitled 'Kalla Fakta' examining the circumstances of the expulsion of the complainant and another individual (Alzery): the two men had been handcuffed when brought to a Stockholm airport; a private jet chartered by the USA had landed and the two men were handed over to a group of special agents by Swedish police. The agents stripped the clothes from the men's bodies, inserted suppositories of an unknown nature, placed diapers upon them and dressed them in black overalls. Their hands and feet were chained to a specially designed harness, they were blindfolded and hooded as they were brought to the plane. They were taken to Egypt where they were handed over to Egyptian authorities, imprisoned and tortured. The UN Committee against Torture found that Sweden had breached Article 3 – the prohibition of sending someone to a country where there is a real risk he or she would suffer torture (CAT 2005).

The case of Alzery was brought before the UN Human Rights Committee and determined in 2005 (HRC 2006). The facts are largely similar to those of Agiza. But by the time the case came before the Committee, the Swedish Parliamentary Ombudsman had published his report on the events on 21 March 2005. According to the Human Rights Committee, the Ombudsman criticised:

> The failure of the Security Police to maintain control over the situation at Bromma airport, allowing foreign agents free hand in the exercise of public authority on Swedish soil. Such relinquishment of public authority was unlawful. The expulsion was carried out in an inhuman and unacceptable manner. The treatment was in some respects unlawful and overall had to be characterized as degrading. It was questionable whether there was also a breach of article 3 of the European Convention. In any event, the Security Police should have intervened to prevent the inhuman treatment.
>
> *(HRC 2006)*

Further, the way in which the Security Police had dealt with the case was characterised throughout by passivity – from the acceptance of the offer of the use of an American aircraft until completion of the enforcement. One example cited was the failure of the Security Police to ask for information about what the security check demanded by the Americans would involve. The Ombudsman also criticised inadequate organisation, finding that none of the officers present at Bromma airport had been assigned command of the operation. The officers from the Security Police who were there had relatively subordinate ranks. They acted with remarkable deference to the American officials. Regarding the foreign agents, the Ombudsman considered that he lacked legal competence for initiating prosecution (HRC 2006).

The European Court of Human Rights (ECtHR) and extraordinary rendition

There have been five cases decided by the European Court of Human Rights (ECtHR) since 2012 on the subject of European state complicity in the CIA extraordinary rendition programme and one case is still pending at the time of writing. The countries in respect to which judgments have been handed down are Macedonia, Poland, Lithuania, Italy and Romania. In each case, the ECtHR found multiple human rights violations and ordered compensation to the victims.

- *El Masri v. Macedonia.* A German national of Lebanese origin was stopped by border guards when entering Macedonia by bus on 31 December 2003 on suspicion about the genuineness of his passport. He was detained by Macedonian authorities in a hotel for 23 days and mistreated including in interrogation about links with Al Qaeda. He was then handed over to a CIA shock capture team which tortured him in Macedonia and then took him to a base in use by the CIA in Afghanistan where he was tortured again, until on 28 May 2004 when he was 'dumped' in Albania from where he found his way back to Germany. The ECtHR found Macedonia had violated Article 3 (prohibition on torture, inhuman and degrading treatment or punishment): (1) on account of the treatment in the hotel in Macedonia; (2) on account of his treatment at the airport in Macedonia (by the CIA team); (3) on account of handing him over to the CIA, thus exposing him to further torture (outside Macedonia) and (4) for failing to carry out an effective investigation into his torture. It further found a violation of Article 5 (right to liberty and security): (1) on account of his detention in the Macedonian hotel; (2) on account of his detention in Afghanistan which was attributable to Macedonia and (3) on account of a failure to carry out an effective investigation. It also found violations of Article 8 (respect for private and family life) and 13 (right to an effective remedy). The ECtHR awarded Mr El Masri €60,000 in non-pecuniary damage.
- *Al Nashiri v. Poland* and *Husayn (Abu Zubaydah) v. Poland*: These two cases are broadly similar. Al Nashiri was 'captured' (or kidnapped) in Dubai in October 2002 and transferred to CIA custody by November 2002. He was transferred to a CIA detention centre in Afghanistan, then to Thailand and from there to a CIA detention site in Poland where he was kept from December 2002 until June 2003. Subsequently, he was transferred to Morocco and then to the CIA site at the US military installation at Guantanamo Bay. He was tortured in every site, though the ECtHR is concerned only with the events at the Polish site and subsequent torture thereafter (as the state hosting the black site knew or ought to have known that there was a real risk that onward transfer by the CIA elsewhere would entail further torture of the victim). Abu Zubaydah was kidnapped in Pakistan in March 2002. He was transferred to Thailand where he was held and tortured until he was moved to Poland in December 2002 until September 2003 where again he was tortured. He was then transferred to the CIA site at the US military installation at Guantanamo Bay. In respect of both men, the ECtHR found that Poland had violated Article 3 (prohibition on torture, inhuman and degrading treatment or punishment) in respect of both men; Article 5 (right to liberty and security); Article 8 (respect for private and family life); Article 13 (effective remedy); Article 6(1) (right to a fair trial); and in respect of Al Nashiri, a violation of Article 2 (the right to life) and Articles 3 and 1 of Protocol 6 (abolition of the death penalty) as Poland knew or ought to have known that he was being transferred to face charges in respect of which the death penalty was applicable. It awarded each man €100,000 in non-pecuniary damages.

- *Nasr and Ghali v. Italy*: In February 2003, Nasr was kidnapped in Milan by a group of unidentified men who took him to the United States Air Forces in Europe, USAFE, in Aviano from where he was taken to Egypt. In Egypt he was tortured in secret detention for several months. His wife, the second applicant, notified the Italian authorities of the disappearance of her husband and the prosecutor undertook a detailed investigation and brought charges against the CIA officers (and their Italian counterparts who participated in the matter) which resulted in convictions. The Italian Government refused to allow extradition requests issued by the Italian courts to be sent to the US authorities for the delivery of the US nationals who had been convicted. The ECtHR found that Italy had violated Article 3 (prohibition on torture, inhuman or degrading treatment or punishment) on account of treatment during the kidnapping and on account of his rendition to Egypt in circumstances where the Italian authorities could not but be aware that he would be tortured again. It also found a violation of Article 5 (right to liberty and security) for the events in Italy and Egypt, Article 8 (respect for private and family life) and Article 13 (effective remedy) in respect of Articles 3 and 8. It found that the Italian authorities had used the principle of 'state secrets' to ensure that those responsible did not have to answer for their actions. It awarded €70,000 in non-pecuniary damages to Nasr and €15,000 to his wife (Ghali) in non-pecuniary damages.
- *Abu Zubaydah v. Lithuania*: In February 2005 Abu Zubaydah was transferred from Poland (see above) to the CIA site in Guantanamo Bay. But in anticipation of the US Supreme Court judgment in *Rasul v. Bush*, 542 US 466 (2004), all the so-called high-value detainees were removed from Guantanamo Bay (where the judgment might have given them rights under the US constitution) and sent to black sites elsewhere. Abu Zubaydah, on a rather circuitous route, ended up at a CIA site in Lithuania from February 2005 to March 2006 where he was tortured. The ECtHR found Lithuania had violated Article 3 (prohibition on torture, inhuman and degrading treatment or punishment) on account of its failure to investigate his allegations and on account of its complicity with the CIA in the detention and torture of Abu Zubaydah. It also found a violation of Article 5 (right to liberty and security) on account of his detention in Lithuania and Articles 8 and 13 (effective remedy). On the facts the ECtHR found that Lithuania had hosted a CIA back site at which Abu Zubaydah had been detained and tortured, it awarded him non-pecuniary damages of €100,000.
- *Al Nashiri v. Romania*: Like Abu Zubaydah, Al Nashiri was rotated out of the CIA site at Guantanamo before the *Rasul* judgment of the US Supreme Court. From April 2004 until October or November 2005, Al Nashiri was held at a CIA black site in Romania where he was tortured. The ECtHR found that the black site had existed and that Al Nashiri had been held and tortured there. It held that Romania had violated Article 3 (prohibition on torture, inhuman or degrading treatment or punishment) on account of the treatment in Romania as well as the onward transfer of Al Nashiri and the failure to investigate his allegations. Article 5 (right to liberty and security) was also violated alongside Articles 8 (respect for private and family life) and 13 (effective remedy in respect of Articles 3, 5 and 8). The right to fair trial (Article 6(1)) was also violated and Articles 2 (right to life) and 3 in conjunction with Article 1 Protocol 6 (abolition of the death penalty). It awarded him non-pecuniary damages of €100,000.
- *Al-Hawsawi v. Lithuania* Application Number 6383/17 (pending). Al Hawsawi, a Saudi national, was kidnapped in Pakistan and handed over to the CIA. He was transferred first to Afghanistan where he was tortured, then moved to Morocco and then to Guantanamo Bay. As result of CIA concerns about the US Supreme Court (see above), he was moved at short notice to Lithuania where again he was tortured.

In all cases (except Italy) the defence of the states was to deny that the applicants had been in their country and that their country had hosted a CIA operated black site for torture. The outright denials made the work of those acting for the victims particularly complicated. Firstly, in many cases their clients were in custody in Guantanamo Bay and unable to communicate with them. Secondly, even where communication was possible, the measures taken by the CIA to hide the identity of the country where the victims were being detained were very extensive (privately chartered flights, blindfolds, earmuffs, sensory deprivation and exclusive US control of the black sites – no local personnel permitted at all), thus the victims did not often know where they were. Thirdly, extraordinarily complicated systems of flight arrangements were devised with layer after layer of private sector involvement in the provisioning of flights etc., multiple and contradictory flight information given to flight control centres around the world which was modified during the flights to hide the actual destinations. Fourthly, on arrival at a black site destination airport, complex arrangements were made with border guard authorities and local military to short circuit all normal controls on arrivals. The role of border guard authorities was crucial as they were responsible for ensuring that every foreigner entering the state was subject to an identity check. They had to be convinced not to check any of the victims on the flights, limiting their checks to crew and US personnel. The victims became ghosts. There was no official record of their arrival or departure to or from the black site or the state. Very substantial sums of money (millions of dollars) were handed out by US agents as largesse at these airports to local staff for illusory services provided. The European Court of Human Rights found that evidence of the presence of the victim on the territory was central to all of the cases and hotly disputed by the states.

This led to very sophisticated analysis of records of air traffic controllers across Europe and the identification of the relevant planes which were being used for the rendition flights. In some cases, the identification numbers of some of the planes were changed and in some cases two planes would be involved with a switch of victim from one plane to another at an intermediate stop before arrival at the end destination. These records were particularly rich, not least because of the frequency with which the CIA moved its victims from one place to another, often more than once a year. Evidence was one of the key issues in all of the cases and in the end the air traffic controllers' records were among the most important and considered sufficiently robust by the ECtHR to find that the victims had indeed been subject to torture on the territory of the defendant state. Among the most important sources of information were documents obtained through freedom of information requests in the USA by US NGOs, documents to which US parliamentary authorities were entitled and requested the reports of CIA oversight bodies. It also led to the ECtHR being required to consider non-traditional evidence, clarify its own standards of proof and assess veracity in a highly contested and politically charged legal challenge.

The evidence

In all of the cases which have come before the ECtHR, the question of evidence was central. In every case, the state authorities denied that the events had taken place, that they had any knowledge of the events or that they or their agents were in any way involved in them. In the face of a wall of denial, all of the courts were faced with a heavy evidential burden to resolve. The burden of proof remains on the applicant/complainant until sufficient evidence is produced to displace it onto the state accused of the action. In a number of the cases, as the applicant/complainant was in prison (detention) in the hands of the US authorities or their allies, obtaining evidence from them directly regarding what they know of their experiences was not possible.

The ECtHR was faced with a most unusual situation where the obtaining of evidence was particularly problematic and the states accused of complicity refused to cooperate. This in itself became a ground on which the ECtHR found a breach of Article 38 (obligation to furnish all necessary facilities for the effective conduct of an investigation) of the European Convention on Human Rights in both cases against Poland. In all cases it called on the relevant governments to carry out an effective investigation into the circumstances. In order to establish the facts in the face of such obdurate silence on the part of state authorities, the ECtHR relied in particular on reports and studies which had been prepared by supranational parliamentary bodies. The first source of particular importance for the ECtHR was the Council of Europe itself. The institutions of the Council of Europe include the Council of Ministers (made up of ministers of the member states) and the Parliamentary Assembly, composed of representatives from the national parliaments of the member states. While the Council of Ministers remained silent on the rendition issue, the Parliamentary Assembly became very active and appointed one of its members, Senator Dick Marty (Switzerland) to carry out an investigation into Council of Europe member State complicity in the extraordinary rendition programme. Senator Marty brought together a team of expert researchers who left no stone unturned in their quest for the truth. The sources used were varied and wide, including many US sources as they became available (Black, Clark and Weizman 2015). On 12 June 2006, Senator Marty presented his first report on rendition and secret detention. Two days later, on 14 June 2006, Council of Europe Secretary General, Terry Davis, published his report on rendition and secret detention, largely supportive of the Marty conclusions but rarely referred to by the ECtHR. Senator Marty's second report was presented on 14 June 2007 which included extensive new evidence of CIA 'black sites' in Eastern Europe. This report is most widely used by the ECtHR to establish the facts of the individual complaints.

Secondly, the ECtHR relied on a second source of evidence, the reports prepared for the European Parliament (Fava Reports 2006–2007). While the EU consists of 27 Member States, most of those states were among those against which complaints of complicity in the CIA programme were brought (the exception is Macedonia which is not (yet) and EU Member State). Claudio Fava, an Italian Member of the European Parliament, was appointed to carry out the European Parliament's special investigation into the operation of the CIA programme in EU states. On 30 January 2007 the Fava Report was published providing evidence strongly supporting the Marty reports regarding complicity of EU states in the CIA programme. This report is widely used by the ECtHR as a reliable source of evidence regarding EU state complicity.

A third major source of evidence used by the ECtHR is the reports prepared by the UN and in particular the work of the UN Committee on Arbitrary Disappearance. The most comprehensive report which the UN has produced is the 2010 Joint Study on Global Practices in relation to secret detention in the content of countering terrorism of the Special Rapporteur on the Promotion and Protection of Human Rights and Fundamental Freedoms, Martin Scheinin, the Special Rapporteur on Torture, Manfrek Nowak, together with the working group on arbitrary detention, vice chair Shaheen Sardar Ali and the working group on enforced or involuntary disappearances, chair Jeremy Sarkin (UN 2010). This report provides a very clear overview of the programme and the states involved in making it possible.

Finally, the Feinstein Report, the executive summary of which was only released in 2014, provides confirmation of many of the facts which the ECtHR had already found in evidence in the earlier judgments. Published in December 2014, it postdates the first three judgments of the ECtHR but is referred to in the next three. It is interesting to note that the ECtHR welcomes the Feinstein Report as an important source of confirmation of facts which it has already determined. It also refers to the code names used in the report for the various sites (each given a colour in the Feinstein Report to hide its actual identity and the responsibility of the state which hosted it). However, it is clear from the way the ECtHR treats the Report that it is primarily a source of confirmation rather than of new evidence important to the determination of the responsibility of the relevant state.

A summary of the key documents used by the ECtHR to establish the facts of the extraordinary rendition programme is as follows:

- Two Council of Europe reports prepared for the Parliamentary Assembly by Senator Marty from 2005;
- The European Union's Parliament – which carried out a number of investigations (all the European states involved (with the exception of Macedonia) were among the (then) 28 Member states of the EU);
- UN Reports and the work of the UN Special Rapporteurs and Working Group on Arbitrary Disappearance, in particular A/HRC/14/42;
- The Feinstein Report the executive summary of which was released in December 2014;

According to the Feinstein Report, all the prisons were closed by May 2006, and the CIA's detention and interrogation programme ended in 2009.

Conclusions

The European complicity in the CIA's extraordinary rendition programme reflects particularly badly on a number of Central and Eastern European countries whose democracies were young at the time. Most of them had only been established after the fall of the Berlin Wall in 1989. The authorities of these states appear to have been unduly influenced by their respect for the USA as the leader of the free world which they had only recently joined. The status of the victims as non-citizens and somehow underserving of treatment reserved for humans is particularly problematic. The case of El Masri stands out as exemplary of this de-humanisation of the victims. Although he was a German citizen, his ethnicity and implied religion outweighed the quality of that citizenship (Balkan states like Macedonia abuse German nationals at their peril, the German authorities can be depended upon to pursue the rights of their citizens – which, eventually, was the case for El Masri). This chapter of complicity is not yet closed as individuals, NGOs and state oversight bodies refuse to abandon their work in revealing the truth of the human rights abuses of that time.

For the purposes of this book on ETOs, the extraordinary rendition programme is a particularly clear case of a state, the USA, taking exceptional measures to avoid national jurisdiction. The elaborate construction of travel, black sites movement of people all took place because the CIA and its legal advisors were confident that they could avoid ETOs by doing so. So far, it seems that their assessment has been correct (leaving aside the negative opinions of the UN Committee on Arbitrary Disappearance). But, in the European case, it has been those states which collaborated with the CIA programme which have been judged and condemned. While the CIA and its officials, for the moment, seem to successfully escape prosecution, they have left a trail of serious legal problems for their allies.

References

Bigo, D., Carrera, S., Guild, E., and Radescu, R. (2015) *A Question for Accountability? EU and Member State Inquiries Into the CIA Rendition and Secret Detention Programme*, LIBE European Parliament.

Black, C., Clark, E. and Weizman, E. (2015) *Negative Publicity: Artefacts of Extraordinary Rendition*, Aperture Foundation, Incorporated; Magnum Foundation.

European Court of Human Rights (ECtHR) (1979-80) *Ireland v. United Kingdom*, 2 EHRR 25.

_______ (2012) *El Masri v. Macedonia*, Application no: 939630/09.

_______ (2014) *Husayn (Abu Zubaydah) v. Poland*, Application no: 7511/13.

_______ (2016) *Nasr and Ghali v. Italy*, ECtHR, Application no: 44883/09.

_______ (2018a) *Abu Zubaydah v. Lithuania*, Application no: 46454/11.

_______ (2018b) *Al Nashiri v. Romania*, Application no: 33234/12.

Fava, G.C. (2006) Report for the European Parliament on the Companies Linked to the CIA, Aircraft Used by the CIA and the European Countries CIA Aircraft Have Made Stopovers (Working Document 8), available at https://www.therenditionproject.org.uk/pdf/PDF%2082%20%5bEP-Nov%202006%20Working%20Document%208%20on%20the%20companies%20linked%20to%20the%20CIA%5d.pdf.

_______ (2006) Report for the European Parliament on 'Extraordinary Renditions' (Working Document 7), available at https://www.therenditionproject.org.uk/pdf/PDF%2086%20%5bEP%202006%20Nov%20Working%20Document%207%20-%20on%20extraordinary%20renditions%5d.pdf.

_______ (2006) Report for the European Parliament on the Testimony by Craig Murray, Former British Ambassador (Working Document 5), available at https://www.therenditionproject.org.uk/pdf/PDF%20189%20%5bFava%20Working%20Document%205,%20Jun%202006%5d.pdf.

_______ (2006) Report for the European Parliament on the Flights Operated by the CIA in Europe (Working Document 4), available at https://www.therenditionproject.org.uk/pdf/PDF%20188%20%5bFava%20Working%20Document%204,%20Jun%202006%5d.pdf.

_______ (2006) Report for the European Parliament on Victims (Working Document 3), available at https://www.therenditionproject.org.uk/pdf/PDF%20187%20%5bFava%20Working%20Document%203,%20Jun%202006%5d.pdf.

_______ (2006) Report for the European Parliament on a Chronology of Events (Working Document 2), available at https://www.therenditionproject.org.uk/pdf/PDF%20186%20%5bFava%20Working%20Document%202,%20Jun%202006%5d.pdf.

_______ (2006) Report for the European Parliament on TDIP Temporary Committee Work Programme (Working Document 1), available at https://www.therenditionproject.org.uk/pdf/PDF%20185%20%5bFava%20Working%20Document%201,%20Feb%202006%5d.pdf.

_______ (2007) Report for the European Parliament on the Alleged Use of European Countries by the CIA for the Transportation and Illegal Detention of Prisoners (Final Report), available at https://www.therenditionproject.org.uk/pdf/PDF%2063%20%5bREP-2007-01-REP%20Report%20on%20the%20alleged%20use%20of%20Europea.pdf.

_______ (2007) Report for the European Parliament on Certain Countries Analysed During the Work of the Temporary Committee (Working Document 9), available at https://www.therenditionproject.org.uk/pdf/PDF%2085%20%5bEP%202007%20Working%20Document%209%20-%20on%20certain%20European%20countries%5d.pdf.

Geyer, F. (2007) *Fruit of the Poisonous Tree: Member States' Indirect Use of Extraordinary Rendition and the EU Counter-terrorism Strategy*. No. 263, CEPS.

Guild, E. (2018) 'The US Senate Select Intelligence Committee Report (Feinstein Report) on the CIA Extraordinary Rendition Programme: Perspectives From Europe' in Guild, E., Bigo, D. and Gibney, M. (eds). *Extraordinary Rendition: Addressing the Challenges of Accountability,* Routledge.

Guild, E., and Bigo, D. (2018) 'Democratic Oversight and the CIA's Extraordinary Rendition Programme in Europe' in Guild, E., Bigo, D. and Gibney, M. (eds). *Extraordinary Rendition: Addressing the Challenges of Accountability,* Routledge.

Johnnston, P. (2007) 'Leaving the Invisible Universe: Why All Victims of Extraordinary Rendition Need a Cause of Action Against the United States', *International Journal of Public Law and Policy* 16, 357–360.

Marty, D. (2007) *Secret Detentions and Illegal Transfers of Detainees Involving Council of Europe Member States: Second Report*, Council of Europe.

Reed, K., (2014) 'Compensation for Extraordinary Rendition: A Comparative Study and the Need for a Domestic Cause of Action in the United States', *Pacific McGeorge Global Business & Development Law Journal* 27, 131–148.

UN Committee Against Torture (CAT) (2005) *Ahmed Hussein Mustafa Kamil Agiza v. Sweden*, CAT/C/34/D/233/2003, available at https://www.refworld.org/cases,CAT,42ce734a2.html [accessed 18 February 2020].

UN Human Rights Committee (HRC) (2006) *Mohammed Alzery v. Sweden*, CCPR/C/88/D/1416/2005, available at https://www.refworld.org/cases,HRC,47975afa21.html [accessed 18 February 2020].

United Nations (2010) Joint Study on Global Practices in relation to secret detention in the content of countering terrorism of the Special Rapporteur on the Promotion and Protection of Human Rights and Fundamental Freedoms, Martin Scheinin, the Special Rapporteur on Torture, Manfrek Nowak, together with the working group on arbitrary detention, vice chair Shaheen Sardar Ali and the working group on enforced or involuntary disappearances, chair Jeremy Sarkin (A/HCR/14/42)

US Senate Select Committee on Intelligence (2014) *Study on CIA Detention and Interrogation Program* (Feinstein Report), US Senate.

US Supreme Court (2004) *Rasul v. Bush*, 542 U.S. 466.

26

Surveillance and cyber operations

Marko Milanovic

Introduction

This chapter examines the extent to and the basis on which human rights treaties apply extraterritorially to state surveillance and cyber operations. Consider only the following examples:

1 The targeted surveillance of a specific individual outside a state's territory – as, for instance, with the operations allegedly conducted by the authorities of Saudi Arabia against Saudi dissidents abroad (see, e.g., Kirchgaessner and Hopkins 2019; Kirchgaessner 2020) (one of which ultimately led to the plot to assassinate the journalist Jamal Khashoggi (see, e.g., Kirkpatrick 2018; for more on the Khashoggi affair, see Callamard 2020; Milanovic 2020), or against the CEO of Amazon, Jeff Bezos, apparently in a rather crude attempt to blackmail him (see Office of the United Nations High Commissioner for Human Rights (OHCHR) 2020).
2 Mass surveillance or bulk collection programmes, such as those run by the US and UK signals intelligence agencies, that syphon the content of electronic communications of millions of people outside the state's territory, or the metadata about these communications, in order to create searchable datasets in which persons of particular interest, e.g. suspected terrorists, can then be found (see Macaskill and Dance 2013).
3 Cyber operations that exfiltrate data on COVID-19 vaccine research, potentially affecting the development of vaccines that could save many thousands of lives (see Akande et al. 2020a).
4 Cyber operations that destroy or manipulate such data.
5 Cyber operations against hospitals or against critical infrastructure, which directly endanger many lives (see Akande et al. 2020b).
6 Cyber operations against media outlets, which disrupt their activities and inhibit their freedom of expression.
7 Online misinformation operations for various purposes, for example, to manipulate the outcome of an election or to destroy public trust in state institutions during the pandemic (see more Milanovic and Schmitt 2020).

DOI: 10.4324/9781003090014-33

The list above is obviously not meant to be exhaustive. What all of these examples have in common, however, is that through entirely digital means states can violate a host of different human rights, from the rights to privacy and the freedom of expression, to the right to life and the right to health, of persons located outside their territories.

The question of the extraterritorial application of human rights treaties has long been a vexing one. It has been especially contentious in situations of armed conflict, for instance, with regard to detention and use of force operations. In my prior work, I have advocated for an expansive and factual approach to the extraterritorial application of human rights treaties, arguing in particular that the *negative* obligation to respect human rights should be territorially unrestricted (see Milanovic 2011, p. 209 et seq.). With regard to extraterritorial surveillance in particular, I have similarly argued that any state surveillance operation that interferes with the privacy of individuals abroad would engage the relevant treaties and would require justification within the human rights framework (see Milanovic 2015).

In this chapter, I will address the extraterritorial applicability both of 'pure' surveillance operations, which only involve the exfiltration of personal data through digital or analogue means, and other kinds of cyber operations, which may affect numerous human rights and not just privacy. The key point in that regard is that if surveillance operations are covered then, *a fortiori*, so are other cyber operations that can have substantially more severe impacts on individuals than the mere exfiltration of data.

The chapter will first proceed to briefly outline how the traditional models of extraterritorial application, the spatial and the personal, would apply to surveillance and cyber operations, examining a few old cases in which the issue was raised, if never properly resolved. It will then look at recent developments that are particularly important in the surveillance and cyber context, even if some of them are not directly apposite: a judgment of the UK Investigatory Powers Tribunal, the advisory opinion of the Inter-American Court of Human Rights on the environment and human rights, the Human Rights Committee's General Comment no. 36 on the right to life and the judgment of the Federal Constitutional Court of Germany on the applicability of the German Basic Law to surveillance operations abroad. The chapter will then finally offer some concluding thoughts on the direction towards which the legal position is likely to evolve, and should evolve, regarding the applicability of human rights law to extraterritorial surveillance and cyber operations.

Surveillance and cyber operations under the traditional models of extraterritorial application

Many human rights treaties, among them the International Covenant on Civil and Political Rights (ICCPR), the European Convention on Human Rights (ECHR) and the American Convention on Human Rights (ACHR), use the notion of state jurisdiction to delineate their scope of application.[1] Human rights courts and treaty bodies have interpreted that notion in two basic ways – as state control over a *territory* in which the victim of the human rights violation is located (the spatial conception or model of jurisdiction), or as state authority, power or control over the *victim* directly, exercised by one of the state's agents (the personal conception or model of jurisdiction) (see more Milanovic 2011, pp. 127–208). Yet, some treaties, like the International Covenant on Economic, Social and Cultural Rights (ICESCR), contain no jurisdiction clauses, and it is even less clear how *customary* human rights law applies extraterritorially, although arguments have been made in favour of the unrestricted application of negative customary obligations (see, e.g., Heyns et al. 2016, p. 823).

How would the two traditional extraterritoriality models apply to surveillance and cyber operations? With one caveat, the application of the spatial model would be reasonably straightforward. If an individual was located in a territory under the effective overall control of a state, even if that territory was not under the sovereignty of that state, the individual concerned would enjoy full protection for their privacy and any other relevant human rights vis-à-vis that state. For example, if a person in Crimea was subjected to electronic surveillance by the authorities of the Russian Federation, the ECHR would apply to that surveillance regardless of the fact that Russia does not possess title to Crimea, an area which nominally remains under Ukrainian sovereignty under international law. If a case presenting such facts were to come to the European Court, it would not need to resolve the disputed question of sovereignty over the territory. All the Court would need to establish was that, as a matter of fact, Russia exercises effective control of the area, regardless of whether that control was obtained lawfully or unlawfully (see, e.g., European Court of Human Rights (ECtHR) 1995, para. 62; see more Milanovic 2015, pp. 122–124).

The spatial applicability of human rights treaties in such circumstances to me seems incontestable. But now for the caveat: it is also possible that human rights bodies would apply the spatial model to scenarios in which the surveillance or cyber operations targets the data of an individual that physically transits or is located in a state's territory, even while the individual themselves is located outside it. Consider the following example: while I am writing this, I am physically located in Belgrade, the capital of Serbia. But were British authorities to conduct a search of my flat in Nottingham, and seize documents or data that they find there even while I am myself out of the country, there would be no doubt whatsoever that the ICCPR and the ECHR would apply to such a search. The more contested issue, which I will turn to in a moment, is the precise conceptual basis of the treaties' applicability, which must be extraterritorial since I, as the bearer of the relevant rights, am outside the state's territory even while the state is interfering with these rights solely by acting on its own territory.

A cyber analogy is reasonably direct. Were the UK to, say, intercept my emails or take control of data located on its own territory, for instance, by syphoning the data from an undersea cable that transits its territory or by seizing it from a UK-based cloud server, the position should be no different than in the example of the physical search of my apartment above. I, at least, see no plausible way of distinguishing the two; if the first is covered, on whatever basis, then so must be the second (see Milanovic 2015, pp. 124–127; Nyst 2013).

This brings us to the applicability of the personal model, that of authority, control, power over the victim exercised by state agents. This is a significantly more complex issue, both generally and with regard to surveillance and cyber operations specifically. In particular, the jurisprudence of the European Court has simultaneously been the most varied and the most restrictive in this regard. It is uncontested that *detaining* a person, i.e. state agents having physical custody over an individual, is an exercise of authority, control or power of them sufficient to create a jurisdictional link between the state and the victim (ECtHR 2014, paras. 74–80). It remains contested whether kinetic uses of lethal force against an individual without detaining them, for example, by firing a missile from a drone, constitutes authority or control over the person.

The most notorious and restrictive such case is of course *Bankovic*, in which the European Court held that an individual would not be within a state's jurisdiction in the sense of Article 1 ECHR solely on the basis that the state dropped a bomb on them from the air, and did so partly on the erroneous basis that the concept of state jurisdiction in human rights treaties had something to do with the concepts of prescriptive and enforcement jurisdiction as aspects of state sovereignty (ECtHR 2001). Other cases followed, some of which implicitly partially overruled *Bankovic*, most notably *Al-Skeini* (ECtHR 2011), but the Court has nonetheless remained reluctant to extend the reach of the Convention to purely kinetic uses of force abroad, as it is morally and logically compelled to do (see generally Milanovic 2012, pp. 127–133). Despite the

Court's holding in *Al-Skeini* that the use of physical force against an individual by a state agent can constitute the exercise of authority or control over that individual, and thus state jurisdiction, and its holding that when a state exercises such authority and control over an individual it only needs to secure those rights of that individual that are relevant to his or her situation, so that rights under the ECHR can be divided and tailored (ECtHR 2011, paras. 136–137), the Court has still preserved the result and conceptual basis of *Bankovic*.

Following the logic of *Bankovic*, if dropping a bomb on someone would not suffice to create a jurisdictional link extraterritorially, then neither would be reading their emails nor the hacking of their phone. But that logic is misguided simply because *Bankovic* was wrongly decided. As I have argued before, the personal conception of jurisdiction as authority, power or control over individuals is prone to collapse to the proposition that negative obligations should apply without any territorial restriction; any purported limits appear to be arbitrary (see Milanovic 2011, pp. 207–208). As a thought experiment to test that argument, consider the following scenarios; suppose that all of them take place in Berlin and involve a hypothetical Angela Merkel:

1. A CIA agent grabs Angela Merkel, disables her escort (assume he is some kind of judo master) and then physically searches her for items in her possession.
2. A CIA agent breaks into and searches Angela's apartment and plants cameras and listening devices.
3. A CIA agent manages to get Angela's phone when she is not looking, and furtively plants a tracking device in it.
4. A CIA agent breaks into Angela's office and hacks into her computer, uploading a virus and downloading sensitive data.
5. A CIA agent observes and listens to Angela using a high-resolution camera/directed mike.
6. A CIA agent observes and monitors Angela's residence from the outside using a high-resolution camera/directed mike, without necessarily observing Angela herself.
7. A CIA agent hacks Angela's phone or computer remotely.
8. A CIA agent intercepts Angela's calls, texts or emails midstream.
9. A CIA agent is able to collect information about whom Angela calls, when, for how long (telephony metadata) or whom and when she mails (internet metadata).
10. The NSA obtains Angela's personal information from its partners in GCHQ, and stores and processes that information.

The scenarios progress from the more physical to the more virtual. There is, in my view, no point along this spectrum that could be picked as some non-arbitrary dividing line between the existence of jurisdiction and the lack thereof. If (1) is covered, then so is (2); if (2) is covered, then so is (3), etc. The personal model simply collapses, with the bottom line being that the state should comply with its negative obligation to respect human rights whenever it is able to do so (see Milanovic 2015, pp. 127–129). Any state surveillance activity abroad, and any cyber operation adversely affected human rights, would therefore be within the ambit of human rights treaties.

Human rights bodies are yet to grapple with this set of issues directly enough. I will canvass some relevant recent developments in that regard in a minute, but first let us briefly look at some of the relevant older, pre-Snowden jurisprudence.

In that regard, the only human rights body to have decided cases dealing with extraterritorial surveillance has been the European Court. Notably, at least two surveillance cases before the Court dealt with situations, we looked at above in which the interference was territorial while the individual was outside any area under the state's control.[2] In the first, *Weber and Saravia v. Germany*

(ECtHR 2006), the applicants lived in Uruguay while their communication was allegedly intercepted in Germany. Germany actually even objected (ibid, para. 66) that the case was outside its jurisdiction under *Bankovic*, but the Court avoided the matter (ibid, para. 72) and dismissed the case as manifestly ill-founded on other grounds. In the second, *Liberty and Others v. the United Kingdom* (ECtHR 2008), two of the applicants were Irish organisations that had communicated with the third, a British one, and their communication was allegedly intercepted in the UK by British authorities. Neither the UK government nor the Court *proprio motu* considered that an Article 1 jurisdiction issue arose with respect to the Irish applicants, i.e. they both assumed that the ECHR applied, and the Court went on to find a violation of Article 8 (see Milanovic 2015, p. 127).

For its part, the UN Human Rights Committee expressed concern about the mass surveillance programmes disclosed by Edward Snowden in its concluding observations regarding the US and the UK. The concluding observations simply assume the extraterritorial applicability of the ICCPR to these surveillance activities, but without articulating a clear basis for doing so.[3] The Committee is yet to hear an individual case that deals with extraterritorial surveillance or other cyber operations.

Relevant recent developments

IPT judgment in Human Rights Watch and Others

The case most directly on point regarding the extraterritorial application of human rights treaties to surveillance actually comes from a domestic court – the UK Investigatory Powers Tribunal, in a case concerning the US and UK mass surveillance programmes (Investigatory Powers Tribunal 2016). Briefly, the Tribunal found the ECHR to be entirely inapplicable to extraterritorial surveillance, directly relying on a *Bankovic* analogy (ibid, paras. 56–61):

> In so far as their claim is founded on belief that their right to respect for their private life has been infringed, neither of [the claimants] allege that, at any material time, they enjoyed a private life in the United Kingdom. Accordingly, under Article 1, the United Kingdom was under no obligation to respect it. The analogy with **Bankovic** is close. ... Accordingly, the retention by GCHQ of information shared with it by the NSA, even in circumstances which do not comply with UK law, could not amount to a breach of the two Claimants' right to respect for their private life.
>
> *(ibid, para. 58)*

If *Bankovic* is correctly decided, at least for ECHR purposes, then the analogy would indeed be hard to resist – it would be absurd to accept that intercepting an individual's email while they are abroad would constitute a jurisdictional link, whereas killing them with a bomb would not. It is thus unsurprising that the Tribunal ruled as it did, and that any corrections to *Bankovic* would have to happen in Strasbourg (cf. ibid, para. 60). The Tribunal also must be right that the applicability of the Convention cannot depend on whether the individual subjected to surveillance is located in the territory of some Convention state party other than the one doing the surveillance, rather than in a third state (ibid, para. 55 referring to the *espace juridique* concept). However, the Tribunal only superficially dealt with the import of the scenario in which interception happens territorially, even if the individual is located outside the state's territory (ibid, para. 59; see more Kim 2016). As of the time of writing, the European Court is yet to address either this scenario or those of 'pure' extraterritorial surveillance, having managed to avoid the extraterritoriality issues in the cases it has examined so far, as I will explain below.

IACtHR Advisory Opinion on the Environment and Human Rights

A more promising development, but less directly apposite, is the 2017 advisory opinion of the Inter-American Court on the environment and human rights (IACtHR) (2017). The opinion has nothing to do with surveillance or cyber operations as such – indeed the Court and the Inter-American Commission are yet to hear any such cases. But the opinion provides us with the first genuinely systematic attempt by the Court to interpret the meaning of the term 'jurisdiction' in Article 1(1) ACHR and the scope of the Convention's extraterritorial application (for detailed analysis, see Vega-Barbosa and Aboagye 2018; Feria-Tinta and Milnes 2018).

In that regard, the advisory opinion is something of a mixed bag. It sets out the *travaux* of the Convention (IACtHR 2017, paras. 71–78) and the relevant international jurisprudence (ibid, paras. 79–81), and (troublingly) endorses the *Bankovic dictum* of the European Court that extraterritorial jurisdiction is *exceptional* and that circumstances giving rise to such jurisdiction should be interpreted *restrictively* (ibid, paras. 81 and 104). Even worse, it endorses the *Bankovic* conceptual confusion between the notion of jurisdiction in human rights treaties and the one in general international law (ibid, para. 90).

But then, when it reaches the bottom line of its reasoning, none of this seems to matter – the Court endorses an *exceptionally* broad approach to the extraterritorial applicability of the ACHR in the environmental context:

> The obligations to respect and to ensure human rights require that states abstain from preventing or hindering other States Parties from complying with the obligations derived from the Convention. Activities undertaken within the jurisdiction of a State Party should not deprive another State of the ability to ensure that the persons within its jurisdiction may enjoy and exercise their rights under the Convention. The Court considers that states have the obligation to avoid transboundary environmental damage that can affect the human rights of individuals outside their territory. For the purposes of the American Convention, when transboundary damage occurs that effects treaty-based rights, it is understood that the persons whose rights have been violated are under the jurisdiction of the state of origin, if there is a causal link between the act that originated in its territory and the infringement of the human rights of persons outside its territory.
>
> In cases of transboundary damage, the exercise of jurisdiction by a state of origin is based on the understanding that it is the state in whose territory or under whose jurisdiction the activities were carried out that has the effective control over them and is in a position to prevent them from causing transboundary harm that impacts the enjoyment of human rights of persons outside its territory. The potential victims of the negative consequences of such activities are under the jurisdiction of the state of origin for the purposes of the possible responsibility of that state for failing to comply with its obligation to prevent transboundary damage.
>
> *(ibid, paras. 101–102)*

To put all of this a bit more simply, if, say, a private company operating in Colombia causes transboundary harm to a person located in Ecuador (e.g. by causing pollution), then that person in Ecuador would be within Colombia's jurisdiction. Although the Court is referring to the effective control of the harmful transboundary activities, it is not saying that the conduct in question has to be attributable to the state, although *a fortiori* the same reasoning would apply if the emitter of the transboundary harm was a state agent. Rather, all of this is based on the *ability* of Colombia, the state of origin, to prevent such harmful acts from occurring (see also ibid, para 104(f)–(h)).

In sum, despite all of the approving references to the jurisprudence of the European Court, the Inter-American Court actually went far beyond anything that its Strasbourg sibling had done. And most importantly for our purposes, whether right or wrong, I also see no plausible way in which this reasoning could be limited to transboundary *environmental* harms. It can just as easily apply to other types of transboundary harms, such as those to privacy (in the surveillance context) or to other human rights, such as life, health or expression (in the context of cyber operations more generally). If, in other words, a state has the ability to prevent transboundary harms to persons in other states that are caused by non-state actors operating from its territory (e.g. a corporation or a hacktivist group), then the victims of such acts would be within the jurisdiction of the state of origin. And again, *a fortiori* the same reasoning must apply to surveillance or cyber operations committed by the agents of the state of origin, such as its security services.

The bottom line of the Court's approach, if applied to surveillance and cyber operations, would be the total elision of any extraterritoriality threshold (not that this is a bad thing). In fact, the Inter-American Court's key reference to the state's *ability* to prevent transboundary harms is redolent of the so-called *functional* approach to the extraterritorial application of human rights treaties, which was recently endorsed, in a somewhat different context, by the UN Human Rights Committee.

HRC General Comment no. 36

The functional approach to extraterritoriality holds that the key question in interpreting the concept of jurisdiction in human rights treaties is not one of state control over the person or over the territory in which the person is located, but one of control over the person's ability to exercise their human rights. One of the foremost academic proponents of such an approach has been Prof. Yuval Shany (2013), who also happened to be the rapporteur, together with the late Sir Nigel Rodley, on the Human Rights Committee's 2018 General Comment no. 36 on the right to life (HRC 2018). And here the Committee reframed its previous approach to extraterritoriality, which did look primarily at control over territory or over the victim, and did so precisely in functional terms:

> A state party has an obligation to respect and to ensure the rights under article 6 [ICCPR] of all persons who are within its territory and all persons subject to its jurisdiction, that is, all persons over whose enjoyment of the right to life it exercises power or effective control.
>
> *(ibid, para. 63; for the Committee's prior position, see HRC 2004, para. 10)*

As with the Inter-American Court's advisory opinion, there is no reason of principle why this approach should be confined solely to the right to life. In other words, if correct, the functional approach should apply to all rights in the Covenant to the extent possible. Thus, if a state exercises power or control over an individual's enjoyment of the right to privacy by subjecting that individual to surveillance, or by processing or disclosing their personal information, the ICCPR should apply. The same goes for cyber operations that would affect other rights, including the right to life. To be clear, the Committee is yet to explicitly say so, but this to me seems to be inescapable consequence of the approach it took regarding the right to life.

German Constitutional Court

This brings us to the final recent development that I wish to examine – the 2020 judgment of the Federal Constitutional Court of Germany in which it held that *all* extraterritorial surveillance activities conducted by German security services had to respect the privacy guarantees in the German Basic Law, even when such activities are conducted against foreigners (Federal Constitutional Court of Germany 2020, para. 87). This is a rich and detailed judgment, most of which deals with the various substantive aspects of how a surveillance regime needs to operate in order to be compatible with fundamental rights, but I will here deal only with the threshold extraterritoriality question.

The extraterritorial application of a state's constitution is formally not an identical issue to the extraterritorial applicability of human rights treaties. It is perfectly possible for constitutional instruments and the jurisprudence built upon them to adopt principles that are significantly different from those in international human rights law, even if many of the underlying policy considerations are the same (for an extended analysis, see Milanovic 2011, pp. 61–82 discussing US and Canadian case law; see also Raustiala 2009; Neuman 1991). Yet, the judgment of the Constitutional Court is remarkable in its internationalist, universalist language and ambition. The Court thus affirmed that German state authorities are comprehensively bound by the Basic Law, regardless of where they act, and that this is mandated by the need to protect human dignity, as a universal ideal, from state power (Federal Constitutional Court of Germany 2020, para. 89). The Court further emphasised the need to read fundamental rights under the Basic Law in the context of internationally protected human rights, and in light of the responsibilities of the German people in a united Europe and the world (ibid, paras. 94–95).

The Court is thus explicit that limiting the applicability of the Basic Law to German territory would undermine universal human rights (ibid, para. 96). Interestingly, the Constitutional Court so found while expressly acknowledging that the European Court was yet to clarify how the ECHR would apply to extraterritorial surveillance (ibid, paras. 97–98), and noting that there was nothing to stop the Basic Law from comprehensively applying abroad even if the European Court were to adopt a narrower approach with regard to the ECHR (ibid, para. 99). Finally, the Constitutional Court rightly noted that the application of the Basic Law abroad was only meant to constrain German public authorities, and that it in no way interfered with the application of the domestic law of the territorial state, imposed any burdens on the organs of the territorial state and did not violate the prohibition of intervention in international law (ibid, paras. 101–103).

Again, if the Court took this approach for extraterritorial surveillance measures by German authorities, it would undoubtedly take the same approach with regard to cyber operations that interfere with rights other than privacy and do so more intensely. While it was explicitly framing its analysis as one of the extraterritorial applicability of domestic fundamental rights, it also directly linked these to human rights as protected by international law, explicitly grounding its analysis in the language of universal human dignity. It moreover did so without referring to the notion of jurisdiction in human rights treaties, which does not appear in the Basic Law, nor to the spatial and personal models of that notion in international case law, but simply chose to bind German authorities comprehensively, without restriction, when they act territorially. And, finally, it seemed to have issued a respectful nudge to the European Court that it should follow its lead, even if it remains far from certain that the Strasbourg Court will do so (see more Reinke 2020; Miller 2020; Çali 2020).

Where should the law go?

It is only appropriate to conclude by looking at where the extraterritoriality case law of human rights bodies should be going with respect to surveillance and cyber operations, and where (and when) it is likely to go. Both the normative and the predictive questions are to my mind reasonably clear, the latter somewhat less so than the former. Normatively, human rights bodies should coalesce around an expansive, factual approach to extraterritoriality, both generally and with regard to surveillance and cyber operations specifically, as the German Constitutional Court has done.

This, of course, is easier said than done. The universality impulse is hard to resist – to paraphrase the Human Rights Committee 'it would be unconscionable to so interpret' human rights treaties as to permit states parties to perpetrate violations of these treaties on the territory of another state, which it could not perpetrate on its own territory (HRC 1981, para. 12.3). But this impulse is offset by considerations of practicality and effectiveness (see Milanovic 2011, pp. 106–117). These are real concerns, but their proper place is on the merits – on *how*, rather than on *whether*, human rights law should substantively govern extraterritorial surveillance and other cyber operations. And it is reasonable to argue, for example, that an extraterritorial regulatory regime should be more flexible than the one the state applies within its territory; if for no other reason, then because it has less capabilities to achieve the legitimate aims it may be pursuing when it is acting outside its territory (see Milanovic 2015, pp. 138–139).[4]

A couple of further points in that regard. First, the nomenclature is less important than the substance. When it comes to the negative duty to respect human rights, it matters little whether human rights bodies choose to approach this issue by applying the traditional personal model of jurisdiction and allowing it to collapse, or by employing a categorical rule that negative obligations are not territorially restricted, or by using some variant of a functional approach. The bottom line will be the same – that all surveillance and cyber operations conducted by state agents outside the state's territory will be covered by human rights law.

Second, however, the question of *positive* obligations is more complex, especially regarding the duty to protect human rights from third parties. Here the differences between the various conceptual approaches become starker. Note, for example, how the German Constitutional Court very carefully said nothing about under what circumstances German authorities would have the duty to protect, under the Basic Law, an individual located outside German territory. Would, for instance, German authorities have a due diligence duty to prevent non-state actors operating from German territory from engaging in conduct that could adversely affect privacy and other rights of individuals outside Germany (see in that regard Milanovic and Schmitt 2020)? We have already seen how the Inter-American Court would seem to answer that question affirmatively.

Under a functional approach, which simply looks at the ability of the state to perform its obligations, the extraterritorial threshold inquiry is elided altogether. Under the approach I have advocated for, positive duties of protection would be limited to individuals within the territorial jurisdiction, primarily in order to make the protective obligation subject to clearer, more bright-line rules. But I am not unhappy with the functional approach to positive obligations if that is where states are willing to go – I am just unsure that they are. A particularly instructive case study in that regard is a scenario in which a state acquires intelligence that an individual's life is in serious and immediate risk while that individual is outside the state's territory. Would, in such a scenario, the state in the possession of the intelligence have to, at a minimum, warn the individual concerned of the danger they are in, in order to comply with an extraterritorial duty of protection?[5]

Third, there are certain argumentative avenues that human rights bodies should avoid. They should not base their extraterritoriality jurisprudence in state control over *cyber infrastructure*, as suggested in an OHCHR paper (OHCHR 2014, para. 34), simply because many potential human rights violations in this context (e.g. hacking a mobile phone to exfiltrate private data *à la* Bezos) require no control whatsoever over infrastructure to implement. They should not base their jurisprudence on discredited concepts such as the European Court's *espace juridique*.[6] Above all, they should follow the German Constitutional Court and not base their jurisprudence on the *citizenship* of the victim, whether as a threshold matter or on the merits, as doing so would be antithetical to universality and human dignity as the core ideas of human rights law (for an extensive discussion, see Milanovic 2015, pp. 87–101; for a discussion in the German context, see Schaller 2018). In short, human rights bodies need to do their utmost to avoid arbitrary line-drawing when no such line-drawing is genuinely sustainable in the long run.

As for the predictive question of whether human rights bodies will in fact adopt an expansive approach, and when they will do so, this is more difficult. Their extraterritoriality jurisprudence has in recent years generally been on an upward trajectory. But whether this trend will continue will depend on numerous attendant circumstances. On a most basic level, cases squarely presenting these issues need to be actually litigated in the relevant forum, with other admissibility issues, most importantly the exhaustion of domestic remedies, being properly taken care of. Similarly, the extraterritorial application of human rights treaties to surveillance and cyber operations is inseparable from other possible state activities, e.g. kinetic uses of force, and human rights bodies will inevitably consider the implications of what they do and try to be reasonably consistent in different categories of cases.

On a bigger picture level, much will depend on the general political climate and on any backlash human rights bodies are subjected to. If that backlash is not catastrophic, eventually they will likely coalesce around a similar, if not identical, approach to extraterritoriality, along the lines that I have suggested above. The known unknown here is the European Court, which has long been the outlier among human rights bodies with its more restrictive extraterritoriality jurisprudence. It is simultaneously the human rights body to which surveillance and cyber cases has and will be brought first, and the one that will do its best to avoid deciding on the extraterritoriality threshold if it does not have to. Thus, for instance, in the *Big Brother Watch* case that is, as of the time of writing, pending before the Grand Chamber of the Court and that concerns UK surveillance programmes, the extraterritoriality issue will almost certainly be avoided because some of the applicants are UK-based organisations (ECtHR 2018, para. 271).

The Court's evasiveness cannot, however, last forever. On the one hand, this is because it has numerous other cases before it that present the extraterritoriality issue and that may compel it to depart from *Bankovic* even more than it has done so far – for instance, the *Bankovic*-in-reverse interstate case brought by the Netherlands against Russia about the downing of the MH17 airliner over Ukraine (ECtHR 2020). On the other hand, that other European Court – the Court of Justice of the European Union – has been much more courageous in striking down transatlantic data-sharing arrangements that unduly impinge on privacy as US surveillance programmes do not provide sufficient safeguards (European Court of Justice 2020). And let us also not forget the gentle German nudge in that regard. It thus seems to me more likely than not that the Strasbourg Court will eventually join its siblings in adopting a more liberal, expansive and factual approach to extraterritoriality.

One final point: arguing that human rights law applies to extraterritorial surveillance and cyber operations does not turn human rights into some kind of all-encompassing regulatory regime for extraterritorial surveillance and cyber operations. In particular, espionage and cyber operations that are limited to *state* data or assets (e.g. the exfiltration of military secrets or the sabotage of air defences systems and the like) would normally not engage the human rights of individuals. The legal interest affected is that of the state, and not of any specific individual, and their protection (if any) is a matter for other rules of international law, such as sovereignty, the prohibition of intervention or the prohibition of the use of force. Conversely, however, it is entirely appropriate for human rights law, focused as it is on protecting individual interests, to operate alongside other parts of international law that appropriately protect state interests.

Notes

1. Thus, under Article 2(1) ICCPR, '[e]ach State Party to the present Covenant undertakes to respect and to ensure to all individuals within its territory and subject to its jurisdiction the rights recognized in the present Covenant,' under Article 1 ECHR '[t]he High Contracting Parties shall secure to everyone within their jurisdiction the rights and freedoms defined in Section I of this Convention,' while under Article 1(1) ACHR 'States Parties to this Convention undertake to respect the rights and freedoms recognized herein and to ensure to all persons subject to their jurisdiction the free and full exercise of those rights and freedoms'.
2. I would personally prefer to deal with such cases on the basis that negative obligations are unrestricted, or under the personal model (which amounts to the same thing), but as noted above they could also potentially be dealt with by a human rights body under the spatial model, even though the person whose rights are being not violated is not actually present in the territory controlled by the state.
3. See HRC (2014) Concluding observations on the fourth periodic report of the United States of America, UN Doc. CCPR/C/USA/CO/4, para. 22 (referring to surveillance 'both within and outside the United States'); HRC (2015) Concluding observations on the seventh periodic report of the United Kingdom of Great Britain and Northern Ireland, UN Doc. CCPR/C/GBR/CO/7, para. 24 (referring to surveillance activities 'both within and outside the state party').
4. This is in fact precisely what the German Constitutional Court has said, by holding that the extraterritorial context may warrant differences in applying the proportionality analysis – see Federal Constitutional Court of Germany 2020, para. 104.
5. An issue directly raised in the case of Jamal Khashoggi – see, e.g., Kirkpatrick 2018; for more on the Khashoggi affair, see Callamard 2020; Milanovic 2020.
6. It would be entirely arbitrary, for example, for the ECHR to apply to the UK spying on an individual in Russia but not one in China, simply on the basis that Russia is, like the UK, an ECHR state party. Even the UK's Investigatory Powers Tribunal thought so – see Investigatory Powers Tribunal 2016, para. 55 referring to the *espace juridique* concept.

References

Akande, D. et al. (2020a) 'The Second Oxford Statement on International Law Protections of the Healthcare Sector During COVID-19: Safeguarding Vaccine Research', *EJIL: Talk!*, 11 August 2020, https://www.ejiltalk.org/the-second-oxford-statement-on-international-law-protections-of-the-healthcare-sector-during-covid-19-safeguarding-vaccine-research/ [accessed 1 January 2021].

Akande, D. et al. (2020b) 'Oxford Statement on the International Law Protections Against Cyber Operations Targeting the Health Care Sector', *EJIL: Talk!*, 21 May 2020, https://www.ejiltalk.org/oxford-statement-on-the-international-law-protections-against-cyber-operations-targeting-the-health-care-sector/ [accessed 1 January 2021].

Çali, B. (2020) 'Has 'Control Over Rights Doctrine' for Extra-Territorial Jurisdiction Come of Age? Karlsruhe, Too, Has Spoken, Now it's Strasbourg's Turn', *EJIL: Talk!*, 21 July 2020, https://www.ejiltalk.org/has-control-over-rights-doctrine-for-extra-territorial-jurisdiction-come-of-age-karlsruhe-too-has-spoken-now-its-strasbourgs-turn/ [accessed 1 January 2021].

Callamard, A. (2020) Report of the Special Rapporteur on extrajudicial, summary or arbitrary executions, UN Doc. A/HRC/41/36 and annex UN Doc. A/HRC/41/CRP.1.

European Court of Human Rights (ECtHR) (1995) *Loizidou v. Turkey*, Application no. 15318/89, preliminary objections.

_______ (2001) *Banković and Others v. Belgium and Others*, Application no. 52207/99.

_______ (2006) *Weber and Saravia v. Germany*, Application no. 54934/00.

_______ (2008) *Liberty and Others v. the United Kingdom*, Application no. 58243/00.

_______ (2011) *Al-Skeini and others v. United Kingdom*, Application no. 55721/07.

_______ (2014) *Hassan v. United Kingdom*, Application no. 29750/09.

_______ (2018) *Big Brother Watch v. United Kingdom*, Application nos. 58170/13, 62322/14, 24960/15, Chamber Judgment.

_______ (2020) *Netherlands v. Russian Federation*, no. 28525/20.

European Court of Justice (2020) *Data Protection Commissioner v. Facebook Ireland Limited, Maximillian Schrems*, Case C-311/18 (Schrems II).

Federal Constitutional Court of Germany (2020) 1 BvR 2835/17, available in English at https://www.bundesverfassungsgericht.de/SharedDocs/Pressemitteilungen/EN/2020/bvg20-037.html [accessed 1 January 2021].

Feria-Tinta, M. and Milnes, S. (2018) 'The Rise of Environmental Law in International Dispute Resolution: Inter-American Court of Human Rights issues Landmark Advisory Opinion on Environment and Human Rights', *EJIL: Talk!*, 26 February 2018, https://www.ejiltalk.org/the-rise-of-environmental-law-in-international-dispute-resolution-inter-american-court-of-human-rights-issues-landmark-advisory-opinion-on-environment-and-human-rights/ [accessed 1 January 2021].

Heyns, C. et al. (2016) 'The International Legal Framework Regulating Armed Drones', *International & Comparative Law Quarterly 65(4)*, 791–827.

Human Rights Committee (HRC) (1981) *Lopez Burgos v. Uruguay*, Communication no. R.12/52, UN Doc. Supp. no. 40 (A/36/40).

_______ (2004) GC 31, UN Doc. CCPR/C/21/Rev.1/Add. 13.

_______ (2014) Concluding observations on the fourth periodic report of the United States of America, UN Doc. CCPR/C/USA/CO/4.

_______ (2015) Concluding observations on the seventh periodic report of the United Kingdom of Great Britain and Northern Ireland, UN Doc. CCPR/C/GBR/CO/7.

_______ (2018) GC 36, UN Doc. CCPR/C/GC/36.

Inter-American Court of Human Rights (IACtHR) (2017) Advisory opinion OC-23/17 requested by the Republic of Colombia, *The Environment and Human Rights*.

Investigatory Powers Tribunal (2016) *Human Rights Watch Inc & Ors v.* The Secretary of State for the Foreign & Commonwealth Office & Ors, UKIPTrib 15_165-CH.

Kim, S. (2016) 'ECHR Jurisdiction and Mass Surveillance: Scrutinising the UK Investigatory Power Tribunal's Recent Ruling', *EJIL: Talk!*, 9 June 2016, https://www.ejiltalk.org/echr-jurisdiction-and-mass-surveillance-scrutinising-the-uk-investigatory-power-tribunals-recent-ruling/ [accessed 1 January 2021].

Kirchgaessner, S. (2020) 'Revealed: Saudis Suspected of Phone Spying Campaign in US', *The Guardian*, 29 March 2020, https://www.theguardian.com/world/2020/mar/29/revealed-saudis-suspected-of-phone-spying-campaign-in-us [accessed 1 January 2021].

Kirchgaessner, S. and Hopkins, N. (2019) 'Saudi Arabia accused of hacking London-based dissident', *The Guardian*, 28 May 2019, https://www.theguardian.com/world/2019/may/28/saudi-arabia-accused-of-hacking-london-based-dissident-ghanem-almasarir [accessed 1 January 2021].

Kirkpatrick, D. (2018) 'Israeli Software Helped Saudis Spy on Khashoggi, Lawsuit Says', *The New York Times*, 2 December 2018, https://www.nytimes.com/2018/12/02/world/middleeast/saudi-khashoggi-spyware-israel.html [accessed 1 January 2021].

Macaskill, E. and Dance, G. (2013) 'NSA Files: Decoded', *The Guardian*, 1 November 2013, at https://www.theguardian.com/world/interactive/2013/nov/01/snowden-nsa-files-surveillance-revelations-decoded#section/1 [accessed 1 January 2021].

Milanovic, M. (2011) *Extraterritorial Application of Human Rights Treaties: Law, Principles, and Policy*, Oxford University Press.

_______ (2012) '*Al-Skeini* and *Al-Jedda* in Strasbourg', *European Journal of International Law* 23, 121–139.

_______ (2015) 'Human Rights Treaties and Foreign Surveillance: Privacy in the Digital Age', *Harvard International Law Journal* 56(1), 81–146.

_______ (2020) 'The Murder of Jamal Khashoggi: Immunities, Inviolability and the Human Right to Life', *Human Rights Law Review* 20(1), 1-49.

Milanovic, M. and Schmitt, M. (2020) 'Cyber Attacks and Cyber (Mis)information Operations during a Pandemic', *Journal of National Security Law & Policy 11, 247-284.*

Miller, R. (2020) 'The German Constitutional Court Nixes Foreign Surveillance', *Lawfare*, 27 May 2020, https://www.lawfareblog.com/german-constitutional-court-nixes-foreign-surveillance [accessed 1 January 2021].

Neuman, G. (1991) 'Whose Constitution?', *Yale Law Journal* 100(4), 909–991.

Nyst, C. (2013) 'Interference-Based Jurisdiction Over Violations of the Right to Privacy', *EJIL: Talk!*, 21 November 2013, https://www.ejiltalk.org/interference-based-jurisdiction-over-violations-of-the-right-to-privacy/ [accessed 1 January 2021].

Office of the United Nations High Commissioner for Human Rights (OHCHR) (2014) Report on the right to privacy in the digital age, UN Doc. A/HRC/27/37.

_______ (2020) 'UN experts call for investigation into allegations that Saudi Crown Prince involved in hacking of Jeff Bezos' phone', 22 January 2020, https://www.ohchr.org/EN/NewsEvents/Pages/DisplayNews.aspx?NewsID=25488 [accessed DATE].

Raustiala, K. (2009) *Does the Constitution Follow the Flag? The Evolution of Territoriality in American Law*, Oxford University Press.

Reinke, B. (2020) 'Rights Reaching Beyond Borders', *Verfassungsblog*, 30 May 2020, https://verfassungsblog.de/rights-reaching-beyond-borders/[accessed 1 January 2021].

Schaller, C. (2018) 'Strategic Surveillance and Extraterritorial Basic Rights Protection: German Intelligence Law After Snowden', *German Law Journal* 19(4), 941–980.

Shany, Y. (2013) 'Taking Universality Seriously: A Functional Approach to Extraterritoriality in International Human Rights Law', *The Law & Ethics of Human Rights* 7(1), 47–71.

Vega-Barbosa, G. and Aboagye, L. (2018) 'Human Rights and the Protection of the Environment: The Advisory Opinion of the Inter-American Court of Human Rights', *EJIL: Talk!*, 26 February 2018, https://www.ejiltalk.org/human-rights-and-the-protection-of-the-environment-the-advisory-opinion-of-the-inter-american-court-of-human-rights/ [accessed 1 January 2021].

27

Arms trade and weapons export control

Marina Aksenova[1]

Introduction

Arms trade is a notoriously opaque sphere of business activity because it involves immense financial flows and is tightly linked to the conduct of governmental agencies granting arms export licenses. The cost-benefit analysis for the state pondering the decision to grant an export license to a certain manufacturer within its borders includes factors such as diplomatic relations with the country receiving the weapons, financial incentives, the relationship with other states supplying arms (especially in the context of consortium producers located in different exporting states), the projection of power in the political arena, and human rights and humanitarian law implications of such decision. Until very recently, the transnational regulation of arms trade has been patchy at best: only a handful of regional instruments of a binding and non-binding nature regulated weapons export control. The Arms Trade Treaty or 'ATT', which entered into force at the end of 2014, changed this status quo (ICRC, 2016).

This contribution explores the implications of the ATT and other legal instruments regulating the trade in weapons in relation to the extraterritorial obligations (ETOs) of states. The discussion expands on the overall starting premise of this volume, namely that the traditional territorial model of attributing human rights obligations is reaching its limits due to globalization and ensuing mutual interdependence of various state and non-state actors. Weapons trade is no exception to this trend. In this regard, it is helpful to refer to the *Maastricht Principles* on Extraterritorial Obligations of States in the Area of Economic, Social, and Cultural Rights (2013) ('*Maastricht Principles*'), which tend to go beyond territorial conception of responsibility by demanding that states act in a way so as to reduce the risk of impairing the enjoyment of rights extraterritorially (Principle 13) and cooperate internationally in realizing these rights (Principle 8(b)). The *Maastricht Principles* call on states to adopt and enforce measures to protect rights in a variety of scenarios, including when the corporation is domiciled in a state concerned (Principle 25(c)).

Weapons trade engages many stakeholders across jurisdictions. It clearly includes states on the supply side of the spectrum that grant licenses and authorizations to producers and manufacturers located on their territory. It is often the case that corporations in question work in consortiums, meaning that different parts of the equipment are produced in different countries.

DOI: 10.4324/9781003090014-34

Weapons are then delivered to a state on the receiving end, which may, in turn, use this equipment in a military campaign in yet another country. Such interrelatedness creates a complex web of mutually reinforcing commitments, which may be difficult to tease apart based on a purely territorial model of establishing human rights obligations. The context of ETOs allows for an expanded analysis of the issue.

This chapter utilizes a specific example to shed light on the nature of obligations arising out of weapons trade: it focuses on potential responsibility of several European arms exporters to the Saudi/UAE-led coalition which is engaged at the time of this writing in an armed conflict in Yemen (Bryk and Saage-Maaß 2019). The communication by the European Centre for Constitutional and Human Rights (ECCHR) filed to the International Criminal Court (ICC) in 2019 alleges potential complicity of corporate and state officials located on the territory of the signatories of the Rome Treaty of the ICC and the ATT, namely Spain, Italy, the UK, Germany, and the United Kingdom, in humanitarian law violations in Yemen for knowingly and purposefully aiding the coalition in the commission of crimes in Yemen.

The following section of the chapter engages with the general legislative framework for weapons trade with the view of establishing standards according to which states grant licenses for exporting military equipment. This section draws links between the *Maastricht Principles* governing states' extraterritorial obligations in the area of human rights (ETOs) and the existing legal regulation of weapons trade. Section 3 focuses on questions of corporate responsibility in the context of arms trade. It engages with the ECCHR submission to the ICC to the extent that some general conclusions – for instance, regarding the standard of knowledge necessary to trigger individual responsibility – may be deduced. The final section of the chapter offers some concluding observations.

Legal framework for states' obligations

International law

The ATT is the key legal document regulating international arms trade at the state level, representing the first comprehensive treaty addressing this issue of global concern. The ATT was initiated in 2006 by the UN General Assembly (UNGA) Resolution in response to the absence of any common international standard for the transfer of conventional arms that might contribute to the devastating human consequences of armed conflict. This regulatory gap undermined peace, reconciliation, safety, security, stability, and sustainable social and economic development (UNGA 2006). Responding to this pressing problem, the UNGA began the process of examining the feasibility of a thematic treaty. The process ultimately resulted in the adoption of the ATT on 2 April 2013. The treaty subsequently came into force on 24 December 2014. At the moment of writing, 109 states have ratified the treaty and 31 states have signed but have not yet ratified it.

In terms of numbers, five out of the world's top ten largest exporters of arms have ratified the ATT. These states are France, Germany, Spain, United Kingdom, and Italy. The United States, which is the number one supplier of weapons in the world, initially signed the treaty but later revoked its intention to be bound by it, as announced by the US administration in 2019 (Brown 2019). The ATT was therefore never legally binding on the US. Nationals of the five countries that ratified the ATT and thus agreed to be subjected to an international review process are currently under scrutiny in the submission filed by the ECCHR to the ICC requesting the Court to open a preliminary examination into the conduct of European arms suppliers.

The main aspiration of the ATT as stipulated in Article 1 is to establish the highest possible common international standards for regulating international trade in conventional arms, which includes combat aircrafts, missiles, large-caliber artillery systems, warships, and other items. There is also a subtler underlying rationale for the treaty, namely, to prevent arms from falling into the 'wrong hands' and thereby to reduce human suffering. The ATT aims to accomplish the overarching goal of establishing a high standard for regulating the arms trade by requiring exporting countries to carry out a thorough and comprehensive risk assessment before engaging in such activity. This requirement strongly resonates with a similar one contained in the *Maastricht Principles*, namely an obligation incumbent on states to avoid causing harm, where such harm is foreseeable (Principle 13) and the accompanying obligation to conduct prior risk assessment of potential impact of state's laws and policies on the extraterritorial enjoyment of rights (Principle 14).

The evaluation procedure under the ATT includes examining the risk of human rights violations in the country of destination (art. 7), the risk of diversion of the exported arms (art. 11), and the possible adverse impact on internal and regional stability (art. 11(2)). In addition to that, and for the sake of transparency, the countries are obligated to report their arms exports and imports annually (art. 13). This latter commitment is echoed in the *Maastricht Principle* 2, which also requires states to observe the principles of transparency and accountability.

Article 6 of the ATT deals specifically with authorizations of conventional arms transfers by the state. It captures a variety of possible scenarios, including a ban on authorizing transfers that would violate measures adopted by the UN Security Council under Chapter VII of the Charter of the United Nations, specifically arms embargoes (art. 6(1)). The arms embargo has indeed been instated with respect to the situation in Yemen; however, it only concerns transfers of weapons to the Houthi rebel groups but not to the coalition (UN Security Council 2015).

Article 6(2) of the ATT also prohibits the supply of arms in cases when such action 'would violate its relevant obligations under international agreements to which it is a Party, in particular those relating to the transfer of, or illicit trafficking in, conventional arms'. This norm appears to be generic in its attempt to cover any activity that falls short of the obligations arising out of the ATT and other instruments relating to arms control, such as the Nuclear Non-Proliferation Treaty, the Biological and Toxin Weapons Convention, and the Chemical Weapons Convention (art. 2(1)(b); EU Council 2008). It is interesting to note that the commentaries to the ATT suggest that a qualifier 'in particular' in the text of Article 6(2) ATT points to the fact that not only thematic treaties but also treaties of a more general application are included within the ambit of this provision, including the UN Charter, which stipulates the principle of non-intervention and the principle of non-use of force under Article 2(4) (Casey-Maslen et al. 2016). The obligations arising from the UN Charter would thus make transfers of weapons to non-state actors illegal given the ruling of the International Court of Justice in *Nicaragua* that 'training, arming, equipping, financing and supplying the contra forces or otherwise encouraging, supporting and aiding military and paramilitary activities in and against Nicaragua' (ICJ 1986, para. 292).

The commentaries also suggest that Article 6(2) ATT may encompass human rights treaties, such as the 1966 International Covenant on Civil and Political Rights (ICCPR) or the European Convention on Human Rights (ECHR) (Casey-Maslen et al. 2016). Article 6 of the ICCPR and Article 2 of the ECHR guarantee the right to life, and weapons transfers may indeed violate this right (Casey-Maslen et al. 2016). That being said, the commentaries further note that the scope of the right to life has been tested in the context of the ECHR when the applicant challenged Italy's supply to Iraq of 'lethal weapons' during the regime of Saddam Hussein. The ruling of the European Court on Human Rights pointed out that no right to have the transfer of arms regulated or other such measures taken by a state party to the ECHR is 'as such guaranteed by the Convention' (ECtHR 1995). It thus remains to be seen how broadly Article 6(2) of the ATT would be interpreted in individual cases.

Finally, and more specifically, the ATT implies a certain level of compliance with the norms of international humanitarian law as it provides in Article 6(3) that a State Party shall not authorize any transfer of conventional arms:

> (…) if it has knowledge at the time of authorization that the arms would be used in the commission of genocide, crimes against humanity, grave breaches of the Geneva Convention of 1949, attacks directed against civilian objects or civilians protected as such, or other war crimes as defined by international agreements to which it is a Party.

It is therefore mandatory in this situation to refuse to grant a license. It is noteworthy that Article 6(3) refers to explicit knowledge existing at the time of the granting of the license that weapons would be used to commit crimes. The earlier draft of the same provision prohibited granting licenses 'for the purpose' of facilitating the commission of international crimes. This initial phrasing presumed an even higher threshold of *mens rea* for the supplying state. The original text was later updated to refer to 'knowledge' rather than 'purpose' due to the difficulty of demonstrating that a state supplies weapons intending the commission of international crimes (Casey-Maslen et al. 2016). Nonetheless, even the knowledge requirement that was ultimately adopted is rather difficult to ascertain when it comes to factual evidence – the degree and specificity of such knowledge remains to be defined on a case-by-case basis. One practical pitfall of such a generalized definition of knowledge is that arms export licenses usually cover a range of products to be delivered over the course of months or even years. It may so happen that the recipient state can plausibly demonstrate that these supplies will be used to pursue legitimate aims. At the same time, it is possible that a certain proportion of the delivered weapons and ammunition would eventually be diverted to the commission of war crimes or crimes against humanity. The question remains as to the degree of scrutiny and vigilance to be exercised by the granting authorities of the ATT State Party in such a scenario.

The ATT provides for an additional safety net when it comes to the requisite knowledge of the granting State Party. Even if the authorities of the supplying state do not meet the standard for awareness described in Article 6(3), they are still obligated under Article 7 ATT to assess the *potential* that the conventional arms could be used to commit or facilitate serious violations of international humanitarian law. If after conducting such an assessment and considering available mitigating measures, the exporting state party determines that there is an overriding risk of such consequences, the exporting state party shall not authorize the export (art. 7(3)). The ATT therefore requires quite a high level of scrutiny when it comes to authorizing weapons exports as it includes both knowledge of the actual crimes committed with the said weapons as well as the risk of their commission.

Regional law

As mentioned in the beginning of this chapter, prior to the entry into force of the ATT the regulation of arms trade had been patchy. Key binding regional instruments include the 2008 European Union (EU) Council Common Position on arms export controls (EU Council Common Position 2008) and the 2006 Economic Community of West African States (ECOWAS) Convention on Small Arms and Light Weapons, Their Ammunition, and Other Related Materials (Kinshasa Convention 2010). There are also non-binding regional guidelines for controlling arms transfers, such as the 2005 Central American Integration System (SICA) Code of Conduct of Central American States on the Transfer of Arms, Ammunition, Explosives, and Other Related Materiel; the 2005 Best Practice Guidelines for the implementation of the Nairobi Declaration and the Nairobi Protocol on Small Arms and Light Weapons; and the 2000 Organization for Security and Co-operation in Europe (OSCE) Document on Small Arms and Light Weapons.

The EU Council Common Position contains obligations similar to those enshrined in the ATT in that it requires the EU member states to assess the recipient country's attitude towards relevant principles established by instruments of international humanitarian law and deny an export license if there is a clear risk that the military technology or equipment to be exported might be used in the commission of serious violations of international humanitarian law (art. 2(2)(c)). Despite the similarity between the ATT and the EU Council Common Position, the latter document arguably contains an obligation of an even higher level of scrutiny of potential risks arising out of arms supplies as compared to the former. The EU Council Common Position requires the risk of serious violations of international humanitarian law to be 'clear'. In contrast, the Article 7(3) of the ATT uses the term 'overriding', which may point towards a higher level of the burden of proof.

The *Maastricht Principles* talk about the 'real' risk of the violations of human rights, which is a 'foreseeable' result of state's conduct (Principle 13). Commentaries to the *Maastricht Principles* further clarify that the term 'real' refers to the probability of a certain result materializing – namely, only ascertainable risks are included. 'Foreseeable result' is then either the result that was actually foreseen or should have been foreseen based on prior assessment (De Schutter et al. 2012). Arguably, both the terms 'clear' and 'real' with reference to potential risks leave considerable amount of discretion in establishing the level of awareness in each specific case.

Domestic regulation

Lastly, domestic regulatory framework for arms exports must be mentioned. National rules usually identify specific competent authorities in each country responsible for granting or rejecting arms export licenses and what additional conditions may apply beyond the common rules of the ATT and the EU Common Position. In this regard, it is peculiar that authorization practice by the EU Member States over recent years exhibits significant divergences. This can be explained by the lack of sufficiently clear regulatory guidance as well as actual deviation from the standards set out in the EU Council Common Position and the ATT (Schliemann and Bryk 2019). Diverse regulatory landscape, which frequently departs from or misinterprets international guidance results in fragmentation. This discrepancy in turn allows the governments excessive flexibility in complying with the rule, prohibiting authorization of arms exports where there is a risk of their subsequent use for violations of international human rights or humanitarian law. Determination of the foreseeability of risk appears to be a normative question open to be resolved by each state according to idiosyncratic criteria.

Such disparity becomes especially apparent in relation to European arms exports to members of the Saudi-led coalition involved in the conflict in Yemen (Schliemann and Bryk 2019). One example of the flexibility afforded to states exporting weapons in the context of the situation in Yemen is a challenge launched in the UK in 2017 by the Campaign Against Arms Trade (CAAT) against the Secretary of State for International Trade. CAAT requested judicial review of licensing decisions relating to military exports to Saudi Arabia, which might later be used in the conflict in Yemen. The claimants argued that the body of evidence available in the public domain not only suggested but also dictated the conclusion that such a clear risk exists, thereby making it unlawful to continue exporting weapons to Saudi Arabia. The UK High Court dismissed the claim (High Court of Justice 2017).

CAAT's subsequent appeal against this decision was partially upheld in 2019 when the UK Court of Appeal ruled that the Secretary acted 'irrationally' by failing to reach a view on whether there had been a pattern of international humanitarian law (IHL) violations by Saudi Arabia and its coalition partners in Yemen (High Court of Justice 2017). This cautious judgment did not determine whether the granting of licenses in this case was lawful or not, but rather focused on the process by pointing out the need to assess the historic pattern of breaches of IHL by Saudi Arabia and its coalition partners. The Court's decision therefore did not suspend any existing licenses but rather invited further scrutiny. Adhering to this ruling, the UK Secretary of State for International Trade pledged to conduct such an assessment. In July 2020, the Secretary of State for International Trade, Liz Truss, announced that following the examination of the relevant data 'there is not a clear risk that the export of arms and military equipment to Saudi Arabia might be used in the commission of a serious violation of IHL'. The UK government therefore recommitted to supplying military equipment to the coalition. The government also withdrew its appeal to the Supreme Court, possibly to avoid further examination of the matter.

CAAT's challenge in the UK courts demonstrates the reluctance of the government to submit to high standard of *mens rea* with respect to granting of the licenses with potential humanitarian or human rights law implications. It also shows the difficulty of litigating human rights law-based claims within the regulatory landscape of arms trade. The following section shifts focus to potential corporate responsibility in the context of arms trade, while retaining the view encompassing states' ETOs.

Obligations of corporate actors

The ECCHR Communication

On 11 December 2019, the ECCHR together with a group of other NGOs submitted a communication to the Office of the Prosecutor of the ICC urging for the opening of a preliminary examination into the conduct of several European companies, based in the UK, Spain, Italy, Germany, and France, that supply weapons to the Saudi/UAE-led coalition ('ECCHR Communication') (Aksenova and Bryk 2020). This document alleges that fighter jets and other military equipment furnished by these companies were used in indiscriminate attacks against civilian objects in Yemen since March 2015. These actions of arms exporters may potentially fall under the definition of several specific war crimes enshrined in the Rome Statute of the ICC, including violence to life and person and directing attacks against the civilian population. More specifically, the ECCHR Communication refers to Articles 8(2)(c)(i), and 8(2)(e)(i), (ii), (iii), and (iv) of the Rome Statute of the ICC.

To provide some context, it is important to note that the war in Yemen started in 2014 when Houthi insurgents took control of Yemen's capital and largest city, Sana'a. They overthrew the government of the Saudi-backed leader, President Abd Rabbu Mansour Hadi, and installed their own rule in large parts of the country including the capital. This takeover prompted a coalition of Gulf states led by Saudi Arabia to launch a campaign in 2015 of economic isolation and air strikes against the Houthi insurgents, with logistical and intelligence support from major world powers including the United States. Other countries, most notably, Spain, Italy, the United Kingdom, Germany, and the UK, also supplied military equipment to the Saudi-led coalition. These parties to the conflict exacerbated what the UN referred to as the world's largest humanitarian catastrophe with estimates of more than 100,000 people killed since 2015 (Global Conflicts Tracker 2020).

Increased focus on responsibility of corporate actors

The timing of the ECCHR Communication to the ICC corresponds to the increasing demand on companies to comply with their obligations under international humanitarian and human rights law. The *Krupp* and *IG Farben* trials by the US Military Tribunal at Nuremberg and the case of *Zyklon B* by the British Military Courts were the first attempts to hold individual industrialists to account for complicity in crimes committed during the Second World War. Despite the fact that several domestic jurisdictions allow for criminal responsibility of corporate entities, international criminal law continued developing along the individual responsibility track ever since the initial industrialists' trials. It is noteworthy that the French proposal to include criminal responsibility of corporations in the Rome Statute of the ICC was not accepted at the conference that drew up the document. Nonetheless, the Statute contains two elaborate articles on modes of liability (arts. 25 and 28) that provide for legal tools to attach responsibility to individuals, including those acting on behalf of corporations.

Recent regional and global developments attest to the fact that the conversation on international corporate criminal liability is not closed. From a sociological perspective, the proliferation of social media activism ensures that increased attention is given to climate change issues and corporate contribution to it. This development invites additional scrutiny of the conduct of multinational corporations in mineral rich areas and the impact of their activities on the environment.

From a legal perspective, additional avenues for prosecutions of corporate entities and individuals are opening up: the Malabo Protocol on Amendments to the Protocol on the Statute of the African Court of Justice and Human Rights adopted on 27 June 2014 and now open for ratifications explicitly extends its jurisdiction to legal persons in Article 46(C) (van Sliedregt 2019). The UN Guiding Principles on Business and Human Rights also instruct corporations to avoid, prevent, and mitigate adverse human rights impacts that are directly linked to their business activities, and in that respect conduct human rights due diligence (Office of the High Commissioner of Human Rights 2012).

The difficulty with the UN Guiding Principles is that they constitute what is called 'soft law' and are therefore not binding under international law *stricto sensu*. The UN Guiding Principles nonetheless provide a solid foundation for the increased recognition of corporate due diligence obligations in the area of human rights incumbent on companies. Moreover, the UNGP also recognize that states have discretion to enact legislation with extraterritorial reach to rein in their corporations. The draft treaty on the human rights obligations of transnational corporations, currently elaborated by a Working Group of the UN Human Rights Council, is testament in this regard (Human Rights Commission 2019). The Working Group is preparing a treaty that will translate some aspects of the UN Guiding Principles into hard law directed at states by prompting them to enact domestic legislation to ensure compliance of corporations with human rights law. It must be noted, however, that the treaty, as it stands now, will address states and is not likely to impose direct obligations on corporations. Thus, even if a treaty is enacted, the UN Guiding Principles will continue to ensure that companies, at the very least, risk high reputational costs for violating due diligence obligations in the area of human rights and international law.

Despite these developments, however, prosecutions, let alone convictions, of individuals acting out of their corporate capacity or corporations as such, for their potential complicity in international crimes, are rare even at the domestic level (Zerk 2013). One widely cited ruling that is relevant for the present discussion is the *Van Anraat* case decided by the Dutch courts in 2005. The case before the District Court of The Hague was brought by the Dutch Prosecutor against *Van Anraat*, a chemicals dealer who sold thiodiglycol to Saddam Hussein's regime, which was used in the production of mustard gas. The Court acquitted Van Anraat of genocide due to the lack of the specific intent but convicted him of complicity in war crimes (District Court of The Hague 2005).

Obligations of corporate actors in the context of arms trade

The ECCHR Communication draws attention to the obligations of corporate actors in the context of arms trade. However, the supply of weapons is only possible due to express authorizations issued by various states. As previously mentioned, the ATT – ratified by all of the states in question – permits trade in weapons but sets out a number of limitations. For instance, Article 6(3) of the ATT expressly prohibits the authorization of the transfer of arms if the state party has knowledge that the arms would be deployed in the commission of international crimes.

Given the complexity of current transnational corporate structures and the varying scope of licenses granted to companies exporting weapons to Saudi Arabia and other coalition members, the degree and specificity of knowledge about the crimes committed with these weapons needs to be evaluated based on factual evidence. The purpose of the ECCHR Communication is thus to invite further scrutiny of the conduct of corporate actors providing continued support to the coalition that includes not only the supply of weapons but also their ongoing maintenance. One of the crucial questions linked to potential responsibility of corporations in this case is the existence of express state authorization in the form of licenses to export weapons.

The lack of coherence at the level of granting authorities has direct impact on businesses engaged in weapons trade as the arms industry is not directly bound by the ATT and the EU Common Position, and thus relies heavily on the decisions by state authorities. State consent may thus be invoked by corporations to eschew due diligence obligations incumbent on companies, which are required to assess the risk of potential human rights violations resulting from their activities. Therefore, the lack of clear regulatory guidance gives rise to divergence from the positive elements of the standards set out by the EU Common Position and the ATT (Schliemann and Bryk 2019). This situation has direct bearing on states' ETOs as it engages the *Maastricht Principles*, which expressly require states to adopt measures to protect rights when the threat of harm originates in their territory or when the corporation facilitating such harm is domiciled in the state concerned (Principle 25(a) and (c)). The *Maastricht Principles* thus impose a positive duty on a state to be proactive in situations when corporations located on its territory are at risk of causing harm extraterritorially.

The challenge with holding corporations accountable for weapons trade lies not only in the existence of state approval for such activity under the licensing regime but also in the nature of business activity as such. Corporations seldom perpetrate international crimes directly since the motive for multinational companies contributing to human rights abuses is usually that of either financial gain or minimization of losses in the context of existing partnerships (Prosansky 2007). The goal is often not to directly engage militarily or support one of the warring parties but rather to conduct successful business operations with a side effect of facilitating violations of human rights. The motive of financial gain obscures the link between specific corporate officials and the ultimate resulting crimes. The connection is further muddled by the fact that companies most frequently knowingly or unknowingly assist in human rights abuses as opposed to being their main perpetrators. Questions of potential complicity thus arise.

Elies van Sliedregt (2019) explains that the level of corporate engagement in international crimes may vary depending on the proximity of corporate influence to the end result. The private military company Blackwater – whose staff allegedly tortured prisoners in Iraq may be on one side of the spectrum, its contribution to a crime being direct (United States Court of Appeals 2006). In contrast, the type of assistance provided by the Canadian oil and gas producer Talisman Energy could be placed somewhere in the middle of the spectrum. This company was charged under the US Alien Tort Claims Act with aiding persecution of civilians in Sudan by virtue of investing in the country's oil industry amidst the civil war. Talisman Energy provided logistical support to state-run militia by building roads and airfields with the aim of protecting its oil reserves (United States Court of Appeals 2009).

Finally, the other side of the spectrum of possible corporate complicity in violations of international human rights and humanitarian law encompasses 'continuous silent approval' by corporations trading with dictatorial regimes. These businesses endorse authoritarian regimes in exchange for the financial benefit they derive from such cooperation (van Sliedregt 2019). In this case, culpability arises from the fact that corporate officials deliberately closed their eyes to what would otherwise have been obvious. In other words, their knowledge may be inferred according to the standard of 'willful blindness', adopted as a form of requisite intent in some jurisdictions (United States Court of Appeals 1992). Arguably, weapons trade frequently falls under the latter category – arms exporters deliberately avoid examining the end use of their products, preferring to focus solely on the relationship between the supplier and the ordering state.

Challenges of holding corporate actors accountable at the ICC

Article 25(3)(c) of the Rome Statute of the ICC is one of the key provisions invoked in the ECCHR Communication as it establishes responsibility of those who:

> ...for the purpose of facilitating the commission of such a crime, aids, abets or otherwise assists in its commission or its attempted commission, including providing the means for its commission.

The question of complicity of corporate actors within the meaning of Article 25(3)(c) appears to be 'ICC specific', yet the implications underlying the ECCHR Communication may have resonance outside of the scope of this specific situation at the ICC as the move by the ECCHR impacts our general understanding of the degree of corporate obligations in the context of weapons trade. In addition to that, the ECCHR Communication may result in an authoritative interpretation by the ICC of some of the key provisions of the ATT, such as Articles 6(3) and 7.

Article 25(3)(c) definition of complicity calls for a 'purposeful contribution' and it differs from the test developed by the ad hoc tribunals requiring that the aider and abettor simply 'knew (in the sense he was aware) that his own acts assisted the commission of the specific crime in question by the principal offender' (ICTY 2002, para. 71). The wording of 'purposeful contribution' appears to have been borrowed by the Rome Statute drafters from Article 2.06(3) of the US Model Penal Code (MPC) demanding that an accomplice aids 'with the purpose of facilitating the perpetrator's conduct'. Interestingly, the MPC does not set out the standard for a minimal contribution to the crime implying that even a marginal contribution can qualify as complicity provided the 'purpose' requirement is met. This peculiarity balances out the conduct requirement (the effect of the assistance) and the enhanced fault requirement. It seems as if the early ICC case law on the matter follows the same balancing exercise between a lower conduct threshold and a higher threshold for the mental element: the ICC in *Bemba* held that the level of contribution under Article 25(3)(c) 'does not require the meeting of any specific threshold' (ICC 2016, para. 93). The ad hoc jurisprudence, in contrast, demanded from accomplices 'substantial contribution to the crime, which the judges clarified to be a fact-based inquiry' (e.g. ICTY 2010, para. 1741).

It remains to be seen how the ICC interprets 'purposeful contribution' in the context of the ECCHR Communication. Interestingly, the question of the standard of 'purpose' vs 'knowledge' discussed in the previous section with respect to the ATT Article 6(3) also arises in the context of individual criminal responsibility at the ICC. It is easier to prove the existence of knowledge that crimes may be committed rather than purpose to facilitate their commission when it comes to arms trade. It remains to be seen whether a *sui generis* approach to *mens rea* within this ambit of human activity will be adopted. In this regard, it is rather helpful that the ICC offers one important generic clarification regarding the nature of 'purpose' in the *Bemba et al.* case: the requirement of 'purpose' only applies to the accomplice's attitude towards their own conduct, whereas a more general awareness of crimes to be committed as a result of this conduct would suffice (ICC 2016, paras. 97–98).

It appears that the financial incentives for corporate officials who continuously carry out arms trade with Saudi/UAE-led coalition members in the presence of general awareness of the crimes committed in Yemen (widely and regularly documented by several NGOs, UN agencies, as well as news outlets) could serve as the evidence of 'purpose'. The question to be further examined is whether express authorizations for arms exports given by the respective states to corporations under the licensing regime obviate the existence of fault in corporate officials. The ECCHR Communication argues that they might not. First of all, the licenses do not create a duty for a corporation to export. Secondly, it is foreseeable to corporations that the weapons they supply to the Saudi/UAE-led coalition in Yemen are likely to be used to commit crimes given the abundance of documentation of serious and repeated violations of international humanitarian law committed by the coalition. Finally, one must bear in mind corresponding duties of the exporting states granting such licenses with the knowledge of potential humanitarian law violations. As explained in the previous section, such activity clearly engages states' extraterritorial obligations to protect human rights.

Conclusion

This contribution examined the legislative framework regulating states' ETOs in the context of arms trade. In addition to that, the chapter purported to shed light on the complex nature of state and corporate involvement in this sector of human activity. It appears that state and corporate responsibility for preventing human rights violations goes hand-in-hand when it comes to supplies of military equipment. Any such equipment has the potential to be used in gross human rights and humanitarian law violations. Questions of risk assessment and knowledge are thus crucial. The ECCHR Communication to the ICC alleging corporate complicity of several European arms exporters in war crimes committed in Yemen served as a case study illustrating specific issues relating to weapons trade.

It is clear that the *Maastricht Principles* strongly resonate with international instruments regulating arms trade. There is a requirement of transparency and risk assessment of potential extraterritorial harm to human rights (broadly conceived) inherent in these documents. The ECCHR Communication to the ICC demonstrates an increasing pull towards holding corporate officials responsible for their complicity in human rights abuses occurring in foreign states. The picture is however incomplete if one omits states' responsibility in regulating corporate activity in the field of arms trade. Ultimately, the decision to grant authorization to export weapons is taken by states. It is then the degree and specificity of knowledge regarding the risks of violations that comes to the foreground. The *Maastricht Principles* impose duties on states to protect rights in cases when harm may result from the activity of corporations domiciled on its territory. They also impose duties on states to conduct risk assessment when their conduct may lead to a real risk of impairing the enjoyment of rights extraterritorially. The *Maastricht Principles* therefore bind together states' obligations to protect human rights irrespective of national borders and corporate activity, which is a very promising endeavor in the context of governing arms trade.

Note

1. marina.aksenova@ie.edu. I would like to thank the editors for their invaluable guidance in preparing this chapter. My gratitude also goes to participants of the ETOs Virtual Authors Meeting of 30 September 2020 and the IE Law Faculty Seminar of 29 October 2020 for their useful feedback on the original draft of this paper. Finally, I would like thank IE student Elvin Gence for her copyediting assistance.

References

African Union (2008) Protocol on the Statute of the African Court of Justice and Human Rights, available at https://au.int/sites/default/files/treaties/36398-treaty-0045_-_protocol_on_amendments_to_the_protocol_on_the_statute_of_the_african_court_of_justice_and_human_rights_e-compressed.pdf, last accessed 23 July 2021.

Aksenova, M. and Bryk, L. (2020) 'Extraterritorial Obligations of Arms Exporting Corporations: New Communication to the ICC', *Opinio Juris,* available at http://opiniojuris.org/2020/01/14/extraterritorial-obligations-of-arms-exporting-corporations-new-communication-to-the-icc/, last accessed 23 July 2021.

British Military Court (1946) *Trial of Bruno Tesch and Two Others*, LRTWC, vol. I, Judgment, available at http://www.worldcourts.com/imt/eng/decisions/1946.03.08_United_Kingdom_v_Tesch.pdf, last accessed 23 July 2021.

Brown, D. (2019) 'Trump Says U.S. 'Will Never Ratify' Arms Trade Treaty', *Politico*, available at https://www.politico.com/story/2019/04/26/trump-arms-trade-treaty-1385303, last accessed 23 July 2021.

Bryk L. and Saage-Maaß, M. (2019) 'Individual Criminal Liability for Arms Exports under the ICC Statute: A Case Study of Arms Exports from Europe to Saudi-led Coalition Members Used in the War in Yemen', *Journal of International Criminal Justice* (17), 1117–1137.

Casey-Maslen, S. et al. (eds). (2016) *The Arms Trade Treaty: A Commentary*, Oxford University Press.

Conference to Review Progress Made in the Implementation of the Programme of Action to Prevent, Combat and Eradicate the Illicit Trade in Small Arms and Light Weapons in All Its Aspects (2006) UN Code of Conduct of Central American States on the Transfer of Arms, Ammunition, Explosives and Other Related Material, A/CONF.192/2006/RC/WP.6, available at http://www.poa-iss.org/RegionalOrganizations/SICA/CentralAmerica-CodeofConduct-English.pdf, last accessed 23 July 2021.

De Schutter, O. et al. (2012) 'Commentary to the *Maastricht Principles* on Extraterritorial Obligations of States in the Area of Economic, Social and Cultural Rights', *Human Rights Quarterly* 34, 1084–1169.

District Court of The Hague (2005) *Public Prosecutor v. Frans Cornelis Adrianus van Anraat*, 09/751003-04, available at http://www.internationalcrimesdatabase.org/Case/178/Van-Anraat/, last accessed 23 July 2021.

European Court of Human Rights (ECtHR) (1995) *Tugar v. Italy*, Application no: 22869/93, Judgment.

EU Council Common Position (2008) 'Defining common rules governing control of exports of military technology and equipment', 2008/944/CFSP, available at https://eur-lex.europa.eu/legal-content/EN/TXT/PDF/?uri=CELEX:32008E0944&from=EN, last accessed 23 July 2021.

Global Conflict Tracker (2020) 'War in Yemen', https://www.cfr.org/global-conflict-tracker/conflict/war-yemen, last accessed 23 July 2021.

High Court of Justice (2017) *Campaign against Arms Trade, R (on the application of) v. The Secretary of State for International Trade*, EWHC 1754, available at https://www.judiciary.uk/wp-content/uploads/2017/07/r-oao-campaign-against-arms-trade-v-ssfit-and-others1.pdf, last accessed 23 July 2021.

Human Rights Commission (2019) 'Legally Binding Instrument to Regulate, in International Human Rights Law, the Activities of Transnational Cooperation and other Business Enterprises', available at https://www.ohchr.org/Documents/HRBodies/HRCouncil/WGTransCorp/OEIGWG_RevisedDraft_LBI.pdf, last accessed 23 July 2021.

International Committee of the Red Cross (2016) Reference for 'Understanding the Arms Trade Treaty from a Humanitarian Perspective', available at https://icrcndresourcecentre.org/wp-content/uploads/2016/11/4252_002_Understanding-arms-trade_WEB.pdf, last accessed 23 July 2021.

International Court of Justice (ICJ) (1986) *Military and Paramilitary Activities in and against Nicaragua (Nicaragua v. United States of America)*, ICJ Rep. 392, Judgment, available at https://www.icj-cij.org/public/files/case-related/70/070-19841126-JUD-01-00-EN.pdf, last accessed 23 July 2021.

International Criminal Court (ICC) (2016) *Prosecutor v. Jean-Pierre Bemba Gombo, Aimé Kilolo Musamba, Jean-Jacques Mangenda Kabongo, Fidèle Babala Wandu and Narcisse Arido*, 'Bemba Judgment', Case ICC-01/05-01/13, Judgment Pursuant to Article 74 of the Statute, available at https://www.icc-cpi.int/CourtRecords/CR2016_18527.PDF, last accessed 23 July 2021.

International Criminal Tribunal for the former Yugoslavia (ICTY) (2002) *Prosecutor v. Mitar Vasiljevic*, IT-98-32-T, Trial Judgment, available at https://www.icty.org/x/cases/vasiljevic/tjug/en/vas021129.pdf, last accessed 23 July 2021.

_______ (2010) *Prosecutor v. Vujadin Popovic*, IT-05-88-T, Trial Judgment, available at https://www.icty.org/x/cases/popovic/tjug/en/100610judgment.pdf, last accessed 23 July 2021.

Maastricht Principles on Extraterritorial Obligations of States in the Area of Economic, Social and Cultural Rights (2013) available at https://www.fidh.org/IMG/pdf/maastricht-eto-principles-uk_web.pdf, last accessed 23 July 2021.

Office of the High Commissioner of Human Rights (2012) The Corporate Responsibility to Respect Human Rights: An Interpretive Guide, HR/PUB/12/02, available at https://www.ohchr.org/documents/publications/guidingprinciplesbusinesshr_en.pdf, last accessed 23 July 2021.

Organization for Security and Cooperation in Europe (2000) Document on Small Arms and Light Weapons, https://www.osce.org/fsc/20783, last accessed 23 July 2021.

Prosansky, B. (2007) 'Mining Gold in a Conflict Zone: The Context, Ramifications and Lessons of AngloGold Ashanti's Activities in the Democratic Republic of the Congo', *Northwestern Journal of International Human Rights* (5), 236, available at https://scholarlycommons.law.northwestern.edu/cgi/viewcontent.cgi?article=1054&context=njihr, last accessed 23 July 2021.

Regional Centre on Small Arms and Light Weapons (RECSA) (2005) Best Practice Guidelines for the Implementation of the Nairobi Declaration and the Nairobi Protocol on Small Arms and Light Weapons, http://www.poa-iss.org/RegionalOrganizations/RECSA/Nairobi%20Best%20Practice%20Guidelines.pdf, last accessed 23 July 2021.

Regional Centre on Small Arms in the Great Lakes Region, the Horn of Africa and Bordering States (RECSA) https://recsasec.org/, last accessed 23 July 2021.

Schliemann, C. and Bryk, L. (2019) 'Arms Trade and Corporate Responsibility: Liability, Litigation and Legislative Reform', *Friedrich-Ebert Stiftung Study*, available at http://library.fes.de/pdf-files/iez/15850.pdf, last accessed 23 July 2021.

The Arms Trade Treaty (2014) 'Treaty Status', https://thearmstradetreaty.org/treaty-status.html?templateId=209883, last accessed 23 July 2021.

UN General Assembly (2015) Resolution 61/89 'Towards an arms trade treaty: establishing common international standards for the import, export and transfer of conventional arms', A/RES/61/89.

UN Security Council (2015) Resolution 2216, available at https://www.undocs.org/S/RES/2216%20, last accessed 23 July 2021.

United Nations (2014) *Arms Trade Treaty, United Nations Treaty Series*, vol. 3013, no. 52373, available at https://www.thearmstradetreaty.org/hyper-images/file/TheArmsTradeTreaty1/TheArmsTradeTreaty.pdf, last accessed 23 July 2021.

United Nations Office for Disarmament Affairs (UNODA) (2010) Central African Convention for the Control of Small Arms and Light Weapons, their Ammunition, Parts and Components that can be used for their Manufacture, Repair and Assembly (Kinshasa Convention), no. 54327, available at http://disarmament.un.org/treaties/t/kinshasa/text, last accessed 23 July 2021.

United States Court of Appeals (1992) *United States v. Campbell,* 977 F.2d 854, available at https://casetext.com/case/us-v-campbell-95, last accessed 23 July 2021.

_______ (2006) *Nordan v. Blackwater Security Consulting, LLC*, 382 F. Supp. 2d 801, available at https://casetext.com/case/in-re-blackwater-security-consulting-llc, last accessed 23 July 2021.

_______ (2009) *Presbyterian Church of Sudan v. Talisman Energy Inc*, 582 5F 3 244, 259, available at http://www.internationalcrimesdatabase.org/Case/43/Presbyterian-Church-Of-Sudan-v-Talisman-Energy/, last accessed 23 July 2021.

United States Military Tribunal (1949) *IG Farben and Krupp Trials*, Law Reports of the Trials of War Criminals (LRTWC), vol. X, available at https://www.loc.gov/rr/frd/Military_Law/pdf/Law-Reports_Vol-10.pdf, last accessed 23 July 2021.

van Sliedregt, E. (2019) 'Regional Criminal Justice, Corporate Criminal Liability and the Need for Non-Doctrinal Research' in Aksenova, M. et al. (eds). *Breaking the Cycle of Mass Atrocities: Criminological and Socio-Legal Approaches in International Criminal Law*, Hart, last accessed 23 July 2021.

Zerk, J. (2013) Report for Office of the UN High Commissioner for Human Rights on Corporate liability for gross human rights abuses: Towards a fairer and more effective system of domestic law remedies, available at https://www.ohchr.org/Documents/Issues/Business/DomesticLawRemedies/StudyDomesticeLawRemedies.pdf, last accessed 23 July 2021.

28

Extraterritorial military action

Vito Todeschini

Introduction

Extraterritorial human rights obligations (ETOs) arise whenever states undertake military action outside national territory. A preliminary question is *when* ETOs apply in relation to military operations. First, states bear ETOs when exercising 'power or effective control' over a person (Human Rights Committee (HRC) 2004a, para. 10), typically in cases of deprivation of liberty. Second, ETOs arise when a state exercises effective control over foreign territory, including in situations of occupation (HRC 2018, para. 63). Third, states have ETOs vis-à-vis any individual whose rights are 'impacted by its military or other activities in a direct and reasonably foreseeable manner' (ibid), e.g., when states carry out airstrikes without 'boots on the ground'. The *Maastricht Principles* on Extraterritorial Obligations of States in the Area of Economic, Social and Cultural Rights (*Maastricht Principles*) incorporate these principles, recognizing that ETOs arise in connection to the exercise of effective control over a person or territory, or when state action has 'foreseeable effects on the enjoyment' of economic, social and cultural (ESC) rights (Principles 9 and 18).

A corollary question is *which* ETOs states are bound by when undertaking extraterritorial military action. Under human rights law, states generally bear three types of obligations (Committee on Economic, Social and Cultural Rights (CESCR) 2000, para. 33). The obligation to respect requires states to 'refrain from interfering directly or indirectly with the enjoyment' of human rights. The obligation to protect prescribes that states must 'take measures that prevent third parties from interfering' with human rights. The obligation to fulfil imposes on states a duty to 'adopt appropriate legislative, administrative, budgetary, judicial, promotional and other measures towards the full realization' of human rights. The obligation to fulfil in turn encompasses the obligations to facilitate, provide and promote (ibid). While within national territory states bear all three obligations, in extraterritorial contexts these various obligations arise depending on the type and degree of control states exercise. As it will be shown, whereas the obligation to respect applies in all circumstances, given that states are always in a position to refrain from interfering with human rights, the obligations to protect and fulfil will apply only when a state exercises effective control over a person or territory. The latter obligations, in fact, require that a threshold criterion be met in order to be triggered (Milanovic 2011, pp. 209 ff.).

DOI: 10.4324/9781003090014-35

At the same time, it is relevant noting that, while the analysis will attempt to identify which of these obligations apply in the various scenarios considered below, the application of and boundaries between such obligations is not rigid.

Section 2 will look at the ETOs arising in connection with deprivation of liberty. Section 3 will focus on the obligations states bear when exercising effective control over territory. Section 4 will then consider the ETOs deriving from use of force against individuals, and Section 5 will briefly delve into what ETOs require when states participate in UN-mandated peace operations. Section 6 will offer an appraisal of the relevance of the *Maastricht Principles* in the area of extraterritorial military action. Section 7 will conclude by highlighting some of the open questions regarding the applicability of ETOs in relation to extraterritorial military action.

Deprivation of liberty and control over persons

Deprivation of liberty constitutes an exercise of 'physical power and control' (European Court of Human Rights (ECtHR) 2011b, para. 136) or 'effective control' (HRC 2014a, para. 63) that brings an individual under a state's jurisdiction, triggering relevant ETOs. This is the so-called 'personal model' of jurisdiction (Milanovic 2011, pp. 173 ff.), according to which a state has an obligation to secure human rights due to the exercise of control over persons. Whether a deprivation of liberty is authorized or lawful is immaterial: exercise of control per se establishes a jurisdictional link between a state and an individual, 'regardless of the circumstances in which such power or effective control was obtained' (HRC 2004a, para. 10).

When exercising *de jure* or *de facto* effective control over a person, states have an obligation to ensure the protection of all the human rights that are relevant to the situation of that individual (ECtHR 2011b, para. 136). Because persons deprived of their liberty are under the complete control of the detaining state, the latter must respect, protect and fulfil the whole range of human rights international law affords to them. This entails, first, respecting their right to life and to be free from torture and other cruel, inhuman or degrading treatment or punishment (ill-treatment), as well as their right to personal liberty and security, including all ensuing procedural guarantees (HRC 2014a, para. 63; 2018, para. 63). A state also has the obligation to protect an individual from violence and other threats to their life while in detention (African Commission on Human and Peoples' Rights (AComHPR) 2015, para. 36). With regard to ESC rights, the *Maastricht Principles* provide that '[a] State exercising effective control over persons outside its national territory must respect, protect and fulfil [the ESC] rights of those persons' (Principle 18). For instance, a state will have the obligation to fulfil the rights relating to adequate food, water, clothing, housing conditions and healthcare (International Covenant on Economic, Social and Cultural Rights (ICESCR), arts. 11–12; UN Standard Minimum Rules for the Treatment of Prisoners, rules 12–35). Whenever a state is unable to fully provide the detention standards required under international law, it nevertheless must guarantee, 'at the very least, minimum essential levels of each of the [ESC] rights' in line with the minimum core obligations entrenched in the ICESCR (CESCR 1990, para. 10).

It is to be noted that, in situations of armed conflict, the rules of international humanitarian law (IHL) governing detention may lead to frictions with a state's applicable ETOs. In particular, IHL allows for the internment of individuals (Geneva Convention (GC) III, arts. 21 and 118; GC IV, arts. 42–43, 78 and 132),[1] namely deprivation of liberty based on security grounds rather than on the alleged or actual commission of a crime. While such form of detention is generally not compliant with human rights law (ECtHR 2011a, para. 100), as it amounts to prohibited 'arbitrary' detention, the HRC has affirmed that '[s]ecurity detention authorized and regulated by and complying with international humanitarian law in principle is not arbitrary' (2014a, para. 64; also ECtHR 2014a, paras. 104–105). In this sense, the standard of 'arbitrariness' is interpreted in light of the rules of IHL, which allow for security detention, rather than human rights law (Inter-American Commission on Human Rights (IAComHR) 1999, para. 42).[2] As a result, carrying out internment in line with IHL does not, in principle, infringe upon human rights law; in contrast, internment that violates IHL implies a corresponding breach of the prohibition of arbitrary detention.

Furthermore, the review of detention under IHL does not necessarily meet the standards prescribed by human rights law. For this reason, the ECtHR has affirmed that the relevant review body, which under IHL may or may not be of a judicial nature, should provide 'sufficient guarantees of impartiality and fair procedure'; furthermore, 'the first review should take place shortly after the person is taken into detention, with subsequent reviews at frequent intervals' (2014a, para. 106). Hence, the ECtHR requires that internment in international armed conflict be compliant with certain essential protections surrounding the right to liberty. On the other hand, IHL also prescribes that interned persons be treated humanely, be protected from torture and ill-treatment and be provided with conditions of detention that safeguard their life and preserve their health (*inter alia*, GC III, arts. 3, 13 and 15; Additional Protocol I (AP I), art. 11; Additional Protocol II (AP II), art. 5). In that respect, IHL prescribes obligations similar to those envisaged under human rights law.

When a state does not have full control over the detention of an individual, its ETOs will be graduated accordingly. For example, if US personnel interrogate a person detained in Afghanistan by Afghan authorities, the state's ETOs arise because interrogation constitutes a form of control over such person, particularly over the enjoyment of their rights (HRC 2018, para. 63). They also apply because of the control exercised by the state over its own agents, who in all circumstances must refrain from engaging in human rights violations (AComHPR 2015, para. 14; Milanovic 2011, pp. 209–210). Accordingly, in such circumstances, the US carries an obligation to respect the detainee's right to life and personal integrity, including by refraining from the use of torture and ill-treatment, in all circumstances.

On the other hand, it is more difficult to determine whether and to what extent the US' obligations to protect and fulfil would apply in such a scenario. One argument could be that, given the US exercises control over the detained individual through interrogation, albeit short of controlling other aspects of detention, it has an obligation to ensure that such a person is not detained arbitrarily by Afghan authorities, and that relevant procedural safeguards are in place. It is more difficult to clearly determine whether the act of interrogation alone is enough to establish that the US has 'effective control' over the detainee for purposes of proactively protecting and fulfilling the ESC rights of the detained individual. Not being the detaining authority, the US would not be directly responsible for securing all the ESC rights the detainee should be accorded, for instance in relation to food and clothing. The fact of the exercise of control through interrogation, however, may raise the question whether the US should ensure that Afghan authorities fulfil their obligations in respect of ESC rights as well, at least during the whole time the US personnel are involved in the detainee's questioning.

Against the background of the same factual scenario, a further question concerns whether the US bears ETOs vis-à-vis a person deprived of liberty when its personnel do not directly interrogate the latter. Certainly, if Afghan agents questioned a person under the direction of US personnel, these would be under an obligation not to engage in any prohibited conduct, such as torture or ill-treatment (Milanovic 2011, pp. 218–219). But what if US personnel witness acts of torture perpetrated by Afghan agents in their presence, without any involvement whatsoever? If the place of detention was under US control while torture is committed by Afghan agents, the US would have the obligation to protect the detainee, as the latter would fall under US' jurisdiction (Committee against Torture (CAT) 2008, para. 16). Yet, if this happens in a place under Afghan control, it can be questioned whether the US carries a legal obligation to prevent or stop such acts. One argument, to be tested, could be that, where US personnel have the ability or power to intervene and stop Afghan agents from torturing an individual, the US must do so as part of its obligation to respect under applicable human rights law.

Occupation and other instances of effective control over territory

ETOs also arise when 'as a consequence of military action – whether lawful or unlawful – [a state] exercises effective control of an area outside its national territory' (ECtHR 1995, para. 62). In this respect, ETOs derive 'from the fact of such control' (ECtHR 2011b, para. 138), giving rise to an obligation to guarantee the human rights of the people located in the area where effective control is exercised. As the HRC has affirmed, '... States parties must respect and protect the lives of individuals located in places, which are under their effective control, such as occupied territories' (2018, para. 63; also International Court of Justice (ICJ) 2004, paras. 109–110; 2005, paras. 178–180, 216–220). This is the so-called 'spatial model' of extraterritorial jurisdiction, according to which effective control over territory, possibly including just an 'area' or a 'place', functions as a threshold criterion that determines when a state has jurisdiction extraterritorially, and thus bears ETOs (Milanovic 2011, pp. 127 ff. and 210).

It is important to highlight that control over territory may vary across a spectrum of intensity. Examples range from full occupation of a territory followed by the displacement of local authorities (e.g., Russia's annexation of Crimea), to temporary control of a limited geographical area (such as a town, a building or even an apartment), to occupation without military presence on the ground (e.g., Israel's closure of the Gaza Strip). In such scenarios, states' ETOs will apply according to the type and degree of control exercised over the territory.

In situations of occupation, where a state exercises effective control over the occupied territory (ECtHR 2021a, para. 196), the degree of control exercised is particularly intense. In such a scenario, a state's ETOs are 'substantially similar to [the obligations] it assumes with regard to situations or persons in its national territory' (De Schutter et al. 2012, p. 1124). The ECtHR has ruled that an occupier is under an obligation to 'secure, within the area under its control, the entire range of substantive rights set out in the [European Convention on Human Rights – ECHR] and those additional Protocols which it has ratified. It will be liable for any violations of those rights' (2011b, para. 138; also HRC 2014b and 2015). The CESCR has also affirmed that states must 'fully guarantee and implement the Covenant [ICESCR] rights for all persons in all territories under its effective control' (2011, para. 3). In addition, the *Maastricht Principles* provide that '[a] State in belligerent occupation or that otherwise exercises effective control over territory outside its national territory must respect, protect and fulfil the [ESC] rights of persons within that territory' (Principle 18). It follows that, in occupied territories, states bear the three obligations to respect, protect and fulfil the human rights of the local population, especially when local authorities have been displaced. Such a principle echoes what is prescribed under IHL, specifically the law of occupation,[3] which derives from the 1907 Hague Regulations (HR), GC IV, AP I and related customary norms. Article 43 HR prescribes that an occupier must 'take all the measures in his power to restore, and ensure, as far as possible public order and safety' which requires, *inter alia*, the maintenance of law enforcement in the occupied territory (Longobardo 2018, pp. 169 ff). This entails, for instance, a due diligence obligation to protect individuals from violence arising from private parties (ICJ 2005, paras. 178–180). The law of occupation also regulates the occupant's duties and responsibilities in relation to ESC rights (Giacca 2014). For instance, article 55 GC IV prescribes obligations in terms of 'ensuring the food and medical supplies of the population', while article 69 AP I imposes an obligation to 'ensure the provision of clothing, bedding, means of shelter, other supplies essential to the survival of the civilian population of the occupied territory'.

Similar ETOs apply when occupied territory is unlawfully annexed (HRC 2015, para. 23; CESCR 2017a, paras. 9–10). The degree of control exercised in such instances is, in fact, equivalent if not more intense than during occupation, given annexation purports to appropriate foreign territory permanently.[4] The ETOs relevant to situations of occupation also apply when territory is controlled by proxy. The ECtHR has found that a state has jurisdiction over foreign territory when, through a subordinate local administration, it exercises 'effective overall control' over such territory (1996, para. 56). In order to establish that such a test is met, it is not necessary to prove that the state 'exercises detailed control over the policies and actions of the subordinate local administration', sufficing to establish that 'the local administration survives as a result of the Contracting State's military and other support' (2011b, para. 138). Accordingly, the controlling state must ensure the whole range of ETOs deriving from the human rights norms binding upon it (ibid). It is further worth highlighting that even military action resulting in the temporary exercise of effective control over a limited geographic area may trigger a state's jurisdiction under human rights law, making relevant ETOs applicable (ECtHR 2004, para. 74; Milanovic 2011, p. 138).

When control over territory is not as intense as in the aforementioned contexts, a state's ETOs will be graduated accordingly (De Schutter et al. 2012, p. 1108). A first scenario concerns occupied territories where local authorities retain some level of control, as in the case of Israel's occupation of the West Bank. The CESCR has specified that Israel 'has positive and negative obligations with regard to the Occupied Palestinian Territory, depending on its level of control and the transfer of authority' (2019, para. 11). In that regard, the occupier's primary obligation is to respect and not to interfere in the local authorities' fulfilment of those rights remaining under their competence (ICJ 2004, para. 112; also CESCR 2011, para. 8). As to the obligations to protect and fulfil, these are retained depending on the degree of control exercised. For instance, the occupier must provide the local population with access to drinking water or necessary healthcare, as prescribed under the ICESCR, to the extent local authorities cannot perform such duties because of the occupation. The occupier, on the other hand, will not be under the obligation to perform those tasks that can be fulfilled by local authorities. For instance, Israel does not have the duty to ensure law enforcement in those areas of the West Bank where such a task falls under the competence of the Palestinian Authority, whereas it retains law enforcement duties wherever the latter cannot exercise its powers. By way of example, Israel must protect Palestinians from threats or violence emanating from Israeli settlers in any area outside Palestinian Authority's control (HRC 2014b, para. 16).

A second scenario where a state's ETOs may be graduated is when effective control over territory is challenged, e.g., when the local population resists the occupation, especially by arms (e.g., as experienced by the United Kingdom (UK) in Iraq). If a state occupies a large area of another state's territory, but the local population still has full control of certain cities, then the occupier does not exercise 'effective control' over the latter for purposes of applying relevant ETOs – bar the obligation to respect, which applies in all circumstances. Limited to such areas, therefore, the occupier will not be under a duty to ensure law enforcement, or provide necessary services to ensure ESC rights. If the local population, on the other hand, is not in full control of certain areas but challenges the occupation through occasional armed actions, then a case-by-case assessment will determine what the occupier is required of in terms of the obligations to protect and fulfil, always in light of the degree of control exercised. A similar example regards situations in which fighting erupts to regain control over territory (e.g., Azerbaijan's military operations to retake Nagorno-Karabakh from Armenia). In such circumstances, ETOs will gradually cease to apply as the occupier loses effective control over territory, particularly in those areas from which it withdraws.

A third scenario concerns effective control over territory exercised without military presence on the ground. In the context of Israel's blockade and closure of the Gaza Strip, for instance, Israel exercises effective control over the land borders, maritime and air space of Gaza, in addition to maintaining its authority over the telecommunications, water, electricity and sewage networks and the population registry. This allows Israel to control all movements of people and goods in and out of Gaza, and to be capable of conducting military operations therein at will. Such conditions make Gaza an occupied territory in IHL terms (UN Human Rights Council (HRC) 2015, paras. 27–30), and amount to exercise of 'effective control' for purposes of ETOs applicability (HRC 2014b; CESCR 2019). In respect of the right to health, for example, barring Gazans from seeking medical treatment outside the Strip, or impeding the import of necessary medical equipment and supplies into Gaza, does not comport with Israel's obligation to respect such right. On the other hand, Israel is not directly responsible for running hospitals in Gaza, a duty that remains incumbent upon local authorities. However, Israel's exercise of control over electricity networks, on which the functioning of hospitals depends, imposes an obligation to provide an adequate amount of electricity, meaning Israel retains certain duties under the obligation to fulfil the right to health. In any case, determining which ETOs states bear when exercising effective control over territory without military presence on the ground requires a case-by-case evaluation in light of the concrete circumstances.

Use of force by distance

When force is used 'by distance', e.g., in absence of territorial control or physical control over a person, ETOs may derive from a state's ability to infringe upon human rights (Hampson 2008, p. 570; Milanovic 2011, pp. 209 ff.). With regard to the International Covenant on Civil and Political Rights (ICCPR), the HRC has affirmed that states must respect and ensure the right to life of:

> all persons subject to its jurisdiction, that is, all persons over whose enjoyment of the right to life it exercises power or effective control. This includes persons located outside any territory effectively controlled by the state, whose right to life is nonetheless impacted by its military or other activities in a direct and reasonably foreseeable manner.
>
> *(2018, para. 63; also AComHPR 2015, para. 14)*

In the HRC's view, the 'direct and reasonably foreseeable' impact on a person's right to life, as a form of exercise of 'power or effective control' over the enjoyment of such a right, is thus a condition that triggers ETOs under the ICCPR. This includes scenarios where force is used by distance without military presence on the ground, such as through airstrikes (HRC 2014c, para. 9(a)). It would also encompass situations where state armed forces are on the ground yet they do not have effective control over the territory in question, for instance during the invasion of a country, or the taking of a city under enemy control. In such contexts, states' ETOs will derive from the ability of its agents to have an impact on human rights.

It is worth noting that the ECtHR has not yet fully acknowledged that use of force by distance suffices to bring an individual under a state's jurisdiction (Joseph 2019, p. 349). In the *Banković* decision, the ECtHR affirmed that, absent effective control over foreign territory, use of force by distance is not sufficient to establish a jurisdictional link between a state and the targeted individual(s) (2001, para. 75). In the ECtHR's view, this would include the 'active phase of hostilities' of an international armed conflict, i.e. where 'armed confrontation and fighting between enemy military forces seeking to establish control over an area' take place (2021a, paras. 136–138). On the other hand, the ECtHR has at times acknowledged that use of force by distance may trigger ETOs under the ECHR (2007a, paras. 54–55; 2008, para. 51; 2011b, paras. 133–137).

When use of force has a nexus with an armed conflict, the protection of the right to life under human rights law intersects with the IHL rules on targeting. IHL imposes on the parties to a conflict to abide by, *inter alia*, the principles of distinction, proportionality and precautions in attack, under which lethal force may be used less restrictively than under human rights law (AP I, arts. 48, 51 and 57; AP II, art. 13). In this respect, the ICJ has affirmed that, to determine whether during the conduct of hostilities a deprivation of life is arbitrary, reference must be made to IHL rather than human rights norms (1996, para. 25; also AComHPR 2015, para. 32). In this respect, the HRC has stated that '[u]se of lethal force consistent with international humanitarian law and other applicable international law norms is, in general, not arbitrary' (HRC 2018, para. 64). On the other hand, 'practices inconsistent with international humanitarian law, entailing a risk to the lives of civilians and other persons protected by international humanitarian law ... would also violate article 6 of the Covenant' (ibid; also AComHPR 2015, para. 32).

ETOs triggered by extraterritorial use of force extend to ESC rights as well. The *Maastricht Principles* provide that states bear ETOs in all situations where their acts 'bring about foreseeable effects on the enjoyment of [ESC] rights' (Principle 9(b)). Similarly, the CESCR has clarified that '[t]he extraterritorial obligation to respect requires states parties to refrain from interfering directly or indirectly with the enjoyment of the Covenant rights by persons outside their territories' (2017b, para. 29; also *Maastricht Principles*, Principle 20). Accordingly, a state has an obligation to respect ESC rights in the context of military action that may have 'foreseeable effects' on their enjoyment, e.g., in relation to the right to health when an airstrike targets a hospital. In this sense, a state must refrain from unlawfully interfering with any ESC right. It is to be noted that even the protection of ESC rights must take into consideration the co-applicability of IHL which, while prescribing less stringent rules on the targeting of objects, also imposes specific prohibitions regarding attacks that may infringe upon certain ESC rights (AP I, arts. 52–54; AP II, arts. 14, 16–17).

While states always have the obligation to respect the right to life and ESC rights, albeit in light of applicable IHL rules, use of force by distance will not trigger an obligation to protect. In fact, in order to protect a person's life or home from threats arising from private parties, states need to exercise effective control over a person or territory, namely a form and degree of control that allows, and requires, to perform such a task. The ability to 'impact' a person's rights may also not be, in itself, a sufficient condition to trigger the obligation to fulfil, as this requires implementing measures – e.g., providing adequate healthcare – a state is not in a position to give effect to, absent effective control over a territory or person.

UN-mandated peace operations

Peace operations are typically established by a United Nations Security Council's (UNSC) resolution, and may be led by the UN (e.g., the MINUSMA operation in Mali), other international organizations such as the North Atlantic Treaty Organization (e.g., the ISAF operation in Afghanistan), or a state. When participating in UN-mandated peace operations, states remain bound by their ETOs (Larsen 2012, p. 185). The HRC has affirmed that the ICCPR applies extraterritorially in respect of persons 'within the power or effective control of the forces [...]

constituting a national contingent of a State Party assigned to an international peace-keeping or peace-enforcement operation' (2004a, para. 10; 2004b, para. 6; also CAT 2008, para. 16). As discussed above, what matters in this respect is the exercise of jurisdiction in the form of 'effective control' over a person or territory, as well as the 'direct and reasonably foreseeable' impact state action may have on a person's rights.

The ECtHR also found the ECHR to be applicable extraterritorially when states contribute troops to peace operations (2014b, para. 152; 2011a, paras. 85–86; 2015, para. 33). However, the ECtHR held that a state's obligations under the ECHR do not apply in relation to UN-mandated peace operations when troops' conduct is attributable to the UN rather than the sending state.[5] In the ECtHR's view, this situation arises when two conditions are fulfilled. First, the UNSC must 'delegate' part of its powers, which occurs when it empowers 'another entity to exercise its function as opposed to "authorising" an entity to carry out functions which it could not itself perform' (2007b, paras. 43, 128–131). Second, the UNSC must retain 'ultimate authority and control' over the peace operation, an assessment to be made on a case-by-case basis, *inter alia* in light of the operation's chain of command (ibid, paras. 133–134).

If such conditions are satisfied, the ECtHR deems the conduct of troops to be attributable to the UN and not to the sending state. This, in turn, excludes the applicability *ratione personae* of the ECHR,[6] precluding a state's ETOs under this treaty from arising in the concrete circumstances. In subsequent case law, the ECtHR has applied this same principle, either reaching the same conclusions in terms of attribution of conduct (*inter alia* 2007c, p. 3), or finding that troops' conduct remained attributable to the sending state for failure to establish that the UNSC had 'delegated' its powers and had retained 'ultimate authority and control' over the peace operation (*inter alia* 2011a, paras. 79–84). Notwithstanding its many critical aspects, such jurisprudence remains part of the *lex lata* within the ECHR (Larsen 2012, p. 164), yet it does not affect the applicability of ETOs in peace operations under different treaties. It is also worth noting that dual attribution, i.e., attribution of the same conduct to more than one entity, may be a possible legal avenue to ensure the applicability of the ECHR in UN-mandated peace operations (ECtHR 2011a, para. 80; Larsen 2012, pp. 151–156).

Besides states, in UN-mandated peace operations international organizations may bear human rights obligations as well. The necessary condition in this regard is that international organizations have legal personality (Larsen 2012, pp. 89–90), which makes them bound by international customary and treaty law (ICJ 1980, p. 37). However, given human rights treaties are generally not open for ratification or access to by international organizations, except for the Convention on the Rights of Persons with Disabilities, these will principally be bound by customary human rights law. In this respect, many human rights have attained customary status, including the rights to life and to liberty (AComHPR 2015, para. 14; HRC 2001, para. 11). In absence of authoritative statement on the matter, it is sensible arguing that international organizations will bear ETOs according to the same rules applicable to states, i.e., when exercising effective control over a person or territory or when their action may impact an individual's rights (Engdahl 2012, pp. 69–71).

Extraterritorial military action and the *Maastricht Principles*

Over time, the *Maastricht Principles* have demonstrated their persistent utility when it comes to determining the applicability of ETOs in extraterritorial military action. On the one hand, they have entrenched the interpretation developed by the ICJ and human rights bodies – the 'effective control over a person or territory' criterion – connecting it to the extraterritorial application of ESC rights. On the other hand, they have been forward-looking and expansive in relation to situations that might escape a rigid interpretation of the 'effective control' criterion, particularly in relation to extraterritorial military action where states have no presence on the ground.

With regard to deprivation of liberty, the *Maastricht Principles* confirmed the 'effective control' criterion previously employed by human rights bodies to determine when ETOs apply in this context (Principles 9(a) and 18). The adoption of the *Maastricht Principles* constituted an important step to entrench the interpretation that ETOs relating to ESC rights apply in relation to deprivation of liberty, a context where human rights jurisprudence had primarily considered the protection of civil rights such as the rights to personal liberty and to be free from torture and ill-treatment. Additionally, by spelling out that states must 'refrain from conduct which nullifies or impairs the enjoyment and exercise of [ESC] rights of persons outside their territories' (Principle 20), the *Maastricht Principles* are also capable of encompassing situations where a state does not have full control of a person's detention, yet has the ability to infringe upon a detainee's rights – such as when it interrogates a person detained by another state.

Moreover, the *Maastricht Principles* acknowledge that 'effective control' over territory triggers state jurisdiction under applicable human rights treaties, which in turn gives rise to the obligation to respect, protect and fulfil ESC rights (Principle 18). Particularly when the exercise of effective control amounts to occupation, states 'may be obliged to secure the entire range of substantive rights' (De Schutter et al. 2012, p. 1108). In this sense, the *Maastricht Principles* reflect the consolidated jurisprudence of the ICJ and human rights bodies on the applicability of ETOs in situations of occupation. Remarkably, by further making reference to situations where a state 'otherwise exercises effective control over territory', the *Maastricht Principles* fill possible gaps regarding ETOs applicability in instances where territorial control falls short of occupation (see also ECtHR 2021a, para. 196).

In the context of use of force by distance, the *Maastricht Principles* have been groundbreaking in recognizing that ETOs arise in 'situations over which State acts or omissions bring about foreseeable effects on the enjoyment of economic, social and cultural rights, whether within or outside its territory' (Principle 9(b)). At the time they were adopted, in 2011, the human rights bodies' interpretation that ETOs attach to the impact that state acts may have on human rights, besides the exercise of effective control over a person or territory, had not yet fully consolidated. This would later emerge in the General Comments of the AComHPR, which referred to 'conduct which could reasonably be foreseen to result in an unlawful deprivation of life' (2015, para. 14), and the HRC, which connected ETOs to the 'direct and reasonably foreseeable' impact of military or other activities on the right to life (2018, para. 63). While it goes beyond the scope of this contribution to enquire on whether such language directly draws on the *Maastricht Principles*, the latter have certainly anticipated the interpretive trend later adopted by human rights bodies. In this sense, they have constituted an important step in the expansion of the protection of human rights, including but not limited to ESC rights, in the context of extraterritorial military action.

Outlook

To conclude, it is pertinent to point out – without purporting to be exhaustive – some questions that are still in need of clarification and further research with regard to the application of ETOs in the context of extraterritorial military action. First, there are instances in which it remains unclear whether states bear ETOs at all. One example is that of state A's agents witnessing state B's officials torturing a detainee where state A has no control over the detained person or the area of detention. In that instance, what needs to be explored is whether, under human rights law, a state bears a due diligence obligation to prevent another state from committing a human rights violation, risking to incur responsibility for failure to fulfil such a duty.

Second, in light of the constant resort to human rights mechanisms in order to seek justice for violations occurring in armed conflict, states might start adopting derogations when conducting extraterritorial military action. In this sense, it is yet to be tested to what extent derogations adopted in the context of extraterritorial military operations could comply with the strict requirements prescribed under human rights law (*inter alia* HRC 2001). For instance, how would conducting military operations abroad or contributing troops to UN-mandated peace operations amount to a 'public emergency which threatens the life of the nation', the necessary condition for states to resort to derogations under Article 4 ICCPR?

Third, when conducting extraterritorial military action states have a duty to investigate alleged human rights violations committed by their agents. The Minnesota Protocol on the Investigation of Potentially Unlawful Death provides that '[t]he duty to investigate applies wherever the state has a duty to respect, protect and/or fulfil the right to life, and in relation to any alleged victims or perpetrators within the territory of a state or otherwise subject to a state's jurisdiction' (OHCHR 2016, para. 19). Indeed, a corollary of states' obligation to respect human rights in extraterritorial contexts is that a duty to investigate arises whenever the former is breached, and the specific right violated – e.g., the right to life – calls for the opening of an investigation (Milanovic 2011, pp. 216–217). The ECtHR, for example, has considered the obligation to investigate in the context of extraterritorial military action (2011b, 2014b, 2021a, 2021b). While human rights bodies have clarified that states must carry out effective investigations in connection with extraterritorial military action, some questions remain open. For instance, to what extent should security concerns characterizing armed conflict be taken into account in the assessment of whether a state has fulfilled its duty to investigate in line with international standards (*inter alia* ECtHR 2014b, 2021b)? And how are states supposed to discharge the obligation to investigate when alleged human rights violations are committed in connection with use of force by distance, i.e., in relation to contexts where they have no presence on, and access to, the ground?

Fourth, questions exist with regard to the allocation of ETOs when states conduct military action in partnership with other states or international organizations. This concerns both the fulfilment of substantive obligations – who is responsible for securing which rights to the affected individuals – and the procedural duty to investigate. For instance, when conducting airstrikes, what ETOs does state A bear if its action is limited to the refuelling of aircrafts of state B, the one actually carrying out an attack? Do both states bear the same ETOs, or are these graduated in accordance with the role played by a state in a military operation? Who among such states bears the duty to investigate in case relevant human rights are violated? Or, what ETOs states have in respect of the transfer of arms to another state? Also, can a state be held responsible for complicity in human rights violations in any of these scenarios, and what are the scope and limits of state complicity in this respect?

While nowadays there is no doubt states bring their human rights obligations along when conducting extraterritorial military action, multiple legal challenges still remain. Future practice and research must test the unexplored terrains where human rights protection is at risk, attempting to find solutions that would prevent states from escaping their ETOs when acting militarily abroad.

Notes

1. IHL regulates the grounds for internment and relative procedural guarantees in respect of international armed conflicts only. It remains debated whether IHL also authorizes security detention in non-international armed conflicts. For discussion, see Hill-Cawthorne (2016).

2. This interpretive operation is based on Article 31(3)(c) of the Vienna Convention on the Law of Treaties, or equivalent provisions included in certain human rights treaties, which requires, in the interpretation of a treaty, to take account of 'any relevant rules of international law applicable in the relations between the parties'. This is known as the principle of systemic integration, which human rights bodies resort to when dealing with the relationship between human rights law and IHL (Todeschini 2018).
3. According to Article 42 HR, '[t]erritory is considered occupied when it is actually placed under the authority of the hostile army'.
4. Annexation, when effected as forceful acquisition of territory, amounts to a prohibited use of force under Article 2(4) of the Charter of the United Nations. Importantly, annexed territory continues to be classified as occupied territory for purposes of IHL applicability; see GC IV, art. 47.
5. Attribution of conduct is concerned with linking the acts and omissions of a physical person to an abstract entity such as a state or an international organization.
6. A treaty's scope of application *ratione personae* circumscribes the subjects it applies to, which are the states parties to it.

References

African Commission on Human and Peoples' Rights (2015) GC 3 on the Right to Life (Article 4), 57th Ordinary Session.

Committee against Torture (CAT) (2008) GC 2 on Implementation of Article 2 by States Parties, CAT/C/GC/2.

Committee on Economic, Social and Cultural Rights (CESCR) (1990) GC 3 on the Nature of States Parties' Obligations (art. 2, para. 1), E/1991/23.

_______ (2000) GC 14 on the Right to the Highest Attainable Standard of Health (art. 12), E/C.12/2000/4.

_______ (2011) Concluding Observations: Israel, E/C.12/ISR/CO/3.

_______ (2017a) Concluding Observations: Russia, E/C.12/RUS/CO/6.

_______ (2017b) GC 24 on State Obligations under the International Covenant on Economic, Social and Cultural Rights in the Context of Business Activities, E/C.12/GC/24.

_______ (2019) Concluding Observations: Israel, E/C.12/ISR/CO/4.

De Schutter, O. et al. (2012) 'Commentary to the *Maastricht Principles* on Extraterritorial Obligations of States in the Area of Economic, Social and Cultural Rights', *Human Rights Quarterly* 34, 1084–1169.

Engdahl, O. (2012) 'Applicability/Application of Human Rights Law to International Organisations Involved in Peace Operations', Proceedings of the 12th Bruges Colloquium.

European Court of Human Rights (ECtHR) (1995) *Loizidou v. Turkey (Preliminary Objections)*, Application no: 15318/89, Judgment.

_______ (1996) *Loizidou v. Turkey (Merits)*, Application no: 15318/89, Judgment.

_______ (2001) *Banković and others v. Belgium and Other 16 Contracting States*, Application no: 52207/99, Decision.

_______ (2004) *Issa and others v. Turkey*, Application no: 31821/96, Judgment.

_______ (2007a) *Pad and others v. Turkey*, Application no: 60167/00, Decision.

_______ (2007b) *Behrami and Behrami v. France*, Application no: 71412/01, Decision and *Saramati v. France, Germany and Norway*, Application no: 78166/01, Decision.

_______ (2007c) *Kasumaj v. Greece*, Application no: 6974/05, Decision.

_______ (2008) *Solomou and others v. Turkey*, Application no: 36832/97, Judgment.

_______ (2011a) *Al-Jedda v. The United Kingdom*, Application no: 27021/08, Judgment.

_______ (2011b) *Al-Skeini and others v. The United Kingdom*, Application no: 55721/07, Judgment.

_______ (2014a) *Hassan v. United Kingdom*, Application no: 29750/09, Judgment.

_______ (2014b) *Jaloud v. The Netherlands*, Application no: 47708/08, Judgment.

_______ (2015) *Pisari v. the Republic of Moldova and Russia*, Application no: 42139/12, Judgment.

_______ (2021a) *Georgia v. Russia (II)*, Application no: 38263/08, Judgment.

_______ (2021b) *Hanan v. Germany*, Application no: 4871/16, Judgment.

Giacca, G. (2014) *Economic, Social, and Cultural Rights in Armed Conflict*, Oxford University Press.

Hampson, F. (2008) 'The Relationship between International Humanitarian Law and Human Rights Law from the Perspective of a Human Rights Treaty Body', *International Review of the Red Cross* 871, 549-572.

Hill-Cawthorne, L. (2016) *Detention in Non-International Armed Conflicts*, Oxford University Press.

Inter-American Commission on Human Rights (1999) *Coard et al. v. United States (Merits)*, Report no. 109/99.

International Court of Justice (ICJ) (1980) Interpretation of the Agreement of 25 March 1951 between the WHO and Egypt, Advisory Opinion.

_______ (1996) Legality of the Threat or Use of Nuclear Weapons, Advisory Opinion.

_______ (2004) Legal Consequences of the Construction of a Wall in the Occupied Palestinian Territory, Advisory Opinion.

_______ (2005) Armed Activities on the Territory of the Congo (Democratic Republic of the Congo v. Uganda), Judgment.

Joseph, S. (2019) 'Extending the Right to Life under the International Covenant on Civil and Political Rights: General Comment 36', *Human Rights Law Review* 19, 347–368.

Larsen, K.M. (2012) *The Human Rights Treaty Obligations of Peacekeepers*, Cambridge University Press.

Longobardo, M. (2018) *The Use of Armed Force in Occupied Territory*, Cambridge University Press.

Milanovic, M. (2011) *Extraterritorial Application of Human Rights Treaties. Law, Principles, and Policy*, Oxford University Press.

Office of the High Commissioner for Human Rights (2016) The Minnesota Protocol on the Investigation of Potentially Unlawful Death.

Todeschini, V. (2018) 'The Impact of International Humanitarian Law on the Principle of Systemic Integration', *Journal of Conflict and Security Law* 23, 359–382.

UN Human Rights Committee (HRC) (2001) GC 29 on States of Emergency (Article 4), CCPR/C/21/Rev.1/Add.11.

_______ (2004a) GC 31 on the Nature of the General Legal Obligation on States Parties to the Covenant, CCPR/C/21/Rev.1/Add.13.

_______ (2004b) Concluding Observations: Belgium, CCPR/CO/81/BEL.

_______ (2014a) GC 35 on Article 9 (Liberty and Security of Person), CCPR/C/GC/35.

_______ (2014b) Concluding Observations: Israel, CCPR/C/ISR/CO/4.

_______ (2014c) Concluding Observations: United States of America, CCPR/C/USA/CO/4.

_______ (2015) Concluding Observations: Russia, CCPR/C/RUS/CO/7.

_______ (2018) GC 36 on Article 6 (The Right to Life), CCPR/C/GC/36.

UN Human Rights Council (2015) Report of the detailed findings of the independent commission of inquiry established pursuant to Human Rights Council resolution S-21/1, A/HRC/29/CRP.4.

29

Cybersecurity and extraterritorial obligations of states

Matthias C. Kettemann and Anna Sophia Tiedeke

Introduction[1]

Be it online or offline, be it in the kinetic world or in cyberspace: we need norms – and have always needed them. 'In the long march of mankind from the cave to the computer', as Shaw puts it in his introduction to international law, 'a central role has always been played by the idea of law – that order is necessary and chaos inimical to a just and stable existence' (Shaw 2021 p. 1). Cyberspace as a truly global infrastructure is governed by rules of international law (some aspects of it are also governed by national law and transnational normative arrangements (Kettemann 2020)), but for the purposes of assessing extraterritorial obligations, this article will focus on international law). Indeed, international law is the only area of law with which global (public) goods can be managed and global public interests protected (Kettemann 2020). The ubiquity of the technology underlying the Internet, which is not restricted by national borders, renders strictly single-state regulation largely ineffective. A failure to ensure cybersecurity in one state leads to less cybersecurity in all states, and therefore has a direct impact on human rights protection across borders. Ensuring cybersecurity within a state, and thereby contributing to cybersecurity extraterritorially, ensures the stability of the international order and thus has to be understood as a key element of the extraterritorial protection of human rights.

Cybersecurity has become a pressing issue for the public as well as the private sector over the last decades. Considering the cross-border character of incidents like the WannaCry Ransomware attack or the hack of the Democratic National Committee, resorting to international law to accord responsibility seems intuitive. Even though political and legal approaches to preventing cyberwar and cybercrime have attracted considerable attention internationally, cybersecurity as a human rights issue has received less attention. In this chapter we will therefore concentrate on cybersecurity as a human rights issue, with a specific focus on the extraterritorial obligations of states and private actors. After taking stock and setting out a comprehensive concept of cybersecurity, we will continue to explain why protecting cybersecurity lies in the common interest of all states irrespective of their borders. We will then outline how extraterritorial obligations of states are conceptually developed, and what obligations states have to ensure an adequate level of cybersecurity and human rights protection. After that, we will identify approaches to improve the protection of cybersecurity in international law. The contribution ends with conclusions.

DOI: 10.4324/9781003090014-36

Taking stock

International law is needed to legitimately and effectively ensure cybersecurity in the common interest of all states; and therefore, international law foresees extraterritorial obligations of states in cyberspace. This is not a new insight.

Already in 2010, in its resolution A/RES/64/211 the General Assembly promoted the creation of a global culture of cybersecurity and expressed concerns in light of growing threats to the reliable functioning of the Internet. The Resolution affirms that states are obliged to deal systematically with these threats and coordinate both with national stakeholders and internationally with the goal of facilitating the achievement of cybersecurity. A similar self-commitment to an international law-based Internet policy was already presented by the European Commission in 2014 (COM/2014/072 final) and is also part of the EU Cybersecurity Strategy for the Digital Decade European Digital Strategy of 2020. Although it might seem evident that without legitimate and effective protection of cybersecurity under international law individuals and societies cannot develop to their full potential, to view these issues as a human rights issue has not been evident until recently. The 2013 UN Group of Governmental Experts (GGE) Report underlined that applying norms derived from existing international law relevant to the use of information and communication technologies (ICTs) by states is an essential measure to reduce risks to international peace, security and stability. The UN Charter is applicable to the whole gamut of socioeconomic activity on the Internet in that it is 'essential to maintaining peace and stability and promoting an open, secure, peaceful and accessible ICT environment' (UN GGE 2013, para. 19).

Applying international law to the Internet lies in the common interest, and safeguarding the Internet as such also lies in the common interest because a stable, secure and functional Internet is essential for international security. Building on this consensus, the GGE Report 2015 confirmed that international law, the UN Charter and international legal principles apply to the Internet (para. 26). Stating *inter alia* that the international community aspires to regulate the Internet in a peaceful manner 'for the common good of mankind' (UN GGE 2015, para. 28 (c)), '[t]he adherence by States to international law, in particular their Charter obligations, is an essential framework for their actions in their use of ICTs and to promote an open, secure, stable, accessible and peaceful ICT environment' (para. 25). After the GGE could not arrive at a decision in 2017, in December 2019 the UN Cybersecurity Groups OEWG (Open-ended Working Group) and GGE held an informal meeting discussing four topics relating to cybersecurity. Apart from threat scenarios, the two groups discussed norms for responsible state behaviour in cyberspace, measures regarding confidence-building and capacity-building. In 2021 the OEWG and the GGE published separate reports, both reaffirming their general commitment regarding the applicability of international law and the UN Charter in cyberspace but also their preference for voluntary norms. The GGE Report 2021 also reiterated the group members' commitment to human rights (para. 36–41).

Ensuring cybersecurity and protecting the Internet's stability, security and functionality in the form of reducing the potential for criminal or terroristic misuses of computers and networks are important in the international fight against cybercrime. Criminals continue to misuse the Internet both for online variants of common scams and for Internet-specific (technology-based) attacks. The size of monetary loss is small compared to the scale of the Internet economy, but the problem is nevertheless serious. Black markets for both buying cybercrime tools (such as complete botnets for as little as 50 USD) and for selling on the proceeds of cybercrime activities (such as credit card information) are increasingly sophisticated, resilient and international (Ablon, Libicki and Golay 2014). This threat requires international cooperation. At the same time, some criminal misuses of the Internet are not direct threats to the Internet's integrity, as criminal networks rely on the Internet to conduct their activities. But other attacks, including Distributed-Denial-of-Service attacks (DDoS attacks) or others not linked to monetary gain – such as attacks to cause social unrest – can amount to substantial threats to the cybersecurity and the Internet's functionality.

Different levels of Internet security awareness and capabilities globally matter to all states because of the interconnectedness of ICTs and the networked nature of the Internet. These are amplified through disparities in national law, regulations and practices. Only international cooperation and the acknowledgement of extraterritorial obligations of states in the protection of the Internet can help to find answers to these challenges. In this context it is important to note with Wilde that '[e]xtraterritoriality is not the displacement of statism with cosmopolitanism', but rather a combination of the two (2016, p. 153). In our globalized world, where the focus of international law is shifting away from governments to (multistakeholder) governance, we need to take a close look at the extraterritorial human rights obligations of states. This will also require a shift of perspective from a territorial protection of human rights towards a functional perspective. This shift 'towards post-territoriality' (Kilovaty 2020, p. 50) is never more apt or more important than when assessing state obligations related to cybersecurity.

While public international law offers useful tools and perspectives on cybersecurity, it also 'suffers from a few fatal flaws that make it a less-than-perfect candidate to stymie the consequences of offensive cyberspace behaviour' (Kilovaty 2020, p. 36). The flaws are rooted in the fact that international law focuses mainly on states that are defined by territory, not on individuals that are affected by breaches of cybersecurity. Transnational legal arrangements, including technical standards and agreements, influence the exercise of power online and shape the normative order in which it is legitimated and contested (Kettemann 2020). Apart from security interests of states, ensuring cybersecurity is closely linked to extraterritorial protection of human rights on the Internet. However, until recently 'the majority of scholarship on transnational cyber operations has focused on the victim state's rights, such as sovereignty and territorial inviolability to delegitimize these operations' (Kilovaty 2020, p. 36). For a long time, human rights have not been in the spotlight of international cybersecurity debates. Looking at cybersecurity from a human rights perspective offers us the opportunity to see all dimensions of a cyberattack or the lack of cybersecurity. A human rights-based view on cybersecurity has the capacity to make the consequences of a lack of cybersecurity visible.

Towards a comprehensive concept of cybersecurity

Cybersecurity is defined very broadly by some states and is a legal (and policy) term that covers risks and threats such as cyberwarfare, cyberterrorism, cybercrime and cyberespionage. There is no doubt that cybersecurity is a crucial part of national domestic, security, foreign and defence policy. As a central theme of Internet policy, cybersecurity is closely linked with the stability, robustness, resilience and functionality of the Internet (Tikk-Ringas, 2015). Cybersecurity can be threatened by cybercrime and cyberterrorism, but also by a lack of legal and technical control of and cooperation between states and a lack of preventive measures, such as developing crisis intervention centres and teams, as well as transnational crisis communication structures for cyber-incidents. But can the term cybersecurity be useful in the context of a human rights discussion? In our view it is still too often the case that (cyber) security is contrasted with (Internet) freedom, and the two concepts are played against each other to the detriment of both. This view misses the point. As emphasized in the German Cybersecurity Strategy of 2016, what matters is that ensuring both freedom and security are among the core duties of the state – offline and online (Cyber-Sicherheitsstrategie für Deutschland 2016, p. 8).

The German Cybersecurity Strategy defines cybersecurity as 'IT security of the networked or network-capable information technology systems in cyberspace'. IT security is understood to be ensuring the 'intactness of the authenticity, confidentiality, integrity and availability of information technology systems and the data processed and stored within these systems' (2016, p. 24). This definition is very technology oriented and too short-sighted in light of how cybersecurity is practically perceived by business and society. The security on the Internet and of the Internet cannot simply be equated with the security of systems and data. Just as security has rightfully been understood more recently as human security, cybersecurity needs to include a human rights perspective.

Protecting cybersecurity lies in the common interest of all states

Already in 1998, experts working for the UNESCO asked the question whether the United Nations General Assembly [could] affirm the principle of regarding cyberspace as 'the common heritage of humanity' (UNESCO 1998, para. 9) and thus safeguard it. In the end, they failed to answer the question, which was well enough, because it was actually the wrong one to be posed in the first place. It is not 'cyberspace' we should concern ourselves with, but rather the Internet itself; and rather than using the concept of common heritage of mankind, which presupposes a certain historical stability the Internet does not have, we rather need to establish why protecting the Internet lies in the global common interest. Though 'common interest' still lacks a clear definition (Feichtner 2007, para. 1), the protection of the Internet's key resources as lying in the common interest is firmly anchored in international documents. It is also in the common interest to protect human rights as the commitment during the World Summits on the Information Society (WSIS) show.

In a statement of the WSIS, which the UN convened in 2003 and 2005 to establish a normative trajectory for the Internet, states affirmed their common desire and commitment to build an information society that is 'people-centred, inclusive and development-oriented' (WSIS 2003, para. 1). Their goal was that individuals, communities and peoples can 'achieve their full potential in promoting their sustainable development and improving their quality of life premised on the purposes and principles' of the UN Charter and respecting fully and upholding the Universal Declaration of Human Rights (UDHR) (WSIS 2003, para. 1). This is a first, clear answer to the question what 'vision' the international community pursues regarding the impact of the Internet. To put it concisely: the Internet is envisaged to serve humankind. Of course, achieving world peace and international security, ensuring human development and respecting, protecting and implementing human rights – as normatively ordered in the UDHR – are in the global common interest.

But is protecting cybersecurity and thus the Internet's integrity essential for reaching these goals? UN Special Rapporteur for freedom of expression, Frank La Rue, in a ground-breaking report on the impact of the Internet on freedom of expression, described the Internet as a 'catalyst for individuals to exercise their right to freedom of opinion and expression'. He called freedom of expression on the Internet itself a 'facilitator of the realisation of a range of other human rights' (paras. 22 and 23). The multiple challenges that the Internet brings for human rights notwithstanding (Jørgensen 2006 and 2019), the absence of the Internet or of an Internet without cybersecurity would seriously challenge the realization of human rights. There are important corollary rights that are premised upon exercising free speech on the Internet, like the freedoms of assembly and association online, and the right to digital education. From all these rights we can also derive a right to access to online information and communication, which is crucial for human development. Similar arguments have been voiced by courts and international organizations (e.g., CoE Res. 1877/2012; ECtHR *Yildirim v. Turkey*, 2012). Even though the Internet simultaneously introduces new threat vectors to human rights, it greatly enhances the potential of people to realize their human rights. It is similarly a facilitator for human security.

In the same vein, the UN GGE report of 2013 determined that the application of norms derived from existing international law is 'essential' to minimize risks to world peace and international security and stability (para. 16). Viewed in the context of information technology challenges, cybersecurity is now one aspect of 'world peace' (para. 16). When analyzing the protection of cybersecurity under international law, the GGE report 2015 that was adopted in consensus by a representative group of governmental experts is very helpful, stating *inter alia* that the international community aspires to regulate the Internet in a peaceful manner 'for the common good of mankind'. Protecting cybersecurity is a common interest of all states. This community interest is not an aggregate of the individual sets of interests; rather, it lies at their intersection. If a protected interest is part of the community interest, this entails consequences relevant to international human rights law. States are therefore responsible to the international community, with regard to cybersecurity according to their judicial authority over critical infrastructures pertinent to it in that 'States should take appropriate measures to protect their critical infrastructure from ICT threats, taking into account General Assembly resolution 58/199 (UN GGE 2021, para. 47–50).

Therefore, to the extent that a state controls Critical Internet Resources (CIRs), e.g., the Internet's backbone infrastructure, Internet protocol numbers, name root servers and the Domain Name System (DNS), it has to exercise this jurisdiction mindful of threats to cybersecurity, and especially the security of these CIRs in a manner that ensures the common interest. To the extent that national politics (and policies) can impact the Internet negatively, a state has to refrain from their formulation and implementation. A state's sovereignty is reduced because of the limits the protection of the Internet as a common interest lays upon it. The US, when it exercised its soft control over Internet key resources, via the Department of Commerce's naming and numbering oversight functions, only exercised 'custodial sovereignty' (Scholtz 2008). This implied that the US had to enter into consultations with other states with regard to the management of CIRs and made sure that the management was transparent and accountable, ideally to the international community and now, after the transition (National Telecommunications and Information Administration (NTIA) 2016), to the global multistakeholder community. All other states, insofar as they can endanger the Internet's stability, security and functionality, are pre-empted from doing so. In assessing whether politics may impact the Internet negatively, it makes sense to suggest the precautionary principle as a guide to decision-making.

A second consequence is that humankind – that is all actors making up the international community, and not only states – has a legitimate interest in making sure that all other actors protect the Internet (or at least do not actively harm it). Though sovereignty oriented states have suggested exclusive sovereignty over national Internet segments, the character of the Internet as protected by international law as a common interest limits their sovereignty. The 2005 Tunis Agenda, though valuable in its description of the normative goals of the information society, still lays down that 'policy authority for internet-related public policy issues' is a 'sovereign right of States' (WSIS 2005, para. 35). The internal and external dimensions of sovereignty relate to the control over territory and individuals, cyberactivity and infrastructure inside that territory and the capacity of states to maintain international relations (Schmitt 2017, p. 4).

This needs to be qualified in light of a common interest approach to protect the Internet, in that the state's policy authority no longer is an exclusively sovereign right, but part and parcel of their sovereignty, to be exercised in the common interest. What sovereignty they have over Internet-related resources has to be understood in light of changing circumstances and the importance of the pursuance of common interests. As far as international law extends to non-state actors, these are also under obligation to conform to, and support, the common pursuance of the global interest in safeguarding the Internet's integrity. This means, for example, that there is an international law-based duty, via the Ruggie Principles of 2011, for companies to respect human rights and rights of victims of business-related abuses and their right to access to remedies. International law has arrived at a point in its development where pursuing the common interest, as Fassbender put it, is the only reasonable answer to its *Sinnfrage* (Fassbender 2002, p. 231). Ensuring a people-centric and development-oriented Internet is one of the key challenges for international law today. To protect human rights effectively, the protection of the integrity of the Internet and the guarantee of cybersecurity as a common interest are essential. The extraterritorial application of political and civil but especially economic, social and cultural human rights, is one of the key measures to ensure the respect for and the protection and fulfilment of cybersecurity, and thereby a people-centric and development-oriented Internet.

Extraterritorial human rights obligations of states

When we talk about extraterritoriality, we think about 'the competence of a state to make, apply and enforce rules of conduct in respect of persons, property or events beyond its territory' (Kamminga 2012, para. 1) and the human rights obligations of states that extend beyond the borders of states' territory. Even though the discussion on extraterritorial obligations has been going on for a long time, what remains undetermined is the substance of these obligations. A strict territorial reading of human rights frameworks would render the protection under these frameworks ineffective, when thinking about the protection of these rights in the context of cybersecurity. This holds true in particular in the area of economic, social and cultural human rights, which 'may directly or indirectly be impaired by cross-border "externalities"'(Askin 2019, para. 1). Even though the ICESCR does not contain a provision on territorial applicability and despite the fact that the ICJ addressed the primarily territorial character of the obligations under the ICESCR in its Advisory Opinion Concerning Legal Consequences of the Construction of a Wall in the Occupied Palestinian Territory (para. 112.), the ICESCR was always interpreted to contain an 'international feature' (Askin 2019, para. 14) and, therefore, an obligation for assistance and cooperation. However, the contours of the obligations remained blurred. In this regard, jurisdiction serves merely as one threshold criterion (Peters 2018, p. 303), especially in cyberspace which presents 'new forms of extraterritorial human rights infringements' (Askin 2019, para. 19). This and other new forms of infringements made revisiting the problem necessary.

The *Maastricht Principles* on extraterritorial obligations of states in the area of economic, social and cultural rights (*Maastricht Principles*) were drafted in 2011 with the intention to finally make some decisive progress. As the preamble of the *Maastricht Principles* 2011 states: 'Drawn from international law, these principles aim *to clarify the content of extraterritorial State obligations* to realize economic, social and cultural rights with a view to advancing and giving full effect to the object of the UN Charter and international human rights' (para. 8 (emphasis added)). The *Maastricht Principles* follow a 'facticist conception of jurisdiction' (Askin 2019, para. 25), envisaged to close the gap in the universal human rights protection, caused by the fact that 'States still interpret their human rights obligations as being applicable only within their borders' (*Maastricht Principles* 2011, p. 3). As cyberspace is the space in which the challenges of extraterritorial obligations are not only most visible but also amplified, clarifying the scope of extraterritorial human rights obligations of states in online settings is of particular importance. However, whereas the extraterritorial obligation of states to protect civil and political human rights is well established by judgments of the ECtHR (*Loizidou v. Turkey; Al-Skeini and Others v United Kingdom; Öcalan v Turkey*) and determined by the 'effective control test', the protection of social, economic and cultural human rights (so called second generation of human rights) has not yet been equipped with a robust framework of hard legal obligations (Askin 2019, para. 7).

Even though the Committee on Economic, Social and Cultural Rights (CESCR) also relied on the effective control test in the context of Crimea (Concluding Observations on the Sixth Periodic Report of the Russian Federation, paras. 9–10), in many regards the contours of the extraterritorial protection of economic, social and cultural rights are still not defined. This fact may have led Wilde to observe: 'The Maastricht initiative notwithstanding, commentary on extraterritorial applicability remains skewed towards coverage of civil and political rights, and the determinations by the CESCR and the jurisprudence of the ICJ notwithstanding, international enforcement remains similarly skewed' (2020, p. 68). Despite this accurate observation, we should not make the mistake to discard the *Maastricht Principles*.

On the contrary, the *Maastricht Principles* are a crucial tool that helps us analyse the different dimensions of extraterritorial obligations of states. The *Maastricht Principles* 'invite us to see human rights as global public good, and a guide for the reshaping of the international legal order' (De Schutter 2012, p. vii). The open character of the *Maastricht principles* offers us a new way of speaking about extraterritorial human rights obligations of states. As De Schutter trenchantly notes, 'they are sufficiently precise to provide a focal point for deliberations as to how to build international regimes – how to regulate trade, how much to protect foreign investors, or how to allocate the responsibilities in combating climate change – yet they are vague enough not to pre-empt the result of these deliberations' (2012, p. vii). By approaching the issue in three steps ('to respect, to protect and to fulfil') (*Maastricht Principles* 2011, p. 8), we will show how the *Maastricht Principles* provide us with a language to formulate standards regarding the obligations of states more precisely. The three different dimensions may, e.g., oblige states to conduct a human rights impact assessment, considering real and foreseeable effects of their conduct abroad, and to put in place measures that ensure that they respect and protect human rights and under specific circumstances fulfil these rights, too. Following the CESCR, in an extraterritorial setting, the main focus lies on the dimension of protection, which means that 'States parties [are obliged] to take steps to prevent and redress infringements of Covenant rights that occur outside their territories due to the activities of business entities over which they can exercise control, especially in cases where the remedies available to victims before the domestic courts of the state where the harm occurs are unavailable or ineffective' (CESCR 2017, para. 33).

Enhancing the effectiveness of extraterritorial human rights obligations in cyberspace

The commitment of the WSIS in 2005 to a 'people-centred, inclusive and development-oriented Information Society' (WSIS 2005, no. 2), to 'the universality, indivisibility, interdependence and interrelation of all human rights and fundamental freedoms, including the right to development, as enshrined in the Vienna Declaration' (WSIS 2005, no. 2), to a stable and secure Internet as a worldwide institution and to the multi-stakeholder approach (WSIS 2005, no. 3) may serve us as guidance in order to identify relevant principles of international law that protects cyberspace as a common interest. We will then show how applying the *Maastricht Principles* can help explain and legitimize a shift towards due diligence in the protection of cyberspace.

Protection of cyberspace as common interest via principles

Particularly relevant to ensuring and promoting cybersecurity are the following principles of international law: sovereign equality, the ban on aggression and intervention, peaceful settlement of disputes, the protection of human rights, the cooperation principle (which draws on the principle of good neighbourliness ('no harm') and the precautionary principle ('due diligence')). Some of these principles have been translated into treaty law in the UN Charter, some are protected under customary international law or are recognized as part of the general principles of international law.

The principle of sovereign equality is a key principle of international law. As a 'pivotal principle' (Besson 2011, para. 1) it is also of special importance for cybersecurity. Each state has jurisdiction and power over its territory and over the ICT infrastructure located there; this also means, however, that it bears a responsibility to ensure that no attacks against other states or institutions, which would infringe on international law, are organized or carried out from its territory.

In addition, the non-intervention principle can be brought to fruition: an intense damage to Internet functionality in another state (e.g., by cyber-attacks) could constitute an intervention, although attribution problems will regularly arise. Only some of the attacks originating from the territory of a state represent an 'intervention' in terms of international law, because most attacks will be attributable to non-governmental protagonists, or to protagonists whose association with governmental agencies cannot be proven (GGE 2015, para. 28 (f)).

The ban on the use of force prohibits states from using measures of power beyond simple 'intervention' (the former being stated in the non-intervention principle). In the context of the Internet, this article could only be applied to especially serious cases of cyberattacks with substantial kinetic effects. The principle of peaceful settlement of disputes is relevant to cybersecurity insofar as any state has the duty, in the event of an incident, to first determine the facts and to collect evidence for attribution of a breach of international law to a particular state. Even if this succeeds, peaceful means of dispute settlement should first be sought. The principle of the protection of human rights is a fundamental principle of international law that is also relevant to cybersecurity. What is problematic under international law are attempts by a state to enforce cybersecurity through an excessive control of the Internet (such as setting up and using surveillance capabilities, or government screening of all Internet communication). The principle of good neighbourliness (UN Charter, Friendly Relations Declaration, art. 74), or 'no harm' principle, can be considered as a global principle in the Internet era. Originally only relevant in terms of the relationship with adjacent states, the principle has been gradually extended. In the Corfu Channel Case, the ICJ described the principle as 'every state's obligation not to knowingly allow its territory to be used for acts contrary to the rights of other states' (p. 22).

The 'no harm' principle has its roots in the *Trail Smelter Arbitration* and *Lac Lanoux Arbitration*. It was formulated in Principle 21 of the Stockholm Declaration of 1972 and Principle 2 of the Rio Declaration of 1992: signatory states are committed 'to ensure that activities within their jurisdiction or control do not cause damage to the environment of other states or of areas beyond the limits of national jurisdiction'. This can be easily applied to other areas in analogy to the environment. The obligation to prevent cross-border damage has crystallized into customary law. Confirmation of treaty consent to this matter can be found in Art. 194 (2) of the UN Convention on the Law of the Sea of 1982 and Art. 20 (1) of the ASEAN Agreement on the

Conservation of Nature and Natural Resources of 1985. Most recently, the ICJ confirmed in the Nuclear Weapons Advisory Opinion (1996, p. 226, para. 29) that the threat to the environment is 'no abstraction but represents the living space, the quality of life and the very health of human beings, including generations unborn'. In accordance with the 'no harm' principle, no state may utilize its dominion in such a manner that would cause damage to other states. In the preventive dimension of the 'no harm' principle, a state must take measures to prevent such hazards. Among other things, a commitment to an appropriate infrastructure, the development of emergency plans and the establishment of an international crisis cooperation structure (and culture) can be construed from this.

The shift towards due diligence

The precautionary principle ('due diligence') is of special importance for cybersecurity. Firstly, the due diligence principle entails information and consultation obligations (Koivurova 2010, para. 3). In the scientific world, it is controversial as to what extent the precautionary principle has a 'due diligence' dimension. or whether the precautionary obligations of states are covered in practice by the 'no harm' principle. The *Maastricht Principles* may give some guidance in this regard, as Principle no. 14 foresees an impact assessment and prevention of adverse effects on economic, social and cultural human rights. Along with state obligations based on individual human rights communicators, recipients and the contents of communications are protected by Art. 19 ICCPR, which has largely crystallized into customary law. Positive obligations related to Internet infrastructure can also be derived from state obligations to provide protection and assurance pertaining to information- and communication-related rights (Kettemann 2020, p. 226). Following the *Maastricht Principles*, states are therefore obliged to respect, protect and fulfil the sustainability and security of the networks in order to allow individuals to realize their human rights, extraterritorially.

With some justification, normative principles for the regulation of cybersecurity can therefore be derived from the principle of due diligence that is reflected in Principle 14 of the *Maastricht Principles*. As a result, the responsibility of states includes not only the duty to prevent and stop cyberattacks originating from their own territory and to (proactively) establish a legal system that ensures and fosters cybersecurity (Schmitt 2015), but also to provide effective remedy in such cases.

All of these are duties which, when translated for cybersecurity, imply certain 'preparatory' duties for states as substantiation of the precautionary principle. We are all neighbours on the Internet, and just as states cannot let their power plants pollute the air in neighbouring states, their ill-secured *national* networks and tools can be misused to attack third countries. They who leave a gun lying around or a car unlocked can be held liable for what happens with the gun or the car. States that fail to adhere to their due diligence obligations leave themselves open to attack and may be held responsible under, e.g., Articles 2 or 9 ASR.

In its preventive dimension, the due diligence principle helps to identify the obligations of states with regard to cybersecurity, particularly with regard to cybercrime, global cooperation and establishment of capacities. Cybersecurity due diligence was described as part of customary international law, whereby particularly the following preventive duties have emerged as recognized obligations under international law: that governments and other stakeholders bolster cybersecurity and develop cybersecurity strategies to protect crucial infrastructures (UN GA Res 64/221), that states (and other relevant stakeholders) work together more closely in the fight against cybercrime and cyberterrorism, and that they ratify conventions such as the Convention on Cybercrime of the Council of Europe, that states conclude treaties promoting cooperation between their police authorities and that states establish confidence-building measures and increase the level of information sharing, generally as well as (and especially) in the event of cybersecurity related incidents (UN GGE 2013, paras 22, 26 et seq.).

This can be fulfilled, for instance, by 'passing stringent criminal laws, conducting vigorous investigations, prosecuting attackers, and, during the investigation and prosecution, cooperating with the victim-states of cyberattacks that originated from within their borders' (Sklerov 2009, p. 62). The GGE also agreed that human rights law applies to cyber activities and that 'States must not use proxies to commit internationally wrongful acts' (UN GGE 2013, paras 20–23). Confidence-building measures are more extensive than obligations under international law, ensuing from the duty of cooperation (OSCE Decision No. 1202, 2016). They are relevant to the evolution of legal norms, however, insofar as they indicate the direction of how obligations under international law are developing.

In fact, the *Maastricht Principles* take the due diligence principle one step further. With the three steps approach, the Principles have contributed to a more concrete understanding of the extraterritorial human rights obligations of states.

The duty to respect is designed as a negative obligation that requires states to directly or indirectly refrain from infringing upon human rights outside their territory. It is widely recognized, and the CESCR in its General Comment No. 14 even uses the language of 'have to' with respect to these negative duties (E/C.12/2000/4, para. 39). This dimension can, therefore, easily be integrated into 'existing human rights architecture' (Askin 2019, para. 31). However, it also poses some challenges in the context of the distinction between positive and negative human obligations of states, and the wide scope of protection carries the risk that these obligations become frayed and thus ineffective.

The duty to protect is a positive obligation. However, it depends on the degree of involvement. The protective ambit increases relative to the state's involvement. The duty to protect may require states to establish mechanisms to ensure that cross border activity of companies has no adverse effects on human rights. This can be understood as a duty to implement a legal framework that ensures 'human rights due diligence in order to identify, prevent and mitigate the risk of violations of the Covenant rights' (CESCR 2017, para. 14). If a state fails to implement an effective legal framework even though it has the capacity, it might violate its due diligence obligations under international law.

The duty to fulfil reflects the third step of effective extraterritorial protection of human rights. The 'obligation of international assistance and cooperation' (ICESCR, art. 2(1)) is to be understood as an obligation of states that have the possibility to assist to do so. This dimension rests controversial (Askin 2019, para. 37) and has merely been considered a secondary dimension of the extraterritorial obligations. A state will not be obliged to fulfil the right to cybersecurity in a third state, but it is obliged to respect it and may be obliged to protect it, depending on the level and intensity of its influence/involvement. This shows that, dogmatically, it is becoming increasingly difficult to differentiate legally between the three dimensions. However, in the multistakeholder setting of cybersecurity, the duty to assist and cooperate could offer an effective tool to ensure a high level of cybersecurity for individuals as well as for states themselves.

Shedding some light on the grey zones

In the light of the importance of the Internet for states, business and society, cybersecurity – as a prerequisite for a reliably functioning and secure Internet and therefore for the protection of human rights – has become a global community interest, which needs protection. The technologicalization and informationalization of many key infrastructure provision functions and of many industry control systems open up new vulnerabilities within states and across territorial borders that can threaten, if an attack is substantial, international peace and security and thereby humans and their rights. Similarly, the increased use of mobile devices and cloud computing and the use of social networks increase the vulnerability of citizens to acts of cybercrime.

Cybersecurity is a key functional condition for an era defined by information and communications technology. States must step up and take on the responsibility through an (effective) extraterritorial application of human rights and the principles and processes of international law. Otherwise, there is no possibility to shed light onto the still existing grey zones of international law in the protection of cyberspace (Schmitt 2017, p. 21). Only if the obligations are clarified, the room for exploitation of grey zones will shrink and, as Schmitt put it: 'The brighter the red-lines of international law as applied to cyber activities, the less opportunity States will have to exploit grey zones in ways that create instability' (2017, p. 21). Kilovaty therefore promotes a 'new' human right, the human right to cybersecurity (2020, p. 52). He envisages a 'robust human right to cybersecurity' (2020, p. 54) that protects individuals from 'carefully tailored cyber operations' and, e.g., establishes encryption in private communication of individuals as a default standard as was suggested by the UN Human Rights Special Procedures, Mandate of the Special Rapporteur in his Encryption and Anonymity Follow-Up Report (p. 4 no. 7 and HRC 2017, para. 9).

Establishing a baseline cybersecurity or more advanced forms are necessary for states to implement in order to meet their obligations under international human rights law: the debate on how best to ensure a stable and resilient Internet for all is far from over – and it is international law that provides the impetus, frame and objective of the debate. The *Maastricht Principles* serve and will continue to serve as guidance for the extraterritorial application of obligations under international law. However, applying the recent judgment of the German Federal Constitutional Court (BND judgment, 2020) and considering the growing body of literature on extraterritorial human rights obligations, especially cyberspace-related activities might emerge as a reference field for the diminishing importance of the difference between acts 'from within' a territory that have extraterritorial applications and acts 'outside of a territory' that have outside (or even inside-of-territory) implications.

Succinctly put: human rights-related extraterritorial obligations of states serve to make this obligation more concrete and are important normative vectors for an increasingly robust protection of cybersecurity by all states, within and outside of their territories. Notwithstanding recent trends towards reterritorialization on the Internet, we are and continue to be all neighbours in cyberspace with a potential *Trail Smelter* lying in each smart refrigerator, home router and unsecure local library network. While the challenges this implies for international law, human rights obligations and international legal scholarship have not all been clearly delineated yet, some key ones are distilled in this contribution.

Note

1. This contribution builds on ideas previously published in Kettemann, The Normative Order of the Internet (Oxford: Oxford University Press 2020). The authors express their thanks to Mark Gibney, Markus Krajewski and Vito Todeschini for valuable comments and to Rike Heyer, Johanna Friederike Stelling (Hamburg) and Ilse Kettemann (Graz) for valuable editorial support.

References

Ablon, L., Libicki, Martin C. and Golay, A.A. (2014) *Markets for Cybercrime Tools and Stolen Data: Hackers' Bazaar*, RAND National Security Research Division.

Agreement on the Conservation of Nature and Natural Resources, (1985) Association of South East Asian Nations (ASEAN)

Askin, E. (2019) 'Economic and Social Rights, Extraterritorial Application', *Max Planck Encyclopedia of Public International Law*

Arbitral Tribunal (1941) *Trail Smelter Case (United States v. Canada)*, United Nations, Reports of International Arbitral Awards 3, 1905–1982.

Arbitral Tribunal (1957) *Lac Lanoux (France v. Spain)*, 12 R.I.A.A. 281, Arbitral decision of 16 November 1957 United Nations, Reports of International Arbitral Awards XII.

Besson, S. (2011) 'Sovereignty', *Max Planck Encyclopedia of Public International Law*.

Charter of the United Nations (1945) 1 UNTS XVI, available at https://www.refworld.org/docid/3ae6b3930.html [accessed 8 October 2020].

Communication by the European Commission to the European Parliament, the European Council (2014) the European Economic and Social Committee and the Committee of the Regions: Internet Policy and Internet Governance, Europe's Role in Shaping the Future of Internet Governance, COM/2014/072 final.

Council of Europe (2012) Parliamentary Assembly Resolution 1877 on the protection of freedom of expression and information on the Internet and online media.

Cyber-Sicherheitsstrategie für Deutschland (2016) Bundesministerium des Innern, für Bau und Heimat.

De Schutter, O. (2012) 'Foreword' in Coomans, F. and Künnemann, R. (eds). *Cases and Concepts on Extraterritorial Obligations in the Area of Economic, Social and Cultural Rights*, Intersentia Publishing Ltd.

European Court of Human Rights (ECtHR) Judgments:

_______ (1995) *Loizidou v. Turkey*, Application no. 40/1993/435/514.

_______ (2003) *Öcalan v. Turkey*, Application no. 46221/99.

_______ (2011) *Al-Skeini and Others v. United Kingdom*, Application no. 55721/07.

_______ (2012) *Yildirim v. Turkey*, Application no. 3111/10.

Fassbender, B. (2002) 'Zwischen Staatsräson und Gemeinschaftsbindung. Zur Gemeinwohlorientierung des Völkerrechts der Gegenwart' in Münkler, H. and Fischer, K. (eds). *Gemeinwohl und Gemeinsinn im Recht: Konkretisierung und Realisierung öffentlicher Interessen*, Akademie Verlag.

Feichtner, I. (2007) 'Community Interest', *Max Planck Encyclopedia of Public International Law*.

German Federal Constitutional Court (BVerfG) (2020) *BND-Judgment*, 1 BvR 2835/17, Judgment.

Human Rights Council (2017) The Right to Privacy in the Digital Age, U.N. Doc. A/HRC/RES/34/7.

International Court of Justice (ICJ):

_______ (1949) Corfu Channel Case (*United Kingdom v. Albania*), Merits.

_______ (1996) Advisory Opinion, Legality of the Threat or Use of Nuclear Weapons, I.C.J. Reports 1996, p. 226.

_______ (2004) Advisory Opinion Concerning Legal Consequences of the Construction of a Wall in the Occupied Palestinian Territory.

International Covenant on Civil and Political Rights (ICCPR) (1966), *United Nations, Treaty Series* 999, 171.

International Law Commission (2001) Draft Articles on Responsibility of States for Internationally Wrongful Acts (ASR), Supplement No. 10 (A/56/10), chp.IV.E.1,

Jørgensen, R.F. (ed). (2006) *Human Rights in the Global Information Society*, Cambridge MIT Press.

_______ (2019) *Human Rights in the Age of Platforms*, Cambridge MIT Press.

Kamminga, M.T. (2012) 'Extraterritoriality', *Max Planck Encyclopedias of Public International Law*.

Kettemann, M.C. (2020) *The Normative Order of the Internet. A Theory of Rule and Regulation*, Oxford University Press.

Kilovaty, I. (2020) 'An Extraterritorial Human Right to Cybersecurity', *Notre Dame Journal of International & Comparative Law* 10(1), 35–55.

Koivurova, T. (2010) 'Due Diligence', *Max Planck Encyclopedia of Public International Law.*

La Rue, F. (2011) Report of the Special Rapporteur on the promotion and protection of the right to freedom of opinion and expression, UN Doc. A/HRC/17/27.

Maastricht Principles on Extraterritorial Obligations of States in the Area of Economic, Social and Cultural, Rights, The Secretariat to the ETO Consortium is currently hosted by FIAN International

National Telecommunications and Information Administration (NTIA) (2016) NTIA Finds IANA Stewardship Transition Proposal Meets Criteria to Complete Privatization, 9 June.

Organization for Security and Co-operation in Europe (OSCE) (2016) Decision no. 1202: OSCE Confidence-Building Measures to Reduce the Risks of Conflict Stemming from the Use of Information and Communication Technologies, PC.DEC/1202.

Peters, A. (2018) 'Global Constitutionalism – The Social Dimension' in Suami, T., Peters, A., Vanoverbeke, D. and Kumm, M. (eds). *Global Constitutionalism from European and East Asian Perspectives*, Cambridge University Press.

Ruggie, J. (2011) 'Guiding Principles on Business and Human Rights: Implementing the United Nations "Protect, Respect and Remedy" Framework', UN Doc. A/HRC/17/31.

Schmitt, M. (2015) *In Defense of Due Diligence in Cyberspace*, Yale Law Journal Forum 125, 68–81.

_______ (2017) 'Grey Zones in International Law of Cyberspace', *The Yale Journal of International Law* 42(2), 1–21.

Scholtz, W. (2008) 'Custodial Sovereignty: Reconciling Sovereignty and Global Environmental Challenges amongst the Vestiges of Colonialism', *Netherlands International Law Review* 3, 323–341.

Shaw, M.N. (2021) *International Law*, 9th Ed., Oxford University Press.

Sklerov, M.J. (2009) 'Solving the Dilemma of State Responses to Cyberattacks: A Justification for the Use of Active Defenses against States Who Neglect Their Duty to Prevent', *Military Law Review* 201, 1–85.

The EU's Cybersecurity Strategy for the Digital Decade (2020) Joint communication of the European Commission and the High Representative of the Union for Foreign Affairs and Security Policy to the European Parliament and the Council Brussels, 16.12.2020 JOIN (2020) 18 final

Tikk-Ringas, E. (ed). (2015) *Evolution of the Cyber Domain: The Implications for National and Global Security*, London Routledge.

UN Committee on Economic, Social and Cultural Rights (CESCR) (2017) GC 24 on State obligations under the International Covenant on Economic, Social and Cultural Rights in the context of business activities, E/C.12/GC/24.

UN Human Rights Special Procedures (2018) Mandate of the Special Rapporteur in his Encryption and Anonymity Follow-Up Report, Research Paper 1/2018.

United Nations General Assembly (UN GA) Resolutions:

_______ (1970) Declaration on Principles of International Law concerning Friendly Relations and Cooperation among States in accordance with the Charter of the United Nations, A/RES/2625(XXV).

_______ (2010) Creation of a global culture of cybersecurity and taking stock of national efforts to protect critical information infrastructures, A/RES/64/211.

UN Group of Governmental Experts (UN GGE) (2013) Developments in the Field of Information and Telecommunications in the Context of International Security, Report of the Group of Governmental Experts on Developments in the Field of Information and Telecommunications in the Context of International Security, UN Doc. A/68/98.

_______ (2015) Developments in the Field of Information and Telecommunications in the Context of International Security, Report of the Secretary General, A/70/174.

_______ (2021) Report of the Group of Governmental Experts on Advancing responsible State behaviour in cyberspace in the context of international security, Advance copy of the consensus report adopted by the Group on 28 May 2021.

UN Open Ended Working Group (UN OEWG) (2021) Final Substantive Report of the Open-ended working group on developments in the field of information and telecommunications in the context of international security, UN Doc. A/AC.290/2021/CRP.2

United Nations Educational, Scientific and Cultural Organization (UNESCO) (1998) Report of the Experts' Meeting on Cyberspace Law, Monte Carlo 29-30, available at http://unesdoc.unesco.org/images/0011/001163/116300e.pdf.

United Nations Environment Programme (UNEP) (1992), Rio Declaration on Environment and Development (UN Doc A/CONF.151/5/Rev.1, UN Doc A/CONF.151/26/Rev.1 Vol.1, Annex 1.

United Nations (UN) Stockholm Declaration of the United Nations Conference on the Human Environment (1972), UN Doc A/CONF.48/14/Rev.1, 3, UN Doc A/CONF.48/PC/6, Principle 21.

Wilde, R. (2016) 'Dilemmas in Promoting Global Economic Justice through Human Rights Law' in Bhuta, N. (ed). *The Frontiers of Human Rights: Extraterritoriality and Its Challenges, Collected Courses of the Academy of European Law*, Oxford University Press.

_______ (2020) 'Pursuing Global Socio-Economic, Colonial and Environmental Justice through Economic Redistribution: The Potential Significance of Human Rights Treaty Obligations' in Binder et al. (eds). *Research Handbook on International Law and Social Rights*, Edward Elgar.

World Summits on the Information Society (WSIS) (2003) Geneva Declaration of Principles, WSIS-03/GENEVA/DOC/4-E.

WSIS (2005) Tunis Agenda for the Information Society, WSIS-05/TUNIS/DOC/6 (Rev. 1).

Part VII

Environment

30

Climate justice and the ETOs

Sara L. Seck

Introduction

The aim of the *Maastricht Principles on the Extraterritorial Obligations of States in the area of Economic, Social, and Cultural Rights (Maastricht Principles)* has been described as to 'clarify extraterritorial obligations of states' (ETOs) on the basis of existing international law, rather than to 'establish new elements of human rights law' (Greenpeace and CIEL 2014, p. 5). Two key questions arise from this ambition in the context of climate crisis and the quest for climate justice. First, can the *Maastricht Principles* be said to have contributed to a clarification of the law so as to assist in conceptualizing the legal obligations of states and other actors to prevent and remedy human rights harms arising from anthropogenic climate change? Secondly, are new elements of human rights law necessary to address the complexity of obligation in the context of climate crisis that go beyond the ETOs?

This chapter will consider both questions in turn. I will first consider some key conceptual issues of relevance to both the ETOs and the quest for climate justice. Second, with reference to several examples, I will illustrate how the concept of extraterritoriality may create confusion rather than clarity, especially in the climate context. I will then explore whether this confusion may be overcome if attention is paid to the precise nature of the relationships at issue to which obligations attach, rather than reinforcing the bright line of politically defined territorial boundaries. In conclusion, I will consider the implications of the right to a safe, clean, healthy, and sustainable environment, including a safe climate system, for ETOs and climate justice.

Conceptual issues

The key sources of international law relevant to the climate crisis are found within the international climate regime, including the 1992 United Nations Framework Convention on Climate Change (UNFCCC) and the 2015 Paris Agreement. Obligations of states under the climate regime are often classified as relating to mitigation or adaptation. Mitigation refers to efforts to reduce greenhouse gas (GHGs) emissions as well as efforts to enhance carbon sinks (UNFCCC (n.d.a)). There are many ways to reduce GHGs, including through decreased use of fossil fuels or by expanding forests to remove GHGs from the atmosphere. Yet, while mitigation of GHGs

DOI: 10.4324/9781003090014-38

is clearly essential to reduce climate harms, and so has a positive impact on the enjoyment of human rights, the development of new green energy projects to replace reliance upon fossil fuels often lead to violations of human rights if undertaken without regard to the rights of local and Indigenous communities, among others (BHRRC 2020). Similarly, the expansion of forest carbon stocks in developing countries as encouraged under the climate regime's REDD-plus has also been associated with violations of the rights of local and Indigenous communities (FOEI 2017). Moreover, as the climate regime encourages both the creation of offsets and the trading of carbon credits, the spatial dimensions of climate mitigation become blurred: from a human rights perspective, how are we to understand the human rights responsibilities of a state that fails to reduce its own emissions (by failing to reduce reliance upon fossil fuels, for example) yet purchases carbon offsets from a developing state (where the forest carbon sink is being developed on lands from which a local community has been forcibly displaced)?

This story is further complicated by the importance of common but differentiated responsibilities and respective capabilities (CBDR) which remains fundamental to the climate regime including under the Paris Agreement even as it has evolved to embrace a pragmatic approach (Galvao Ferreira 2018). The original justice-based version of CBDR under the UNFCCC and Kyoto Protocol informed the central obligations of states to reduce GHG emissions, distinguishing clearly between the obligations of developed and developing states, with the obligation to 'go first' placed on developed states due to both greater capabilities and historic responsibilities (Galvao Ferreira 2018, pp. 34–35). However, this version of differentiation was seen as compromising universal participation by some developed countries who then expressed objection to the exemption of emerging economies with significant emissions from emissions reduction obligations (Galvao Ferreira 2018, p. 36). As a result, the Paris Agreement refers to 'common but differentiated responsibilities and capabilities, in light of different national circumstances' and all state parties are now required to 'formulate, communicate, and update their nationally determined contributions' with regard to emissions reductions (Galvao Ferreira 2018, pp. 38–40). Yet, from a human rights perspective, it is not obvious how to reconcile the Paris Agreement's voluntary approach to emissions reduction targets (mitigation), with the obligations of states under international human rights law to reduce GHG emissions 'within the shortest possible time frame both nationally and through international cooperation and assistance' with the move to zero carbon emissions by developed states to ideally happen by 2030 (Khalfan and Liguori 2020, p. 15). This is especially so if attention is paid, as it should be, to responsibility for historic emissions, and related issues of climate justice.

Adaptation, on the other hand, may be defined as 'adjustments in ecological, social, or economic systems in response to actual or expected climatic stimuli and their effects or impacts' (UNFCCC (n.d.b)). Again, there is no single adaptation response; rather adaptation actions can range from early warning systems to flood defences to drought-resistant crops, and much more. Adaptation measures may successfully reduce climate harms and so have a positive impact on the enjoyment of human rights of some, yet adaptation initiatives may at the same time be implemented in a manner that disregards the human rights of others.

While loss and damage initially emerged as a component of the Cancun Adaptation Framework, it has developed as a distinct area since its incorporation into the Paris Agreement (Doelle and Seck 2020, p. 670). Loss and damage are defined in the literature as comprised of two categories of harm: permanent (an irrecoverable loss); and reparable (recoverable damage) (Doelle and Seck 2020, p. 669). Whether or not loss and damage occur is dependent upon both mitigation and adaptation: some loss and damage impact today may have been 'avoided' by mitigation efforts, while future loss and damage may be 'avoidable' should mitigation be enhanced or adaptation undertaken. Where future efforts cannot prevent loss and damage, however, it is 'unavoidable' (Doelle and Seck 2020, p. 669). From a human rights perspective, are violations of human rights arising from climate loss and damage to be understood as resulting from the failure of a state (or a non-state actor) to reduce greenhouse gas emissions (or purchase equivalent offsets), or from the failure of a state (perhaps a different one) to implement effective adaptation measures, or both? There is then the reality that climate change is the result of cumulative emissions, raising complex but not insurmountable questions of allocation and attribution (Heede 2014).

To understand the human rights implications of climate changes requires moving beyond the climate regime, given the sole reference to human rights is found in the preamble of the Paris Agreement. Sources of international human rights law are increasingly grappling with climate change (United Nations General Assembly (UNGA) 2019, pp. 15–17), including the July 2019 Safe Climate report by David Boyd, the Special Rapporteur on the issue of human rights obligations relating to the enjoyment of a safe, clean, healthy, and sustainable environment (UNGA 2019). The Safe Climate report first canvasses the devastating impact of the climate emergency globally on the enjoyment of human rights, then clarifies state obligations and business responsibilities, concluding with practical recommendations on what is required to protect a safe climate. Among the rights identified by Boyd that are currently 'threatened and violated' by climate change 'are the rights to life, health, food, water and sanitation, a healthy environment, an adequate standard of living, housing, property, self-determination, development and culture', as well as the rights of the child and others who are especially vulnerable (UNGA 2019, p. 10). Importantly, while those who have contributed most to the problem have the greatest responsibility to solve it, and have also 'reaped immense economic benefits', people living in poverty have contributed minimally to the problem, yet 'lack the resources to protect themselves or to adapt to the changes' (UNGA 2019, p. 10). Thus, as documented by the Special Rapporteur on extreme poverty and human rights, 'the adverse impacts of climate change disproportionately affect people living in poverty', and, the world faces 'a future of climate apartheid, where the wealthy pay to shield themselves from the worst impacts of climate change while the poor suffer immensely' (UNGA 2019, p. 10). However, a rights-based approach to climate change has the potential to contribute to solutions by highlighting 'principles of universality and non-discrimination, emphasizing that rights are guaranteed for all persons, including vulnerable groups' (UNGA 2019, p. 10).

What might this mean for state obligations, and in particular our understanding of their 'reach'? And what of business responsibilities? The Safe Climate report does not refer to the ETOs or 'extraterritoriality', rather framing state obligations in accordance with the 2018 *Framework Principles on Human Rights and the Environment* put forward by the former Special Rapporteur John Knox (United Nations Human Rights Council (UNHRC) 2018), as falling into three categories: 'procedural, substantive, and special obligations towards those in vulnerable situations', a framework that 'can be operationalized in the context of climate change in order to respect, protect and fulfil human rights' (UNGA 2019, p. 17). With regard to substantive obligations, Boyd clarifies:

> States must not violate the right to a safe climate through their own actions; must protect that right from being violated by third parties, especially businesses; and must establish, implement and enforce laws, policies and programmes to fulfil that right. States also must avoid discrimination and retrogressive measures. These principles govern all climate actions, including obligations related to mitigation, adaptation, finance, and loss and damage.
>
> *(UNGA 2019, p. 18)*

These human rights obligations are 'reinforced by international environmental law', as according to the 'do no harm' principle, 'States are obliged to ensure that polluting activities within their jurisdiction or control do not cause serious harm to the environment or peoples of other States or to areas beyond the limits of national jurisdiction' (UNGA 2019, p. 18). Consequently: 'Given the foreseeability of increasing climate impacts, this well-established "no harm" rule of customary international law is being violated as a result of greenhouse gas emissions, which, regardless of where they are emitted, are contributing, cumulatively, to adverse effects in other States, including small island developing States' (UNGA 2019, p. 18). This framing accords with the conceptualization of climate change as a common concern for all states, in keeping with the UNFCCC, and one that is a shared responsibility and requires international cooperation (Seck 2011a, pp. 180–181). Indeed, according to the Safe Climate report, the 'obligation to cooperate to achieve a low-carbon, climate resilient and sustainable future' extends to the sharing of information, transfer of climate-friendly technologies from wealthy to poorer states, the honouring of international commitments, and the need to ensure 'fair, legal and durable solutions for migrants and displaced persons' (UNGA 2019, p. 19). With regard to finance, Boyd clarifies the importance of funds to low-income countries being in the form of grants rather than loans: 'It violates basic principles of justice to force poor countries to pay for the costs of responding to climate change when wealthy countries caused the problem' (UNGA 2019, p. 19). He concludes the assessment of state obligations with reference to the work of the Committee on Economic, Social, and Cultural Rights who warned states in 2018 that:

> a failure to prevent foreseeable human rights harms caused by climate change, or a failure to mobilize the maximum available resources in an effort to do so, could constitute a breach of their obligation to respect, protect and fulfil all human rights for all. States must, therefore, dedicate the maximum available financial and material resources to shift to renewable energy, clean transport and agroecological farming; halt and reverse deforestation and soil deterioration; and increase adaptive capacity, especially in vulnerable and marginalized communities.
>
> *(UNGA 2019, p. 19)*

Another crucial clarification in the Safe Climate report is the responsibility of businesses, in line with the 2011 UN Guiding Principles on Business and Human Rights (UNGA 2019, p. 19). Accordingly, businesses 'must adopt human rights policies, conduct human rights due diligence, remedy human rights violations for which they are directly responsible and work to influence other actors to respect human rights where relationships of leverage exist' (UNGA 2019, p. 19). Specifically, businesses have five main responsibilities in relation to climate change:

> to reduce greenhouse gas emissions from their own activities and their subsidiaries; reduce greenhouse gas emissions from their products and services; minimize greenhouse gas emissions from their suppliers; publicly disclose their emissions, climate vulnerability and the risk of stranded assets; and ensure that people affected by business-related human rights violations have access to effective remedies. In addition, businesses should support, rather than oppose, public policies intended to effectively address climate change.
>
> *(UNGA 2019, pp. 19–20)*

The identification of duty-bearers beyond states in the Safe Climate report is important given the complexity of climate change, and the prominence of attribution science that measures the greenhouse gas emissions from carbon major companies (whether private or state-owned) since the industrial revolution (Heede 2014). These studies serve as the foundation for an increasing number of climate litigation cases against fossil fuel companies, arguably an important piece of the quest for climate justice and accountability (Ganguly, Setzer and Heyvaert 2018).

ETOs and climate justice: Clarity or confusion?

While the discussion of state obligations in the human rights and climate change space may not refer explicitly to the *Maastricht Principles* or the concept of extraterritoriality, it is arguable that these are implicit in the way in which the human rights obligations of states are conceptualized in clarifications such as the 2019 Safe Climate Report. Nevertheless, it is important to ponder whether the lack of embrace of ETOs' language is incidental or deliberate, and, importantly, whether it might matter or not. In this part I will first briefly consider the relevance of ETOs to human rights and climate change and then offer a few examples which suggest that the language of extraterritoriality itself may create confusion rather than add clarity when contemplating climate obligations, and so is perhaps best avoided. Instead, I will argue that relational language that intentionally speaks to the nature of the relationship to which the obligation attaches hold more promise for the realization of climate justice and accountability.

How might ETOs contribute to solutions to climate change and assist those most vulnerable to climate harms in seeking climate justice? According to a report on the *Maastricht Principles* and climate change authored by Greenpeace and CIEL, *Maastricht Principle* 13's 'Obligation to avoid causing harm' is directly relevant to transboundary and global environmental issues such as climate change, by confirming the extraterritorial reach of state obligations to refrain from actions or omissions that risk the nullification or impairment of the enjoyment of social, economic, and cultural rights (Greenpeace and CIEL 2014, p. 6). This obligation is engaged when the harm is foreseeable and may not be justified on the basis of a lack of certainty, in keeping with international environmental law's precautionary principle. *Maastricht Principles* 28 and 29, read in relation to Principles 30–35, 'reiterate the obligations of States to take deliberate, concrete and targeted steps, separately and jointly through international cooperation, to create an international enabling environment conducive to the universal fulfilment of ESCRs, including in matters of environmental protection' (Greenpeace and CIEL 2014, p. 6). In addition, *Maastricht Principle* 17 provides that states 'must elaborate, interpret and apply relevant international agreements and standards in a manner consistent with their human rights obligations, including those pertaining to environmental protection', while *Maastricht Principles* 23–27 elaborate the state 'duty to regulate to ensure that non-State actors do not nullify or impair the enjoyment of economic, social and cultural rights' whether by 'administrative, legislative, investigative, or adjudicative measures' (Greenpeace and CIEL, p. 6). In sum, the report claims that the '*Maastricht Principles* provide an excellent tool for holding governments accountable for extraterritorial violations of human rights on the basis of their existing obligations under international law' including those that require them to 'regulate and hold private corporations accountable for human rights violations resulting from their activities abroad and provide remedies to victims' as well as the 'use [of] their influence in international policy fora to create an enabling environment for the realization of human rights, including those relating to the right to a healthy environment, and cooperate internationally to mitigate the negative effects of eco-destruction and climate change' (Greenpeace and CIEL 2014, p. 10).

In practice, however, it is not so easy to apply the concept of extraterritoriality to the climate context as will be shown below with reference to a few examples. Indeed, as I have argued elsewhere, it may be important to move beyond the language of extraterritoriality (the 'e-word') in a time of climate and planetary crisis, so as to consciously avoid reinforcing the mythical image of the bounded autonomous state which flows from the unconscious adoption of the image of the bounded autonomous individual (liberal man) as a model for the sovereign nation state (Seck 2019a). The key point is that (in my own words) language which 'reinforces a vision of the territorially bounded sovereign state as an independent, autonomous being [...] in a time of global ecological crisis, is not only unhelpful, but undermines the critical importance of building mutually supportive relationships that acknowledge the reality of our ecological interdependence' (Seck 2019a, pp. 57–58). It is true that *Maastricht Principle* 8 defines ETOs as encompassing both 'obligations relating to acts and omissions of a State, within or beyond its territory, that have effects on the enjoyment of human rights outside of that State's territory' and 'obligations of a global character that are set out in the Charter of the United Nations and human rights instruments to take action, separately, and jointly through international cooperation, to realize human rights universally'. Clearly, the Maastricht ETOs embrace a vision of ETOs that includes support for global relationship building. Yet, I worry that conceptualizing this as 'extraterritorial' is nevertheless problematic.

To explain, the 'e-word' is associated under principles of public international law with the illicit exercise of jurisdiction beyond the foundational basis of state jurisdiction: territoriality. The problem rests in part with the fact that 'extra'-territorial, as the binary opposite of 'territorial', allows for no nuance. So, while the ETOs aim to clarify the extraterritorial nature of state obligations in the context of the primary rules of international human rights law, as distinct from the permissive exercise of jurisdiction under rules of public international law, the reality is that many states express discomfort with the exercise of state jurisdiction in the first place, often claiming concern that they may infringe the sovereignty of other states (Seck 2008). This discomfort may equally be attributable to the state's failure to acknowledge that certain state actions already have implications beyond borders to which human rights obligations must attach (Seck 2011b). If it is commonly believed that it may be impermissible to even exercise jurisdiction in a particular context, how can one then have a serious conversation about obligations to do so?

Legitimate exercise of jurisdiction from a public international law perspective is based on territoriality jurisdiction, or nationality (active personality) jurisdiction, with other more contested possibilities including passive personality jurisdiction, effects (a version of territoriality), as well as universal jurisdiction in limited instances. There is no public international law doctrine that legitimizes the exercise of extraterritorial jurisdiction per se, and so it is crucial to refer back to some other basis to legitimate the reach of state law. Moreover, the exercise of state jurisdiction could be prescriptive (legislative), adjudicative (judicial), investigative, or in relation to enforcement, and the legitimacy or illicitness of the jurisdictional reach will differ with each context. Finally, rules of private international law are crucial in determining how a court understands its role, and whether or not the case before it is one that it should hear, and to which it should apply forum or foreign law, or whether it is a case best heard in a foreign jurisdiction with a closer connection, where a foreign court may then choose to apply its own law as the most closely connected, or the law of another forum. In short, judicial analysis of legitimate exercise of jurisdiction can be complex. My concern is that the *Maastricht Principles*, which invoke the language of 'extraterritoriality', albeit in the context of state obligations under international human rights law, may inadvertently reinforce the muddiness of waters that might otherwise be at least slightly clearer.

As an example, in the corporate accountability context, the *Kiobel* litigation under the US *Alien Tort Statute* (ATS) is notorious for having led to a limitation in the potential for ATS litigation against multinational corporations (United States Supreme Court (USSC) 2013). The United States Supreme Court based its decision on the presumption against extraterritoriality, a doctrine that provides that unless a statute explicitly indicates that it applies beyond the realm, it is to be construed in a territorially bounded manner. On the facts the connection between the multinational enterprise and the US was less strong than it would have been had the head office of the enterprise at issue been located in the US. Nevertheless, it did indeed carry out business in the US, and the sweeping scope of the majority's decision made no distinction in any case. Conceptualizing the relationships at issue as extraterritorial undermines the ability to draw attention to the transnational nature of economic relationships, which would enable a more nuanced analysis of responsibility flowing from existing interdependence and aligning with calls for transnational access to justice (Seck 2013a). A different point is that responsibilities of non-state actors under international law, including transnational businesses, are increasingly captured by reference to the umbrella term of transnational law, arguably another version of relational responsibility (Seck 2013b). The phrase transnational obligations would therefore seem more appropriate; after all, we do not call them extraterritorial corporations or extraterritorial enterprises.

The *Kiobel* litigation has unfortunately inspired US courts charged with litigation brought by cities against fossil fuel companies in the climate context to similarly invoke the presumption against extraterritoriality even in cases where there is no statute to be interpreted, with the allegations resting on state nuisance law (Rudyan 2019). Much litigation later, the litigation continues over whether the cases should be heard in federal or state courts with outstanding issues of personal jurisdiction over foreign corporations (United States Court of Appeals for the Ninth Circuit (n.d.), summary). Nevertheless, there is no question that the harms alleged are harms in the United States – indeed, harms to specific cities – a solid territorial connection that is quite distinct from the facts of *Kiobel*.

Another example is the carbon majors case before the Philippines Human Rights Commission (Greenpeace Philippines 2015). The petitioners framed the problem with reference to the *Maastricht Principles* on ETOs. Yet, clearly harm to Filipinos in the Philippines provides a clear territorial nexus from which to justify an investigation by the Philippines Human Rights Commission, even if multiple defendant corporations locate their head offices or operate their businesses outside the Philippines, or if the emissions responsible for the harm originate from all over the world (Seck 2019a, p. 56). The undeniable territoriality of the climate harms, whether to people or the environment physically located in the Philippines, establishes a real and substantial connection between the allegations and the territory, sufficient to establish subject matter jurisdiction even if each individual defendant might contest the exercise of jurisdiction over them by the Commission by claiming a lack of personal jurisdiction as indeed many did (Seck 2019a; Seck 2017). At the end of the day, the Commission continued its public inquiry and the final outcome has not yet been released. However, it is unclear whether it was helpful or possibly confusing to raise the ETOs and so indirectly the e-word in relation to this investigation. Clearly, a domestic human rights commission should – must – hear claims relating to local human rights harms, even if some or most of those alleged to have caused the harms are not based within the forum territory. The effectiveness of such an inquiry at the end of the day is quite a different question from the obligation to hold the inquiry in the first place. For example, while Ecuadorean courts in the notorious litigation over oil pollution in the Amazon issued a multi-billion-dollar judgment against Chevron and in favour of the plaintiffs, seeking enforcement of this judgment in foreign courts where corporate assets are held has proven to be extremely challenging (Seck 2013b, p. 193).

Similar curious reference to extraterritoriality is found in other climate contexts. For example, the Committee on the Elimination of Discrimination Against Women released a periodic report on Norway in which it stated that Norway should (as I have described previously):

> review its policies on energy and climate change so as to ensure its policy on oil and gas extraction "takes into account the disproportionate negative impacts of climate change" on the rights of women, especially those in poverty who are "more reliant on natural resources for their livelihoods"
>
> *(Seck 2019a, p. 56)*

This statement is found in a section entitled: 'Extraterritorial state obligations'. Yet, the negative impacts of climate change on the human rights of women are also felt in Norway – perhaps most especially by members of the Indigenous Sámi (Prior and Heinämäki 2017). This is not to say that increased emissions arising from increased exploitation of fossil fuels will not have a disproportionate impact on the rights of women living in poverty outside of Norway; nevertheless, it is curious that the reference here is made only to women outside of Norway, and not to those within: Why not all poor women reliant upon natural resources for their livelihoods irrespective of where in the world they live? What does framing this as an issue of ETOs add?

A possible answer might be that where impacts outside the state are more severe, these could bolster arguments to stop harmful activities before they have begun. Yet, commentators reflecting on the *People v. Arctic Oil* case before the Norwegian Supreme Court have also queried the usefulness of the concept of 'extraterritoriality' (Duffy and Maxwell 2020). This case was brought by a coalition of environmental groups who claimed that the Norwegian government's issuance of a block of oil and gas licenses to explore for undeveloped fossil fuel deposits in the Barents Sea violated the Norwegian Constitution's right to a healthy environment, as well as Articles 2 and 8 of the ECHR, by failing 'to exercise due diligence to protect against the human rights implications of climate change' (Duffy and Maxwell 2020). According to Duffy and Maxwell, the Norwegian Court of Appeal's decision, finding against the plaintiffs, held that Norway's jurisdiction was limited to 'the risks of harm within Norway, *inter alia,* as the state is not responsible for impact on rights beyond its borders' (Duffy and Maxwell 2020). The case raised geographically complex facts, as the allegations were that Norway should be responsible for all GHG emissions arising from the exploration, extraction, and production within Norway of the fossil fuel resource, as well as the GHG emissions that would arise from combustion of these resources once exported outside of Norway. Yet, Norway and every other country in the world would be affected by the GHG emissions as each stage of release would contribute to the global climate change problem. Ultimately, according to Duffy and Maxwell, the Court of Appeal held that:

> the global consequences of climate change were beyond the scope of the state's obligations under the ECHR, such that it could only assess the projected impacts of climate change *in Norway* (which it found to be "serious", but "more limited and of a different nature than the global effects", even at warming of 4.5°C). Second, it found that there was no "real and immediate" risk of harm to life of persons within Norway, and no "direct and immediate link" between the impugned decision and resulting harm.
>
> *(Duffy and Maxwell 2020)*

While Duffy and Maxwell initially describe this outcome as being about 'the extent to which the Convention applies "extraterritorially"', they subsequently query whether this is the right framing:

> That said, the Norwegian case also prompts a more preliminary question: is the case really "extra-territorial" at all? The claimants allege that it is not. The impugned conduct – the

> grant of government licenses – takes place within the state, in respect of exploration and drilling that would also take place on Norwegian territory, but where its *effects* would be inextricably internal *and* external. The ECtHR's "exceptional'" extra-territorial jurisprudence, by contrast, developed in situations where state agents operated beyond its borders and allegedly violated the rights of persons also situated outside the state's territory. One could query whether this makes a difference, given the wording of the jurisdiction clause and its focus on persons within the state's jurisdiction? Brief regard to ECtHR practice suggests, however, that it may.
>
> *(Duffy and Maxwell 2020)*

These examples raise the question of whether there is a systemic, conceptual problem with human rights obligations beyond borders (ETOs) per se or only with respect to their mobilization and interpretation in the climate context. As noted above, I have concerns about the use of the word 'extraterritorial' to describe state obligations in the transnational corporate accountability context, recommending instead that the description of the obligation reflect the nature of the relationship to which the obligation attaches. In the climate context, these relationships are often both geographically and structurally complex. For example, in the Philippines petition, the concern was over harms to people in the Philippines, and the responsibility of emitters primarily outside the Philippines including transnational enterprises and their home states. On the other hand, in the Norwegian *Arctic Oil* case, the concern was with preventing conduct in Norway (and subsequent conduct outside of Norway), so as to prevent harm both to those within and outside of Norway. Moreover, in the climate context, the problem is both that the global climate system is shared by everyone, and that the cause of the harm is cumulative GHG emissions from everywhere – yet those most vulnerable to harms are often those who have least contributed to the problem, and climate attribution science is increasingly able to clarify the percentage contribution to global GHG emissions of specific state and non-state carbon majors. The problem is best conceptualized as one of climate justice, which requires recognition of the deeply interconnected nature of earth systems and people everywhere, including transnational economic relationships, even as responsibilities and capabilities are differentiated.

The right to a safe, clean, healthy, and sustainable environment - safe climate

Having said all of this, the reality is that ETOs – at least as understood as transnational, transboundary, common concern, cross-border, or global climate harms – are most certainly relevant, and applicable to the climate change context. Indeed, *Maastricht Principle* 27 frames the obligation as one of cooperation: 'All States must cooperate to ensure non-state actors do not impair the enjoyment of economic, social and cultural rights of any person. This obligation includes measures to prevent human rights abuses by non-state actors, to hold them to account for any such abuses, and to ensure an effective remedy for those affected'. This is undeniably true in the climate context, yet remains elusive in practice.

According to a detailed analysis of state responsibility for human rights violations in the context of climate change by Ottavio Quirico (2018), the international recognition of a human right to a healthy environment could have implications for the analysis of both extraterritoriality and policy discretion in climate litigation. It is true that there are always external implications to recognition of internal human rights obligations in the climate cases examined by Quirico, as a 'merely internal duty to take adequate adaptation and mitigation policies against climate change' has 'beneficial extraterritorial effects' for 'citizens of other countries, because of the global common nature of the atmosphere' (Quirico 2018, pp. 196–197). While this is useful if the arguments are focused on mitigation and adaptation to climate change, the problem of remedy for diagonal human rights harms necessitates additional work. This could be accomplished with systemic integration of human rights and climate regimes through a general state duty to prevent climate change in line with the Paris Agreement's 1.5-degree threshold quantified in accordance with a fair share (Quirico 2018, pp. 209–210). If a sustainable environment (safe climate system) were conceptualized as both an *erga omnes* duty and right, this 'would contribute to overcoming the discrepancy between the territorial scope of application of human rights and the transboundary nature of GHG emissions' with 'the universal scope of the claim' also aligning with notions of intergenerational justice, and so protection of future generations (Quirico 2018, p. 211).

Substantive environmental rights are clearly receiving increased attention in regional human rights mechanisms, and through international initiatives pushing for recognition. Among notable developments is the Inter-American Court of Human Rights (IACtHR)'s Advisory Opinion on Environment and Human Rights, issued in response to a request from Colombia to clarify the scope of state responsibility under the American Convention on Human Rights with regard to environmental harm (IACtHR 2017). While the request may have been motivated by activities other than climate change, the resulting judgment clearly embraces the idea that states 'have a duty to prevent transboundary environmental damage that could impair the rights of persons outside their territory' on the basis of effective control over activities (Banda 2018), an idea sometimes described as invoking diagonal rights (Feria-Tinta and Milnes 2018). Notably, while the English translation of the Advisory Opinion does use the language of extraterritoriality in its analysis, it avoids the term in its conclusions, where the court specifies that under the American Convention, the concept of jurisdiction 'encompasses any situation in which a State exercises effective control or authority over a person or persons, either within or outside its territory' (IACtHR 2017, para. 104(e)). 'States must ensure that their territory is not used in such a way as to cause significant damage to the environment of other States or of areas beyond the limits of their territory' (IACtHR 2017, para. 104(f)); and 'States are obliged to take all necessary measures to avoid activities implemented in their territory or under their control affecting the rights of persons within or outside their territory' (IACtHR 2017, para. 104(g)). The approach of the IACtHR is also endorsed by Duffy and Maxwell (2020), suggesting that it 'leads the way in firmly rejecting the idea that human rights obligations are inapplicable based on formalistic notions of territorial or personal control'.

Beyond the scope question, the Advisory Opinion is also noteworthy for having 'recognized the existence of an "autonomous" right to a healthy environment' under Article 26 of the American Convention, a right that arguably 'protects the environment *per se*' (Banda 2018). This opens the door to the justiciability of claims absent evidence of harm to humans, a development that reflects relational world views, as well as the importance of intergenerational justice. In this light, it is interesting to see how youth petitioners have framed their claims in a Communication to the Committee on the Rights of the Child (2019). While the petition was deliberately crafted to ensure that there was a petitioner who was either a national or resident of each respondent country, they nevertheless carefully state that 'all petitioners, however, are within the jurisdiction of each respondent because the petitioners are all victims of the foreseeable consequences of the carbon pollution knowingly emitted, permitted, or promoted by each respondent from within their respective territory' (CRC Communication 2019, para. 241). Moreover, the actions of each respondent are said to be 'causing and perpetuating the climate crisis and violate the petitioners' rights' (CRC Communication 2019, Part IX).

Conclusions

This chapter has considered two key questions: first, can the *Maastricht Principles* be said to have contributed to a clarification of the law so as to assist in conceptualizing the legal obligations of states and other actors to prevent and remedy human rights harms arising from anthropogenic climate change? Secondly, are new elements of human rights law necessary to address the complexity of obligation in the context of climate crisis that go beyond the ETOs?

With regard to the first question, it is clear that invocation of the *Maastricht Principles* without careful consideration of whether or not the climate problem at issue is one that involves extraterritorial obligation has led to confusion rather than clarity. However, it is also evident, given the geographic and structural complexity of climate claims, that binary distinctions between territorial and extraterritorial obligations may not be terribly useful in any case. This concern may be somewhat mitigated by reference to obligations in relation to global harms combined with duties of international cooperation, and it is arguable that more explicit relational language such as invocation of obligations to prevent and remedy transboundary, cross-border, transnational, or common concern environmental human rights harms (depending on the context) may be preferable (Seck 2011a, pp. 163–181). Nevertheless, ultimately it is important to not lose sight of the climate justice dimensions at issue despite the failure of the international climate regime to explicitly acknowledge the responsibility and liability of historically high-emitting developed states for climate loss and damage even as experienced by the most vulnerable and least-responsible developing states.

An evolving question is whether new elements of human rights law are necessary to address the complexity of obligation in the context of the climate crisis, such as through explicit and universal recognition of a right to a safe climate system through recognition of a right to a safe, clean, healthy, and sustainable environment. A different but equally important question is whether what is necessary is a paradigm shift in terms of how the 'human' who is the holder of rights is understood: if all humans were conceptualized as ecologically embedded relational individuals, although differentially situated, as I have argued elsewhere (Seck 2019b; Seck 2021), then the same result could be reached without waiting for universal state recognition of a right that is in essence to not be subject to anthropogenic planetary destruction. Moreover, ecologically embedded relational individuals – which we all are – are found everywhere – from corporate boardrooms to investment advisors to politicians to climate refugees. While we all require a safe climate in order to thrive, those most vulnerable to climate harms are whose rights are already violated due to race, poverty, disability, age, gender, and/or indigeneity, among other identities. Transformative re-imagining of the 'human' with attention to difference may be a key part of the climate justice puzzle.

References

Banda, M.L. (2018) 'Inter-American Court of Human Rights' Advisory Opinion on the Environment and Human Rights', *ASIL Insights* 22(6) https://www.asil.org/insights/volume/22/issue/6/inter-american-court-human-rights-advisory-opinion-environment-and-human [accessed 12 January 2021].

Business & Human Rights Resource Centre (BHRRC) (2020) 'Renewable Energy & Human Rights Benchmark: Key Findings from the Wind & Solar Sectors', https://media.business-humanrights.org/media/documents/files/Renewable_Energy_Benchmark_Key_Findings_Report.pdf [accessed 12 January 2021].

Committee on Economic, Social, and Cultural Rights (CESCR) (2018) 'Climate change and the International Covenant on Economic, Social, and Cultural Rights', available at www.ohchr.org/en/NewsEvents/Pages/DisplayNews.aspx?NewsID=23691&LangID=E [accessed 12 January 2021].

Communication to the Committee on the Rights of the Child (2019) in the case of *Sacchi et al. v. Argentina, Brazil, France, Germany & Turkey*, available at https://childrenvsclimatecrisis.org/wp-content/uploads/2019/09/2019.09.23-CRC-communication-Sacchi-et-al-v.-Argentina-et-al.pdf [accessed 12 January 2021].

Doelle, M. and Seck, S. (2020) 'Loss & Damage From Climate Change: From Concept to Remedy?', *Climate Policy* 20(6), 669–680.

Duffy H. and Maxwell L. (2020) 'People v. Arctic Oil before the Supreme Court of Norway – What's at Stake for Human Rights Protection in the Climate Crisis?', *EJIL Talk! Blog, 13* November 2020, https://www.ejiltalk.org/people-v-arctic-oil-before-supreme-court-of-norway-whats-at-stake-for-human-rights-protection-in-the-climate-crisis/ [accessed 12 January 2021].

Feria-Tinta, M. and Milnes, S. (2018) 'The Rise of Environmental Law in International Dispute Resolution: Inter-American Court of Human Rights issues Landmark Advisory Opinion on Environment and Human Rights', *EJIL:Talk! Blog, 26* February 2018, https://www.ejiltalk.org/the-rise-of-environmental-law-in-international-dispute-resolution-inter-american-court-of-human-rights-issues-landmark-advisory-opinion-on-environment-and-human-rights/ [accessed 12 January 2021].

Friends of the Earth International (FOEI) (2017) 'REDD+ The Carbon Market and California-Acre-Chiapas Cooperation: Legalizing Mechanisms of Dispossession', https://www.foei.org/wp-content/uploads/2018/01/REDD_The-carbon-market-and-the-California-Acre-Chiapas-cooperation.pdf [accessed 12 January 2021].

Galvao Ferreira, P. (2018) 'Differentiation in International Environmental Law: Has Pragmatism Displace Considerations of Justice' in Craik, N., Jefferies, C.S.G., Seck, S.L. and Stephens, T., (eds). *Global Environmental Change and Innovation in International Law*, Cambridge University Press.

Ganguly, G., Setzer, J., and Heyvaert, V. (2018) 'If at First You Don't Succeed: Suing Corporations for Climate Change', *Oxford Journal of Legal Studies* 38(4), 841–868.

Greenpeace and Center for International Environmental Law (CIEL) (2014) 'Extraterritorial Obligations in the Context of Eco-destruction and Climate Change', *FIAN International for the ETO Consortium*, https://www.fian.org/fileadmin/media/publications_2015/ETO_and_climate_change.pdf [accessed 12 January 2021].

Greenpeace Philippines (2015) 'Petition to the commission on human rights of the Philippines requesting for investigation of the responsibility of the carbon majors for human rights violations resulting from the impacts of climate change', available at https://www.greenpeace.org/static/planet4-philippines-stateless/2019/05/5a38951a-5a38951a-cc-hr-petition_public-version.pdf [accessed 12 January 2021]

Heede, R. (2014) 'Tracing Anthropogenic Carbon Dioxide and Methane Emissions to Fossil Fuel and Cement Producers 1854-2010', *Climatic Change* 122, 229–241.

Inter-American Court of Human Rights (IACtHR) (2017) The Environment and Human Rights (State Obligations in Relation to the Environment in the Context of the Protection and Guarantee of the Rights to Life and to Personal Integrity – Interpretation and Scope of Articles 4(1) and 5(1) of the American Convention on Human Rights), Advisory Opinion OC-23/18, Series A no. 23, English translation available at https://www.corteidh.or.cr/docs/opiniones/seriea_23_ing.pdf.

Khalfan, A. and Liguori, C. (2020) 'Amnesty's approach to climate change and human rights' in Ismangil, D., van der Schaaf, K. and van Troost, L. (eds). *Climate Change, Justice, and Human Rights*, Amnesty International Netherlands.

Oslo District Court, Borgarting Court of Appeal and Norwegian Supreme Court (n.d.) *Greenpeace Nordic Ass'n v. Ministry of Petroleum and Energy,* summary, Climate Change Litigation Databases http://climatecasechart.com/non-us-case/greenpeace-nordic-assn-and-nature-youth-v-norway-ministry-of-petroleum-and-energy/ [accessed 12 January 2021]

Prior, T.L. and Heinämäki L. (2017) 'The Rights and Role of Indigenous Women in the Climate Regime', *Arctic Review on Law and Politics* 8, 193–221.

Quirico, O. (2018) 'Climate Change and State Responsibility for Human Rights Violations: Causation and Imputation', *Netherlands International Law Review* 65(65), 185–215.

Rudyan, A.B. (2019) 'Extraterritoriality in Common Law Climate Actions: Judicial Restraint or Judicial Error', *Pace Environmental Law Review* 37(1), 177–209.

Seck, S.L. (2008) 'Unilateral Home State Regulation: Imperialism or Tool for Subaltern Resistance?', *Osgoode Hall Law Journal* 46, 565–603.

_______ (2011a) 'Transnational Business and Environmental Harm: A TWAIL Analysis of Home State Obligations', *Trade, Law & Development* 3(1), 164–202.

_______ (2011b) 'Conceptualizing the Home State Duty to Protect Human Rights' in Buhmann, K., Morsing, M. and Roseberry, L. (eds). *Corporate Social and Human Rights Responsibilities: Global Legal and Management Perspectives*, Palgrave Macmillan.

_______ (2013a) 'Kiobel and the E-word: Reflections on Transnational Environmental Responsibility in an Interconnected World', *Law at the End of the Day Blog,* 5 July 2013, http://lcbackerblog.blogspot.ca/2013/07/sara-seck-on-kiobel-and-e-word.html [accessed 18 July 2021]

_______ (2013b) 'Transnational Judicial and Non-Judicial Remedies for Corporate Human Rights Harms: Challenges of and for Law', *Windsor Yearbook of Access to Justice* 31, 183–202.

_______ (2017) 'Revisiting Transnational Corporations and Extractive Industries: Climate Justice, Feminism, and State Sovereignty', *Transnational Law & Contemporary Problems* 26(2), 383–413.

_______ (2019a) 'Moving Beyond the E-Word in the Anthropocene' in Margolies, D.S., Özsu, U., Pal, M. and Tzouvala, N. (eds). *The Extraterritoriality of Law: History, Theory, Politics,* Routledge.

_______ (2019b) 'Relational Law: Re-imagining Tools for Environmental and Climate Justice', *Canadian Journal of Women and the Law* 31(1), 151–177.

_______ (2021) 'A Relational Analysis of Enterprise Obligations and Carbon Majors for Climate Justice', *Oñati Socio-Legal Series: Climate Justice in the Anthropocene* 11(1), 254-284 https://opo.iisj.net/index.php/osls/article/view/1217 [accessed 18 July 2021].

United Nations General (UNGA) (2019) Report of the Special Rapporteur on the issue of human rights obligations relating to the enjoyment of a safe, clean, healthy and sustainable environment: Safe Climate, A/74/161.

United Nations Framework Convention on Climate Change (UNFCCC) (n.d.a) 'Introduction of Mitigation', available at https://unfccc.int/topics/mitigation/the-big-picture/introduction-to-mitigation [accessed 12 January 2021].

_______ (n.d.b) 'What do adaptation to climate change and resilience mean?', available at https://unfccc.int/topics/adaptation-and-resilience/the-big-picture/what-do-adaptation-to-climate-change-and-climate-resilience-mean [accessed 12 January 2021].

United Nations Human Rights Council (UNHRC) (2018) Report of the Special Rapporteur on the issue of human rights obligations relating to the enjoyment of a safe, clean, healthy and sustainable environment: Framework Principles, A/HRC/37/59 (annex).

United States Court of Appeals for the Ninth Circuit (n.d.) *City of Oakland v. BP p.l.c.,* summary, Climate Change Litigation Databases, http://climatecasechart.com/case/people-state-california-v-bp-plc-oakland/ [accessed 12 January 2021]

United States Supreme Court (USSC) (2013) *Kiobel v. Royal Dutch Petroleum Co.*, 133 S. Ct. 1659.

31
Cross-border pollution

Antal Berkes

Introduction

Environmental pollution can be defined as '[a]ny alteration in the character or quality of the environment which renders it unfit, or less fit, for certain uses' (United Nations Economic and Social Commission for Western Asia (UN ESCWA) 2012). The environment can be affected by any of its components, including by the air, land, water, atmosphere, etc. Cross-border pollution is understood as the introduction, directly or indirectly, of hazardous substances into transboundary components of the environment (Economic Commission for Europe 1990, Definitions/I(c)) that causes harm 'in the territory of or in other places under the jurisdiction or control of a State other than the State of origin, whether or not the States concerned share a common border' (International Law Commission (ILC) 2001b, art. 2, Commentary para. 9). State practice has recognised the close connection between pollution, and more broadly environment degradation on the one hand, and human rights in general (UN Conference on the Human Environment 1972, para. 1; Inter-American Court of Human Rights (IACtHR) 2017, paras. 47–55), and economic, social and cultural rights in particular (International Covenant on Economic, Social and Cultural Rights (ICESCR) 1966, art. 12(2)(b); Committee on Economic, Social and Cultural Rights (CESCR) 2000, para. 15; African Commission on Human and Peoples' Rights (ACommHPR) 2001, para. 51), on the other.

Various provisions of the 2011 *Maastricht Principles* on Extraterritorial Obligations in the Area of Economic, Social and Cultural Rights (MP) reflect the state practice on extraterritorial human rights obligations in respect of cross-border pollution, while others constitute progressive development of international law. There are finally few provisions that can be criticised and subject to further amendments. This is especially the case of Principles 24–27 that provide for the state's obligation to take preventive measures to ensure that non-state actors do not impair the enjoyment of the economic, social and cultural rights of any persons abroad. Taking into account the recent practice of treaty monitoring bodies, the extraterritorial obligation to protect against the conduct of non-state actors should be specified with clearer thresholds, especially to answer the question which human rights and against what kind of polluting corporate activities states are expected to protect.

DOI: 10.4324/9781003090014-39

The chapter argues that while the *Maastricht Principles* constitute a good basis for extraterritorial obligations regarding human rights violations arising from cross-border pollution, prescribing more punctual threshold criteria could have better reflected positive international law. The Chapter proceeds as follows. Section 2 explains, in the light of state practice, what kind of threshold criteria human rights obligations in matter of cross-border pollution should satisfy. Sections 3–5 analyse in detail what state conduct the obligations to respect (2), protect (3) and fulfil (4) require in matter of cross-border pollution under the MP and state practice. Among those obligations, the MP incorporate a detailed guidance as to the content of the states' obligations to protect against human rights violations by third parties (such as private persons, corporations, other states) that set a higher standard of regulation than that required by the present state of international law as reflected in existing state practice. Therefore, they reflect a progressive development of international law especially in interpreting the obligations to protect. The MP, however, are necessarily flexible and vague as they do not provide appropriate guidance as to the threshold criteria, especially as to the minimum severity of the risk of a human rights violation and causality.

Uncertainty about thresholds

As the minimum threshold of gravity of a harm that cross-border pollution produces cannot be determined with certain qualifications (e.g. 'significant', 'serious', 'grave') other than on a case-by-case basis (ILC 2001, art. 2, Commentary para. 4), legal instruments regulating cross-border pollution all have an inherent unease to define a minimum threshold of harm that instigates state obligations. In fact, not every level of environment pollution can instigate state obligations, especially if the pollution is detectable but does not result in a real detrimental effect on matters such as, for example, human health, industry, property, environment or agriculture in other states (ILC 2001, art. 2, Commentary para. 4). The International Law Commission set this minimum threshold in its draft articles on prevention of transboundary harm from hazardous activities as activities causing a risk of 'significant transboundary harm' (ILC 2001, art. 1 and art. 2(a)). Likewise, the International Court of Justice has concluded in environmental law cases that the obligation of prevention arises when there is risk of 'significant damage' (International Court of Justice (ICJ) 2010, 55–56, para. 101; ICJ 2015, 720, para. 153).

International human rights monitoring bodies have also required a minimum threshold of severity of the human rights impact when addressing complaints about environmental pollution. When examining cases of alleged interference in private life caused by pollution, the European Court of Human Rights (ECtHR) found a violation in some exceptional cases even in the absence of any evidence of the serious danger to people's health if the pollution adversely affected the individual' quality of life, right to home or family life (ECtHR 1994, para. 51; 2012, paras. 104 and 108). Most often, however, the Court requires a certain minimum degree of the degradation of the individual's well-being, insofar as the ECHR does not include a right to a healthy environment (ECtHR 2005, para. 68; 2011, para. 105; 2016, para. 15). For the Court, the adverse effects of the environmental pollution on human rights must attain a certain minimum level if they are to be considered a violation of the ECHR; the assessment of that minimum is relative and depends on all the circumstances of the case, such as the intensity and duration of the nuisance, and its physical or mental effects (ECtHR 2005, para. 69; ECtHR 2011, para. 105; 2009, para. 100). For instance, the Court required 'a level of severity resulting in significant impairment of the applicant's ability to enjoy her home, private or family life' (ECtHR 2011, para. 58). Thus, the ECtHR has examined the impact of the environmental harm on the individual, rather than the risk that exists for the environment or the level of environmental degradation. The Inter-American Court of Human Rights (IACtHR) has followed this logic and concluded that 'States must take measures to prevent significant harm or damage to the environment, within or outside their territory' (IACtHR 2017, para. 140). The IACtHR considered '[a]ny harm to the environment that may involve a violation of the rights to life and to personal integrity' as significant harm (ibid). In a recent case concerning the positive obligations of the state within its own territory without any foreign element, the Court considered the 'right to a healthy environment', derived from Article 26 of the American Convention on Human Rights, as an autonomous right that protects the environment 'even in the absence of the certainty or evidence of a risk to individuals' (IACtHR 2020, paras. 202–203). The IACtHR generally recognised that environmental damage can cause a violation of additional human rights but did not require any threshold. It is unclear how this precedent, rendered in an extremely divided decision (three to three, with the President's deciding vote), would be applied to extraterritorial cases that are likely to address the required degree of the impact of environmental pollution on human rights.

Another question of threshold is the link between the harm and the state conduct: not any state has extraterritorial obligations towards individuals affected by cross-border pollution outside its borders, but only the state whose conduct has certain causal connection to the harm to the victims (ECtHR 2019, para. 106). There are often complex factual links between the state's conduct and its extraterritorial consequences, as other factors may influence the environmental pollution (ECtHR 2019, para. 160). Causation is linked to questions of foreseeability and proximity or direct harm (ILC 2006, 79, para. 16). Human rights monitoring bodies have applied certain tests to better specify this link: the ECtHR required 'direct and immediate link' in Article 8 cases; 'direct and immediate cause' (ECtHR 2008); 'sufficiently proximate repercussions' (ECtHR 2004, para. 317); 'real and immediate risk' (ECtHR 2010, paras. 286 and 296); while the Human Rights Committee required 'a direct and reasonably foreseeable impact on the right to life' (Human Rights Committee (HRC) 2019, para. 22). The IACtHR, in its Advisory Opinion on extraterritorial human rights obligations related to environmental pollution, required a threshold of 'real and immediate risk' (IACtHR 2017, para. 120), but only with respect to the protection of the right to life. To serve legal certainty, and in conformity with the Court's intention to interpret cases of extraterritorial jurisdiction restrictively (IACtHR 2017, paras. 81 and 104), the minimum proximity of the factual/causal link should be formulated more generally as a threshold criterion of the required extraterritorial nexus.

The practice of treaty monitoring bodies, authoritative interpreters of the respective human rights treaties, thus confirms that cross-border pollution only instigates the state's extraterritorial obligations when: (1) a direct link between the environmental pollution or degradation and an impairment of a protected right is established, and there is a causality between the action or omission of a state, on the one hand, and the pollution, on the other; (2) the adverse effects of the pollution on human rights must attain a certain minimum level if they are to fall within the scope of international human rights law (ILC 2017, para. 82). The assessment of that minimum standard is relative and depends on the content of the concerned right and all the relevant circumstances of the case, such as the intensity and duration of the nuisance, and its physical or mental effects.

Principle 13 MP seems to address, at least impliedly, the proximity threshold, but not severity when it refers to 'a real risk of nullifying or impairing the enjoyment of economic, social and cultural rights extraterritorially' and 'a foreseeable result' of state conduct. To instigate extraterritorial obligations, the provision requires a 'real risk' as opposed to merely hypothetical or theoretical risks (De Schutter et al. 2012, p. 1113). The principle also implies that the threshold is not the strict *conditio sine qua non* theory but a state conduct that produces 'foreseeable' harm 'even if other, intervening causes, also played a role in the violation' (De Schutter et al. 2012, p. 1114). The link between the foreseeability of the harm and the risks of such harm is occurring is that only the foreseeable risk instigates the state's obligations, while the state is not expected to prevent unforeseeable risk of human rights violations. Therefore, the proximity requirement complies with the case law of the above-mentioned international human rights monitoring bodies, although a more meticulous wording would be welcome. Such a more specific threshold could be that used by the Human Rights Committee as a universal standard, that of 'direct and reasonably foreseeable' harm, as it further highlights that a remote causal link is insufficient to instigate state obligations (ECtHR 1999).

As to the severity requirement, Principle 13 does not 'establish a threshold of severity or intensity of the risk: it refers to the probability of the risk materializing, not to the consequences that might follow from such materialization of the risk' (De Schutter et al. 2012, p. 1113). While it may imply that the MP allow, like the ECtHR, a case-by-case analysis of the impact of the environmental pollution on the individual, state practice shows that a certain minimum threshold of seriousness is necessary at the level of all economic, social and cultural rights (below). As the positive obligations to protect and fulfil will indicate (Sections 4–5), the instigation of extraterritorial human rights obligations with regard to the risk created by non-state actors is the most compelling in case of *jus cogens* norms and human rights protecting the physical integrity of the person.

Obligations to respect

Under the obligation to respect, states shall refrain from: (i) any practice or activity that denies or restricts access, in equal conditions, to the requisites of a dignified life, such as adequate food and water, and (ii) unlawfully polluting the environment in a way that has a negative impact on human rights; 'for example, by dumping waste from state-owned facilities in ways that affect access to or the quality of potable water and/or sources of food' (IACtHR 2017, para. 117).

These duties have an extraterritorial dimension too. Customary international law prohibits a state from allowing its territory to be used to cause damage on the territory of another state (USA-Canada Arbitral Tribunal 1941, 1965; ICJ 1949, p. 22; ICJ 2010, p. 55–56, para. 101). At the level of persons and bodies whose conduct is attributable to the state, this obligation imposes at the very least a negative conduct not to violate the rights of other states. In international human rights law, the obligation to respect has been interpreted as an obligation not to violate human rights of individuals outside the state's territory. It requires the state to 'refrain from unlawfully polluting air, water and soil, e.g. through industrial waste from state-owned facilities' (CESCR 2000, para. 34).

Violations of the obligations to respect are 'State actions, policies or laws that contravene the standards set out' in binding international norms protecting socio-economic rights (CESCR 2000, para. 50). Examples include 'the suspension of legislation or the adoption of laws or policies that interfere with the enjoyment of any of the components of the right to health'; or 'the failure of the state to take into account its legal obligations regarding the right to health when entering into bilateral or multilateral agreements with other states, international organizations and other entities, such as multinational corporations' (CESCR 2000, para. 50).

It is understandable that treaties on the protection of environment provide mainly on positive obligations of states parties 'to prevent, reduce and control pollution' rather than to refrain from polluting (Convention for the Protection and Development of the Marine Environment of the Wider Caribbean Region 1983, arts. 4(1)–(2), 5–10; Convention on the Protection of the Black Sea Against Pollution 1992, art. V(1), VII–XII;), as the latter are absorbed by the former.

Therefore, highlighting positive measures within the obligation to respect by the MP is a welcome development: beyond the principles 20–22 that focus on negative obligations, Principle 19 provides that

> All states must take action, separately, and jointly through international cooperation, to respect the economic, social and cultural rights of persons within their territories and extraterritorially, as set out in Principles 20 to 22.

This principle cannot be read as amending the mainly negative conduct that obligations to respect require: the state shall refrain from polluting the environment that violates socio-economic rights, while taking measures against pollution by third parties is a conduct expected under the obligation to protect. If consistently reading the obligations to respect, 'taking action' under Principle 19 can be interpreted as 'requiring that the state redress any violation attributable to it' (Gould and Shelton 2013, p. 577). In other words, once the state violates its obligation to respect, it is required to take action to avoid, counter and mitigate the impact of the pollution (CRC Concluding observations: Islamic Republic of Iran 2016, para. 74; Special Rapporteur on the adverse effects of the illicit movement… 2008, para. 54). Due to the spill-over effect of cross-border pollution, joint coordination of positive measures to counter and mitigate the harm is crucial and is confirmed in international environmental law (UN Conference on the Human Environment 1972, Principle 24; ILC 2001b, art. 4). Human rights monitoring bodies have confirmed the mainly negative obligation not to violate human rights outside the state's territory through transboundary pollution, together with a positive obligation to mitigate such a risk (CEDAW 2018, paras. 43 and 46(a); CRC Committee 2013, para. 31).

Other rules of the MP further specify the obligations to refrain in various scenarios that might play a role in cross-border pollution. Principle 20 provides on this duty in situations where the conduct of the state has a potential impact on the enjoyment of economic, social and cultural rights without the involvement of any third party (other state or international organisation) in the situation that leads to nullification or impairment of the enjoyment of these rights (De Schutter et al. 2012, p. 1128). Principle 21 requires states to refrain from a conduct that impairs the ability of another state or international organisation to discharge their international obligations. It also expects states not to aid, assist, direct, control or coerce another state or international organisation in breaching its international obligations regarding economic, social and cultural rights. More relevant in cross-border pollution is Principle 22 which requires the state to refrain from adopting measures, such as embargoes or other economic sanctions, which would result in nullifying or impairing the enjoyment of economic, social and cultural rights. An example is the non-respect of obligations of the state under international humanitarian law protecting natural environment (CESCR 2002, para. 22), for instance, the use of chemical, incendiary or bacterial weapons (Protocol Additional I to the Geneva Conventions 1977, arts. 54(2) and 55).

Obligations to protect

The obligation to protect requires states parties to prevent third parties, that is other states, international organisations, non-state actors such as individuals, civil society organisations, national or transnational corporations from interfering in any way with the enjoyment of human rights (CESCR 1999, para. 15; CESCR 2000, para. 51; CESCR 2002, para. 23). Contrary to the obligations to respect as formulated in the MP which comply with state practice, its provisions on the obligations to protect human rights extraterritorially from the conduct of third parties have been contested by several states. However, protection against non-state conduct is particularly important in cross-border pollution where most incidents result primarily from private conduct (Bodansky et al. 2008, p. 6).

Principle 24 provides that

> [A]ll states must take necessary measures to ensure that non-state actors which they are in a position to regulate, as set out in Principle 25, such as private individuals and organisations, and transnational corporations and other business enterprises, do not nullify or impair the enjoyment of economic, social and cultural rights. [...]

Under Principle 25, the state is required to adopt mainly regulatory measures in any of the following scenarios:

a the harm or threat of harm originates or occurs on its territory;

b where the non-state actor has the nationality of the state concerned;

c as regards business enterprises, where the corporation, or its parent or controlling company, has its centre of activity, is registered or domiciled, or has its main place of business or substantial business activities, in the state concerned;

d where there is a reasonable link between the state concerned and the third party's conduct;

e where the conduct impairing economic, social and cultural rights constitutes a *jus cogens* violation.

Among those principles, the last one, related to *jus cogens* violations is unproblematic as it is recognised in general international law that all states are obliged to cooperate to bring to an end through lawful means any serious breach of a peremptory norm (ILC 2001a, art. 41(1)). The other scenarios, however, are contested.

In general international law, the standard of due diligence is the legal basis for an obligation to protect the rights of other states where the state knew or should have known that activities unlawful under international law were perpetrated on its territory and caused damage to another state (ICJ 1949, p. 18). Compared to the standard of due diligence, also considered as a customary norm (ICJ 2010, pp. 55–56, para. 101) or general principle of law (ICJ 1949, p. 22), the MP performed two major moves: first, they protect not the rights of other states but human rights of individuals outside the territory of the state; and second, the harmful activities are not necessarily perpetrated entirely on its territory, but may be perpetrated (partly) abroad by a third party to which the state has certain nexus, such as the social centre of activity or the place of registration or other reasonable link.

As it is well-analysed, human rights obligations of the state towards persons outside its territory relate to the question of jurisdiction under human rights treaties, defined as the main criterion for the applicability of international human rights treaties, the nexus between the state and the individual's human rights violation, that is, factual control, power or authority that the state exercises over a given individual, territory or situation (De Schutter et al. 2012, p. 1102; Milanovic 2011, p. 39). In the dominant case law of international human rights law, the state can have extraterritorial jurisdiction if it has effective control over the territory where the violation occurs, or over the victim and/or the perpetrator, that is, state agents commit the human rights violation abroad (ECtHR 2011, paras. 133–140; IACtHR 2017, paras. 79–80). However, one might ask whether extraterritorial jurisdiction would cover cases where the state has control neither over the victim nor over the perpetrators, nor over foreign territory, but over activities within its own territory that lead to foreseeable harm being caused abroad. This is the scenario of the home state's control over its corporate nationals that violate human rights abroad. In those cases, it is a third party (a non-state actor) and not the state's agents that violates human rights abroad, and one may ask how far such breaches may fall within the jurisdiction of the state.

The UN Guiding Principles on Business and Human Rights (UN HRC 2011a, Principle 1; UN HRC 2011b, para. 1) commented the idea of such an extraterritorial obligation to regulate the extraterritorial conduct of corporate nationals as follows:

> At present states are not generally required under international human rights law to regulate the extraterritorial activities of businesses domiciled in their territory and/or jurisdiction. Nor are they generally prohibited from doing so, provided there is a recognized jurisdictional basis.
>
> *(UN Human Rights Council 2011a, Principle 1)*

Several states, especially developed home states, have opposed a recommended obligation to regulate the extraterritorial conduct of their corporate nationals, while other states, typically developing host states, expressly supported it.[1] The case law of the ECHR has never recognised such an obligation either (European Commission of Human Rights (ECmHR) 1995), especially as the Court avoids to admit 'a "cause-and-effect" notion of "jurisdiction"' (ECtHR 2010, para. 64; ECtHR 2001, para. 75).

Nonetheless, since the adoption of the MP, human rights monitoring bodies have gradually interpreted human rights treaties as entailing the home state's obligations to regulate such conducts (Convention on the Elimination of All Forms of Discrimination Against Women (CEDAW) 2013, para. 12(b); CESCR 2017, paras. 25–35; CRC Committee 2013, paras. 43, 45 and 50). Recently, the Human Rights Committee provided in its General Comment no. 36 (2018) on the right to life that states parties:

> […] must also take appropriate legislative and other measures to ensure that all activities taking place in whole or in part within their territory and in other places subject to their jurisdiction, but having a direct and reasonably foreseeable impact on the right to life of individuals outside their territory […] are consistent with article 6.
>
> *(HRC 2019, para. 22)*

This marks the recognition of the causality-based jurisdictional link by the most universal treaty body. In the domain of cross-border pollution, this entails, for instance, the state's obligation to take appropriate legislative and administrative measures to prevent acts of transnational corporations registered in the state party which negatively impact on the enjoyment of rights of indigenous peoples to health and an adequate standard of living in other states (e.g. CERD Concluding observations: UK 2011, para. 29; CERD Concluding observations: USA 2014, para. 10(d)).

In its Advisory Opinion on *The Environment and Human Rights*, the IACtHR was the first human rights court to recognise a new extraterritorial jurisdictional link based on effective control over domestic conducts. The Court accepted a jurisdictional link 'when the State of origin exercises effective control over the activities that caused the damage and the consequent human rights violation' (IACtHR 2017, para. 104(h)). It is based on the factual – or, as the Court formulates, 'causal' – nexus between conducts performed in the territory of the state and a human rights violation occurring abroad (IACtHR 2017, paras. 95, 101 and 102). As noted above, the Court limited its finding to interpret state obligations to respect and to ensure the rights to life and to personal integrity in relation to damage to the environment. The African Commission on Human and Peoples' Rights also interprets the right to life as imposing extraterritorial obligations where 'the State engages in conduct which could reasonably be foreseen to result in an unlawful deprivation of life' (ACommHPR 2015, para. 14). This requires the state to adopt measures 'to protect individuals and groups from real and immediate risks to their lives caused either by actions or inactions of third parties', including 'preventive steps to preserve and protect the natural environment' (ACommHPR 2015, para. 41). In the *Issa Yassin and Others v. Canada* case (2017), the Human Rights Committee also confirmed that 'there are situations where a State party has an obligation to ensure that rights under the Covenant are not impaired by extraterritorial activities conducted by enterprises under its jurisdiction' (HRC 2017b, para. 6.5).

It is striking that the most authoritative treaty interpretation, especially the IACtHR advisory opinion and recent general comments, requires states parties to protect against extraterritorial violations by corporate nationals in the context of the right to life and the right to physical integrity. Given the general international law obligation to cooperate to bring to an end any serious breach of a peremptory norm (ILC 2001a, art. 41(1)), one can add the freedom from torture and the right to self-determination of people. For those human rights, an interpretation requiring the obligation to protect against extraterritorial corporate violations is not accepted by most states parties but constitutes the progressive development of international law. This means that the respective human rights treaties should be interpreted according to this authoritative reading of their monitoring bodies that may also contribute to the formation of a customary human rights norm. It is questionable whether treaty bodies will extend this reading beyond the protection of the right to life and the right to physical integrity to other rights affected by pollution such as the rights to adequate food, to water and to take part in cultural life – as the IACtHR interpreted an autonomous right to a healthy environment in a non-extraterritorial context (IACtHR 2020, para. 207).

International human rights treaty bodies have confirmed that the obligation to regulate requires, as Principle 25 MP provides, a wide range of measures such as 'administrative, legislative, investigative, adjudicatory and other measures'. In the matter of cross-border pollution, monitoring bodies specified that the right to health expects from states 'the prevention and reduction of the population's exposure to harmful substances such as radiation and harmful chemicals or other detrimental environmental conditions that directly or indirectly impact upon human health' (CESCR 2000, para. 15). The IACtHR expects from states the obligation 'to supervise and monitor activities within their jurisdiction that may cause significant damage to the environment' (IACtHR 2017, para. 154). Preventive measures should be broadly conceived, as they should address both the source of the pollution, i.e., the environmental damage and its impact on human rights (ACommHPR 2015, para. 41). States were recommended

- 'to enact or enforce laws to prevent the pollution of water, air and soil by extractive and manufacturing industries' (CESCR 2000, para. 51);
- 'to take reasonable and other measures to prevent pollution and ecological degradation' (ACommHPR 2001, para. 52);
- 'to make use of a wide range of administrative and quasi-judicial mechanisms, many of which already regulate and adjudicate aspects of business activity in many States parties', such as 'consumer and environmental protection agencies' (CESCR 2017, para. 54) or 'environmental tribunals' (CRC Committee 2013, para. 30);
- to impose administrative sanctions on corporate national such as the denial of awarding of public contracts in public procurement regimes to companies that have not provided information on the environmental impacts of their activities (CRC Committee 2013, para. 50);

- to adopt preventive measures such as effective regulation and monitoring of the environmental impact of business (CRC Committee 2013, para. 20);
- to establish and implement regulations to ensure that the business sector complies with environment standards (CRC Committee Concluding observations: New Zealand 2016, para. 13(a));
- to hold corporate nationals 'accountable for any adverse impacts on the rights of indigenous peoples and other ethnic groups, in conformity with the principles of social responsibility and the ethics code of corporations' (CERD Concluding observations: Norway 2011, para. 17; CRC Committee Concluding observations: Canada 2012, para. 28).

This list of recommended best practices is non-exhaustive: according the standard of due diligence, the state is expected to take all reasonable measures within its capacity. It is a case-by-case evaluation of what reasonably available measures the state can take to ensure the prevention of the environmental damage and its impact on human rights.

The drafters of the MP have thus remarked (De Schutter et al. 2012, pp. 1136–1137) and at the same time anticipated this progressive interpretation by international human rights treaty bodies. It is regrettable that the MP do not provide for any minimum threshold on the severity of the risk of environmental impact on economic, social and cultural rights. The above-mentioned limitation of those extraterritorial protective obligations to the rights protecting the physical integrity of the person and *jus cogens* norms would constitute a sound basis, while extending them to other rights such as the right to property (e.g. restriction of the communal property of indigenous people because of environmental pollution) or the right to adequate housing (e.g. housing estates damaged by environmental pollution) seem to run against the dominant practice of monitoring bodies and States. The reason for the priority given to rights protecting the physical integrity of the person and peremptory norms of human rights law is that they constitute the most fundamental human rights; human rights treaty monitoring bodies also recognised that certain rights, especially non-derogable human rights require a higher degree of diligence than other rights (ACommHPR 2006, para. 155; ECtHR 2004, para. 334). This would be in line with the focus of general international law on 'significant transboundary harm' or 'significant damage' in formulating the obligation to protect against cross-border pollution (Section 2). Therefore, the instigation of extraterritorial obligations to protect against polluting corporate activities is the most compelling in case of *jus cogens* norms and human rights protecting the physical integrity of the person. This would also create a legitimate compromise between an activist claim to oblige the state to protect any human rights anywhere around the world affected by the conduct of its corporate nationals, on the one hand, and the fear of developed home States of the restriction of their economic and investment policies, on the other.

Obligations to fulfil

The obligation to fulfil requires states to take necessary steps, to the maximum of their available resources, to facilitate and promote the enjoyment of human rights. It may require allocating resources to the elimination of cross-border pollution or seeking business cooperation and support to implement economic, social and cultural rights (CESCR 2017, para. 23). While these duties are programmatic as they depend on the state's available resources and capacities – except the minimum core obligations – the state must move as expeditiously and effectively as possible towards 'achieving progressively the full realization of' economic, social and cultural rights' (CESCR 1990, para. 9).

Principle 29 on the obligation to create an international enabling environment has found also echo in the practice of human rights monitoring bodies. The Committee on Economic, Social and Cultural Rights confirmed that states shall undertake to encourage corporate actors whose conduct they are in a position to influence to ensure that they do not undermine the efforts of the states in which they operate to fully realize (CESCR 2017, para. 37; CESCR 2011, para. 6). International frameworks to fulfil might be, for instance, the environment standards of the OECD Guidelines for Multinational Enterprises (OECD 2011, pp. 42–46) or the European Pollutant Release and Transfer Register (EU 2006). The measures taken under Principle 29 aim at leading to the universal fulfilment of socio-economic rights also in matter of environmental protection. For instance, the right to health has been interpreted as including an obligation of states to 'formulate and implement national policies aimed at reducing and eliminating pollution of air, water and soil, including pollution by heavy metals such as lead from gasoline' (CESCR 2000, para. 36). The right of the child to the enjoyment of the highest attainable standard of health entails an obligation to 'combat disease and malnutrition [...] through, *inter alia*, [...] taking into consideration the dangers and risks of environmental pollution' (Convention on the Rights of the Child 1989, art. 24(2)(c)).

Principle 34 provides on the obligation to seek international assistance and cooperation as a means to fulfil socio-economic rights. This has a strong positive law basis as certain human rights treaties provide on the obligation to implement the convention 'through international assistance and co-operation, especially economic and technical' (ICESCR 1966, art. 2(1); American Convention on Human Rights 1969, art. 26). In case of cross-border pollution, the duty to internationally cooperate is recognised in international environment law and constitutes a customary international norm (IACtHR 2017, paras. 183–184).

While one can criticise the MP on the obligations to fulfil by saying that their programmatic and resource-dependent character makes them empty, in fact their follow the logic of state practice in matters of economic, social and cultural rights. The emphasis on extraterritorial obligations to fulfil reflects certain realism: Principle 31 provides that 'the fulfilment of economic, social and cultural rights extraterritorially' is 'commensurate with, *inter alia*, its economic, technical and technological capacities, available resources, and influence in international decision-making processes'. This standard, 'commensurate with' capacities, is as flexible as the state's obligation to fulfil economic, social and cultural rights in its territory 'to the maximum of its ability' (MP 31), as both depend on the state's capacity to assist and cooperate. As opposed to the obligation to fulfil in the state's own territory, however, the extraterritorial one 'cannot be achieved by any one state on its own' (De Schutter et al. 2012, p. 1151), but expects the state to 'cooperate to mobilize the maximum of available resources for the universal fulfilment' (MP 31).

Conclusions

Cross-border pollution is a clear global challenge as it requires by definition positive action by more than one state: beyond the state of origin, all states affected by the pollution are potentially human rights duty-bearers, given the connection between environmental pollution and socio-economic rights. The MP provide in detail on extraterritorial obligations to respect, protect and fulfil economic, social and cultural rights outside the state's territory. Its principles provide a sound and detailed framework for the obligations to respect (Principles 19–22) and fulfil (especially Principles 29, 31 and 34), and thus reflect the dominant state practice in international environment law and international human rights law.

Other rules of the MP, however, incorporate a progressive development of international law especially in interpreting the obligations to protect, in line with the evolving interpretation by most international human rights treaty bodies. However, the obligation to regulate corporate nationals' conduct abroad lacks appropriate guidance as to the threshold criteria, in particular as to the severity. Principles providing on the 'risk' of a harm (Principles 13–14) should be read as referring to a clear, direct and reasonably foreseeable negative impact of the pollution on economic, social and cultural rights abroad. Furthermore, the required threshold of severity should be expressed. Principles 24–27 provide for the state's obligation to take preventive measures to ensure that non-state actors do not impair the enjoyment of the economic, social and cultural rights of any persons abroad. Taking into account the recent practice of treaty monitoring bodies, the extraterritorial obligation to protect against the conduct of non-state actors should apply to polluting conducts that have a clear, direct and reasonably foreseeable negative impact on the rights protecting the physical integrity of the person and *jus cogens* norms.

Note

1. See, opposing: CEDAW (2017b) General Recommendation No. 35 written comments of states: Australia, paras. 13-16; Norway; HRC (2017a) General Comment no. 36 Written comments of States: Austria; Canada, para. 7; Germany, para. 21; Netherlands, paras. 18 and 29; France Comment submitted after the adoption of the General Comment, paras. 16-18; Norway; U.S.A., para. 13; in support of: WTO Communication from China, Cuba, India, Kenya, Pakistan and Zimbabwe 2002, para. 21.

References

ACommHPR (2015) GC 3 on the Right to Life.

African Commission on Human and Peop'es' Rights (ACommHPR) (2001) *The Social and Economic Rights Action Center and the Center for Economic and Social Rights v. Nigeria*, Communication 155/96.

Bodansky, D. et al. (eds) (2008) 'International Environmental Law: Mapping the Field', *The Oxford Handbook of International Environmental Law*, Oxford University Press.

Committee on Economic, Social and Cultural Rights (CESCR) (1990) GC 3 on the nature of states parties' obligations.

_______ (1999) GC 12 on the right to adequate food, UN Doc. E/C.12/1999/5.

_______ (2000) GC 14 on the Right to the Highest Attainable Standard of Health, UN Doc. E/C.12/2000/4.

_______ (2002) GC 15 on the right to water, UN Doc. E/C.12/2002/11.

_______ (2011) Statement on the obligations of States Parties regarding the corporate sector and economic, social and cultural rights, UN Doc. E/C.12/2011/1.

_______ (2017) GC 24 on State obligations under the ICESCR in the context of business activities, UN Doc. E/C.12/GC/24.

Committee on the Elimination of Racial Discrimination (CERD) (2011) Concluding observations: United Kingdom of Great Britain and Northern Ireland, UN Doc. CERD/C/GBR/CO/18-20.

_______ (2011) Concluding observations: Norway, UN Doc. CERD/C/NOR/CO/19-20.

_______ (2014) Concluding observations: United States of America, UN Doc. CERD/C/USA/CO/7-9

Committee on the Elimination of Discrimination against Women (CEDAW) (2017a) General recommendation no. 30 on women in conflict prevention, conflict and post-conflict situations, UN Doc. CEDAW/C/GC/30.

_______ (2017b) General recommendation no. 35 on the Gender-related dimensions of Disaster Risk Reduction in a Changing Climate, written comments of states, available at https://www.ohchr.org/EN/HRBodies/CEDAW/Pages/DraftGRDisasterRisk.aspx [accessed 24 September 2020].

_______ (2018) General recommendation no. 37 on the gender-related dimensions of disaster risk reduction in the context of climate change, UN Doc. CEDAW/C/GC/37.

Committee on the Rights of the Child (CRC Committee) (2012) Concluding observations: Canada, UN Doc. CRC/C/CAN/CO/3-4.

_______ (2013) GC 16 on State obligations regarding the impact of the business sector on children's rights, UN Doc. CRC/C/GC/16.

_______ (2016) Concluding observations: New Zealand, UN Doc. CRC/C/NZL/CO/5.

De Schutter, O et al. (2012) 'Commentary to the *Maastricht Principles* on Extraterritorial Obligations of States in the Area of Economic, Social and Cultural Rights', *Human Rights Quarterly* 34(4), 1084–1169.

Economic Commission for Europe (1990) Code of Conduct on Accidental Pollution of Transboundary Inland Waters (Decision C (45)), UN Doc. E/ECE/1225, ECE/ENWA/16.

European Commission on Human Rights (ECmHR) (1995) *Rasheed Haje Tugar v.Italy*, no. 22869/93, report of 18 October 1995 on the admissibility.

European Court of Human Rights (ECtHR) (1994) *López Ostra v. Spain*, Application no: 16798/90, Judgment.

_______ (1999) *Jean Asselbourg and 78 Others and Greenpeace Association-Luxembourg v. Luxembourg*, Application no: 29121/95, decision on the admissibility.

_______ (2001) *Banković and Others v. Belgium and 16 other States*, Application no: 52207/99, decision on the admissibility.

_______ (2004) *Ilaşcu and Others v. Moldova and Russia*, Application no: 48787/99, Judgment.

_______ (2005) *Fadeyeva v. Russia*, Application no: 55723/00, Judgment.

_______ (2008) *Georgia Andreou v. Turkey*, Application no: 45653/99, decision on the admissibility.

_______ (2009) *Leon and Agnieszka Kania v. Poland*, Application no: 12605/03, Judgment.

_______ (2011) *Dubetska and Others v. Ukraine*, Application no: 30499/03, Judgment.

_______ (2011) *Grimkovskaya v. Ukraine*, Application no: 38182/03, Judgment.

_______ (2012) *di Sarno and Others v. Italy*, Application no: 30765/08, Judgment.

_______ (2016) *Otgon v. the Republic of Moldova*, Application no: 22743/07, Judgment.

_______ (2019) *Cordella and Others v. Italy*, Application nos: 54414/13 and 54264/15, Judgment.

European Union (EU) (2006) European Pollutant Release and Transfer Register (E-PRTR) Regulation, available at https://ec.europa.eu/environment/industry/stationary/eper/legislation.htm [accessed 24 September 2020].

Gould, A. and Shelton, D. (2013) 'Positive and Negative Obligations' in Shelton, D. (ed). *The Oxford Handbook of International Human Rights Law*, Oxford University Press.

Human Rights Committee (HRC) (2017a) ICCPR GC 36 on Article 6 – Right to life, Written comments of States, available at https://www.ohchr.org/en/hrbodies/ccpr/pages/gc36-article6righttolife.aspx [accessed 24 September 2020].

_______ (2017b) *Basem Ahmed Issa Yassin et al. v. Canada*, Communication no. 2285/2013, Views of 26 July 2017, UN Doc. CCPR/C/120/D/2285/2013.

_______ (2019) GC 36 on Article 6: right to life, UN Doc. CCPR/C/GC/36.

Inter-American Court of Human Rights (IACtHR) (2017) The Environment and Human Rights (State obligations in relation to the environment in the context of the protection and guarantee of the rights to life and to personal integrity – interpretation and scope of Articles 4(1) and 5(1) of the American Convention on Human Rights), Advisory Opinion OC-23/17 of November 15, 2017. Series A no. 23

_______ (2020) *Indigenous Communities of the Lhaka Honhat (Our Land) Association v. Argentina*, Series C no. 400, Judgment (Merits).

International Court of Justice (ICJ) (2010) *Pulp Mills on the River Uruguay (Argentina v. Uruguay)*, I.C.J. Reports 2010, Judgment.

_______ (2015) *Certain Activities Carried Out by Nicaragua in the Border Area (Costa Rica v. Nicaragua) and Construction of a Road in Costa Rica along the San Juan River (Nicaragua v. Costa Rica)*, I.C.J. Reports 2015, Judgment.

International Law Commission (ILC) (2001a) Articles on Responsibility of States for Internationally Wrongful Acts, with commentaries, *Yearbook of the International Law Commission 2001* vol. II, Part Two.

_______ (2001b) Draft articles on Prevention of Transboundary Harm from Hazardous.

_______ (2006) Draft principles on the allocation of loss in the case of transboundary harm arising out of hazardous activities, with commentaries, *Yearbook of the International Law Commission 2006*, vol. II, Part Two.

_______ (2017) Fourth report on the protection of the atmosphere by Shinya Murase, Special Rapporteur, UN Doc. A/CN.4/705.

Milanovic, M. (2011) *Extraterritorial Application of Human Rights Treaties: Law, Principles, and Policy*, Oxford University Press.

Special Rapporteur on the adverse effects of the illicit movement and dumping of toxic and dangerous products and wastes on the enjoyment of human rights (2008) Report of the Special Rapporteur Okechukwu Ibeanu, Mission to Ukraine, UN Doc. A/HRC/7/21/Add.2.

United Nations Conference on the Human Environment (1972) Declaration of the United Nations Conference on the Human Environment.

United Nations Human Rights Council (2011a) Report of the Special Representative of the Secretary-General on the issue of human rights and transnational corporations and other business enterprises, John Ruggie, Guiding Principles on Business and Human Rights: Implementing the United Nations "Protect, Respect and Remedy" Framework, UN Doc. A/HRC/17/31.

_______ (2011b) Resolution 17/4 Human Rights and Transnational Corporations and Other Business Enterprises, UN Doc. A/HRC/RES/17/4.

World Trade Organization (WTO) (2002) Communication from China, Cuba, India, Kenya, Pakistan and Zimbabwe: Investors' and home Governments' obligations, WTO, Working Group on the Relationship between Trade and Investment, WT/WGTI/W/152.

32

ETOs and biodiversity

A right to food perspective on the intersection of human rights and environmental law

Philip Seufert and Sofía Monsalve Suárez

Introduction

The rapid and dramatic loss of biodiversity is one key manifestation of the deep ecological crisis that humanity and the planet are currently facing, the other key issue being global warming. Several scholars and activists have pointed out that the world is currently facing a new mass extinction – the sixth in the history of planet Earth, this time caused by us, humans. The rapid destruction of biodiversity affects the lives and livelihoods of people all over the world and has direct consequences on the enjoyment of human rights. The emergence of the novel coronavirus SARS-CoV-2 in 2020 has forced us once more to critically consider our societal relationship with nature.

On the following pages, we will discuss the close interrelatedness between biodiversity and the realization of human rights, focusing particularly on the extraterritorial component of states' obligations in this regard. We will identify some areas that are critical to addressing both human rights violations and ecosystem destruction and line out ways in which states are required to act in order to comply with their obligations under international human rights and environmental law. Our analysis and proposals are based on our work as human rights practitioners and, in particular, our close work with rural people and their organizations, especially organizations of small-scale food producers and indigenous peoples.

Biodiversity and human rights: A multifaceted relationship that stretches beyond borders

Biodiversity and human rights are closely interrelated. Firstly, biodiversity and functioning ecosystems are necessary to realize a number of human rights, such as the rights to food, water, health and culture (Knox 2017). Food production and the availability of nutritious, healthy and culturally adequate food fundamentally depend on functioning, biodiverse ecosystems as well as humans' ability to live in concert with other living beings – plants, animals, insects and microorganisms. Biodiversity is also a critical component of natural water cycles as well as the access

DOI: 10.4324/9781003090014-40

to safe water for consumption, food production and other household uses. For the billions of people who directly depend on the cultivation and harvesting of food and other natural materials, the diversity of living nature is the basis for their right to work. Healthy ecosystems prevent pathogens and dangerous diseases to spill over to humans. In addition, millions of plants, animals and microorganisms are the basis for drugs and treatments that ensure physical and mental health and wellbeing. Finally, ecosystems, animals, plants and all of living nature are the basis of many forms of cultural expressions and spiritual life that people and communities celebrate around the world.

While biodiversity and healthy ecosystems are essential for the survival and wellbeing of all people, they are particularly important for all those people and communities who live in close relationship with living nature, such as indigenous peoples, peasants, pastoralists, artisanal fishers and forest dwellers. For these groups, the natural environment is not only the basis of their livelihoods, but also the source of their dignity and self-determination. A second crucial aspect of the intersection between human rights and biological diversity therefore is the respect, protection and fulfilment of the rights of these people, as a precondition to ensure the preservation of biodiversity and functioning ecosystems. This understanding has consistently evolved over the last years and has led to an increased recognition that the protection of our living environment is not mainly an issue of conservation, but that communities and people play critical roles as custodians and stewards of ecosystems (Boyd 2020). What is more, conservationist approaches that are based on the assumption that nature and biodiversity can only be protected if humans are excluded, have led to the expulsion of rural communities and indigenous peoples from their lands and territories in many parts of the world (Tauli-Corpuz 2016).

This two-way relationship between human rights and biodiversity relates to states' obligations under international law, both within their national territory and beyond borders. Indeed, whereas the preservation of biodiversity and the management of ecosystems have a strong local component – e.g. local communities managing a given landscape or forest – they are also fundamentally transnational issues. As the former UN Special Rapporteur on human rights and the environment has noted, 'many of the components of biodiversity, the threats to biodiversity and the benefits biodiversity provides have transboundary or global dimensions' (Knox 2017). For instance, many ecosystems, such as not only oceans, rivers or lakes, but also terrestrial ecosystems, are transboundary. Moreover, however local their management may be, ecosystems and landscapes are linked regionally as well as globally. One example are migratory birds who connect ecosystems across continents. In addition, the destruction of ecosystems that are relevant for the entire planet, such as the deforestation of the Amazon rainforest or the dying of coral reefs, affect people all around the world. Finally, several of the key drivers of ecosystem destruction and biodiversity loss need to be understood and addressed as transnational issues.

Factors of biodiversity loss and related human rights violations

Based on FIAN's documentation of violations of the human right to food and nutrition around the world for more than 30 years, we have identified a number of factors leading to the destruction of biodiversity and adverse human rights impacts. The emerging patterns are confirmed and complemented by the findings of human rights bodies and authoritative scientific evidence regarding the drivers of biodiversity loss (IPBES 2019). It should be stressed that biodiversity loss/destruction is one aspect of broader environmental harm or degradation, and is often linked to other forms thereof (e.g. pollution through toxic substances, soil degradation, etc.).

Among the first factors causing biodiversity loss and human rights violations are deforestation and the destruction of land and water ecosystems for the expansion of industrial agriculture, in particular monoculture plantations of globally traded cash crops such as soy, sugar cane, maize etc. Conversion of forests, grasslands and arable land as well as destruction of water bodies also occur in the context of industrial/extractive projects, such as mining, oil and gas extraction, manufacturing, etc. All these activities cause major destruction of ecosystems and, in many cases, displace local communities and people. They further lead to significant pollution of water, soils and air, including through the use of pesticides, industrial runoff, emissions etc., which negatively affect biodiversity and lead to the impairment of human rights (FIAN et al. 2018). In the context of marine ecosystems, industrial fishing and intensive aquaculture are main factors leading to overexploitation, pollution and the destruction of biodiversity, while negatively affecting small-scale fishers, fish harvesters and fish workers (Ertör and Ortega-Cerdà 2018). ETO issues arise through the involvement of transnationally operating corporations in extractive activities, their financing and/or the trade of raw materials and products resulting from such activities. In addition, ETOs arise in the context of state policies (e.g. in the field of food, energy, trade and finance) that promote such activities in other countries.

Another important driver of the destruction of land and water ecosystems as well as the loss of land, fisheries and forests are large-scale infrastructure projects, such as dams, highways, large ports and real estate development. In several cases, such projects are part of broader policies aiming at establishing special economic zones to boost economic development (Guttal and Chrek 2016). ETOs become relevant in cases where such projects affect other countries (e.g. dams on transboundary rivers), and whenever foreign public or private actors are involved in the financing and/or implementing of such activities, including international/regional development banks, development cooperation or companies involved in construction.

Biological diversity, in particular agricultural biodiversity, is also reduced through the promotion of a limited number of homogeneous and uniform crops and varieties through agricultural policies, in particular a push for industrial, hybrid seeds of a limited number of high-yielding crops, as well as genetically modified organisms (GMOs). According to the UN Food and Agriculture Organization (FAO), this has led to the loss of some 75 percent of plant genetic diversity over the last century (FAO 2005). Genetically uniform industrial varieties and GMOs cannot be adapted by peasants and indigenous peoples to changing climatic and environmental conditions. In this context, human rights and ETO issues arise, among others, because of development cooperation and/or the expansion of intellectual property rights (IPR) regimes (e.g. through trade agreements), which limit the use and conservation of seeds, as well as their adaption by peasants and indigenous peoples to the local environment (De Schutter 2009). In addition, the global industrial seed and agricultural input market is dominated by a few transnational corporations whose operations directly impact biodiversity and peasants' and indigenous peoples' rights over seeds around the world.

It must further be noted that there is a close relationship between the rapid loss of biodiversity and global warming. Climate change, rising average temperatures and changing rainfall patterns strongly affect biodiversity. In parallel, declining biological diversity reduces the resilience and adaptability of ecosystems to changing climatic conditions, and, consequently, of societies in general. This results in adverse impacts on the right to food and nutrition as well as other human rights. A clear example that shows the interlinkages between biodiversity loss and climate change is deforestation, which is a critical factor of biodiversity loss, while also being an important driver of global warming. Consequently, states' ETOs in the context of climate change are also highly relevant in the context of biodiversity (refer to chapter on climate change in this volume).

Importantly, women (in particular rural women) and other gender groups are particularly affected by the destruction of ecosystems and biodiversity and its impacts on communities' and families' livelihoods. These often add to existing structural discrimination and marginalization. In many countries and regions, rural women play an important role as custodians of biodiversity, conserving a vast array of species, breeds and varieties (both domesticated and wild), including when these are no longer used to generate income. Another group that is particularly affected in the context of ecosystem destruction are human rights defenders working on land and environmental issues (EHRDs) who are the target of different forms of violence (Global Witness 2020). EHRDs often operate in remote areas and thus have more difficult access to protection mechanisms and justice. In many instances, they are members of already marginalized groups, including ethnic minorities. Individuals and communities opposing ecosystem destruction also frequently face risks linked to the existence of significant power imbalances. States' ETOs in the context of human rights and biodiversity therefore require them to take into account the impacts on women and EHRDs in the contexts mentioned above.

What this list of key factors of biodiversity destruction and related human rights violations shows is that states' obligations related to biodiversity, and specifically their ETOs, require them to take action in a range of policy fields, including:

- Food and nutrition;
- Seeds and biotechnologies;
- Development cooperation, including in the context of environmental protection and governance of land and natural resources;
- Trade, investment and finance, including corporate accountability;
- Energy;
- Climate change;
- Protection of human rights defenders;
- Women's rights and gender equality.

States' ETOs related to biodiversity

As said before, biodiversity has a clear transboundary and global dimension, regarding its components, the factors that drive its loss and the benefits that arise from it. Therefore, the impacts that states' acts and omissions may have beyond their national territories require special attention in the context of their obligations under international law. As the previous section has shown, states' ETOs are relevant to address the rampant destruction of biodiversity through economic activities and to protect affected people. In addition, ETOs require states to cooperate in order to support the realization of human rights and the preservation of biodiversity and ecosystems. This section will develop further on states' ETOs in this context, building on the general and specific obligations of states under human rights law as well as the way these have been summarized and clarified in the *Maastricht Principles* (MP).

Obligation to respect

In general terms, states are required to respect, protect and fulfil human rights as well as apply the principles of non-discrimination, non-retrogression and accountability. In the context of ETOs, this requires states, firstly, to respect human rights by avoiding to cause harm in other countries. This means that they must take measures to prevent their acts and omissions, including their policies and laws, from directly or indirectly interfering with the enjoyment of human rights and from contributing to biodiversity loss (MP 13, 20 and 21). Direct interference refers to the involvement of public entities in contributing to biodiversity-related human rights violations.

One example is development cooperation policies or programs supporting conservation initiatives that result in the dispossession of indigenous peoples or other rural people. Also the support of land policies in other countries, which focus on the promotion of land-based investments may lead to dispossession and ecosystem destruction, especially when there are no adequate safeguards in place. Another example is the public financing of infrastructure projects in other countries, e.g. through (national, regional or international) development banks.

Indirect interference encompasses conduct that reduces the ability of another state to comply with its human rights obligations. This can occur through trade and investment agreements, which reduce the policy space of states to implement measures required to ensure the preservation of biodiversity and ecosystems. A critical issue in the context of biodiversity are provisions requiring the establishment or tightening of IPR regimes, which are frequently part of trade agreements and limit farming communities' rights to conserve, use, exchange and sell seeds (Berne Declaration 2014). This example points to possible tensions with other international agreements, for instance, in the framework of the World Trade Organization's (WTO) Agreement on Trade-Related Aspects of Intellectual Property Rights (TRIPS) or the World Intellectual Property Organization (WIPO). In such cases, the principle of the primacy of human rights as well as the special attention that needs to be given to vulnerable and marginalized groups must guide states to prioritize their human rights obligations.

One important procedural element of avoiding harm in other countries is to conduct prior human rights, social and environmental impact assessments as well as to monitor the extraterritorial impacts of policies, laws and practices where the risk of adverse impacts on human rights and biodiversity is high (MP 14). States are thus required to carry out *ex ante* assessments and to put in place monitoring mechanisms in the context of their policies in the above-mentioned policy fields. It is of crucial importance that prior assessments are conducted by an independent body and with public participation, and their results be made public. Monitoring of existing policies should focus on human rights compliance and involve independent human rights bodies/experts (including national human rights institutes in affected countries) as well as those affected by policies. The outcomes of prior and *ex post* assessments need to inform measures to prevent, cease and remedy harm.

Obligations in the context of international agreements and cooperation

The duty to avoid harm also requires states to elaborate, interpret and apply international agreements in a manner consistent with their human rights obligations (MP 17). This includes agreements in the area of environmental protection and conservation, food, trade, investment, finance, development cooperation and climate change. In the context of biodiversity, this also refers to the need to comply with states' obligations under international environmental law, specifically the Convention on Biological Diversity (CBD) and its protocols as well as the International Treaty on Plant Genetic Resources for Food and Agriculture (ITPGRFA). These agreements further need to be implemented according to the highest human rights standards and based on the principle of the primacy of human rights. This requires states, among others, to rigorously apply the precautionary principle in the context of GMOs and biotechnologies. It also requires them to support the implementation of peasants' and indigenous peoples' rights over seeds, as recognized by the ITPGRFA, and to refrain from interpreting these rights in a manner that restricts them to the benefit of IPR. This duty is also relevant in the context of the establishment of market-based mitigation and offsetting schemes under international environmental and climate agreements (sometimes subsumed under the term 'nature-based solutions'). Such schemes usually have transboundary or extraterritorial components (e.g. because restoration measures in one country can be used to compensate for ecosystem destruction in another state) and entail risks of dispossessing local people as well as aggravating ecosystem destruction and biodiversity loss (African Centre for Biodiversity 2020).

The UN Special Rapporteurs on human rights and the environment have emphasized the need for cooperation between states in the context of biodiversity, stating that while 'international cooperation normally plays only a supporting role in the protection of human rights, [...] the effective protection of biodiversity, like the effective mitigation of climate change, is possible only with international cooperation' (Knox 2017, para. 36). This resonates with MP 29 and 32, which clarify states' obligation to participate in good faith in international governance processes in order to create a conducive environment for the universal realization of human rights, as well as to ensure that their policies and practices respect human rights principles and priorities when engaging in international cooperation. The latter includes prioritizing the rights of marginalized and disadvantaged population groups, observing the right to participation and self-determination, as well as the principles of non-discrimination and equality, including gender equality, and avoiding retrogressive measures. These obligations require states to ensure that their positions in international negotiations and policy spaces are in line with their human rights obligations as well as their commitments under environmental law, especially in those areas that entail risks of causing or facilitating ecosystem destruction and biodiversity loss (see list of policy issues above). Whereas the duty to cooperate applies to all countries, the Special Rapporteur on human rights and the environment has pointed out that wealthy states in particular must 'contribute their fair share towards the costs of conserving, protecting and restoring healthy ecosystems and biodiversity in low-income countries, in accordance with the principle of common but differentiated responsibilities' (Boyd 2020, para. 74).

Obligation to protect

Regarding their protect obligations, states' ETOs require them to establish the necessary regulatory mechanisms to ensure that non-state actors that they are in a position to regulate do not impair the enjoyment of human rights in other countries (MP 24). This means concretely that states must adopt and enforce measures to protect human rights and biodiversity from harm caused by transnationally operating corporations, wherever a corporation has its centre of activity, is registered or domiciled or has its main place of business or substantial business activities, in the state concerned. As has been described in the previous section, corporate activities related to industrial agriculture, intensive aquaculture, mining, infrastructure development, energy production, etc. are the main drivers of biodiversity loss and related human rights violations, and often the harm is caused in other countries than corporations' home states. Rural people such as peasants, indigenous peoples, artisanal fishers, pastoralists, forest dwellers and rural workers are particularly affected by ecosystem destruction and human rights violations resulting from such activities. Special attention needs to be put on the biodiversity and human rights harm caused by toxic substances, such as pesticides. Another relevant example are transnational seed companies that use aggressive marketing practices and their economic power to impose the use of industrial/commercial seeds and GMOs on rural people, thus undermining local seed and peasant seed systems, which are crucial for the conservation of agricultural biodiversity and the realization of the right to food and nutrition (Global Network for the Right to Food and Nutrition/ Global Convergence of Land and Water Struggles – West Africa 2017).

Another way in which corporations impair rural people's rights over seeds, breeds and other genetic resources is related to the use of digital technologies. Technological developments of the last decades allow the sequencing of genetic material and its storing in digital format in huge data bases (in policy debates, this is often referred to as digital sequence information, or DSI). Biotechnologies, such as gene editing, allow introducing the respective traits into the genome in order to create varieties with desired characteristics (e.g. resistance to drought). In combination with intellectual property rights in the form of patents on genetic sequences, digitalization further restricts the rights of peasants and indigenous peoples over seeds and biodiversity, even though most of the genetic material that forms the basis of digital sequencing has been collected in their fields and they detain the associated traditional knowledge. DSI and patents are also likely to further increase the concentration of the industrial seed sector, which is currently dominated by four companies (ETC Group 2019). These examples point to the fact that effective measures to regulate transnationally operating corporate actors and hold them to account need to be a critical element of states' efforts to preserve biodiversity and ensure its sustainable use. Such regulation is particularly important in the light of the high level of concentration in the industrial seed and agricultural input sector.

As part of their ETOs, states must, moreover, cooperate in regulating and holding TNCs and other non-state actors accountable for human rights abuses and ensuring effective remedies for those affected (MP 27). This is particularly important in the context of the increasing financialization of the economy, which entails, among others, complex financing schemes – 'investment webs' – of extractive activities, involving many different actors (companies directly involved in the operations as well as different forms of financers, such as shareholders, banks, investment funds, pension funds etc.). Such investment webs typically stretch over different countries, implying finance flows across borders (FIAN et al. 2020). It is therefore important to stress that measures to regulate corporate actors need to include the legal duty on parent companies to exercise due diligence by controlling their subsidies, as well as addressing involved actors throughout investment webs.

In addition to corporations, the Special Rapporteur on Human Rights and the Environment has pointed out to the role that conservation organizations play in the context of biodiversity, including in the context of human rights impairments and violence through exclusive conservation activities (Boyd 2020, paras. 78–79). In the context of their protect obligations, states must therefore also monitor and regulate the activities of conservation organizations that they are in a position to regulate as well as conditioning financial support to such organizations to effective respect of human rights.

As mentioned above, EHRDs are among the groups that are particularly at risk of human rights impairments in the context of biodiversity and ecosystem destruction. States therefore need to put a particular emphasis on ensuring their protection – especially in cases where actors are involved that they are in a position to regulate – and are required to cooperate with other countries in this regard, including through diplomacy.

Obligation to ensure effective remedy

States' ETOs require them further to put in place effective accountability mechanisms to ensure that individuals and communities affected by human rights violations related to biodiversity loss and ecosystem destruction have access to effective remedies, including judicial remedies where necessary (MP 37 and 38). Important components of this duty are to cooperate with other states to this effect (MP 27) – in particular those states where the harm has been caused – and to ensure remedies in cases of impairments caused by the transnational operations of corporations or conservation groups. Given that moral-duty-based and non-judicial grievance mechanisms have in many cases proven to be ineffective in addressing human rights abuses, state-based judicial remedy is crucial and human rights obligations call for states to advance their judicial system, opening it up and guaranteeing full access to civil, administrative and criminal effective justice systems to all victims of corporate human rights abuses, wherever they occur, including in the context of biodiversity and ecosystem destruction. As emphasized before, states should also take specific measures to ensure the protection of EHRDs, which includes ensuring effective remedy in cases of human rights impairments.

Bringing together human rights and environmental law

The description of states' ETOs in the context of biodiversity and human rights in the previous section is based on an integrated reading of states' obligations under international human rights law on the one hand, and international environmental law on the other. Both fields of law provide critical procedural and normative guidance for states, but have historically developed on separate tracks – though not entirely disconnected. The understanding of their close interrelatedness has advanced only recently and is still in the building. This applies to the interconnection of biodiversity and human rights in general as well as in particular their implications for ETOs. Indeed, the extraterritorial component of states obligations at the intersection of biodiversity and human rights is a field that requires further attention.

Human rights

Regarding human rights, it is worth noting that the Universal Declaration on Human Rights as well as the two human rights Covenants are largely silent on nature and biodiversity, with the exception of Articles 1.2 of both the International Covenant on Civil and political Rights and the International Covenant on Economic, Social and Cultural Rights, which establish the principle that peoples have sovereignty over their natural resources. They do not, however, explicitly address the relationship between nature and human dignity as a core objective of human rights. However, the fact that the realization of several of the rights enshrined in these documents require biological diversity and functioning ecosystems has been recognized by some of the General Comments (GCs) issued by the Committee on Economic, Social and Cultural Rights, in particular GCs 4, 12, 15 and 21. The Committee on the Elimination of Discrimination Against Women's General Recommendation no. 34 on the rights of rural women is more explicit about biodiversity, underlining states' obligations to address threats posed by loss of biodiversity (para. 12) and clarifying that seeds and land are fundamental human rights (para. 56). It should be noted that all these documents also refer to ETOs (sometimes referred to as 'international obligations'), but without going into detail regarding the biodiversity-related components. Based on the discussion in the previous chapter, it is noteworthy that GC 24 on state obligations in the context of business activities refers to environmental impacts of such activities and contains comprehensive guidance on states' ETOs related to the regulation and monitoring of transnational corporations.

In recent years, the Human Rights Council's universal periodic review process as well as the treaty bodies have been increasingly highlighting the human rights impacts of damage to ecosystems and biodiversity, in particular in the context of deforestation and economic activities (Boyd 2020, paras. 62–63). It should be noted, however, that the observations and recommendations issued so far do not explicitly refer to extraterritorial aspects in this regard.

Human rights that are closely tied to biodiversity are also enshrined in regional human rights agreements, including the African Charter on Human and Peoples' Rights as well as the American Convention on Human Rights and its Additional Protocol in the Area of Economic,

Social and Cultural Rights (Protocol of San Salvador). The latter also explicitly recognizes the right to a healthy environment (art. 11), which is also enshrined in several national legislations. Additional regional agreements that are important in the context of human rights and biodiversity are the Regional Agreement on Access to Information, Public Participation and Justice in Environmental Matters in Latin America and the Caribbean ('Escazú agreement') as well as the Aarhus Convention. None of these instruments, however, is very explicit about the extraterritorial components of these rights.

Environmental law

Regarding international environmental law, the most important reference in the context of biodiversity is the CBD, which was adopted during the 1992 United Nations Conference. It is worth noting that the CBD does not focus on environmental rights of people or communities, but rather on the way in which states must ensure the conservation and sustainable use of biodiversity that are present in their national territories as well as the use of such biological resources by other countries. However, it recognizes certain rights of indigenous peoples and local communities and states' obligations in this regard, namely to respect, preserve and maintain knowledge, innovations and practices of indigenous and local communities relevant for the conservation and sustainable use of biological diversity (art. 8(j)), as well as to protect and encourage customary use of biological resources in accordance with traditional cultural practices (art. 10(c)). Article 5 underlines the importance of cooperation in the context of biodiversity conservation and article 22 clarifies that obligations under other international agreements need to be implemented in a way that does not damage biodiversity.

The CBD has two protocols that provide further normative guidance. Firstly, the Nagoya Protocol establishes that states must take measures to ensure that traditional knowledge associated with genetic resources that is held by rural people and communities is accessed with their prior and informed consent or approval and involvement, and that mutually agreed terms have been established (art. 7). In addition, states are required to respect indigenous and local communities' customary laws with respect to traditional knowledge associated with genetic resources, and to not restrict the customary use and exchange of genetic resources and associated traditional knowledge within and amongst indigenous and local communities (art. 12). Secondly, the Cartagena Protocol is the main international agreement on biosafety for GMOs and further specifies states' obligation under the CBD to implement measures to regulate, manage and control the risks associated with the use and release of living modified organisms resulting from biotechnology (art. 8(g)). The Cartagena Protocol reaffirms the precautionary principle as one of the cornerstones of environmental laws (art. 1) and contains provisions regarding the transboundary movement, transit, handling and use of GMOs, as well as guidance on risk assessments, monitoring and safeguards for the environment and human health (Annex III, art. 4). The CBD's emphasis on states' international obligations apply also to both protocols, in particular where access to genetic resources involves actors from more than one country, as well as in the context of transboundary movement of GMOs.

Building on the CBD, the ITPGRFA recognizes the rights of peasants and indigenous peoples over seeds. It recognizes the access to and use of plant genetic resources for food and agriculture as key elements of food security. A key element of the treaty is the recognition of peasants' and indigenous peoples' rights over seeds, based on the recognition of their past, present and future contribution to the preservation and sustainable use of plant genetic resources (preamble). In article 9, the Parties recognize these rights (referred to as 'farmers' rights'), including their rights to the protection of traditional knowledge relevant to plant genetic resources for food and agriculture; the right of peasants to equitably participate in sharing benefits arising from the utilization of plant genetic resources for food and agriculture; and their right to participate in making decisions on matters related to the conservation and sustainable use of plant genetic resources for food and agriculture (art. 9). It further stresses that Parties shall not limit peasants' and indigenous peoples' rights to save, use, exchange and sell farm-saved seed/propagating material (art. 9.3). These provisions directly relate to states ETOs, given that the ITPGRFA refers to the importance of international cooperation in its implementation and does not limit its scope to national jurisdictions.

An integrated interpretation of human rights and environmental law

Even though international human rights and environmental law have developed in a somewhat disconnected manner, recent years have seen important efforts aiming at bringing both together, including in the context of biodiversity. The creation, by the UN Human Rights Council, of a dedicated mandate on human rights and the environment has contributed to developing a better understanding of the interlinkages between human rights and environmental issues.[1] This refers specifically to the understanding that the protection of the natural environment, including biodiversity, is indispensable for the effective enjoyment of a number of human rights.[2] The former Special Rapporteur on Human Rights and the Environment has developed Framework Principles, which are based on his analysis of the interrelatedness between environmental issues and human rights and aim to 'facilitate the implementation of states' human rights obligations relating to the enjoyment of a safe, clean, healthy and sustainable environment' (Knox 2018, para. 7), including biodiversity. As his successor explains, these framework principles refer to three categories of state obligations, namely: 1) procedural obligations; 2) substantive obligations; and 3) special obligations towards those in vulnerable situations (Boyd 2020, para. 68). In the light of the fundamentally transboundary and global dimensions of biodiversity (see Section 2), these have all extraterritorial components. The Special Rapporteur has particular highlighted states' duty to ensure that activities within their jurisdiction or control do not cause harm to the environment or peoples of other states, as well as their obligation to cooperate internationally (ibid, paras. 73 and 74).

The procedural obligations identified by the Special Rapporteur are based on and reaffirm international standards regarding access to information and transparency; effective participation of rights holders; environmental, social and human rights impact assessments; access to justice and remedies; gender equality; as well as the protection of environmental human rights defenders. 'Each of these obligations applies to measures that affect biodiversity in ways that threaten the full enjoyment of the human rights that depend on its components' (Knox 2017, para. 28).

The substantial obligations are based on 'a general duty to protect biodiversity' (Knox 2017, para. 35) and require states to not violate the right to a healthy environment or other human rights related to healthy ecosystems and biodiversity through their own actions; to protect those rights from being violated by third parties, in particular businesses; and to establish, implement and enforce laws, policies and programs to fulfil these rights (Boyd 2020, para. 70). In this context, the framework principles emphasize in particular the need to rigorously apply the precautionary principle and to avoid discrimination and retrogressive measures.

Finally, the special obligations in the proposed Framework Principles refer to states' particular obligations towards marginalized and vulnerable groups, in particular indigenous peoples, peasants and other rural communities (Boyd 2020, para 72). As discusses above, these groups directly depend on functioning ecosystems and biodiversity and are therefore particularly affected by environmental harm in general, and biodiversity loss in particular. It is in this context that the adoption of the UN Declaration on the Rights of Indigenous Peoples (UNDRIP) as well as the UN Declaration on the Rights of Peasants and Other People Working in Rural Areas (UNDROP) are highly relevant. Both recognize the specific rights of rural people and clarify states' obligations in this regard, including concerning their rights to natural resources, land, seeds, biodiversity and a healthy environment (arts. 5, 17, 18, 19 and 20). Article 2 of the UNDROP specifically points to states' ETOs by underlining their duty to uphold their human rights obligations in the context of international agreements and international cooperation, as well as to regulate corporations and other non-state actors that they are in a position to regulate.

The two Declarations provide an opportunity for a more holistic reading of some key instruments of environmental law from a human rights perspective. The CBD, for instance, is built upon the premise that states have sovereignty over the biodiversity in their national territory. The question that arises from the recognition of specific rights of indigenous peoples and other rural people related to such resources by UNDRIP and UNDROP then is: what do states' sovereign responsibilities entail in terms of obligations to protect and guarantee communities' and people's rights? An important part of the answer to this question is that the effective protection of indigenous peoples' and other rural peoples' tenure, management, production and knowledge systems are key to addressing the rapid decline of biodiversity (Boyd 2020, para. 72). In this context, also specific normative guidance has been developed in the UN system on issues that are critical for the conservation of biodiversity. Instruments such as the Voluntary Guidelines to Support the Progressive Realization of the Right to Adequate Food in the Context of National Food Security, the Voluntary Guidelines on the Responsible Governance of Tenure of Land, Fisheries and Forests in the Context of National Food Security, as well as the Voluntary Guidelines for Securing Sustainable Small-Scale Fisheries in the Context of Food Security and Poverty Eradication, all refer to the need for sustainable management of natural and genetic resources and emphasize the importance of international cooperation in this regard. The Guidelines on the Responsible Governance of Tenure also contain specific paragraphs that clarify states' obligations to regulate and hold accountable corporations operating abroad (para 3.2) as well as to ensure that their own land-related investments abroad are consistent with human rights (para 12.15).

Conclusion

The rapid decline of biodiversity in the context of the deep ecological crisis that the world is facing has increased awareness about the complex relationships between human societies and their natural environment, and sparked efforts to bring together human rights and environmental law. It is now understood that a failure to comply with obligations to preserve biological diversity entails an elevated risk of human rights violations, and that addressing structural drivers of human rights violations critically contributes to the preservation of biodiversity.

It is important to stress that the cross-fertilization between the two spheres of law is already happening, especially in national and regional legislation and jurisprudence.[3] Interesting lessons can be drawn from numerous examples of recognition and implementation efforts regarding the right to a healthy environment in national legislation (Boyd 2018, paras. 30 ff.). A particularly interesting case is a judgment of the Inter-American Court of Human Rights in February 2020, which recognizes the violations of the rights to food, water, a healthy environment and cultural identity of indigenous communities in Argentina. This judgment can be seen as a concrete example of integration of different sources of law, recognizing their interdependence and applying a holistic approach to human rights.[4] Some countries have also recognized rights of nature in their legal frameworks. Such developments at national and regional level should inspire and guide further developments in international law. Indeed, the previous and current

Special Rapporteurs on Human Rights and the Environment have been calling for the explicit recognition of a human right to a healthy environment by the UN General Assembly, of which biodiversity is one critical component.

Despite increasing awareness of the important nexus between human rights and biodiversity and the recognition of its transboundary and global dimensions, more work is needed to clarify and develop the concrete ETOs that arise for states in this context. The understanding of biodiversity as a 'global commons' is much less well established as compared to climate change. Even though the preamble of the CBD affirms that the conservation of biological diversity is a common concern of humankind, states have maintained a strong stance that the conservation of biodiversity is, primarily, an issue of national sovereignty. Increasing awareness on the critical importance of the impacts that states' acts and omissions can have on biodiversity, ecosystems and people beyond their national territories will be critical in order to advance in this regard and to address the current ecological crisis.

Notes

1. It should be noted that this work has been complementary to the work of the Special Rapporteur on the implications for human rights of the environmentally sound management and disposal of hazardous substances and wastes. See https://www.ohchr.org/EN/Issues/Environment/ToxicWastes/Pages/SRToxicWastesIndex.aspx.
2. For more information, see: www.ohchr.org/EN/Issues/Environment/SREnvironment/Pages/SRenvironmentIndex.aspx.
3. Interesting resources are https://climate-laws.org/litigation_cases and http://climatecasechart.com/non-us-climate-change-litigation. Although the focus lies on climate change, the cases compiled there are also relevant in the context of biodiversity.
4. For more information, see www.corteidh.or.cr/docs/comunicados/cp_24_2020_eng.pdf.

References

African Centre for Biodiversity (2020) 'Nature-based Solutions or Nature-based Seductions?', www.acbio.org.za/en/nature-based-solutions-or-nature-based-seductions [accessed 30 July 2021].

Berne Declaration (2014) 'Owning Seeds, Accessing Food. A Human Rights Impact Assessment of UPOV 1991', available at www.publiceye.ch/fileadmin/doc/Saatgut/2014_Public_Eye_Owning_Seed_-_Accessing_Food_Report.pdf [accessed 30 July 2021].

Boyd, D. (2018) Report of the Special Rapporteur on the issue of human rights obligations relating to the enjoyment of a safe, clean, healthy and sustainable environment, available at https://undocs.org/pdf?symbol=en/a/73/188 [accessed 30 July 2021].

_______ (2020) 'Human Rights Depend on a Healthy Biosphere', Report of the UN Special Rapporteur on Human Rights and the Environment, available at https://undocs.org/A/75/161 [accessed 30 July 2021].

De Schutter, O. (2009) 'Seed Policies and the Right to Food: Enhancing Agrobiodiversity and Encouraging Innovation', Report of the Special Rapporteur on the Right to Food, available at https://undocs.org/A/64/170 [accessed 30 July 2021].

Ertör, I. and Ortega-Cerdà, M. (2018) 'The Expansion of Intensive Marine Aquaculture in Turkey: The Next-to-Last Commodity Frontier?', *Journal of Agrarian Change*, 1–24, available at https://onlinelibrary.wiley.com/doi/abs/10.1111/joac.12283 [accessed 30 July 2021].

ETC Group (2019) 'Plate Tech-Tonics. Mapping Corporate Power in Big Food', available at https://etcgroup.org/content/plate-tech-tonics [accessed 30 July 2021].

FAO (2005) 'Building on Gender, Agrobiodiversity and Local Knowledge', available at www.fao.org/3/a-y5956e.pdf [accessed 30 July 2021].

FIAN International, Rede Social de Justiça e Direitos Humanos and Comissão Pastoral da Terra (2018) 'The Human and Environmental Cost of Land Business. The Case of MATOPIBA', htttp://bit.ly/MATOPIBALandGrab [accessed 30 July 2021].

FIAN International/Transnational Institute/Focus on the Global South (2020) 'Rogue Capitalism and the Financialization of Territories and Nature', available at https://www.fian.org/files/files/Rogue_Capitalism_and_the_Financialization_of_Territories_and_Nature_(1).pdf [accessed 30 July 2021].

Global Network for the Right to Food and Nutrition/Global Convergence of Land and Water Struggles – West Africa (2017) 'Business profits or diverse food systems? Threats to peasant seeds and implications in West Africa', available at http://www.fian.org/fileadmin/media/publications_2018/Reports_and_guidelines/180329_FIAN_FFM_BurkinaFaso_EN_Web.pdf [accessed 30 July 2021].

Global Witness (2020) 'Defending Tomorrow. The climate crisis and threats against land and environmental defenders', www.globalwitness.org/en/campaigns/environmental-activists/defending-tomorrow [accessed 30 July 2021].

Guttal, S. and Chrek, S. (2016) 'An Overview of Large-Scale Investments in the Mekong Region. Focus on the Global South', available at http://bit.ly/LargeScaleInvestmentsMekong [accessed 30 July 2021].

Intergovernmental Science-Policy Platform on Biodiversity and Ecosystem Services (IPBES) (2019) Global Assessment Report on Biodiversity and Ecosystem Services. https://ipbes.net/global-assessment [accessed 30 July 2021].

Knox, J. (2017) 'Human Rights Obligations Relating to the Conservation and Sustainable Use of Biological Diversity', Report of the UN Special Rapporteur on Human Rights and the Environment, available at https://undocs.org/A/HRC/34/49 [accessed 30 July 2021].

_______ (2018) Report of the Special Rapporteur on the Issue of Human Rights Obligations Relating to the Enjoyment of a Safe, Clean, Healthy and Sustainable Environment, available at https://undocs.org/A/HRC/37/59 [accessed 30 July 2021].

Tauli-Corpuz, V. (2016) 'Conservation Measures and their Impacts on Indigenous Peoples' Rights', Report of the UN Special Rapporteur on the Rights of Indigenous Peoples, available at https://undocs.org/A/71/229 [accessed 30 July 2021].

Part VIII
Conclusion

33

Conclusions

The future of extraterritorial human rights obligations

Gamze Erdem Türkelli, Mark Gibney, Wouter Vandenhole and Markus Krajewski

As this is being written, the worldwide COVID-19 pandemic continues to rage, and some important extraterritorial lessons – some good and some bad – have emerged from this pandemic. The first and perhaps most obvious is that communicable diseases do not respect national borders. What began in Wuhan, China soon spread to every corner of the globe, even as states quickly responded by attempting to close themselves off from the rest of the world. If the pandemic teaches us nothing else, it should teach us that each one of us is potentially far more connected with the rest of humanity than we had ever imagined.

There is, however, another lesson from the response to the pandemic and it relates to the development of a COVID vaccine and its distribution. Of particular concern is whether the states of the Global North will only recognize an obligation to protect their own citizens, thereby leaving large swaths of humanity to fend for themselves. If this is the case, the pandemic will most assuredly take the lives of that many more individuals. Yet, what we seem to be witnessing is that in the face of a global vaccine shortage combined with desperate domestic demand, few seem to think in terms of states having human rights obligations to people in other lands.

The present crisis will pass, sooner or later. But what remain are many other political, social, economic and ecological events that will continue to have a comparable global impact. The most notable of these events is climate change. In the case of climate change, as with the pandemic, the human rights consequences will not – and cannot – be restricted by national borders. However, and continuing with the pandemic analogy, some states will be better positioned to cope with the devastating crises that will ensue than others. In blunter terms, people will either live or die depending on where they happen to be born. Yet, is this kind of situation all that much different from the world as it exists today?

What has propelled the push to recognize extraterritorial obligations (or to use different terminology, human rights beyond borders) is the understanding that an exclusively or predominantly territorial approach to human rights has left large parts of humanity unprotected. And what has always been difficult, if not impossible, to reconcile is the self-proclaimed "universality" of human rights with a system of protection that is the antithesis of universality, one where a state's human rights obligations end suddenly and, in our view, rather arbitrarily at its own

DOI: 10.4324/9781003090014-42

domestic borders, while at the same time, giving states license to operate under a completely different set of human rights standards depending on whether they were operating at home or abroad.

Perhaps these crises, and others, will be used to further question the utility and even the legitimacy of human rights (Moyn 2010; Hopgood 2013; Posner 2014). The charge that most assuredly will be made by these critics is that all the international human rights law in the world could do little in the face of the most tragic and devastating cataclysms facing us. Our answer is that what has attempted to pass itself off as human rights is not truly "human rights," but rather, reflects the biases and interests of a small segment of states and a small segment of the world's population.

As climate change and the COVID-19 pandemic remind us, human rights protections must be effective and available to individuals and communities also when individuals and communities are faced with border-defying political, social, economic or ecological problems that render the very idea of territorially bound human rights obligations obsolete. In order to realize the emancipatory potential of human rights, we also need a reckoning within international law that concedes the shortcomings of state-centricity and of legal straitjackets such as predominantly territorially based understandings of jurisdiction and primarily causality-based conceptualizations of legal responsibility. To that end, we see the need to critically re-engage with the fundamentals of the debate around both primary and secondary norms. The key axes of that reengagement should centre on moving beyond territorial jurisdiction, recognizing global obligations and conceptualizing a more expansive understanding of responsibility.

Moving beyond Territorial Jurisdiction

The 'state-centricity of traditional human rights mechanisms and the near obsession to link human rights obligations to jurisdiction in its narrowest conception' (Erdem Türkelli 2020, p. 36) is a core impediment to the idea of universal availability of human rights protections to each and every rights-holder (Roxtrom and Gibney 2017). Many human rights treaties, even when they have a jurisdiction clause, do not solely limit jurisdiction to a state party's territory, for instance, by referring not only to a state ensuring relevant rights *within its territory* but also rights *subject to its jurisdiction* (Milanovic 2013).

The enforcement of human rights obligations beyond borders, as the contributions to the Enforcement section highlight, has not followed a uniform approach across different systems. The work of the UN Treaty Bodies have been pivotal in establishing a narrative around operational ETOs and global obligations of states, in pushing further for human rights-based international assistance and in clarifying how states ought to interact with private actors and international institutions (Pribytkova in this volume).

The European regional human rights enforcement system under the European Court of Human Rights (ECtHR), on the other hand, has been particularly reluctant to concede a reading of jurisdiction beyond borders in (what it deems "exceptional") circumstances of effective control (Haeck, Burbano-Herrera and Ghulam Farag in this volume). Nonetheless, the ECtHR has allowed for an extraterritorial exercise of jurisdiction in such cases, having recognized that not doing so would create 'a regrettable vacuum in the system of human-rights protection' as it would 'remov[e] from individuals … the benefit of the Convention's fundamental safeguards and their right to call a High Contracting Party to account for violation of their rights in proceedings before the Court' (ECtHR 2001, para. 78). ECtHR's own reasoning that has motivated this overture is an important reminder about the purpose of human rights law and of enforcement mechanisms that should seek to make human rights entitlements available to rights-holders in practice. In order to do so, human rights enforcement mechanisms should focus on 'enabling outsiders' access to domestic and international courts by removing formal and practical barriers or equipping judicial bodies with the adequate means to analyse situations that occurred far away' (Müller in this volume).

The Inter-American system has in fact been a pioneer in providing extraterritorial human rights protections (Wilde in this volume) and recognizing state obligations to rights-holders beyond territorial borders. As the Inter-American Court of Human Rights reminds in its Advisory Opinion 23 on environment and human rights, "jurisdiction" is not circumscribed by the territorial borders of a state. In fact, each time a state engages in conduct with human rights impacts (within or outside of its territorial borders), it also exercises its jurisdiction (para. 78). States' obligations may include preventing third parties within their territory from causing environmental harm or damage within and outside of their territory as well as themselves avoiding activities within their territory or control that may impact rights-holders within or outside of their territory.

The African Charter on Human and Peoples' Rights does not delimit the application of the Charter to a specific territory, geography or legal space. While the African Commission has previously accepted both the spatial and the personal models of jurisdiction, the Court and the Committee have yet to build jurisprudence on the matter (Oloo and Vandenhole in this volume).

The necessary de-coupling of territory and jurisdiction would overcome a binary narrative as regards human rights obligations being territorial versus extraterritorial (Seck in this volume).

Towards Obligations beyond borders: Recognition of "global obligations"

The cross-boundary nature of some of the most pressing global problems and the global nature of harms necessitates moving past constructed binaries when conceptualizing human rights obligations. At this juncture, the notion of global obligations, distributed in a differentiated fashion, becomes critical to addressing gaps in human rights protection.

Global obligations, as several authors in this volume including Skogly, Müller and Seck note, are a means through which human rights obligations may be conceptualized more broadly and in ways that fill current protection gaps. Global obligations are not constrained by territorial boundaries and will be particularly helpful in addressing not only truly global problems such as climate change or pandemics, but the transboundary impacts on human rights of various issues and themes tackled in this volume: digitalization (Dentico) and cyber technologies (Milanovic; Kettemann and Tiedeke), migration (Gammeltoft-Hansen; Gombeer and Smis; Jegede), finance and financial assistance (Herre and Backes; de Moerloose, Erdem Türkelli and Curtis; Khulekani; Scali; Chenwi), investment (Augenstein; Van Ho), trade (Sellin; Aksenova) or tax systems (Michelmore), pollution and environmental degradation (Berkes; Seufert and Molsave Suarez).

A widespread recognition of global obligations necessitates the evolution of international law in general and human rights law in particular. As Skogly astutely points out in her contribution to this volume, the legal basis for recognizing global obligations is already found in the United Nations Charter, which protects the fundamental rights of the person and subsequent treaties that elaborate on the obligations contained therein. Recognizing that states have global human rights obligations does not in and of itself preclude the differentiated attribution of these global obligations based on capacity or historical contributions to global political, social, economic or ecological problems with adverse human rights impacts, with a view to contributing to global justice and equity (Skogly in this volume; Seck in this volume; Salomon 2007; Shelton 2009; Vandenhole 2018).

A More Expansive Understanding of Responsibility

Global obligations attributed on a differentiated basis and obligations borne by 'plural and diverse duty-bearer[s]' (Vandenhole 2015) naturally necessitate an international legal responsibility regime that allows for the attribution and distribution of shared responsibility for wrongful acts or omissions resulting in human rights violations among different states (as well as other international legal actors, including international organizations, non-state actors and hybrid public-private actors). Both the existing international responsibility frameworks under the Articles of Responsibility of States for Internationally Wrongful Acts (ARSIWA) and the Articles of Responsibility of International Organizations (ARIO), and the *Maastricht Principles* fall short of formulating adequate responses in this regard (Vandenhole 2018).

The reformulation of responsibility under international law and particularly in reference to human rights law should overcome the main shortcomings of existing responsibility frameworks. These include:

1 The use of international legal personality as the single benchmark for duty-bearing and consequently being legally responsible for the breaches of these duties;
2 The constrained scope of responsibility determined by the restrictive attribution of conduct to an international actor (defined as a state or an international organization or a combination thereof) either through its agents or organs, requiring a direct relationship between acts or omissions on the one hand and breaches of international obligations on the other (putting into question whether responsibility may be applied to less direct or indirect relationships, as noted by both Schechla and Todeschini in this volume or through a broader designation of attribution beyond the conduct of agents or organs);
3 The attribution of shared responsibility limited to situations of "aiding and abetting" or more colloquially put, complicity (which, as Guild points out in this volume, may require a high burden of proof by the rights-holders, rendering human rights protections moot);
4 A lack of recognition of how responsibility should be attributed and distributed for differentiated human rights obligations;
5 A liability-based (ex post facto) outlook that ties international legal responsibility to specific harms and does not factor in "forward-looking" perspectives of responsibility (echoing Young 2006).

Recent developments in the domain of shared responsibility that have culminated in scholarly attention respond to some of these shortcomings, for instance, by proposing to expand the scope of responsibility (Erdem Türkelli in this volume). While welcome, these developments do not push the boundaries of the law enough to accommodate the differentiated attribution and distribution of responsibility for differentiated obligations, to challenge the constraints of international legal personality or to conceptualize responsibility in forward-looking ways.

Promise may be found in alternative understandings of responsibility, inspired by both legal and non-legal approaches. In this regard, expanding the boundaries of legal responsibility to incorporate relationships beyond causality is the first step. Salomon (2007), for instance, links responsibility for systemic or structural violations to failing to act with due diligence and with an adequate standard of care. Similarly, Young's (2006) forward-looking model of political responsibility does not delimit responsibility to causality or to liability for harms but to actions or lack thereof in the face of foreseeable harms or injustices.

The second step is to recognize the various bases for the differentiated attribution of responsibility to various duty-bearers that also determines the distribution of responsibility among these duty-bearers. For Young (2006), these included power and influence, relative privilege gained due to structural injustice, vested interests and collective ability to prevent, resolve or contribute to the harms. For Salomon (2007), likewise, the bases for a differentiated attribution of responsibility should comprise power and influence over and benefits resulting from global processes leading to violations and the capability to assist. Additionally, Salomon invokes differentiation on the basis of a given actor's contribution 'to the emergence of the problem' (2007, p. 193).

In the third step of operationalizing, a more expansive understanding of responsibility, the idea of a polycentric governance framework for responsibility may function to offer rights-holders a multiplicity of venues for holding various state and non-state duty-bearers to account for their human rights impacts by overcoming obstacles linked to international legal personality and by bypassing causality based and liability-focused responsibility regimes (Erdem Türkelli 2020). The polycentric governance of responsibility also calls for legal, political and social responsibility mechanisms to be developed – when found to be lacking – to respond to the needs of rights-holders (Erdem Türkelli in this volume).

The state-centric myopia of international law on the one hand and the roots of an international legal system that has favoured the politically, economically and militarily more powerful states on the other have created obstacles to realizing the transformative potential of human rights. International law's legal fictions that obscure asymmetric power relations between different states informed by historical extraction patterns have prevented both less powerful states and individuals and communities living outside of these powerful states from claiming the same level of protection that is accorded to powerful states and even private actors such as companies under international legal regimes such as through investment law. We have a choice. We can continue to view human rights as we have in the past and live in a world where there is human rights protection for a few but little for the many. Or we could think of human rights as they should be: as the means of protecting all of us – by all of us.

References

Erdem Türkelli, G. (2020) *Children's Rights and Business: Governing Obligations and Responsibility*, Cambridge University Press.

European Court of Human Rights (ECtHR) (2001) *Cyprus v. Turkey* (Application No. 25781/94) Judgment.

Hopgood, S. (2013) *The Endtimes of Human Rights*, Cornell University Press.

Milanovic, M. (2013) *Extraterritorial Application of Human Rights Treaties: Law, Principles, and Policy*, Oxford University Press.

Moyn, S. (2010) *The Last Utopia: Human Rights in History*, Harvard University Press.

Posner, E. (2014) *The Twilight of Human Rights Law*, Oxford University Press.

Roxtrom, E. and Gibney, M. (2017) 'Human Rights and State Jurisdiction', *Human Rights Review* 18, 129–150.

Salomon, M.E. (2007) *Global Responsibility for Human Rights*, Oxford University Press.

Shelton, D. (2009) 'Describing the Elephant: International Justice and Environmental Law' in Ebbesson, J. and Okowa, P (eds). *Environmental Law and Justice in Context*, Cambridge University Press.

Vandenhole, W. (2015) 'Obligations and Responsibility in a Plural and Diverse Duty-Bearer Human Rights Regime, in Vandenhole W. (ed) *Challenging Territoriality in Human Rights Law*, Routledge.

_______ (2018) 'De-Growth and Sustainable Development: Rethinking Human Rights Law and Poverty Alleviation', *Law and Development Review* 11(2), 647–675.

Young, I.M. (2006) 'Responsibility and Global Justice: A Social Connection Model', *Social Philosophy & Policy Foundation* 23(1), 102–130.

Index

For Product Safety Concerns and Information please contact our EU
representative GPSR@taylorandfrancis.com
Taylor & Francis Verlag GmbH, Kaufingerstraße 24, 80331 München, Germany

www.ingramcontent.com/pod-product-compliance
Lightning Source LLC
LaVergne TN
LVHW080802011026
849160LV00015B/1513
* 9 7 8 0 3 6 7 5 4 6 5 7 1 *